A Host of Opportunities: An Introduction to Hospitality Management

R

**FIRST
EDITION**

n to

H

M

L

Gary K. Vallen
Northern Arizona University

IRWIN

Chicago • Bogotá • Boston • Buenos Aires • Caracas
London • Madrid • Mexico City • Sydney • Toronto

© Richard D. Irwin, a Times Mirror Higher Education Group, Inc. company, 1996

Irwin Book Team

Publisher: *Rob Zwettler*
Executive editor: *Kurt L. Strand*
Sponsoring editor: *John Biernat*
Senior developmental editor: *Libby Robenstein*
Developmental editor: *Maryellen Krammer*
Editorial assistant: *Kim Kanakes*
Marketing manager: *Heather L. Woods*
Project editor: *Amy E. Lund*
Production supervisor: *Dina Genovese*
Manager, graphics and desktop services: *Kim Meriwether*
Designer: *Matthew Baldwin*
Cover photographer: *Sharon Hoogstraten*
Compositor: *Wm. C. Brown Publishers*
Type: *10/12 Times Roman*
Printer: *R. R. Donnelley & Sons Company*

Times Mirror
Higher Education Group

Library of Congress Cataloging-in-Publication Data

Van Hoof, Hubert B.
    A host of opportunities: an introduction to hospitality
management / Hubert B. Van Hoof.
        p.   cm.
    Includes index.
    ISBN 0-256-18058-X
    1. Hospitality industry—Management.   I. Title.
TX911.3.M27V38   1996
647.94′068—dc20   95–44281

To our students:
- who will dedicate their lives to providing customers with comfort, shelter, entertainment, and service.
- who will balance technical expertise with a concern for people and quality.
- who will lead the hospitality industry into the 21st century.

Preface

This book is meant to be an introduction to the hospitality industry and hospitality management and is designed for introductory courses. We feel it is unique in various ways. Besides being an introduction to the hospitality industry, it is also an introduction to hospitality management education. The 16 chapters in this book reflect not only the extent and diversity of the industry, but they also reflect what is taught at 40 of the largest and most prominent hospitality management programs in the United States. We compared the programs of these leading programs and looked for similarities and differences in their curricula and course descriptions. We found that many schools teach the same kinds of classes. They all have classes on accounting, automation, human resource management, and travel and tourism, just to name a few. Classes at various programs may have different names, but they have surprisingly similar contents. Each of the individual chapters, therefore, represents those courses in some way. In fact, each of the chapters could be considered an overview of a course taught at a university or a junior college.

The book is unique because it reflects what recruiters and industry practitioners consider important in hospitality education. While all education should aim for relevance, hospitality management education in particular should be highly relevant and closely tied to the reality of hospitality management. Increasingly, the industry has indicated that future management candidates should have a sound theoretical background coupled with practical industry experience.

The hospitality industry would like its managers to have good communication and interpersonal skills and more or less expects them to have the necessary technical skills. This book responds to this alliance of skills; some chapters emphasize human skills whereas others focus on more technical aspects.

The book is divided into six parts, each with a particular focus. Part I, "Tuning in to Hospitality and Management," looks at the concept of hospitality and discusses what it means to be a manager. It provides students with a checklist to determine whether they are made of the right material. Part II, "Introduction to Components of the Travel and Tourism Industry," highlights several growing components of that industry. Casino management, resort management, and the relationship between the travel and tourism industry and the hospitality industry are all discussed. Part III, "Introduction to Lodging Management," looks at the history of the lodging industry and both "front" and "back" of the house operations. It emphasizes the role of the lodging industry within the broader market parameters of supply and demand. Part IV, "Introduction to the Food and Beverage Industry," describes the various aspects of restaurant and bar management, and looks at the intricacies of food production. Part V, "Introduction to Hospitality Operations," addresses some of the more technical skills required of a hospitality manager. Topics included are human resource management, accounting and finance, marketing, law, and automation. Part VI, "Hospitality Management Career Opportunities," proposes some strategies students can apply in obtaining employment in the hospitality industry. It suggests ways to research potential employers and offers suggestions in regards to writing résumés and conducting job interviews. Each section is preceded by a brief overview introducing the topics discussed in the section.

We included 16 individual chapters in the text, since regular semesters at most programs roughly encompass 16 weeks of instruction. Each of the chapters follows the same pattern. They introduce their particular topic area, discuss the topic matter, and present students with several questions for consideration. These questions are fairly broad in nature and are primarily intended to stimulate student interest in the topic. Additionally, each chapter, within the framework of the topic, discusses four issue areas that have become increasingly important in the hospitality industry in recent years. Under the heading "Eye on the Issues," each chapter discusses "hot" issues in environment, technology, ethics, and the international arena. Words in **bold block** represent keywords; words in ***bold italic*** are core concepts.

Being educators ourselves, we know that the order in which we have presented the material may not suit everyone's needs. However, we have attempted to present the material in a logical and coherent flow, with sufficient flexibility built in to allow educators to change the order in which they present the material.

This text is accompanied by an Instructor's Guide that includes additional materials designed for those using the text.

Hubert B. Van Hoof
Marilyn E. McDonald
Lawrence Yu
Gary K. Vallen

Acknowledgments

Without a doubt, this book could not have been developed without the help, patience, and cooperation of a great many people. We would like to acknowledge the following people and extend to them our sincere gratitude: David A. Williams and Galen Collins for their moral support of a project that took nearly three years to complete; Debbie James, Rebecca Levitt, and Thomas Combrink for their logistical assistance; Kurt Strand, John Biernat, Amy E. Lund, and Heather Woods for their guidance and help, especially during the final "hectic" stages; and James L. Morgan for his artistry with a camera. We also greatly value those colleagues across the country who shared their time and expertise through their helpful reviews and constructive criticisms; the hospitality industry executives and companies who contributed useful advice and materials; and all of our colleagues, who offered us words of encouragement and challenge. We cannot miss this opportunity to also thank our students, for testing (and inspiring) us daily; and our families, for their support and understanding. Lastly, we acknowledge and thank *our* teachers, for their patience, high standards, encouragement, and example. It is our pleasure to recognize these contributions and give full credit for the assistance we received en route to publication.

We would like to extend a special thank you to the following individuals who reviewed this book:

Agnes L. DeFranco
Conrad N. Hilton College,
University of Houston

David V. Pavesic
Georgia State University

Lynn Huffman
Texas Technical University

Michael Sciarini
Michigan State University

Howard Adler
Purdue University

Contributions

We would also like to acknowledge the following contributors to *A Host of Opportunities: An Introduction to Hospitality Management.* As experts in their own fields they have made unique and valuable contributions to this book.

William E. Miller, EdD	Chapter 2:	*Managerial Leadership for the Hospitality Industry.*
Paul J. Wiener, MBA	Chapter 4:	*Resorts, Clubs, Attractions, and Events.*
Emery H. Trowbridge, EdD	Chapter 5:	*Casino Management.*
Philip P. Pappas, MPS	Appendix A:	*Tourism Development*
Richard G. McNeill, MIM	Chapter 6:	*Lodging: History, Supply, Demand, and Structure.*
Marja J. Verbeeten, MHM	Appendix B:	*Hospitality Development.*
Samuel N. Powell, MA	Chapter 8:	*Hotel Operations.*
Christine Lynn Jaszay, PhD	Chapter 9:	*Food Service Management.*
	Chapter 11:	*Human Resource Management.*
Wallace L. Rande, EdD	Chapter 10:	*Food Preparation.*
James T. Murphy, MS	Chapter 12:	*Hospitality Accounting and Finance.*
Bruce S. Urdang, JD	Chapter 13:	*Hospitality Law.*
Lenka M. Hospodka, MBA	Chapter 14:	*Hospitality Automation.*
Richard M. Howey, PhD	Chapter 15:	*Hospitality Marketing.*
Lizette Melis, MA	Chapter 16:	*Career Opportunities and Job Search Strategies.*
Eileen Mahoney, MA	Chapter 16:	*Career Opportunities and Job Search Strategies.*

Note to the Student

On behalf of the authors, welcome to *A Host of Opportunities: An Introduction to Hospitality Management.*

The hospitality industry, in all its diversity, is an exciting, challenging, and demanding environment. If you are looking for a future career in this industry, be prepared to be challenged, to hustle, to enjoy yourself, to learn, and to persist. It will take many steps before you get where you would like to be, whether it be manager of a restaurant, general manager of a hotel, president of a hotel chain, or owner of an out-of-the-way bed and breakfast operation.

However, you have already taken the first steps in fulfilling your dream of becoming a hospitality industry manager: you have shown your willingness to learn by enrolling in a hospitality management program and by purchasing this book! You can expect to learn a lot from the people who have written this book: all of the authors have worked in the industry, come from a variety of backgrounds, and taught students like yourself for many years. They know what the industry and what education are all about.

We feel that we can safely assume the following: at this stage in your life, you have either made up your mind to become a hospitality manager, you are playing with the idea of becoming one, or you don't know what you really want to do. Whatever the case may be, this book can help you make some decisions about your future. We, the authors, know how exciting the hospitality industry is and how rewarding a good education can be. We are anxious to help you learn and share our knowledge and enthusiasm with you. We truly hope that our appreciation for the industry shows throughout the book and that it will rub off on you. So, welcome to the world of hospitality. Let's get busy . . .

Contents

PART II

Introduction to Components of the Travel and Tourism Industry

10 Food Preparation 316

PART V

Introduction to Hospitality Operations

11 Human Resource Management 349

Tuning in to Hospitality and Management

Part I opens the window for you, the potential hospitality manager, to look through onto the horizons that stretch before you if you choose a career in the fast-paced world of hospitality. Through the open window blow breezes from around the globe, breezes that can carry you to exciting multicultural experiences in many contexts. Your career might include managing an officers' club in the South Pacific; arranging catering for Air Force One; planning the next Woodstock; providing faultless accommodations for a papal visit; coordinating the events surrounding a national play-off; or owning your own bed and breakfast. The scope of opportunity is truly enormous, as you will see in Chapter 1, ''The Essence and Scope of Hospitality.'' There, you'll also learn about the lifeblood of hospitality—service—and the attitude that makes it possible.

Chapter 2, ''Managerial Leadership for the Hospitality Industry,'' provides a thorough look at the skills and characteristics of managers and invites you to see how you measure up. Through the use of hypothetical questions and case studies, it recaps the kinds of decisions and situations faced by managers, and emphasizes the importance of ethics in business—and in life in general.

Together, these two chapters provide an excellent introduction to career opportunities that may surprise you in their breadth and depth.

CHAPTER

1 The Essence and Scope of Hospitality

This chapter, ''The Essence and Scope of Hospitality,'' introduces you to the important concepts of *identity* and *service,* both of which are bedrocks of the hospitality industry. It also emphasizes two skills closely linked to service—communication and teamwork. The chapter also relates hospitality management to the times of millenial changes—in the workforce, in the customer base, and in the global marketplace. After establishing the complex diversity hospitality managers will encounter, the chapter describes diverse components of the industry ranging from club management to ownership of a bed and breakfast operation.

Outline

Introduction

"Party of one? Right this way."

Welcome to the world of hospitality, a world that offers a host of opportunities. It is no accident that this text opens with a welcome, for in no other profession is the concept of welcoming as essential as in this one—where a host of an inn, a restaurant, or an attraction steps forward to warmly greet his or her guests.

Your hosts for this text, the writers of the chapters ahead, are more than successful professors. They are, by design, individuals who have also *worked as hospitality professionals*—who have lived, eaten, and breathed the subject matter they present to you. Each has brought hands-on experience to the teaching arena and is able to present it in a doubly useful way—with a practitioner's savvy and an educator's perspective. As teachers, they know that you have not chosen to pursue a degree in hospitality management with the idea of becoming a speck in the sea of 9 million food service workers and nearly 2 million lodging workers. You have chosen this major with your eye on management and advancement. You have taken stock of your abilities and attitudes and seen a future for yourself as a leader. You have conducted a kind of personal inventory and matched your strengths with this group of careers. If you haven't, pay close attention to Chapter 2 and Chapter 16—they'll get you started!

Identity Drives Planning

Taking stock of yourself is closely tied to one of the most important concepts in this wide-reaching industry: identity. Identity is an all-important guideline in business, and in the hospitality business in particular. There are more than

900 significant chains listed in the American Hotel and Motel Association's most recent *Directory of Hotel and Motel Companies.* Many of these companies have one or more ''products,'' name brands, or ''identities.'' Choice Hotels International, for example, offers seven under its umbrella: the Quality, Comfort, Clarion, Sleep, Rodeway, EconoLodge, and Friendship chains. In the face of such diversity, defining a market identity or ''niche'' becomes essential.[1]

Let's make this example personal. Suppose you decide to host a party in your home. Perhaps you'd like to be able to invite Madonna, the president, and a Jackson or two—but you realize that your two-bedroom apartment isn't likely to attract such stellar guests. Setting your sights a little more realistically, you consider inviting a few professors and your supervisor from work, but again you adjust your thinking. Would you be comfortable entertaining them amidst your neon milk-crate furnishings, using NFL tumblers from a long-ago burger promotion? (This is not to suggest that you cannot have style on a shoestring; college students are known for their inventiveness.) Reality sets in. What alternatives do you have, given your income, budget, and facilities?

In many ways, your facility, that is, your home, dictates your party-planning decisions. Its lavishness affects, perhaps, your guest list; its roominess, the number you can invite; its kitchen area, the type and amount of food you are able to prepare and serve, and so on. In other ways, your personal identity affects your party options. Perhaps your preference runs to small groups of intimate friends with a background of New Age music and whale songs. Maybe you prefer the jostle of wall-to-wall people vibrating to sub-woofer-enhanced tunes. All these elements are part of your identity and must be factored into your plans.

Similarly, a hotel's, attraction's, club's, or restaurant's identity drives its planning. Everything about its inventory, staffing ratios, marketing, price structure, furnishings, and so on hinges on the elements of its identity. A coffee shop manager, secure in his or her unit's identity, feels no compulsion to stock calamari or lobster, whereas a seafood restaurant manager might consider them essential. A midmarket hotel purchasing agent, concerned about durability, might buy bath towels in a 14 percent polyester/86 percent cotton blend, while a resort's executive housekeeper might hear complaints if guest towels were anything less than 100 percent super-absorbent cotton terry. A 30-room mountain inn might or might not find it profitable to advertise in the nearest metro area's high-end home-and-garden magazine—depending on how rustic it is and how appealing its location.

Many such considerations, though linked to marketing, precede it. Self-definition—identity—can be both the child and the parent of marketing (see Exhibit 1–1). An owner or manager may set an establishment's identity as, say, ''a retreat'' or ''a rendezvous.'' It then becomes the marketing department's job to expand upon and enhance this identity, and the job of management and staff to provide the promised environment. A property or unit that tries to market itself at cross purposes to its identity seldom produces the

Exhibit 1–1

*Self-definition—
identity—can be both
the child and the
parent of marketing.
In the first example,
Outlet A's facilities
(or location or
budget) control its
identity. It must
market itself based
on those limitations
(or strengths).
Property B evidently
has greater
flexibility. Depending
on how it chooses to
market itself, it can
potentially shape its
identity to fit into one
of several niches.*

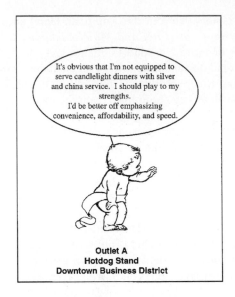

**Outlet A
Hotdog Stand
Downtown Business District**

**Property B
40-cottage lodging property,
45 miles outside metropolitan area.**

satisfied return customers that are essential to success. This is true because identity also stimulates customer expectations.

A customer's expectations vary depending on price and environment. According to Susan Clarke of Motivation, Unlimited:

> [For a $5 tab] . . . you would expect your meal to be a ''no frills'' experience—ready fast, hot or cold enough, probably wrapped in paper, handed to you from a counter, to be eaten with disposable utensils in a Formica-dominated landscape . . . [for a] $20 meal your expectations will be both different and greater. This time you'll be looking for a china plate, a tablecloth, glassware, metal flatware, and personal table service. How about a $50 meal? You'll surely have greater expectations, but now the increments have more to do with nuance and grace—the decor is more elegant, the service more attentive, the food more fashionable. Perhaps the china will be fine ''bone,'' and the table linens true linen; the goblets may be crystal, the cutlery actually silver.[2]

Thus, identity suggests a value to be expected. It becomes part of a transaction between the customer and the seller. This often unspoken transaction may include expectations of quality, speed, ambience, price, attitude, reliability, or flexibility, just to name a few. How well you, as a responsible manager, arrange to meet such expectations, through your efforts and the efforts of your staff, will determine your success. This is the element of ''service,'' the meeting of guest expectations. And that is the decathlon of the hospitality industry—the multievent trial that demands excellence from ''A'' for amenities to ''Z'' for zoo concession management. *Amenities* vary among

EXHIBIT 1–2

Customer expectations are often based on menu selection, value pricing, and high-quality food operations.

Courtesy: Taco Bell Corporation, Irvine, California. Photo by James L. Morgan, 85283.

EXHIBIT 1–3   **Top Seven Guest Room Personal Care Amenities (by rank)**

Deodorant soap	Mouthwash
Shampoo	Hand and body lotion
Facial bar soap	Hair conditioner
Toothpaste	

Source: American Hotel and Motel Association, *Lodging Guest Research Report*. Presented by Prof. Lee M. Kreul at the International Hotel, Motel, and Restaurant Association Annual Convention.

businesses and can be defined as the services, gifts, or ''grace notes'' a client receives as part of doing business with the company. At the simplest level, amenities are actual products provided for guest use. In hotels, they can include soap, shampoo, hand lotion, shoe shine cloth, and an in-room coffee machine (see Exhibit 1–3). Resorts customarily raise the ante with upscale amenities that may include high-quality bathrobes for in-house use, cosmetic-quality skin care, sun block lotion, complimentary newspaper, and gourmet chocolates. Airlines may provide toothbrushes, toothpaste, sleep masks, or slippers for long-distance flights.

In a larger sense, amenities can also be seen as including a range of guest services, from in-room check-out via ''smart system'' technology, to concierge or business services, to even extra leg room on commercial flights. All of these may contribute to a guest's comfort and satisfaction, though they are usually supplemental to the essential nature of the business in question.

Service

Why Is Service Important?

When it comes right down to it, there are only two reasons to provide good service: because you perceive it as ''right'' or a ''good,'' or because it somehow pays you to do so in the marketplace. (You'll learn more about the importance of managerial values in Chapter 2.) Businesses, such as the notorious ''last chance for gas'' station seen in cartoons, might opt for a profit by gouging on prices or ripping off travelers for repairs, because they have no competitors. In the absence of competition, the marketplace ceases to *be* a market, offering little or no financial incentive for service, fairness, or integrity. In such an environment, the customer must take what he or she gets. You can almost hear the operator's mental wheels turning: ''Why should I smile at these pigeons? Smiling won't make the gas tank hold more gas,'' or ''These customers will never be back and if they *did* come back, this will still be the only game in town, heh, heh.''

Such unscrupulous scenarios have been played out many times on lonely stretches of highway, on frontiers, and in socialist economies (where state-run operations have no competitors). When we encounter fair-minded operators under such circumstances, we can appreciate and admire them even more for adhering to higher personal standards of behavior, despite the temptations of "all that the market will bear." And it is these operators who, all other things being equal, are likely to withstand competition when it does arrive. This was brought home to the American economy during the ultracompetitive 1980s.

Studies by the Strategic Planning Institute (SPI) of Cambridge and the Technical Assistance Research Programs Institute of Washington, D.C., showed that customers were extremely dissatisfied with mediocre and unresponsive service. While some companies tried to offset poor service with lower pricing, most Americans rejected such tactics. Service, it seems, is an indispensable part of the free market equation. In fact, Ron Zemke, in *The Service Edge,* cites SPI's discovery that superior service providers can charge, on average, 9 to 10 percent more than their inferior service–providing competitors—and still gain market share![3]

So What Is Superior Service?

Service starts with an attitude. This attitude prompts you to "make it ready, make it right, make it to the customer's satisfaction, and do so with courtesy and professionalism." Your goal—regardless of your hourly wage or salary, regardless of whether a tip will be forthcoming, regardless of whether this is the 1st or 70th time you have performed the task—is to leave the customer feeling pleased that he or she has done business with you. Zemke refers to this quality as "earnest(ness)." It can't be faked. It requires attentiveness and responsiveness beyond (and in addition to) any technical skills.

Some other words often heard in relation to good service are:

- On-time
- Attentive
- Polite, personable
- Gave full value
- Went beyond the call of duty
- Friendly
- Dependable
- Knowledgeable
- Respectful
- Anticipative
- Follow through
- Resourceful
- Accurate

- Convenient
- Competent
- Well trained

If you enjoy identifying and satisfying customer needs, your choice of a career in the hospitality industries will be especially rewarding, particularly if you enjoy the challenge of bringing details together into a successful whole. Harvey Mackay, in *Swim with the Sharks Without Being Eaten Alive,* offers this truism: "Little things don't mean a lot; they mean everything."[4]

Empowerment

Superior service encompasses all the above earmarks and then builds upon them, usually through creativity and empowerment. While you may be familiar with the kind of creativity that drives chefs to carve dolphins out of ice blocks or flowers out of radishes, you may not yet have been exposed to the essential concept of empowerment. **Empowerment** is the placing of the authority to *do* in the hands of employees so that when an occasion for creativity or problem solving or crisis handling arises, an employee can act. Empowerment gives the employee confidence that his or her solution, whether it be a refund, a "comp" (providing a service at no charge, that is, "complimentary"), or a decision to evacuate the basement, will be supported by management.

The concept of empowerment grew in popularity during the 60s, 70s, and 80s when it was first applied to the rights of minorities, the poor, and women. Senator Jack Kemp spoke of it as: "Giving people the opportunity to gain greater control over their own destiny . . . " Some of this sense carries over into the managerial use of the term. For instance, more recently, David Statt's *Concise Dictionary of Management* noted that an empowered employee "*owns* the task she has been entrusted with and accepts full responsibility for it, being inspired to extend herself by the force of the vision and commitment she is shown rather than by any kind of coercion."[5]

Now we begin to see some of the give-and-take upon which empowerment is built. Trust is a major factor. In the example above, if the employee does not have reason to believe that management will back her decision, she will decline the responsibility of acting. On the other hand, management must trust her ability to make good judgments (and make sure she has been provided with the tools, such as training and vision, to make such judgments). This implies an "enlightened" organization that values its employees. William D. Hitt, in *The Leader-Manager,* suggests that "inasmuch as empowerment treats people as *persons,* they will put forth their best effort—go beyond what is expected of them."[6] And best effort is yet another component of superior service.

Communication and Teamwork

Service has come to be seen less and less as something unmeasurable or intangible and more and more as a salable *product*. Some companies even promise to demonstrate their commitment to service through objective performance. Thus we see them promise their guests that, "Our cashier will greet you with a smile and make eye contact with you or we'll . . . " and "If we don't greet you by name, your breakfast is on us." And guess what? Often times these by-the-book approaches pay off in better service. One reason is that some behaviors (such as smiling, nodding when listening, calling guests by name) are proven signals of attention—and guests perceive them positively.

Another reason is that when management conveys specific guidelines to employees, it is communicating in a very strong way what the organization holds important. If management were to assign as an organizationwide goal that all employees take every opportunity to *overcharge* guests, that, too, would send a message, stronger than any memo or voice mail announcement. Such straightforward communication brings results—and a corporate culture evolves to meet it—upward or downward, depending on the message. When Hilton Inns, Inc., introduced its quality service effort, "Priority 1," the name alone left little doubt about the organization's intended direction.

Internal communication is an essential part of providing superior service. It does a chef little good to prepare an amazing meal, cooked to perfection, if the server has gotten the order wrong. An indifferently cleaned guest room can negate a five-month selling effort by the sales department, undo the efficient handling provided by a crack bellstaff, and undermine the front desk's friendly and accurate check-in. A catering company will lose not one, but many, clients if the hostess who hired it falls faint from an allergic reaction to mushrooms—a fact noted in the contract, but not communicated to the kitchen.

One assistant general manager of an upscale suburban hotel has a succinct way of describing the need to communicate important details—sometimes both verbally and in writing. She calls it the ***Mack truck theory.*** Her explanation:

> Carrying around important information "in your head"—not logging it in because you think you'll be on duty the next day to take care of it—is dangerous. What if you were run over by a Mack truck on your way to work? There'd be no way to deliver what you promised because the details exist only on your mental bulletin board. And the guest who relied on you is the one who would suffer, not to mention employees who stepped up to fill in for you. There's no reason to risk letting people down like that when a little communication is all it takes.

In the hospitality industry, poor service in one area inevitably reflects badly on all other areas. Once the "spell" of efficiency and responsiveness has been broken, the client becomes hypersensitive to other weaknesses. One

EXHIBIT 1–4

The 1990s have shown an increase in tourism that celebrates history, cultural heritage, and nostalgia. This has been a boon for rural areas, which can benefit from ''outside'' money brought into their economies by visitors. Shown here, the Auburn•Cord• Duesenberg Museum, virtually the only tourist attraction in De Kalb County, Indiana, acts as a tourism ''magnet.'' In a recent year, the museum, housed in a 1930s vintage art deco building, saw nearly 67,000 visitors. The museum also markets itself regionally as a banquet and wedding facility to generate further funding.

Courtesy: the Auburn•Cord•Duesenberg Museum, Auburn, Indiana.

only has to review comment cards at any hotel to know that guest dissatisfaction is prone to snowballing. What starts as a complaint about a lost reservation soon picks up into a laundry list of the ''slow, scuffed-up elevator, the housekeepers' noisy vacuums at 8:30 AM, and wobbly legs on the banquet chairs.'' Instead of one department called on the carpet, four have been implicated!

At busy facilities with many departments and round-the-clock shifts, communication is a must. In fact, in interdependent organizations such as convention centers, hotels, and clubs, the service orientation we've discussed must be extended *from one employee to another* for a seamless, well-oiled performance.

Jonathan Tisch, president of Loews Hotels, has often compared the performance aspect of hospitality to show business, emphasizing the need for teamwork among all the supporting players. When any member of the production, no matter how small his or her part, flubs a line, drops a sandbag, or sews a seam improperly, the whole performance suffers; the audience's enjoyment is jarred, and ticket sales drop. That's bad news, but it also brings up another important point. There is another factor in this all-important service equation, namely the underlying need for profit.

The Need for Profit

During a brainstorming session on college hotel/restaurant management (HRM) program requirements, an enormously successful hospitality entrepreneur remarked, "But when do you teach them how to make a profit?" Technical skills, a commitment to service, training, vision, and people skills are all important characteristics for managers to have, but at the end of the day, the season, the year, or the decade (depending on your organization's perspective), management's goal is to show "black ink" in satisfying quantities. To do so, managers must balance the ideal (the goals and essentials mentioned throughout this chapter) with reality (expenses, a stalled economy, taxation, regulation, dwindling labor force). After all, *manager* is a title based upon the verb *manage*. It refers to an activity, not to a lease on a roomy office. So we must add to all the other prerequisites the understanding of how to make an operation profitable.

Fortunately, during the mid-90s, the hospitality industry is poised for a period of increased profits. The economies of the world's major nations—once based on agriculture, then based on manufacturing—have shifted into economies based on services. Columnist George F. Will captured the transformation he saw in the United States as follows: "McDonald's has more employees than U.S. Steel. Golden arches, not blast furnaces, symbolize the American economy." Of course, there is much more to the service sector than simply fast food, and a great deal of it falls under the umbrella of hospitality. Leisure, travel, tourism, recreation, and, in some cases, entertainment are often linked with hospitality in forecasts and projections of national income and employment. When so compiled, these enterprises emerge as a giant, outshining almost all other sectors of the economy.

But hospitality profitability is not all smooth, downhill skiing. Because it draws upon a global pool of customers, it is tied to the health of not only local economies but also to the economies and exchange rates of international trading partners. In fact, for nearly the past decade, much of the lodging segment of the industry struggled to remain solvent. The late 80s found much of America "overbuilt" with hotels, many of them burdened with excessive debt. (**Overbuilding** occurs when a market area has far more rooms than it has customers and usually results in low occupancies and rate "wars.") This resulted in an aggressively competitive market. Chains and independents alike "woke up" to the need for clearly defined identities and corporate cultures based on service, as discussed at the beginning of this chapter. To return to the opening metaphor, for the past 10 years, the lodging industry has survived by putting one foot in front of the other, much more like cross-country skiing or even snowshoeing than the relative effortlessness of a downhill glide.

An International Industry

While the lodging industry has been flat in America, investors have looked abroad for opportunity. Holiday Inn, Best Western, Hilton, Ramada, and Sheraton are just a few of the major companies whose logos may be seen around the globe. Restaurants have made even more media waves than hotels; much ado was made about McDonald's appearance in Moscow and Beijing, KFC's presence in Tokyo and Shanghai, and Baskin-Robbins in Vietnam. Naturally, an international marketplace requires a vast employee network to support it. In 1991, the World Travel and Tourism Council estimated that travel- and tourism-related enterprises employ more than 112 million people worldwide, or 1 in 15 employees. In fact, the internationalization of hospitality has become so important that each of the upcoming chapters will discuss how it relates to the subject under consideration.

Travel Shrinks the World

In 1983, Somerset R. Waters reported an estimated $652 billion for worldwide spending on domestic and foreign travel combined.[7] By 1993, that estimate had risen to $3.47 trillion. Both figures are happily significant in the fact that they exceed the estimated worldwide spending on military defense (the latter by almost three times) and give support to the argument that tourism promotes peace. This is but one effect of the long-awaited ''shrinking'' world en route to the ''global village'' predicted by sociologist Marshall McCluhan. As borders have opened, travel restrictions have been relaxed and improved economic conditions have allowed more international travel than ever before. In 1994, more than 45.7 million visitors traveled to the United States, spending nearly $73 billion. In return, Americans are estimated to have spent close to $56 billion while visiting foreign countries during the same period.[8] Chapter 3, ''The Travel and Tourism Industry,'' will provide a more in-depth look at the enormity and complexity of international travel.

Cultural Sensitivity.   Internationalization has more than only economic consequences. It requires that students pursuing hospitality careers develop sensitivity to persons of other cultures, not only as guests or customers, but as co-workers and senior managers. With more and more corporations expanding internationally, managers can expect opportunities and assignments far from their familiar surroundings. Indeed, some international companies advocate overseas experience for ambitious managers. The experience of being a stranger in a strange land promotes empathy and perspective faster than any book-learned understanding of cultural difference ever could. And one need not be transferred to a European or Asian country to find oneself working under a managing director from foreign shores. Multinational companies weren't invented in the United States, nor have they limited their expansion to non–North American sites. For this reason, many schools offering hotel, restaurant, institutional, or tourism management programs emphasize not only geography and international commerce, but also cultural diversity and organizational theory.

A Change in the Demographics of Hospitality

The make-up of hospitality management has changed greatly in the last two decades. According to Elaine Grossinger Etess, the first female president of the American Hotel and Motel Association (AH&MA), ''During the early 70s schools of hospitality management were bastions of male dominance with the occasional few 'token' women in each class. Today, however, most of our colleges report that over 50 percent of those matriculated are women.''[9] Etess also noted that up to that time, ''women (held) the usual entry-level positions—maids, waitresses, and switchboard operators. Management positions were almost always filled by men. Men had 'careers' as hoteliers; women had 'jobs in hotels.' '' Fortunately, the industry has moved toward a better balance.

Women Making Strides

In American business in 1992, women represented 41 percent of all professional and managerial positions.[10] *Working Woman* also reports that, despite this visibility, on average, college-educated managers who are women earn approximately 20 percent less than their male counterparts. According to a recent *Lodging* magazine article, the hospitality industry has a somewhat better track record, paying women hospitality managers about 15 percent less than men in equivalent positions.

Women continue to gain ground in this area. In fact, McDonald's reports that over the past few years, the number of its women operator/owners has tripled. Nita Lloyd-Fore, a director of sales for national accounts with Hilton, wrote that in the late 60s, when she joined Hilton, there were only four women ''who held the job of director of sales at our properties. Today, . . . more than 60 percent of those positions are held by women.''[11] Still, not all the news is so promising. When Joan Sills was named president of Colony Hotels (a Radisson subsidiary) in early 1992, she became the first woman to preside over a major lodging chain. Nationwide, across business and industry, it's estimated that only 5 percent of top-level executive positions are held by women.

Altered Labor Pool

While women have made visible progress, similar strides must be made to pursue balance in opportunity for minorities and the differently abled (the latter being the preferred way to refer to those who used to be called *disabled* or *handicapped*). The legislation known as the Americans with Disabilities Act (ADA), which became effective in 1992, is intended to prevent employment inequities to the disabled. Many consider this legislation not only overdue philosophically, but also timely in terms of America's shifting employment pool. The president's Committee on the Employment of People with

Disabilities estimates that the ADA will bring to notice an untapped pool of nearly 23 million potential employees at a time when industry is facing a nearly stagnant growth rate in available labor. The hospitality industries will be one of the hungriest if what Marvin Cetron predicts is true. His prediction: "By the year 2000, one out of every 10 people in the United States will be working in the hospitality industry."[12]

Changing Commitment to Work

Human resource experts also see a change in the value placed on work and success. The days of sacrificing family life in favor of "workaholic" success seem to be over. Fewer young managers indicate a willingness to work 75+ hours a week, even with the promise of rapid advancement. More companies are being asked to provide child-care plans for working parents. One study found that 71 percent of the corporate women surveyed were more interested in balancing work and family than in building a "supersuccessful" career. An increasing number of male managers agree. Family time is no longer being seen as a luxury, but as a necessity.

Adjustments will undoubtedly be made. With the demand for qualified hospitality employees increasing and the labor pool dwindling, employers are motivated to make their employment packages attractive and competitive. In the meantime, employers are looking at another answer to labor shortages: older citizens. A study that included Days Inns Hotels found that workers older than 55 are as productive and cost effective as their younger counterparts. Employers characterize the group as having very low rates of absenteeism, often coupled with graciousness and politeness skills honed by having been in the workforce for decades.

Customer Profiles Change

As the people behind the scenes have changed, so have the people who consume hospitality services. Let's look at a few examples:

1. The much-described **baby boomers** (people born between 1946 and 1964) are today estimated at 77 million strong, representing about half of the working U.S. population. Now at the peak of their earning power, they will begin retiring in 10 to 15 years, shaking all leisure-time norms to date. By the year 2000, 13 percent of the population will be 65 years or older. In some Sunbelt areas, there are already communities in which more than half of the population consists of "seniors." This group, as a whole, has both discretionary income and the leisure time in which to spend it, making it a force to be reckoned with. Raymond Goodman, Jr., of the Whittemore School of Business and Economics, University of New Hampshire, has estimated that today's population age 50 and older owns more than 77 percent of all the financial assets in America, spends more on travel and recreation than any other age

group, and eats out about three times per week. These are the people hospitality operators want to ''reach out and touch.''

2. The business traveler has changed. In the last 10 years business travel by women has increased dramatically, so that they now represent nearly 29 percent of business travel. Hoteliers have been spurred to pay attention, since female corporate travelers are among the most loyal repeat customers when satisfied with their accommodations.

3. Another significant change is the increase in families choosing to vacation together, kids included, at resorts and upscale hotels. As William Lucas, managing director of the Westin La Paloma Resort, put it, ''Yuppies had puppies!—and they want to bring them along on vacation.''[13] This has brought about a need to review activities, menus, and facilities for child appropriateness. This has become so common that a new category of resort is being market tested: couples-only resorts. As humorist Dave Barry puts it, these ''do not allow you to bring your children, the theory being that it is difficult for you and your spousal unit to get into a romantic mood if one of you has to pause every 45 seconds to shout, 'Jason! I told you not to squirt sun block into Ashley's ear!' ''[14]

4. Researchers have also noted an increasing preference of travelers for ''experiential'' vacations—trips that offer more than sightseeing and sunbathing. The popularity of Elderhostel, spa vacations, bed and breakfasts, wine country safaris, and ''real cowboy'' excursions are just a few examples of this consumer trend.

Needed: A Comfort Level with Technology

No matter how you arrive at your first hospitality position, you'll do well to develop a comfort level with technology. With the growth of electronic keying devices, point-of-sale devices, and property management systems, it's virtually impossible for employees of any service area to spend a day untouched by high tech. Telephones have become increasingly complex—to the point that one desktop phone can do more than entire switchboards of days gone by. Yet how many times have you witnessed businesspeople fumbling with their phone buttons, warning that they might lose you if they transfer your call? How many times have you heard people muttering about their ''dumb computer''?

The solution to such occurrences is training. People hate to be frustrated while trying to accomplish something, yet frustration is common around unfamiliar technology. While there is a significant amount of clumsy or quirky equipment out in the marketplace, grumbling about it is usually not the best response; *mastering* it is. Most will be extremely useful as a tool or as a mechanical assistant.

A word about word processing and spreadsheets. Many students preparing for management careers scoff at learning these two basic types of software, believing they will have a secretary who will ''take care of all that.'' Reality suggests: Don't kid yourself. These are essential skills, even if you do rise to a position supported by a secretary. Timely communication is extremely important. With a word processing program you can put down your thoughts at two or three times the speed it takes to handwrite them. Why would you want to slow yourself down by refusing to use an easily acquired skill?

Technology has given the hospitality industry a huge boost in efficiency, simplifying reservations, guest billing, forecasting, climate control, energy consumption, inventory control, scheduling, sales and marketing functions, and research. It is so important that each of the upcoming chapters will discuss its applications in greater detail, and a whole chapter (Chapter 14, ''Hospitality Automation'') has been dedicated to it.

Where the Wings of Hospitality Can Take You

Chances are, as you considered a career in hospitality, you imagined yourself as the manager or executive chef of a fine restaurant, a general manager at a luxury hotel or resort, or maybe even a pit boss at a casino. These are all possibilities, but your choices are wider than perhaps you ever dreamed. A hospitality management degree and experience can connect you to a network of careers in leisure, travel, tourism, and recreation, simply because of the scope of these related enterprises. Though you'll get more details in appropriate upcoming chapters, here's a preview.

Lodging

Hotels and resorts have been compared to miniature cities in the way that they incorporate life support systems—light, heat, water, food, shelter, security, and sanitation facilities. As such, they often include within their ''city limits'' elements of food service, recreation, entertainment, and personal services for travelers. There are close to a dozen major categories of lodging facilities, ranging from tiny bed and breakfasts to the latest development, megaresorts. The niches in between these extremes include commercial hotels, airport hotels, economy properties, suite hotels, residential hotels, conference centers, casino hotels, and resorts. The tiniest cousin in this family had its debut in Japan: the sleeping tube, which takes the airport hotel to an extreme by providing the guest with space little larger than a closet in which to sleep. Chapter 6, ''Lodging: History, Supply, Demand, and Structure,'' will discuss some of the differentiating characteristics of lodging categories and their markets.

Gaming, which has traditionally been associated with the lodging industry, has expanded its scope since 1987, when legislation opened up opportunities for Native American–owned gaming facilities. Since then, freestanding and riverboat casinos have flourished. Experts at Harrah's, the famous casino company, estimate that by the year 2000, casino gambling will be legal in 40 of the 50 states. Americans made an estimated 92 million visits to casinos in 1993 betting

Exhibit 1–5

Gaming chains have formed partnerships with Native American tribes to promote gaming on reservations.

Courtesy: Harrah's Ak-Chin Casino, Pinal County, Arizona. Photo by James L. Morgan, 85283.

nearly $400 billion. A closer look at Chapter 5, ''Casino Management,'' will give you an estimate of how much of this fortune ended up in hospitality coffers, by virtue of a tidy trick called the *casino advantage*.

Perhaps in response to increased gaming competition from nonhotels, casino hotels in Las Vegas have begun impinging on the attractions market by creating theme parks and megahotels that are attractions in themselves. The MGM Grand, and the Egyptian-themed Luxor are two striking examples. A Star Trek park planned by the Las Vegas Hilton will have the capacity of handling 1,000 visitors per hour, at a $10.00 per person fee. Gaming is indeed trying ''to boldly go where no one has gone before.''

On a more down-to-earth level, campgrounds and recreational vehicle parks form a distinct subcategory of their own within the larger definition of lodging. A relatively new usage of a perennial form of lodging has been developed around college dormitories. Though primarily residential units for three-fourths of the year, such facilities are now being actively marketed for transient occupancy by study groups (such as Elderhostel) and attendees of educational summer camps.

Food Service

The preparation and delivery of food to guests and travelers is another seemingly omnipresent category closely connected with lodging, travel, and recreation. Beyond the obvious area of familiar restaurants lies institutional food service in hospitals, businesses, colleges, and correctional facilities.

Exhibit 1–6

Hospitality management is nothing if not creative. The proprietor of Bogen's Bar and Grill in Blacksburg, Virginia, was one of the first to see the potential of offering Internet services to his customers. The "cyberbar" was an immediate success, gaining both loyal patrons and national newspaper coverage for the tavern.

Courtesy: Bogen's Inc., Blacksburg, Virginia.

Recently a new category has been recognized in the form of "commuter food," which is different still from traditional food service offered on trains, planes, and ships. Commuter food operations are often located in or near subway stations, train depots, and bus stops. Workers on their way home pick up restaurant-style entrees in take-out packaging. Sbarro, Inc., known for its food-court stores, has worked to develop this market.

Food service also encompasses everything from snack bars, festival and arena vending, discos, coffee houses, and picnic packing (popular in California), to the new "smart drug cocktail bars" featuring health drinks loaded with vitamins, amino acids, and other nutrients believed to enhance memory and mental clarity. Each of these unique categories has its own challenges and strengths, but all share the common need for responsible management. Chapters 9 and 10 discuss some of the issues that affect every food service operation.

EXHIBIT 1–7

Ethnic foods have entered the ''quick serve'' market competing with traditional burgers and chicken. The Tokyo Express chain menu includes sukiyaki, noodle dishes, and sushi.

Courtesy: Tokyo Express, Phoenix, Arizona. Photo by James L. Morgan, 85283.

Institutions

Until recently, hospitality managers working in institutions were primarily involved with food service in hospitals, prisons, school cafeterias, and so on. In the last few years, opportunities have expanded to include health care management and retirement center management. Managers in these positions oversee a whole spectrum of guest services, including activities, housekeeping, food service, transportation services, special services, and guest satisfaction. This promises to be a growth area as America's famous baby boomers age and seek out such facilities.

Transportation

Lodging and feeding guests along their journeys would be irrelevant without the essential means of getting them to their destinations. This area includes not only airlines, cruise ships, ferries, trains, motor coaches, limousines, taxis, and shuttle buses, but also rental car operations and service station facilities, not to mention airports and terminals. One might even include parking facilities, horses, trail mules, rick-shas, and golf carts in this category. Transportation is closely linked to **infrastructure,** the system of roads, harbors, bridges, tunnels, airports, and so on necessary for vehicle movement. Infrastructure also includes other services required by residents and visitors:

- Utilities, such as water, electricity, and gas.
- Health care.
- Sanitation and sewer.
- Services, such as traffic control, police, and emergency personnel.

Travel and Tour Arrangements

Within this detail-driven area there are travel agencies, reservation systems, and tour-planning, retailing, and wholesaling operations. We might also include guide services, rating and accreditation associations, and **destination-management companies (DMCs)** in this collection of enterprises. DMCs provide stress-relieving services for meeting planners responsible for meetings in distant locales. Because DMC specialists know the high points of their area and patronize subcontractors they have found to be reliable, they can arrange for speakers, entertainers, shopping excursions, airport pick-ups, VIP welcomes, and many of the tiny-but-important details an out-of-towner would find time consuming or difficult to arrange.

Tourism Marketing and Promotion

The task of creating consumer interest in a city, region, state, or country falls not only on the shoulders of the marketing staff of individual hotels and attractions but also on agencies such as national tourism authorities, state or provincial tourism offices, chambers of commerce, and convention and visitors bureaus. These entities work to promote awareness of their areas as multifaceted destinations, with the purpose of attracting visitors who will stay for several days or even weeks. Their work is often important to the economic health of their city, state, and so on because of the ***ripple effect*** of outside money (also called the *multiplier*). Because of tourism's ripple effect, one dollar spent effectively to promote tourism can result in two or three dollars reaped in direct or indirect return.

To provide a simplified example: The money visitors spend in a town for accommodations or meals also indirectly supports the businesses that supply the hotels and restaurants they patronize. (These could include food and liquor wholesalers, carpet-cleaning companies, local newspapers, rental car agencies, florists, and so on.) Local retailers consistently benefit as visitors shop for pleasure or essentials. In popular tourist areas, many companies prosper to the point of needing additional employees to serve increased demand for their products and services. Governments also profit through the taxes collected on increased sales. This helps explain why governments and businesses see tourism as a cash cow, and are willing to fund tourism marketing agencies. Not to be forgotten, however, is the other side of the coin: the costs of tourism. These are touched on in several upcoming chapters.

Club Management

Club managers face a different set of tasks than others in hospitality, largely because they deal with a clientele composed of members who usually have invested significant sums in the form of dues or initiation fees. Members patronize their club's facilities frequently and may have a voice in how they are operated. To serve these familiar customers, club managers must find a happy medium between variety, in terms of menu offerings and special events, and predictability, in terms of consistent, excellent service.

Club management is a growing field within the industry and includes opportunities in military installations and public or private facilities.

Activities and Attractions

Tourism stakeholders benefit through the availability of unique or attractive activities. These can include events, expositions, fairs, and festivals, whether cultural, ethnic, political, sport related, religious, artistic, or for "fans." Many of these are outdoor affairs that require festival grounds, stadiums, tracks, and so on, while others take place indoors at civic centers. Thousands of events are held each year ranging from polka festivals to Star Trek convocations. This category also includes the enormous field of meetings, conventions, and trade shows. A whole subset of enterprises has grown to support these activities, including contract services for everything from security to parking services, from exhibition and audiovisual rental agencies to portable toilet

EXHIBIT 1–8

*Developers of
Biosphere II never
imagined that a
science-related
attraction would
prove so popular that
they would have to
add lodging, food
and beverage, and
retail outlets.*

Courtesy: Arizona Office of Tourism, Phoenix, Arizona.

vendors. Chapter 4, ''Resorts, Clubs, Attractions, and Events,'' discusses relevant management challenges for this area.

State, national, and regional parks also serve as activity magnets to millions each year. So popular are such scenic and play areas that in some areas they are in serious danger of overuse. Park management has become a difficult specialty. Managers must walk a fine line between serving the traveling and recreation-minded public and controlling the negative physical impacts caused by millions of park users.

Akin to park recreation are those enterprises that provide leisure and sports facilities such as golf courses, bowling lanes, tennis, and other private or public clubs. In Japan, entrepreneurs have taken this category to new heights by building the world's largest indoor ski slope, 25 stories high, and as long as five football fields!

Shopping

Travelers seem born to shop, and every aspect listed above has its own specialized league of merchants associated with it. The pursuit of purchases has far outstripped traditional souvenir buying. The popularity of shopping has now escalated to the point that some shopping areas can accurately be described as tourist destinations by themselves (Rodeo Drive, Beverly Hills; Mall of America, Minneapolis; Fifth Avenue, New York; Champs D'Elysée, Paris, to name a few). Other communities flourish through the marketing of art and/or crafts, sometimes by emphasizing the cultural or ethnic specialties of the locale. The U.S. Travel and Tourism Administration (USTTA) estimates that of the 18 most popular activities foreign visitors participate in, shopping ranks first, engaging 83 percent of all tourists.

Services and Miscellaneous

Hospitality's wings extend to specializations within the scope of standard business. As in other enterprises, there are needs for human resources managers, training specialists, accountants, controllers, financial planners, purchasing agents, clerks, office managers, physical plant engineers, cleaning and maintenance experts, and so on.

Miscellaneous specialties tied to hospitality include those of restaurant critics, travel writers, travel publishers, and hospitality consultants.

Hospitality and Corporate Citizenship

Hotels, restaurants, airlines, casinos, spas, and amusement parks are bombarded with requests from their communities for donations to be used as prizes or in charity auctions or raffles. More often than you would expect, they participate in these community-minded events . . . for several reasons.

Hotels, attractions, theaters, amusement parks, and, in some cases, airlines have what can be called **perishable inventories.** This means, in the case of a hotel with 200 rooms, that on a given night there are 200 perishable opportunities for revenue. Come night time, if the room has not been sold, the hotel has lost the revenue it might have earned. By making tax-deductible donations of accommodations during known slow periods, the hotel can lessen its revenue losses while helping worthwhile charities. Even if the financial benefit is small, the hotel also gains public relations points for being a good citizen. The hotel may pick up bonus revenue if the ''comped'' guests patronize its restaurant or lounge. There is also excellent potential for positive word of mouth, since human nature prompts people to talk about great deals to their friends and to recommend businesses with whom they have had personal experience.

The same principle applies to airline seats, theater tickets, Ferris-wheel rides, and so on. The plane must still fly and the show must still go on even if seats are empty. The cost to the donating company is minimal, yet the benefits are positive. In the case of a restaurant, most of these principles apply, though the cost to the donor may be somewhat higher, percentagewise, since the food that is consumed must be replaced—slightly different from a seat that may be sold over and over again.

This partially explains the mechanism by which hospitality enterprises can and do benefit from donating inventory to charitable causes. But there are philosophical and psychological reasons as well.

It's common in many corporate segments of the hospitality industry for managers to be transferred every few years. Since home changes with regularity, smart managers often try to involve themselves in their new communities as soon as possible after arriving. This is a good psychological strategy for preventing a feeling of rootlessness. Most major cities have local chapters of professional organizations such as the American Hotel & Motel Association (AH&MA), National Restaurant Association (NRA), Hotel Sales and Marketing Association International (HSMAI), and Meeting Planners International (MPI), and these offer outlets for community involvement. This is the personal side of the coin of good citizenship.

Corporate philosophy is the other side of the coin. Enlightened corporations believe they have a responsibility to their communities. In some cases they have even built a commitment to humanitarian acts into their business or action plans. This is why it is common to see hotel associations collecting old sheets and towels for homeless shelters, and restaurants and banquet facilities contributing unused meals to charity dining rooms. In Canada, when Canadian Pacific Hotels' (CPH) housekeeping staff expressed their dislike of throwing out slightly used bars of soap and partially used bottles of shampoo and conditioner, the company sought a solution. The result was a relationship with

EXHIBIT 1–9

Participation in high-profile charitable events gives hotels, resorts, and restaurants a "win-win" way to support their communities. Celebrity chefs, such as Jacques Pepin, support events like these with their presence and participation.

Courtesy: Jacques Pepin.

Global Ed-Med (GEM), a group that specializes in sending medical supplies to the Third World. In remote areas not serviced by GEM, CPH seeks out local charities with a need for such amenities.

According to Rick Van Warner, "the nation's restaurant operators are finding ways not only to contribute to a wide variety of fund-raisers but also on a *daily basis* to get their perishable leftovers into the mouths of people who need them."[15] America's food-service operators are using their resources to respond to the problem of hunger. (Statistics show that 20 million people in the United States go hungry each day—including one out of every eight children under age 12.)

An easy way for students to get started in hospitality citizenship is to become active in student organizations while on campus. These include:

- Club Managers Association of America (CMAA).
- Hosteur.
- Hotel Sales and Marketing Association International (HSMAI).
- International Food Service Executive Association (IFSEA).
- International Student Organization (ISO).
- Eta Sigma Delta.
- International Association of Hospitality Accountants (IAHA).
- Professional Convention Management Association (PCMA).
- Educational Institute (EI).

Student chapters often undertake such projects as canned-goods drives, ''Caring Is Sharing'' programs, ''adopt-a-highway'' commitments, tutoring, and scholarship fund-raising.

Environmental Concerns

The 1990s brought awareness of environmental responsibility to all major industries, hospitality included. Hotels and restaurants have been forced to examine their energy use, waste management, and commitment to reducing nonrecyclables. The ''green'' trend has even become a selling point, with some meeting planners requesting that no Styrofoam coffee cups be used and that recycling bins for aluminum cans be placed near break tables.

Airlines have also been pressured to reconsider their meal packaging, which generates tons of garbage daily. Noise pollution has become a major consideration in airport expansion and route assignment. Desert-zone golf courses have received criticism for their use of water resources. Golf courses everywhere have had to examine their use of fertilizers and pesticides. Tourism developers have learned the hard way that they must consider not only physical environmental impacts, but also sociological ones, particularly in Third World locations or in sites with fragile ecosystems. You'll read more about environmental concerns as they apply to specific areas in upcoming chapters.

Eye Openers

It's Not All Resorts and Disney Worlds

Discussions of trends in hospitality customarily focus on the corporate side of the industry. This is the visible and often more glamorous part of the iceberg. Fewer facts and figures are known about the independent side, one-unit enterprises, ''mom-and-pop'' operations, and so on. That doesn't lessen their importance or potential desirability as career options. Independence or I-want-to-do-it-my-way entrepreneurship may be your work style or lifestyle. Thousands of corporate restaurant managers and chefs have been heard to dream aloud of owning their own restaurants. Still other managers long for a low-pressure, non-urban lifestyle in towns that cannot support luxurious operations.

Smaller Operations

Let's not ignore the options of smaller operations, whether they be total independents or franchises of modest chains. As owner or general manager of

Exhibit 1–10

At the opposite end of the spectrum from megahotels and resorts, bed and breakfasts offer a personal slower-paced option for travelers.

Courtesy: Dena Dierker, Dierker Design, 86001.

a small property, *you* are the boss, *you* set policy, and *you* set your hours. (Of course, the hours you set yourself may, of necessity, be quite demanding.) When making your career plans, don't overlook this huge, but less well-publicized side of the industry as a small restaurateur, hotelier, or bed and breakfast owner. *So You Want to Be an Innkeeper . . .* offers these thoughts:[16]

> There is a timeless quality to innkeeping. The work never seems to be done, interrupted by the phone, sporadic eating patterns, late-night arrivals, a water heater that burns out when the inn is full, a travel writer who arrives unannounced when the septic tank is being pumped.
>
> . . . Your whole idea of how to use time is changed . . . Time off tends to be in snatches; the concept of a "weekend" grows increasingly foreign; "quitting time" disappears.
>
> On the other hand there are opportunities to sit down and enjoy pieces of the day most nine-to-fivers don't have: a late breakfast in the garden on a slow weekday . . . evening wine with interesting guests.

Private owners need the same arsenal of management skills as corporate managers. Accounting, financial, marketing, leadership, and problem-solving skills are still needed—and often need to be augmented with "fix-it" skills, since there is no handy engineering department to call upon. By the same token, hands-on ability must pick up where theory leaves off. A private owner often has to do his or her own market research, copy writing, menu planning, health-code compliance, bookkeeping, and so on. For many, this can be a satisfying combination that complements individual personality or lifestyle preference.

Conclusion

Hospitality management covers an enormous scope of opportunity across many enterprises ranging from the more familiar hotel and restaurant arena to the realm of adventure tourism or stadium management. To a great degree, all these enterprises can be categorized as service industries, since they deliver an intangible product different from the more concrete products of manufacturing or agriculture. The concept of service has been extended to mean an overall attitude displayed by all employees and designed to ensure guest satisfaction.

The industry is fast moving and international in scope, with good growth potential projected for the next 10 to 20 years. It has gained respect in the past 25 years for its positive economic impact and as a nationally and internationally significant provider of employment.

Hospitality continues to embrace technology as a means of providing improved service. Technology, which, 100 years ago, was limited to guest room

telephones (a big deal when New York City's Netherlands Hotel installed them in 1894), now includes worldwide reservations systems, one-button customer account information access, and "smart" guest room technology. Hospitality has jumped on the Internet, too. In 1994 Pizza Hut pioneered a World Wide Web log-on order connection that received customers' orders through a Wichita, Kansas, clearinghouse and routed them back to the chain's nearest outlet.

The diversity included in hospitality, leisure, recreation, travel, and tourism enterprises offers career opportunities of interest to those with managerial, technical, or creative priorities. It offers a satisfying stage for those who want to star in service.

Each of the upcoming chapters will focus in on important areas of the industry, giving you your first glimpse of what goes on (in and out of public sight) to enable delivery of superior service. So, if you'll step this way, we've made a reservation for you, and everything is ready . . .

Keywords

overbuilding   13
baby boomers   16
infrastructure   22

destination-management companies   22
perishable inventories   26

Core Concepts

amenities   8
empowerment   10

Mack truck theory   11
ripple effect/multiplier   23

Discussion Questions

1. Why is it important for a company to have a clear understanding of its identity? Why should managers be quite clear on their company's identity?

2. Describe three ''signals of attention'' that can be used effectively with guests. Suggest another one, not listed in the chapter, that you think would also be effective.

3. Describe the gender shift in hospitality manager roles since 1970.

4. What are two demographic groups being recruited in the face of labor shortages?

5. Give a short description of baby boomers and their characteristics. List four baby boomers with whom you are personally acquainted. Do they appear to fit the description?

6. List 10 amenities that might be found in resort guest rooms. Brainstorm three amenities not listed in the chapter. Remember to keep cost in mind.

Managerial Leadership for the Hospitality Industry

This chapter introduces you to the skills, responsibilities, attitudes, and ethical behavior needed by hospitality managers. It includes an outline for appraising your personal assets as well as your personal liabilities. Other sections describe what managers do and identify the knowledge and competencies needed by managers in the hospitality industry at present and into the next two decades. A particularly important competency is that of *ethical competency,* a characteristic that enhances every manager's merit and quality of life.

Outline

Introduction: Measuring Yourself for a Management Career

By enrolling in a program designed to prepare you for managerial leadership responsibility in the hospitality industry, you have positively identified yourself as a dreamer with direction. While you dream of managing a hotel or restaurant—or perhaps something more—you also understand that fulfilling your dream will take professional preparation.

It is a rare individual who has not thought at some point that he or she could do a better job than those they've observed managing a business in the hospitality industry, be it a country club, a theme park, a resort, or some other enterprise that caters to guests. When you visualize yourself as such a smooth and effective manager, what do you imagine? Someone who:

- Consistently demonstrates a set of qualities called leadership skills?
- Is sensitive to people and inspires them toward accomplishment of common organizational goals?
- Possesses a combination of integrity, loyalty, and accountability?

This snapshot of managerial traits sounds pretty formidable, but developing these characteristics is far from impossible. Ordinary men and women in managerial leadership positions in the hospitality industry demonstrate them time and again.

Succeeding as a manager in the highly competitive hospitality industry is no snap. Economic conditions, labor trends, ethical implications, demographic shifts, and many other factors often create complexities that look relatively simple from the outside. But success is possible—in fact, probable—if you can weld two vital elements together. Good managers superglue their classroom learning (analytical and decision-making skills) with leadership skills, solid character traits, and good old-fashioned management ethics. Fusing these critical elements is essential if you want to succeed.

This chapter explains the main factors you'll need to consider in deciding whether hospitality management is right for you. This includes an outline for appraising your personal resources, talents, skills, strengths, potentials, and weaknesses. Later sections describe four basic management functions shared by all managers: planning, organizing, leading, and controlling. Let's translate these into active terms.

- *Planning.* Setting objectives and deciding how the organization is to accomplish its goals.
- *Organizing.* Developing a structure within which the work to be done is defined and coordinated.
- *Leading.* Inspiring people to achieve goals with high performance.
- *Controlling.* Evaluating performance towards achieving an organization's goals.

These functions are set against a background that will allow you to judge your affinity for them. A case study will even let you test-drive them—before you decide whether to pursue a hospitality industry management career.

This chapter will not put you in charge—that's something you must do for yourself. Its contents, however, will certainly give you insights into the strengths needed for success. Like a *Mobil Guidebook,* it will note attractions and warn against chancy detours. Beyond that, it will show you the exciting industry that awaits you—one that offers a profession filled with integrity, service to others, honor, loyalty, and self-satisfaction. We expect a solid increase in the need for college-educated hospitality industry managers into the 21st century. By the time the century changes, you could be well on your way to success.

Your Most Important Assets

From the moment you decide to become a manager, you have chosen to put yourself in charge—to make positive things happen. Before you reach that awesome point, though, you will have to do several things. Some of them are fairly obvious, such as learning to express yourself and learning to plan, organize, lead, and control in a business setting. Yet, long before you even start all that, you need to do something else: Step back and ask yourself, "Am I the right person to do this?"

The Heart of the Dream

We are all conditioned by our culture to dream about managing a business as being the ultimate career goal. That, in many minds, is having it made. Many of us have been spoon-fed success stories about Conrad Hilton, Ellsworth Statler, Howard Johnson, Donald Trump, J. W. Marriott, and Ray Kroc (the

EXHIBIT 2–1

A business conduct guide demonstrates a corporate-level concern that all members of management act in a legal and ethical manner.

Certificate of Compliance

Marriott Corporation
Business Conduct Guide

Marriott

Date _____

Mr. J.W. Marriott, Jr.
President
Marriott Corporation
One Marriott Drive
Washington, D.C. 20058

Dear Mr. Marriott:

I certify that (i) I have read the Marriott Corporation Business Conduct Guide including CP-43 set forth in the appendix, and (ii) I am and will continue to be in compliance with the policies referred to therein.

Signed,

SIGNATURE _____

PRINT NAME _____

PRINT TITLE _____

Please print your name and title under your signature and return no later than two weeks following your receipt of the guide.

Courtesy: Marriott Corporation, Marriott Drive, Washington, DC 20013.

founder of the McDonald's empire). The mystique of going from ''scratch'' to success on such a scale is really the nucleus of this dream—a carrot-on-a-stick wish for many who wonder about going into the hospitality business.

Though only a tiny few will ever do so fantastically well, many among the millions of men and women in management earn comfortable incomes for themselves and their families. And they do so without the extraordinary luck of good timing or the unusual insight that has contributed to some of the super successes. They achieve their success with hard work, careful planning, and a realistic grasp of their own abilities and the world around them. Rest assured, they know their own resources, their personal strong points, and their limitations quite well.

Many Approaches

There are several ways to go about appraising your personal resources. The only one of real importance, though, is a thorough and careful self-examination. You can seek opinions of friends, relatives, and associates, but be wary—they aren't any more objective than you are. If you want to go to the effort and expense, you can consult experts to test various aspects of your personality and intelligence. Your campus may have career or testing counselors available to help you. If not, you will find specialists under psychologists or psychometric services in the classified listings of an urban telephone directory. Such opinions and test results should be considered only a double-check on what you conclude about yourself. Facing up to yourself and saying: ''I'm good at this and this; not good at that and that; and so-so on these,'' is essential. You have to know what you can do, and you have to know yourself before you can determine that.

We hope to offer you some guidance on how to go about such a self-appraisal. Much research has been done to identify the character traits of the successful business manager. One study identified them as:

- Drive
- Thinking ability
- Human relations ability
- Communications ability
- Technical knowledge

Another study identified them as:

- Perception
- Boldness
- Persistence
- Persuasion
- Ethics

You can devise your own checklist to rate your personality and capabilities, perhaps using a scale of 1 to 10. But be honest—you will not be fooling anyone but yourself.

Environment

Managers are role models, whether they like it or not, and whether they believe it or not. Announcing a recycling plan is all very good. Giving awards and certificates to recyclers of the month is admirable. But one of the true engines of a recycling program is the visible participation of management. When your employees see you using scratch paper made from last week's promotional flyer or carefully taking your soda can to the nearest ''blue'' box, the message sinks in.

Personality Inventory

The following list of 11 traits and capabilities is a good place to start a personal inventory. After each, there are some nuts and bolts questions to help you bring the trait into focus.

• **Initiative.** Are you a self-starter, even on tasks that aren't pleasant, or do you tend to procrastinate? Do you have to be reminded to take out the trash and mail your bills, or do you anticipate and prepare for such chores?

• **Leadership.** Do you enjoy directing the efforts of others, inspiring positive responses? Or do you hate to boss people around? Do you find yourself constantly impatient with people's imperfections? Can you stand up and direct what must happen, even if it is unpopular?

• **Sensitivity.** Do you genuinely like people and enjoy being involved with them? Do you think you could continue to feel ''people positive'' if you had to deal with intolerant and abusive guests? With less than motivated or competent employees? Are you outgoing, or do you tend to be introspective and enjoy being alone? Are you willing to concentrate your efforts on pleasing the 5 percent of your guests and employees who are critical and discriminating in their tastes? (If you can do that, the other 95 percent will probably take care of themselves.)

• **Responsibility.** Do you like being counted on to deliver, or would you prefer that others bear that burden? Do you want to be considered dependable, reliable? Can you accept blame when something goes wrong, even though you may not be directly responsible?

• **Organizational ability.** Do you readily see what needs to be done to accomplish a job and how to go about it? Do you like to plan activities and see them carried out, or do you consider yourself more of an ''idea person'' who would rather leave all the administrative details to others?

EXHIBIT 2–2

Conrad N. Hilton (1887–1979), one of America's hospitality pioneers, combined exceptional leadership skills with high personal standards to develop one of the world's best-known hotel chains.

Courtesy: Conrad N. Hilton Archives, University of Houston, Houston, Texas.

• **Industry.** Do you like to work and can you do it for long hours, or do you expect to work less when you are the manager? Can you concentrate on a task and stay with it until it is done, or do you typically walk away from a job the minute you get bored?

• **Decisiveness.** Do you like to make decisions? Do you make them thoughtfully, carefully, firmly, and promptly—or do you tend to shoot from the hip, let things work themselves out, or perhaps pass the buck to others? (Deciding not to decide is a decision in itself.)

• **Health status.** Are your body and mind together? Do you have the physical stamina and emotional stability to take the hard labor and mental stress that are part of managing? Can you take disappointment and frustration, or are you easily discouraged and inclined to become depressed easily? Or would you prefer not to sweat and worry at all?

• **Moral character.** Are you a person of character who is trustworthy, treats people with respect, is responsible, is fair, is caring, and is a good citizen? Or are you considering a management career to take advantage of the ''fools'' that comprise the paying guests? Do you plan to use ''do unto others before they do it unto me'' as a management philosophy? You will have to decide whether you are going to follow that route or hold fast to the Golden Rule: ''Do unto others as you would have them do unto you.''

• **Knowledge and intelligence.** Do you have skills or technical knowledge that you can use in the industry, and do you have the ability and willingness to learn the things you do not know? Are you willing to study and listen to advice, or do you think you know everything? Do you have the open-mindedness it takes to grasp new ideas and new areas of knowledge, or are you satisfied to consider only what is comfortable?

• **Self-image.** Do you like yourself and take pride in your appearance and ability? Do you have confidence in yourself? Or do you figure that how you look is nobody's business? Do you worry that people might not like you, or that you might not be smart enough to make it as a manager?

This self-assessment could go on forever, of course, and for some it could become an easy way of talking oneself out of doing anything. The greater risk, though, would be sidestepping a full and realistic self-evaluation.

Step Back and Look

No matter what method you choose or what criteria you use, holding the mirror to yourself in honest appraisal is a forerunner to success. If you take inventory now and identify a weakness, such as poor speaking ability, you can take steps to improve. If you wait until the time you finally realize you need a skill, you'll be hard-pressed to acquire it overnight.

Here are some questions to ask the mirror: Do you hate to plan and organize and do paperwork? Do you dread such office work because your strength lies in socializing with guests? If so, you might think twice about pursuing upper management. As a manager, you can count on spending a great deal of time and energy on planning, organizing, and so on. This isn't optional and it isn't temporary. It will be a constant throughout your career. If you enjoy that kind of work or at least recognize the need for it enough to tolerate it—but feel unsure how to go about some of it—do not worry. You can learn quickly enough in most cases.

EXHIBIT 2–3

Ask yourself, can I live up to Ritz-Carlton's standards?

THREE STEPS OF SERVICE

1

A warm and sincere greeting. Use the guest name, if and when possible.

2

Anticipation and compliance with guest needs.

3

Fond farewell. Give them a warm good-bye and use their names, if and when possible.

"We Are Ladies and Gentlemen Serving Ladies and Gentlemen"

THE RITZ-CARLTON

CREDO

The Ritz-Carlton Hotel is a place where the genuine care and comfort of our guests is our highest mission.

We pledge to provide the finest personal service and facilities for our guests who will always enjoy a warm, relaxed yet refined ambience.

The Ritz-Carlton experience enlivens the senses, instills well-being, and fulfills even the unexpressed wishes and needs of our guests.

THE RITZ-CARLTON BASICS

1 The Credo will be known, owned and energized by all employees.

2 Our motto is: "We are Ladies and Gentlemen serving Ladies and Gentlemen". Practice teamwork and "lateral service" to create a positive work environment.

3 The three steps of service shall be practiced by all employees.

4 All employees will successfully complete Training Certification to ensure they understand how to perform to The Ritz-Carlton standards in their position.

5 Each employee will understand their work area and Hotel goals as established in each strategic plan.

6 All employees will know the needs of their internal and external customers (guests and employees) so that we may deliver the products and services they expect. Use guest preference pads to record specific needs.

7 Each employee will continuously identify defects (Mr. BIV) throughout the Hotel.

8 Any employee who receives a customer complaint "owns" the complaint.

9 Instant guest pacification will be ensured by all. React quickly to correct the problem immediately. Follow-up with a telephone call within twenty minutes to verify the problem has been resolved to the customer's satisfaction. Do everything you possibly can to never lose a guest.

10 Guest incident action forms are used to record and communicate every incident of guest dissatisfaction. Every employee is empowered to resolve the problem and to prevent a repeat occurrence.

11 Uncompromising levels of cleanliness are the responsibility of every employee.

12 "Smile – We are on stage." Always maintain positive eye contact. Use the proper vocabulary with our guests. (Use words like – "Good Morning," "Certainly," "I'll be happy to" and "My pleasure").

13 Be an ambassador of your Hotel in and outside of the work place. Always talk positively. No negative comments.

14 Escort guests rather than pointing out directions to another area of the Hotel.

15 Be knowledgeable of Hotel information (hours of operation, etc.) to answer guest inquiries. Always recommend the Hotel's retail and food and beverage outlets prior to outside facilities.

16 Use proper telephone etiquette. Answer within three rings and with a "smile." When necessary, ask the caller, "May I place you on hold." Do not screen calls. Eliminate call transfers when possible.

17 Uniforms are to be immaculate; Wear proper and safe footwear (clean and polished), and your correct name tag. Take pride and care in your personal appearance (adhering to all grooming standards).

18 Ensure all employees know their roles during emergency situations and are aware of fire and life safety response processes.

19 Notify your supervisor immediately of hazards, injuries, equipment or assistance that you need. Practice energy conservation and proper maintenance and repair of Hotel property and equipment.

20 Protecting the assets of a Ritz-Carlton Hotel is the responsibility of every employee.

1092

Do you tend to throw yourself wholeheartedly and single-mindedly into whatever you are doing? You might want to take another look at your prospects, particularly if you have a family. You must keep in mind that you and your family must have time together, not just to eat and sleep, but to *be* with each other. Some sacrifices may be required, but asking your family to live on pure hopeful dedication is unfair and unwise.

On Being a Manager

Being a manager means being involved in several different types of relationships—with guests, employees, owners, vendors, bankers, accountants, and, yes, government officials. Some of these relationships will be as equal to equal; other relationships will require you to take a dominant, dependent, or subordinate role. You will have to determine what each of your relationships should be. This may mean:

- Acknowledging that, as a manager, you will answer to owners who may not always be fair, or even sensible.
- Realizing that while guests may be unreasonable, you cannot talk back to them.
- Accepting the fact that a supplier may leave you absolutely ''hanging'' through sheer stupidity.
- Understanding that your employees may not share your work ethic or your standards.
- Being willing to admit you have made a mistake, and doing whatever is necessary to correct it.

If any of these relationship realities seem unacceptable to you, perhaps you should reconsider your dream of becoming a manager, because unreasonable guests, unreliable suppliers, and your own mistakes are inevitable factors in managing any business.

Successful managers, in a sense, make the fewest, smallest, and least costly mistakes. Everyone is going to make errors; the difference is this: A successful manager will minimize the damage and learn from the experience. The professional perfectionist—the person who cannot stand to make the tiniest little mistake—does not belong in the imperfect world of managerial leadership.

Devil's Advocate

In a similar vein, a manager runs a great risk of failure if he or she cannot face up to and cope with his or her own areas of weakness. In many cases, a manager may be unwilling or afraid to hire someone to handle a function about which he or she feels insecure or inadequate. Even if he or she does hire someone, it may be with the subconscious wish that the person will fail, since failure would remove the perceived threat. How do you think you would react in such a situation? Do you think you could see past your insecurity and realize that the whole objective of hiring a qualified person is to improve the performance of the business? If not, maybe you should not think of management as a career—or limit yourself to managing a business with no growth potential and no need to hire new employees. Unfortunately for you, that latter category would pretty much exclude the hospitality industry.

We have been playing the devil's advocate a bit here with these negative questions, but some students find this approach helpful. It's hard to pose questions to yourself about situations you've never been in. It's also hard to know what specialty suits you best when you have no clear conception of the traits that will help you shine or make you stumble in a given area. Listing your strengths and weaknesses will not only help you make the basic decision about becoming a manager; it will also help you decide which segment of the hospitality industry suits you best.

There are a couple of simple tests that will help you decide. One is to ask yourself, What can I offer the marketplace?

- If you have a food production background and the drive it takes to coordinate a food service program, perhaps you'd shine in some sort of managerial position in the food and beverage area.
- If you are gregarious and persuasive, but not particularly strong in operations-related knowledge, perhaps some managerial position in the marketing department of a major resort would be a good goal.
- If you like serving people and enjoy seeing their pleasure at being entertained, perhaps an attraction management position in a theme park would best suit your personality.
- If you like planning large events with themes, music, lights, atmosphere—and clockwork timing—perhaps you'll find your place in the sun as a catering manager.

Study Others

Look around at the people who are already in the hospitality industry. Are you like them? Would you enjoy being around them, competing with them, and working with them to solve industry problems? That would be a plus, since there is a good chance you will be involved in trade associations, chambers of commerce, or other business groups. Beyond that, how would you feel about being labeled? Your customers and your suppliers will closely identify you with what you manage. You may find yourself called a *foodie* or *hotelie* (with varying degrees of admiration attached). If the thought bothers you, it is time to be thinking of something else—or to be re-examining your values.

A final note: Hospitality is not homogenized. Be aware that persons of every age, color, religion, and political persuasion, with an overwhelming array of physical, mental, and emotional disabilities, are managing things and leading people in the hospitality industry—successfully. If you are used to being surrounded by people just like you, you may find this stimulating, startling—or both.

EXHIBIT 2–4

If you have a food production background and the drive it takes to coordinate a food service background, perhaps you would shine in some sort of managerial position in the food and beverage area.

Ethics

What will you do when you find yourself in your first real office, with a door to close and no time clock to punch? Will you strive to be on time every morning? Or will you perhaps be one of those managers who uses the hour or so before the official workday begins to get a head start on the day?

Will you treat your employees with respect regardless of their rank, or will you emphasize in subtle (or blatant) ways that you are the boss? Will you back up your employees when they make decisions in your absence—even when you may not agree with them? Is it more important to honor their decisions (in areas you've made them responsible for) or honor your own interior feelings on the subject? Think about it . . .

The basic personal requirements for successful managers are these:

- The ability to express yourself.
- The desire to succeed.
- A willingness to serve.
- Possession of appropriate leadership skills.
- Good old-fashioned integrity.

If you can develop these requirements in the classroom and on the job, we just might be able to breathe a little more easily about the future of the hospitality industry and, for that matter, the future of our society. Possessing these traits will certainly bode well for *your* future.

What Managers Do

To be a successful manager of a hotel or restaurant, you must focus obsessively on service and quality. To achieve these objectives will require that you lead every employee in your organization to a conscious goal of implementing quality and service in every contact with every guest. That will not happen unless you, the manager, know where you are going with your hotel or restaurant. You cannot know that until you establish a plan for your business that includes specific goals, policies, and procedures—and systems for meeting them.

Let us begin our overview of what managers do by thinking through the operation of a hotel or restaurant with a mind towards setting policies in every one of the several major areas of management responsibility.

As many of this text's chapters will indicate, it is not enough merely to set policies—you must also establish systems and procedures to enforce them, which means setting up adequate measurements and records to tell you how well your staff is complying with them.

Systems, procedures, and records exist to improve the efficiency of the organization; they are the basic tools in the manager's decision-making process. If you do not use these tools, you will be rowing your hotel or restaurant upstream without a paddle.

The Business's Character

Every business in the hospitality industry has a personality of its own, reflecting the nature of the business and the personality of the manager. This is commonly referred to as the *character* of the business. A business's character can, to some extent, be established consciously. A logical and effective way of doing it is to define policies carefully and objectively.

It is better to set these policies as you begin and change them if experience dictates than to set them as you go along. If you start out vaguely, you will end up not knowing where you are going, and the business will be running you—ragged and rudderless—into the bleak night of bankruptcy.

Setting policy standardizes your operation, and permits you to exercise what is sometimes called the **exception principle** of effective business management: When you and your employees know and follow policies, systems, and procedures, it frees you to handle the exceptional situations, the ones that do not fit the plan. If the plan is well developed, this can be a powerful approach to creative management.

Hard-Nosed Positivism

Policy has to be set in the context of the world around you, including the customs in your city or region, the economic conditions, and the sea of government rules and regulations on which your business will be floating.

You may think that in these days of consumerism and environmentalism—with all the elements of employee health, safety, morale, equal rights, sexual harassment, downsizing, inflation, and taxes—that there is little policy-setting discretion left to the manager. This is hardly the case.

First, all these areas of regulation impose only an extra layer of need for policies; the basic need for policy exists even without them. Second, you cannot blame the rules if you do not succeed. The competition has to live under pretty much the same rules. Creative, aggressive managers approach regulation as a challenge, and set their business policies to (at least) minimize the detrimental effects of regulation, and to (at best) turn the rules to profitable advantage.

Hard-nosed positivism is the best approach to setting policy. Be optimistic, upbeat, and positive as you look at any policy-setting area, but at the

EXHIBIT 2–5

Ray Kroc, founder of McDonald's, had the vision to imagine a chain of golden arches across America. He, like virtually all "super successes," combined his vision with hard work, careful planning, and realism.

Courtesy: McDonald's Corporation, Oakbrook, Illinois.

same time put it through the most critical test of all: Look at it through the eyes of your toughest customer.

Policy Areas

Here is a summary of 11 major management areas for which policy needs to be set:

• *Sales.* Without sales you have no revenues, and without revenues, you have no profit. That sounds simple, but sales do not just happen. They are the result of planned and systematic action. Since they are not an activity beyond your control, you must set policy regarding them. What you decide will, for instance, determine if your approach will be hard sell, highly personalized, low key, high volume, or customer driven. The sales policy will be one of the key areas in setting the style of your operation.

• *Credit.* When you set up your credit policies, you'll find that some of your decisions have been made for you in the form of limits. How far will your suppliers trust you? How long will they carry you without charging late fees or interest? What is the ceiling amount they will let you charge on account? If you have to delay payment, how much will it cost you—in interest or carrying charges, or forgone cash discounts, and so on? You might also set guidelines for your use of credit. It's a dangerous thing to use credit for payroll, but a necessary thing to use it for elevator repair. Beyond that, you will need to reach some agreement with yourself, either cautioning yourself—for example, "I will be especially watchful about how much credit I take advantage of, since I tend to spend too much that way"—or giving yourself permission—for example, ''I have to relax a little and learn to live with buying on credit without worrying, since using credit is necessary to the success of the business.''

• *Purchasing.* Buying goods and services for your business may seem to be a simple matter: Buy at the best price and on the best terms you can get, right? Wrong.

As a management policy, you need to know how much of what to buy from whom, when, and how. As you manage your business, you must find suitable sources of supply, negotiate terms (such as cash-and-carry discounts, credit arrangements, and returns), establish and maintain favorable relations with suppliers, and set up delivery arrangements.

One of the first policy questions a manager faces with regard to purchasing is: Do I diversify purchases, or concentrate them? In a small motel or café, particularly a young one, it is probably better to concentrate buying in one or a few places, while retaining the option to change readily if needs dictate. Here is where your personal character can be a particular asset. By concentrating your purchases with one or two suppliers, you can build credibility (based on your character) as well as creditability (based on your payment history).

If you run a larger property, you will likely have the budget or the clout to deal with vendors or negotiate contracts on your own terms. Be wary, though, of getting locked into contracts that tie you up. Economies of scale are very important, but sometimes a contracted price break can turn out to be a management shackle. **Economies of scale,** in this case, simply mean you receive the advantage of volume discounts in purchasing supplies, equipment, and advertising.

• *Prices.* What you charge for your food, services, or rooms will be determined in part by your chosen policy. You can decide that your profit margin is going to be 5 percent or 100 percent, depending on a combination of what it costs you to provide the product or service and how much it is worth to the guest. If the two do not match, something will have to change, or you will be out of business soon.

• *Inventory.* Managing stock, particularly in the restaurant business, amounts to an exercise in the juggling arts—knowing when to order products so they are available when you need them, not long before nor too late after. Experience is the best teacher, but considerable thought must be given to the subject before you fill the first bin. Here are some factors that may affect your inventory policy.

It costs money to maintain inventory. Expenses include the basic cost of the goods, plus interest on credit, handling costs, depreciation, taxes, insurance, and storage. Such extras can add up to as much as 25 percent of the basic inventory investment. In short, you do not want too much stock just sitting around. On the other hand, carrying too little inventory may be expensive in other ways, particularly if it results in expensive rush orders, service delays, or running out of an item.

Inventory problems can be avoided to a great extent by establishing a system of control. Much of the intricacy of inventory control has been simplified through technology and electronic recordkeeping, but part of it still lies in the realm of management ''arts.'' This is an ability separate from science: the art of anticipating supply problems. Though it may seem that some managers have a sixth sense about such things, they more likely have an excellent grasp of conditions in the supply market that helps them anticipate shortages, delays, or other management problems that suppliers may have upcoming.

• *Personnel.* Any business is only as good as the people who work in it. Elements of personnel policy range from whom you hire to how you fire. They also include pay, benefits, training, working conditions and hours, promotions, morale, and labor relations—all in the context of state and federal regulations.

Training requires a conscious policy effort. Even a skilled person deserves an introduction to your way of doing the job. Morale does not make or maintain itself. It requires constant attention. Part of that attention is communication. It's good policy to know when to communicate on the ''broad band'' and when to use the ''closed circuit.'' Praise publicly, but criticize privately. Remember the axiom that in all human relations, most major problems result from neglected minor grievances.

• *Quality control.* In your planning, you should be conscious of the need for quality control and performance standards in your operation. Traditionally, quality control has been thought of as a management technique for manufacturing operations, but the concept can be applied just as readily to the hospitality industry. No matter what you are running, you need some system to assure you that your staff is not only meeting, but anticipating your guests' needs; you have to see to it that the quality of product and service is up to your reputation.

Total quality management (TQM) has been introduced into the hospitality industry by such companies as Ritz-Carlton, Embassy Suites, and Domino's Pizza. Many other companies have adopted its principles to different degrees. Exhibit 2–6 summarizes the seven quality principles commonly included in successful TQM approaches.

Eye on the Issues

International

As a manager you may find yourself working with department heads from foreign cultures—cultures that have different values than you are used to. If someone in the United States behaves in a way that is consistent with such values, you may, perhaps, take issue with their behavior, especially if it conflicts with the law or with accepted business practices. Suppose, though, that it is you who are assigned to a foreign country. How will you react to an environment where, for instance, bribery is an accepted business practice? Or where, perhaps, you must develop and exploit personal connections with someone (a government official, a vendor, and so on) to get things done? Perhaps you will witness women or foreign nationals being treated in what are, to you, unacceptable ways. All these things are possible when you accept overseas assignments.

EXHIBIT 2–6   Seven Principles Common to Successful TQM Approaches

1. **Customer orientation.** The customer defines quality and is the focus of improvement processes.
2. **Empowering leadership.** Management is committed to leading change toward a shared objective and gives authority and resources to individuals so that they may bring about improvement.
3. **Across-the-board employee involvement.** All staff members, at every level, are involved in strategic planning and continuous quality improvement training.
4. **Education and training.** Employees are given opportunities to better understand their jobs and roles. They are given a bigger picture of their part in the organization's processes and encouraged to focus their energies on producing a superior product.
5. **Team approach.** This is the heartbeat of TQM. Here the focus is on collaboration. The team approach solicits multiple perspectives (on product, processes, customer satisfaction, and so on) and capitalizes on each individual's strengths.
6. **Process control.** The team must gain full knowledge of processes and systems, including knowing whether a given process is in control or out of control. Decisions made are based on facts.
7. *Continuous quality improvement* **(CQI).** The organization should no longer be satisfied with meeting an established threshold or endpoint but will strive constantly to provide a higher quality of care and services.

Source: J. Folstad and R. Small, ''The Journey to Total Quality Management,'' *P&T Journal* 18, no. 11 (November 1993), pp. 33–37.

• *Insurance.* Insurance is inescapable, but policy helps decide early on what coverages you will take. It is helpful to think of insurance as an aspect of management called *risk management,* a process for handling liabilities of any kind (physical, legal, financial, and so on). It is possible to reduce some risks by taking precautions; in other cases, the risk can be transferred to someone else for a price less than the potential loss. This is where insurance comes in.

The basic rule here is not to risk any more than you can afford to lose. Nobody can free a business of all risk, but you should not retain any risk you cannot afford to take. It makes no sense to risk heavy possible loss to save a little in premiums, nor is it cost effective to pay insurance for high-probability small losses (like petty pilferage) that cannot be eliminated.

Though there are many types of insurance, you'll find that most of your concerns will fall under one of these five categories of coverage:

- Loss or damage to your property or operation.
- Loss or damage to your own personal property.
- Bodily injury and property damage liability.
- Business interruption coverage.
- Protection against death or disability of key executives.

• *Public relations.* No matter what your business is, it will have an image in your industry and in your community. It is within your power to set and maintain that image as a matter of policy. Public relations policy will cover everything from advertising and promotion programs, which are essential for generating sales and for community relations in both civic and trade association terms, right down to a policy on customer complaints. Doing business means interacting with people, in groups and individually. If you do not make a constructive effort to organize and control your side of those interactions, there may not be another side.

• *Records.* Call it bookkeeping, busy work, a blasted nuisance, paper shuffling, or whatever, keeping records is crucial in the management of a hotel or restaurant. Look back, and you will see the need for records to keep track of where you are in every one of the policy areas this chapter has outlined.

If you do not keep good records, you cannot really tell how your business is doing—and that is inviting disaster. Managing a business without records is the same as traveling from Seattle to Miami without gauges on your dashboard. You may make it, but it is going to be by sheer luck. Ignorance will get you in the end.

On the other hand, there are risks in overorganizing. You should know yourself well enough by now to tell if you will be inclined to swamp yourself or your staff with paperwork.

Some new managers start out with the mistake of reinventing the wheel when it comes to setting up recordkeeping, designing all sorts of tailored forms, files, and complex systems.

Forms can be useful, but they must be designed properly. The best test of a form is to trace its working path from inception to disposition. If it gets tangled up somewhere, back up and rethink the process. Forms should convey something essential, and do so simply, quickly, and clearly. They are management tools, not an end unto themselves.

• *Regular review.* We tend to ignore what our records are telling us, hence the need for another policy: Decide right now that you will create a regular and thorough system of review for your policies, systems, procedures, and records. As your business grows and changes, needs for updating and revision will become apparent. Notice them before it is too late by studying the situation on an established, periodic basis.

• *Planning and budgeting.* There's yet a larger area of management policy that we have not covered—planning and budgeting—though we've hinted at it. It looms behind all the systems, procedures, and records we've talked about establishing. If you do not know by now that you have to forecast your business's activities as accurately as possible and manage them in the context of your budget and management plan, you have not been paying attention. Policies, procedures, systems, and records give form and substance to goals and objectives; they tell you where you have been and where you are. Without them, you are going to have a hard time knowing where you are going.

Becoming a Manager: The American Dream Awaits

Considering all the ground we have covered, it might seem that all there is left to do is simply apply for that general manager's job at the Ritz and move into the executive offices. You may be eager to rush through your education and pursue that dream of managing a hotel or restaurant. Or you may be a little daunted at just how much there is to learn.

Eye on the Issues

Technology

Are you computer literate yet? The sooner you become so, the better. Your hotel/restaurant/institutional management program will no doubt include some required computer courses. Don't just take them to get through them, though; take them with the idea of taking advantage of the tools they'll provide you. When you move out into the industry, you'll encounter people at high levels who are not comfortable with computers. This is often because their training and preparation took place in a time when personal computers were not widely available—or even affordable to average managers. These people, for whatever reason, never had or took the chance to learn how to use a PC.

Other department heads or employees may want to learn to use new programs they've heard about. Newly promoted employees may now have jobs that require them to use PCs and programs, but may feel intimidated by computers. The point is, appreciate your computer skills, be ready to learn new ones, but, as a manager, show compassion for those who haven't had your opportunities. And, if you can, provide training opportunities and encouragement for your staff members. Once they gain proficiency in even one program or activity, they will be willing to try others. By helping them grow, you'll encourage their loyalty to you and your operation.

Executing the Fundamentals

Taking charge. Being the boss. Doing a better job than Joe Schmoe. That is just about where we came in. Right now, management may look like a lonesome world—the thought of being in charge may be awesome when you contemplate everything involved.

Do not talk yourself out of it. Go back now and review the ground we have covered. Think how much you have learned—about yourself, about evaluating your chances to make it happen.

Part of what you have accomplished during this chapter falls under the heading of *critical thinking.* Critical thinking involves comparing, contrasting, balancing what is known with what is theorized, looking at alternatives, weighing possible outcomes, and anticipating reactions and consequences. (See the critical thinking case study in Exhibit 2–7.)

Keep in mind that becoming a manager of a hotel or restaurant is, like any other aspect of life, a matter of executing the fundamentals—fundamentals

Exhibit 2–7 Critical Thinking Case Study

The following case study asks you to apply critical thinking to the management issues involved below. Base your responses on the text and the successful manager character traits identified earlier in this chapter.

Getting into Management

Ms. Labell, the front office manager of a 350-room suburban hotel, has been asked to choose one of her employees for promotion to a managerial position. She has narrowed the choice to either Ms. Kain or Mr. Stull, but is uncertain about the final selection. Ms. Labell jots down the following information as she considers who to recommend:

Ms. Kain	*Mr. Stull*
Leads department in productivity	Has department seniority
Has a college degree	Above-average productivity
Confident	Demonstrates concern for others
Somewhat assertive	Somewhat lacking in personal confidence
Demands high performance of others	High ethical standards
Female	African-American

No matter what happens, Ms. Labell knows that she will have a human relations problem with the employee not selected. Additionally, she knows that she will be evaluated by the hotel general manager on the basis of how successful the new manager performs. Ms. Labell comes to you for advice.

1. Which individual would you select?
2. Upon what factors would you base your decision?

that you can learn in the classroom, on the job, and through self-examination. Be pragmatic. Be realistic. Be objective as you prepare yourself for the promises and pitfalls of a management career in the hospitality industry.

Who Knows What Is Right or Wrong?

Most people in the hospitality industry agree on what is absolutely right—saving someone's life, helping the needy—and what is absolutely wrong—murder, theft, torture. If an employee is caught coming out of the back entrance of a hotel with a shopping bag filled with towels and a manager says, ''You are stealing!'' both employee and manager know exactly what is meant. Lying and stealing are wrong in precisely the same way in the hospitality industry as they are throughout society. The moral and ethical problems of the hospitality industry are essentially the same as the problems of society at large.

Despite their certainties about right and wrong, men or women who value integrity and principle will, however, experience situations on the job that may challenge their perception of those absolutes. In the workplace there are many shades of gray, even in routine, ethical decision making. Many of these gray area decisions are made in the context of economic and professional pressures that compete with ethical principles and often result in deception, cover up, concealment, or blame shifting.

The Language of Ethics

A person may understand very well what the term *ethics* means, but may not be able to define it. Conversely, a person may be able to define *ethics,* yet not know exactly what it means. To make sure we're all on the same wave length, let's look at some thoughts on what this essential term means.

> **Ethics** is the name we give to our concern for good behavior. We feel an obligation to consider not only our own personal well-being, but also that of others and of human society as a whole.
>
> Dr. Albert Schweitzer

> **Ethics** concerns standards of behavior consonant with values that we hold to be important.
>
> Kirk Hanson, director, The Business Enterprise Trust

Hospitality ethics, then, is the study of ethics as it applies to our segment of the business world, the hospitality industry. It aims at developing reasonable ethical standards for our industry. A **code of ethics** is a written standard of conduct consisting of rules or principles (values) on which we've agreed. Having such a code helps us live and work together with a certain level of confidence. It allows us to depend upon and better trust our fellow workers. See Exhibit 2–8 for an example of such a code.

The term *values* refers to learned attitudes or beliefs that individuals consider to be important. The values that we hold are inward motivations that drive our outward actions. Values that relate to our beliefs about *right* or *wrong* (e.g., honesty, integrity, fairness) are ***ethical values.*** Values that are ethically neutral (e.g., ambition, happiness, pleasure) are ***nonethical values.***

Why Should the Hospitality Industry Be Concerned with Ethics?

With increasing frequency we are being bombarded by headlines targeting questionable and sometimes criminal behavior in the hospitality industry:

- ''48 Biltmore Hotel Investors Sue Accountants for $15 Million''
- ''Hooters Restaurant Chain Is Sued: Ex-Waitresses Say They Were Harassed''
- ''Holiday Inns Danced the Tax-Avoidance Two-Step''
- ''Bob Evans Farms Family Restaurant Executive Quits after Pot Raid''

EXHIBIT 2–8

*A code of ethics
developed*

CODE OF ETHICS
HOSPITALITY SERVICE AND TOURISM INDUSTRY

1. We acknowledge ethics and morality as inseparable elements of doing business and will test every decision against the highest standards of honesty, legality, fairness, impunity, and conscience.

2. We will conduct ourselves personally and collectively at all times such as to bring credit to the service and tourism industry at large.

3. We will concentrate our time, energy and resources on the improvement of our own product and services and we will not denigrate our competition in the pursuit of our own success.

4. We will treat all guests equally regardless of race, religion, nationality, creed or sex.

5. We will deliver all standards of service and product with total consistency to every guest.

6. We will provide a totally safe and sanitary environment at all times for every guest and employee.

7. We will strive constantly, in words, actions and deeds, to develop and maintain the highest level of trust, honesty and understanding among guests, clients, employees, employers and the public at large.

8. We will provide every employee at every level all of the knowledge, training, equipment and motivation required to perform his or her tasks according to our published standards.

9. We will guarantee that every employee at every level will have the same opportunity to perform, advance, and will be evaluated against the same standard as all employees engaged in the same or similar tasks.

10. We will actively and consciously work to protect and preserve our natural environment and natural resources in all that we do.

11. We will seek a fair and honest profit, no more, no less.

©1989 IIQEST

Source: International Institute for Quality and Ethics in Service and Tourism Limited (IIQEST).

During the 1980s and early 1990s, ethical misconduct was at the core of many business calamities at companies including Dow-Corning, Phar-mor Drugs, Drexel Furniture, and dozens of savings and loans. The names of executives such as Boesky, Milkin, Helmsley, and Keating were splashed across headlines. The hospitality industry was not immune during this period—as chronicled by the headlines cited—nor were the major accounting firms of Arthur Andersen, Ernst and Young, or Price Waterhouse—all of whom are active in the hospitality industry.

EXHIBIT 2–9

Customer convenience sometimes takes a back seat to ethical considerations, as shown at this Wendy's Restaurant in the Columbus, Ohio, Zoo.

Courtesy: Wendy's International, Dublin, Ohio. Photo by James L. Morgan, 85283.

There are three primary reasons why the hospitality industry and its future managers should be concerned with ethics:

- *Self-interest.* Scandals are expensive. Beyond the fact that they are public relations disasters, they can result in fines, penalties, and possible jail terms.
- *Most people are inclined to act ethically.* Our self-esteem and self-respect depend to a great extent on the private assessment of our own ethical behavior. Most people will alter their conduct if they discover it is inconsistent with their company's culture.
- *TQM programs may expose internal ethics problems.* The employee involvement and empowerment programs being implemented throughout the hospitality industry demand an unprecedented degree of integrity and honesty within a company. These processes often bring to light ethical shortcomings.

Most of you have entered your first jobs with a personal value system in place and a fairly well-developed character. You *want* to be ethical; you *want* to be proud of yourself and what you do for a living. Your self-esteem and self-respect depend on your private assessment of your own character. Very few people are willing to accept the fact that they are not ethical.

If those who manage in our industry convey the idea that adherence to a high standard of personal and professional ethics is a necessity—not an option—in our industry, employees at all levels will get the message.

I Am Just a College Student.
Why Talk to Me about Hospitality Ethics?

Recent studies conclude that the ethical quality of society has worsened in the last few decades. In fact, evidence suggests there is a continuing downward spiral with regard to the ethical and moral behavior of the college-age generation.

A comprehensive report by the Josephson Institute of Ethics titled *The Ethics of American Youth: A Warning and a Call to Action* concluded that an unprecedented proportion of today's youth has severed itself from the traditional moral anchors of American society.[1] Honesty, respect for others, personal responsibility, and civic duty were all found lacking. It might make you angry to hear these things said about your age group, but here is the evidence the report cites:

- *Dishonesty.* Cheating in college is rampant (about 50 percent at most colleges). Anywhere from 12 to 24 percent of résumés contain materially false information, and there is an increasing willingness to lie on financial aid forms and in other contexts where lying benefits the applicant.
- *Civic duty.* Young people are detached from traditional notions of civic duty. They are less involved, less informed, and less likely to vote than any generation previously measured.
- *Violence and disrespect.* Assaults on teachers are up 700 percent since 1978 even though the number of students has gone down; 59 percent of urban teachers have been subjected to verbal abuse by students. In 1986–87, *on school grounds,* there were 3 million incidents of attempted or completed assault, rape, robbery, or theft. More than one in four college women report they have been the victim of rape or attempted rape, 86 percent by dates or acquaintances. Shocking proportions of young men acknowledge predatory attitudes towards women—in one study, 50 percent of the males said they would force a woman to have sex if they were sure they would not get caught.
- *Ethical values.* A significant proportion of the present 18- to 30-year-old generation exhibits an attitudinal shift away from the traditional moral principles of honesty, respect for others, and personal responsibility. Today's youth, when asked, stress personal gratification, materialism, and winning at any cost.

Further evidence of ethical and character erosion in America is found in the book *The Day America Told the Truth—What People Really Believe about Everything That Really Matters.*[2] This treatise, based on a national survey, takes a statistical look into the heart and soul of America. The authors' findings are disturbing. Four of their conclusions are particularly relevant to the hospitality industry:

- The number one cause of business decline in America is unethical behavior by executives.
- The majority of Americans goof off, fake illness, or abuse substances in the workplace.
- Americans have little respect for the property of others. They have a tendency to take anything that is not nailed down—from work, at stores, and on the road.
- The majority of female workers are more ethical and trustworthy than their male counterparts. They are less likely to steal, to fake being sick, to lie to their bosses, to leave work early, and so on. It is imperative that women be looked to for leadership in American business right now.

The Core Consensus Ethical Principles

Managers and supervisors in the hospitality industry routinely face decisions with ethical implications. How they handle those decisions can have a significant impact on the profits, productivity, and long-term success of an organization.

The Josephson Institute of Ethics advocates 10 ethical principles as standards for the kinds of behavior in which an ethical person should and should not engage.[3] The institute believes these core *consensus ethical values* transcend cultural, ethical, and socio-economic differences. The 10 core values are honesty, integrity, trustworthiness, loyalty, fairness, concern and respect for others, commitment to excellence, leadership, reputation and morale, and accountability. These are discussed in more detail in Exhibit 2–10.

The Notion of Stakeholders

A person concerned with being ethical feels obliged to consider the ethical implications of all decisions in light of their possible effects on others. Each person, group, or institution likely to be affected by a decision is a *stakeholder*—a little like a planet circling a sun. Depending on the sun's behavior, a planet may become too hot or too cold, experience violent storms and earthquakes, be knocked out of its orbit, and so on. Unlike the sun, a decision maker can (and must) choose his or her behavior. Those who do not actively and consciously make choices cannot honestly call themselves decision makers; they'd more accurately compare themselves to lemmings or sheep.

The stakeholder concept helps managers examine their particular solar system of interested parties in such a way as to bring about the greatest good. It asks managers to make all reasonable efforts to foresee possible consequences and to take reasonable steps to avoid unjustified harm to innocent stakeholders—an ethical decision maker should never inadvertently cause harm.

EXHIBIT 2–10   **Ten Core Ethical Principles for Hospitality Managers**

Honesty—
Hospitality managers are honest and
    truthful. They do not mislead or deceive
    others by misrepresentations.

Integrity—
Hospitality managers demonstrate the
    courage of their convictions by doing
    what they know is right even when
    there is pressure to do otherwise.

Trustworthiness—
Hospitality managers are trustworthy and
    candid in supplying information and in
    correcting misapprehensions of fact.
    They do not create justifications for
    escaping their promises and
    commitments.

Loyalty—
Hospitality managers demonstrate loyalty
    to their companies in devotion to duty
    and loyalty to colleagues by friendship
    in adversity. They avoid conflicts of
    interest; do not use or disclose
    confidential information; and should
    they accept other employment, they
    respect the proprietary information of
    their former employer.

Fairness—
Hospitality managers are fair and
    equitable in all dealings; they do not
    abuse power arbitrarily nor take undue
    advantage of another's mistakes or
    difficulties. They treat all individuals
    with equality, with tolerance for and
    acceptance of diversity and with an
    open mind.

Concern and Respect for Others—
Hospitality managers are concerned,
    respectful, compassionate and kind.
    They are sensitive to the personal
    concerns of their colleagues and live the
    "Golden Rule." They respect the rights
    and interests of all those who have a
    stake in their decisions.

Commitment to Excellence—
Hospitality managers pursue excellence
    in performing their duties and are
    willing to put more into their job than
    they can get out of it.

Leadership—
Hospitality managers are conscious of the
    responsibility and opportunities of their
    position of leadership. They realize that
    the best way to instill ethical principles
    and ethical awareness in their
    organizations is by example. They walk
    their talk!

Reputation and Morale—
Hospitality managers seek to protect and
    build the company's reputation and the
    morale of its employees by engaging in
    conduct that builds respect and by
    taking whatever actions are necessary to
    correct or prevent inappropriate conduct
    of others.

Accountability—
Hospitality managers are personally
    accountable for the ethical quality of
    their decisions as well as those of their
    subordinates.

These 10 ethical principles listed were adapted from a publication of the Josephson Institute of Ethics,
Marina del Rey, California.

Even so, decision makers sometimes deliberately decide to do (or authorize) things they know are wrong. Michael Josephson suggests that there are three major reasons why fundamentally ethical people do things that conflict with their own code of ethics:[4]

- Unawareness or insensitivity.
- Selfishness, self-indulgence, or self-protection.
- Defective reasoning.

Understanding the stakeholder concept does not always lead to good ethical decisions or, for that matter, to ideal conduct. It is, however, a powerful analytical tool that helps decision makers reason through the ethical implications of a decision.

How Do You Decide What Is Ethical?

The Business Roundtable concluded in a recent report that ethical considerations are at stake:

- When people are affected.
- When interests collide.
- When choices must be made between values.[5]

As you might imagine, for people in business that means nearly all the time. This means that you, as a manager, will be constantly choosing between "goods" and "bads"—and sometimes among goods. Which good will you choose? To whom will you listen? Accountants? Lawyers? Owners? That little voice inside? Admiral Arleigh A. Burke, U.S. Navy (Retired), concluded: "Individuals are responsible for their own integrity. They will be influenced by many people and events but, in the end, their integrity quotient is of their own making."

In Exhibits 2–11, 2–12, and 2–13, you'll find some models for thinking through and resolving ethical issues. If you find yourself confused about a decision, try applying each of these models to your problem. Chances are, they will help you understand what is the right thing to do.

EXHIBIT 2–11   The Golden Rule

This most basic and perhaps the most practical of all ethical theories is as valid in business decisions as it is in personal ones. **The Golden Rule** (also called the *rule of reciprocity*) simply states: "Do unto others as you would have them do unto you."

Variations of the Golden Rule are found in the revered writings of Christians, Muslims, Jews, Hindus, and Buddhists, as well as in the works of philosophers and social theorists dating back to 500 BC.

EXHIBIT 2–12   **The Ethics Check Questions**

- Is it legal?
    Will I be violating either civil law or company policy?
- Is it balanced?
    Is it fair to all concerned in the short term as well as the long term?
    Does it promote win-win relationships?
- How will it make me feel about myself?
    Will it make me proud?
    Would I feel good if my decision were published in the newspaper?
    Would I feel good if my family knew about it?

Source: K. Blanchard and N. V. Peale, *The Power of Ethical Management* (New York: William Morrow and Company, 1988), p. 27.

EXHIBIT 2–13   **The Josephson Institute Ethical Decision-Making Model**

- All decisions must take into account and reflect a concern for the interests and well-being of all stakeholders. (This is simply an application of the Golden Rule.)
- Core *ethical* values and principles always take precedence over *nonethical* ones.
- It is ethically proper to violate an ethical principle only when it is clearly necessary to advance another true ethical principle that, according to the decision maker's conscience, will produce the greatest balance of good in the long run.

Source: M. Josephson, *Making Ethical Decisions* (Marina del Rey, CA: Josephson Institute of Ethics, 1992), p. 35.

Conclusion

The reason we have seen so much emphasis on ethics in the hospitality industry recently is not that hospitality managers and employees are any less ethical than managers and employees in other industries. It's more an outgrowth of a changing focus. Until recently, the hospitality industry had not thought much about the concept of corporate culture. Whatever was *was*. This approach had its drawbacks, including high turnover and low employee loyalty. In the last decade or so, companies have realized that they can remodel their corporate cultures and improve their work environments. Many have chosen to build in rewards for positive ethical behavior.

Positive ethics means concentrating on doing what you should do simply because it is the right thing to do. It is knowing the difference between what is right and what is expedient. (*Expediency* is summed up in the phrase, the end justifies the means.) As a manager you will occasionally experience business situations that challenge your commitment to your values. You will have to choose between expediency and responsibility. You will be asked to win at all costs and told, through explicit or subtle messages from your superiors, to meet your quotas or face the consequences. These pressures will often be difficult to handle. Sometimes the only good answer may be confrontation or even a change of employment. It isn't always easy to be ethical—but the best businesspeople are.

The ethical reputation of the hospitality industry is determined by the separate actions of the managers and employees in lodging, food service, and allied businesses. *Your* actions are important on an individual level because those actions, combined with those of your colleagues, establish and define the ethical reputation of the hospitality industry in general.

Two Ethical Problems for Discussion

1. Lynn, a store manager for a small Midwest restaurant chain, is, by all performance measures, the top-rated manager of the chain's restaurants.

   An external audit team discovered that Lynn was pocketing cash from customers and not entering the sales into the cash register. Further investigation determined that Lynn was not personally keeping the money, but was using it to reward her staff with perks, bonuses, and other incentives. This puts Lynn in clear violation of the company's code of ethics.

   As Lynn's district manager, what action should you take to resolve this ethical dilemma?

2. Two HRM majors were talking about the issue of employee theft. Chris asked Kelly if she would steal $1,000,000 if no one else in the world would ever find out. Kelly asked who the money belonged to. Should that make a difference? *Does* that make a difference? Would it be OK to steal the million dollars if it belonged to sadistic terrorists? What if it belonged to no known person (was found just sitting on a table in the student union)?

Keywords

Core Concepts

Discussion Questions

1. What kinds of personality traits or characteristics do you suppose a successful manager should possess? Do you have any of these traits or characteristics?

2. Can a person be taught managerial skills and competencies?

3. Do you agree or disagree with the following statement: "The secret of business success is not *who* you know; it's *what* you know."

4. How would you describe the difference between a leader and a manager?

5. Name 11 major management areas for which policy needs to be set.

6. Four findings from *The Day America Told the Truth—What People Really Believe about Everything That Really Matters* are listed in this chapter. Give one example (from your personal experience or knowledge of current public events) to illustrate each of the four findings.

7. Do you think it is acceptable to be dishonest or to commit criminal acts so long as you accept responsibility for them and are willing to pay the penalty?

8. Suppose you inherited a $20-million company whose wealth was based on whaling (which you abhor) and that has been responsible for decimating the world's whale population. What would you do? (If whaling is not a troublesome venture for you, substitute illicit drug smuggling or production of landmines and assault weapons as the company's source of wealth.)

References

Blanchard, K., and N. V. Peale. *The Power of Ethical Management.* New York: William Morrow and Company, 1988.

Folstad, J., and Small, R. "The Journey to Total Quality Management." *P&T Journal* 18, no. 11 (November 1993), pp. 33–37.

Josephson, Michael. "Teaching Ethical Decision Making and Principled Reasoning." In *Ethics: Easier Said Than Done,* Winter 1988, pp. 29–30.

Josephson, Michael. *Making Ethical Decisions.* Marina del Rey, CA: Josephson Institute of Ethics, 1991.

Josephson Institute of Ethics. *The Ethics of American Youth: A Warning and a Call to Action.* Marina del Rey, CA, October 1990.

Patterson, J., and Kim, P. *The Day America Told the Truth—What People Really Believe about Everything That Really Matters.* New York: Prentice Hall, 1991.

Rest, James R. "Can Ethics Be Taught in the Professional Schools?" *The Psychological Research Journal,* 1988, p. 42.

PART II

Introduction to Components of the Travel and Tourism Industry

There are many hospitality career opportunities that sometimes escape the notice of hospitality management students. This section discusses some of those by placing the hospitality industry within the broader context of travel and tourism.

Each of the many service-oriented businesses discussed in this book contributes to making a tourist's travel experience more satisfactory. The hospitality industry is not only a sector of, but also an integral part of, the travel and tourism industry. It offers travelers comfortable overnight stays and memorable dining experiences. As a hospitality manager, therefore, it is important to know the functions of and relationships among the different sectors in the travel and tourism industry. Once you view the travel and tourism industry as a functional system, you will be in a better position to anticipate changes in the industry and predict how they will affect your operation. Knowledge about people's travel behavior will give you a ''leg up'' on the competition. Such foresight will enable you to plan and position your business better.

Chapters 3, 4, and 5 discuss many aspects of the travel and tourism industry. Chapter 3 stresses the importance of understanding the travel and tourism industry as a functional system. It studies the travel history in both Western and Eastern civilizations and defines the terminologies commonly used in travel and tourism studies. The transportation sector and the travel agency operations are specifically discussed in this chapter, and the working relationship between hoteliers and travel agents is emphasized.

Chapter 4 focuses on the specialized world of resorts, clubs, attractions, and events. It compares resort hotels with nonresorts and offers insight into the unique management aspects associated with seasonal resorts. This chapter also opens the door to a segment often overlooked by hospitality programs—

that of private club management—one of the fastest growing hospitality specialties. Resorts, clubs, attractions, and events have the drawing power to pull tourists to destinations, and are vital to the success of the tourism industry.

Chapter 5 explores casino and gaming management, the fastest growing segment of the hospitality industry in the United States. It starts out by tracing the history of gaming, explains how governments are involved in the regulation of the gaming industry, and discusses current gaming developments, such as Indian gaming and riverboat gaming. The second part describes the games commonly played in casinos and analyzes management responsibilities associated with operating and controlling them. Students interested in management opportunities in gaming will find this an interesting introduction to this dynamic segment of the industry.

The appendix at the end of this section offers a look at the processes and concerns involved in developing a tourist destination. It demonstrates a community-oriented development approach that has proven effective when developing tourism for a particular destination area, including a detailed assessment of tourism resources and tourist markets, and emphasizing cooperation among a wide range of agencies, developers, and hospitality and tourism operators.

All three chapters will touch on current issues facing the travel and tourism industry and offer unique and realistic perspectives on these issues.

The Travel and Tourism Industry

Travel and tourism is offered as either a required or an elective course in most hospitality management schools. It introduces hospitality management majors to the complexity and interdependence of various aspects of the travel and tourism industry. It focuses on historical travel development, types of visitors, transportation systems, and travel agency operations. The chapter presents an overview of the travel and tourism industry, and emphasizes the importance of a good working relationship between hoteliers and travel agents.

Outline

Introduction

The travel and tourism industry is highly diverse and fragmented. It encompasses all aspects of the hospitality industry that serve the needs and wants of people who are away from home. *Travel and tourism* is thus an umbrella term that includes all businesses that offer travel products and services directly and indirectly to the travelers.

The ***travel and tourism industry*** is a system with mutually interdependent components. This concept can be best understood by considering the spring break trip to Miami you may have taken last year. Before you started traveling, you first went to **Campus Travel** to purchase an airline ticket and make a car rental reservation. Then you flew **American Airlines** to Miami and picked up a **Budget** rental car at the airport. You then drove to the beachfront **Holiday Inn** and checked into your hotel room. In the evening, you met your friends and had dinner at **China Coast** (a chain of Chinese restaurants developed by General Mills). After dinner you strolled along the beach and bought several small souvenirs at a retail shop called **Little Havana.** This description of your first day in Miami vividly demonstrates that your travel needs could not be met without the services of travel agents, airlines, car rental companies, lodging accommodations, food services, and other retail services.

From the perspective of the travel and tourism industry, every segment of the industry depends on the others to provide a complete and satisfactory travel service and experience to tourists. Such interdependence illustrates the complex nature of the travel and tourism industry and presents a challenge to hospitality managers. If you, as a future manager, do not understand the interconnections between all segments of the travel and tourism industry, you cannot anticipate the changes occurring in other parts of the industry and the ripple effects of those changes on the whole industry.

This is indeed the main reason why a travel and tourism course is normally offered to hotel and restaurant management majors. The understanding of travel and tourism as a functional system can enhance students' perspectives on the whole industry, enable them to analyze industry trends better, and develop aggressive and successful working relationships with other sectors of the industry.

A Brief Travel History

Travel can be traced back as early as humanity's first existence. However, in the modern sense of the word, travel did not occur until the Agricultural Revolution (around 8000 BC) when human beings became settled farmers and built their permanent homes. Travel came to be understood as encompassing activities away from home. Because of their novelty and/or significance, major historical travel events have been outlined and discussed ever since the Agricultural Revolution.

The Ancient World

Travel in the ancient world was limited to certain people in society. The word *travel* has a French origin, *travail,* meaning "toil and labor." Travel thus meant adventure, hardship, and risk, especially in ancient times. Ancient people traveled for various purposes, such as pleasure, trade, scientific exploration, and religious pilgrimage.

The ancient Romans and Greeks were the most famous ancient pleasure seekers. Travel in Europe during Roman times was fast, easy, and safe compared to earlier times. The Romans introduced a network of more than 50,600 miles (over 81,000 kilometers) of well-maintained stone-paved and metaled roads. An additional 125,000 miles (about 200,000 kilometers) of secondary roads spread from the North Sea to the Sahara Desert, and from the Atlantic Ocean to Mesopotamia. This well-developed road system facilitated leisure travel in the Roman Empire, and more than 100 miles (160 kilometers) a day could be covered during good weather.

The summer vacation evolved as Romans sought to escape the summer heat of Rome. Greece was a popular destination for educated Romans. Spas located at natural hot springs were also popular destinations due to their curative value. Inns were stationed about every 20 miles (32 kilometers) along the major roads.

Commercial trading also made ancient people travel from one place to another. Ocean-going ships were in use by 4000 BC (about the same time that the wheel and cart came into use) when Sumerian ships were trading with Indians via the Persian Gulf. By 1000 BC, Phoenician ships had rounded the southern tip of Africa for commercial trading.

The search for scientific knowledge was another major motivation for travel in the ancient world. The discipline of geography is generally traced back to the early Greeks, who were the first people within the Western cultural tradition to compile geographic information of the world. The first regional geography book was written around 475 BC by Hecataeus. Another Greek, Herodotus, later traveled extensively throughout the Mediterranean and Near East. His nine histories gave the first accurate description of the world known to the eastern Mediterranean people.

Ancient people traveled for religious purposes as well. Possibly the oldest religious travel story is the epic of Gilgamesh, a story told by King Gilgamesh of Ur of southern Mesopotamia in which the hero crossed deserts, mountains, and oceans in his search for eternal life. After many hazardous encounters, he arrived at the Island of the Blessed. The search for a spiritual paradise was a driving force for travel in the ancient world.

The Middle Ages

After the decline of the Roman Empire, Europe fell into the Dark Ages when organized religion dominated everyday life. Travel became difficult and dangerous because of the deterioration of the roads and bandits' rampant attacks on travelers. Religious pilgrimage was the dominant travel motivation at the time since organized religion was the dominant power in society. The famous *Canterbury Tales* by Geoffrey Chaucer is a good description of religious travel in Europe at that time.

At the same time, travel was increasing in the eastern part of the world, particularly in China. The peak of Chinese civilization was the Tang Dynasty

EXHIBIT 3–1

A popular attraction, such as Mount Rushmore, also capitalizes on the history of the United States.

Photo by Amy E. Lund

(AD 618–907). Changan, the capital of the Tang Dynasty, was the terminal point of the famous Silk Road, and merchants from many foreign countries traded there. Changan was also the political center in the region, and bright young Japanese students were sent there to study Chinese imperial government administration. In addition, Buddhist pilgrims traveling between China and India provided an important source of contact between the two regions. The famous Chinese Monkey King stories were based on such Buddhist pilgrimages.

The establishment of the Mongol Empire by Genghis Khan (AD 1271–1368) was a major event in east–west travel and contact. The creation of a single empire stretching from the borders of Europe into South Asia and to the Pacific Ocean enabled an incredible freedom of travel through Asia. It was at this time that Marco Polo made his famous journey through Asia and brought back fascinating and beautiful descriptions of places and people he encountered.

The Age of Exploration

As Europe grew out of the Middle Ages, its peoples became increasingly curious about the outside world and its nation states became ready to exert themselves as world powers. The desire to explore, discover, and understand other places and peoples drove many explorers and scientists to travel in many directions. The sailing of Christopher Columbus in 1492 is credited as the beginning of the great **age of exploration,** which also marked the advent of capitalism and modern scientific thought. This period was characterized as the opening of sea travel.

Travel for cultural and artistic purposes became increasingly popular in Europe in the 17th and 18th centuries. It became fashionable for the upper classes to visit the European cultural, artistic, musical, and government centers to sharpen their intellect through an increased knowledge of the world. This so-called Grand Tour of Europe was the beginning of European travel.

The Industrial Revolution

The beginning of the Industrial Revolution was marked by the invention of the steam engine by James Watt in 1765. The subsequent application of the steam engine to ships and locomotives made oceans and railroads the primary modes of travel. Distant travel by sea and expanding railroads contributed greatly to the rapid growth of travel. In 1830, the Liverpool and Manchester Railway opened in England. In 1838, the *Sirtus* became the first steamship to cross the Atlantic. This technological development, together with economic and social changes in Western industrial countries, generated rapid growth in the travel industry.

Environment

Environmental concern has been a trendy concept in the travel and tourism industry. The contact between tourists and the physical environment may cause the degradation of the attractiveness of the local community, through the littering of scenic sights, pollution of air and water, damage young trees while camping, the illegal hunting of animals, and so on. Travel agents can help reduce negative impacts by educating the traveling public through their brochures and pamphlets, and by promoting natural or ecotourism. Travel agents can also be actively involved in the beautification and maintenance of natural attraction programs in the local community. These business and civic activities can enhance both tourists' and local residents' awareness of environmental conservation and protection.

These topics of emerging importance are essential to the success of your business in the next century. The public perception of your operation in these areas can affect your business directly. Your technological competence and global competitive strategy can give you a leading edge in your business. Your ethical standards and environmental awareness can win the trust of customers.

At this time, a British Baptist preacher, **Thomas Cook,** saw great potential for travel business. He realized that there was a great need, desire, and motivation for travel in industrial societies, and he immediately capitalized on this by establishing the first world travel agency to serve the emerging leisure travel market. He initiated the concept of the all-inclusive group tour. His first organized tour, on July 5, 1841, included a group of 570 people taking a train excursion between Leicester and Loughborough north of London. Later, Cook's tours expanded to many other foreign destinations, such as Egypt, the United States, and the Orient. Now, Thomas Cook Travel has become one of the largest multinational travel operations in the world, and Thomas Cook is recognized as the father of modern travel agency operations.

Modern Travel

It wasn't until after World War II that tourism became a worldwide industry and leisure experience. Contemporary mass tourism emerged as the result of a series of major technological, economic, and social changes during the first 50 years of the 20th century.

Technologically, the introduction of commercial jet airplanes made travel fast and comfortable. The automobile meant another revolutionary technological advance in the history of travel. The development of the freeway system in the United States and Europe made automobile travel even more convenient, to the extent that automobile travel nowadays has become the landmark that reflects freedom of choice for the individual traveler.

Disposable incomes in the industrialized nations rose steadily in the past, with the financial ability to pursue travel and leisure activities creating a great

EXHIBIT 3–2

The development of commercial passenger airplanes.

Courtesy: The Boeing Company, Seattle, Washington.

demand for travel products and services. The wealthy industrial countries have always been the major tourist-generating countries and top spenders.

Socially, there has been a gradual shortening of the work week and an increase in the length of paid vacations in the Western industrialized nations. For example, the Monday holiday plan in the United States stipulates that whenever a major holiday falls in the middle of the week, it is celebrated on Monday. These changes have given the average person more free time for recreation and travel.

The tradition of travel is as old as humankind. The history of tourism, as described by Professor Joseph Fridgen of Michigan State University, ''is filled with social, economic, and political currents that move the industry forward. Central to understanding tourism's history are the mix of people's motivations and availability of attractions. Travel patterns change with times, technology, and policies, but do not stop.''[1]

Current Tourism Developments

Travel and tourism has grown into one of the largest industries in the world. The growth of the global and domestic tourism industry has had a significant economic impact on countries that have made tourism development an economic priority. Revenue generation, job creation, and infrastructure improvement are always heralded as the major economic benefits to the destination areas. According to the World Travel and Tourism Council's (WTTC) 1993 report, the travel and tourism industry now accounts for more than 6 percent of the world gross domestic product (GDP), employs 1 in every 15 employees, and accounts for 7 percent of the world's capital investment and 13 percent of consumer spending worldwide.

EXHIBIT 3–3   **World Industry Ranking by Industry Output**

	World Ranking	
	1993	*1992*
Electronics	1	1
Telecommunications	2	2
Engineering	3	3
Construction	4	5
Travel and tourism	**5**	**8**
Agriculture	6	4
Chemicals	7	10
Petrochemicals	8	7
Automobiles	9	6
Banking/insurance	10	9
Pharmaceuticals	11	12
Utilities	12	13

Source: World Travel and Tourism Council, ''Travel & Tourism: The World's Largest Industry,'' *WTTC Progress and Profiles—1993* (Brussels, Belgium: World Travel and Tourism Council, 1993), p. 22.

The travel and tourism industry was ranked the fifth largest industry in the world in 1993, up three places from 1992 (Exhibit 3–3). It is expected to become the leading global industry by the turn of the century and to double in size by 2005. A closer examination of tourism development in the world and the United States reveals the rapid growth of the industry.

World Tourism Development

International tourism has witnessed dramatic increases in both visitor arrivals and receipts since 1950 (see Exhibit 3–4). International tourist arrivals increased 174 percent between 1950 and 1960, and international tourist receipts over the same period were up by 227 percent. Such rapid growth can be explained by the increased wealth, education, and leisure time in industrialized societies; by the technological development of transportation and information systems; and by the improved political relations among countries. This growth has been interrupted only in 1982 and 1991 due to the economic recessions in major Western industrial countries.

Today, as the world economy has become more integrated, more countries have relaxed their entry restrictions for foreign tourists. In addition, more developing nations have become newly industrialized nations, such as the four ''Asian Tigers'' (South Korea, Taiwan, Hong Kong, and Singapore) in the Far East. Residents of the newly industrialized countries are now able to make overseas trips. This development will, to varying degrees, change the world

EXHIBIT 3–4   **World Tourism Growth, 1950–1992**

Year	International Tourist Arrivals (thousands)	Percent Change	International Tourist Receipts (U.S. $ millions)	Percent Change
1950	25,282	—	2,100	—
1960	69,296	174.09	6,867	227.00
1961	75,281	8.64	7,284	6.07
1962	81,329	8.03	8,029	10.23
1963	89,999	10.66	8,887	10.69
1964	104,506	16.12	10,073	13.35
1965	112,729	7.87	11,604	15.20
1966	119,797	6.27	13,340	14.96
1967	129,529	8.12	14,458	8.38
1968	130,899	1.06	14,990	3.68
1969	143,140	9.35	16,800	12.07
1970	159,690	11.56	17,900	6.55
1971	172,239	7.86	20,850	16.48
1972	181,851	5.58	24,621	18.09
1973	190,622	4.82	31,054	26.13
1974	197,117	3.41	33,822	8.91
1975	214,357	8.75	40,702	20.34
1976	220,719	2.97	44,436	9.17
1977	239,122	8.34	55,631	25.19
1978	257,366	7.63	68,837	23.74
1979	273,999	6.46	83,332	21.06
1980	287,906	5.08	102,372	22.85
1981	289,784	0.65	103,750	1.35
1982	289,177	−0.21	97,880	−5.66
1983	292,177	1.04	98,695	0.83
1984	320,142	9.57	109,004	10.45
1985	329,636	2.97	115,424	5.89
1986	340,808	3.39	149,811	29.79
1987	366,758	7.61	171,577	14.53
1988	393,865	7.39	197,743	15.25
1989	427,884	8.64	210,837	6.62
1990	455,594	6.48	255,074	20.98
1991	455,100	−0.11	261,070	2.35
1992	475,580	4.50	278,705	6.76

Source: Compiled from various tourism statistical yearbooks by World Tourism Organization, Madrid, Spain.

travel pattern that has been dominated by the traffic flow generated from Western industrial countries up to now.

U.S. Tourism Development

Travel and tourism plays an important part in the U.S. economy. The industry is the country's second-largest employer after health services. Approximately 5.95 million people were employed in travel-related jobs in 1991. The food service and lodging sectors provide the most jobs, with 1.745 million and 1.050 million employees, respectively. Travel industry employment has risen consistently every year since 1958.

Tax receipts from domestic and international travelers totaled $47 billion in 1991, with $41 billion generated by domestic travelers and $6 billion generated by international tourists, an increase of $2.2 billion from 1990.

In 1991, domestic and international travelers spent $360 billion in the United States, an increase of 3 percent over 1990. This amount includes spending for transportation (including payments to U.S. airlines by international visitors outside the country), lodging, food, entertainment, and incidental purchases directly related to travel.

A very significant contribution of tourism to the national economy is the travel expenditures by foreign tourists. International tourism is now the largest U.S. business service export, accounting for 11 percent of total U.S. exports of goods and services. In 1989 the United States for the first time had a **travel surplus** in its travel account balance of payments, because international tourists visiting the United States outspent the U.S. tourists visiting overseas by $3.1 billion. In other words, the United States received more travel revenues from foreign tourists than its citizens spent on and during overseas trips. There were more revenues than expenditures in the country's travel account. This travel surplus continued to increase from $11 billion in 1990 to $17 billion in 1991. The travel surplus is a good indicator of the United States becoming a popular and leading tourist destination in the world, and reflects the success of the vigorous marketing efforts by both the government and the travel industry. With the news media often alarmingly reporting the U.S. huge trade deficit, the public may not be aware that the travel and tourism industry creates exports and generates a trade surplus for the national economy.

The U.S. travel and tourism industry presently ranks third in retail sales based on business receipts, after motor vehicles and groceries. The industry will definitely continue to grow because of the country's diversity of tourism resources, the changes in the population, and the ever-increasing number of international tourists.

Definitions

Because of the large economic, sociocultural, and environmental impact made on the destination areas, tourism and travel has been studied by various academic disciplines, government agencies, and industry sectors. Generally, tourism study and policy analysis recognize two major factors: the person and the trip. Consistent and universally accepted definitions of *visitors* and *trips* enable the industry and researchers to measure the magnitude of the tourism industry better and to develop a data bank for tourism analysis and planning.

Eye on the Issues

Ethics

The travel and tourism industry is a people-oriented service industry. Managers make daily decisions that deal with people, and they must factor ethical considerations into the everyday business decision-making process. For example, tour company managers may be asked by local souvenir shops to send tour groups to their retail store, even though the handicrafts sold there are not authentic or of good quality. In return, the shop owner might offer gift certificates and cash rewards for each busload of tourists sent to the store. Many business decisions carry ethical overtones.

For the purpose of defining and classifying *travelers,* the classifications developed by the World Tourism Organization in 1981 have thus far been the best guidelines (see Exhibit 3–5). This classification system identifies all people who travel; they are divided into visitor and nonvisitor groups. The study of travel and tourism focuses primarily on the visitor group, which is further divided into two major types: tourist and excursionist. A **tourist** is then defined as someone who visits a destination for any reason other than for an occupation, and spends at least 24 hours (overnight stay) at the destination. A person visiting a place for leisure, business, health, visiting friends and relatives (VFR), or other reasons, and spends one night, is thus counted as a tourist by the destination. An **excursionist** is any person who visits a destination area for less than 24 hours. This definition includes visitors on cruise and train excursions, and day visitors who only visit the destination, but do not use the local lodging accommodations for an overnight stay.

The other unit of tourism study is the **trip,** which can be measured by distance and length of stay. The distance factor is measured in various ways by different countries. For instance, the United States Travel Data Center defines a *person-trip* as a person who travels away from home for at least 100 miles (160 kilometers) one way. This measurement is commonly used by many government agencies and the travel industry for compiling and writing tourism reports. However, Statistics Canada defines a trip as anyone who travels a minimum of 50 miles (80 kilometers). Obviously, there are disparities among different countries in measuring a trip. Therefore, tourism reports should be interpreted with caution: Are the data in the tourism reports measured by the same definitions?

Length of stay is an important indicator of economic impact on the destination areas. The longer tourists stay at the destination, the greater the economic contribution tourists make to local residents, because tourists spend

EXHIBIT 3–5 Classifications of Travelers

Visitors		Nonvisitors
Tourists	*Excursionists*	*Nonvisitors*
Leisure:	Day visitors	Border workers
Holidays	Cruise passengers	Nomads
Culture	Crews	Refugees
Sports		Armed forces
VFR		Diplomats
Professional:		Transit
Meeting		Immigrants
Mission		
Business		
Other		

Source: *Technical Handbook on the Collection and Presentation of Domestic and International Tourism Statistics* (Madrid: World Tourism Organization, 1981).

more on local lodging, food, entertainment, and other retail businesses the longer they stay. Length-of-stay data are particularly important to destinations for planning and developing tourist products and services. Short-stay excursionists, for instance, generate fewer demands on local lodging accommodations, whereas long-haul tourists create greater demands on local transportation systems, hotels, food services, attractions, and shopping facilities. The longer the stay, the greater the demand, and the more money tourists will spend on goods and services.

Measuring the economic benefits generated by tourists is always a focus of study for travel and tourism, particularly with regard to what is called the *economic multiplier effect.* The economic multiplier examines how tourist spending filters through the local economy and stimulates the growth of other sectors. As discussed in the introduction, tourism is a highly fragmented industry, part of and directly affecting many other sectors of the economy. Tourists use and consume many different products and services. Products and services are purchased from companies specializing in the tourist business, from companies in other industries, and from businesses that may have no direct contact with the tourists.

For example, a tourist spends $80 for accommodations in a ski resort. This amount is counted as sales to the local hotel. The hotel owner uses part of the tourist's spending as employee wages. A hotel employee spends part of her salary on rent. The landlady then pays her dry cleaning bill with the rent collected from the hotel employee. Thus, the dry cleaner also benefits from tourist expenditures even though there may be no direct business contact with the tourist.

This example demonstrates the circulation of a tourist's initial expenditures and the economic multiplier effect. Clearly, tourist spending goes through several rounds in the local economy. As the initial tourist spending filters through the local economy, various businesses benefit. This is indeed a very distinctive characteristic of the tourism industry, and is of great interest to destination developers and policy makers.

Travel Motivations and Tourist Attractions

Travel is motivated by two major factors: the so-called *push factor* and *pull factor*. The push factor is the driving force away from your everyday life and work environment. To get away from everyday life and routine work schedules, you need to escape from it all for a period of time, to relax and recharge the battery. This factor is usually determined by income and education levels. People with different incomes show distinctly different preferences in selecting travel destinations.

The pull factor is the drawing power of the destination area. Beautiful scenery, friendly people, nice climate, and gourmet food entice potential travelers to visit the destination. This drawing power is strengthened by vigorous promotional and marketing efforts of the destination and the travel industry. You are thus made aware of the attractions and services offered by the destinations and motivated to visit the place. The image and quality of the destination therefore play an important role in influencing your choices of destinations.

The push and pull factors always work together to motivate your desire to travel. Your travel behavior often results from the influence of various motives. However, at any one time, either the push or the pull factor may be a driving factor to a potential traveler, and this dominant factor influences the decision-making process in selecting a destination.

In the United States, the purposes of travel are studied and grouped into five categories: visiting friends and relatives (VFR), sightseeing and entertainment, business and convention, outdoor recreation, and others. In 1991, VFR had the largest share of the domestic travel market, accounting for 38 percent of the total travel volume. The sightseeing and entertainment group ranked second with 25 percent of the total market. Business and convention was third, showing 16 percent of the total market, and 13 percent traveled for outdoor recreation. The category of others accounted for the remaining 8 percent.

This is just one way in which the purpose of travel can be examined and analyzed. Grouping tourists by travel purposes can provide important planning data for destination developers and policy makers. However, one thing to remember when interpreting data on travel purpose is that business travelers and VFR visitors often combine their trips with leisure activities. There has been a growing tendency for multipurpose trips in the travel industry. Therefore, the study of travel purpose needs to be examined with a critical eye and account for those trends.

Courtesy: Grand Canyon Travel in Flagstaff, Arizona; the Carlson Travel Network.

Tourist Attractions

Tourist attractions are another important area of study for destination planning and development. The planned assessment and development of tourist resources will enhance the destination's attractiveness and create a positive image for the destination. The study of attractions generally has three major aspects: physical (or natural) attractions, cultural/historic attractions, and theme parks.

Natural Attractions.   Natural attractions primarily include natural wonders and physical amenities. Natural wonders are the nationally or internationally recognized features, and most spectacular physical features in the destination area, such as mountains, rivers, glaciers, waterfalls, and canyons. The Grand Canyon and Redwood Forest are examples of attractions of natural wonders (see Exhibit 3–6). The national parks in the United States are a very good example of this type of attraction. The national parks protect and manage the most spectacular natural wonders in the country for the enjoyment of tourists, and they are now the prime physical attractions visited by millions of domestic and international tourists every year.

In addition to famous natural wonders, other physical amenities, such as lakes, creeks, forests, and beaches, can also be fully utilized for tourist sight-seeing and recreational activities. Natural attractions lure travelers because of the beauty, recreation, and inspiration they provide.

Cultural and Historic Attractions.   Cultural and historic attractions are the tangible and intangible forms of human cultures found in various parts of the world. The tangible buildings and artifacts reflect the cultural values and aspirations of a particular group of people inhabiting a place. The intangible forms, such as music and customs, reveal the way of life of a particular society. Cultural and historic attractions are appealing tourist resources that transmit cultural meanings to tourists.

Cultural and historic attractions are extensive. They can be permanent-site attractions or temporary events. Permanent-site attractions are available for tourist visitation on a year-round (or long seasonal) basis. These can include sites like a historical museum, a temple, the Empire State Building, the Washington Monument, the Hopi Reservation, or New York City. Each of these attractions presents the culture and history of the place and its people. For example, the Temple of Heaven in Beijing, China, used to be a sacred religious building where Chinese emperors came to pray to the God of Heaven for good weather to sustain agricultural production in the country (see Exhibit 3–7).

Temporary event attractions are staged for tourists at a specific time, such as Mardi Gras in New Orleans, the Chinese New Year Parade in San Francisco, and even the Super Bowl (see Chapter 4 for a more detailed discussion of events development and management). Cultural and historic attractions appeal to those who are inspired to learn about contemporary and/or long-vanished civilizations.

Theme Parks.   Theme parks are specifically developed for tourist consumption. They are also called *manmade attractions.* Theme parks offer visitors a highly themed and packaged travel experience that is filled with fun, excitement, and thrill. The Walt Disney attractions, Universal Studios, Knott's Berry Farm, Sea World, and Six Flags attractions are well-known theme parks in the United States. However, the popularity of the Disney experience is not limited to the United States; it is now an international attraction with establishments in Tokyo and France. There have been some emerging themes for park development in the past few years. One of the fastest growing sectors of attraction development in theme parks has been water parks, which combine water slides and wave pools. Education and patriotism have also been important themes for attraction development in recent years.

Natural, cultural/historic, and theme park attractions act as magnets for destinations. They are the mainsprings that have driven much of humanity to travel for centuries. A good assessment and understanding of tourist attractions will enable a destination to fully utilize its resources and increase its travel business.

EXHIBIT 3–7

Pictured here is the Temple of Heaven in Beijing, China.

Transportation Systems

As described in your spring break vacation to Miami in the introduction, a major aspect of the travel and tourism industry concerns the movement of people by airplanes and rental cars. The movement of people away from their permanent residences is facilitated by various modes of transportation. From the horsedrawn carriages in the Roman Empire to the mail coaches in England and Wales in the 18th century, and to contemporary commercial jet airplanes, the development of transportation systems has had a tremendous impact on the changing landscape of the travel and tourism industry.

International

Political and economic changes are removing many of the existing barriers to international travel, and it is expected that these changes will continue. As demonstrated in this chapter, international tourists have already generated a great demand for many travel products and services in the United States, such as RV rentals and motorcoach tours. The rapid increase in the number of foreign tourists to the United States presents new challenges to the travel and tourism industry: Understanding cultural preferences of various nationalities and learning foreign languages are two good examples. Future hospitality managers must have an enhanced global perspective.

Speed and **accessibility** are two distinct contributions that modern transportation has made to the rise of travel and tourism. Speed of movement is an important factor of travel because of the time constraints on many travelers. With the introduction of the jet engine airplane, coast-to-coast travel was shortened to hours. The high speed of movement enables tourists to visit many destinations in a relatively short time.

The rise of jet travel, automobile travel, and high-speed train travel has also opened up more and more destinations across the globe. These modes of transportation have great impact in improving access to various regions in the world. Accessibility is essential in long-haul leisure travel and holiday destinations. The nature of available transportation strongly impacts a location and even influences the type of recreational pursuits. The jet airplane, the automobile, and the speed train have thus redrawn the world map of travel and tourism since World War II. For example, the nonstop maiden flight of PanAm to China in 1977 trumpeted the opening of this self-centered and mysterious country to the outside world. In the West, modern highways in Europe have now made it possible to drive all the way from northern Germany to Sicily. These different forms of transport have put most regions of the world within the reach of many tourists.

Automobile Travel

According to the 1992 report of the *Travel Industry World Yearbook,* most travel in the world, both domestic and international, is **automobile travel.**[2] Over the years, the growth of world travel has been paralleled by the growth of passenger car registrations. The United States has the highest concentration of automobile ownership, and accounts for 34 percent of the world's registered passenger cars. Automobile travel in the United States reached 2.1 trillion passenger miles on highways in 1991, an increase of 1.3 percent over the previous year. Travel by car accounts for more than four out of five of all intercity passenger miles in the United States.

In addition to family cars, there are other forms of motor vehicles used for travel purpose: recreational vehicles (RVs) and sightseeing motorcoaches. The Recreation Vehicle Industry Association reports that there are about 8.5 million privately owned RVs in the United States and about 25 million people who use RVs regularly. The annual average travel distance is estimated at 5,900 miles (9,495 km) per RV, and the average travel time per RV is 23 days. The RV rental market has been a fast-growing business in the last decade, with an average annual increase of 2.5 percent since 1980. This market has been largely driven by the increased number of foreign tourists to the United States. In 1990, nearly a half-million overseas visitors rented recreational vehicles.

Motorcoach tours cater to both one-day excursions and multiday tours. About 77 percent of the passengers who took motorcoach tours were on one-day excursions. The typical traveler on an escorted tour is over 55 years old. Another major market for motorcoach tours is again the overseas tourist. The motorcoach tours industry sees a bright future for its business as the U.S. population is aging and more and more foreign tourists are coming to visit the country.

Railway Travel

The demand for **railway travel** has been on the rise in the last decade. The elegance and nostalgia of rail travel attract more tourists to travel by rail. High-speed trains can now transport visitors quickly and comfortably to their destinations. Many regions in the world are developing rail service at a record rate. The major rail systems of Europe plan to spend $100 billion in the next 10 years to develop more-efficient high-speed rail lines. The opening of the tunnel under the English Channel (the Chunnel) has significantly expanded the network of high-speed trains now linking major European cities. France first built the 186 mph (299 kph) lines between Paris and Brittany in 1989, and it is planning to extend the service to Spain. Italy, Sweden, Switzerland, and Spain are all investing heavily in upgrading the quality of their railways.

Rail travel is still the main mode of long-haul transportation in many eastern European and Asian countries. The famous Orient Express, for instance, links many destinations in Western and Eastern Europe, Mongolia, and China. The collapse of the Communist system in the eastern European countries will help increase rail travel there, where foreign investment and technological and managerial assistance are badly needed to upgrade the rail infrastructure and provide services at international standards.

Rail travel has only recently regained popularity in the United States, via the Amtrak system. Founded in the late 70s, Amtrak now carries more than 23 million passengers per year, and recently reported a 3.5 percent increase in ticket revenues. During the past 20 years, Amtrak has transformed a disintegrating passenger-rail network into a respectable component of the U.S. transportation system with ticket booking available through a network of more than 30,000 travel agencies. In 1992, Amtrak began the promotion of the company's first continental train service, which links Los Angeles with Miami via three trains per week. The 58-hour route crosses eight states and features Amtrak's modern, double-decked superliner coaches, considered among the most comfortable in the world.

Air Travel

The world airline industry is a multibillion dollar industry. According to Boeing Company's estimates, the world growth of **air travel** during the next 15 years is expected to average about 5.2 percent per year, and the passenger volume will double to about 2.2 billion by the end of the century. Such rapid development of the world's commercial airline industry will create great demand for airport infrastructure development, aircraft manufacturing, and lodging and food service businesses worldwide.

With the emergence of new world travel markets, the patterns of international air transportation will be adjusted accordingly. Based on the forecast of the International Airline Transport Association (IATA), the Pacific Rim area will hold a 40 percent share of all international air passenger traffic by the end of the century. The Pacific Rim market has already become a target market for rivalry among the U.S. carriers. Tokyo, Hong Kong, and Singapore have become major gateway cities to the region.

Russia and other Eastern European countries are making great efforts in upgrading their commercial aircraft and introducing Western-style management and operations. Russia Air has ordered new aircraft from Western countries and has signed several joint-venture agreements with Western countries for technology transfer and service management expertise. With the introduction of Western-standard technology and service management, the Eastern European countries will surely have great impact on the international air transportation industry.

Domestically, the three major airlines—American, Delta, and United—still dominate the air travel market. In recent years, the airline industry has experienced cut-throat competition, especially in airfares and frequent-flier programs. As a result, the public now enjoys better service and lower fares than it did several years ago. Some successful, limited-service regional airlines have emerged, such as Southwest and Alaska Airlines. These airlines are operated regionally and have low operating costs because of their no-frill service approach. They compete very successfully with the country's giant air carriers.

Travel Agency Operations

Since Thomas Cook's first train excursion in 1841, travel agency operations have developed into a full-fledged component of the travel and tourism industry. Travel agencies now play very important roles in shaping potential tourists' perceptions of destinations and in influencing their holiday decisions. Travel agencies are used extensively by travelers for travel advice and price shopping. Once a travel agent makes a recommendation, most travelers usually stick to the advice. Therefore, travel agents can substantially influence consumers' vacation plans and help them decide what travel products and services to purchase. This role of the travel agents needs to be fully realized and understood by other hospitality businesses, because a good working relationship with the travel agents can increase business sales.

Travel agency operations fall into two functional categories: tour wholesalers and tour retailers. The function of the ***travel wholesaler,*** also known as a *tour operator* or *tour wholesaler,* is to consolidate transportation, accommodation, meals, and sightseeing services into one package. These package tours are then marketed by the wholesaler and also by a retail network—the tour retailers. A tour wholesaler can be an independent tour company, such as American Express, Thomas Cook, Carlson Wagonlit Travel, a tour unit of an airline, or a tour operator of motorcoach tours.

The role of the ***travel retailer*** is to bring seller and buyer together, and receive a commission from the supplier for the sales. Traditionally, travel retailers sold only tours and tickets for wholesale suppliers. However, many tour retailers now diversify their operations by offering their own package tours or working with local organizations to promote some specific package tours. Despite this small diversification, the bulk of tour retailers' income is still derived from selling tours and tickets for tour wholesalers and other hospitality suppliers.

Travel agency operations can also be classified by their business specializations. Leisure travel, corporate travel, and group and incentive travel are the major travel specialties. Incentive travel has grown and continues to grow rapidly, to the delight of travel agencies, which handle the bulk of it. Perhaps the least well-known specialty, incentive travel is used by many companies to reward their top performers or incite them to work harder. Trips to destination resorts serve as an incentive for outstanding performance.

Most retail travel agencies sell leisure vacations almost exclusively. Their services include selling sightseeing tours to various destinations, arranging modes of transportation, and serving the travel needs of independent tourists and families.

Travel agencies specializing in corporate travel offer a full range of business travel services, such as making arrangements with air, hotel, car rental, and other vendors. Some travel agencies are primarily engaged in group travel for meetings. Since business corporations and professional associations hold meetings and conferences on a regular basis, their regular and reliable business is welcomed by travel agents.

Travel agency operations have some very distinctive business characteristics. They share some operational functions with other segments of the hospitality industry, but they have their own unique aspects of business operation.

Relative ease of entry into the business, computer applications, geographic knowledge, people and marketing skills, and relationships with hoteliers are essential functions of travel agency operations.

<hr>

Eye on the Issues

Technology

The speed and extent of the implementation of new technology in the travel and tourism industry have been phenomenal. As a travel agency manager, you would need to be aware of the latest technological developments in your field such as the global distribution systems that enable you to make airline, car rental, and hotel reservations instantly around the world. As an agency owner or operator you will need to explore available technology and discover to what degree your competitors are using it. More and more travel agencies are investing in satellite ticket printers to expedite the reservation and ticketing process. You must decide if this would be feasible for your operation. By being technologically competent, you will be better able to manage a successful operation in a highly competitive business world.

Relative Ease of Entry

The travel agency business is characterized by its relative ease of entry. The up-front investment is minimal, as compared to other hospitality businesses, such as hotels and restaurants. Office space and furnishings, and a computerized reservation system are the only major requirements for starting the business. Usually, a prospective travel agent only needs to obtain one business license from the local government.

However, the travel agent has to receive several professional certifications (called *appointments*) from transportation associations to be able to sell tickets, such as an appointment from the International Air Transport Association (IATA) for international airline ticket sales, one from the Air Traffic Conference (ATC) for domestic airline ticket sales, and from railway and shipping groups.

Another very important group is the **Airlines Reporting Corporation (ARC),** a professional group representing airlines for collecting airline ticket sales and remitting commission payments to the travel agents. As a clearinghouse, ARC appoints a local bank as an area settlement bank for travel agents to deposit all airline ticket sales. Every 10 working days, ARC collects the airline ticket sales less commissions from the travel agent's account in the area settlement bank. In addition, ARC regularly publishes the *Industry Agents' Handbook,* which describes the requirements of reservations, ticketing, and reporting for travel agents to follow. At present, approximately 37,000 travel agencies in the United States are members of ARC.

Computer Applications

The management and operation of a travel agency require sound computer skills (see Exhibits 3–8a and 3–8b). Every travel agency leases at least one automated central reservation system (CRS) from a major airline. All major U.S. airlines have their own central reservation systems for ticket reservations, flight scheduling, and ticket prices, as shown below.

American Airlines	SABRE (Semi-Automated Business Records Environment)
United Airlines	Apollo
Trans World Airlines	Worldspan
Continental Airlines	System One
Delta Airlines	Datas II System

In Europe, Amadeus is the major airline reservation system; Abacus is used by many Asian airlines.

Many airline and car rental central reservation systems nowadays have been enhanced to include hotel information, so that travel agents can book lodging accommodations. Systems that combine airline, car rental, and hotel central reservation systems are known as *global distribution systems* (GDSs). Many hotel chains can now afford to have instant communication with all the major GDSs. For instance, Wizcom's ResAccess, owned by Avis, can provide room availability, rates, and other information including booking confirmation to travel agents around the world electronically, and without manual processing or costly follow-up telephone calls.

Another technological device that is widely used in travel agency operations is the **satellite ticket printer** (STP). An STP in the office of a corporation can print out tickets when the travel agent activates it through a telephone line hookup. Thus, the business traveler in that corporation can conveniently pick up the ticket in-house and the travel agent saves time and money too. In 1991 7,359 travel agencies were equipped with STPs, about 20 percent of all travel agencies in the United States.

Geographic Knowledge

Travel agents need to have good geographic knowledge of the United States and certain other regions of the world. Travel agents market and sell holiday vacations to various domestic and international destinations. In order to effectively promote the attractions and accommodations of the destination to potential tourists, travel agents must have a thorough knowledge of the hospitality industry, and the local culture and society in the destination area.

There has been a tendency toward geographic specialization in travel agency operations, with many travel agencies now specializing in promoting certain regions of the country or the world, such as the Southwest or Northeast

EXHIBIT 3–8a

Carlson Wagonlit Travel Agency in Paris is one of the largest travel wholesalers in the world.

Courtesy: Carlson Wagonlit Travel, Minneapolis, Minnesota.

EXHIBIT 3–8b

Travel agents at work in Carlson Wagonlit Travel Corporate Business Center in Phoenix, Arizona.

Courtesy: Carlson Wagonlit Travel, Minneapolis, Minnesota.

in the United States, or Asia, Europe, or South America for international travel. This geographic specialization and expertise of a particular region enables the travel agents to serve customers better.

To increase such geographic knowledge, travel agents are often invited by destinations to participate in familiarization tours (''fam'' tours), that is, to visit an area's tourist attractions and stay in a variety of hotels. Fam tours give travel agents first-hand knowledge of the destination. The fam trip perk is also a major draw to people considering a travel agency career.

People and Marketing Skills

Travel agents must have the essential business operations skills required in any other hospitality businesses: people skills and marketing skills. The travel agency business has only recently become a very competitive business with very small operational profit margins. To be successful in the business, the travel agent cannot afford any errors in his/her operations. Quality service as reflected in caring for customers' needs can win repeat business and positive word-of-mouth publicity. Good communication skills and a detail-oriented work style are vital for satisfying the customers. Creative marketing—offering attractive tour packages, and incentives to travel—can give the travel agency a competitive edge and increase its business. These two basic hospitality operations skills, people and marketing, can enable the travel agency to run a very competitive business.

Relationship with Hotelier

A good working relationship between travel agents and hoteliers must be emphasized. As discussed earlier, travel agents are influential in shaping the potential tourists' holiday decisions and in directing a large volume of travel traffic. They can be very influential and be a sales force for hoteliers. In Europe and Asia, travel agents sell approximately 50 percent of all hotel rooms. Hoteliers and travel agents both enjoy a good relationship and run profitable businesses.

However, the relationship between hoteliers and travel agents in the United States has been an uneasy one due to some misconceptions. Some hoteliers consider the travel agents a middle person who chips away a portion of the room revenues in the form of commissions. Those room sale commissions are often not promptly paid to the travel agent, which is the main complaint by travel agents working with the hoteliers. Some hoteliers are reluctant to forge strong ties with travel agents. As a result, hotel room sales by travel agents in the United States are lower than cruise, airline, railway, coach tours, and car rental sales generated by travel agents.

Some hoteliers are missing sales opportunities by not developing strong relationships with travel agents. Travel agents now advise approximately 60 percent of potential travelers in their hotel selections.[3] It is vitally important, therefore, for hoteliers to establish a good working relationship with travel agents, who are a greatly underutilized sales force. If possible, hotels should introduce travel agents to their hotel products and services, and should pay agents' sales commissions promptly. In this way, the hoteliers and travel agents can be true partners in profits.

A recent promotion and appreciation program launched by Ramada Hotels did just that: it improved the working relationship between the company and travel agents. During the last four months in 1993, Ramada Hotels in the northeastern United States placed a thank you gift in the rooms of guests referred to them by the travel agents. The gift, along with a card, expressed appreciation of the guests' stay on behalf of the travel agents who booked the rooms. This program was designed to thank travel agents for referring their clients to Ramada Hotels and promote further business with the travel agents.

Social Costs of Tourism Development

We have thus far discussed the positive aspects of tourism development, particularly the economic benefits. But we must realize that each coin has two sides. Tourism development, if unplanned and unregulated, can have negative impacts on local communities: the quality of life of the local residents can be affected by the increased number of tourists. The *social cost of tourism* development is a commonly discussed repercussion of tourism.

An increased number of tourists can put great pressure on local infrastructure and services, such as parks, shopping malls, and parking lots. This crowdedness obviously affects local residents' daily lives and often leads to local resentment of tourists. This resentment then develops into actions that discourage tourists from coming to their communities. In the summer of 1991, the state of Oregon aired some humorous radio commercials to advise Oregonians to be courteous to tourists. The ads said that instead of ramming a car with California license plates into the guard rail, or directing an RV from British Columbia to the nearest landfill, Oregon residents should be nice to tourists regardless of their accent or dress. The commercial clearly illustrated the social cost stemming from the conflict between the local residents and tourists.

Increased tourism may also increase crime. The shooting of foreign tourists in Miami in 1993 shocked the whole world and had a devastating impact on the tourism industry in south Florida. Robberies of tourists are often reported in different parts of the world. Tourism-related crime tarnishes the image of a particular community and has a direct impact on the quality of life of the local residents.

Conclusion

Travel and tourism is a highly diverse and fragmented industry that encompasses all of the businesses serving the needs of people who are away from home. Every hospitality business is an integral part of the travel and tourism industry. Mutually supportive, all segments of the industry combine to form one of the leading industries in the United States and in the world. The great economic impact of the industry will continue to draw enthusiastic interest and preferential support from communities around the world.

In terms of potential career development, the travel and tourism industry is one of the largest job generators in the world and offers a great variety of career opportunities: transportation-related businesses, government tourism agencies, travel wholesalers or retailers, various nonprofit travel associations, private marketing and consulting firms, or simply as an entrepreneur starting your own hospitality business. (Chapter 16, "Opportunities in Hospitality," discusses the breadth of options in greater detail.)

A sound knowledge of hospitality management and operations may enable you to move both vertically and horizontally in career development. The fundamentals of hospitality management, such as managing people, money, and technology, are transferable to other segments of the industry because of similarities in the hospitality industry sectors and the interdependence of all the business functions.

The wisdom of both Western and Eastern civilizations points to the enlightenment of travel: "Travel broadens one's mind" is often heard in the Western world while "Traveling 10 thousand miles equals reading a thousand books" is a popular saying in Chinese culture. If you enjoy travel, meeting new people, and learning about other cultures, you will benefit tremendously from working in the travel and tourism industry because the industry offers frequent travel opportunities. These opportunities for travel agents to visit various destinations each year are often the main incentives that draw people to this profession. Personal and intellectual growth through travel is immeasurable.

As seen throughout history, travel is deeply ingrained in all the cultures of the world. Travel demands change with the political, social, and technological trends of time. However, travel as a contemporary cultural pursuit and business activity will continue to grow at a rapid pace. The travel and tourism industry beckons you to join a growing and rewarding industry, and to lead that industry into the next century.

Keywords

age of exploration   69

Thomas Cook   70

travel surplus   74

trip   75

length of stay   75

tourist attraction   78

accessibility   81

automobile travel   81

railway travel   82

air travel   83

Airlines Reporting Corporation (ARC)   85

satellite ticket printer   86

Core Concepts

travel and tourism industry   66

tourist   75

excursionist   75

economic multiplier effect   76

push factor   77

pull factor   77

travel wholesaler   84

travel retailer   84

global distribution systems   86

social cost of tourism   89

Discussion Questions

1. Discuss the complex and interdependent characteristics of the travel and tourism industry.

2. By studying the history of travel, what future can you picture for the travel and tourism industry?

3. What is the significance of international tourism to the U.S. balance of accounts in travel since 1989?

4. Can you describe the operational functions of travel agency management?

5. Why is it so important to develop a good working relationship between the travel agents and the hoteliers?

References

Bush, Melinda. "Understanding the $130 Billion Customer." *Hotels,* October 1993, p. 74.

Emmer, Rita Marie; Chuck Tauck; Scott Wilkinson; and Richard G. Moore. "Marketing Hotels: Using the Global Distribution Systems." *The Cornell Hotel and Restaurant Administration Quarterly* 34, no. 6 (December 1994), pp. 80–89.

Fridgen, Joseph D. *Dimensions of Tourism.* East Lansing, MI: The Education Institute of the American Hotel and Motel Association, 1991.

Waters, Somerset R. *Travel Industry World Yearbook: The Big Picture.* New York: Child & Waters, 1992.

World Tourism Organization. *Yearbook of Tourism Statistics.* Madrid, Spain: World Tourism Organization, 1992.

World Travel and Tourism Council. "Travel & Tourism: The World's Largest Industry." In *WTTC Progress and Profiles—1993.* Brussels, Belgium: World Travel and Tourism Council, 1993.

Resorts, Clubs, Attractions, and Events

The tourism and hospitality industry is a highly diversified industry offering a spectrum of career opportunities. This chapter elaborates on four important aspects of the tourism and hospitality industry—resorts, clubs, attractions, and events—and discusses the management and operations of these exciting businesses. Based on the past and present successes of such entities as Disney and the city of Las Vegas, the expected future growth of such hospitality operations is tremendous. If you are interested in exploring career opportunities in these challenging fields of hospitality management, the job market for qualified managers should be strong.

Outline

Introduction

Resorts, clubs, attractions, and events are exciting businesses holding special niches in the world of hospitality. While resorts have many similarities with hotels in their basic functions, they are significantly different in other ways—and not just on the glamor side. Also, future managers are often pleasantly surprised to learn that the skills they will acquire in what they've thought of as a hotel-and-restaurant curriculum are equally applicable to the management of private, public, or military clubs; to planning and managing festivals and other events; or to running a theme park, museum, or other attraction. Let's take a look at opportunities that are a little like the proverbial horse of a different color. They're recognizable as hospitality operations—with quite a few interesting differences.

Resorts

Resort hotels are associated with leisure activities and travel for pleasure. A number of resort hotels operate very successfully in the meeting and convention market, but the main difference between resort and nonresort properties is the emphasis on leisure and pleasurable activities.

Resorts offer a vast array of leisure destinations, with different activities and amenities geared toward pleasing guests who have a range of values and lifestyles as well as different budgets.

Hospitality students often dream of a career in resort management without realizing that its demands are often far more taxing than those of management at city hotels or other nonresort properties. Managers with considerable experience at nonresort properties have found their first resort experience to be a real challenge. Resorts have a different momentum, a different style from other operations, and their operating challenges are different, too. Most resorts

Courtesy: Hyatt Hotels & Resorts, Chicago, Illinois.

experience a wide variation in activity levels during the changing seasons. This impacts revenues, staffing, and marketing, and may even result in completely different types of guests from one time of year to another. Who goes to ski resorts when there is no snow or to beach resorts when it's cold?

This section offers a brief history of resort development, differentiates between the operational challenges of resort and nonresort hotels, and emphasizes the major aspects of resort operations.

A Brief History

Resorts go back as far as civilization, when the rulers and aristocracy of Rome went to villas on the Island of Capri, or when Mogul rulers escaped the heat of the Indian summer by withdrawing to mountain palaces in Kashmir, India, in the 1300s. Europe had its beach, lake, and mountain resorts, and developed health resorts (also called **spas**) in locations with natural hot springs believed to have curative powers. One of the most famous ones, The Spa Resort, was established in Belgium in the 13th century, and it continues to operate today.

The New World continued the European spa tradition, with development of spa-related properties in Saratoga Springs, New York; White Sulphur Springs, West Virginia; and elsewhere. The development of the railroads in the 1800s provided convenient access to a number of areas that had previously

Exhibit 4–2

*Hyatt Regency
Cerromar Beach
Resort at Dorada,
Puerto Rico.*

Courtesy: Hyatt Hotels & Resorts, Chicago, Illinois.

been difficult to reach. Resorts in New England, upstate New York, and Atlantic City, New Jersey, became more accessible and grew into popular destination resorts. Atlantic City became America's first resort city, and made an
important move to broaden its customer base by including not only the
wealthy, but also the middle class among its clientele.

Prior to Atlantic City's development as a seaside resort, resorts were the
exclusive domain of the wealthy and powerful. That customer base did not
really expand until Sir William Butlin began the family-oriented Butlin Holiday Camps in Britain in 1936. After World War II, the economic growth of
the United States and the increase in family income led to increased demand
for vacation and leisure destinations and resorts. The recovery of the Western
European economies a decade or so later led to parallel increases in demand
throughout Europe and the Mediterranean. The development of jet passenger
aircraft in the 1950s made travel to such destinations even more feasible. When
jumbo jets and wide-body passenger aircraft reduced operating costs and lowered airfares, international travel and visits to resorts—for both pleasure and
business—boomed.

Increased prosperity and reduced airfares led to another phenomenon, that
of group travel and mass tourism. Quantity discounts and the buying power
of large groups encouraged the development of charter and tour operators who
were able to negotiate low prices for entire aircraft, large blocks of rooms,

and deep discounts on amusements and activities for their group travelers. Resorts catering to these mass leisure travelers were built in the most desirable physical locations around the world.

Resorts versus Nonresorts

The difference between resorts and nonresorts can be discerned in two aspects: location and function. Resorts are normally located in the most desirable physical locations, as compared to urban hotels. Islands, mountains, deserts, and lakefront sites are usually the prime locations for resort development. Functionally, resorts offer more than just lodging and food and beverage services to their guests. They provide guests with luxury accommodations, numerous food and beverage outlets, lavish entertainment, and exciting recreational activities, such as golf, tennis, skiing, and various water sports.

Resorts can be characterized in two ways: destination resorts and activity-based resorts. A **destination resort** implies a place or location, rather than a single property. Resort cities, such as Miami, Orlando, and San Diego, are popular destinations because they offer a wide choice of activities, entertainments, and other diversions—along with their mild climates, beaches, and golf courses. In these cases, the location or the city itself is considered a resort, and individual properties are part of the total inventory of attractions that make the destination desirable. There may be a major attribute or activity that is at the core of the area's attractiveness, but the total array is what comprises the destination.

Eye on the Issues

Environment

Each of the four areas discussed in this chapter have impacts on the physical environment: the development of an attraction, the set-up of an event in a particular location, and the operations of a golf resort or club. Resorts, since they are often located in remote locations, need to consider how their buildings will fit into the natural landscape. Intrusive architecture or overly prominent positioning of construction (sometimes called "architectural pollution") may destroy much of the attractiveness of an area, causing local resentment and opposition.

Resort developers must examine local resources before building large facilities that might strain existing facilities. Some resorts, in areas with water shortages, have found it necessary to build and operate their own sewage and water treatment plants, since existing plants are adequate to serve only a small, spread-out population. It is also entirely possible that the amount of trash and solid waste generated by a resort could outmass that of an entire small community. For resorts to be good neighbors, they must be sensitive to the carrying capacity of local utilities and aware of such things as drainage and run-off. The lush landscaping of some golf courses and resort grounds often requires large quantities of fertilizers, pesticides, and other chemicals. These toxins can contaminate ground water and damage vegetation in surrounding areas.

An **activity-based resort** focuses on a single aspect of a destination or property as the key to identity. Aspen, Colorado, and Killington, Vermont, are known primarily as ski resorts. Palm Springs, California; Scottsdale, Arizona; and Pinehurst, North Carolina, are well known for golf. Hilton Head Island Beach and Tennis Resort, as the name suggests, focuses on tennis and water fun.

One of the challenges that specific activity-oriented resorts face is developing attractions for seasons when their primary activity is impossible or uncomfortable. How, for instance, can guests be persuaded to stay in Aspen in the summer, or in upstate New York in the heart of winter? Another issue facing these resorts is that guests often travel as families, and the enthusiasm of one family member for golf, skiing, or scuba diving may not be shared by everyone else. What can guests do the rest of the time? Are there alternatives that will make the resort experience a pleasure for the rest of the family, and are there things to do off the golf course, the beach, or the ski slope?

An issue for resort developers is the level of difficulty of their golf courses and ski terrain. Professionals, experts, and the trade press love the more challenging and difficult locations. The average vacationer tends to be just that—average. She or he wants to enjoy vacation time, get some satisfaction out of being active, but may not necessarily want to test him- or herself in a world-class competitive arena.

There are a few resorts that are narrowly focused and aimed at only the dedicated enthusiasts. Helicopter skiing in the Bugaboos, remote hunting and fishing camps, or far-flung islands that offer outstanding diving make no attempt to cater to everyone. Most resorts are not so intentionally unique; they try to attract a broad range of clientele. Like other operators in any competitive business, resort developers and marketers must differentiate themselves, make themselves stand out as special, without becoming so specialized that they appeal to so few people that they cannot be run profitably.

Seasonality.   One of the key aspects of resort management is *seasonality.* Many resorts have a high season, a low season, and what is called a *shoulder season.* The **high season** is the time when demand, occupancy, and rates are highest, and when the resort's attractions are at their peak, staffing is at its highest level, and activity and revenue crest.

Shoulder seasons are the periods before and after the high season. During the shoulder, properties are usually gearing up for or gearing down from the high season, and weather and activities are often attractive, but not prime. During these weeks or months, occupancies and rates are somewhat lower than during high seasons, but still reflect the desirability of the location and property at that season. Markets may shift a little during the shoulder season, moving more toward groups and individuals who are more price sensitive than high-season guests.

Low season offers the greatest challenge to the resort operator. High-season attractions are usually not available or may not be particularly enjoyable during these periods. The normal strategy to attract business during this time is to offer discounts to attract enough business to meet operating costs. Fixed costs have to be paid each month, whether revenue is down or not. Selling a room that normally goes for $325 at a discounted rate of $110 may not generate profit, but it will probably cover obligations to the bank, the utility companies, the government, and essential vendors.

Successful resort operators are those who have been able to extend their high and shoulder seasons, find new markets for their low seasons, and develop special events and activities to draw guests at times that used to be slow. Successful resort operators reduce their costs when revenues are down, but find ways to keep key employees working yearround. This is often accomplished by adjusting the number of employees based on seasonal needs (in other words, laying off and hiring on as needed). The trick is to do so without compromising high-quality guest service. Resort managers have to be good at recruiting and training people, particularly at the start of each high season, when they must get new employees up to superior performance levels quickly. Many resort managers and hourly employees like the rhythm of the seasons, with their changes in pace and activity, and would grow bored with the relatively even pace of many nonresort properties.

Length of Stay.　　Resort guests usually stay longer than guests in nonresorts, except for those who seek out such long-stay products as Guest Quarters or Residence Inns. *Length of stay* often has a relationship to travel time, distance, and costs in that the further the guest travels to the destination, the longer he or she is likely to stay. A typical destination resort may have an average stay of 5.5 days, whereas the typical ''transient hotel'' has an average stay of only 1.5 to 2 days.

For resort managers, this means being prepared to handle most check-ins and check-outs on one or two days, rather than having them spread more evenly throughout the week. It also means that the resort must provide a lot more variety in its food and beverage outlets and available activities. Otherwise, guests will grow tired of the same choices and take their trade and money off the property. This aspect of longer stay requires resort managers to be more creative, and to rely on their activity directors, chefs, and catering directors to develop special events, menus, and divertisements.

Extent of Property.　　In addition to having multiple food and beverage outlets, resorts usually also offer swimming pools, health clubs, and facilities for tennis, golf, or other activities, and are often more spread out than conventional hotels. It is not unusual for rooms to be located in several buildings, all of which are connected by extensive landscaping. This means housekeeping and maintenance operations become more complex. Supplies and trash must be moved around the property without offending guests. Single-structure hotels usually have no problem separating front-of-the-house areas from areas guests should not enter. In multibuilding resorts this is harder to accomplish.

Staffing.   Resort staffing presents some challenges that many urban hotels don't have to face. As mentioned, seasonality is an issue, both with respect to keeping qualified staff despite the threat of layoffs, and matching availability of seasonal help, such as students on summer vacations with the dates of high-season business.

City hotels have a large population base from which to draw and a large housing market available to employees. Cities often have public transportation systems for those who lack personal transportation. By contrast, many resorts are in rural areas with small local populations, no public transportation, and a shortage of available and affordable housing. Resort managers often find themselves recruiting from far away and having to provide or assist employees with housing and transportation.

Resort Marketing

Think about planning a vacation. How do you decide where and when to go and how long you will stay? What do you want to do? If you are a member of a couple or a family, how do you work around your various preferences? Resort marketers have to understand their potential customers' wants and needs and project how these will affect their decision-making processes. What will cause customers to choose *their* resort over another? What is the best way to communicate information that will make customers believe that their resort will satisfy their needs? Will they choose their destination first and then decide where to stay? What balance of marketing will promote the destination as well as the resort?

Marketers use research to help them answer these questions. Resorts constantly conduct research to determine who their customers are, where they come from, and how they make their leisure travel decisions. Modern data processing, hotel guest histories, credit card spending information, questionnaires, and surveys all help marketers identify major source markets. When they know where the majority of their guests come from, they can focus their efforts on buying heavier media coverage in those areas.

Many resort destinations market through a convention and visitors bureau, a chamber of commerce, a resort association, or some other partnership of entities interested in promoting the destination. Airlines often cooperate with resorts in promoting destinations along their routes. Credit card companies, who make money on commissions on purchases by cardholders, are often willing to cooperate in advertising resort destinations where cardholders spend significant sums. Such joint efforts also maximize valuable marketing dollars.

Marketers also must consider whether they are better off marketing to a geographical area (perhaps ZIP codes identified as common to many guests) or to an interest group (such as readers of golf, skiing, or scuba magazines).

A third avenue is through travel agents or tour operators. These groups must be paid commissions and offered discounts, but they often deliver business a resort has no easy way to reach. Good marketing may bring guests to a resort the first time, but good management and friendly, efficient staff are the keys to creating a resort experience that will bring guests back for repeat visits, the backbone of all successful resorts.

The People Factor at Resorts

Due to the unique mix of features in a resort environment, managers must be adaptable to serving guests who have different motivations and behavior patterns than business travelers. Guests who stay for pleasure are less focused on efficiency than on enjoying their experience. They are in and out of their rooms several times a day, perhaps changing between activities, perhaps taking a nap, or maybe just lounging on the balcony or patio. Resort guests tend to sleep later than business travelers, and front desk managers must often diplomatically decline late check-outs to guests who'd like to linger. If they don't, arriving guests won't be able to check into the clean and ready room they expect.

Guests are on the property for several days or longer and, as a result, have more time to develop relationships with staff. These relationships are also a big part of the resort experience and can greatly influence repeat business. Club Med has taken this guest–staff interaction further than any other chain, but even more traditional resorts recognize the importance of hiring employees who have good communication and social skills as well as technical ability.

It's not uncommon for resorts to double the size of their staff as the high season approaches, then cut back again when the high season is over. This provides its own problems regarding service levels and excellence. It's hard to provide the same quality of service at one-third the high-season price—and with half the staff.

Eye on the Issues

Ethics

Although managers of events, attractions, and resorts face ethical challenges, club managers may encounter them more frequently given the close relationship they have with their client base, who are also indirectly their bosses. For instance, a club manager may be approached by a very influential member who is a prominent local business owner. This member may try to convince the manager to purchase his/her products for the club without using fair bidding practices. Managers may also find themselves unwilling participants in political struggles between power groups within their club's membership. Dealing with such situations requires a high standard of ethical conduct. Sometimes it may be hard to sort out the rights and wrongs or weigh the best interests of the club, its members' satisfaction, and its board of directors' policies. Integrity and honesty should always come first.

Courtesy: Club Med, New York, New York.

Summary

Resorts are challenging, but exciting places to work. Customer focus is different from that of city, suburban, or airport hotels. Guests are there to enjoy themselves, and successful resort managers create memorable and diverse resort experiences for their guests. Demographic and social trends are providing more leisure time and more opportunities to travel, which results in increasing demand for leisure services, activities, and facilities.

A specialization in resort operations and management can provide challenging and satisfying career opportunities. With the right skills, experience, and adaptability, would-be resort managers can look forward to working in a wide variety of locations, climates, property sizes, and specialized recreational facilities.

Club Operations

Private clubs have long been places for people of similar interests to support the activities they like. They provide an environment where like-minded people can share each others' company and congenial activities. The history of clubs has been one of exclusivity and social privilege, with many clubs traditionally excluding women and minorities. The Civil Rights Act of 1964 forbids exclusion on the basis of race, creed, religion, gender, or national origin, and a series of court cases has made the point that private clubs may exclude individuals for various reasons, but not for any of the above characteristics.

There are many types of private clubs serving the social and recreational needs of their members. The study of club management has long been overlooked by many academic hospitality programs. However, the club industry has grown rapidly in many regions of the United States and provides many managerial opportunities for hospitality graduates. This section describes the different types of private clubs and discusses the management functions involved in this specialty.

Types of Clubs

Clubs are generally categorized in one of three ways:

By location	Country clubs, city clubs, or beach clubs.
By activity	Golf clubs, tennis clubs, yacht clubs, health or athletic clubs, road and gun clubs, or hunting clubs.
By ownership	Membership-owned equity clubs; individual- or company-owned clubs; a club owned by a corporation for its own employees; or U.S. government–owned military clubs.

The members in an **equity club** buy a share in the ownership of the club's assets. Most clubs own valuable land and buildings, and each member thus owns a proportional share of the assets. Since the purpose of such clubs lies not in the seeking of profits but in the service of its members, they are usually exempted from income taxes. An example of an equity club is the famous Brookline Country Club in Massachusetts, one of the oldest country clubs in the United States.

The **development club** is a profit-seeking entity. A company develops a club and then sells membership to the public. Members have no control over club operations. The Dallas-based Club Resorts of America is a leading company in developing and managing such clubs. Many development clubs are associated with real estate development. The presence of the club adds value to residents' homes and offers them amenities as homeowners. The initiation fee for club membership is usually the purchase of a lot within the development. After the development company sells a certain proportion of the property within the development, it will often deed the club to the property owners, who then gain control of its operations.

A club owned by a corporation is used for its own executives, managers, and employees. Such facilities promote employee morale and build friendships among managers and workers. A good example is the DuPont Country Club, which has more than 10,000 members, most of whom are employees of the DuPont Company.

The U.S. government also operates clubs for military personnel around the world. Many of these military clubs have excellent facilities and offer a wide range of recreational and travel services. They often seek civilian personnel to manage these facilities, offering attractive salaries and fringe benefits.

Club Membership

Most of the private clubs in the United States are member-owned equity clubs. More than 50 percent of these are country club or golf club operations. Members pay a one-time initiation fee to become a member of the club, then pay ongoing dues to maintain membership and receive services. The membership structure in private clubs can be very complicated. Following is only a partial listing of commonly encountered membership categories:

Type of Membership	*Description*
Regular	Members pay full initiation fee and membership dues. They enjoy the full privilege of using club facilities and services. They have voting rights.
Social	Members pay reduced initiation fees and membership dues. In turn, their access to club facilities and services is limited. For instance, most social members are permitted to use the clubhouse for social and dining functions only. They must pay additional fees if they use golf or tennis facilities. In most clubs, they have no voting rights.
Junior	Most clubs offer junior membership for the children of regular members. Junior members are usually 21 to 30 years old. Dues and initiation fees are lower than those of regular members but they are entitled to use all club facilities. They seldom have an equity interest in the club or a right to vote on its operations.

Some clubs offer a range of limited membership categories for nonresidents, senior citizens, and spouses of former club members. A member from

EXHIBIT 4–4

*Management
hierarchy at a
private club*

Members

Board of Directors
|

Standing committees - - - - - - - - - - - - - - - General Manager
| Assistant Manager

Membership   Clubhouse Manager
Finance & Budget   Controller
Clubhouse   F&B Director
Athletic   Membership Service
Entertainment   Golf Superintendent
                           Golf Professional
                           Tennis Professional

Ad Hoc Committees
(one-time committee for specific issue/activity)

one category may also switch categories (such as from social to regular member) when openings become available. Most private equity clubs limit their membership to keep from overcrowding their facilities. Many prestigious country clubs have waiting lists of more than 10 years, and many eager candidates for membership.

Club Organizational Structure

The organizational structure of clubs differs from that of most hotel operations. In hotels, the general manager is the chief operating officer, at the top of the management hierarchy. In private clubs, the management hierarchy is quite different, as shown in Exhibit 4–4.

As Exhibit 4–4 demonstrates, the members are the owners of the club and they are the decision makers. The members elect a board of directors for overseeing club operations, formulating club rules and bylaws, and hiring the general manager. The board of directors also appoints various standing committees to work with the GM on appropriate management aspects. The GM attends the monthly board of directors' meeting and reports on club operations. He or she must work with the standing committees and supervise the management team. The ultimate goal for a club manager is to satisfy the needs of the membership. Such positions are very challenging due to the combination of masters the GM must serve, directly and indirectly.

Club Finance

The main source of club revenues is membership dues. Exhibit 4–5 shows the average percentage of each revenue source and how expenses are allocated for both country and city clubs in the United States. Clubs have a pool of customers that is limited to members and guests. If members don't generate sufficient revenue to support the club's operations, alternate measures must be taken. Typically, clubs' choices in such cases are limited to increasing membership, trying to increase fees, or assessing members a one-time fee to cover deficits. In a member-owned club these can be sensitive issues. In effect,

EXHIBIT 4–5   **Club Revenue Sources and Expense Categories**

Club Revenues	Country Club	City Club
Dues	46.2%	39.8%
Food	26.6	40.1
Beverages	8.3	9.4
Rooms	—	1.8
Sports	14.1	—
Others	4.8	8.9
	100%	100%

Club Expenses	Country Club	City Club
Operating supplies and expenses	32.9%	28.5%
Payroll	47.9	46.0
F&B costs	11.8	16.5
Real estate taxes and insurance	6.0	6.3
Balance available for debt service, capital improvements, etc.	1.4	2.7
	100%	100%

Source: *Clubs in Town and Country,* Pannell Kerr Forster Worldwide, 1993, pp. 10, 21.

the board of directors must ask members to charge themselves more or risk overcrowding their facility—always a tough proposition.

A number of clubs set a minimum revenue level by charging their members a minimum monthly fee to increase the use of club food and beverage services. Members who don't frequent the club often enough to spend the minimum amount pay it nonetheless. This makes them more likely to patronize the club, rather than waste their money.

Eye on the Issues

International

The United States is now the second most visited tourist destination in the world. Increasing numbers of international tourists will continue to flock to American attractions, resorts, and events. In the past, many foreign tourists traveled in groups with guides and translators. In recent years, however, more and more foreign tourists are traveling in couples or families, as independent travelers. This is becoming increasingly true of Asians. Managers can be proactive in preventing difficulties for such visitors by using international signage, collecting a list of bilingual speakers who may be called in emergencies, or translating important information into the languages of the nationalities who most commonly patronize the operation. Exhibit 4–7 shows some of the common international icons used worldwide.

EXHIBIT 4–6

California Country Club is a privately owned country club located in the City of Industry. The Club offers an outstanding location, superior golf course, ample acreage, abundant water, and membership potential.

Courtesy: California Country Club, Whittier, California.

EXHIBIT 4–7

International icons

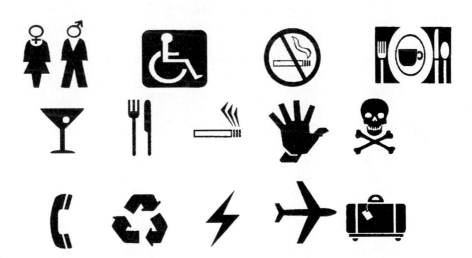

Individuals have different tastes and opinions as to how things should be done. Club members are no exception, and one of the challenges club managers face is reconciling differing opinions. A constant source of club discontent involves the level of fees, which most members want to minimize. Still, periodic major replacement of worn and broken equipment is a necessity, as is good preventative maintenance. Managers must work with board of directors' decisions on these matters, which can sometimes be counterlogical.

Club Operations

Club management and operations are a specialized career within the hospitality industry. Just as students get tired of dorm food, long-time club members want variety. Club managers often find themselves juggling the priorities of those who want things just as they've always been, and members who want things changed or improved.

Club employees often develop relationships with members over time. This can complicate matters when members interfere in issues involving managers and staff members. Members may also feel their ownership gives them the right to express complaints directly to the board, bypassing the normal chain of command and magnifying small offenses.

Club members usually consider the club as an extension of their living room. Every club member feels that the club belongs to him or her and acts accordingly. This sometimes requires a diplomatic juggling act from managers as they seek to offer a balance of events aimed at different generations and special interest groups within the membership. Club managers face a real challenge in trying to deliver fresh and interesting services and products to the same members, at acceptable prices, over extended periods of time.

Attractions

Most of us have visited an attraction at one time or another. An ***attraction*** is a place, structure, building, or scenic point that draws people for a tourist or business purpose. The source of the attraction may be a natural phenomenon or it may be a human creation. For instance, the Grand Canyon and Niagara Falls have been natural wonders for centuries, whereas the Eiffel Tower in Paris was originally built for a World Exposition at the end of the 19th century. Despite the difference in their origins and age, all these are referred to as *attractions*.

Attraction Ownership

Attractions fall into three funding-source economic categories: (1) attractions that are privately funded and operated for a profit, (2) those that are publicly

EXHIBIT 4–8   Three Major Classifications of Attractions Based on Funding

Private for Profit	Public/Nonprofit	Quasi-Public
Recreation	**National, State, Tribal, County, or Municipal/City**	
Miniature golf	Parks	Convention centers
Canoe rentals	Forests	
Rifle ranges	Monuments	Theaters
Go cart tracks	Buildings	Performing arts centers
Carnivals	Marine areas	Symphony halls
Theme parks	Battlefields	
Water parks		
Zoos		
Museums		
Art	Art	
Cultural	Historical	Heritage and cultural centers
Educational		
Historical		
Religious		
Spectator sports		
Baseball		Ball parks
Basketball		Coliseums
Boxing		
Football		Sports fields
Hockey		Sports domes
Race tracks		
Participation sports		
Bowling		
Flying		Airports, glider ports, heliports
Golf		
Sailing		Harbors, marinas, lakes, and
Skating		waterways
Swimming		
Tennis		

funded and operated as nonprofit operations, and (3) those that are quasi-public; that is, they combine private and public funding, usually for the profit of the private entity(s). Exhibit 4–8 shows some examples of each economic classification.

The lists in Exhibit 4–8 are not intended to be complete, and any number of other attractions could be added to them. Some of those traditionally classified as public may have been developed privately and later sold to governmental agencies. Often land owned by one government agency can be transferred to another government agency to become a public attraction. For instance, a U.S. Army coastal artillery training site, Camp Monomoy, on Cape Cod in Massachusetts became the Cape Cod National Seashore Park in the 1960s.

Seasonality of Attractions

Another important consideration in managing an attraction is its seasonality. Climatic conditions imposed by the changing seasons often dictate the attractiveness and the demand for hospitality services. Many attractions are only open in the summer when weather is warm and the attraction is physically accessible. Others, like Death Valley National Monument, in California, may curtail operations in the summer because of excessive heat. Managers of attractions are constantly using their ingenuity to find ways to extend their operational season and thus increase revenues. Some successful examples include ski areas that have installed Alpine slides or promoted their ski lifts as scenic rides during the summer.

Admissions

A significant feature of most attractions is their paid admission. Admission is physically controlled by entry gates to events or facilities. Tickets, often available based on inclusive or exclusive fee structures, serve as additional control devices by specifying what options visitors may access without further charge. A visit to the observation deck at the Empire State Building in New York City or a visit to a local horse racing track, movie theater, miniature golf course, or other recreation attraction requires a paid admittance. It is these fees that generate the revenues that, at least partially, cover the operational costs of running the attraction. The fees require a form of documentation such as tickets, vouchers, or passes that are accounted for (usually by serial numbers). Management can project revenues from the sale of these tickets and employ a set of accounting principles that together make up the operation's internal controls. These controls protect its revenues and record its expenditures. The average amount spent per guest/visitor is referred to as the *per capita admission expenditure*. Other per capita figures can be computed by dividing total guest/visitor expenditures on food, beverage, gifts, sundries, and souvenirs within the attraction by the total admission counts.

Visitation

A concern all attractions and hospitality operations have is to encourage repeat visitation by their client/guest base. Many hospitality operations depend on

EXHIBIT 4–9

An example of a popular theme park is Cedar Point in Sandusky, Ohio.

Courtesy: Cedar Point Amusement Park, Sandusky, Ohio.

The theme park concept has also been adopted in Europe. One of the largest theme parks is De Efteling near Tilburg, Holland.

EXHIBIT 4–10

Of the original seven wonders of the ancient world, the Egyptian pyramids are the last ones remaining. They are one of the world's most popular tourist attractions.

Photo by Phil Pappas.

repeat guests for their survival. Hotels often report greater than 85 percent repeat visitation; however, at some attractions repeat visitation dips below 10 percent. A person may only visit the Eiffel Tower or Grand Canyon once in his or her lifetime but patronize a hotel many times.

The challenge for managers of attractions or hospitality operations within, near, or as part of an attraction is to create a perceived value in the minds of guests. It is important that guests feel they have received a significant value for the money they have spent. The idea is to create an experience so perfect, with so much perceived value, that the guest will want to return. More importantly, attraction managers want their guests to boast about their experience to family, friends, and associates. This is the most treasured of all marketing achievements and is known as *word-of-mouth advertising*. Achieving this target guest experience and favorable word of mouth requires close attention to detail in every operational function of an attraction. Operators continuously look for new amenities to add to their attractions to increase return patronage.

Marketing

Marketing the attraction is a major operational concern. Marketing begins with the original vision of the attraction. From this a mission statement and marketing philosophy are created. A marketing position statement is developed to emphasize the unique aspects of the attraction. In today's market, maximum emphasis should be placed on the eco-tourist, cultural, and other socially desirable aspects of the project. Marketing should also accent the overall experience and its high perceived value to satisfied guests.

Marketing approaches are devised to persuade guests to visit the site. These approaches carry the advertising message and project an identity to potential visitors. Some of these channels include public relations, merchandising, and advertising in media such as radio, TV, newspapers, magazines, and billboards. Public relations efforts may include contests or civic contributions (such as nonprofit event sponsorships or donation of experience packages to foundations like Make a Wish). Contests and promotions are often coupled with advertising to reinforce perceived value. Hosting celebrities or recognized sports tournaments are other effective promotional tools.

Sales representatives are employed to call on potential sources of bulk business such as corporations, organizations, and associations. They attend trade shows, fairs, and tourist expositions. They will often cooperate with regional chambers of commerce or tourist bureaus to conduct sales blitzes in various geographic areas of the country. Here they will be selling the region and their property's role within the region rather than only their attraction. It is only logical that a region's attractiveness may far outweigh an individual operation as a magnet for visitors.

Eye on the Issues

Technology

Technology has been reshaping the operations of the tourism and hospitality industry at a rapid pace. Attraction and event management have been dramatically influenced by new technologies in lighting and sound. Theme parks, stadiums, and arenas often host incredible exhibitions with light shows and pyrotechnics. Festivals often feature live music, fireworks, or miles of strung minilights, especially during holiday celebrations. All these technologies require caution and concern for the safety of guests and participants. The incredible safety record of Disney, one of the pioneers of nightly light and fireworks spectacles, is due to training, security, and constant attention.

Wholesale and retail tour brokers, travel agents, and travel planners can also be an effective sales force for attractions. Listings in trade and tour directories, subscribed time on computer information networks, and placement on airline and major hotel reservation networks are all essential, since most brokers and agents use electronic computer networking to book 90 percent or more of their tours.

Miscellaneous activities such as logo gifts, novelties, premiums, clothing, and amenities can also work well for attractions. Other marketing strategies include rack brochures, direct mail, and telephone solicitation. As described in Chapter 15, "Hospitality Marketing," marketing never ends. It is a cycle that begins with research to discover guest needs, develops services to meet those needs, delivers the services to the guest, and follows with more study.

Merchandising

Closely linked to marketing is the ***merchandising*** of the attraction itself. Merchandising involves integrating all the products and services so that they are best displayed for consumption by visitors. Successful merchandising is a direct result of the master planning of the project. It includes the placement and layout of the rides, view points, food and beverage outlets, gift shops, rest areas, and entertainment. The design should subtly orchestrate the guests' maximum contact with revenue-producing areas. Included in merchandising are staff members—hosts, characters, and employees who meet and greet the visitors. They make up a large part of the value perceived by the guests. For instance, Walt Disney theme parks view all employees as actors, all uniforms as costumes, and their parks as theaters. There is no crossing the line between acting and reality. The guest must always believe in the fantasy he or she is experiencing. Merchandising encourages guests to explore more of the fantasy or to take the fantasy home with them in the form of souvenirs. Guests should feel drawn to explore around the next corner or to find out what lies behind the barker, not quite visible through the half-closed tent flap. It is management's job to make sure that guests maintain their sense of perceived value as they move from one attraction, booth, or display to the next.

Human Resource Management

Human resource management of attractions is one of the most difficult aspects of operations. Often remoteness, seasonality, and the theme of the attraction may make it extremely difficult to recruit, select, train, and motivate employees. Seasonality and remoteness may mean employees must be housed at the site and that all the traditional services must be provided—shopping areas, food, clothing, lodging, medical, schools, security, recreation, fire protection, and transportation.

Remoteness requires significant pre-employment and on-the-job training so that employees are knowledgeable about the environment to protect themselves and the guests. The theme of the attraction may require managers to continually motivate employees so that they do not destroy the image, fantasy, and perceived value guests must experience. Motivation requires managers to relay to the staff that each guest is to be viewed as a first-time visitor and that the guest experience must be perfect to assure the long-term success of the attraction. Pay and benefits must be equal to or better than other nearby facilities or employers.

A steady recruiting source for new employees must be arranged by human resource managers, and a constant attempt must be made to reduce turnover. Turnover can best be curbed in attractions by cross-training, rotation of jobs, appropriate scheduling, incentive programs, and employee benefits. Exit interviews should be employed to uncover sources of employee frustration.

Other Revenue Centers

The operation of attractions also includes some other areas that relate to revenue. Revenue centers often seen in conjunction with attractions are: food and beverage operations, merchandise and souvenir shops, rides, and games. Attraction managers need to find effective ways to blend these revenue centers into their attractions to avoid clashing with the environment they've so carefully constructed. For example, managers of a Victorian village attraction would probably match their setting with a period teahouse operation rather than with a 1950s-style diner. Their souvenir vendors would offer potpourri, Sherlock Holmes hats, and quaint music boxes rather than endangered-species tee-shirts and cartoon-character neckties.

Attraction managers also have the responsibility to provide surroundings that are not only enjoyable, but also safe for both visitors and employees. Failure to do so can lead to guest injury, lawsuits, and, far worse, negative publicity.

Running a tourist attraction is extremely complex. The management of attractions requires, just as any other hospitality operation, excellent people, financial, marketing, and many other technical skills. The challenge is great, but you can imagine the self-fulfillment managers experience when they see happy visitors coming into their attraction full of anticipation—and leaving the attraction wholly satisfied.

Events

Events, shows, expositions, and fairs are just some of the more familiar activities that attract multitudes of people to a particular place for a particular period. They are often essential to the tourism promotion of an area. Like attractions, events are largely for the enjoyment of the people who attend them. The main difference between events and attractions is that attractions are permanent and events are temporary. An event may be a one-time affair or one that is repeated periodically. Many large events take place annually and last from one day to a few months. Their relative success over time will ultimately determine the size, length, and frequency with which they occur. Events often travel from area to area depending on the season, much as traveling circuses did during earlier years. Events are held for many reasons. Some broad classifications of events include:

- Religious
- Cultural
- Technical
- Economic
- Amusement
- Political

- Historical
- Sporting
- Social
- Recreational

Events can also be classified on the basis of geographical locations and degree of importance. For instance, internationally known mega-events include world's fairs and the Olympics. Regional events include state fairs and other such events, while local events are generally city or community sponsored.

Obviously, many events evolve around a theme, as do attractions. It is this overriding theme that the guest wishes to experience and remember after departure. The theme (and the experience of it) becomes a silent salesperson through word-of-mouth advertising and is responsible for motivating other visitors to share the event's experience. Event managers have the responsibility to assure that the theme is carried throughout the operation.

Events generate significant revenues through admissions, seating charges, food and beverage sales, souvenir programs and publications, recorded music sales, and other items. The most difficult to manage is the food and beverage aspects. As part of the event, sufficient food and beverages must be available to serve the visitors' needs. Since attendance is highly unpredictable due to weather, type of event, and competition from other nearby activities, the concession manager must rely on historical data and a lot of luck.

Since most events are outdoor activities and last only short periods of time, a good deal of temporary or portable concession equipment and stands must be used. Employees must be recruited from nearby communities to work at the concession stands, prepare and deliver the food, and care for and clean the facilities. Only a limited amount of time is available to train these employees, so concessionaires employ a permanent cadre of department managers to train and oversee them.

Cash management is extremely important, and a staff of security and money runners must constantly collect the cash from the stands and deliver it to the counting room. Accounting for food and beverages sold is accomplished through elaborate stock sheets and cash registers, where available. Each food item and drink cup has a value. An inventory procedure is used to track consumption. Since each item has a value, those missing from inventory are considered consumed and a like amount of money for their value must have been received in cash.

Vendors may be employed to roam through the crowds selling food, drinks, and souvenirs. They operate from vending stations and account for their items in a similar fashion. Most vendors are paid a cash commission based on their sales. They must provide their own change bank and pay a reduced price for their items before they sell them. Care must be taken to be sure that vendors do not sell items for prices higher than the price set by management. To prevent this, badges, signs, and item packaging must clearly display the prices. Often these items will be a combination refreshment/souvenir. At the Kentucky Derby, for instance, mint juleps are vended in a take-home high-ball glass. A recent trend in coliseums and sports parks is the availability of recognized franchise food outlets. Pizza Hut, McDonald's, Wendy's, Orange Julius, KFC, and Taco Bell may be represented in a food pavilion area. These may all be owned and operated by the concessionaire, leased, or operated individually.

Conclusion

This chapter touched on four major aspects of the tourism and hospitality industry. It outlines many potential exciting career opportunities for hospitality graduates in club, resort, attraction, and event management. Although each area has it own focus and specialization, the common denominator is hospitality service. A hospitality graduate with good people skills and appropriate preparation in finance, technology, and management can excel in any of these areas.

Keywords

spa   94
destination resort   96
activity-based resort   97
high season   97

shoulder season   97
low-season   98
equity club   102
development club   102

Core Concepts

resort hotels   93
seasonality   97
length of stay   98
private clubs   102

attraction   107
merchandising   113
event   114

Discussion Questions

1. Discuss the differences between resorts and nonresorts. Mention at least one from each of the following areas:
   a. Marketing
   b. Guest motivation
   c. Housekeeping
   d. Food and beverage

   Now add one more difference *from an area not included in a, b, c, or d.*

2. What are the effects of seasonality on resort pricing, marketing, staff, and operations?

3. With what do resort managers in remote locations have to deal that city hotel operators do not? Discuss staffing, transportation, utilities, and environmental impacts.

4. Discuss how consumers' hotel choices differ when they book a resort hotel as opposed to deciding where to stay in a city.

5. What departments might exist in a resort that are not typically found in city and suburban hotels?

6. What differentiates an equity club from a development club?

7. How does the club organizational structure differ from that of most midsize hotels?

8. What are the major sources of club revenues? Of club expenditures?

9. Why do many clubs impose a minimum monthly fee on their members?

10. Identify the revenue centers of attraction operations.

11. What are three of the major operational challenges for a concession manager in managing an event?

Casino Management

This chapter is devoted to casino management and the operational aspects of gaming. It addresses all of the current issues in gaming that have transpired from its early history—the prevention of fraud, government control, the Indian Gaming Regulatory Act, how the games are played, and how the casinos market their facilities. Future hospitality and casino managers need to be aware of the peculiarities and challenges of this exciting and continuously evolving segment of the hospitality industry.

Outline

Introduction

Casinos and gaming are growing in popularity. Almost all states and many Indian reservations now have some form of gaming activity, and the number of facilities is increasing continually. From charity bingo to high-stakes table games, the growth potential of this segment of hospitality—and the management opportunities it offers—is unmatched.

Casinos differ from more traditional hospitality operations such as hotels, restaurants, and recreation centers in that guests willfully involve themselves in risky activities. Casinos play upon the feeling of elation that guests experience from taking those risks. The "rush" often intensifies as players win, then lose, then win again. The exposure to risk and the defiance of odds in a casino game are not unlike the feeling one gets when "pulling G's" on a carnival ride. It's scary (partly because you are not in control), but temporary—when the ride ends, everything will be back to normal. Unlike a carnival ride, though, if guests can demonstrate some skill in playing casino games, they have some control over the outcome of their experience.

Contrary to popular belief, casinos make a profit even when guests win. In return for giving guests the privilege of gambling, casinos collect a share of the amounts wagered. They do so, "invisibly" to most players, by paying less than the correct odds to winners. This is called the *casino advantage* and will be discussed later. For now, let us look at a scenario that demonstrates a few truths about odds and winning.

Suppose Carl from Kansas enters a casino and decides to try his luck at the card game of Blackjack (also known as *21*). He spots a seat at a table where the dealer looks friendly. After watching the play for a few minutes, Carl sees that the object of the game is to score as close to 21 as possible—without going over. He sits down and exchanges a $100 bill for twenty $5.00 tokens, then places $10.00 worth of chips on his space. The dealer deals him two cards that total 20 points. At one point less than 21, 20 points is a good score. In fact, it would be risky to ask for another card, since only an ace would prevent his total from going over the limit of 21. For Kansas Carl to lose this hand, the dealer would have to beat Carl's score. Carl "holds" pat at 20 points.

The dealer deals more cards to the other players. He then turns over his own cards, which total 11 points. The dealer, by rule, must take one more card, which comes up a face card (10 points). Carl winces. The dealer's total is 21—and Carl and most of the other players have lost their bets to the dealer. In subsequent hands, Carl's fellow players win and lose. Even Kansas Carl wins a few hands, but after a while he decides to quit, having lost his entire original $100.00. During this time the dealer has been collecting lost bets and paying them back out to winning players. Thus, the winners are being paid with the losers' money. Though this doesn't cost the casino anything, neither does it generate a profit—and profit is a necessity.

To make a profit, the casino charges a percentage of the winnings it pays out. Each game in the casino has its own percentage based on the probability of playing and winning the game (the true odds of winning). To this, a casino adds a fee structure, and from this combination the casino odds are established. When a player wins, he or she is paid based on this casino odds percentage.

The casino retains the difference between the true odds and the casino odds—and this is where it takes its profit.

These profits from gaming separate casinos from other hospitality businesses. They are so large that other auxiliary services, such as lodging, food and beverage, entertainment, and recreation, become secondary and are frequently operated at a minimum profit (or even a loss) in order to support more profitable gaming activities. Because of their overwhelming profits, gaming departments often give away or "comp" services to attract gamblers.

A comp is a marketing technique used to encourage players to wager more money in order to qualify for certain complimentary awards. These awards are based on the levels of gaming activity and can include show tickets, meals, special dining, accommodations, transportation, and special guest status. A comp is usually a service or product of another department in the casino complex.

In fact, the gaming department often pays other internal departments retail value for their services. For instance, suppose Kansas Carl would have paid $69 for his room at the casino's hotel. If the gaming department comps Carl's room, it would then pay the rooms department the $69 room rate Carl would have paid. This is accomplished through transfers from the promotion expense account of the gaming department. Many casinos compete for big-spending gamblers by offering free rooms, meals, transportation, show entertainment, and recreation activities. The profits from gaming enable them to do so without bankrupting the other departments.

The management of the other hospitality activities in a casino requires the same amount of care and devotion as in freestanding hotels and restaurants. In fact, casino guests, particularly losers, are sometimes more demanding than average guests, since they assume their lost wagers pay for the extravagant and opulent surroundings. Moreover, casinos are often called upon to provide services not typically requested by guests in traditional hotels, such as amusement parks, extravagant shows, and 24-hour feasts. This requires increased staffing and greater departmentalization. While most traditional hotels have an employee-to-guest ratio of .5 or 1 to 1, hotel casinos often have three or four employees for every one customer. The resulting organizational structure is very large and consequently complicates management's tasks. Let's take a closer look at some of the specifics involved in managing the rapidly evolving and growing field of gaming.

Casinos

Gaming is without a doubt the most rapidly growing segment in the hospitality industry. As more states legalize gaming and many Indian tribes exercise their sovereignties to conduct gaming, management opportunities in this segment will be unsurpassed. This section will discuss the history of gaming, government regulations on gaming, and the management of various gaming activities. Notice that the term *gaming* has come to be preferred over its synonym *gambling*.

Gaming History

In the United States, gaming and wagering can be traced back to the days of the Revolutionary War. Lotteries were used to finance George Washington's Continental Army, and to build roads (turnpikes) and bridges. Gambling centers such as Saratoga, New York, and Newport, Rhode Island, were largely created as recreational amenities to the spas and medicinal and recreational facilities that attracted the wealthy class. In the western territories it was part of the culture at the turn of the 18th century and gambling saloons flourished in many cities, such as Tombstone, Arizona Territory.

During the 19th century, gambling halls flourished in New Orleans and on the paddle wheel steamers of the Mississippi River. In 1835, the Palace of Fortune was operated successfully in Washington, D.C., and even President Buchanan sometimes visited the facility.[1]

Gaming's popularity and social acceptability waxed and waned over the years, depending on prevailing morality and economics. During the Great Depression of the 1930s, Nevada and many other states were hard hit. Nevada, however, saw gaming as a way to raise much-needed revenue for the state and to control the illegal gambling that already operated within its borders. In 1931, Nevada legalized gaming in a legislative gamble that paid off handsomely. Not long afterward, when the development of the Hoover Dam outside Las Vegas brought many workers to that remote area with no place to spend their pay, the nearby casinos were soon overcrowded.

World War II brought a multitude of travelers to Nevada, and many new gaming facilities were built. By the late 1940s, the Flamingo, the Last Frontier, the El Cortez, and the El Rancho were in operation in Las Vegas, which continued to grow. Today, it has more casinos and hotel rooms than any other city in the world.

The next four decades saw gaming develop as a primarily adult form of entertainment. In the late 1980s and early 1990s, this focus shifted in ways gaming pioneers would have never foreseen. With the opening of the 5,001-room MGM Grand in December 1993, the trend in Las Vegas changed from adult-oriented gaming thrills to multifaceted entertainment in which gaming is only one aspect. Theme parks, movie stunt spectaculars, circus acts, theme entrances (such as Treasure Island's pirate ship battle, Luxor's Sphinx and pyramid, the Mirage's erupting volcano, and Excalibur's castle) have transformed Las Vegas into a giant fantasy land targeting the family travel market.

EXHIBIT 5–1

A modern pyramid of glass and steel rivals the ancient structures—but for different reasons.

Courtesy: Luxor Hotel Casino, Las Vegas, Nevada.

Environment

The ecological impact of new and exiting casinos must be closely monitored by sponsoring communities. Impact on wildlife, flora, fauna, water resources, and air from potential pollutants and environmental stress should be assessed before new ventures will be allowed. Casinos attract a large number of guests whose concerns are far from environmental. Casino managers will bear responsibility for actions by their guests.

The surge in casino construction on Native American tribal lands, in particular, has caused concern about access and traffic management on roads that previously received minimal use. Additionally, the volume of visitors descending upon reservation casinos has grown enormously, causing unforeseen littering problems. It's now accepted that adequate waste management and recycling efforts must be built into future developments.

The other major gaming center in the United States is Atlantic City, New Jersey. In 1976, the state legalized gaming in the restricted geographic area of Atlantic City with the objective of economic development. At the time, Atlantic City was a city of high unemployment, deteriorating infrastructure, and urban decay. Carefully crafted casino regulations and building-size requirements allowed a casino company, Resorts International, to virtually monopolize Atlantic City for the first years of legalized gaming.

Today, Atlantic City has many large casinos, and its location near the major metropolitan areas of the northeast has given it a unique market. Most of its visitors are "turn around" gaming customers, arriving and departing by bus, playing only for short periods of time. This differs from Las Vegas, which relies on "destination" or longer visitor stays.

Recent entries into low-stakes gaming include the towns of Blackhawk, Cripple Creek, and Central City, Colorado; and Deadwood, South Dakota. Gaming has recently received approval in Chicago, Illinois, and a major casino development is under construction in New Orleans, Louisiana.

Government Regulation

Regulation and control of gaming are an individual state issue. Under the Tenth Amendment, police powers are granted to all states by the U.S. Constitution. Therefore, each state's legislature has the right to enact or ban gaming within its borders. A recent act of Congress, the *Indian Gaming Regulatory Act* (IGRA), recognized the sovereign status of Native American tribes and their right to conduct gaming. Once enacted, legalized gaming may be licensed and regulated by the state and some tribes through a casino control commission. Each state enacts regulations that are then interpreted and enforced by a casino control board (as in Nevada) or other government agency.

When Native American gaming became legal in 1987 with the IGRA's passing, Indian tribes saw gaming as a way to encourage economic development and provide employment. The U.S. Congress saw Indian gaming as a potential source of income for the tribes and as a way for the federal government to reduce tribal subsidies. The act specified that final gaming approval rests with the individual states in which federally recognized Native American reservations are located. States were directed to enter into compacts in good faith, and to allow gaming on the reservations. The result was that almost all states where federally recognized tribes reside have, or are negotiating, compacts.

To gain themselves a piece of the casino action, some states have entered into financial participation with tribes. Connecticut, for instance, where table games were allowed and slot machines forbidden, reversed its slots policy for a percentage of the slot take at the Foxwood's Casino in Ledyard. In return, this casino, which until the opening of the MGM Grand in Las Vegas was the largest in the world, is guaranteed to be the only casino in the state.

Gaming can be classified as high stakes or low stakes. High-stakes gaming has no limits on the amounts that may be wagered and is found in Nevada, New Jersey, and in some Native American casinos. Low-stakes gaming, with bet limits on each game, predominates elsewhere. Each type of gaming requires its own level of licensing and enforcement. States often introduce legalized gaming within certain geographic locations under the banner of economic development because of the likelihood of increasing local employment, increasing income, and generating tax revenues. In return for granting these privileges, the states receive large tax revenues and license fees.

Low-stakes gaming has been authorized by some states along the Mississippi and other rivers. These states have authorized a fixed number of river boats on which gaming may be conducted. They have also limited port locations, number of departures, and the stakes in each game.

Other states have authorized so-called *floating casinos* (see Exhibit 5–2). Here the only requirement is that the casino actually floats. No requirement exists with regard to river or waterway navigability. The result is that cities like Tunica, Mississippi, have massive casinos built *on the shore* of a waterway. Before entering the casino, guests cross over a bridge. Once the water has been crossed, all classes of gaming are available and legal.

In Iowa, any riverboat may apply for a casino license. The few restrictions include that the vessel must accommodate a minimum of 500 people; that the maximum of 30 percent of the space on the boat be designated for gaming; that there be one table game for each 20 slot machines; and that bets do not

EXHIBIT 5–2

*Riverboat gaming,
once popular in the
19th century, is
seeing a revival. One
of the most popular
gaming venues in
New Orleans is
Hilton's Flamingo
Casino on the
Mississippi.*

Courtesy: New Orleans Hilton Riverside.

exceed $5.00 with a $200.00 loss maximum per individual player. Illinois and Louisiana have similar regulations though they have limited the number of vessels and facilities.[2]

Casino Operations

Gaming is generally categorized into three types. Laws define Type I gaming as games that are played as part of a heritage and culture, such as lacrosse, long-distance running, and games of physical dexterity. Type II gaming includes bingo, pull tabs, lotto, and punch boards. Type III gaming involves the nonbanked games such as slots, keno, race and sports book, and banked games such as craps, roulette, and 21.

All casinos share certain characteristics. To be successful, casino games must give a winning advantage to the house. As indicated earlier, this is called the *casino advantage* and represents the percentage that the house keeps from all gaming transactions. This is their charge to the players for the privilege of gambling. This advantage is difficult to pinpoint with accuracy because it fluctuates based on the number of players, amounts wagered, and the number of gaming transactions. The casino will always pay off at a percentage slightly lower than the correct odds. *Correct odds* are defined as the true statistical

EXHIBIT 5–3   **The Game of Roulette**

> In the game of roulette, there are 18 ways to win by playing either red or black, and 20 out of 38 ways to lose. (The roulette wheel displays 38 numbers: 18 are black, 18 are red, and 2 are green zeros.) The odds expression of 20 to 18, as a percentage against the player, is 52.6 percent and represents the casino advantage (20/38 = 52.6%).

Source: J. Gollehon, *Casino Games* (Grand Rapids, MI: Gollehon, 1988).

odds of a given occurrence in a number of repetitions. (There is no advantage or disadvantage to correct odds.)

As a general rule of thumb, the casino advantage is closer to the actual **odds of winning** on a game than to the correct odds. However, even this expression is subject to misinterpretation, since odds are really expressed as the "odds of losing." For instance, suppose Kansas Carl knows that the odds are 20:1 if he plays Big Six Wheel. He places a $10 chip on the $20 portion of the wheel, thinking he has a 20:1 chance to win. If he understood the odds expression 20:1, Carl would know that the first number expresses the number of times he will lose, while the second number equates to the number of times he will win. The sum of the two numbers is the total number of all probabilities. Thus, Carl might expect to win once in 21 plays. Expressed as a percentage, these odds mean that a player will win 4.76 percent of the time (1/21 = 4.76%) instead of the perceived odds of 5 percent (1/20 = 5%). A further example is given in Exhibit 5–3.

One can be assured, then, that in the long run, the casino will always win.

Win, Drop, and Hold PC

Win, drop, and *hold percentage* are terms the casino uses to monitor its financial performance. Even though each game has a determined payout (casino odds) to winners, each game has many ways (combinations of winnings paid out) in which the casino advantage is applied. To consolidate all of these advantages, the casino adopts the term *hold PC*. To determine the PC, other amounts must be tracked. They are the *win* and the *drop*.

The concept of *win* is the result of subtracting the original amount of money to bankroll a game from the *drop,* or the amount of money exchanged for chips (tokens with various monetary denominations that are used to place wagers) at the game. Casinos use these two amounts to compute a hold percentage (hold PC) with which they monitor the performance of the games. To compute the hold PC, the win is divided by the drop. The objective of every casino, then, is to obtain the largest drop available, as Exhibit 5–5 shows.

The drop for the various games depends on casino location, game mix, volume of play, and type of players. Casinos go to elaborate lengths to monitor the performance of individual games, slot machines, and even casino dealers.

Exhibit 5–4

A common sight in many casinos.

ROULETTE WHEEL

THE ROULETTE WHEEL has 36 numbers from 1 to 36, plus a "0" and a "00". The numbers are alternately colored red and black, with the "0" and "00" green.

Play begins when the players have placed most of their bets by putting their chips on the numbered layout.

The Dealer then spins the small white ball in the opposite direction of the spinning wheel. Bets may be placed until the ball is about ready to leave the track and the Dealer signals no more bets. The Dealer then points out the winning number and bets are paid accordingly.

Checks (chips) can be bought in stacks of 20 from the Dealer. Each player is given different colored checks. You may bet money as well as checks and make as many bets as you wish, (up to the table pay off limit).

0	00

1 to 18	1st 12	1	2	3
		4	5	6
		7	8	9
EVEN		10	11	12
	2nd 12	13	14	15
		16	17	18
		19	20	21
		22	23	24
ODD	3rd 12	25	26	27
		28	29	30
19 to 36		31	32	33
		34	35	36
		2 to 1	2 to 1	2 to 1

EXHIBIT 5–5   The Drop and Hold PC Concept

Drop = All cash in the drop box

Win = Drop − (Table fills − Table credits)

Win ÷ Drop = Hold PC

Dealers are assigned their own hold percentage (based on performance) and their contributions to the games' drop are tracked. Since some dealers have better skills (in terms of contribution to drop) at some games than at others, casinos rotate them to games where they contribute the greatest drop. Over a period of time each game and each dealer will produce a consistent hold percentage. In an honestly run casino the hold percentages over 30 days will be roughly:

Game	Hold
Craps	20%
21	26
Roulette	30
Baccarat	10
Big Six	80

Source: J. Scarnes, *Complete Guide to Gambling* (New York: Simon & Schuster, 1986).

Eye on the Issues

Ethics

During the emergence of gaming in the years following World War II, casinos were infiltrated by underworld figures. These characters have been portrayed in Hollywood productions as *The Godfather, Bugsy,* and others. The stigma of the underworld influence has dominated the perception of the gaming industry and the unethical practices then condoned. "I'll make you an offer you can't refuse" was not atypical of the way business was conducted. By the late 1960s most of the crime syndicates had been bought out by legitimate businesses. Howard Hughes and others helped Nevada casinos lose their bad image.

Today, this image has been largely erased and a family atmosphere has been created. Casino management companies are among the best run and ethically concerned hospitality firms. Certainly, occasional favors are done for guests who have influence or are high rollers, but most of them are done as comps and are accepted business procedure. A person entering a career in the casino business today can be assured that the company will treat him or her ethically and expect ethical behavior in return.

This means that if customers bet $1 million on craps during one month, the casino, which has a hold percentage of 20 percent on craps, will make $200,000.

The hold percentage is not entirely profit. The cost of operating a casino is greater than that of other hospitality businesses. Two of the greatest costs are fixed expense (such as lease and mortgage payments) and labor. (As mentioned earlier, employee-to-guest ratios are very high: often 5 to 1 or higher). All these expenses are deducted from the total moneys collected as casino hold. The hold is a little like gross sales revenues of other businesses. If a pizza outlet sells $1 million in pizzas, it doesn't make a profit of $1 million. It must subtract the cost of paying its employees to make the pizzas, the cost of ingredients, and its expenses for rent, utilities, and so on before it can even begin to estimate its profit. Likewise, a casino must subtract its costs of doing business from its total hold income before it can compute profit. This is not a perfect analogy, but it does offer a simple explanation of the difference between total moneys collected and total profit.

Gaming Marketing

Marketing is the secret to success of any casino operation. Casinos must not only identify their guests but also design ways to satisfy them and get them to patronize their operation. Casinos use the same techniques as other hospitality operations, differing only in their tendency to use more promotions, packages, celebrities, contests, and *static attractions,* such as golf, shows with big-name entertainers, fine restaurants, and deluxe accommodations. Casinos spend a great deal of money on their marketing, often more than 7 percent of gross revenues, which is substantially higher than the lodging industry average of 5.2 percent.

Since guests must visit the casino to gamble, many different techniques are used to attract them, to enhance their visit, and to encourage them to remain at the property after they arrive. One of the newest methods used to attract guests is family entertainment. For many years, Las Vegas relied on gaming and adult entertainment to draw visitors to its casinos. However, the introduction of legalized gaming in a number of states and on Native American reservations has caused Nevada's casinos to shift their marketing efforts dramatically.

Characterized as a type of adult Disneyland in the past, Las Vegas has taken entertainment in a different direction. Whereas in the past, casinos relied on celebrities to attract guests into the showroom and onto the casino gaming floor, they have now shifted to permanent family-oriented attractions such as the white tigers at the Mirage and the theme park at the MGM Grand. Their marketing emphasis highlights a total entertainment package. The strategy is to generate more revenues from the entertainment side and to maximize nongaming as well as gaming revenues. This has proved successful for the Circus Circus Enterprises, the MGM Grand, the Mirage, Luxor, and others. Not only has nongaming revenue increased, so has the average guest's length of stay.

Ironically, the emergence of gaming in other states and on Native American reservations has spawned a type of breeding ground for future Las Vegas visitors. Once people have tried low-stakes gaming in nearby casinos, they are more willing to visit Las Vegas and its gaming action with their new sense of skill and game mastery. The intimidating atmosphere of Las Vegas is waning as more confident visitors elect to vacation in this once forbidden city.

The entertainment attraction, as a marketing tool, has extended beyond the casinos—it has become part of their exteriors. Now erupting volcanoes and pirate ship battles are free attractions at the entrances of casinos in an effort to draw more people onto the gaming floors. At Caesar's a moving walkway takes guests from the "strip" (the term given to Las Vegas Boulevard, the site of most casinos) into the casino. As might be expected, the casinos make no provision to shuttle people back to the strip.

Each casino attempts to provide each visitor with what is termed a ***total guest experience*** (TGE). This experience is a culmination of service, gaming, entertainment, food and beverage, guest rooms, and amenities enjoyed by the guest. It is this TGE that becomes the ultimate marketing edge and dominates a casino's marketing philosophy. If the TGE is successfully overwhelming, guests go home gushing to their families and friends. These positive word-of-mouth exclamations ultimately bring more guests to the casino.

Las Vegas casinos also employ the services of a convention and visitors bureau to help them attract more guests. Conventions represent a major market for the casinos, and Las Vegas's new family-style entertainment has made it an acceptable convention site to many organizations that had steered clear of the city in years past. The Las Vegas Convention and Visitors Authority has divided the market into six target-market segments: conventions, corporate meetings and incentives, international travelers, special events and travel wholesalers, retail travel agents, and individual consumers.[3] Each of these segments represents a significant contribution to the casinos' revenues.

In addition to the physical layout, amenities, and atmosphere, casinos employ hosts to make sure guests are enjoying themselves. Hosts are responsible for tracking a guest's gambling activity and issuing complimentary goods and services. A system of rating gambling activity exists at most casinos, and guests are given comps based on their rated gaming activity (see Exhibit 5–6). The higher the rating, the more comps are given. Rating forms are filled out by casino executives.

Competition among casinos to offer comps becomes an important factor in "high-roller" gamblers' decisions to patronize one casino over another. Casinos may give away penthouse suites, show tickets, and dining privileges, and even provide transportation by private jet for their better customers.

Casinos also employ sports figures and other celebrities to act as their hosts in the hopes of attracting their fans. Tournaments and promotions are often used to lure guests to a casino by offering large jackpots or prizes. Most of these theme events are promoted over media channels to gain publicity for the casino. In the long run, guests who participate in these events will normally gamble away as much as they win in the jackpots.

EXHIBIT 5–6

Casino hosts are employed to rate guests' gaming activity. These ratings are used as a basis for awarding "comps."

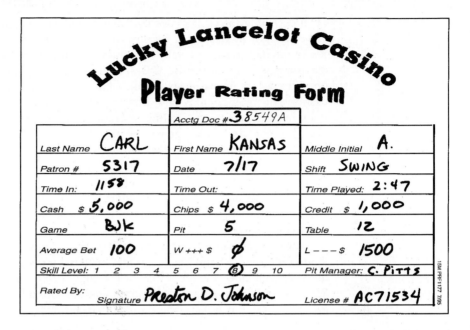

Until recently, casino executives often employed or contracted with "junket masters" to bring high rollers to their casinos. These junket masters were well-connected with the wealthy and speculative set in most large cities. It was their role to size up clients' creditworthiness, arrange their travel to the casino, and provide them with their initial bankroll. At one time, junket action represented a large percentage of casino drops, but it has faded for several reasons. The first is expense. Casinos must pay a junket master a percentage of the profit they make on each of his or her players. The second reason is tied to the emergence of megacasino resorts. Most of these now have their own in-house high-roller development staff and no longer require the services of junket masters.

Control Issues

Credit approval, the protection of a casino's bankroll, and control of the games are the most important responsibilities of a casino manager.

Casino Credit.   The credit policy of a casino affects its total drop. Since many wealthy guests return repeatedly, the casino can extend gambling credit to these individuals without a great deal of risk. Since the money is already in the casino, it takes very little effort to loan it to approved customers. Of course, elaborate tracking techniques need to be in place and control policies need to be established. A liberal credit policy, however, can add millions to a casino's total drop.

How does a player get credit? Suppose Carl from Kansas drives to Las Vegas, a stranger to one and all without any large amounts of cash. Carl can obtain credit at the casino cage by filling out a casino credit application (just as he would when applying for any credit transaction). The casino cage will verify the information (usually by computer link) to credit bureaus and agencies such as Dun & Bradstreet. Based on the information obtained, Carl will be given a line of credit upon which he can gamble. Once established, the casino will track his play and draws against the credit line. They will also track his repayments to this line of credit. For this privilege the casino will charge a monthly percentage on any unpaid amounts.

Credit can be granted either before play from the casino cage or at the table. Credit granted at the table during play is termed **rim credit** and is given to players who have established a credit line with the casino. As each set of gaming tables makes up a "pit," control of the rim credit must be handled from this pit. The pit boss (pit supervisor) is responsible for verifying and approving the credit.

Casinos also have policies to deal with guests who may have exceeded their credit limits. Some casinos offer "walking money," which assures that the guest can enjoy the rest of his or her stay in Las Vegas and return home. Strong-arm tactics are avoided and reputations are protected. For some premium casinos, a bad debt is just another risk of doing business.

Protection of Casino Bankroll.   The *casino bankroll* is a term given to the money that is placed out in the banks of individual games and machines. For instance, at an average-sized casino, a 21 game might have a bank of $50,000, while a craps table would likely have a bank of $250,000. It is from these banks that winners are paid. The casino manager is charged with protecting this bank from theft and misuse. All these banks, together, constitute the casino bankroll, which can be likened to a large petty cash fund found at most hotels. All draws against and issues to table banks are recorded, and the total must balance at all times.

The drop (all the money that has been exchanged for chips at the table) is collected from the tables three times a day; this is a highly regulated and monitored activity. In the casino-cage vault room, TV cameras monitor each box as it is opened and counted. Each box number and its monetary contents are read off verbally and videotaped. This counting procedure is referred to as the *soft count*. (Coins from the slot machine drop boxes comprise the "hard count.") The Casino Control Commission has representatives present during these counts and retains the videotapes. No owners or operators are allowed in the count room. This is to prevent the possibility of **skimming** (stealing money before it is counted). After the money is counted, the casino bankroll is replenished, and the remaining money is packaged for deposit to the bank.

Control of Games.   The casino manager has the responsibility of controlling the games and protecting the casino bankroll from unsavory guests and employees. The manager is helped with elaborate security devices and gaming controls. His or her greatest assistance, however, comes from other casino executives.

Exhibit 5–7

Native American tribes are using gaming and tourism revenues as forms of economic development.

Courtesy: Cow Creek Indian Gaming Center, Canyonville, Oregon.

Eye on the Issues

International

As the travel market becomes more globalized, managers of casinos will need to appeal to international visitors, even more than they've done in the past. This can be done through multilingual and multicultural presentations and services. Multilanguage brochures and videotapes with foreign language subtitles should be available on site. Also, a foreign game offered in a casino may have some drawing power for visitors from that country or region; for example, the mahjong game would draw many visitors from Asia. A host or hostess with the language and cultural knowledge of certain countries should greet the tour groups from these foreign countries when they first arrive at the casino, assisting them in learning the casino's guest features and services. Attention to and respect for international tourists will help assure high attendance and guest satisfaction.

Casino executives oversee dealer activity. Control and protection of casino cash is most difficult in table games because an accurate counting of the total amount wagered (termed the **handle**) is not possible. Control is exercised initially by the dealer (employee who deals the game), the **floor walker** (the manager responsible for antitheft), and the pit boss.

The pit may contain any mix of tables, but generally has a number of tables whose total dealer positions are divisible by three. Dealers work 40 minutes "on" and 20 minutes "off" per hour. By using three as the divider, positions are covered during the entire shift. Usually, a senior dealer will act as the relief dealer. Following is a detailed discussion of how the major banking and nonbanking games are operated and controlled.

Control of Banked Games.   This part will describe the operations and control of the major banked games: craps, big six wheel, roulette, 21, and baccarat.

Craps.   Craps requires four employees, two dealers (to receive bets and pay winners), a ''stickman'' (who controls the dice), and a ''boxperson'' (who controls the bankroll), as illustrated in Exhibit 5–8. Depending on the volume of activity at the craps table, a floor walker may double as a dealer or boxperson. The stickman controls the speed of the game. Great care is taken to keep the play moving, because the speed of play can greatly improve the drop at a craps table. Normally, the quicker the play, the greater the excitement, which generally leads to larger drops.

Dealers have to take bets, issue chips, calculate winnings, and pay off winners rapidly. Because they handle so much money (in the form of chips), their behavior is scrutinized to prevent fraud. A mirror on the inside edge of the table allows the boxperson and floorwalker to monitor the exchange of money and chips between players and dealers. Craps dealers who attempt to steal conspire with a collusion partner who poses as a player. Their methods often include paying off more than actually won by concealing larger-value chips under smaller-value chips or handing chips directly to their agents when the boxperson or floorwalkers are preoccupied. The opportunity for fraud extends to the other side of the table—since guests may attempt to substitute tainted (''loaded'') dice into the game (see Exhibit 5–9). The stickman watches for this. Before every roll, the dice must be passed to the boxperson for inspection and approval. These measures effectively reduce fraud by players and employees.

An Inside Look at Craps

Casino Dice
Each die is six-sided and .750 millimeters wide. The dots are actually drilled indentations painted and smoothed to a finished surface.

The Play
Any number of players may play.

The game is played on a felt-covered table with solid railings that are padded on the inside.

The player throwing the dice is termed the *shooter*. The dice pass from right to left as new shooters take their turns.

Two casino dice are thrown by the shooter so that they bounce off the padded side of the table furthest from the shooter. This first roll is termed the *come out roll*.

If, on this roll, the shooter obtains a 7 or 11, the roll is a winner and is called a *natural* or a *pass*.

If the shooter obtains a 2, 3, or 12 on the come out roll, the roll is a loser or a ''crap.''

EXHIBIT 5–8

*Can you identify the
stickman, boxperson,
and dealers?*

EXHIBIT 5–9   Tainted Dice

Some of the most common ways of tainting dice
include:

Drilling a hole and inserting weights.

Rounding the edges of dice.

Applying heat with an iron to one side of a die.
When the die cools, it will return to its normal size
and shape.

If the shooter throws a 4, 5, 6, 8, 9 or 10, the roll is called his/her *point*. The player continues throwing the dice until he/she either throws a point again or throws a 7, which is now a loser or ''miss out.''

The casino advantage is always better than the true odds on all wagers made.

Most Common Bets

All bets must be made before the dice are thrown. Bets are made with the dealers and overseen by the boxperson.

Right bet. ''Right bettors'' bet with the shooter that he will roll a natural on the come out roll or establish a point before rolling a seven. Players place their wagers on the ''pass line.''

Wrong bet. ''Wrong bettors'' bet against the shooter that the dice ''don't pass.'' Players place their wagers on the ''don't pass line.''

Come bet. This bet is made after a point is established and the player is betting with the shooter to roll the point again before a seven.

Don't come bet. This bet is the same as a come bet except now the player is betting against the shooter, that he or she will shoot a seven before his point.

Big six and big eight. With these bets a player is wagering that a six or eight will be thrown before a seven.

Field bets. An even money bet that the numbers 3, 4, 9, 10, or 11 will be rolled and a double-the-money bet on 2 or 12.

Proposition bets. These are so-called *side bets* and are either ''hard way bets'' (obtained by rolling pair combinations) or ''horn bets,'' which are one-roll bets on the numbers 2, 3, 11, and 12 at the same time.

Big Six Wheel and Roulette.   Big six wheel and roulette both involve numbered wheels spun by a dealer. Big six uses a large wheel mounted vertically, while roulette uses a smaller, horizontally mounted wheel. Both games require only one dealer. Each game has a corresponding table upon which bets are placed.

An Inside Look at Big Six (often known as wheel of fortune)

Any number of players may play.

The game is played on a vertically mounted wheel with 50 sections around the outer rim. Forty-eight of these sections have U.S. dollar denominations ranging from $1.00 to $20.00. The two remaining slots have a joker or flag as a symbol.

There are seven corresponding betting spaces on the betting table. A wager on any of the dollar face amounts will pay that amount. The flag and joker pay 40 to 1.

The players place their bets and the dealer spins the wheel. A leather thong on top of the wheel clicks through each place on the wheel until it stops. The bill face in which it stops is the winner. The casino odds on this game are over 18 percent to the casino's advantage.

An Inside Look at Roulette

A small ivory ball dances inside the spinning wheel to land on a black, red, or green number.

Any number of players may play.

The roulette wheel is mounted horizontally on a felt-covered table upon which the players place their bets. The wheel and corresponding table felt have 38 spaces. The numbers alternate red and black from 1 to 36. There is also one green zero and one double green zero for a total of 38 spaces.

The wheel is spun clockwise and play begins when the dealer spins counterclockwise a small white ivory ball in a track inside the edge of the spinning wheel.

The players are allowed to bet up until the ball begins to drop out of the track and onto the numbers. The numbers are painted inside slots separated by small metal edges called *ferrets*. There are also diamond-shaped "canoes" on the wheel's surface that act to deflect the ball.

The ball lands in a number that is declared a winner. A marker is placed on the number on the felt and the dealer first pays off all "outside" bets and then all "inside" bets according to the odds established by the casino.

The casino advantage at roulette is approximately 5.26 percent, which is one of the best odds for the player in a casino.

Blackjack (or 21). Card game dealers follow set dealing procedures and their every move is recorded by hidden TV surveillance cameras located above their tables (called the **eye in the sky**). For example, 21 dealers, before leaving the table to go on breaks, must show both sides of their hands to the camera to prove that they do not have any concealed chips. Any deviation from the normal procedures will prompt security personnel to investigate.

Most theft by dealers occurs from "subs" (derived from *submarine*). This is a method of stealing chips by dropping them into hidden pockets in clothing. Since most chips are made of clay, they make a specific noise when struck together. Floorwalkers, attuned to the sound, are often alerted by the distinctive clicking made when the thief drops stolen chips into his or her pocket. As a precaution, most casinos require dealers to wear shirts and aprons without pockets.

Card game dealers also steal by employing **agents** or "confederates." Floorwalkers become suspicious of these agents because they tend to play only with their colluding dealer. They also notice when players play with lower denomination chips but routinely cash in large value chips. Casino executives refer to this as a *tell* (an activity after the fact that tells them some illegal action has occurred).

EXHIBIT 5–10

Blackjack and craps are two of the most popular games in casinos.

Courtesy: Gold River Resort and Casino, Laughlin, Nevada.

Most card game theft involves manipulating the cards to the thief's advantage. Playing cards must be routinely changed to reduce opportunities for thieves to mark cards or to prearrange them to their advantage.

Casino executives must also be aware of card counters (and wheel clockers). Both employ methods of stealing that may involve some sort of computer device and are used by players in an attempt to gain an advantage over the casino. State gaming regulations prohibit any electronic device that may help players.

Wheel clockers will watch a roulette wheel for hours on end and make detailed entries in a log. Later they will enter these observations into a computer to determine if there are any numbers in which the ball might land more frequently than allowed for by odds. The technique is not unlike that used by scientists in the space program to determine where unmanned satellites may be expected to return to the earth. Usually, these players can be spotted by their betting patterns. Because they have accumulated illegal (but useful) information, they will bet large amounts when they have an advantage and small amounts when the house has the advantage. By acting on this special knowledge, they may give themselves away.

Casinos have also caught players wired with elaborate computer and counting devices. One player had the computer's input device attached to his toe and the output device (a mild electric shock) wired to a sensitive part of his body. The casino was tipped off when the output device malfunctioned and the player agitated excessively in his seat.

Baccarat.   Baccarat is a card game in which only two hands are dealt. Nine or 12 players (depending on the size of table) may bet on one of two hands—the banker's or the players'. Those who bet on the players' hand are betting that the **bank hand** will lose. Those betting on the bank hand are charged a 5 percent commission to exercise this option. Most games are played with cash and large-value chips.

Since players can wager on the bank's hand or the players' hand, only two hands are dealt per game and usually fewer than eight cards are shown. The casino dealers pick up and distribute the cards and wagered money or chips by using long paddle devices. This gives the game a certain mystique and is perhaps why the game is often featured in movies where casino action is depicted.

Baccarat is actually very easy and is often played with variations. In a version called *chemin de fer,* players may elect to bank a hand (provide the stakes against which other players may wager). This gives them an opportunity to win greater amounts. Of course, the risk of losing more is also possible as they must pay all winning players if they lose.

EXHIBIT 5–11   Ways to Defraud the Casino: A Baccarat Scam

One elaborate Baccarat scheme involved the following: During play, several sets of hands were carefully recorded. The cards were picked up in the exact order dealt and stowed in the discard tray. When the cards were reshuffled, the dealer faked shuffling this particular set of hands. It then became a ''slug.'' When the first hand of the slug reappeared in the game, the rest of the hands were known until the end of the slug. The dealer and his agents were able to steal millions from the casino before they were caught.

Eye on the Issues

Technology

A casino's competitiveness may, in the future, hinge even more upon how (and how fast after development) it employs technological advances. Guests are fascinated by technological wizardry such as that of the statues in the Forum Fountain in Caesar's Palace in Las Vegas that move, talk, laugh, and play instruments. Guests are also flocking to try virtual reality technology in games and amusements. Enterprises that install and promote such hot technologies will have a competitive advantage over neighboring enterprises that don't.

Baccarat requires four employees, two dealers who control the game, a ''croupier,'' and a floorwalker known as a ''ladderperson'' (so called because he or she sits in a high chair with a view of the entire table). The ladderperson must ensure the game is dealt correctly and that the players are awarded the correct winnings. Using a check sheet, dealers must also track the 5 percent commission due to the casino from players who bet the bank to win. The commission is collected at the end of play. As in the game of 21, management must be alert to prearranged, switched, or marked cards (see Exhibit 5–11).

Control of Nonbanked Games.   As discussed earlier, nonbanked games include slots, keno, bingo, poker, card rooms, and race and sports book.

Slots.   The slot handle (total amount played) is always known because each coin is metered when it enters the machine and when it is paid out. Most payoffs are paid mechanically by the machine. Large jackpots are hand-paid by bank draft, and the machine is opened by a casino executive to verify that it was not tampered with. Slot wins are easily tallied and the slot hold percentage readily determined. Slot drop is collected three times a day, and elaborate accounting procedures are followed. Coins are initially weighed to determine their monetary value. This is termed the *hard count*. The casino

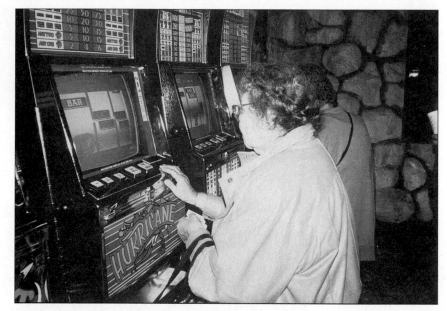

Courtesy: Wildhorse Gaming Resort, Pendleton, Oregon.

bankroll is replenished with rolled coins, and the excess is bagged (usually in $500 amounts) and tagged for bank deposit (see Exhibit 5–12A and B).

Slot theft does occur in casinos, but newer electronic machines are more secure and the old techniques of stealing have become largely ineffective. The biggest theft problem occurs with illegal slot keys, making elaborate control of keys mandatory.

Slot operations require several different types of employees. Slot mechanics are needed to keep the machines functioning. Change booths and change sellers are needed to supply coins to customers. The most prominent employee is the change person on a high platform stationed in the center island of a group of slot machines who acts as a type of carnival barker to encourage guests to play certain machines.

The slot mix (the types, denominations, and layout of machines) is important. Machines are generally placed in groups of 250 to 400 units. Since a certain segment of slot play is impulse driven, machines must be located in the main guest circulation areas of the casino. Casino regulations require a minimum payout (usually 85 percent), but the casinos often program certain strategically located machines to pay more in an effort to attract more players to the other machines. These ''looser'' machines may pay out as much as 97.5 percent of what was deposited. Needless to say, the location of the loose machines is a carefully guarded secret.

Slot aisles must feel like destinations and spark a take-a-peek excitement that draws guests through the slot areas with a desire to **peek** and see around

EXHIBIT 5–12B
Continued.

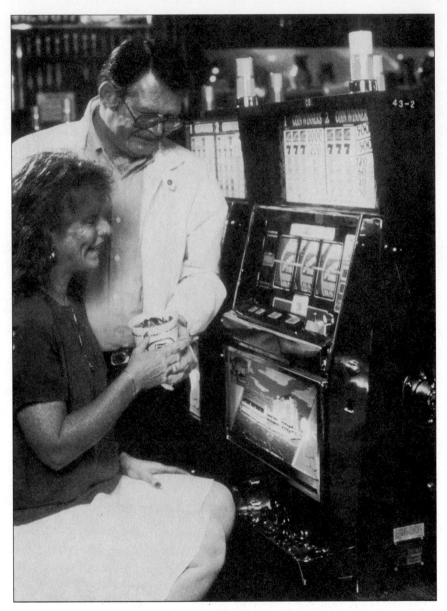

Courtesy: Gold River Resort and Casino, Laughlin, Nevada.

a corner or just ahead, and then create a desire to experience the next group of slot machines.

Keno.   Keno is the only game in the casino that one can play while enjoying other activities, such as dining or sitting in the lounge. Numbered balls are blown about in a hopper-like apparatus until 20 balls blow up into two rabbit ears, each capable of holding 10 balls. The numbered balls represent the winning numbers. The numbers are shown on electronic boards placed in strategic locations throughout the casino. Players follow the progress of the game by watching the numbers being displayed. Each game lasts approximately 10 minutes, but games take place around the clock.

Keno requires a minimum of three employees. Tickets are sold at the keno window or by keno runners (employees who roam certain casino stations and sell keno tickets). A second employee collects tickets at the keno desk. The third employee controls the operation of the game. The game consists of 20 numbers drawn from a selection of 80 possible numbers. Players can mark combinations in any number of ways. These tickets are called **way tickets** and will pay winners depending on the way the numbers are selected. Tickets are made out in duplicate with the original ticket submitted to the casino and the duplicate returned to the customer.

The keno handle is always known, and the keno drop is a function of total tickets sold rather than of the amount wagered. Specific controls require the microfilming of tickets and taking pictures of the winning numbers. Care must be taken to make sure that no tickets are accepted after the numbers are drawn. A recent innovation is the touch-screen video terminal that accepts wagers and issues tickets. Players who win via this method must cash in their tickets at the keno cashier cage.

Bingo.   Bingo requires somewhat different controls. The game is played on reusable cards having 24 numbers in five rows and five columns. Columns are marked so that *bingo* is spelled across the top of the card. The center space in column N is free. Each column (except N) contains 5 numbers from 15 possibilities: column B, 1–15; column I, 16–30; column N, 31–45; column G, 46–60; and column O, 61–75.[4] Players initially purchase cards. Floorwalkers sell a system of validation stickers for marking the cards. Each card and validation sticker is serial numbered.

Seventy-five balls (numbered to correspond to the bingo cards) are blown about in a machine. As the numbers are drawn, they are called out over a public address system and displayed on electronic boards. Guests mark off numbers on their cards and yell ''bingo'' when they have covered five numbers in a row, column, or diagonal track. (Other versions may require covering more numbers.) The prize value remains high for the first 50 numbers drawn but diminishes rapidly in value as the number of balls drawn reaches 75. Jackpots roll over to the next game if not won.

In this game, the casino's main revenue comes from the sale and resale of the cards. The total drop is the amount of card sales, and the win is the drop less the prize value. Most bingo operators retain 50 percent of their card sales. Controls are necessary to ensure that all cards and validation tickets are accounted for. This is accomplished by using sequentially numbered cards and stickers that are usually disposable and valid only on the date issued. Winning numbers are photographed and the names of the winners are kept in a log.

Poker and Card Rooms.   In the poker room, the casino acts as a host by providing a dealer and a place to play cards. Players pay a seating fee. The dealer handles the cards and conducts the play. He also controls the **pot** (amount wagered in each hand) and assures that the casino gets a percentage

EXHIBIT 5–13   **Black Sunday**
Sometimes (not often) the oddsmakers majorly miscalculate.

Not too many years ago, Nevada casinos' sports books offered favorable odds on the teams in the Super Bowl. Weeks prior to the game, casino oddsmakers attempted to balance the wagers between teams in order to make a profit no matter which team won. As it turned out, the amount of wagers made on the early odds were greater than those made closer to game day. The point spread was not great enough on game day (the point spread was made), and the casinos had to pay off on both teams. This cost the casinos millions, hence the name Black Sunday.

of the hand as a **rakeoff.** It is also common for the winning hand to pay a percentage to the casino. As with the other games, dishonesty by players is a concern and dealers must be alert for card cheats.

Race and Sports Book.   The race and sports book activities of casinos do not contribute significantly to the drop. They are primarily there as a way to attract sports enthusiasts who wish to wager on races and games. Once inside, the casino can expect sports fans to bet on the table games and play the slots where the casino advantage is a lot greater. The handle and drop in the race and sports book are always known. The win is predictable in the race book area because the casino offers approximately the same odds as the tracks and takes an additional fee for handling the bets.

The sports book is somewhat more risky as the casino must employ professional handicappers who establish the **morning line** (the odds the casino will pay on any specific sporting event). Since bets are accepted over a period before the event, the casino is obligated to pay the original odds on early bets even though the odds may have changed by the date of the event. A casino can win handsomely if it can correctly predict and adjust the odds. Since it can't, it ends up losing because more bets are written earlier at the original odds. This happened on a Super Bowl football game several years ago. The day has since been called ''Black Sunday'' by many sports and race book managers.[5] See Exhibit 5–13. Wagers on all events are consolidated and termed the *total write*. With the introduction of computer ticket write and cashier functions, it is virtually impossible to defraud the casino in this area.

Conclusion

Casinos are becoming more than just places to gamble. As the proliferation of gaming continues throughout the United States, casinos are looking for more ways to attract guests. While gambling will still represent the greatest profit center, megaresorts and entertainment facilities that have mastered the art of creating a

TGE will offer stiff competition. Facilities that have broadened their appeal and effectively targeted their markets will steal customers away from those that offer limited or gambling-only activities.

The successful casino of the future will provide the kind of unforgettable experiences for which guests crave and to which they respond. Casinos will use emerging high technology to create ever-more-thrilling attractions. Guests will be the silent sales agents of the casino by telling all of their friends, who in turn will tell their friends. The constant stream of guests dazzled by the lights, awed by the scene, thrilled by the rides, and wined and dined to satisfaction will be more than willing to drop thousands and thousands of dollars into the gambling sector. Entertainment is the fastest growing sector in the economy, and the large gaming meccas of Las Vegas, Atlantic City, and now New Orleans want to capture the family market business that Disney has commanded for many years. This is the biggest gamble yet by the gaming industry, but after all, isn't that their business?

Keywords

rim credit   132
skimming   132
handle   133
floor walker   133
eye in the sky   137
agents   137

bank hand   139
peek   141
way ticket   143
pot   143
rakeoff   144
morning line   144

Core Concepts

Indian Gaming Regulatory Act   123
casino advantage   125
correct odds   125

odds of winning   126
static attractions   129
total guest experience   130

Discussion Questions

1. Define the term *casino advantage*.
2. Identify the revenue mix of casinos.
3. What are the major operational challenges for a casino manager in managing games of chance?
4. What prompted Nevada to legalize gambling in the 1930s?

5. Describe the various measures for controlling the banked games and nonbanked games.
6. Describe marketing techniques, past and present, of Las Vegas casinos.

References

Crutchfield, James. Comments made in conversation with the author, 1994.

Gollehon, John. *Casino Games.* Grand Rapids, MI: Gollehon, 1988.

Leonard, Saul. "Study of Financial Reports on Casino Operations." In *U.S. Gaming Industry.* Los Angeles: Saul Leonard, Inc., 1992.

Rowe, Megan. "Las Vegas—Big Gamble." *Lodging and Hospitality,* February 1994.

Scarnes, John. *Complete Guide to Gambling.* New York: Simon & Schuster, 1986.

APPENDIX A
TOURISM DEVELOPMENT

Outline

Contrary to what is commonly assumed, the definition of *tourist* is not limited only to those people who travel for pleasure. Business travelers, once they are outside their geographic area, are also often considered tourists. When combined, pleasure and business travelers form the two main segments of the tourism market.

Travelers within each segment not only have their own needs and desires with regard to the destinations they visit; they also have varying financial means. Business travelers on expense accounts will stay at different hotels and eat at different restaurants as compared to retired people who travel for six months out of the year on a limited budget.

Knowing what the needs and the means of the different kinds of tourists are is extremely important, not only for established tourism destinations, but also for those towns, regions, or communities that want to develop themselves into tourism destinations. If a destination can understand what travelers in the various segments would like, what they are willing to pay, and then provide those things at the right price, it can attract a very lucrative source of revenue. Areas that have been hard hit economically (by losing sources of revenue and employment such as factories, mills, and air bases) can use tourism revenues to become prosperous again.

Tourism development comes at a price, though. Tourists put a strain on the resources of an area. For example, they congest roads, create additional pollution, and may destroy the very things that originally attracted them. Tourism may affect an area's lifestyle to the extent that local residents feel their quality of life has deteriorated. It may also cause real estate prices to rise, ultimately making a region unaffordable or unlivable for its original inhabitants.

Sensible and careful tourism development therefore requires finding a balance between the positives and negatives associated with it. Tourism development means more than simply creating attractions and waiting for tourists to come, spending money right and left. Tourism development also means creating techniques and regulations to control its negative consequences. Look at what more and more of this country's national parks are considering: limiting the number of tourists who are permitted to visit some parks for fear that overuse will destroy what they have been charged to preserve for future generations. This, too, is tourism development.

This appendix also attempts to show the difference between rampant and planned development by discussing the steps through which conscientious tourism development can emerge. In previous chapters you've read about the past and present of tourism as it relates to the hospitality industry. We now look at the future of tourism, which most believe will depend upon "sustainable tourism."

Opportunities for New Kinds of Tourism

As new tourism segments begin to emerge, they expand opportunities for tourism development. The New Age movement, for example, has created a tourism segment of travelers interested in places offering spiritual or cosmic "vibrations" or "vortexes"—a hard-to-prove (or disprove) quality that many communities are now marketing. Other new segments, such as **ecotourism** (tourism aimed at travelers whose main objective is to experience some aspect of the environment as part of their vacation) and **experiential tourism** (for tourists whose main objective is to learn and experience the history and culture of the area they visit), have prompted communities and individuals alike to develop attractions they hope will because a tourism destination attracts visitors, and visitors have to eat and sleep. Investors, entrepreneurs, and local communities alike know they can make money when tourism is developed. A developer may be the individual who would like to turn his or her house into a bed-and-breakfast operation, a local community that can raise revenues through fees and taxes on tourist expenditures, or a consortium of investors who would like to develop a large shopping mall with a luxury hotel attached.

Tourism and hospitality development are therefore closely related. This appendix discusses some steps communities may find useful when seeking to develop tourism. The second part will discuss the process of developing a hospitality project that might take advantage of the subsequent increased numbers of visitors. Theme parks, state parks, and historical attractions, as well as restaurants and hotels, do not come into existence out of the blue. It takes a good idea, hard work, determination, and luck to become successful.

Assessment of Attractions

Tourism development is often regarded as a good alternative form of economic development. In some cases, the infrastructure requirements necessary for tourism development are less costly to put in place than those required for some other type of development. In other cases, though, substantial changes must be made to the existing infrastructure before any thought can be given to allowing a massive influx of people into a region. Whatever the case, before any tourist development can take place, certain procedures should be followed to ensure that the development enhances, rather than destroys, the existing environment and culture. The **assessment** process is one in which a community looks at its assets, liabilities, and opportunities.

The first step taken in tourism development is generally the creation of a council or committee consisting of concerned individuals and businesses that will address development issues. This committee follows a prepared agenda or process that allows for systematic analysis. The process starts by analyzing the current tourism situation by determining what currently attracts tourists to the area. This assessment includes questions regarding both natural and cultural attractions. In terms of the natural features of a particular area, the assessment asks questions such as:

1. What is the climate like? Does the area have seasonal extremes, or is it fairly temperate?
2. What is the geography like? Does it change drastically? Are there mountains, forests, deserts, lakes, beaches?
3. Are there unique wildlife and other natural phenomena? Is there a lake in the area that has ideal fishing conditions? Are there canyons or caves that may attract interest?

In terms of the cultural features of a region, the assessment might seek to determine:

1. What historic attractions, if any, there are in the area.
2. What traditional cultural activities and events are currently available for tourists to participate in or watch. Are there rodeos, battle reenactments, or other local events that may attract visitors?
3. What attractions of modern culture are available for the visitor. These might include team sports, performing arts, galleries, and museums.

The most convenient way to undertake such an analysis is to use inventory forms (Exhibit A–1). Using a form will allow the group or committee doing the inventory to assess the current state of development for each item objectively. Maybe there is a historic train, but the tracks need a lot of repairs, or maybe there is a museum, but only fit for limited visitation. Additional forms would be used to assess the current state of the infrastructure, but once again with two goals in mind: to find out what is available and to determine what condition it is in.

Current State of Development

Visitation Analysis. The next step in the process is to determine the present state of tourism to the area, by conducting what is called a *visitation analysis.* There are a number of sources from which information about visitation to a particular region can be gathered. In most cases these will be state offices of tourism, local chambers of commerce, or federal tourism authorities. A visitation analysis typically determines the

EXHIBIT A–1   Product Analysis

Historical, Cultural, and Ethnic Attractions	Community	Region
Antique shops		
Archaeological sites and ruins		
Art galleries		
Battlefields		
Birthplaces of famous people		
Burial grounds		
Conservatories		
Crafts		
Ethnic celebrations		
Famous historical buildings		
Ghost towns		
Historic tours		
Historical markers		
Mansions		
Missions		
Monuments		
Museums		
Native American culture		
Native American reservations		
Native folklore		
Old forts		
Pioneer churches		
Pioneer homes		
Prehistoric items		
Reconstructed historical towns		
Reenactment of historical events		
Special ''nationality'' days		
Trading posts		

One (**1**) means the attraction exists but is minimally developed.
Two (**2**) means the attraction exists and is well-developed for tourism.
P stands for potential; the attraction is not currently developed, but has the potential for future development.

numbers and types of tourists who visit the area. The analysis looks at:

1. Historical data on visitation. How many people have visited the area over the years?
2. Seasonal patterns of visitation. What are the high and the low seasons of visitation?
3. Tourist traffic by port of entry. What are the major points of entry to the area for visitors? Is there an airport, a train depot, a harbor? How many people enter the community at each place?
4. Occupancy data. These are excellent indicators of seasonality and level of visitation to an area and should include local campgrounds, RV parks, and inns as well as hotels and motels.

A visitation analysis also tries to determine what type of visitor the area receives. Data obtained through this analysis are typically divided to describe tourism segments. By identifying segments (groups with similar characteristics), an area can clarify what kinds of ''product'' might be best received by those segments or how existing products might be tweaked to appeal to them. If the visitation analysis determines a lot of young people visit an area, it is important to have appropriate entertainment available for them.

The first step in determining the type of visitor to an area is to identify the segments into which visitors fall. Commonly accepted segments include: pleasure/ leisure; business; recreation; shopping; and conventions. For a more detailed description of these segments and their motivating characteristics, please see Chapter 6.

Once the types and numbers of tourists to the area have been determined using some or all of the methods mentioned above, the next step is to develop a visitor profile for each of the segments frequenting the area. Each profile of the typical visitor should include information on demographics (such as average age, gender, number of people in the party, income, education, and family composition) and other important characteristics of the segment (such as average length of stay, location of stay, main seasons for visiting, mode of transportation, destinations visited, activities, expenditures for each activity, and impressions). The town of Sedona, Arizona, has successfully positioned

EXHIBIT A–2

During the summer, roads in Sedona, Arizona, are congested and traffic jams have become inevitable. Yet the city resists building or broadening existing roads and making changes in its infrastructure, concerned that it will change its inherent character and affect its quality of life.

itself in the tourist market by addressing the needs of New Age tourists, as Exhibit A–2 shows.

Infrastructure and Facilities.   After the process of identifying and characterizing the tourist segments has been completed, it is necessary to examine the infrastructure of the area in order to determine exactly what is currently in place and what must still be developed to attract visitors. (Exhibit A–3.)

This examination looks at:

1. How many and what kind of lodging and tourism facilities are available.

Exhibit A–3   Infrastructure Inventory Lodging

Name of Property	Chain Affiliation	Number of Rooms	Age of Property	Quality of Ranking (A, B, C, or D)	Rate Category (A, B, C, or D)	Best Guess Level of Annual Business (A, B, C, or D)	Classify Level of Service (A, B, C, or D)	Guest Profile: Major Portion of Business Comes From					What Meeting Facilities Are Available?	List the Available Amenities	Disabled Access? (Y/N)
								Families/ Leisure	Business/ Corporate	Govern- ment	Tour Groups	Other Groups			

2. The quantity, quality, and variety of restaurants and bars in the area.

3. The recreational opportunities available, and how they are rated.

4. Transportation for tourists (availability of air transportation, rental cars, and taxis; the quantity, quality, and accessibility of public transportation; the types of water transportation available; and the types of guided tours that are available).

5. The dependability of the communication services in the area.

6. The reliability of mail and parcel shipping services.

7. The variety and quality of radio, television, and cable TV.

8. The accessibility of tourist information services, especially those geared to foreign visitors.

9. The dependability of basic utilities and public services.

10. The reliability of existing public safety measures and the availability of medical services.

11. The presence of travel agents to assist visitors with their travel needs.

12. The opportunity for tourists to go shopping.

Promotional Activities.   Another area to examine during the assessment is the types of promotional activities that are currently used to advance the tourism industry. Promotional efforts for an area fall into three categories: public support, such as a state or federal tourism office; regional and cooperative promotion efforts; and private efforts.

Developers want to know what overall budget is available for promotional activities, and what activities are currently taking place (these could range from media campaigns involving print and broadcast advertising, promoting media familiarization trips, and representation at trade shows, to joint campaigns with neighboring areas to reduce the cost.

Availability of Labor.   When planning tourism development, planners often neglect the human resource issues that face the industry. Of utmost importance is a steady, reliable supply of trained workers (at all levels, not just front-line staff). So it is important to know where the workers are coming from, if there is affordable housing for them, what the wage levels are in the area, whether education programs are available for tourism workers, and the general skill levels of the workers. (Chapter 8 ''Hotel Operations,'' discusses ways of finding labor in a tight market.) There is no better way to lose a visitor than have someone respond to the question ''So, what's there to do around here?'' with the answer, ''Nothing.'' If a community has decided upon a course of economic development through tourism, it is essential that every member of the community realize that they have the potential of being in the ''tourist business''—from the server at the local coffee shop to the cashier at the general store to the attendant at the gas station.

Financial, Legal, and Environmental Aspects. Another realm of concern to the visitor and developer alike is the financial, legal, and regulatory environment of the area. Financial concerns may include the availability of local currency if the intent is to attract a lot of foreign visitors. Legal ramifications center around customs regulations such as those that allow or prohibit the importation of certain products, immigration rules that require visitors to obtain visas before entry, and the local hospitality-related ''bed, board, and booze'' taxes that can increase the price of a hotel room significantly. Bed, board, and booze taxes can be any combination of additional taxes placed on the visitor for hotel, restaurant, or liquor charges. Additionally, liquor regulations, closing times for bars and nightclubs, zoning requirements, environmental protection regulations (such as the added cost of enforced recycling), and water-use restrictions may all either contribute to or detract from the amount and type of tourism development that may take place.

A final issue (and one that has historically been neglected during infrastructure assessments) is an examination of the environmental quality within the area. Air, land, and water quality should be examined. There is little that will detract more from a panoramic vista than to drive or fly into an area that exhibits a yellow haze over the horizon. Likewise, littered rivers, waterways, and roads detract from the tourist experience. The environment has become a major concern in today's society, and is a prime motivator in the tourism industry. Visitors want to travel to areas that are, if not pristine, at least well tended and presentable. As eco-tourism develops, you will see why potential developers must be aware that this is one of the fastest growing markets in the travel industry and that the tourist in general has become much more aware of environmental concerns.

Summary Analysis and Strategy Development

Analysis

Once both types of data collection, the attraction inventory and the infrastructure inventory, have been completed, the developer must create a summary analysis of the current tourism situation. This includes comparing the area inventories (infrastructure, attractions) with the market segment profiles to determine how and where they match (or don't match). This is followed by a discussion of what still needs to be developed.

Consider an example. It has been determined that an area is ideal for bus travelers to stop, have lunch, and view the gardens that attract monarch butterflies. Two major questions that tend to be forgotten until the first load of buses come through are: Is there parking available for the buses, and are there enough public restroom facilities to handle the increased numbers? The needs of the travelers for entertainment and nourishment may have been met, but additional facilities are needed to make the area accessible to increased levels of tourism.

Promotion

The next step in the process is to develop a program for promotion. Promotional options will evolve as a direct result of budgetary constraints. If dollars are few, it is unlikely that the options will include blasting television advertising across the United States. This is where research into current promotional efforts on the part of various organizations comes into play. What kind of promotion will best attract the type of visitor that is wanted? If most of the visitation is on a drive-through basis, perhaps it would be efficient to create an easily accessible and attractive visitor information center. If most of the people arrive by plane, it would be helpful to provide information at the airport or possibly en route in seat-back publications.

Coupled with the problem of planning a promotional strategy is the issue of where to find more tourists or visitors. The obvious starting point is to determine where they are currently coming from, what has attracted them in the first place, and what new promotional strategies might attract additional visitation—or extend visitation of the existing market. After completing the inventory, promoters might seek to identify new attractions that can be coupled with others, with the goal of extending a three-hour stay to an overnight. If a community lacks enough punch to package effectively, it might link with one or two nearby communities to jointly market the area, perhaps encouraging those who would have simply overnighted to stay on another day or two. They might also look at opportunities to develop new festivals that run over a weekend. These options can all create low-cost opportunities to help additional tourism dollars to flow into the local economy.

Extending visitation is only one answer to the problem. As tourism research continues to mature, new market segments continue to emerge. Tourists are no longer defined simply by the purpose or length of their visit; researchers now look at cultural and societal dimensions. Several new markets have come into existence and all need to be considered for development.

Ecotourism.   There are numerous definitions of the term *ecotourist*. Some state that it represents a tourist who is looking to become totally submerged in the natural experience, that is, go trekking through the outback, camp, or enjoy nature without the trappings of civilization anywhere in view. Others define it as anyone participating in an adventure-style recreation, be it hiking or viewing desert flora and fauna. For our purposes, ecotourism is that segment that has an interest in exploring how nature plays a part in our overall understanding of our culture. Thus, a group of bird watchers can be considered ecotourists in the same way that a group that arranges to be left in the tundra with plans of hiking out is considered ecotourists.

Cultural Tourism.   This group is interested in observing, and to some extent participating in, the native cultures they have traveled to see. In the United States, this is exhibited as an increased interest in the Native American cultures, weekends among the Amish, and

Exhibit A–4

The ecological integrity of beaches, such as this one on the Gulf of Mexico, can be threatened by incautious development.

Courtesy: Phil Pappas

Exhibit A–5

The Mayan ruins at Chichén Itza, Mexico, attract tourists interested in cultural and historical attractions.

escapes into the Bayou. In Australia this would mean observing Aboriginal ceremonies, and in Peru, visiting the ruins of Machu Picchu. The level of interest varies, from wanting to totally immerse oneself in the culture, to spending a week traveling among Mayan ruins in tents, yet ending the vacation at a resort in Cancun.

Existential Tourism. Existential tourists look to immerse themselves in a new culture. They typically do not venture to acknowledged tourist areas, but rather go off and live for a period of time within the culture itself.

Experiential Tourism. Rather than become one with the culture, these tourists seek to understand the ''essence'' of the culture. For example, prior to a visit to the village of Oraibi on the Hopi reservation in Arizona, this group may start by reading everything they can find on Hopi history, religion, art, and family life. Once they arrive at their destination, they would probably seek to discuss what they have learned with people from the village to better understand what they have seen.

Experimental Tourism. This group is willing to try any new experience. This might range from skydiving to sampling local cuisines. They want to *sense* rather than *observe.*

Recreational Tourism. This group is looking for personal enjoyment. They are not particularly interested in an educational experience. Examples of personal enjoyment include boating, fishing, shopping, and attending rodeos.

Diversionary Tourism. These tourists do not want adventure. They seek to maintain the same diversions they have always pursued: sitting by the pool, exploring museums, seeing the sights, and so on.

There is still another set of definitions for the new tourist, ranging from big spenders who want to be catered to and who enjoy luxury, to the ''Antitourist,'' who doesn't consider him- or herself a tourist at all. These new definitions for tourism may be useful in helping to develop a strategy for promoting an area and local communities. For example, unless there are luxury resorts in the vicinity, it is unlikely that there will be a large influx of big spenders. On the other hand, forested areas with recreational opportunities may attract several of the other segments.

The Final Proposal

The final task for the local development committee is to bring all the information together and formalize proposals for specific projects and actions. This would include statements on:

1. Which groups are targeted and what the profiles of each group are.
2. Which attractions and facilities exist that will attract the target groups.
3. Which promotional plans are best suited to the budget.
4. Which facilities still need to be developed to attract the target groups.
5. What the proposed time line is to complete the development.

Once this action plan has been completed, the committee would work with city, state, or federal governments on securing the necessary funds for development. As with any planning process, development is cyclical in nature. While the plan is being implemented, it should be constantly reviewed and updated. Change occurs quickly. Consider the Gulf War of 1991, for example. The possibility of terrorist attacks at airports played an important part in how the travelers planned their vacations. International visitation was down. Communities that had well-developed action plans could adjust to this change, and many in fact switched their focus from attracting long-term stays of seven or more nights, to attracting weekend visitors. As events happen, committees should be ready to adapt and modify their plans.

If the committee does an outstanding job, performs an extensive assessment of the area, and wins support for its plan, some parts of the development strategy can be put into immediate action. For example, the local chamber of commerce (with financial help of local businesses) can start a promotion campaign to have tourists stay overnight, instead of just visit for the day. Businesspeople who were involved in the planning process will probably have already begun working on certain projects of their own. And new investors, attracted by the potential of the area, will come up with further plans and money.

By following this thorough plan of inventory and assessment, a local area may prepare itself for development based on awareness and avoid the growth of weedy, unplanned, and uncontrolled development.

Keywords

PART III

Introduction to Lodging Management

This section introduces you to management opportunities in the lodging industry. The lodging industry greatly impacts a country's economic, social, and cultural development. It contributes significantly to national, regional, and local economies in terms of generating employment and government tax revenues. For example, in the United States in the early '90s, the lodging industry generated $63 billion in sales, provided jobs for 1.6 million full- and part-time employees, paid $19 billion in wages and salaries, and generated $6 billion in federal taxes.

The lodging industry also greatly affects local communities and cultures. It seems that almost every city or community, no matter how large or small, has its own ''grand hotel'' that serves as an anchor of the local community. Important gatherings and celebrations are often held in hotels. Many new ideas and fashion styles are introduced in and disseminated from hotels and millions of travelers visit them each year.

Staying in hotels has become a part of our way of life. Hotels, as part of the physical landscape, reveal ''secrets'' of our cultural landscape; if studied by anthropologists of another century (or even another planet), they would give insights about our habits, beliefs, and characteristics.

Developing and managing hotels can be of tremendous economic, social, and cultural significance. Besides the opportunity associated with potential career growth, there are also important societal responsibilities. The three chapters in this section discuss in detail the career opportunities, management responsibilities, and challenges in the lodging industry.

The first chapter traces the historical development and structure of the lodging industry by offering a unique and innovative perspective. It analyzes the lodging industry from an industry-supply-and-market-demand point of view and demonstrates how supply and demand are linked. It describes in detail the varied lodging products (supply) in today's lodging industry and explains why these products are developed to satisfy guests' demands and needs. The chapter emphasizes that supply and demand can (and must) be matched effectively by a hotel's marketing and sales department.

The second chapter in this section focuses on the rooms division of a hotel—the "front of the house." The chapter explains the important functions this division performs in a hotel and outlines its managerial and supervisory positions. Every step of the guest cycle is discussed: from making a reservation to check-in, to check-out.

The third chapter discusses three additional functions in hotel management and operations: housekeeping, maintenance, and engineering—the "back of the house." These functions focus on the physical side of hotel operations—the comfort, cleanliness, and safety of guest rooms and public areas. It elaborates on the operational procedures of a hotel's housekeeping department and emphasizes the challenging management responsibilities of this department. It identifies the major operational functions of the maintenance and engineering departments and stresses the needs and importance for environmental awareness and energy conservation.

This section closes with an appendix that walks students through the processes involved in developing a lodging project (or other hospitality projects). It explains the importance of feasibility studies and analyzes the five steps involved in development. After considering the hurdles that must be overcome before a project "flies," students will better understand that hotels, resorts, and restaurants that have seemingly popped up overnight have actually taken the work of many months, and sometimes years.

After completing this unit, you will have a more complete understanding of the different types of lodging facilities, their market demand, and the various aspects of a hotel's operation.

Lodging: History, Supply, Demand, and Structure

An Overview

This chapter follows a framework that presents both lodging supply and travel demand. It first discusses lodging supply: industry scope, current development, categories of hotels, types of hospitality business organizations, and typical hotel organizational structures. It then describes the various travel markets that place demand on lodging products and services and shows how hotel sales departments serve as a link between lodging supply and travel demand. The chapter ends with a brief discussion of some current issues that face the lodging industry.

Outline

Introduction

The goal of all businesses is to link or match supply with demand; hotels (who have supply) want to sell rooms and other services to guests (who provide demand). Bringing supply and demand together to make a profit is essential for any business.

Supply, in a service industry like lodging, is a **holistic** concept; that is, it must be considered as a whole—or system—not simply as disconnected pieces of a puzzle. **Supply** consists of tangibles, such as hotel type and physical amenities, and intangibles, such as the many personal services provided by the lodging staff.

Demand, or customer wants and needs, is always changing and varied. There are many customer groups or market segments that demand certain types of lodging facilities to satisfy their specific needs. The lodging industry has adapted by designing and building many types of facilities to appeal to different segments.

Today, if you want to climb the corporate lodging ladder, you must intimately understand the link between customer needs and the services your company can provide. And you must understand something about the dynamics of the world's tourism system, since the lodging industry is a subset of it.

There are two important premises to state before this discussion continues:

- Lodging exists in an increasingly competitive environment.
- Customers are becoming increasingly demanding.

Given these two conditions, you can see that, in order to succeed, hotels must consistently provide quality experiences to demanding customers. If they do not, their competitors will. Since customer demands are continually increasing, hotels must continually improve their services, or they will fall behind.

Suppose customer couple X loved your hotel and its service when they stayed there five years ago. Even if you could somehow wrap your staff and building into a magical cocoon and keep it unchanged for five years, couple X, if they visited again, would probably find it lacking in some ways. It wouldn't be simply a case of lagging technology, or not-quite-stylish room decor; Couple X would be slightly disenchanted because they have had half a decade to become more sophisticated. Their needs have changed. Perhaps, five years ago, they had no children. Consequently, your lack of a Nintendo room and baby-sitting services went unnoticed. Perhaps, when last they visited, they were focused on business meetings and didn't care that there was no nearby shopping Mecca to explore. Whatever the reasons, while you were tucked away in your cocoon, you lost touch with your customer base and are now no longer attuned to its needs.

Successful lodging facilities and their managements are not only attuned to their customers, they know how to acquire them and, most importantly, how to keep them. To be a successful lodging facility manager, you must become a marketing- and customer-oriented person. This chapter can assist you in reaching this goal; it provides information organized around five discussion sections.

The first section of the chapter gives an overview of the lodging industry's supply. First we discuss the tourism system and the lodging industry's place within this system. Second we present the scope of the lodging industry. Here we discuss the size of the industry, occupancies, and various other descriptive statistics. Third we will talk about the specific products and services of this industry, including:

- Lodging chains and independent organizational structures.
- Hotel categories, such as city-center or urban hotels, suburban hotels, and airport hotels.
- Some of the newer forms of lodging facilities that market to specialized market segments, such as group/convention customers and business transient customers.

The second section of the chapter covers hotel business organizational structures: hotel chain operations versus independent hotel operations. We look at franchising and management contract company operations and finally present a typical organizational structure of a hotel.

In the third section, we examine the demand side of the lodging industry. Here we discuss demand characteristics by using a marketing segmentation approach. We discuss both group and individual traveler demand in both the business travel segment and the pleasure travel segment. Understanding customer needs, wants, and other characteristics is necessary because it is these needs and wants that dictate what types of lodging facilities will be built. The idea of first asking what customers need and then creating the right product is a fundamental principle of effective marketing.

The fourth section briefly describes how marketing provides the link between and brings together supply and demand. We illustrate the marketing process by describing the organization and operations of a typical hotel sales department.

In the final section to this chapter we discuss current issues facing the lodging industry. Environmental, ethical, international, and technological issues will be examined.

EXHIBIT 6–1

The tourism system

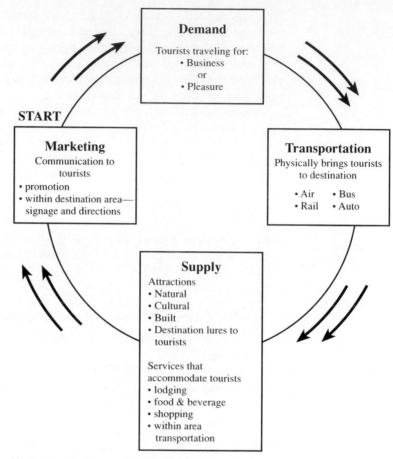

Modified from R. C. Mill and A. M. Morrison, *The Tourist System: An Introductory Text* (Englewood Cliffs, NJ: Prentice Hall, 1992).

The Tourism System and Lodging Supply

The Tourism System

Before discussing the supply side (the specific products and services offered by the lodging industry), let's consider an overview of the *tourism system* to see the lodging industry's location in this broader system (see Exhibit 6–1). Note that supply consists of two elements: attractions, which lure travelers, and service facilities, which include the lodging industry. Demand, as illustrated, consists of travelers and can be grouped into such segments as business travelers and pleasure travelers.

Marketing is a process that builds a link between supply and demand. Without such a link, demand would be ignorant of the products and services provided by supply; that is, the customer would be unaware of attractions and the service facilities that support them. As Exhibit 6–1 also shows, without the physical link provided by transportation, demand would not reach supply to consume or experience its offerings.

All of the components of this system are interdependent, and changes that occur in one area affect the others. For instance, if the price of jet fuel jumps up, airlines may raise their fares. With higher plane fares, fewer people will be able to afford travel to distant vacation spots. Thus, demand is decreased and there is excess supply in such destinations. Let's now look at the marketing linkage system in more detail.

The tourism marketing system maps how supply attempts to communicate with demand (see Exhibit 6–2). Note that supply companies have several alternative ways in which to send their products and services message to the demand.

- They can have their direct sales force talk *directly* to potential customers through personal interactions.
- They can have their sales force talk *indirectly* to potential customers by first selling to wholesale intermediaries (such as tour operators or independent meeting planners) who might, in turn, sell to retail travel agencies, who might then sell to the final customer (demand).
- They can sell *impersonally* through marketing promotional tools such as advertising and public relations.

Exhibit 6–2 also shows a less common ''hopscotch'' method whereby wholesale intermediaries skip over retail intermediaries to sell directly to the final customer. This is represented by the broken line between wholesale intermediaries and final customers.

Eye on the Issues

Environment

With the growing concern for the environment, customers and other interested parties have begun making environmental demands upon the lodging industry. Two primary areas of environmental concerns for the lodging industry are ''site pollution'' and internal operational ecological considerations. Site pollution concerns arise when the lodging facility is built without regard for the surrounding natural environment, the architecture is incompatible with the natural surroundings, signage is too large, the facility's grounds have been overdeveloped, and so on.

Internal operational ecological issues have to do with how the facility conserves resources. Recycling of paper products and other materials, use of new supplies made from recycled materials, disposal of waste products, and use of excess food from restaurants (given to local food banks and shelters for the homeless) are some examples of lodging facilities becoming environmentally conscious.

Exhibit 6–2

*The tourism
marketing system*

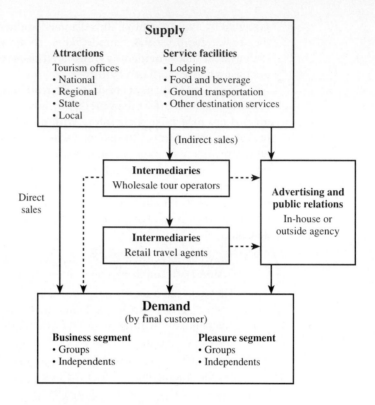

History

The hospitality industry is an old one. References to tavernkeeping have been found as early as 1800 BC where the Code of Hammurabi decreed death as the penalty for watering beer. As will be seen, the lodging and hospitality industry generally follows the growth of business and trade. Its forms and locations respond to the evolution of transportation. It arose and evolved in response to the needs of travelers throughout history. As described by Lundberg, the following is a brief overview of the forerunners of today's lodging industry.[1]

Early inns and taverns supplied food, drink, and a place to sleep for travelers. As early as the fifth century BC, ancient Greek taverns featured these basic amenities, and occasionally provided musicians and other entertainment for guests.

During this same period, travelers throughout present-day Turkey, Iran, Afghanistan, and northern India stayed at **caravanserais,** the predecessors of the stagecoach inn (and later the motel). These lodging facilities served the needs of caravans and other travelers and consisted of an enclosed courtyard for animals and spartan rooms for the traveler.

At its peak, the Roman Empire (Ascendancy: 27 BC to AD 395; Fall: AD 476) had conquered lands surrounding the Mediterranean and large parts of today's Europe. To connect this empire, the Romans established excellent road systems that were used by business, pleasure, and military travelers. Inns and taverns were established every 30 miles along the more than 51,000 miles of road. Major cities had larger sized hotels that were usually owned and managed by the municipal government. The ruins of Pompeii, destroyed in AD 79, reveal many *hospitea* and *caupona* (inns or hotels that provided lodging, and sometimes a basic menu of wine, bread, and meat). With the fall of the Roman Empire, protection for travelers was nonexistent and trade and the innkeeping business came to a standstill. For the next several hundred years, Euro-Asia's innkeepers no doubt wished they had chosen another line of business.

During the Dark Ages, AD 476 to 1000, which followed the fall of the Roman Empire, religious pilgrimage became the primary travel motivation. Monasteries and other religious houses accommodated the few travelers throughout Europe during this age of intellectual stagnation, widespread ignorance, poverty, and cultural decline.

The Crusades, beginning in 1095 and continuing over the next two hundred years, precipitated a social revolution. The resulting increase in trade led to the rise of a middle class, and travel and inns were once again in demand. Beginning in Northern Italy around 1282, guilds of innkeepers flourished and established rules and regulations for themselves and for their guests. Innkeeping became a solid business.

Between 1400 and 1600, Europe entered a period known as the Renaissance, or rebirth and revival of art, literature, and learning. This also was known as the age of discovery, when Columbus, Magellan, and Da Gama explored the ''edges'' of the world. This period was characterized by colonization of the world by major European countries, the emergence of strong cities and nation states, and a rapid increase in commerce and trade. The lodging industry began to expand in response to the needs of travelers and traders.

In England, innkeeping began to grow rapidly and gained reputable standing around the 15th century. (Earlier inns had primarily been ale houses offering scant accommodations.) By the mid-1400s, however, some inns had as many as 30 rooms. English common law formalized the industry, declaring inns to be ''public-houses'' and imposing responsibilities on innkeepers regarding their guests' well-being. The law required that an inn receive all who presented themselves in reasonable condition and were willing to pay a reasonable price for accommodations.

In 1539, King Henry VIII fostered a rapid growth of innkeeping when he decreed that church lands had to be given away or sold. This action stripped religious orders of monasteries and churches and took away a convenience travelers had counted on for several hundred years. Travelers turned to public houses, and inns and taverns flourished.

Beginning with the growth of roads and stagecoach travel and government-sponsored postal service in 1784, the coaching era of inns flourished through the early 1800s. Inns were called upon to provide not only food, drink,

Courtesy: Palmer House Hilton, Chicago, Illinois.

lodging, and entertainment for their guests but also spare coach horses, fodder, and stables.

Trade accelerated as the Industrial Revolution began in England around 1760 and spread throughout northwestern Europe over the next 60 years. In America, the impact of this revolution began to be felt around 1850.

In 1825, the English railroad began operations. This revolution in transportation was the beginning of the rapid demise of the country coaching inns as travelers chose more direct and faster conveyance. Railroad transportation stimulated the development of railroad lodging facilities that were located near train stations, usually near the center of cities. In 1838, Parliament dealt the death blow to the coaching inns by giving the postal service business to the railroads.

America's innkeeping industry, though it started later than Europe's, inevitably paralleled its English predecessor. Colonial America saw its earliest taverns beginning in 1634; the first in Boston was called Coles Ordinary. These taverns primarily offered food and drink and occasionally rooms. As in England, in the countryside and along the roads, taverns expanded their accommodations to serve the needs of stagecoach travelers. The first regular stagecoach route was established in 1760 between New York City and Philadelphia. By 1838, 2,500 miles of roads and turnpikes (toll roads) stretched throughout the east, served by numerous stagecoach inns. Larger hotels grew up in the wharf districts of cities on navigable rivers and coasts. As had occurred in England, the development of U.S. railroads, in the mid-1800s, led to a new era for the lodging industry. New and larger hotels established themselves near train stations in city centers.

In the 1900s, U.S. and world trade was significantly interrupted by World War I, 1914 to 1918; the worldwide depression of the decade of the 1930s; and World War II, 1939 to 1945. Beginning in the late 1940s and through today, domestic and international travel has undergone unparalleled growth. This was accompanied by equally dramatic developments in the lodging industry. Travel for business purposes increased as U.S. and world trade boomed. After the sacrifices of World War II, people were ready to travel for pleasure, and returning soldiers who had been exposed to international travel fed the excitement with tales of their experiences. In response to this pent-up demand, the phenomenon of mass tourism was born. Both business and pleasure travel were further assisted by rising disposable personal income in industrialized countries, advancing technology and reliability in air transportation, increased automobile ownership, and improved highways.

As the close of the 20th century approaches, recent changes in the world order have continued to advance travel and growth in the lodging industry. The breakup of the Soviet Union and Eastern Europe and their adoption of market-based economies have opened new business and trade opportunities. In the Asian-Pacific region, the opening and development of China and other smaller countries have further expanded world trade activity. Globalization of business and trade has led to expanding globalization of the lodging industry.

Scope and Categories of Lodging Supply

The discussion of lodging categories in this section gives some specific historical background on the development of American lodging as it grew to meet the needs of pleasure and business travelers.

The Scope of the Lodging Industry.   As indicated in Exhibit 6–5, lodging facilities are a component of total tourism supply. The lodging industry is made up of more than simply resorts, hotels, motor hotels, motels, and bed and breakfast inns; it also incorporates alternative lodging forms such as cruise ships, tourist courts, sporting and recreational camps, motor home parks, pensions, hostels, and campsites for transients. These alternative forms have widely varying operating structures from hotels and motels, and most lodging industry analysts do not include these categories in their statistics. Consequently, this section will focus upon the hotels, motels, and resorts in the United States.

There are about 100,000 hotel and motel properties in the world; about 45,000 of these are in the United States. Hotels with more than 200 rooms number about 3,000 in the United States and about 7,000 in the rest of the world; most hotel properties have less than 200 rooms. In the United States, 68 percent of the properties have fewer than 75 rooms.

EXHIBIT 6–4

The Palmer House Hilton Hotel is a perfect example of a property that combines elegance, history, and detail. It is the longest continuously operating hotel in the United States.

Courtesy: Palmer House Hilton Hotel, Chicago, Illinois.

Eye on the Issues

Ethics

Every day, hotel managers are faced with a variety of business decisions with ethical implications: Should we ''bump'' an already reserved guest, because we want to book a large and profitable group? Should we hire undocumented workers at substandard wages? How do we treat minorities, women, older employees, people with AIDS, and so on. To help address these ethical concerns, Stephen S. J. Hall, founder of the International Institute for Quality and Ethics in Service and Tourism (IIQEST), has proposed an ethics code for hotels.

This code has 11 points that provide guidance to hotels. The areas covered include: acknowledgment of ethics as relevant to doing business, personal ethical behavior, a commitment to continuous improvement of ethical concerns, nondiscriminatory practices, commitment to quality products and services, development of a safe and congenial working environment for employees and customers, and equal employee advancement opportunities. Keep this in mind when you need guidance.

EXHIBIT 6–5   **Tourism Supply Components**

Services	
Destination Transportation	**Accommodations**
Ferry and ship	Lodging
Bus	Hotel, resort, motel
Rail	Motor home
Auto, taxi, and limousine	Cruise ship
	Camp, trailer, hostel
	Food and beverage facilities
Shopping	**Other Services**
Gifts and souvenirs	Banks and foreign exchange
Arts and crafts	Medical
Marketplaces	

Attractions	
Natural	**Cultural**
Climate	Business centers
Geography	Visiting friends and relatives
	Historical sites
	Festivals
Built	**Other Attractions**
Theme parks	Sporting events
Conventions	Concerts
Museums	
Gambling	

According to the American Hotel & Motel Association, in the United States, only 9 percent of properties have room rates above $85 per night. Properties with room rates under $30 per night make up 38 percent of total lodging facilities. In 1992, average U.S. room rates were $59.82, up from $53.01 in 1987.

In the United States, the lodging industry is presently recovering from a period of overbuilding and underperformance. Prior to tax reforms in 1986, building was stimulated by federal tax deductions for large real estate investments. Many properties were built solely as real estate investments, without regard for demand or competition. Tax reform ended these large deductions. Underperformance was caused by both the oversupply of properties in the market and the fact that many were operated by inexperienced real estate developers or wealthy owners who cast themselves as managers.

Exhibit 6–6 shows that, for the past few years, average occupancy has been steadily climbing. From a low of 61 percent in 1991, average occupancy

Exhibit 6–6

Average occupancy

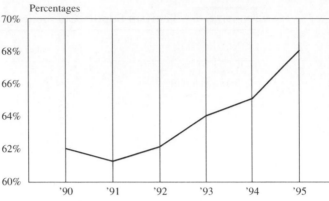

Source: *USA Today*, September 29, 1993.

Exhibit 6–7

New rooms

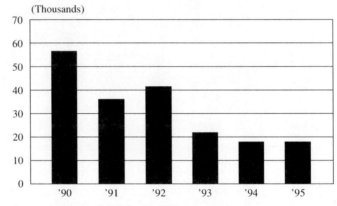

Source: *USA Today*, September 29, 1993.

rose to 64 percent in 1993, and is projected to hit 68 percent in 1995. This is because the number of people needing hotel rooms (demand) is finally catching up with supply. (As a result of the overbuilding, supply increased by 111,000 hotel rooms in 1988. By contrast, in 1993, only 23,000 new hotel rooms were built.) Exhibit 6–7 illustrates this downward trend in the recent past.

Significantly, the lodging industry has returned to profitability. For the first time in 12 years, the industry will experience overall profit. See Exhibit 6–8.

Hotel Categories.   Contemporary hotels can be categorized by price, service levels, guests or market segments served, and location. Many hospitality publications, such as *Lodging Hospitality* magazine, consulting firms, and lodging industry analysts categorize hotels by location, and this chapter will follow their lead. Some newer forms of lodging facilities will also be discussed.

EXHIBIT 6–8

Percentage of hotels losing money

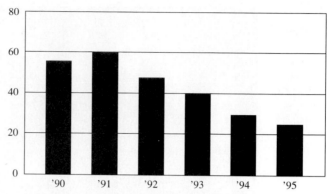

Source: *USA Today,* September 29, 1993.

The most generally recognized hotel categories and their percentages of total United States' lodging properties are:

City center or urban hotels	8.2%
Resort hotels	6.5
Suburban hotels	33.3
Highway hotels/motels	47.9
Airport hotels	4.1

City Center Hotels.   By the end of the Depression of the 1930s, most medium to large cities had at least one downtown hotel. Major cities like New York and Chicago had many downtown hotels. These hotels were typically built near railroad stations, which, for convenience sake, were usually located near the center of a city's business district. Other downtown hotels were built near centers of government, such as city halls and state capital buildings. Prior to the beginning of World War II, most business took place at city centers. Downtown hotels primarily catered to the needs of local and visiting businesspeople.

After World War II, some business activities began to shift from downtown areas to suburban areas. This was a result of a change in the favored means of transportation—airplanes were rapidly replacing trains as a mode of long distance travel. Because of space requirements, airports were built in outlying suburban areas. As roads improved and more Americans bought automobiles, the suburbs beckoned to businesses. From 1945 to the mid-1960s, as business activity decreased in city centers, so did the number of downtown hotels. But during this period, another lodging sector grew tremendously: As American families increased their mobility, the motel sector took off.

EXHIBIT 6–9

Two examples of city center hotels. The contemporary Marriott in Washington, DC, and the Waldorf-Astoria in New York City.

Courtesy: Marriott Corporation, Washington, DC.

EXHIBIT 6–9

Continued.

Courtesy: Waldorf-Astoria, New York, New York.

Beginning in the mid-1960s and continuing through today, building new (and restoring old) downtown hotels became the trend. This followed the re-birth of downtown areas as locations for general business activity and as locations of major convention centers. It is an interesting fact that 54 percent of all city center hotels were constructed in the last 10 years; only 16 percent are older than 50 years and have been renovated. Still more interesting is that only about 16 percent of city center hotels are chain affiliated.

City center hotels derive about 75 percent of their business from commercial and convention guests, with the remaining 25 percent coming from pleasure and leisure guests. In 1991, city center convention hotels averaged a 70 percent occupancy level and a $106 average daily rate (ADR).

The distinguishing characteristics of modern city center hotels are similar to those of other full-service facilities. Most of these include rooms, coffee shops and restaurants, a minimum of one cocktail lounge, room service, laundry and valet services, news stands, gift shops, and a health club. Many older downtown hotels have no parking on site. Where available, parking is very expensive, ranging from approximately $15.00 per day in Chicago to $30.00 a day in New York City.

Resort Hotels.   Resorts are primarily built to satisfy the pleasure or vacation needs of travelers. A large percentage of their revenue is derived from group meetings that combine business and pleasure. ***Resort hotels*** are generally found in destinations that are desirable vacation spots because of their climate, scenery, recreational attractions, or historic interest. In the United States, most new resorts are being built in the sun states and in ski areas. Usually, resorts have lavishly landscaped grounds and golf, tennis, and health club facilities. Most resorts are full service with restaurants, cocktail lounges, gift shops, room service, laundry, and concierges to assist guests with off-property activities.

In the past, resorts generally operated in the summer only. Today most operate year-round. Usually, resorts and hotels in resort destination areas have a wide range in ***seasonality;*** that is, they have strong high seasons where guest demand is great and they have weak low seasons where demand is limited. This seasonality attracts very different customers, largely because of price. For example, resorts in Palm Springs, California, have a high or expensive season from January through April when daytime temperatures are in the 70s and much of the nation is in a deep freeze. The high season is characterized by high room rates and high occupancy rates. Palm Springs' low season runs from May through early September, when daytime temperatures might be over 110° Fahrenheit. Resort occupancies and room rates tend to be low. During the so-called shoulder season, September through December, rates toe the middle line.

Resorts attempt to fill their rooms throughout the year by adjusting their prices. In the low season, price-sensitive customers are attracted by deeply discounted rates. In the high season, more affluent customers welcome the upscale halo effect and exclusivity brought about by high rates. By appealing to different customer categories and catering to different needs, resorts keep their average occupancies comfortably high.

In addition to being located in destinations with natural physical beauty, resorts have also been built near human-made attractions such as theme parks: Disneyland and Walt Disney World are good examples of such attractions. Furthermore, casino operations in Las Vegas and Atlantic City also attract resort development.

EXHIBIT 6–10

The concierge has become a valuable service for hotel guests.

Courtesy: Four Seasons Hotels & Resorts, Toronto, Canada.

Generally, resorts achieve high occupancies and high sales per room. In 1991, the resort hotel category averaged a 66 percent occupancy and ADR of $120 (the highest ADR of all hotel categories). Resorts, however, are the most expensive properties to operate. For instance, to provide appropriate service, they must have larger staffs. On average, resorts have 1.6 employees per room, as compared to a standard full-service hotel that averages less than one employee per room. In other words, a resort with 100 rooms would likely have 160 employees, while a standard full-service hotel might have 93.

Today's resorts are attracting more individual business travelers than in the past. Approximately 40 percent of resort business is comprised of business travelers and 75 percent of these are at the resort to attend meetings and conferences. With this increase of business guests, many resorts are adding amenities such as facsimile machines, secretarial services, and on-site travel agencies. This trend of an increased number of business travelers staying at resorts is projected to continue into the future.

Suburban Hotels.   As mentioned in the discussion on city center hotels, the American economy rapidly expanded following the end of World War II. As downtown areas used up available land for the construction of office towers, real estate prices more than tripled. Many corporations did not want to pay these higher prices; to them the suburbs seemed a better and less expensive alternative. With the increased growth in suburban-based businesses, strong demand for nearby hotels arose. The suburban hotel category continues to expand today, as businesses and housing sprawl outward from city centers. In 1991, full-service hotels in this category averaged an occupancy level of 63 percent and an ADR of $74.

Eye on the Issues

International

Globalization was already well underway when the walls surrounding the Soviet Union and Eastern Europe tumbled. Rapid business and trade expansion in Asia, Europe, the United States, and other areas of the world have required that the international lodging industry grow to accommodate business travelers' needs.

On a monthly basis, *Hotels Magazine* reports the news regarding the rapid international expansions, acquisitions, and mergers of the lodging industry. Today, there are hotel chains in the United States that operate globally—Sheraton operates hotels in 61 countries. ACCOR, based in France, operates in more countries (66) than any other hotel chain and owns Motel 6, which was founded in the United States. Clearly, international hotel ownership and geographic areas of operations are expanding. Today's and tomorrow's hotel managers must be "internationalists."

Hotels in this category are distinguished by the tendency to be midsize, and they are likely to be chain affiliated. With an average size of 250 to 300 rooms, they are usually smaller than city center hotels. About half of all suburban hotels are chain affiliated. Their major source of revenue is conference and meeting business. Their facilities often include swimming pools and sports and health equipment. Additionally, suburban hotels often serve as the focal point of their communities, hosting local events and weekly meetings of organizations such as the Lions and Rotary Clubs.

Highway Hotels/Motels.   In the 1920s, America began to develop its highway system. Small tourist courts began to spring up along these highways, though the earliest were somewhat crude. They usually consisted of a row of simple, easily accessible cabins offering travelers a parking space directly in front of the room. Many were without a private bath.

In these early days, motels were small (averaging 20 rooms) and were usually operated and/or owned by a couple living on the premises. Food and other services were not offered. Tourist cabins and motels evolved and slowly grew larger throughout the 1920s. They even managed growth during the Depression of the 1930s and through World War II.

After the war, with pent-up demand for automobiles and travel, the motel business began to grow rapidly. With this increase in travel, the older form of tourist cabin motel came to be seen as unsatisfactory. Entrepreneur Kemmons Wilson recognized the changing needs of post-WWII travelers and created the first Holiday Inn in Memphis, Tennessee, in 1952. His innovations included putting a restaurant in the property, which upgraded its status by making it more like a hotel.

While retaining drive-up accessibility to the sleeping rooms, the motel/tourist court evolved to the motor hotel. This evolution continues. Though today's highway hotels often offer many of the same facilities as suburban and city hotels, they have distinct characteristics. The distinguishing characteristics include plentiful parking space and a highway location that features a large, bright sign designed to be easily readable by passengers in fast-moving automobiles. Most highway hotels offer ice machines, vending machines, and a swimming pool.

Airport Hotels.   Travel by passenger airplane began in the 1920s. However, this form of travel was only available to the more affluent. After World War II and in the 1950s, more people began traveling by air, but it was not until after 1959 that mass travel by air began. The Boeing 707, the first successful passenger jet aircraft, inaugurated a new era of air travel for America's large middle class. To accommodate these changing modes of travel, hotels popped up around airports, just as hotels had earlier developed around train stations and highways.

Airport hotels tend to offer the same full-service accommodations as city center and suburban hotels, but with a narrower target market: they are aimed primarily at the individual business traveler. Airport hotels are also designed to accommodate business meetings, and they are often popular sites for corporate training meetings. This category generally has a high occupancy rate and does most of its business on weekdays during business travel periods.

Newer Forms of Lodging Facilities.   In addition to the preceding categories of hotel properties, many newer forms have recently evolved. Analysts often include these facilities in the statistics of the five categories above for convenience. In reality, though, these newer, specialized or hybrid forms of lodging are interesting in their own right. These properties were created and built to serve the specific needs of clearly categorized groups of customers, or *market segments.* Market segmentation, discussed further in Chapter 15, ''Hospitality Marketing,'' drives the need for such innovation.

Conference Centers.   Surprisingly, the **conference center** concept has its roots in both academia and high-tech industry. In the mid-1950s, corporate in-house conference centers were typified by IBM's Homestead facilities (1954), G.E.'s Croton-on-the-Hudson Development Center (1955), and AT&T's Lisle Training Center and Hopewell Training Center (both 1955). These corporate centers were freestanding facilities with audiovisual systems and other sophisticated meeting amenities. However, their customer base was exclusively internal; they were dedicated to the training needs of their owners' employees.

During this same period, universities were operating on-campus conference centers for university and adult continuing education needs. The university centers had broader missions; they also hosted nonuniversity affiliated meetings. Attendees of these meetings stayed at dormitories and ate in college cafeterias. But business meetings attracted a more upscale type of attendee, with higher expectations. This was a new form of demand, and it evoked a new kind of supply. Posh private executive conference centers were born in 1964.

The Tarrytown House in Tarrytown, New York, a renovated mansion, became the first commercial conference center. Tarrytown House incorporated technologically advanced meeting facility features within an elegant setting. Later in the same year, the Arden House opened its doors. The Harrison Houses followed these successful conference centers by opening similar concept facilities first in Glen Cove, New York (1968), and then in Lake Bluff, Illinois (1970). These early conference centers were designed to serve fewer than 100 executive-level attendees, were situated in remote but conveniently accessible locations, and had a *think tank* feel to them. By the mid-1970s, conference centers had rapidly refined their market segments and offered a unique product.

Early pioneers in this expansion included Stonebridge Conference Center in Snowmass, Colorado (1973), the Woodlands Inn and Conference Center near Houston, Texas (1974), the Scottsdale Conference Center and Resort in

EXHIBIT 6–11

Both the Cheyenne Mountain and Scottsdale Conference resorts supply a growing conference market.

Courtesy: International Conference Resorts of America, Phoenix, Arizona.

Scottsdale, Arizona (1976), and Scanticon near Princeton, New Jersey (1981). The success of these conference center pioneers spawned rapid development of pure conference centers throughout the 1980s and 1990s. Existing hotels, eager to cash in on the concept, added conference center features to their properties.

Today, conference centers have evolved into four basic types:

- Executive conference centers specialize in meetings for middle- to upper-level management.
- Corporate conference centers are of two types: those owned by a corporation and exclusively for that company's meeting use and those primarily for the owner company's use but also available for outside organizations.
- Resort conference centers are designed for meeting use by any organization.
- Nonresidential conference centers do not offer sleeping rooms and are often developed by not-for-profit organizations, such as colleges and universities.

The defining characteristic of a conference center is that the majority of its revenue comes from conferences and meetings held by various organizations. It is not unusual for a conference center to generate 95 percent of its revenue from group meetings. Other distinguishing characteristics include special pricing structures (usually room rates that include meals and meeting room charges); a high proportion of meeting and function rooms relative to the number of sleeping rooms; access to sophisticated audiovisual equipment; specialized staff (called *conference coordinators* or *convention service managers*) who are assigned to each organization holding a meeting at the property; and the ability to accommodate meetings ranging in size from fewer than 10 to several hundred attendees.

While pure conference centers cater almost exclusively to the group meeting business, many commercial hotels and resorts have adopted the features of this specialized niche. In essence, they add an "ancillary conference center" to their property. This variation on the conference center category generates 30 to 60 percent of revenue from group business, with the remainder of revenue coming from individual business and pleasure travelers.

All-Suite Hotels.   The all-suite concept was pioneered in the late 1960s by Bob Woolley, a builder and founder of Granada Royale Hometels (owned now by Holiday Inns). The *all-suite hotel* was initially designed for the extended-stay business traveler, who wanted more room to spread out. It also was designed for the relocation market; new or transferred employees and their families used it as a temporary home base while house hunting. Today, this concept enjoys extraordinary popularity, and many hotel chains have added all-suite hotels to their product lines. Major corporate chains such as Hilton, Hyatt, and Marriott all have all-suite divisions.

Defining characteristics of all-suite hotels are kitchen facilities, complete with cookware and serving utensils; videocassette players with a selection of movies; and sports centers with fully equipped health clubs. They may also offer complimentary breakfasts and cocktail hours. All-suite properties attempt to create a ''homey'' and temporary residence atmosphere by designing social gatherings for guests. They are competitive with standard hotels because they eliminate many costly hotel features, such as extravagant lobbies, multiple restaurants, entertainment facilities, and extensive group meeting space.

In 1991, this category of hotels averaged a 71 percent occupancy level and had an average daily rate of $69.

Market Segmented Chain Products.   In the early 1980s, Robert Hazard became the president of Quality International. Over the years, this chain had accumulated a diverse range of properties ranging from barely acceptable, through mid-scale, to higher scale. The problem was that they all carried the Quality International label: Customers were confused because they all carried the same name yet differed greatly. Robert Hazard acted to remove this confusion by grouping this hodgepodge into categories:

- An economy class, called Comfort Inns.
- A middle class, called Quality Inns.
- An upper class, called Quality Royale (currently named Clarion).

The result was a market segmented by product. This move eliminated customer confusion and resulted in the lodging industry discovering market segmentation (a concept discussed further in Chapter 15).

This practice was successfully followed by many hotel chains, notably the Marriott Corporation, which also created segmented hotel product lines. Marriott's Fairfield and Courtyard products appeal to the price-sensitive customer; Residence Inns were designed to appeal to customers who stayed longer than a few nights and needed a more homelike environment; and Marquis hotels appeal to the more upscale traveler.

Hotel Business Organizational Structures

Chains versus Independent Hotels

Every summer, *Lodging Hospitality* magazine publishes an annual survey entitled ''The Top 400 Performers.'' These are the most successful hotels in the United States. Hotels are ranked by such variables as occupancy percentages, total sales per room, payroll expense per room, employees per 100 rooms, and total sales per employee. The following provides an approximate overview of the ownership characteristics of these top 400 lodging facilities:

Independently owned	42%
Franchise affiliated	29
Corporate owned chain	14
Chain managed	13
Consortium and referral group	2

Note that the above classifications are not mutually exclusive. For example, a hotel can be owned by an individual or a corporation, carry a franchise affiliation, and at the same time be operated by a separate hotel management company. In one Sun Belt tourist mecca, for instance, there is a suburban hotel owned by a real estate developer that carries the Hilton franchised name and is managed by a small Missouri hotel management company. The following is a discussion of these various forms of ownership and management arrangements as they exist in the lodging industry.

Independently Owned Hotels.   Hotels in this category are usually independently owned and managed by an individual or corporation. A distinguishing characteristic of independents is that they are neither chain owned nor carry a franchised chain name. Since these hotels have no chain affiliation, they generally have less name recognition to the traveling public. They are further isolated, because they are seldom part of a national or international reservation system. They usually solve this lack of reservation system by allying with a referral or marketing association, such as Preferred Hotels, Leading Hotels of the World, or Best Western International. These arrangements are also known as *consortia* and provide central reservation systems and marketing networks to independent hotels, giving them an instant link to the world. Referral and association arrangements are not the same as franchise agreements. The only affiliation any of these properties have is that all of them are part of a common reservation and marketing system.

Gone are the days when an American traveling to Europe wrote a letter a year in advance to reserve a week's stay at a posh European hotel. Today's traveler wants instant (computer) confirmation of a reservation. The electronic reservations revolution has spawned giant consortia, giving independents access to markets they had never dreamed of being able to tap. Most attract business by offering independent hotels access to the global travel market through computerized central reservation systems (CRS), which we discuss in Chapters 7 and 14.

Chain Hotels.   Most people are familiar with chain hotels. All of us recognize the familiar Marriott, Hilton, Hyatt, Travelodge, and Holiday Inns chain names and logos. Hotel chains usually operate in the form of a business known as a corporation. A corporation operates hotels in several ways: It owns and operates its own hotels; it franchises hotels, or allows someone else to use its corporate name for a fee; and it may supply management personnel for a fee (a management contract arrangement) to actively operate someone else's hotel property.

Corporate chain hotels usually are owned and operated by the corporation. These hotels carry the chain logo and are managed by personnel from that chain. Franchised chain hotels are usually owned by a company that is different than the corporate chain that provides the franchise. Management contract chain hotels are usually owned by one company and managed by a hotel management team employed by a separate company.

Variations of these basic arrangements often occur and in recent years, simple chain ownership and/or franchising have become more complex. Sometimes individually owned hotels are both franchised and managed by a chain. Other times, an individually owned hotel might carry a chain franchise and be self-managed, or it may hire an independent hotel management company to run the hotel.

For example, in 1993, *Hotels* magazine reported that the New Jersey–based Hospitality Franchise Systems (HFS) became the world's largest hotel company. HFS is a corporation that owns thousands of hotel properties that are operated under franchise agreements from several different corporate hotel chains. HFS owns hotels, but it does not operate these hotels under the HFS logo; the HFS hotels carry the logos of other chain hotels via franchise agreements. HFS operates 3,413 hotels with 354,997 sleeping rooms in seven countries and planned to open 605 more hotels by 1994. Franchise names included under the HFS umbrella are Ramada Hotels, Howard Johnson, HoJo Inns, Days Inns, and Super 8.

Today's chain hotels also have a global ownership and presence. According to the annual 1993 survey by *Hotels,* the French chain ACCOR (which owns Motel 6) has hotels in 66 countries, more countries than any other chain. This is followed by U.S.–based ITT Sheraton, which has properties in 61 countries; and Holiday Inns Worldwide, which has a presence in 55 countries.

The 200 largest corporate chains account for 31 percent of the world's hotel inventory. They own 3,508,974 rooms in 24,173 hotels. Sixty-six percent of the largest hotel chains (132) are based in foreign countries.

Franchising

Franchising in the hotel and restaurant business dates back to around 1900, when the Ritz Development Company first franchised the Ritz-Carlton name to a hotel in New York City.

A *franchise* is the authorization given by a company to another company or person to sell that company's unique products and services. The granting company, or franchisor, grants to another company, the franchisee, the right

EXHIBIT 6–1

Residence Inn is a good example of a chain that attempts to standardize room types across its entire system.

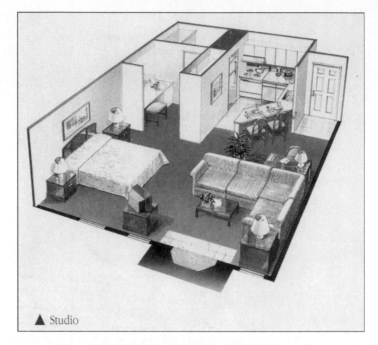

▲ Studio

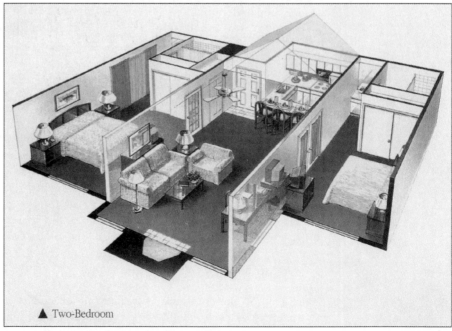

▲ Two-Bedroom

Courtesy: Residence Inn, Washington, DC.

to conduct business based upon certain guidelines for a contracted period of time and in a specified place. For example, the Hilton Corporation grants to an independent owner of a hotel the right to use its name, to use Hilton's reservation systems, to participate in Hilton national advertising for a specified time, in a specified place, and according to guidelines and standards outlined by Hilton. Under the franchise agreement, the franchisor, Hilton, grants all of this to the franchisee, the independent hotel owner. For the privilege of using the franchisor's name, the franchisee must pay a fee. There are typically two types of fee arrangements: an initial fee upon signing the franchise agreement and ongoing fees.

Eye on the Issues

Technology

The issue of technology in the lodging industry includes the application of computerized methods to replace processes previously done by hand. Surprisingly, when compared to other industries, the lodging industry has been a latecomer in computerizing its operations. Today, rapid change is occurring throughout all functional departments of hotels: reservations and front office, engineering, housekeeping, food and beverage operations, marketing and sales, accounting, and general management operations.

Individual hotels are embracing computerized "yield management" systems, which assist in setting the best room pricing structures for a given period. Their marketing and sales departments have computerized communications, client databases, customer account filing systems, and computerized time management capabilities. Sophisticated hotel management systems assist general and departmental management in more effective operations. And, of course, both chain-affiliated and individual independent hotels are linked to national and international markets through computerized reservation systems.

Initial fees will vary according to the franchisor's determined value of its goodwill or reputation and prestige; the market potential of the trading area or territory being discussed; the franchisor's average cost of finding, recruiting, and training a new franchisee; and the hard costs of signs, plans, and so on. It should be obvious that the goodwill value of a McDonald's franchise would command a higher fee than that of a lesser known fast food chain. Similarly, a Sheraton franchise may have higher initial fees than that of a lesser known hotel chain. Hilton Inns, for example, charges an initial fee of approximately $25,000, while another chain charges about $15,000.

Ongoing fees are usually calculated as a percentage of the franchisee's gross revenue. These fees also vary: Holiday Inns charges approximately 4 percent of gross revenue and Days Inn has an annual fee of about 6.5 percent.

There are advantages and disadvantages in franchising—both to the franchisor and the franchisee. The primary advantage to the franchisor is that it can rapidly expand business throughout the United States and the world by signing up hundreds of franchisees who must raise most of the necessary investment capital to start the business. Primary disadvantages to the franchisor are ensuring that the quality and standards of the product and services being franchised are maintained; making sure that few, if any, of the franchisees fail; and surrendering a certain amount of control to the franchisees. It is harder to make changes in the operating and marketing procedures of a franchised property than those of a company-owned property.

Advantages from the view of the franchisee may include:

- Site selection assistance.
- Construction expertise.
- Fixtures and equipment assistance.
- Good training.
- Initial and ongoing support from the franchisor.
- Marketing assistance, which includes access to international computerized hotel reservation systems and a national and international group business sales force.

Disadvantages for the franchisee may be related to restrictive operating policies mandated by the franchisor, unwanted marketing efforts by the franchisor, unprotected sales and trade territories, inadequate training programs, and ''no guarantee of renewal'' clauses in the franchise contract that allow the franchisor to decline to renew the franchise after the term of the contract (typically 20 years).

Management Companies

A management contract is a written agreement between an owner and an operator of a hotel or motel. The owner employs the operator as an agent (a kind of employee) who assumes full responsibility for operating and managing the property. There are basically two types of hotel management companies: chain affiliated and independent management.

Hotel chain corporations usually have a separate division that specializes in providing operating expertise and management services to privately owned hotels under the chain's franchise. These are chain-affiliated management arrangements.

Independent management companies are nonchain affiliated, privately owned, and focus upon providing hotel operating expertise to independent properties. These independent management companies can contract to operate hotels that have a chain franchise affiliation or to operate an independently owned and nonfranchised hotel.

There are three provisions common to most management company contracts:

1. The management company has the exclusive right to manage the property without interference by ownership.
2. The owner pays all operating and financing expenses and assumes all ownership risks.
3. The management company is held harmless from its actions except for gross negligence or fraud.

Owners pay management companies for their expertise in managing hotels and for the convenience of having them handle most operating decisions for the hotel. Fees are negotiable but generally fall into three areas: (1) technical assistance fees that cover the time and expertise of the operator; (2) pre-opening management fees that are generally paid before the property is open, since this requires more extensive work than managing an established property; and (3) ongoing management fees. Ongoing management fees are usually based on some kind of fee structure. These can include a basic fee only, an incentive fee only, or a basic fee plus performance incentive.

Type of Fee Arrangement	Ownership Pays Management Company
Basic fee only	W% of gross revenue to manage
Incentive percentage only	X% of net revenue if certain performance standards such as occupancy or daily rate levels are met
Basic fee plus a performance incentive	Y% of net revenue to manage + Z% of gross revenue if certain performance standards are met

Most management companies use a basic fee plus a performance incentive. Basic fees usually range from 3 percent to 5 percent of the hotel's gross revenue. Incentive percentages are in the 2 percent to 5 percent range and are dependent on the operation's profitability.

Hotel management companies are most prevalent in the United States. *Hotels* magazine's 1993 survey reports that among the world's largest 100 hotel management companies, only 7 were located in foreign countries. The largest management company in the world is Denver, Colorado–based Richfield Hotel Management, Inc., which controls 33,351 rooms in 164 hotels. Their management portfolio of franchise names includes Hilton, Radisson, Sheraton, Regal, Comfort, Quality, and Clarion. Richfield also owns 10 hotels.

In recent years, hotel management companies have had a difficult time as hotel owners have set more demanding standards of performance. Hotel overbuilding, followed by an industry recession from the mid- to late 1980s, caused owners to want quick action in improving their properties' performances. The operating climate for management companies changed as owners expected better and faster returns and declined to negotiate long-term contracts.

Management contracts have advantages and disadvantages from the perspective of both the owner and the management company. Advantages from the owner's viewpoint include being freed from daily operating responsibilities and having access to the expertise of established hotel operators with a proven track record. A major disadvantage is that ownership carries most of the property's financial burden. If the management company performs poorly or if the property requires expensive repairs, it is the owner's money that is tied up and he or she must make up for losses or find funds to make repairs.

The main advantage from the management company's perspective is that it can control many properties without the large investment and financial risk of ownership. Disadvantages, as viewed by the management company, are related to the financial health of the owner. Management companies grow by having a good operating reputation. This reputation can be jeopardized if the owner does not supply needed shortfalls in revenue, which could result in substandard hotel facilities and services. Also, performance incentive fees provide the majority of a management company's profits; hotels in poor condition do not do very well.

Whether or not an individual lodging property is corporately owned by a chain, independently owned and operated, has a franchise affiliation, or is operated by a management company, most properties follow a similar organizational hierarchy and structure.

Management/Organization Structure

The organization structure of a full-service hotel represents most of the functional departments that are possible in all hotel categories discussed earlier. Exhibit 6–13 depicts a typical organization structure. Note that there is considerable variation in organization, structure, number of personnel, and so on, depending on the type of property. For example, this organization chart would be typical of a large, city center property. A specialty property, such as a Marriott Residence Inn or a small airport property, would be represented organizationally by some of the same but fewer positions.

Lodging Facility Market Demand and Segments

The different types of hotels are designed and created to be responsive to different travelers' needs and demands. These needs determine the types of accommodation facilities found in the lodging industry. Total demand for a lodging product is sometimes envisioned as a whole pie that can be cut into many pieces or segments. In Exhibit 6–2 we showed that suppliers can either sell to end-user demand or intermediary demand. Using the analogy of a pie,

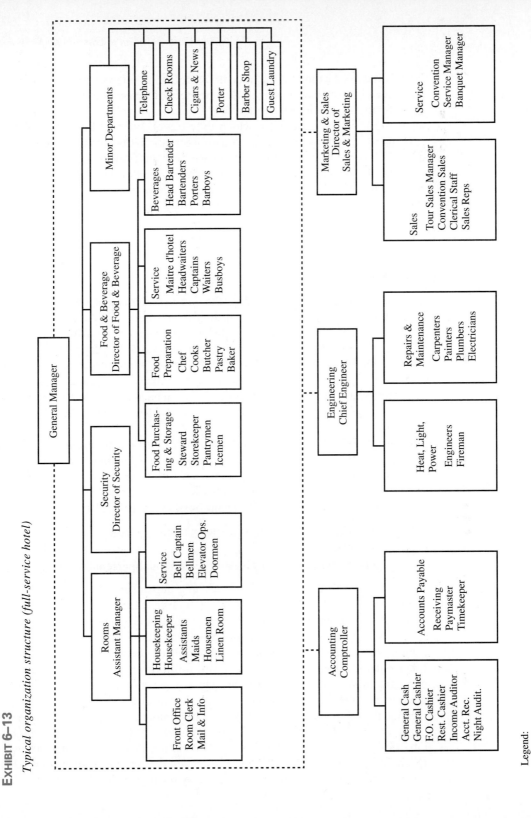

EXHIBIT 6–13

Typical organization structure (full-service hotel)

Legend:
———— Line departments
------- Staff departments

we could describe the lodging industry as being cut into two halves: the travel end-user segment and the travel market intermediary segment.

The discussion in this section first examines travel end users by looking at the purposes or reasons for which they travel. We will look at two broad reasons for travel: business and pleasure/recreational/personal. Looking more deeply into the habits of end users, we will investigate how business or pleasure travel takes place: in groups or through independent travel. The last examination of end-user demand will be accomplished by a detailed look at these groups and independent travelers, using a variety of categories and classifications. Following the discussion of the travel end-user segment, we will describe the travel market intermediary segment.

Travel End-User Demand

The lodging industry typically cuts the end-user demand segment of the pie into additional smaller pieces according to a single segmentation variable, purpose of travel. This variable is a behavioral category described in Chapter 15, "Hospitality Marketing." Lodging marketers simply ask prospective travelers: "What is the purpose of your trip?" These purposes create natural categories of travelers. Each of these categories, slices, or segments has unique needs and wants. Thus, additional questions can be asked of these more refined segments, so that the lodging facility can further refine its products and services.

The two major end-user market segments defined by purpose of travel (*business/organizational* and *pleasure/recreational/ personal*) are illustrated in Exhibit 6–14. Both of these segments can be further divided into group and independent travel subsegments. The subsegments of most interest to a hotel sales force are those that involve group business, specifically:

* Conventions and meetings (a subsegment of business/organizational travelers).
* Tours (a subsegment of pleasure/recreational/personal travelers).

Hotel sales forces focus their efforts on group business because the "piece of business" involved in each sale is much larger than for an individual sale. One convention group sale (for example) might bring a hotel 200 sleeping-room assignments for three or four nights. In addition, the group may contract for several luncheons and banquets, play golf on the hotel's course, and use other hotel services, which produces still more revenue. A sale to a tour bus company might seem smaller (with 40 guests per bus) but usually involves a contract for several months. Whenever the tour company brings a bus tour through the region (weekly, biweekly, etc.) 40 more passengers will stay overnight. Over a three-month contract, this could total more than 500 room nights. Obviously, courting group business is a better use of sales staff than trying to reach independent/individual pleasure travelers and independent/individual business travelers. For this, most hotels rely on advertising.

EXHIBIT 6–14

Lodging market demand by "purpose of visit."

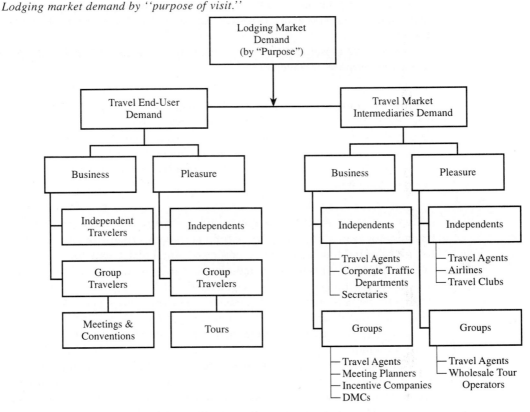

Segmenting by the variable purpose of travel is the most common way hotels categorize demand. Other segmentation variables that can be used include:

• Demographic variables such as age, income, gender.
• Geographic variables such as region, density.
• Psychographic variables such as social class, personality, lifestyle.
• Behavioral variables such as frequency of travel, benefits sought.

Remember that the above slices, categories, or segments represent the total potential demand pie. No single lodging facility is capable of addressing all of these. It must choose a few target segments based upon its resources. Research helps lodging facilities select which segments to pursue. Making a good match involves not only matching physical resources (such as facilities, location) but also matching a client's needs in terms of price and availability. If a group needs space for an annual Fourth of July meeting, the hotel must have the space available then, not in December.

As you can see, there are many ways to segment customer markets. Creative lodging marketers are continually looking to identify the special needs of new segments and accordingly design innovative products to address those needs.

Let's take a closer look at some of the major segments of the demand pie, divided by purpose of travel.

Business/Organization Segment.   This segment is composed of demand from businesses and organizations of all types. Group demand comes from corporations, associations, social groups, educational groups, government groups, religious groups, and so on. Independent demand comes from individual members of these businesses and organizations who are traveling for business purposes.

Groups.   Groups attending meetings and conventions are a large source of business for the lodging industry. Group sizes may range from 10 attendees to groups of thousands, and these groups occupy hotel rooms for an average of three nights. Groups in the business/organization segment meet for a variety of reasons, including training; management development; executive and board of director retreats; national and regional sales conferences; and international, national, regional, and state association conventions. They select lodging facility meeting sites based upon the facilities' ability to satisfy the purposes of these meetings.

Individual attendees do not select the lodging facility where these meetings will be held; thus, lodging sales forces must identify and work through group decision makers. These include organizational executives or intermediaries such as independent meeting planners and sometimes travel agencies (see Exhibit 6–14).

Independents.   Individuals traveling for business purposes make up a large portion of lodging industry revenues. In addition to having the potential for frequent repeat business, they are easier to identify and reach than pleasure travelers. Thus, lodging facility sales forces are able to contact the organizations from which these travelers depart and/or the local organizations where they will visit in order to offer accommodations and services. Most lodging facilities have one salesperson specializing in obtaining this type of business. Additionally, advertising may be heavily used to attract this group.

Business/organization independent travelers are motivated to travel in order to carry out economic requirements of their businesses. Generally, business travelers are well-educated and affluent, have high-level jobs, and tend to fly often. Given the increasingly national and international geographic nature of modern business, this category of traveler will remain a dominant segment in the future.

We'll turn now to a discussion of yet another segment, that of the pleasure/ recreational/personal end user (Exhibit 6–14).

Pleasure/Recreational/Personal Segment.   The pleasure/recreational/personal traveler is motivated by four factors:

- *Physical.* These motivators are related to physical rest, sports participation, beach recreation, relaxing entertainment, and other activities connected with health.
- *Cultural.* These motivators are related to the desire to know about the culture of other areas. These include history, current social organization and institutions, music, architecture, art, folklore, dances, language, and religion.
- *Interpersonal.* Travel in this category is motivated by a desire to visit friends or relatives, meet new people, make new friends, and escape daily routines.
- *Status and prestige.* These motivators come from a desire for recognition, attention, appreciation, knowledge, and a good reputation as perceived by other people. This travel includes trips related to the pursuit of education, business, and hobbies.

Like the business/organization segment, the pleasure segment can be further subdivided into group demand and independent demand.

Group.   The pleasure/recreation/personal segment is motivated to take trips and does so in a group form known as tour packages. Tours became an important travel segment following World War II and have expanded rapidly since 1960. Tours offer the traveler the advantage of security and greater affordability.

Tours are put together by knowledgeable tour wholesalers. These wholesalers can offer vacation packages to the traveling public at prices lower than individual travelers would be able to arrange by themselves. Wholesalers buy travel services such as transportation, hotel rooms, sight-seeing services, airport transfers (ground transportation), and meals in large quantities at discounted prices, then package the components, add a markup, and resell this package to a group of individual travelers. All retail travel agencies offer packages for sale ranging from traditional trips through the United States and Europe to exotic packaged tours to the rain forests of Brazil.

Independents.   The travel motivators mentioned earlier (physical, cultural, interpersonal, and status and prestige) also influence the independent pleasure/ recreational/personal segment. This category, like the independent business traveler, can be further subdivided by variables other than purpose of travel.

In their 1985 book, *The Tourism System,* Mill and Morrison refer to eight representative segments of independent travelers in the United States:[2]

Resort travelers.

Family pleasure travelers.

Elderly travelers or senior travelers.

Singles and couples.

Minority pleasure travelers.

Travelers with disabilities.

Gaming travelers.

Other growth travelers.

An understanding of the needs and wants of the end-user customer is imperative to lodging-facility managers. By knowing what the target customers want, marketers and managers can custom-design a product and services package that will initially attract the targets and then work to increase the possibility that they will become repeat customers.

Management's job doesn't end by scoping out relevant end-user customers. Managers also need to understand a second population of lodging facility demand: travel market intermediaries.

Intermediary Demand

Intermediaries are part of the demand for the lodging industry because often hotels cannot sell directly to the end users we have previously discussed. Often hotels must first sell their supply to these intermediaries, who afterwards sell it to the end users. Thus, for the lodging facility to be successful, it must address the needs and wants of another group of customers, the travel market intermediaries. Since these intermediaries also serve the same end users, their needs and wants are similar to those of the end users—with one additional need: to satisfy their business objectives.

Exhibit 6–2 on page 162 shows that when a hotel sells *indirectly* to end-user demand, it must first sell to an **intermediary.** Exhibit 6–14 shows that travel market intermediaries consist of two types: those that deal mainly with business end users and those that deal mainly with pleasure/recreational/personal end users. Some intermediaries serve both groups of end users.

Business Segment Intermediaries.   This category of intermediaries works to match lodging facilities with business and organization end-user demand.

For the group business subsegment there are several types of business intermediaries that act as interfaces between hotels and end users from business and organization groups. These include meeting planners, travel agents, incentive travel specialists, and destination management companies (DMCs).

Independent business end users have several kinds of intermediaries from which to choose when purchasing travel services. They may make travel arrangements through a travel agency, through an in-house travel department called a *passenger traffic department,* or through their secretaries and assistants. These intermediary gatekeepers can be valuable allies for lodging marketers who make the effort to communicate the benefits of their hotel's products and services.

Pleasure/Recreational/Personal Segment Intermediaries.   These intermediaries differ from the preceding business travel intermediaries in that they help lodging facilities to attract end-user demand that is traveling for pleasure.

Group travel for pleasure/recreational/personal end users can be arranged and sold directly or indirectly by wholesale tour operators, inventoried and sold by retail travel agencies, or arranged and sold by travel clubs (Exhibit 6–14).

Travel agencies are the most dominant link between travel service suppliers and the independent pleasure traveler. Credit card companies are another intermediary for reaching the independent traveler. Visa, MasterCard, American Express, and most major oil company cardholders, for example, usually have access to special pricing and discounts for tourism services.

Demand for tourism services, in general, and the lodging industry, in particular, can be viewed as consisting of travel end-user demand and travel market intermediary demand. (See Exhibit 6–2.) Because tourism suppliers often sell directly to the end user, a clear understanding of their needs and wants is necessary for effective marketing efforts. Alternatively, tourism suppliers often sell indirectly to the end user. That is, they must first sell to travel market intermediaries who then sell to end users. Again, marketers must understand the needs and wants of this intermediary demand in order for their tourism products and services to pass through the pipeline and eventually reach the consuming end user. The needs and wants of both end-user demand and intermediary demand will influence the design and nature of products and services offered for sale by the lodging industry.

Marketing and Sales Bring Lodging "Supply" and "Demand" Together

We now turn to a discussion of how the process of marketing (and sales, a subcomponent of marketing) links lodging supply and lodging demand.

Marketing

As you will learn in Chapter 15, "Hospitality Marketing," the marketing concept asserts that the key to achieving organizational goals lies in determining the needs and wants of target markets and delivering the desired satisfiers more effectively and efficiently than competitors. The marketing concept rests on four main pillars: a market focus, customer orientation, coordinated marketing, and profitability.

Marketing is a process that links supply and demand. Marketing principles suggest a logical path toward courting demand:

1. *Segment* or divide the demand pie into many pieces.
2. *Target* or choose which segment or piece of the pie to serve with its products/services.
3. *Position* or promote and communicate the characteristics of the organization's product/services to these selected target customers in a way that helps customers understand how these products and services would be of unique benefit.

Positioning is the part of marketing where the familiar activities of selling, advertising, pricing, and so on take place. To give a practical illustration of this activity, we will now examine how a hotel sales department is organized and operates to link supply and demand.

The Hotel Sales Department: The Link between Supply and Demand

Personal sales is only one part of marketing a property. Referring back to the four Ps of marketing, the sales department and the act of selling are considered part of promotion. Promotion is communicating the company's products and services to potential customers. The personal sales process occurs in the same fashion as does the full process of marketing. Salespeople must first locate potential customers, ask about their needs and wants, and then match their company's products and services, or supply, with this demand.

Exhibit 6–15 shows the organization structure of a hotel sales and marketing department. This specific example represents a specialty conference center property that has more than 300 rooms and earns 90 percent of its revenue from corporate and association group business. While different properties have widely varying revenue structures and niche markets, this model serves to illustrate most group-directed sales and marketing functions.

Marketing management is generally the responsibility of the director of marketing (DOM) who delegates the specific management of the salespersons (Exhibit 6–15) to the director of sales (DOS). In some properties, these two management functions are handled by a single manager, the director of sales and marketing (DOS&M). In some small properties, the DOS&M also is the primary salesperson; in fact, the marketing department may consist of only one person. Whatever arrangement is used, all functions must still be accomplished.

In our illustration, the DOM delegates the sales management responsibility to the DOS, who reports to the DOM. The DOM is primarily responsible for advertising, which is used to attract individual lodging guests and as a support tool to the group sales efforts. Additionally, the DOM oversees telemarketers, conference coordinators, and other support staff and represents the

EXHIBIT 6–15

Structure of hotel marketing department

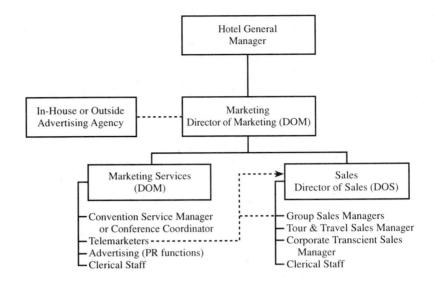

sales and marketing department to the hotel general manager. Telemarketers primarily locate solid potential customers and then turn these leads over to the experienced salespeople. Conference coordinators are specialists who make sure that groups meeting in the hotel receive effective service before, during, and after their meetings.

The director of sales directly designs the sales force and manages it on a daily basis. Often, the DOS also does a limited amount of personal selling. Designing a sales force entails setting sales objectives, devising a selling strategy, deciding the appropriate size and compensation for the sales team, and structuring appropriate selling territories. Once the DOS has recruited and trained the right people for the sales force, he or she can begin managing them. This includes directing their actions on a daily basis, motivating them, and, finally, evaluating their performance.

Exhibit 6–15 shows *three types of sales managers* (the term for sales-people in the hotel business) found in a typical sales department. *Corporate transient sales managers* are responsible for attracting individual business travelers. *Tour and travel sales managers* deal strictly with wholesale tour operators and retail travel agents. Finally, *group sales managers* specialize in corporate or association meetings. The discussion below concentrates on the duties of group sales managers in order to demonstrate how they match group meeting demand with hotel meeting service supply.

Group sales managers generally specialize in corporate or association meetings. Their territories are most commonly structured around geographic guidelines—usually East Coast, mid–U.S., and West Coast markets. Sometimes their workload is organized according to industry. For example, a sales manager may concentrate on pharmaceutical corporations, oil companies, or accounting firms. Association business may be segmented by industries or memberships that they represent: trade associations, insurance, medical and professional, scientific, and so on. The territory or workload structure is dependent upon the overall strategy designed by the DOM and DOS.

Effective sales managers bring supply and demand together through the selling process. This process entails four steps:

1. *Prospecting and qualifying.* Sales managers must locate potential customers and determine if they have a reasonable probability of contracting with the lodging facility. Prospecting involves sifting through the names of hundreds of corporate and association meeting planners. This is usually accomplished by telephone. **Qualifying** involves asking these prospects a number of **screening questions.** As shown in Exhibit 6–15, sales managers are sometimes assisted in this step by telemarketers.

2. *Pre-approach and approach.* After a qualified prospect has been identified, more preparation is needed before the sales manager actually attempts to meet with or telephone the prospect. For example, if companies in the same industry have held meetings at the hotel in the past, the sales manager might review how successful they were or how good the feedback from them was. He or she may try to discover personal attributes of the prospect. This is necessary because buying decisions are made both on a rational needs and benefit basis and on an emotional level. It is important to establish a good personal feeling between both the buyer and the sales manager. This is best begun through knowledge.

3. *Presentation and demonstration.* This is the step where the sales manager actually presents the benefits of the property's supply and demonstrates how these benefits satisfy the buyer's demand or needs. In the hotel business, this presentation is usually accomplished by having the potential buyer visit the property. This is a way of having the buyer actually sample the product. While this is the ideal method to make a presentation, this cannot always be arranged. Presentations by telephone, supported by sales brochures and videos, or in the prospect's office are alternative methods.

During this step of the sales process, the sales manager will invariably encounter objections to points that are made in the presentation. Answering and overcoming these objections is an art and comes with experience. Additionally, the sales manager must ''ask for the order'' or attempt to close the sale by obtaining a signed contract. Since this is a big moment, it sometimes makes sales managers anxious, but, obviously, it is an imperative action.

4. *Follow-up.* After people make a purchase, they sometimes experience a phenomenon known as *buyer's remorse.* This means that they must periodically be reassured that they made the right decision. An effective sales manager is sensitive to this and will maintain a relatively close contact with the customer before the meeting, during the meeting, and immediately following the meeting. Since the sales manager would like this customer to hold the same meeting at his/her property the following year and have the customer speak favorably of the hotel property, this single important step goes a long

way in creating positive customer feelings regarding the professionalism of the hotel's operations.

Consistent with the marketing concepts discussed earlier, hotel group sales managers are minimarketing organizations unto themselves. They must effectively perform all the basic steps of marketing in order to bring hotel supply and customer demand together. They first prospect and qualify (which is the equivalent of doing market research to discover customer needs and market segment characteristics). Then, through the approach and presentation steps, they communicate or promote the benefits offered by their hotel. Finally, by staying in contact with the customer prior, during, and after the meeting, they attempt to achieve the essence of effective marketing—acquiring and retaining customers.

Marketing, like so many other hotel departments, is symbiotic and interdependent with a hotel's other functional areas. Marketers will try hard to sell a dead horse—and if anyone could succeed, it would be them. But the point is that marketers do best when they have a healthy horse to sell, one with a shiny mane, proudly arched neck, and spirit. Marketing departments rely on the rooms division and property management to have clean, functioning rooms ready on time for their assigned occupants. They rely on the food and beverage staff to prepare and serve beautiful banquets and provide relaxing lounges and restaurants for clients eating ''on their own.''

By the same token, other departments rely on the sales and marketing department to communicate as precisely and solicitously with them as they do with clients. Every promise or guarantee sales managers make to their clients should be documented and communicated to all departments affected by the ''ripple'' of the promise. If the client is told that an atrium balloon drop (first prize, a trip to the Riviera) will take place at 10:30 PM, all affected departments should be consulted—*before* the promise is made!

If internal communication is given only a token nod, the best laid plans of mice and meeting planners can go drastically astray. In the case of the balloon drop, suppose no one communicated with the plant maintenance people and they picked that afternoon to flood the atrium flower beds. Picture all the guests in black tie and taffeta trundling through the muddy planters in search of the winning balloon! Imagine the day that one sales manager books the north atrium for a Siamese cat show and another books the south atrium for the Animal Dander Allergy Sufferers Association (shown on the books only as the ''ADASA'' luncheon). You can paint your own comedy of errors, but be assured, if they happen on your property, they won't seem very funny.

The underlying preventative for such problems is internal communication with and respect for the functions of other departments. Marketing departments, with their staff of communication experts, can lead the way in encouraging consultation and cooperation between all lodging departments. This is essential even in the smallest properties, and only grows in importance as property size increases.

Conclusion

This chapter has presented an overview of the lodging industry from a marketing philosophy standpoint—the essence of successful business operations is the successful exchange of products/services for value (usually monetary). Instead of simply describing components and elements, it views the industry as a dynamic interaction and exchange between supply (products/services) and demand (the customers' needs). It systematically discusses:

1. Lodging facility supply, the tourism system, and lodging product types.

2. Lodging facility market demand and segments.

3. Hotel business organizational structures.

4. How a marketing subcomponent, personal sales, links the market segment, group/convention customers, with the lodging product.

5. Current issues surrounding the lodging industry: environmental, ethical, technological, and international.

Keywords

holistic   158
supply   158
demand   158
caravanserais   162

conference center   176
intermediary   192
qualifying   196
screening questions   196

Core Concepts

tourism system   160
resort hotels   172
seasonality   172
market segments   176

all-suite hotel   178
consortia   180
franchise   181
three types of sales managers   195

Discussion Questions

1. Describe and interrelate the tourism system components. Why must members of the lodging industry be knowledgeable about changes that occur within this system?

2. Why are tourists motivated to travel? Include in your discussion both business and pleasure travelers—groups and independent travel.

3. How does a hotel salesperson (sales manager) systematically make a sale?

4. Describe the organization of a sales and marketing department at a full-service hotel.

References

Lundberg, Donald E. *The Hotel and Restaurant Business.* New York: Van Nostrand Reinhold, 1989.

Mill, R. C., and A. M. Morrison. *The Tourism System.* Englewood Cliffs, NJ: Prentice Hall, 1985.

APPENDIX

ONE DAY IN THE LIFE OF HANS WILLIMANN, GENERAL MANAGER

Guests are upset. Waiters call in sick. There's trouble at home. Just another GM's day.

Hans R. Willimann
General Manager, Four Seasons Chicago

5:30 AM

The all-news station abruptly wakes me from my deep stupor with the latest state of the crumbling evil empire. Gorbachev is out, Yeltsin is in, unrest in Latvia, the Moldavians fight rebels. Byelorussia is voting for a new capital. I don't know which is worse—being awakened at this ungodly hour before the crack of dawn with chaos in the republics, or dreaming about being chased around the kitchen by the executive chef at knife point.

6:00 AM

Tiptoeing down the stairs, I am greeted by my only friend at this uncivilized hour—my golden retriever. Che will fetch the newspaper—for a low-cholesterol, imitation bacon strip.

The digitally programmed coffee machine is the highlight of the moment, and, after a cup of hot brew, I am ready to join some 500,000 commuters to do my daily battle in Chicago.

6:35 AM

My reliable car starts with a Bavarian *hummm.* My journey brings me through the quiet, not yet awakened suburb of Wilmette to the grid-locked inbound Edens highway. During the next 30 minutes, I am closer to God than even my insurance agent can fathom. Who was the sarcastic politician who named this six-lane concrete race track "The Edens"? "Paradise Lost" is more appropriate.

6:40 AM

I turn to the rock-and-roll station to be humored by disc jockey Johnny B. I expect a racy joke, but he's making an early morning celebrity wake-up call to the venerable sister hotel just across from our own. Frantically I am trying to call my friend who is manager there. Still sleepy, he inquires about my health.

"Do you know that a radio station is trying to wake-up the rock star VIP in your hotel?" I yell into the mobile phone. "He is already in the elevator. . . . Get your security to intercept him. . . . Throw him out. . . . Get even. . . . Don't let him get away with it."

"Why are you so upset this early?" my colleague retorts. I guess there are advantages to living in the hotel versus inching your way through the Kennedy junction.

My pulse is racing over 180, and I start to question the wisdom of our company physician who insists I do cardiovascular exercises. Clearly, my heart gets all the exercise and excitement it needs by being on this highway and listening to the disc jockey's antics.

7:11 AM

Our doorman stands in the middle of the street frantically waving down any taxi who would be so good as to dignify us with its presence. How many angry guests, I ponder, are going to call me this morning because even the doorman's aggressive hustling didn't get them their timely cabs? I contemplate giving cabbies a free car wash voucher if they respond to our doorman's lively trilling.

As I pull into the hotel, I see the milk truck is obstructing the entrance to and from the garage. I also see that the dock master is yelling; the department store truck cannot exit the receiving turntable; and the grease truck is on the wrong dock.

7:15 AM

The milk truck finally leaves, and I ascend to the eighth floor in the parking garage. Through the guest elevator I finally enter my serene and elegant hotel lobby. The oversized flower arrangement of snow-white daisies greets me. I make a mental note not to forget to spray the lobby with floral scent to complete our guest's impression of a multi-sensual experience.

My first concern is Roomservice. We are running a full house of demanding radiologists in town for meetings.

Pandemonium. Two waiters called in sick. One elevator is broken down. The repair service was notified at 6:15 AM, but their voice mail directed us to press the right extension or the pound sign. We do not know the right extension and are pounding the phone. The service contract covers us only for the hours of 8 AM to 6 PM. Anything before or after those appointed hours would cost us $150—for starters.

7:20 AM

Where is the Food and Beverage Director? Oh, I forgot. He worked the Governor's function last night until the wee hours, and I told him he should sleep in. So I call Banquets to check if they can help us out. Yes, two waiters are on their way.

Taking the emergency stairs, I am huffing and puffing up to Housekeeping. The Executive Housekeeper's face seems flushed. I worry that she is close to a coronary.

"How do you expect me to make up the rooms?" she queries.

"What's wrong with the emergency stairs?" I timidly ask.

"Have you ever carried a bucket, vacuum cleaner, assorted sheets, pillowcases, soaps, shampoos, not to mention 12 terry-cloth bathrobes up three flights of stairs without a cart?" she answers.

What can I say?

7:25 AM

My telephone rings. "Are you the manager?"

"Yes sir. My name is . . . "

"I don't care about your name. Just tell me why it should take 31 minutes for a lousy slice of dry toast and lukewarm coffee to be delivered to my room. Do you know how to run a luxury property? My corporation will never again stay in any of your miserable establishments."

"Please, sir, I would like to apologize for the lapse in service." Too late; he hangs up. I remind myself that the customer is always right.

I check with Roomservice. Yes, Room 4305 was very angry and did not leave a tip. I check with the Front Desk. Yes, they know the gentleman in 4305. He didn't have any credit cards, and when the Assistant Manager tried to get cash in advance, he could not be found. I check with Security. Yes, the gentleman in 4305 has his car in the garage—a 1978 Nova filled to the brim with wallpaper sample books. This guest arrived on our doorstep at 11 last night, relocated from another hotel.

I call the doorman. "Do not deliver room 4305's car without my personal approval or the guest's full payment on his account."

7:51 AM

The Chief Engineer is calling to inform me that the couple in Room 3802 seems to prefer taking a shower outside the bathtub, and the people in Room 3702, directly underneath, are complaining that their bathroom ceiling is leaking. "How could this happen in a luxury hotel?" they ask. "Did you use a cheap plumbing contractor?"

7:57 AM

Finally I head for breakfast. I order my usual fare—carrot juice to lower my cholesterol, yogurt with fresh berries and our alternative cuisine bran/carrot muffins. Twenty minutes later my healthy victuals have not yet arrived at my table. The maitre d' informs me that the new Pantry Cook, who just arrived, had no idea how to squeeze a carrot. I settle for orange juice, and make a mental note to talk to the Human Resources Director about taking pictures of all the menu items for new staff members.

8:23 AM

The Planning Committee is meeting with all Division Heads. I am late. The Director of Human Resources reports that at the end of our first operating year, of the 18,000 individuals screened and interviewed, we hired 532. Our full-time head count is 498, and 76 positions have turned over and over and over. Should we increase our wages or contract this service? The new Americans with Disabilities Act (ADA) mandates new employment practices which require rewriting of all of our job descriptions.

The Controller says we are surpassing our advertising budget, and the Marketing Director notes that the direct mail campaign brought us only weekend business with a quadruple occupancy. We need to purchase more roll-away beds, and the guests all think the bathrobes and hair dryers are freebies.

I report that the Mayor and Alderman are very grateful for our participation in the Clean Sweep Program for Chicago. Could we also participate in the Adopt-a-Street Program and donate items for the annual food drive? By the way, the City Council passed a resolution to increase the room tax and the telephone tax.

The fire alarm interrupts the briefing. We spring to action, dispersing to our assigned emergency stations. The fire trucks come howling down the street. Guests file down staircases and out doorways. The firefighters storm up to the 36th floor with fire axes in hand. Only then do we discover that a young child pulled the fire alarm by mistake.

People are upset, yelling about incompetent management. And—you guessed it—they threatened to stay at the venerable hotel across the street. "It doesn't happen over there," says one. "I'm going to miss my million-dollar merger meeting," says another. "You will certainly hear from my lawyer." "I want a rebate." I humbly beg their pardon, hand out my business card, and the beat goes on.

9:53 AM

Back to the meeting. We are going through the high balance report on all the guestrooms. And here's our

old friend in Room 4305. Seems he called Roomservice again, but this time he ordered $400 worth of champagne and caviar, with no credit cards. Let's call the police before this bird flies the coup.

10:29 AM

Eleven messages wait on my desk and one is holding. A prominent charity in town wants what every other charity in town wants—a weekend for two at the hotel. Naturally, they note in their very pleasant letter, it's tax deductible.

Here's a note from my very best friend Don Schmo. "Remember me? We met in the St. Louis airport four years ago when our planes were delayed. You gave me your card and said that if I need a room in Chicago . . ." Funny, I've never been to St. Louis, and even if he were my best friend, due to a computer breakdown, we are 40 rooms overbooked. But of course, he insists, don't GMs always have a room up their sleeves?

11:06 AM

The Chef wants to resign. He has had it with the menu changes in our Lounge . . . three times in two days. And a regular guest sent back her hamburger saying that she wanted it cooked black and blue, not bloody.

Speaking of employment, an executive search firm has been calling for the last three days wanting to know if I'd be interested in working in Hong Kong at twice my salary, living in. I decline, but make a mental note of their number.

12:00 Noon

The vintner's luncheon is 30 minutes late. We will be doing a vertical tasting of the most exciting Cabernet Sauvignons. I hope to make it through without going horizontal.

My wife calls to remind me that I promised to babysit the kids at 8 PM while she attends a parent-teacher association (PTA) meeting. And could I donate a raffle prize for the teacher's union? "Does that guarantee that my 7-year-old's teacher will not go on strike?" I snap.

12:15 PM

I am scanning the 15 guest comment cards. Twelve guests find that the attitude and service at the hotel is exceptional. One guest didn't like the decor, and one guest is allergic to feather pillows. I make a note to include the guest's wishes in our guest history.

12:30 PM

The press and the vintner are waiting for me. So is the goose liver and port luncheon. Into the third course, all the problems of the day seem so far away. However, by dessert, reality looms. My guilt button triggers remorse for not having worked out today, and I drag myself back to my office.

3:30 PM

The Regional VP invites me on an inspection tour of all guest corridors. Carpets need shampooing, walls need touch-up, baseboards could do with repair, and the sand in the ash urn needs to be changed. And whoever puts the hotel logo in the sand needs to press a little harder. The Regional VP mentions the impending inspection of the Area VP. "Do I have to be more explicit?" he hints with one eyebrow raised.

4:16 PM

I start working on the profit-and-loss statement for the last month. The cash flow is terrific. The bottom line has increased, and our guest retention is starting to become acceptable.

7:11 PM

The Mayor is supposed to arrive at the hotel. Could I escort him up to the dinner party? I am delighted. How many members of the press are waiting at the front door?

7:45 PM

The Sheik would like to extend his visit one more week. He needs 20 rooms. We're sold out. I start calling my hotel colleagues to round up some empty rooms.

8:15 PM

I am going through my mail and see my medical report. I need to lose 10 pounds, have excessive cholesterol, and should exercise at least three times a week for 50 minutes. Furthermore, I should cut out sodium if I would like to see my children reach age 20.

8:25 PM

I leave the hotel and by 8:55 PM find my way back to Wilmette seeing all the morning sights in reverse. I pull into the garage, walk through the kitchen door, and wham. If looks could kill, I'd be one dead GM.

"What have I done?" I ask my wife in all innocence.

"Remember that PTA meeting? Remember the raffle prize for the teacher?" she says.

I slink into the den and turn on CNN just in time to see that Yeltsin is getting $500 million in American aid. Che, my golden retriever, looks at me with sad and knowing eyes and signals to me that he is looking forward to fetching the paper at 5:30 AM.

Source: Hans R. Willimann, "One Day in the Life of Hans Willimann," *Hotels,* August 1992, pp. 63–64, 66.

Rooms Division

If, later in your studies, you take an overview course on rooms division operations, you'll be introduced to all aspects of hotel front-of-the-house management. Such courses familiarize you with manual rooms division methods as well as automated computer applications. Specific areas of study generally will include: an understanding of each job position found within the rooms division, the reservation stage of the guest cycle complete with a discussion of both in-house and central reservations functions, the guest arrival and check-in stage including all associated tasks, the visitation stage of the guest cycle, and a thorough understanding of the intercommunication between departments. You'll also likely be exposed to detailed customer-service training modules, basic accounting knowledge appropriate to the night audit and guest folio posting, and information relevant to the guest check-out and billing stage of the guest cycle. This chapter will give you a sneak preview of the rooms division and its importance in the lodging experience.

Outline

Introduction

Welcome to the exciting world of hotel customer service. Once you are familiar with the interesting positions and activities of the rooms division, you will have an enticing new option for a life-long career. Your future as a rooms division manager awaits you. This chapter will acquaint you with several key departments within the lodging sector of the hospitality industry.

Hotels and motels, the primary components of the lodging sector of our industry, are usually quite different from each other in terms of physical, procedural, and operational characteristics. However, different as most operations are, there are also a number of similarities. One common aspect between hotel and motel operations is the *departmentalization of the rooms division.*

All hotels, regardless of size or price, have a **rooms division.** The rooms division is different from other hotel departments because of its extensive responsibility. In fact, the rooms division is generally considered to house three separate departments: *reservations, front office,* and *uniformed services.*

In larger hotels, these three departments are quite sizable, consisting of several hundred or more employees; in smaller operations (such as motels, for example), these three departments may be so small that they are adequately handled by just one or two individuals. No matter the number of employees or the size of the hotel, the rooms division generally handles a wide variety of responsibilities and functions. This chapter examines the three departments of the rooms division and explains their specific responsibilities.

Important Departments for Interested Students

One reason the rooms division is an interesting area of study in hospitality education is because so many students find employment there. The rooms division offers students a variety of job positions while attending college. These positions may include front desk clerk, reservationist, uniformed bell-person, cashier, and/or night auditor. Students like working in the rooms division of hotels because such jobs generally offer flexible schedules, good pay ranges, and exciting personal contact with guests.

More importantly, rooms division positions are frequently available to college students who possess little or no lodging experience. In many cases, the college student need not even be 21 years of age. Although they are generally considered entry-level jobs, rooms division positions offer students an excellent opportunity to gain valuable experience and a chance to advance up the corporate ladder. The rooms division is so exciting that some students who originally planned to pursue other college majors ultimately opt to pursue hotel management degrees instead.

Important Functions to Concerned Managers

As interesting as the rooms division proves for many college students, it is of paramount interest to hotel general managers. The three departments of the rooms division are important to hotel general managers because they are the **pivot points** around which the entire hotel operation revolves. The rooms division is the pivot, the lifeline, of hotel operations for three main reasons: economics, customer service, and departmental forecasting.

Economics.   The rooms division is the pivot point in terms of economics because it is responsible for most, if not all, of the property's revenue. In small, **economy- or budget-lodging operations** (e.g., Motel 6, Sleep Inn, EconoLodge), the rooms division generates practically 100 percent of every dollar earned by the motel. After all, other than the sale of rooms, there are few additional *revenue centers* in a budget property. As Chapter 6, ''Lodging: History, Supply, Demand, and Structure,'' explained in its discussion of segments and niches, by definition, budget-lodging operations do not have restaurants, lounges, convention centers, or health spas. Therefore, other than a few small revenue centers like soda-vending machines, pay telephones, newspaper stands, or video-arcade games, the rooms division represents the vast majority of income in budget-lodging operations.

Unlike budget properties, **full-service lodging** operations generate considerable revenues from other departments. Yet even in full-service lodging operations (e.g., Four Seasons, Marriott, Sheraton), the rooms division generates substantially more than half of the hotel's revenues. (See Exhibit 7–1.) Indeed, even in casino properties where gaming is the clear income leader, the rooms division is the second most important department (gaming revenues generate roughly 66 percent of all income, the rooms division is next with about 20 percent of income, and all other departments generate the remaining 14 percent of income) and many executives are quick to point out that the casino would not earn nearly as much revenue if the rooms division were not supplying rooms for tired gamblers.

Customer Service.   Customer service is as critical to the rooms division as food is to the restaurant. It is truly the staple of the rooms division. No other department or functional area of the hotel has as much guest contact as the rooms division. Indeed, the rooms division represents both the customer's first and last impressions of a hotel.

EXHIBIT 7–1

Full-service hotel department income ratios to total revenues. This statement demonstrates that the rooms division (rooms + telephone) is responsible for about 70 cents out of every customer dollar. For economy- or budget-lodging operations, the rooms division generates about 97 cents out of every customer dollar.

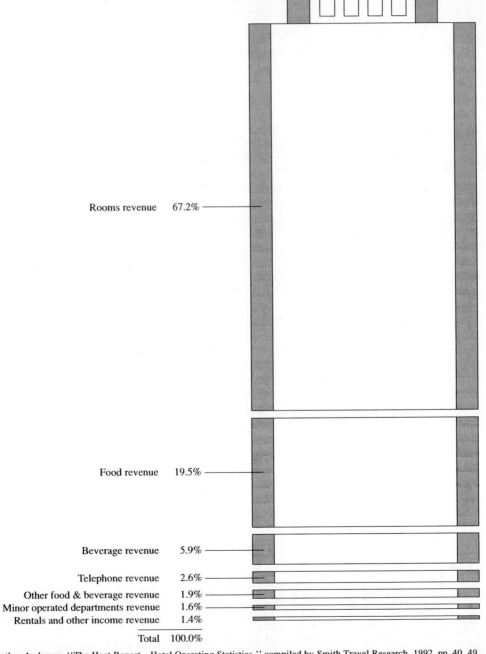

Rooms revenue	67.2%
Food revenue	19.5%
Beverage revenue	5.9%
Telephone revenue	2.6%
Other food & beverage revenue	1.9%
Minor operated departments revenue	1.6%
Rentals and other income revenue	1.4%
Total	100.0%

Source: Arthur Andersen, ''The Host Report—Hotel Operating Statistics,'' compiled by Smith Travel Research, 1992, pp. 40, 49.

EXHIBIT 7–2

A pocket-sized card depicting the mission statement and guest service creed for employees of Omni Hotels

OMNI
HOTELS
MISSION

OUR MISSION IS TO BE
THE HOSPITALITY COMPANY
MOST PREFERRED BY
DISCERNING CUSTOMERS,
DEDICATED ASSOCIATES AND
INVESTING PARTNERS
WHO SHARE OUR VISION

Omni Service Tradition

THE
POWER
OF
ONE

OMNI HOTELS' ASSOCIATES WILL

1. Think! Use common sense
2. Know and satisfy our customers' expectations
3. Greet customers immediately with our undivided attention
4. Smile and make eye contact
5. Make the first and last 30 seconds count
6. Be natural and appropriately friendly
7. Use customers' names whenever possible
8. Promptly answer telephones with a smile in our voice
9. Determine the needs and wishes of our customers and make decisions that benefit them. Bend the rules sometimes.
10. Take ownership of our customers' needs and wishes and personally follow through on their complaints
11. Escort customers whenever possible

12. Stay up! Be energetic! Take good care of ourselves.
13. Wear our uniforms and name tags in an immaculate manner.
14. Take personal responsibility for cleanliness and safety.
15. Be ambassadors for our hotel and promote it enthusiastically.
16. Be a team player
17. Protect and maintain all hotel assets and equipment
18. Always remember that we are hospitality professionals
19. Always maintain your smile even though our customers may not.

*"We are hospitality
professionals serving
our customers"*

Courtesy: Omni Hotels, New York, New York.

In fact, the entire rooms division is designed towards providing full guest service. The rooms division in many fine hotels provides bellpersons, front desk personnel, concierges, and the like—all with the goal of providing the highest possible level of guest service. Most experts agree that the quality of service and guest contact provided by the rooms division is a crucial factor in the overall guest experience. (See Exhibit 7–2.)

Departmental Forecasting. Throughout the hotel, department managers prepare their employees' schedules one to two weeks in advance. However, advanced scheduling requires accurate knowledge about upcoming business activity. Managers need to know how busy or slow the hotel expects to be so that they can staff their departments accordingly. Forecasting information related to upcoming business levels is a primary responsibility of the reservations department of the rooms division.

Because the reservations department knows the expected numbers of guests and types of rooms needed each day, it is responsible for providing accurate forecasting information to every other hotel department. This makes sense, because business in every other operational department is primarily a function of the number of rooms sold. The restaurant, for example, will sell more breakfasts the morning after a full house than it will during slower occupancy periods of the hotel. Business levels in the lounge, health spa, casino, or any other department are likewise closely related to the number of hotel rooms sold.

Environment

Today's hotels seek to conserve water, energy, and resources not only for financial reasons but because of genuine environmental concern. Certain aspects of conservation fall specifically to the rooms division for implementation.

Water Conservation

The largest use of water in any hotel is the guest room. Guests staying in hotels are often unconcerned about the amount of water and energy they use. After all, they're not paying the utility bills. To combat misuse of water in the guest room, most hotels have installed *water flow restrictors* in guest showers, sinks, and toilets. Few guests notice the slight reduction of water flow, but the net result can be hundreds or thousands of gallons of water (and dollars!) saved per day.

Another application of water conservation finding acceptance in today's newer hotels is *brown water* recycling. Although brown water is "used" water, it is clean enough to meet minimum irrigation standards of local agencies. Sources of brown water in hotels include guest room sinks and showers, some in-house laundry cycles, and certain kitchen applications. Hotels route this used water into large cisterns where it is stored for future use in irrigation and plant watering.

Energy Conservation

The most exciting form of conservation is energy conservation in the guest room. Through the use of computer technology, today's newest hotels are installing a number of energy saving systems in the guest room. These systems include such items as *infrared* and *motion sensor detectors* that are programmed to monitor the room's occupancy and shut down nonessential electrical and heating, ventilating, or air-conditioning (HVAC) systems when the room is vacant.

Less sophisticated systems require the guest to insert the room key into a special slot that activates the room's nonessential electrical systems. Although the key is required to activate certain energy applications like the television, the air-conditioning, and bedside lamps, other electrical sources continue to work without the key. In this way, the room attendant has ample light to clean the room and access to active electrical outlets and the guest has enough light to enter and exit the room before and after insertion of the key into the special energy slot.

Past, Present, and Future

The rooms division is not immune to the technological changes taking place across the entire hospitality industry. In fact, the rooms division is often the point of introduction for new devices, software applications, and hardware components used in hotels. Other chapters touch on such new applications as electronic locking systems, property management systems, self-check-in and check-out terminals, and in-room technologies including safes, television interfaces, and minibars.

New technologies have forever altered the way the rooms division functions. Years ago, literally every aspect of the rooms division was manual. The entire **guest cycle,** including reservations, arrival, check-in, visitation, check-out, and billing, was performed manually. Today, some hotels have automated every step of the guest cycle, using such new technologies as:

- Central reservations systems with a host of new applications.
- Self-check-in terminals built directly into airport courtesy vans for registration during the arrival process.
- Fully integrated property management systems that monitor billing activity during the guest's visit.
- Automated minibar systems that immediately charge the guest's account for each item removed from the refrigerator.
- In-room television interfaces where the guest can view the account and check out from the privacy of the hotel room.

Few hotels have this degree of automation today. Many properties simply cannot afford a great deal of expensive technology; other hotels are skeptical of experimenting with new forms of technology; and still other operations are convinced that automating too many steps of the guest cycle will cause a decline in one-on-one guest service.

Though technology is surely the wave of the future, most students should be prepared for a mixed bag of rooms division applications. Most hotels have some form of rooms division technology interlaced with plenty of good old-fashioned manual applications.

Job Positions in the Rooms Division

Hotels generally divide job positions into **front of the house** and **back of the house.** Front-of-the-house job positions are considered more guest-service oriented than their back-of-the-house counterparts. Front-of-the-house job positions usually afford the employee direct and frequent contact with the guest. The actual quality or amount of guest contact varies with the specific job position. Rooms division jobs generally have some of the highest incidence of guest contact. This contact requires the front-of-the-house employee to be well versed in such guest-service skills as handling complaints, providing local and hotel-specific advice and suggestions, and providing a well-rounded customer experience. Because of this constant contact with the guest, rooms division positions are critical links in the hotel's efforts to provide quality guest service to all patrons.

This does not mean that back-of-the-house job positions are not equally important links in terms of quality guest service. They truly are, because they are responsible for preparing and maintaining the guest product. Although they are generally considered guest-support rather than guest-service positions, back-of-the-house employees do have ample opportunities to communicate with the customer. Examples of contact between guests and back-of-the-house employees might include a groundskeeper who assists a guest with directions, a housekeeper who performs the evening turn-down service, or a banquet set-up person who rearranges a room according to a client's request.

Practically every job position listed in the rooms division is considered front of the house. In fact, almost the entire guest cycle involves some component of the rooms division. It is easy to see why most general managers consider the rooms division the critical key to creating a climate of quality guest service throughout the operation. In the following subsections, we will examine job positions within the three departments of the rooms division: reservations, front office, and uniformed services. Please refer to Exhibit 7–3 for a chart of the rooms division hierarchy.

The Reservations Department

In most cases, the reservations department is the first contact the guest has with the hotel. The overall quality of this initial experience is often a key factor in the guest's selection of one particular hotel over another. A reservationist who has a pleasant voice, actively answers guest questions, and markets special features of the hotel has a better chance of booking a reservation than someone who merely acts as an order taker. A positive reservation experience is the first step in ensuring quality guest service.

Aside from ensuring a quality service experience, the reservations department is charged with two other key tasks: selling rooms and communicating forecast statistics. The first of these tasks, selling rooms, is critical to the economic health of the hotel. As we have already discussed, room sales is the number one source of revenue for most hotels. It is the reservations department's responsibility to sell rooms in an efficient manner. In terms of this discussion, *efficiency* translates into maximizing occupancy and maximizing the average room rate. A reservations department that fills as many hotel rooms as possible at the highest rate possible is worth its weight in gold. A more detailed discussion of efficiency is available later in this chapter under the heading ''Yield Management.''

The third primary responsibility assigned to the reservations department is forecasting room sales statistics. As suggested earlier in this chapter, all departments in the hotel rely on the reservations department to provide them with accurate 10-to-14-day forecasts. These forecasts become the basis for business projections by all the other departments in the hotel. When the reservations department predicts a full house next week, all departments staff accordingly—the food and beverage department will be busy in its various restaurants and lounges, the housekeeping department will clean a maximum number of rooms, and the front desk will have to deal with a great number of check-ins and check-outs. In a casino property, even the gaming departments respect the reservations department's forecasts as an accurate barometer of business levels.

EXHIBIT 7-3

The rooms division staffing hierarchy. This staffing chart shows the customary positions found in most large full-service hotels.

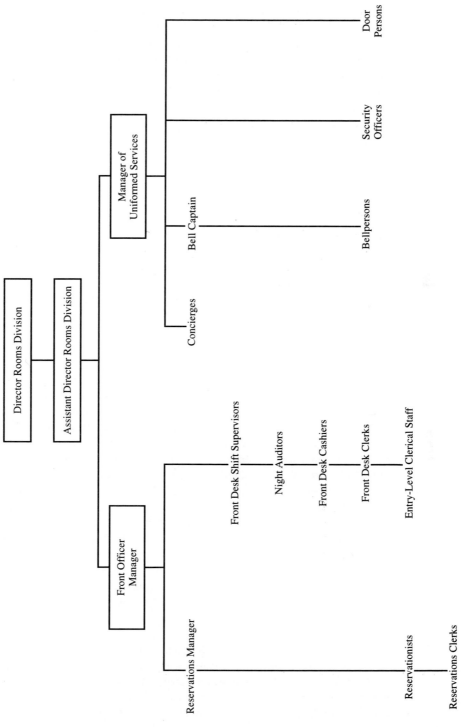

Job Positions in the Reservations Department.   There are relatively few distinct positions in the reservations department. In fact, many operations treat these positions as training grounds for future advancement into the front office. The reservationist's experience in dealing with guest service, selling rooms in an efficient manner, and providing business-level forecasts provides a good foundation from which to advance to other positions in the hotel. The reservations department is responsible for taking, canceling, monitoring, and accounting for all reservations.

Positions in the in-house reservations department generally include, in descending order of responsibility, reservations manager, one or more reservationists, and one or more reservations clerks.

The Front Office

The **front office** is the second of the three departments in the rooms division. The front office is the primary guest service department of the entire hotel. Generally, no other hotel department has the opportunity for as much guest contact as the front office.

Although there are a number of very specific duties accruing to the front office, most can be categorized in the following list of generic tasks and front office activities: greeting the guest; performing guest check-in and registration; selecting and assigning guest rooms; establishing credit and method of payment; opening, posting, and closing the guest account; cashing personal checks, travelers' checks, and foreign currency, and issuing safe deposit boxes; listening to and solving a full-spectrum of guest complaints; communicating guest information between departments; performing guest check-out and farewell; and ensuring quality service across all of these tasks and activities.

Just as the rooms division is divided into three departments (reservations, front office, and uniformed services), the front office department is often divided into three functional subdepartments: the front desk, the cashiers, and the night audit.

Job Positions at the Front Desk.   The front desk is responsible for the initial contact with the guest through greeting, registration, and room assignment. In addition, most guest problems, room changes, information requests, or other guest contacts are generally handled by the desk clerks.

Positions within the front desk functional subdepartment generally include a front desk manager, one or more front desk shift supervisors, one or more front desk clerks, and some entry-level clerical positions.

Job Positions of the Cashier Staff.   The front office cashiers are responsible for opening guest accounts, posting charges to the account during the guest's visit, and closing the account upon departure. Since the closing of an account is the final stage in the guest cycle, front office cashiers have most of their contact with the guest during the check-out phase of the guest cycle. Likewise,

EXHIBIT 7–4

Front desk staffing is universal, as this example from Hotel François in Paris shows. In this case the front desk clerk and the supervisor are on duty.

Courtesy: Hotel François, Paris, France.

Eye on the Issues

Ethics

Because the rooms division is a profit-generating operation, it must practice strategies and make business decisions that some guests perceive as unethical. Several generally accepted lodging practices that guests construe as unethical include overbooking, seasonal room rate adjusting, and yield management.

In terms of overbooking, the hotel has a legal obligation to accommodate confirmed reservations. Therefore, many guests believe that hotels should not overbook deliberately. But hotels use overbooking as a technique to enhance their occupancy in a world they consider full of potential no-shows. Hotels deliberately overbook by the number of rooms they expect to no-show. Sometimes the hotel's estimate is inaccurate, and guests are "walked" to another hotel. For the walked guest, this may be a question of ethics. For the hotel, it is more a question of economics.

The practice of increasing room rates during busy seasons or holiday periods as a means of max-imizing revenue during periods of high demand is also dimly viewed by guests. Many guests have a difficult time understanding why a room rate would jump $100 between Thursday night and Friday night. According to these guests, it is unethical to raise the rate just because Friday night is the beginning of a busy holiday weekend.

A final example can be found in yield management practices industrywide. Through the introduction of yield management technology, room rates fluctuate according to a variety of factors. Some guests have a difficult time understanding why the same room costs significantly more just because it was booked at the last minute or because it was one of the few such rooms remaining in the hotel. These guests don't understand the practice of altering rates according to demand. If the hotel is nearly 100 percent occupied, the hotel can easily raise the rate and squeeze a few extra dollars out of the remaining rooms available.

though most complaints are handled by front desk clerks, monetary complaints or problems associated with the *guest folio* (also known as the *guest bill* or *guest account*) are handled by the front desk cashiers.

Many hotels cross-train their clerks and cashiers. A cross-trained employee is capable of serving as either front desk clerk or cashier at any given moment. This makes a great deal of sense in terms of quality customer service. After all, when the desk is busy with arrivals, there are relatively few guests checking out; therefore, most cashiers can be temporarily reassigned to serve as front desk clerks. During busy check-out periods, there are relatively few guests checking in; therefore, most front desk clerks can be temporarily reassigned to serve as cashiers. Not only does this make sense from the guest's point of view, but the hotel also realizes significant labor cost savings by operating with a relatively smaller, well-trained staff, ready to take on any challenge. (See Exhibit 7–5.)

Positions within the cashier subdepartment may include the cashier supervisor and the cashier.

Job Positions of the Night Audit Staff.   The night audit is the third functional subdepartment found at the front desk. The **night audit** is so-called because it is a nightly audit of hotel accounts and departments. The night audit is generally conducted between the hours of 11 PM and 7 AM (this shift is generally referred to as the **graveyard shift**) because this is the slowest period for the hotel.

Because it is basically an accounting activity, the night audit seeks employees who are naturally adept with numbers and accounting practices (as well as employees who can function during late-night hours). Because of these unique skills (and the fact that the graveyard shift offers rather unappealing hours) the night auditor is the highest paid hourly employee at the front desk.

The night auditor must also perform all front desk clerk and cashiering duties that may arise during the graveyard shift, although there is usually little such activity during the late hours of the audit. The bulk of the night auditor's shift is spent posting room charges and tax to all rooms, verifying and balancing accounts for all guest rooms and hotel departments, and preparing a series of summary reports about departmental revenue activities from the preceding day.

Positions within the night audit subdepartment may include the night audit shift supervisor and the night auditor.

Uniformed Services

The third department included in the rooms division is **uniformed services.** The uniformed services department is also known as the guest services department or the hotel services department. The uniformed services department is so called because employees of this department wear distinct uniforms to assist the guest in identifying them as hotel front-of-the-house employees.

EXHIBIT 7–5

To an inexperienced cashier, foreign travelers cheques look very similar to domestic ones.

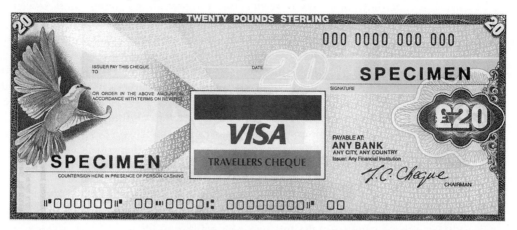

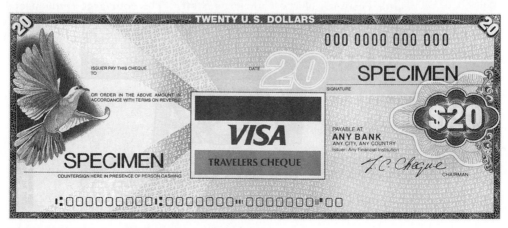

Courtesy: Visa U.S.A., Inc., San Francisco.

These uniforms help identify uniformed services employees as members of the bell staff, the concierge staff, the hotel security force, or doorpersons. Each of these positions is responsible for providing quality guest service to all customers.

The size of the uniformed services department varies according to the size and type of hotel. Because this department is so labor intensive, small economy- or budget-lodging operations can ill afford such positions. Guests do not expect to find uniformed services employees in economy- or budget-lodging operations. Instead, guests understand that there is a necessary trade-off between service and price. They are willing to be somewhat inconvenienced (for example, they must carry their own luggage) and to receive less service (they may have to find answers to their own questions instead of asking a concierge) in exchange for a lower hotel room rate.

On the other side of the spectrum are luxury and full-service hotel operations. These properties, by their very nature, provide a full range of uniformed services employees. The guest who is willing to pay a higher average room rate can expect the full-service hotel to provide a bell staff, a concierge staff, hotel security, and doorpersons.

Job Positions of the Bell Staff.   The bell department is responsible for carrying luggage and escorting guests to rooms during the check-in and check-out stages of the guest cycle, handling baggage for groups, and promoting the various facilities within the hotel to guests. (See Exhibit 7–6.) In many hotels, the bell department also operates the complimentary airport and local shuttle service. In addition, bellpersons maintain cleanliness in the lobby areas and provide information to guests in the absence of a concierge. Bellpersons are also commonly asked to assist hotel management with various errands as they arise.

Positions within the bell department usually include a bell captain and several bellpersons (also known as the *bellman* or *bellboy*).

Job Positions of the Concierge Staff.   The **concierge** (pronounced kon′-syerzh) is a relatively new position in America that has gained popularity since the early 1970s. The concierge originated in medieval Europe as little more

EXHIBIT 7–6

*Bellman assisting
guests upon arrival.*

Courtesy: The Ritz-Carlton Hotel Company, Atlanta, Georgia.

than a doorkeeper. Today, concierges are polished professionals charged with the delivery of guest service in a myriad of forms.

The concierge is the hotel's expert with regard to local activities and attractions. The concierge may be the individual who helps the guest secure tickets to a sold-out performance or sporting event, who recommends a special restaurant or museum, who gives directions or secures transportation, and who arranges tours and baby-sitting. Stories abound of concierges who have provided unique service under unusual circumstances. These stories include finding and decorating a guest's room with 100 dozen white roses; securing freshly laid, brown farm eggs each day for a famous actress; and finding a dentist to pull a tooth for a miserable guest at 2 AM.

In most hotels, the concierge position works as a specialized counterpart of the bell staff by providing an extra component of service and information away from the hectic pace of the bell desk. Indeed, in those operations that

Courtesy: Los Angeles Hilton & Tower, Los Angeles, California.

do not provide concierge service, most functions of this position fall to the bell department. In such cases, it is the bell department that arranges transportation, finds tickets, and makes appropriate recommendations.

In full-service hotels that staff the concierge position, these services are usually provided in two distinct ways. One method for providing concierge services is to limit access to the higher paying guest. Hotels limit access to these services by providing **concierge floors** or wings. In this manner, only those guests staying on the more expensive concierge floors or wings are allowed to enjoy the services. Although these rooms may be somewhat more upscale than other rooms in the hotel, the guest is primarily paying a surcharge for access to concierge services. In rough numbers, this surcharge averages about $50 per room night. The second method is to establish concierge services in the lobby of the hotel. (See Exhibit 7–7.) In this way, access to the concierge is provided to all hotel patrons. Other hotels offer some combination of these two techniques.

Job Positions of the Security Staff.   Along with providing clean and comfortable accommodations, the rooms division is also responsible for providing a safe haven to guests. Guest safety includes room key security; the prevention of burglary, forced entry into the room, or personal harm; fire safety; deterrence of prostitution and drug use; and control of minor inconveniences like excessive noise at late hours. These issues pose a big responsibility for the security staff.

Today's electronic hotels, however, are simplifying and streamlining the role of the security staff. Closed-circuit cameras aid the tracking of unauthorized individuals throughout the hotel; fire safety systems assist with constant monitoring of fire prevention equipment; electronic locking systems remove the threat of lost room keys and unwarranted break-ins; and electronic guest history systems provide information related to medical problems or personal information that might assist security personnel in an emergency.

The size and scope of this department are a function of hotel size and type. Very large hotel operations have an entire department dedicated to security and headed by the director of security. Average-sized hotels may employ only one or two such officers per shift. Smaller operations often contract this function to independent professional security companies. In any case, the bell staff is frequently called upon to assist the security department.

The security officer is responsible for making rounds throughout the hotel and assisting guests and staff during emergency situations. Most hotels require this position to have at least minimal life-safety training.

Other Job Positions in the Uniformed Services Department. Again, the number and types of other uniformed positions are a function of the size and type of hotel. Other common positions may include doorpersons who meet, greet, and assist the arriving and departing guests under the *porte cochere,* covered arrival area; van and shuttle drivers who pick up and return guests to the airport and other transportation terminals; and valet parking attendants who park and retrieve guest automobiles.

Two other, historically common, uniformed services positions have been fully replaced in today's modern hotels. Elevator operators, who once played an important role in quality guest service, and pages, who delivered messages to guests before the advent of electronic paging systems, are no longer part of today's uniformed services departments.

Eye on the Issues

International

The rooms division of the hotel deals with a truly international scope of guests. Many hotel employees are immersed in multicultural guest communication on a fairly regular basis. Therefore, well-trained rooms division employees should be culturally aware and sensitive to the needs of foreign visitors.

This is especially true in today's rapidly changing world. Historically, international tourists restricted their travel to major international cities like Los Angeles and New York; today they are just as likely to visit rural America. Historic battlefields, national parks, Native American villages, and white-water rafting are all included on their lists of exciting things that America offers.

In many full-service hotels, training in cultural awareness is expanded to include knowledge about foreign currency exchange policies (see Exhibit 7–5). Many international visitors appreciate the convenience an in-house foreign currency exchange provides. In this way, they can convert their British pounds, French francs, German deutsche marks, or Japanese yen into American greenbacks without the added hassle of locating a bank or currency merchant elsewhere in the city.

EXHIBIT **7–8**

The guest cycle

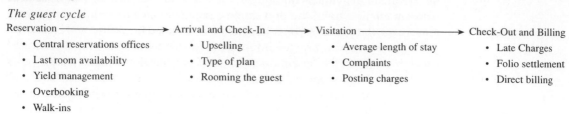

Reservation ⟶ Arrival and Check-In ⟶ Visitation ⟶ Check-Out and Billing

• Central reservations offices	• Upselling	• Average length of stay	• Late Charges
• Last room availability	• Type of plan	• Complaints	• Folio settlement
• Yield management	• Rooming the guest	• Posting charges	• Direct billing
• Overbooking			
• Walk-ins			

The Guest Cycle

The three departments that comprise the rooms division of a hotel share a vast set of tasks and responsibilities. Entire textbooks are dedicated to the multitude of functions associated with the rooms division. Therefore, no single chapter can completely outline each aspect of every job position within the rooms division. Indeed, even employees who have worked in the hotel industry are still amazed at the degree of variety and change associated with their jobs on a day-to-day basis.

Furthermore, each lodging operation conducts tasks in a very individualized fashion. Learning the specific routine at one establishment is no guarantee that you will be able to perform effectively at a different property. The only guarantee is understanding that all hotels and rooms divisions perform roughly the same general functions. As a student, you must visualize the big picture in terms of understanding the primary functions of the rooms division.

This section presents an overview of the rooms division by paralleling the guest cycle. Understanding the guest cycle is an excellent way to gain insight into those functions common across all hotels. By examining each logical step of the guest cycle—reservations, arrival and check-in, visitation, and check-out and billing—we can better understand the role of the rooms division. (See Exhibit 7–8.) The first stage of the guest cycle is the reservation.

Reservations

Although there are a variety of reservation types, they all have the same basic purpose. An advanced reservation is designed to match the guest's need for accommodations with the hotel's ability to provide accommodations. If the two parties—guest and hotel—agree on the date, room type, price, and length of stay, then a reservation can be made.

There are a number of ways in which a reservation is communicated to the property. Let's examine one straight-forward example of a reservation: The guest telephones the property directly and asks for the in-house reservations department. The hotel's in-house reservationist answers the phone call and discusses the reservation's particulars with the guest. The reservationist then checks hotel room availability (either manually in some type of log book or chart, or electronically through a computer reservations screen) for the specific date. If the date is available, the reservationist quotes the guest a rate (rates are usually quoted from the highest rate downwards, offering one room category at a time until the guest makes a selection) and tries to book the reservation. Even if the date is not available, the reservationist will usually suggest an alternate date in an attempt to convert the call into a future booking.

The reservation process remains roughly the same across all types of reservations inquiries. Other types of reservations inquiries include such possibilities as requests by mail, by a travel agent, as part of a larger convention or tour group, or as part of a complete travel package booked through an airline. The most popular type of reservations request, however, is through a chain or independent central reservations office.

Central Reservations Offices.   Most hotels today are affiliated with a central reservations office or central reservations system. If the hotel is a chain property (e.g., Holiday Inn, Hilton, or Quality Inn), the guest calls the 1-800 phone number for the **central reservations system (CRS).** Even if the hotel is not affiliated with a chain or referral organization, it may be linked to a private central reservations system.

Because the CRS is answering phone calls for all properties within the chain or membership, the actual physical location of the CRS is unimportant. Guests who call to make a reservation for a given destination rarely know the actual location of the 1-800 CRS to which they are speaking. For example, imagine that a prospective guest who lives in Los Angeles, California, has called 1-800-331-3131 to seek accommodations at a Residence Inn by Marriott in Orlando, Florida. This guest has no idea that the Marriott CRS reservationist on the other end of the phone is actually located in Omaha, Nebraska. In point of fact, one popular chain's CRS is actually staffed by incarcerated prisoners at a women's correctional institute in Phoenix, Arizona!

Central reservations systems act on behalf of the hotel by taking reservations and forwarding the information to the specific property. This is an important service and one of the leading reasons hotels choose to franchise or affiliate with a well-known brand. Indeed, some properties receive upwards of 75 percent of all their reservations through a CRS. It is easy to see why so many hotels depend, in part, upon CRSs to book a portion of their reservations.

However, CRS services are incredibly expensive. Complex central reservations systems capable of handling several million telephone calls per year may cost upwards of $250 million for development and implementation. The high cost of such a system is passed on to the individual member hotel in the form of annual charges and flat fees for each room night booked on the CRS. Depending on the chain or CRS service, reservation fees run somewhere around $2 to $6 per room night if booked across the CRS.

Last Room Availability.   Today, the CRS is one of the fastest growing areas of new technology in the hotel industry. Most major lodging chains have either replaced or significantly updated their CRSs in recent years. Current CRSs offer a number of advantages over the outdated systems of yesteryear.

The old-fashioned central reservation systems (1960s through 1980s) required constant manual updating between the hotel and the CRS. The hotel in-house reservations department was responsible for tracking the number of rooms sold by the CRS and calculating how many rooms still remained available for a given date. The CRS would continue ''blindly'' selling rooms until they were notified by the hotel to *close* room sales. In other words, the CRS never knew how many rooms were available at the individual property; it only knew that they were still *open* with regard to room availability.

This placed an important responsibility on the in-house reservationist to notify the CRS when room availability was tightening. This notification became an exercise in timing and forecasting; as often as not, mistakes were made. Sometimes the hotel in-house reservationist closed rooms with the CRS too early, other times too late. If the reservationist closed rooms with the CRS too early; then rooms were still available for sale; if so, those remaining rooms became the responsibility of the in-house reservations department. Many times the in-house reservations department could not generate enough reservations activity to fill the house, so the date would come and go with several rooms left unsold. On the other hand, if the in-house reservationist closed the rooms too late, the hotel became overbooked.

Commonly referred to as ***last room availability*** or *full-duplex systems,* today's CRSs offer on-line, two-way communication with all affiliated hotels. No longer a hit-and-miss game of guessing when the last room will be sold, modern CRSs can literally sell the very last room at any hotel. This is because the CRS now has on-line real information about the actual status of rooms at every hotel within its system. This is significantly more efficient because it allows the CRS more opportunities to sell every room without either underselling or overselling the hotel. In addition, last room availability technology is a necessary first step in providing an automated yield management system to the chain.

Yield Management.   Probably the biggest buzzword to enter the hotel industry over the last several years has been ***yield management.*** Although yield management in itself is not a new concept, the technology behind automated yield management is very new. Indeed, the ability to link yield management technology into national central reservations systems is leading-edge technology.

In simple terms, yield management is the process of controlling rates and occupancy in order to maximize gross room revenues. This is certainly nothing new; hotels have always increased their rates when demand was high and decreased rates to generate more sales when demand was low. After all, a ski resort that discounts rooms in the summer and charges full price in the winter is utilizing a simplified form of yield management. The big difference today is that yield management is no longer a manual guessing game. The current systems are so accurate and sophisticated that they have made a drastic difference in how hotels successfully sell rooms.

Today's yield management technology uses artificial intelligence computer systems that actually adjust rates and occupancy restrictions on behalf of the reservations department. Without any assistance from the reservationist, the yield management system literally changes rates and updates room occupancy restrictions automatically. The system is able to make expert decisions because it has been programmed to employ strategies and thought processes similar to an expert human yield manager. Just like a human yield management expert, the automated system considers:

- Past years' history (How well did the hotel do in past years for the same period in question?).
- The types of rooms and guests currently being booked (Are our high-end rooms selling as strongly as our low-end rooms? Is our corporate demand as strong as our leisure demand?).
- Group historical pick-up rates (If group business has been booked for these dates, what are the group's historical pick-up statistics in terms of rooms requested versus rooms actually delivered?).
- How far in advance are we of the date in question (the closer we get to a given arrival date, the more drastic the rate variations must be to make an impact)?

As the statistics for a given date improve, the yield management system will begin raising the average rate and may also add simple occupancy restrictions. Common occupancy restrictions include requiring a minimum length of stay (usually a two- or three-day minimum) and closing certain dates to arrival (only allowing for stayovers). The goal behind accurately predicting demand for a given date is to sell the most possible rooms for the highest possible rate to attain the greatest possible yield. Yield is defined as average daily rate (ADR) times the number of rooms sold ($Y = ADR \times$ Number rooms sold). For example, a 200-room hotel that sells 65 percent of its rooms at an average daily rate of $78.53 yields $10,208.90 in rooms revenue.

Overbooking.   Yield management systems also consider the ***quality of the reservation*** when determining rates and occupancy restrictions. The quality of a given reservation is its likelihood of actual arrival at the hotel. For example, advanced deposit reservations that are secured by the guest's prepayment have a much stronger likelihood of arrival than, say, a 6 PM reservation that is nonguaranteed and held under the guest's name until 6 PM.

A discussion of the quality of the reservation includes three basic types:

1. **Advanced deposit reservations** are prepaid by the guest in an amount generally equal to the first night's room and tax. Advanced deposit reservations are the highest quality; they have the highest likelihood of arrival.

2. **Guaranteed reservations** are guaranteed either to the guest's credit card or to the guest's corporate account. In either case, if the guest fails to arrive, the hotel may charge the guest for one night's room and tax. Because guests understand they will be charged for a **no-show,** guaranteed reservations are of fairly high quality. They have a very strong likelihood of arrival.

3. **Nonguaranteed reservations,** also known as **6 PM hold reservations,** are not secured with a deposit or any other form of guarantee. If the guest fails to arrive by 6 PM, the hotel has the right to sell the room to someone else. However, if the hotel is unable to resell the room, it has no recourse against the guest. As a result, nonguaranteed reservations are the lowest quality; they have the lowest likelihood of arrival.

Because of these varying degrees of quality, many hotels try to compensate for no-shows by **overbooking** their rooms. In other words, they take more reservations than the actual number of rooms they have available. Although this is risky, it is a generally accepted practice in the hotel industry. Here is a simple example:

Suppose a 200-room hotel has 50 rooms whose guests are staying over from the night before and 150 rooms for sale that day. Of the 150 rooms available for sale that day, 50 of them have advanced deposit reservations (with a 100 percent arrival rate); 50 have guaranteed reservations (with a 96 percent arrival rate); and 50 have nonguaranteed reservations (with a 70 percent arrival rate).

By projecting reservations against the arrival statistics, the hotel determines it still has 17 rooms to sell. In other words, if estimates are accurate, there will be 50 advanced deposit reservations (50 × 1.0), 48 guaranteed reservations (50 × .96), and 35 nonguaranteed reservations (50 × .70). As a result, there will also be 17 no-show reservations.

200 −	50	−	50	−	48	−	35	=	17
	stayover		advanced deposit		guaranteed		nonguaranteed		available for sale

The question is how accurate are the arrival statistics for any given day? If the hotel feels confident that the estimate is accurate, they might try to sell some of the 17 rooms to walk-in guests during the day. **Walk-in guests** are guests who arrive without a reservation and hope to find an available room. But this is risky.

Selling an extra 17 rooms in the example above is risky because it assumes today's arrival patterns will be similar to past history. However, if some of those projected no-shows actually do arrive, the hotel will find itself overbooked. There will be too many guests arriving for the number of rooms available at the hotel. In this case, the hotel will have to **walk** the few overbooked guests to another hotel.

Technology

The rooms division of the hotel has probably seen more technological advancements in the past 10 years than any other single area in the entire industry. As a result, today's front office employee must be knowledgeable in many new forms of automation. The breadth of this automation extends from the guest's reservation to the check-in process and even to the selection of in-room technologies.

The guest reservation process is one excellent example of change in recent years. Guests now receive up-to-the-minute room rate and occupancy quotes via last room availability systems interfaced with corporate yield management software.

The check-in process has also undergone significant change over the past 10 years, as more and more hotel front offices have shifted their focus from manual processes to automated property management systems (PMSs). Examples of applications provided by today's fully automated front desks include: guest history databases that track personal and hotel utilization information, housekeeping interfaces that automatically detail daily housekeeping schedules, electronic locking systems that prepare a new key combination each time the room is sold, and additional modules that post bills from and share front-office data to a number of other integrated departments.

Another major technological change occurring in the hotel industry is the acceptance by many guests of self-check-in and self-check-out terminals. Corporate guests are especially pleased to find an increasing number of these terminals. Instead of waiting in long front desk lines, guests can help themselves by inserting their credit card and following the steps outlined by the terminal.

Full-service hotels that do not offer self-service terminals may provide a similar service via the in-room guest television. These in-room television systems also allow the guest access to a number of other services, including ordering room service ordering directly from the television menu, viewing telephone messages, purchasing items from the gift shop or catalog, and even programming a morning wake-up call.

A hotel finds itself in a rather unfortunate situation when it walks a guest. Not only is the guest upset and inconvenienced, but the hotel has essentially broken its promise to deliver a room. As a result, most hotels extend a number of courtesies to the walked guest. These courtesies generally include transporting the guest to another equal or higher-quality hotel, paying the difference in room rate if the second hotel is more expensive, absorbing the cost of a few long-distance phone calls so the walked guest can let others know about the situation, transporting the guest back to the original hotel the next day, and possibly even buying a meal or placing a fruit basket in the room as an expression of apology. As you can see, walking a guest is an expensive undertaking.

Arrival and Check-In

During the arrival and check-in stage of the guest cycle, several functions occur simultaneously: the guest arrives, a room is selected, and the guest is registered into the hotel. During this stage, the guest is likely to come into contact with a number of front-of-the-house rooms division employees. The guest may meet a shuttle van driver at the airport, be greeted by a doorperson under the *porte cochere,* be checked in by a front desk clerk, and roomed by a bellperson. This stage of the guest cycle has some of the highest potential for quality guest-service contact of any time during the guest's visit.

During the actual check-in process, the guest is registered and provided an opportunity to ask questions and be sold on various attributes of the hotel. During this period, the guest's personal history information is verified, a method of payment is established, the check-out date is determined, and a room is selected. In most hotels, these functions are automated via the property management system (PMS).

Upselling.   During the check-in process, the front desk clerk will try to match the most appropriate room with the guest. At this point, clerks are encouraged to *upsell* the guest by offering nicer accommodations at a slightly higher cost. Many guests are pleased to have the option of purchasing a better-quality room. In turn, the hotel is pleased to sell the more expensive room because it represents higher revenues to the operation. In fact, upselling guests to a more expensive room is such a profitable practice that many hotels provide their employees with bonuses associated with an improved average room rate.

You see, the cost of cleaning a room is roughly the same for a standard or a deluxe accommodation. Therefore, when the hotel can earn an extra $25 or so by upselling the customer, almost all of that revenue is extra profit. Extra revenue per room translates to a higher *average daily rate* (also known as *average room rate*). Average daily rate (ADR) is calculated by taking total rooms revenue for the day divided by the actual number of rooms sold.

Generally, as ADR increases, the profitability of the hotel increases. This is true because variable costs for a given hotel room remain relatively constant no matter what the ADR might be. As the ADR increases, there is more and more revenue above the variable costs to apply towards the fixed costs and the overall profitability of the operation.

Plans.   Another consideration of the average daily rate is the type of *plan* the hotel provides. Many lodging operations offer a meal plan as part of the quoted room rate. Although full meal plans (two or three meals per day) are generally found only in resort hotels, many transient operations have started offering breakfast with the room. Hotels that include three meals per day (breakfast, lunch, and dinner) in the room rate are referred to as **American plan** properties. Those that offer two meals per day (breakfast and dinner) are known as **modified American plan** hotels. However, most guests are accustomed to staying in hotels that offer lodging only without any meals included in the rate. These operations are providing **European plan** accommodations (room only).

In recent years, more and more hotels have begun to offer a complimentary breakfast to their guests. This change is due, in part, to the proliferation

EXHIBIT 7–9

EXHIBIT 7–9

A key to successful upselling is matching the needs of the guest to the available room types. Families often enjoy suites.

Courtesy: Residence Inn, Washington, DC.

of all-suite lodging operations which almost always offer some form of breakfast included in the basic room rate. As a result of the success of all-suite properties, many standard, limited-service hotels and motels have begun to provide complimentary continental breakfasts to their patrons. Hotels that include a simple continental breakfast in the room rate are providing the **continental plan.** Those hotels that offer a more substantial full breakfast meal are providing the **Bermuda plan.**

Rooming the Guest.   Following the check-in process, many hotels provide bell service to assist in rooming the guest. During the rooming process, the bellperson explains the various highlights of the hotel, carries the guest's luggage, checks the room for cleanliness and function, makes suggestions, and answers pertinent questions. Most guests tip the bellperson in exchange for the quality service he or she provides.

Because rooming the guest presents the greatest opportunity of receiving a gratuity, most bell departments work on a rotating basis. The bellperson who most recently roomed a guest is relegated to the back of the rotation pecking order until all other bellpersons have had their opportunity to room a guest. The bellperson who has been rotated to the front of the line, in other words, the position next in line to room a guest, is referred to as a *front.* The bellperson who last finished rooming a guest and is now at the back of the line is referred to as a *last.*

Visitation

The visitation stage of the guest cycle refers to the actual period of time the guest spends at the hotel between the time of check-in and the time of checkout. For some types of operations (e.g., transient hotels), the average length

EXHIBIT 7–10

*A well-trained bell-
person showcases the
guest room features.
Indeed, lighting the
fireplace may reflect
the ultimate in guest
service.*

Courtesy: Residence Inn, Washington, DC.

of stay may only be one night. Other operations (e.g., destination resorts) have an average length of stay of at least a week.

It is during the visitation stage that most of the communication on behalf of the guest occurs between departments. Literally every department in the hotel has a need to communicate with the front desk at some time or other. Each day, for example, the housekeeping department will need to know the status of the guest's room. The housekeeping department will need to know if the room is scheduled for check-out or as a stayover so it can be cleaned accordingly. Other departments, like the gift shop or cocktail lounge, need to know the status of the guest's account. Specifically, they need to know if the guest is allowed to charge purchases to the room account, or if the guest is a ''cash only'' customer.

Handling Guest Complaints.   Just as the front desk communicates with other departments, it also communicates directly with the guest. Although most of the contact with the guest occurs during the check-in and check-out stages, there are plenty of opportunities to deal with the guest during the visitation stage. For example, guests may interact with the telephone (PBX) department (for phone calls, messages, and wake-up calls); the front desk (for special requests or room changes); or the cashiers (for billing, credit, or account issues).

Another common reason guests approach the front desk during their stay is to complain about a problem. The front desk receives significantly more guest complaints than any other front-of-the-house department in the hotel. Because the front desk is the most visible customer-service department, it is the most likely place where a guest will go to complain. Therefore, as likely as not, the complaint handled by the front desk will deal with a problem in

EXHIBIT 7–11   **Steps to Properly Handle Guest Complaints**
Front-of-the-house employees should be carefully trained to handle
the complaint. Adherence to this process ensures satisfaction to
most guests.

1. Listen to the guest to learn the facts. Take simple notes if necessary.
2. Never argue with the guest. Never interrupt nor defend hotel practices.
3. Sympathize and apologize calmly to the guest.
4. Summarize your understanding of the events.
5. Ask what action the guest would like you to take. Offer appropriate suggestions to resolve the situation.
6. Take immediate action to resolve the problem. You are personally responsible for getting it done.
7. Follow up directly with guest to ensure his or her complete satisfaction.

some other department. In this way, the front desk is charged with handling problems on behalf of all hotel departments.

Customer complaints are not necessarily bad things. In fact, complaints provide a series of opportunities to the hotel. They provide an opportunity to see the guest's point of view in a given area or with regard to a particular hotel policy. Complaints provide the opportunity to fix a problem or oversight that, if left uncorrected, might affect future guests. And complaints provide the hotel with an opportunity to convert a dissatisfied guest into a loyal customer.

By human nature, most guests will choose not to complain. Either they are too busy, they see the problem as too minor, they are too shy, or they just don't wish to be bothered. Whatever the reason, few guests actually complain. Therefore, each voiced complaint the employee hears actually represents a number of other guests who chose not to complain. That is why even the silliest complaint should be handled seriously and professionally.

Most hotels carefully train their front desk clerks in the proper steps of handling a guest complaint. Once trained, many hotels will empower their employees with the authority to handle the complaint in a manner that the employee deems appropriate. Indeed, one major luxury lodging chain empowers its hourly wage employees to personally handle complaints up to a value of $3,000. Now that's empowerment! Refer to Exhibit 7–11 for an understanding of the simple steps for properly handling a guest complaint.

The Guest Folio and the Night Audit

Guests pay for their room nights and other charges (e.g., telephone, restaurant charges, in-room movies) in many ways. Most guests use a credit card; others pay by cash, travelers' check, or hotel credit card. Still others have their account directly billed to a prearranged corporate account. Whatever the method of payment, the guest's account or *folio* is opened, maintained, and closed by the front desk cashier. It is the front desk cashier who ultimately settles the guest's folio during the check-out stage of the guest cycle.

Posting Charges.   Because hotels are 24-hour operations, posting charges to the guest folio is a full-time responsibility. Charges come to the front desk either electronically (through the property management system) or manually (in the form of departmental room charge vouchers) from an assortment of different departments at all hours of the day and night.

It is important to understand that departmental charges to the guest room represent only those charges the guest wishes to be included on the folio. The front desk has no accounting responsibility for sales in other departments when the guest chooses to pay cash for the purchase at the time of sale. To illustrate this point:

> Imagine two guests, Mr. George Harrison (room 2102) and Mrs. Joanne Lennon (room 1616). Mr. Harrison eats dinner one night in the hotel dining room ($29.47) and charges the meal to his room. That amount, $29.47, will be posted to his folio and will be part of the total bill for which he is responsible at check-out from the hotel. On the other hand, Mrs. Lennon chooses to pay cash for her dinner ($31.16) and will not see any related charge on her folio. The front desk has no responsibility for accounting for Mrs. Lennon's cash transaction. Indeed, even during its night audit, the front desk will not account for a cash purchase in another department.

Late Charges.   Charges to the guest's folio come from any and all departments in the hotel at any and all hours of the day. Likewise, the guest has every right to check out of the hotel and demand the folio at any and all hours of the day. Therefore, the front desk cashier must constantly remain up-to-the-minute with room charges in order to present the guest an accurate folio on demand.

Mistakes happen, however, and it is possible for a cashier to present the guest with an incomplete folio. For whatever reason, it is not unusual for certain charges to arrive late either electronically or manually to the front desk. Unfortunately, these **late charges** are difficult to collect after the fact. In situations where the guest is a cash-only customer, the hotel might never receive payment for the late charge. In other circumstances (say when the guest uses a credit card or corporate direct bill), collection is more certain though costly and difficult.

The Role of the Night Audit.   Due to the 24-hour nature of the hotel industry, it is important for hotels to remain up-to-the-minute with the entire front office accounting ledger. On a daily basis, most hotels balance all of the guest folios against all of the departmental room charges. This daily process of balancing hotel guest accounts is known as the *night audit*.

The purpose of the night audit is to verify that room charges from each of the various hotel departments have been received by the front desk and accurately posted to the appropriate guest folios. Although this accounting function is the primary purpose of the night audit, it is not the only duty assigned during this front desk shift. Night auditors are also responsible for posting room and tax to each guest's folio, producing end-of-day managerial status reports, preparing the list of tomorrow's arrivals, and performing all other front desk functions that may arise during the shift.

Check-Out and Billing

The check-out and billing cycle is just the reverse of the guest arrival and check-in pattern. For the most part, the same rooms division positions that assisted the guest at arrival now assist the guest at departure. The bell department retrieves the guest's luggage from the room, the cashier checks the guest out of the hotel, the doorperson offers a fond farewell, and the shuttle driver returns the guest to the airport.

It is during the check-out stage that the guest is asked to close the folio. The folio can be closed in two basic ways: either the guest pays the bill (by cash, travelers' check, or credit card) or the guest delays payment of the bill. In other words, the folio is either settled on the spot or it is deferred to the guest's corporate account for settlement in the future.

If it is settled on the spot, the cashier posts the payment and hands a *zero balance* folio to the departing guest. In such a case, no further action is warranted—the account is closed and the hotel has received payment in full. Guests who defer payment to their corporate account for monthly billing are another story. These guests are asked to sign the bottom of the folio and are then handed a copy of the unpaid bill. The unpaid folio is then routed to the hotel's accounting department where it is held until the next corporate direct billing cycle. At this point, the accounting department monitors the folio until payment is eventually received from the corporation owing the money. Once the money is received, the payment is posted and the folio shows a final zero balance.

We've now reviewed the basic guest cycle from beginning to end. Each of these steps is far more complicated than can be described within the scope of this chapter. Later in your curriculum you will learn much more about the rooms divisions in such classes as guest service management and hospitality automation.

Conclusion

A career in hotel management is not necessarily suited to everyone. Certain traits and skills are required to succeed in this challenging field. When these traits are present, rooms division managers love their job. They love the rooms division because it offers them a high degree of challenge, stimulus, variety, and autonomy. These are unique aspects that most jobs do not provide.

On the other hand, when such traits as compassion, high energy levels, self-motivation, and an eye for detail are not present, many managers grow to dislike their jobs. Without these traits, they often become jaded to their customers, depersonalized to their employees, and emotionally exhausted from the physical and psychological challenges of the position.

Therefore, if you are interested in becoming a rooms division manager, gather plenty of personal experience before deciding on this specific career path. (Chapter 2, ''Managerial Leadership for the Hospitality Industry,'' suggests some self-knowledge exercises that may help crystallize your thinking about such a career.) If and when you do select this calling, you will not be disappointed. Imagine having the opportunity to host the president of the United States and house several hundred secret service staff members—now that's an honor. Imagine reserving an entire floor for several nights while a rock band is performing in town—now that's a thrill. Imagine staying for free at other sister properties of your chain as a regular advantage of your position—now that's a perk.

Or imagine just a regular old day. You are exhausted after handling a morning of check-outs and an afternoon of rooming several hundred guests and accommodating two large groups. Your day wasn't exactly error-free, and you handled your share of guest problems and complaints. The day is over, you are pleasantly tired, and you head towards the door. Just then an elderly couple approaches you and asks if you are the rooms division manager. You respond yes, while you secretly brace yourself for the complaint that's sure to come. Instead, they proceed to tell you what a marvelous property you run. They've stayed in lots of hotels but you have the friendliest, most accommodating staff they have ever met. As they finish their compliment, they ask if you will still be here the next time they come through. You respond yes, as you realize you truly love your job. Although you are still tired, you feel like a million bucks as you head for the exit door.

Keywords

Core Concepts

Discussion Questions

1. From the student's viewpoint, the rooms division may be the most important department in the entire hotel. Jobs in this department provide both high visibility to hotel management and plenty of one-on-one contact with the guest. Discuss three other aspects of rooms division jobs that make them appealing and beneficial to students interested in a career in hotel management.

2. In terms of yield management, some experts argue that it is unfair to charge higher rates for last-minute room reservations than for reservations reserved weeks or months in advance. Generally, what type or market of consumer makes room reservations well in advance? Conversely, what type or market of consumer makes room reservations at the last minute—just days or hours before arrival? Explain why hotels charge last-minute reservations higher rates than those with longer lead times.

3. Late charges create hardships for corporate guests who expect the folio they receive at check-out to be a complete and accurate representation of their visit. Several days later, if they receive a new folio reflecting some type of late charge (say a late breakfast that posted after they checked out), they may have to completely rewrite their corporate expense report. Develop a list of several reasons why late charges occur and decide if you agree with the statement "too many late charges indicate a poorly managed hotel."

4. Hotels overbook their room reservations to compensate for no-shows and cancellations. However, by regularly overbooking, the hotel runs a grave risk of severely inconveniencing the guest. Maybe, instead of overbooking, the hotel should establish more rigid reservation policies. If you were the reservations manager, what types of policies might you employ to minimize the need for overbooking?

5. Using the guest complaint exhibit (Exhibit 7–11) as a backup resource, develop a role-playing exercise with a classmate. Let the classmate take the part of an upset customer. Your job is to defuse and resolve the argument. Have fun, but be realistic in your complaints.

APPENDIX B
HOSPITALITY DEVELOPMENT

Outline

In 1993, more than 10,000 new rooms were added to the 80,000 rooms that already existed in Las Vegas, Nevada, by the opening of several so-called *megaresorts*. Luxor, Treasure Island, and the MGM Grand all opened in the same year. The MGM Grand alone added over 5,000 new rooms and four gigantic casinos to the Las Vegas market.

Development of these new properties required enormous investments. Estimates for the development of the MGM Grand property, for instance, range from $800 million to over $1 billion! Yet, all the people and companies that invested in these properties felt safe in committing money and resources to these new ventures. Apparently, they were sure that all those new rooms would be filled and that more and more people would be willing to travel to Las Vegas to gamble and visit the amusement parks that were developed alongside the casinos and hotels.

Similar stories can be told about food service operations. Some of the largest fast-food chains in this country, like McDonald's, Taco Bell, and Burger King, open new stores daily, not only in the United States but also in Europe, Asia, and everywhere else in the world. These companies still feel that there is room for growth in an already crowded market. Very often, fast-food chains open up new stores right next to the competition—and they do so on purpose. Nowadays, we can buy Whoppers, Big Macs, and tacos all within one city block. Competition can apparently be positive.

Why is it that lodging and food service operators and investors feel safe in committing money and resources the way they do? Why do some restaurants and hotels fail where others succeed? And was E. M. Statler, one of this country's most important hospitality entrepreneurs, right when he said that "location, location, and location" were the three most important aspects in developing and successfully operating a new hotel property? The following pages will attempt to answer these and other questions, questions that deal with the concept of *hospitality development.*

Hotels, motels, resorts, and fast-food and full-service restaurants do not appear with the snap of a finger. Years of hard work, the investment of lots of time and money, patience, and a great deal of both common sense and imagination precede their openings.

The hospitality development phase is an important part in the success, or failure, of a hotel or restaurant. It is far more complex than initially meets the eye. No longer can someone start a restaurant based on the concept of "everybody loves my cooking, so why not open a restaurant?" or open up a small motel because "I like staying at motels myself and I know what I want." Too many restaurant and hotel failures are proof that these approaches no longer work.

Several stages can be distinguished in the development process, ranging from the initial idea or concept of developing a food service or lodging operation to looking at a potential market and making the actual decision about how to manage and operate a restaurant, hotel, or resort.

EXHIBIT B–1

The five phases of the hotel development process

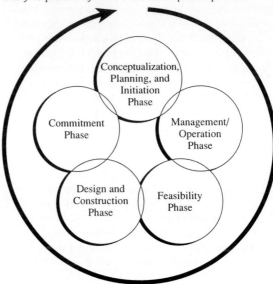

Courtesy: Laventhol & Horwath.

A restaurant or hotel is developed by taking it one step, or stage, at a time. The five stages are:

1. Conceptualization.
2. Feasibility study.
3. Commitment.
4. Design and construction.
5. Management/operation.

Although these stages will be discussed in this order, it does not mean that one stage begins where another one ends. As Exhibit B–1 shows, all stages in hospitality development are intertwined. For example, during the **conceptualization** stage, when an idea about developing a hospitality operation takes shape, developers already think about where and how to raise the necessary funds. And the decision on how to manage and operate the property is normally taken at least a year before the operation opens its doors, during the design and construction stage or perhaps even earlier. It is known for a fact that when the major investor in the MGM Grand project in Las Vegas began to develop his ideas, he already had several people in mind who would actually develop and operate the property.

Conceptualization

The first stage in developing a lodging or food service operation is conceptualization, the stage in which a concept or idea about a particular project to be developed takes form. An individual or a group of individuals then takes the initiative of transforming the abstract idea into a concrete plan.

The people developing the concept should have some idea of the type of food service or lodging operation they wish to create in these initial stages of the process. They might be able to answer questions such as: Is it going to be a full-service or fast-food restaurant? Are we looking at developing a roadside motel or a five-star resort?

The concept on which everything else is based might be very vague or it might be based on nothing more than a "gut feeling." Alternatively, it might be fairly concrete, indicating a possible site for development, the type of hotel or restaurant to be developed, the preferred operator, or even some of the physical characteristics of the property. Whatever the case may be, eventually objectives need to be established during the conceptualization stage. Developers have to have financial goals, operational deadlines, and governmental guidelines to work with.

One of the major problems encountered during this initial phase of the development is that of commitment. Developers at times attempt to develop a project without knowing each other's levels of commitment to the project or without knowing where and how to find adequate financial backing. When there are multiple developers interested in the project, it may happen that no one developer is willing to commit financially to the project until the others do so as well. A lack of coordination and commitment can at times drag out this initial stage to the extent that some investors may lose interest or find other opportunities.

Ideally, in this initial stage of the development process, many specialists are also brought into the project. Just having the money, the initial commitment, and an idea are not enough for successful development. Legal and financial experts are needed to provide assistance, as well as marketing experts, architects, designers, interior decorators, contractors, and engineers. If the developers feel they would like to become part of a national restaurant or hotel chain, they will begin to involve representatives of those management companies or franchises at this stage. They, too, will voice their desires and opinions.

In all, the first stage in the development process is often the critical one. Negotiations tend to move from the general to the specific. If people can agree on the major issues, they can usually agree on the minor ones. So if this huge organizational effort can bring all the necessary funds and expertise together, if it succeeds in convincing those involved that the project will eventually generate money, and if it creates solid lines of communication between all parties involved, the chances that the project will actually be developed will increase dramatically. Only with a solid belief in success, a will to succeed, and good communication between all the parties involved can a project, whether it be a 20-room motel, a 5,000-room megaresort, or a 50-seat, full-service, fine dining restaurant, be completed.

Feasibility Study

Lodging and food service development should not be based on gut feeling. Most developers and most of the institutions that lend developers money require a feasibility study before they commit to a project. As its name indicates, a **feasibility study** attempts to determine whether or not a particular project is feasible—whether it has a chance not only to survive, but to have sufficient revenues to cover all expenses and make a profit.

A developer may speculate that a certain hotel or restaurant may be successful in a particular location. Speculation alone, though, will not attract investors. They may have the money to invest, but they may not have the same gut feeling. What a feasibility study does is either confirm or reject those speculations, based on hard facts and research. Carried out by an independent consultant, a feasibility study will give both the developer and the lender a good idea as to what can be expected in terms of income, expenses, and profit. If a bank, pension fund, insurance company, or any other money lender invests in a project, it needs to receive a respectable **return on investment (ROI).** (ROI can be compared to the interest charged to borrowers on a car loan or a mortgage that accrues to the lender by virtue of its risk.)

The feasibility study gives the lender an indication of the ROI that can be expected. Obviously, if the study determines that the income from the project is going to be very low, the lender will be hesitant to provide financing. Moreover, the riskier the venture looks on paper, the higher the interest rate the lender will demand from the developer: The price of money goes up as the risk goes up. If the outlook is good, though, the lender will be more willing to come up with the cash and the interest rate will be lower.

A feasibility study attempts to accomplish two things. First, it attempts to determine the present and future demand for the lodging or food service facility to be developed. It tries to answer the question: Is there a market for the proposed product? Second, based on the estimate of the future demand for the product, it attempts to determine the property's operating income for several years after it starts operation. Investors and developers would like to know if an operation will survive after several years, not just one or two years, since the costs are high in the initial years of operation. Those high start-up costs will negatively affect the operation's bottom line in the beginning, so it is the long-term outlook that really counts.

There are several reasons why hospitality entrepreneurs decide to have a consultant conduct a feasibility study. As stated earlier, a positive feasibility study can help them obtain the necessary funds for the development of the project. Banks, for instance, will not even consider lending someone money without a feasibility study done by a consultant with a good reputation. Moreover, the study might help the developer obtain a franchise or management contract. Major hotel or restaurant chains do not like to be associated with poorly operated or unprofitable properties. And although the study is not a guarantee of success, it may serve as a blueprint for financial potential.

A feasibility study may also help create a good relationship between developers and local officials. If the site for the facility and its size, type, and impact are known to local officials, they can determine in those initial stages whether or not the developer is aware of and intends to adhere to laws and regulations, what the operation's impact will be on the local economy, and how it will affect the local infrastructure. A proposed hotel or restaurant will not only mean additional traffic; it will also create an additional demand for electricity and water. More importantly, a proposed hospitality development will almost always provide a boost to the local economy, adding employment or tax revenues, or both.

With regard to the relationship between developers and local government officials, an additional aspect has to be mentioned. In some communities, the law requires developers to file an environmental impact statement (EIS) with local officials. The EIS is pivotal to obtaining permission to build a hotel or a restaurant in a certain area. It describes in detail what the effects of the property will be on the surrounding area, particularly if the area is environmentally fragile. Only after the EIS has been approved by local authorities can construction begin.

A feasibility study consists of several specific steps that can be grouped under two headings: assessment of market support and financial analysis.

Assessment of Market Support

In order to determine whether or not there is sufficient demand for the product, a feasibility study will attempt to identify a potential market. The only thing a consultant normally knows is the location of the proposed hotel or restaurant. The questions he or she asks at this stage are: What kind of people will visit the proposed hotel or restaurant? What are their desires? What are they willing to spend? Where do they come from? And how will they get there? The local chamber of commerce, the local economic development office, and the state's office of tourism might be helpful in supplying some of this useful demographic and per capita data.

Second, the study will try to determine how many people will visit the proposed restaurant or hotel. This is normally done by looking at the general population and at the existing facilities in the area. Questions asked at this stage are: What is the general customer base? How much and what kind of business does the competition do? A consultant will also determine whether or not similar hotels or restaurants are planned in the same area, catering to the same market. These might be a threat to the profitability of the proposed property in the long run.

Once it has been determined that there is a potential market for the product, and after that potential market has been quantified, the study will attempt to predict what kind of facility might appeal to that market and what size the facility should be. As far as lodging facilities are concerned, the study will try to determine what type of lodging facility is appropriate: Does the location and market allow for a luxury five-star hotel or would an economy-class property be more appropriate? The study will also determine the number of additional rooms a particular market can handle. As with the development of the Las Vegas megaresorts, research found that the city could, in fact, handle another 10,000 rooms. Nowhere else in the country, though, would that have been likely.

Feasibility studies for food service facilities try to pinpoint what type of restaurant could be established in a particular location. By looking at existing restaurants and residents of a particular area, a consultant or developer can decide to make a new restaurant completely different from what is offered and hope for new business. On the other hand, knowledge of what the customer wants may also just as easily lead the consultant to recommend developing a restaurant similar to existing ones. And, as with lodging development, after the type of restaurant has been determined, one has to decide on size. Will the market sustain a 200-seat restaurant or will 50 seats be the maximum that can be added?

Feasibility studies also incorporate an estimate of the suitability of the site for development. They consider the site's accessibility, the existing zoning regulations, the site's physical characteristics, the need for major changes in its infrastructure (water, sewage, electricity, roads), its surrounding areas, and any other existing plans that might affect the site.

Once the potential customer base has been established and the costs for the actual development have been determined, the feasibility study will go into the second phase, the financial analysis. More than anything else, potential financial backers are interested in this part of the study.

Financial Analysis

In its financial analysis, the feasibility study will present the developer with an estimate of how much revenue can be generated by the property, what the expenses will be, and what profit can be expected. What the consultant will do is produce what is called a *pro forma* income statement that tells the lender exactly how and where monies will be earned and spent, and how much will be left over.

Revenues, expenses, and profits will not only be presented in dollars but also in percentages of sales and investment. Using percentages is important because it enables those involved to compare the

proposed operation to similar existing operations and to industrywide averages. For example, labor cost percentages for the food service industry in general are close to 30 percent of sales. If the feasibility study shows a labor cost percentage of 38 percent (that is, 38 percent of total revenue), this might be cause for concern and developers might want to investigate ways to trim expenses in this particular area. This is more meaningful than trying to compare payrolls in two very different locales. Imagine being given a report that expressed labor costs only in dollar amounts. Would you be able to knowledgeably compare $56,000 a year to the $1,800,000 that is spent on labor each year by a Las Vegas resort or casino? Based on the financial analysis, the investors will decide whether the risk of developing the property is acceptable, what the interest rates are going to be on the loans, and, in general, whether or not to go ahead with the development of the property.

Feasibility Study—Additional Remarks

Finally, a few additional remarks with regard to the feasibility study need to be made. First, a positive feasibility study is not a guarantee of success. Factors beyond the control of the consultant might change to such an extent that a hotel that looked good on paper will go under within a year. Most studies therefore have a disclaimer on one of the first pages of the report that states that the consultant cannot be held accountable for any mishaps. The overall economy cannot be controlled, and he or she has to rely on the information that was available. If the economy falters or if the data the consultant worked with were incorrect, the actual picture might look completely different from the projected one.

Second, there is a tendency among developers and consultants alike to produce positive feasibility studies. Developers would like their hunches to be confirmed, and consulting companies look much better when they produce positive reports. Since the study is only an estimate, those estimates can easily be adjusted upwards or downwards as the case may be. It is up to the ethical judgment of the person carrying out the study to be honest about a proposed development and advise against a project if it does not appear feasible. At the same time, those who read and use the study must also be prudent and use common sense in their judgments; it never hurts to do some cross-checking and look for some other sources of information.

Third, in one case, a feasibility study that indicated that a town had room for an additional 400 hotel rooms convinced several developers. This resulted in 2,000 additional hotel rooms being developed since five companies decided to open up a hotel based on the same study. The feasibility study was not wrong, but the fact that it was sold to several people caused several properties to perform poorly. In this case, the ethics of the consultant and/or the prudence of the developers might have been questionable. It may take several years for room demand to catch up with the supply of rooms and for the original predictions made in the feasibility study to come true. The old saying ''buyer beware'' applies here too.

Commitment

Once the commitment phase of hospitality development is reached, it is assumed that the necessary monies are available and that the results of the feasibility study were positive. What then is the commitment phase? Investors and developers are often wary of investing their capital in an operation if others are unwilling to do so. However, with a completed pro forma financial analysis, an estimate of the cost of design and construction available, and a preliminary timetable set up, it is time to put the final package together (the commitment phase is sometimes also referred to as the *package phase*). Major financial backers will now commit themselves and their money to the project. It is time to sign the contracts.

The commitment phase involves some the following:

- Site acquisition.
- Selection of potential franchise or affiliation.
- Selection of architect(s)/engineer(s) for design.
- Selection of contractor or builder.
- A complete determination of all costs involved.
- An agreement on how to finance the operation.
- An agreement on how to operate the facility.
- A determination of ownership structure, based on how the financing of the project has been

arranged and what can be expected in return for the investment (ROI).
- The necessary environmental documentation.
- A development schedule.
- A complete knowledge of all laws and regulations applying to the proposed site and property.[1]

Those involved would like all of the above to be legal and binding, so most of these commitments will be in the form of contracts or letters of intent. Yet, even though contracts are signed, sealed, and delivered, they always include clauses that protect the parties involved and will allow investors to withdraw at various stages of the game.

The most important step in this phase of the development is making sure that the financing for the project is secure. Financing for hospitality development normally has to cover (1) construction of the property (which includes the purchase of land, materials, and equipment; and salaries for constructors, builders, and designers) and (2) what is called *permanent financing*. Permanent financing generally applies to the arrangements that are made to cover operational losses in the first few years. It is not uncommon for lodging and food service operations to operate at a loss initially, and lenders and developers are aware of that. This does not necessarily mean the restaurant or hotel is poorly managed. It can also be the case that, as we saw earlier, start-up costs are so high that it is unrealistic to expect a profit or even to break even. Nevertheless, bills have to be paid. Permanent financing will make sure that the financial backing exists to tide the property over in those initial years until it has firmly established itself and until it no longer has to worry about start-up costs.

Costs for development can also be categorized very generally into direct and indirect costs. Direct costs of development include the purchase of the land and construction. Indirect costs include legal and other consulting fees, interest paid on loans during development, fees paid for licenses and permits, monies paid for inspections, and salaries paid to designers.

As in the other phases of the development process discussed so far, commitment to a particular project does not happen all at once; it happens in stages. Yet, once most of the initial financing has been arranged, the design and construction arrangements slowly take shape and building can start.

Design and Construction

Design

Space allocation is the key word when it comes to designing a hotel or restaurant. Space is expensive. It is not surprising that so many high-rise properties are built in downtown areas. The price of land in downtown New York, Los Angeles, or Chicago has skyrocketed in the last few decades, and it would simply be infeasible for a hotel property to spread out and take up a few city blocks as resorts located on lower cost land can do. Building vertically is the most cost-effective solution for downtown properties.

Beyond the fact that space is expensive, designers of hotel and restaurant properties have to work within some generally accepted boundaries. A hotel room is normally between 200 and 400 square feet, depending on the type of hotel. Guests have come to expect a certain amount of square footage, and designers must accommodate that expectation. Someone who pays $300 a night expects a spacious room and spacious public facilities. Restaurant seats, too, need a certain amount of space. In general, 8 to 10 square feet of space are needed for people to be seated comfortably and for servers to do their jobs well.

Another commonly accepted norm is that at least 50 percent of the total space available in a commercial hotel should be dedicated to bedrooms, since the rooms division is the revenue center in commercial hotels (see Chapter 7 on rooms division management). However, this can vary depending on the type of facility to be developed: Where budget properties allocate up to 90 percent of the space available to guest rooms, resort properties may dedicate less than 60 percent to guest rooms. Exhibit B–2 gives some examples of space allocations.

The design phase must also consider all the legal requirements related to design, in particular, those that deal with safety and security. The five areas that are of importance in the design stages of a hotel property are site (landscape), guest rooms, public areas (the front of the house), support services, and administration (the back of the house).

EXHIBIT B–2   Room Space Allocation as a Percentage of Total Space by Hotel Type

| Property Type | Space Allocation | | |
	Number of Rooms	Service Level	Percent of Space for Guestrooms
Motel	100	Economy	85 to 95%
All suite	200	Midprice	75 to 85%
Hotel	300	Luxury	75 to 85%
Resort	400	Luxury	65 to 75%
Conference center	200	Midprice	55 to 65%
Convention hotel	2000	First class	65 to 75%

Beyond space allocation for the inside of the property, landscaping and parking are important considerations for a property's outside area. Landscaping is determined primarily by the type of property. Luxury resort guests have come to expect lavish gardens and fancy driveways. Motel guests, on the other hand, hardly expect anything in terms of the outside appearance of the property.

Parking space allotment is primarily determined by a property's location. However, the type of property is also a factor, because it determines the modes of transportation of the guests and the employees. The farther away a property is from any means of public transportation, the more likely it will be for patrons and employees to use their personal cars to get to the hotel or resort, and the more parking space must be allocated. Some rules of thumb that apply to allotment of parking space are: one space for every room, one space for every three to four restaurant seats, one space for every three employees. Some cities regulate the minimum number of parking spaces (and disabled accessible spaces) that operations must provide.

As far as restaurant design is concerned, several additional considerations must be taken into account. Beyond space allocation for a dining room and a preparation area, and the landscaping and parking, design must incorporate receiving and storage spaces and make sure that these areas are linked to each other in the most economical and efficient way.

EXHIBIT B–3

The Luxor Hotel/Casino under construction.

Courtesy: Luxor Hotel/Casino, Las Vegas, Nevada.

Specialists are often employed to design kitchens. The flow of food from storage through preparation to the dining area is of utmost importance in providing the customer with a good product and a good overall dining experience. (See Chapters 9 and 10 for more on this subject.) Additionally, restaurant and kitchen design must also incorporate safety and security regulations. Exhibit B–4 presents a typical restaurant design.

Too little space allocated or an incorrect design can severely limit the success of an operation. The back of the house, in particular, tends to be neglected at times in the design stages. The rationale seems to be that the ''guest does not see this anyway'' and, as we said before, ''space is expensive.'' However, inadequate space allotment in the back of the house can be just as harmful to the operation as too little space up front. On the other hand, too much space allotted can prove to be an economic burden. It is often a thin line that separates a good from a poor design.

Construction

After all the design decisions have been made, it is up to the construction manager to make sure that the project is finished in time and on budget. A project's contractor must see to the following:

- Administer and initiate contracts.
- Develop working drawings and specifications.
- Secure permits and approvals.
- Direct the bidding selection process and conduct negotiations with subcontractors.
- Keep an eye on construction progress.
- Handle claims and disputes.
- Coordinate on-site facilities.

EXHIBIT B–4

Typical restaurant design

Reprinted from ''A Guide to Preparing a Restaurant Business Plan'' (1992) with the permission of the National Restaurant Association.

- Schedule construction activities.
- Obtain a certificate of occupancy upon completion.
- Bring in the project in time and on budget.[2]

The above list will suffice to describe some of the aspects of construction. One observation is in order: Very seldom do projects come in on time and within budget. Even outstanding planning, strict construction control, and efficient communication will not guarantee success. There are so many variables involved that Murphy's Law might apply in this situation: If something can go wrong, it probably will. And every time it does, time is lost and money is wasted.

Management/Operation

Although this is the last phase in the hospitality development process, this does not necessarily mean that it is the last phase chronologically. As Exhibit B–1 shows, developers may already have an idea at the conceptualization stage as to how they are going to operate or manage their property and who is going to do it for them. In general, it can be said that this phase begins about a year before the property opens.

The most important goal of this phase of the development is to ensure the long-term success of the operation. Success requires an experienced management team. Since many developers or owners do not have sufficient experience in the hospitality industry but develop properties as any other real estate undertaking, it is common practice to have a hospitality management company or a hospitality chain operate the enterprise.

In the food service industry, it is often the case that the owner is also the operator of the property. He or she is directly responsible not only for the day-to-day management of the restaurant but also for the long-term financial aspects. His or her operational skills directly affect how quickly loans can be paid off.

In the lodging industry, on the other hand, the operators are normally not the owners or developers of the property. This may result in friction between developer and operator. If the operation does not generate enough revenue to pay the interest on the loan that was taken out to develop the property, the owner will end up paying the difference and blame the operator for poor management. Yet, if owners are not willing to pay for maintenance because it costs too much and the hotel loses business because of deteriorating facilities, the operators have cause to blame the owners. Whatever the case, a poor working relationship can be very destructive to the ultimate success of the property.

If owners and developers prefer not to work with independent or small operating companies, they can instead work with large management companies and hospitality chains (Hyatt, Marriott, and Hilton in the hotel industry, and Taco Bell, Red Lobster, and McDonald's in the restaurant industry) that have the expertise to make almost any operation a successful one. Many owners and developers turn to them for operational assistance through franchise agreements.

A franchise agreement is an agreement between a franchisee (in this case, the developer of the new hotel or restaurant) and a franchisor (a renowned hospitality chain). The franchisor grants the franchisee the right to sell food or rooms under the franchisor's name. Along with the name, the franchisee gets marketing assistance, operational guidelines, and, most important, a tested and successful operational approach. Hilton and McDonald's know how to sell rooms and hamburgers, respectively, and their selling and operational techniques have been proven successful.

An additional benefit to the franchisee in the lodging industry is the central reservation system (CRS) that ties the hotel chain together. Potential customers from all over the world can use the chain's toll-free number to make reservations for a particular property. The CRS can assist a hotel when it wants to compete globally and can provide it with market analyses based on its own reservations data. Traditionally it has been very difficult for individually owned and operated hotels to get that kind of national and international exposure. This is changing with the development of reservations networks for independents, though these still lack the "identity" associated with franchise CRSs.

In return for the use of the name and the assistance, the franchisee pays the franchisor a franchise fee. Depending on the agreement, the franchisee pays certain royalty fees (which are normally a part of gross sales or operating income), will contribute to the advertising budget of the franchise, and rents or purchases equipment from the franchisor (in the case of certain food service franchises). Additionally, the franchisee will have to abide by the operational rules of the franchisor, rules that cover detailed requirements for the physical plant, the number of telephones in a room, the color of the tiles in the bathroom, or the number of employees per guest.

For the owner/developer, joining a franchise may be beneficial for several reasons: (1) The property acquires a national image and reputation almost overnight and (2) the property increases its chances for success since it will employ tested marketing, sales, and other operational procedures. Joining a nationally or even internationally known chain is obviously not a guarantee of success, but it will generally increase the property's chances for survival. What the owner/developer will ultimately have to decide is whether the benefits of joining a chain are worth the additional financial burden. He or she will compare costs and benefits and do what is called a *cost-benefit analysis*.

Keywords

This chapter focuses on the operational functions of the physical plant of the hotel. It combines the operations of housekeeping, maintenance, and engineering since these functions strive for the same goal: providing a clean and comfortable lodging environment for the guests. It discusses the managerial and operational aspects of these three functions in great detail and introduces current operation issues.

Outline

Introduction

Management in hospitality is well aware of the priority guests put on clean, comfortable guest rooms with well-functioning facilities. Keeping a hotel clean and all the equipment working properly is an important job. Without professionally competent staff in these areas the hotel's "product" will be undesirable and/or unsafe—and all the king's horses and all the king's men (in the form of marketing, sales, and central reservations) will be unable to keep sales up.

This chapter will explore the functions of the housekeeping department, including its structure, staffing, training, and operations. Managing the housekeeping department, often a hotel's largest in terms of number of employees, requires a high level of people management skills. This chapter will also explain and define the responsibilities of the engineering and maintenance department, including the types of skilled labor needed for successful operation of hotel buildings.

The goal of this chapter is to discuss the many internal activities that occur deep within hotel buildings. For a hotel to be successful, a guest must find a clean, comfortable, well-maintained building in which all the building systems are working properly. Guests must also feel that they are safe and secure while under the hotel's roof. Not surprisingly, housekeeping, engineering, and maintenance staff are positively involved with hotel environmental, safety, and security issues. Beyond guest security, the protection of the hotel's assets—both human and property—is another area of great responsibility.

Housekeeping

The following section of this chapter will discuss the housekeeping department of a hotel, its areas of responsibility, job descriptions, and total organizational structure. It will explore day-to-day operations, including purchasing and laundry procedures, and discuss how reliable procedures are developed. By the end of the chapter you will understand why housekeeping is much more than a maid cleaning a guest room. The management of the housekeeping department is a challenging job that is critical to the success of the hotel.

The primary (and often most visible) function of the housekeeping department is the cleaning of guest rooms. It is also responsible for cleaning public areas such as foyers, lobbies, public rest rooms, and the dining room; and back-of-the-house areas such as employee break rooms, rest rooms, and locker areas, and the laundry.

The importance of the cleanliness of the guest rooms, the public rest rooms, the dining room, and lobby cannot be stressed enough. A hotel guest demands the highest standard of cleanliness. He or she is buying a well-made bed with fresh linen and a clean bath/shower room. The cleanliness of an establishment can make the difference between being sold out or going out of business.

EXHIBIT 8–1

Housekeeping is more than a maid cleaning a guest room; it is the heart of the hotel operation.

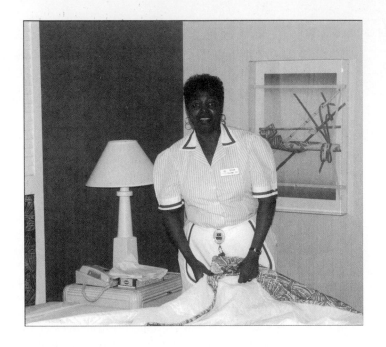

Departmental Organization

Depending on the size of the property, the number of housekeeping employees can range from two (in a small budget motel with fewer than 20 rooms) to hundreds (in a thousand-room resort.) The person in charge of this department, the **executive housekeeper,** must therefore be a good manager of people.

Because of the size of the housekeeping department and the importance of the job performed, the role of the executive housekeeper is pivotal to the success of the hotel. The position of executive housekeeper is, in most cases, a middle management position, as shown in Exhibit 8–3.

The organizational chart in Exhibit 8–2 clearly shows the positions under the executive housekeeper. The number and types of positions are determined by the size and type of hotel.

Integration and Communication

The housekeeping department is fully integrated with all other areas of the hotel operation. Front desk, maintenance, engineering, catering, food/beverage, banquet, and security all depend on lines of communication with the housekeeping department. The front desk sells the rooms, so it must know which rooms are clean and available for check-in. Housekeeping provides the front desk with updates on the changes in status of guest rooms, ranging from ''checked out'' to ''room ready.''

No well-run housekeeping department will ever release a room to the front desk for check-in before it is ready—not even with the expectation that the

Exhibit 8–2

The various positions in the housekeeping department.

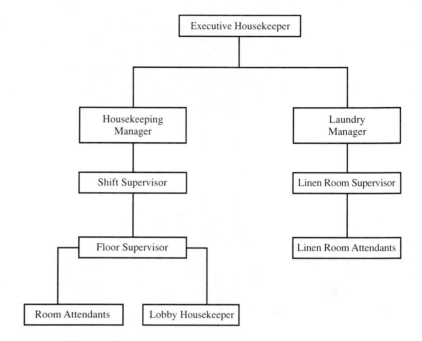

room will be ready in five minutes. If the front desk checks a guest into a room that is not made-up, everyone looks bad. The guest will be disturbed, the front desk will be embarrassed (and then angry), and the property's image will suffer. Once a guest develops a negative feeling towards a hotel, it is a hard job to turn those feelings back into positive ones.

The front desk gives housekeeping a written (or electronically transmitted) document called a **rooms report,** which indicates the number of guests checking out or staying over. Also included in this document are any special requests from guests (such as a late check-out or early wake-up). Housekeepers use the rooms report to prioritize rooms and schedule the workload.

The front desk also provides housekeeping with a list of rooms that have been vacated and that, therefore, can be made up first. As the business day continues, communication flows back and forth between housekeeping and the front desk. The front desk updates housekeeping on check-outs, and housekeeping notifies the front desk when a room is ready to be sold.

As explained above, the flow of communication between housekeeping and the front desk is two-way and constant so that both operations can run at maximum efficiency all the time. This cooperation allows the hotel to fulfill guests' needs and generate the maximum room revenue possible.

Terminology and language are also important. Professionals never refer to a room as "dirty." Instead, you will hear a room described as "not made up" or "on change." "Dirty" would sound negative to a guest. How employees speak to each other in the presence of guests has a definite effect on the hotel's image.

EXHIBIT 8-3

Hotel organizational structure

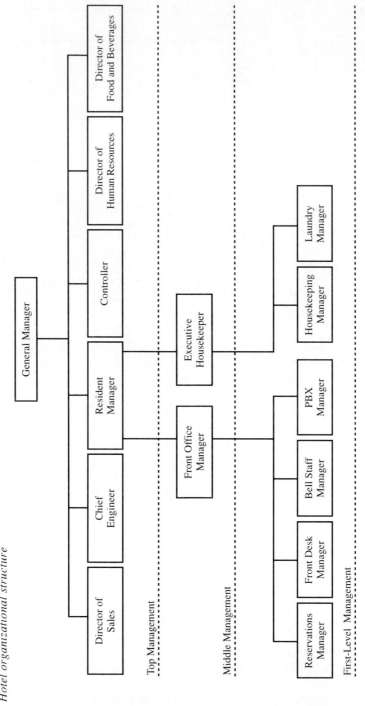

Eye on the Issues

Environment

Energy Management

Energy management is the responsibility of the engineering and maintenance department. Monitoring how energy is used to heat and cool the property is an ongoing process. Performing energy audits, section by section, may reveal old energy-wasting equipment in need of updating. In older properties, some equipment *bleeds* energy. Replacement is often very cost effective.

Water-conserving shower heads and low-flush toilets are rapidly becoming standard. We can expect to see high-efficiency motors and longer-lasting fluorescent light bulbs. HVAC components will use less energy and incorporate environmentally friendly air-conditioning refrigerants. Properties will be better insulated to reduce heat/cold loss. All these changes, whether passive or active, will lower operating costs.

Recycling

The hospitality industry can contribute to the world's recycling in a major way. There are tons of materials that can be recycled in hotels over the course of a year.

Plastics are used all over the hotel—and most of them can be sorted and recycled. A number in an embossed triangle appears on the bottom of most plastic containers, indicating recyclability. Employees can be trained to sort by number, and they often wholeheartedly support recycling, even

though it adds a step to cleaning up. Kitchen patrols will find plastic milk- and dairy-product packaging; the dishroom will yield dishwasher detergent tubs. Housekeeping will yield cleaning supply bottles and used shampoo and conditioner (amenity) containers.

Newsprint and other paper generated by a hotel are easily recycled. Computers with printers can pile up mountains of paper. Most upscale hotels provide each guest with a daily newspaper. This can add up to hundreds of pounds of newspaper weekly.

Aluminum cans are the most commonly known recyclables. Any property with a soda machine will soon have pounds of crushed cans. Steel coffee, tomato paste, and other cans can also be recycled and are always to be found in commercial kitchens.

Liquor, beer, and wine bottles are a leading source of recycled glass. Glass is sorted by color, generally clear, green, and brown.

As with all policies, leadership should be shown at the top. If employees see managers recycling, they will see how serious the property really is about conservation.

Hotels may also contribute to environmental responsibility by getting their guests involved in their recycling programs. There are now attractive recycling bins suitable for placement on property; these give guests the opportunity to participate and, as a side effect, subtly enhance a hotel's public image.

Management Aspects

The next section of this chapter deals with the everyday aspects of management, which include staffing, training, and scheduling. These are the areas that managers in hospitality deal with on a day-to-day basis.

Staffing.   One of the biggest challenges an executive housekeeper must face is staffing—finding the right people to perform the department's jobs. The entry-level position of room attendant or housekeeper is one of the most difficult to fill. Low pay, low status, and hard physical work best describe a

EXHIBIT 8–4

Twenty-four-hour maid service: a growing necessity but difficult to staff and schedule

Courtesy: Four Seasons Hotels & Resorts, Toronto, Canada.

housekeeper's job. Cleaning guest rooms and public areas, working in the laundry, and performing all the "dirty work" in the hotel is what a housekeeper does.

The geographic location of a property has a great deal to do with the people who apply for work within it. A property in a remote location, such as a ski resort high in the mountains or a guest ranch in a remote desert area, may have to provide housing for employees. A hotel located in a downtown area with easy access to public transportation has a much easier time getting employees. Most people who work at minimum wage jobs find it difficult to afford a car and so rely on public transportation to get to work. Some hotels, out of necessity, set up van pools to transport their employees. In some cases the same van that is scheduled to drop off guests at the airport early in the morning can use a return route to the hotel that passes by designated pick-up points for hotel employees. This benefits the hotel in two important ways. First, all the employees, not just housekeepers, have a reliable way to get to work and be on time. The second benefit deals with the hotel's public image. Employee transport programs contribute to reduced traffic and lower pollution; by providing them, a hotel is seen as environmentally conscientious—a public relations plus.

If a hotel or resort wants to attract the best potential applicants for its housekeeping department, it must first evaluate the wages and benefits offered by other competing hotels. Obviously, if the property down the street pays a dollar an hour more or offers some type of health insurance, people will prefer to work for the competition. Market forces oblige hotels to make their wages and benefits competitive if they want to attract capable workers. Knowing what the competition pays enables you to equal or exceed it.

With the transportation problem addressed and the wages and benefit package set, the next area to define is where to locate housekeeping labor. The easiest place to start looking for employees is internally. Current employees may have a friend or relative in need of a job who would suit the hotel's needs nicely. The same network of friends and relatives is also valuable for passing word along to *their* circle of friends. To take advantage of this network, job openings are posted on a bulletin board and present employees are encouraged to share the news. Some properties even go as far as paying bonuses to employees for finding help. By using internal resources to fill job vacancies, a hotel can save a great deal of time and money.

If the internal posting fails to produce applicants, some type of external search will have to be undertaken. This can be as simple as posting a help wanted sign in front of a small motel or as extreme as running a radio commercial advertising for help with an offer of free transportation and lodging.

The demographics of the local community may also affect the ***demographics of the applicant pool.*** Depending on the area, the labor market may include, but not be limited to, housewives, single parents, students, retired persons, the differently challenged, and immigrants. The last group may be difficult to reach because of language obstacles, but do not discount them simply because they do not speak English. They may already have the experience and work ethic a hotel is looking for. If so, they may welcome the chance to learn English. A hotel may even offer an English language program as an employee benefit.

The size and structure of the property will influence the extent to which an executive housekeeper will be responsible for hiring. A large resort hotel has thousands of employees and a very structured hiring process. In this case, the human resources department is normally responsible for hiring. One of the main functions of the human resources department is to screen applicants and conduct interviews, as explained in the human resources chapter. At smaller properties with fewer employees, the job applicant will be interviewed directly by the owner, manager, or executive housekeeper.

The housekeeping department has the highest turnover rate of any department in the hotel. The hard work, low pay, and lack of respect are reasons for housekeeping turnover. If some time and research are applied to hiring the right applicant from the start, turnover can be reduced. Turnover is very expensive to any business. Time taken placing ads and interviewing applicants takes managers away from other duties. The ideal situation is to be able to hire the best qualified person with the most stable work history. In reality, though, circumstances may force a manager to hire the first person who walks in the front door looking for work.

Training.   Once housekeeping positions have been filled, the most important job undertaken by a manager becomes training. A training program starts with the assumption that the trainees have never before done the work at hand. A training program starts with the basics and builds from there; just because a new housekeeper spent 10 years at XYZ Motel does not mean he or she knows how to do things the way your property requires.

A room attendant's job is a hands-on physical activity. The best form of training comes in the form of on-the-job training, also known as *OJT*. An experienced housekeeper is paired with a new hire who learns by watching and doing. It is very important that the trainer is not only an outstanding performer as a housekeeper but also a good teacher. Training programs may last from two days to two weeks. The progress of the new employee should be monitored by the supervisor or area manager. If there is some type of problem, this is the time to correct it.

In addition to guest room cleaning procedures, training should also include attitude, conduct, appearance, safety, security, and guest relations. The new employee must be aware that he or she is part of the hospitality industry. How an employee conducts him- or herself on the property and around guests reflects on the image of the hotel. Guests will remember friendly, helpful people who helped make their stay more enjoyable. Ultimately, it does not cost anything to be thoughtful and courteous to guests, but it may cost the hotel everything if employees fail to make guests feel pampered.

Appearance is also an important part of training. An exclusive resort supplies housekeepers' uniforms and may have a strict policy about make-up, hair length, jewelry, and type and color of footwear. The locally owned small property may require only a tee shirt and blue jeans. Research has shown that **codes of appearance** can positively affect employee attitudes, because people who take the time to make sure they look good generally have more confidence and self-esteem. This can add to the feelings of belonging and team spirit needed for the housekeeping department to perform at maximum efficiency.

An important part of training often overlooked is that of orienting a new employee to the entire property. The new housekeeper should know what facilities are used most by guests and where they are located. When the housekeeper is able to assist guests by recommending one of the hotel's restaurants, the whole property benefits. Guests will often stop the first person in sight to ask directions to the pool, spa, club house, business center, banquet offices, and so on. Often, the first person they see will be a room attendant or houseperson. If the hotel does not take the time to train these employees and make them familiar with the property, guests may feel that ''nobody knows anything around here.''

Scheduling.   The housekeeping manager's next challenge is that of scheduling. The main problem in *scheduling employees* relates to the hospitality industry's nonstandard work calendar; many employees must work when the general population is off (weekends, holidays, and evenings). Hotels are open every day of the year. This includes all weekends and holidays. Some properties do the majority of their business between Friday and Monday. Finding people willing to work when their friends or family is off is difficult. From

EXHIBIT 8–5

Housekeeping is responsible for maintaining in-room amenities, such as irons and ironing boards.

Photo by James L. Morgan, 85283.

the first interview, the employee should be aware that working weekends and holidays will be a job requirement.

There are some important factors in developing a housekeeping schedule. The schedule should be posted in a highly visible area as far in advance as possible. The schedule is always subject to change because of fluctuations in room occupancy. The schedule should be fair, in the sense that weekend and holiday work should be assigned as equitably as possible. Good recordkeeping counteracts complaints that the schedule favors one individual over another. If possible, employees should have input in the scheduling process. People will be much more cooperative if they have a say in what weekends and holidays they work. It is desirable to make sure the same employees are not working Christmas, New Year's Eve, or Thanksgiving unless they choose to.

One type of schedule to keep housekeepers happy is a workweek of four 10-hour days. This schedule allows for a forty-hour work week and three days off. Once again, the idea is to rotate the days so that each employee works the same number of weekends. Another way to schedule is to give people the same days off every week; some employees prefer two days off in the middle of the week. Most properties use some type of seniority system to determine who picks first. That is, the employee with the most time on the job is awarded the first pick for days off. The privilege of first pick for days off may also be given as a reward for outstanding job performance.

Employees of different religious backgrounds may observe holy days unfamiliar to management. When they request time off to observe such days, management must be sensitive. Respect for how others worship will go a long way in gaining employee loyalty. It may be helpful to request a calendar of holy days for religions represented in your department. We are automatically sensitive about asking employees to work on traditional Christian holidays; it is courteous to be aware of the special days of other religions.

The challenge of scheduling is to achieve the employee coverage necessary to get the job done while being fair to all parties involved. This is an area of management where the manager in charge is limited only by his or her own imagination and courage to try new and different ideas. It is possible to make changes in scheduling that increase morale and increase productivity without resulting in a reduction in quality.

Eye on the Issues

Ethics

Housekeeping management faces ethical concerns in two distinct areas. The first lies in the super-visor–employee relationship and reveals volumes about the entire organization's human relations philosophy. A housekeeping department that shows respect for its employees (many of whom are entry-level workers facing barriers of language and trans-portation) sets a positive ethical tone. Even the lowest-paid members of the staff are entitled to fairness in the areas of scheduling, promotion, ben-efits, and penalties. An example of an unfair pen-alty for housekeepers is the practice of holding them responsible for items stolen from guest rooms by guests. Properties who use this policy often post signs in their guest rooms as a means of shaming theft-minded guests into honest behavior. While theft of guest room items can be a problem, this sweatshop practice is an unfair solution, since housekeepers have no control over guests' honesty.

The second area of ethical concern, which ap-plies not only to housekeepers, but also to main-tenance workers and engineering staff (and every other staff member who has guest-room access), is respect for guest property and privacy. Employees should be trained not to handle guest property except within clearly spelled-out guidelines.

Standard Operating Procedures

Establishing how things are done on the property is the next area of impor-tance. A **standard operating procedure** (SOP) is a clear, concise description of how to perform a specific task. Standard operating procedures include many housekeeping tasks such as:

- How to enter a guest room.
- How to make a bed.
- How to clean a bathroom.
- How to report lost and found articles.
- How to stock a housekeeping cart.
- How to mop a floor.

SOPs include all equipment needed and all safety precautions that need to be taken. They may include specific guidelines dealing with how to handle cleaning chemicals and the disposal of hazardous material. A certain type of equipment may require a certain number of hours of training to operate. A programmable washing machine, commercial ironing machines, and a carpet cleaning machine all require some training before they can be operated properly.

The reason for creating standard operating procedures is to ensure that the same tasks are performed exactly the same way throughout the property. This will ensure a uniform standard of cleanliness. The guest rooms' "finish" should look the same from the basement to the penthouse. Each public rest room, hallway, stairwell, and public area should be cleaned the same way.

Standard operating procedures can be as finicky as specifying what station will be preset on the guest-room clock radio or as general as "vacuum the lobby." These procedures take many things into consideration—safety, speed, time of day, appearance, and productivity. They must be written so they can be followed easily. They must also be adaptable to changes. If an employee finds a faster or easier way to perform a task, the procedure should be re-written. Most standard operating procedures can be improved. The approach of "we have always done it this way" does not guarantee success. Allowing employees to try to improve existing procedures may be beneficial to the hotel and make the employees feel appreciated. The future of management is worker empowerment, and the most important way employees can contribute is to find new solutions to old problems.

Departmental forms are often a part of SOPs. Forms are standardized ways to transfer information needed for the hotel to function. Information generally flows from the general to the specific. The night auditor's report to house-keeping is a form that summarizes the status of all the rooms in the hotel. (Symbols commonly used include C/O for "checked out," O/C for "on change," S/O for "stay over," OOO for "out of order," and R/R for "room ready.") Depending on the size of the property and its staff, the executive housekeeper will use this information to apportion work to senior house-keepers (who will then assign it to individuals or teams) or to make direct assignments. In a very large property the information from the night auditor's report may go through several layers of organization, each with its own daily work forms, before it reaches the hands of the housekeeper who will actually clean the rooms.

Key control is another area where SOPs are of use. This will be explained in more detail in the section of this chapter dealing with security. At this point, though, it is important to note that it is very important to have a strict SOP for issuing keys to housekeepers (and other staff members) who need them for their daily tasks. Ideally, all departments that need access to guest rooms and storage areas should use the same procedures for signing pass keys in and out. That way, the managers of those areas will know who has the keys, and when and where the keys were given out.

Two other areas that require good SOPs are the lost and found operation and guest loan items. Both involve writing down information that will be shared by the front desk and housekeeping department. For example, if a housekeeper finds a pair of gold earrings in a vacated guest room, he or she should bring them back to the housekeeping office. Here, the date, time, and room number are recorded and passed on to the front desk on a form. When the guest calls back to the front desk to ask if anyone has found the earrings, the information can easily be found.

Similarly, if the front desk lends an item to a guest, such as an iron, and the housekeeper finds the iron after the guest checks out, it is recorded and placed back into the loan item area. Housekeeping lets the front desk know that the iron has been returned so the guest will not be charged for it.

Time card control is another good area for SOPs. Time cards keep track of how much hourly personnel are paid. To ensure that the actual time worked is paid to the worker, controls must be in place. Employees should be instructed from the first day of work what these procedures are. Most businesses have rules about time cards, such as:

Time Clock Rules

Only punch your own time card.

Do not punch other employees in or out.

Do not come to work a half-hour early and punch in.

Remember to punch out when you leave at the end of your shift.

If you have forgotten to clock in or out, notify your supervisor as soon as possible so adjustments can be made.

Still another common area for SOPs is control of inventory. Just as the hotel kitchen and bar departments need inventory control, so does housekeeping. Only a limited number of employees should have access to valuable items. These employees need to record the number and type of articles they remove from storage or equipment bays. Using such controls is a sound business practice that reduces employee theft and speeds up the process of taking inventory.

One last SOP is the guest room inspection routine. To achieve the best quality control, a standard guest inspection checklist is given to those who supervise the inspection of guest rooms before they are released to the front desk as ready to sell. This type of SOP ensures that each room passes the same inspection quality checks.

Used correctly, standard operating procedures will result in uniform and consistent performance.

Laundry

Hotels have two choices regarding laundry: hire a contract service or use an on-premises laundry. There are positive and negative sides to both options.

International

In a career that may take you to all parts of the world, it's important to pay attention to local laws and customs. Local labor laws may influence the number of hours per day and days per week during which workers may be scheduled. Religious practices and local customs may affect uniform selection; how closely males and females may work together; and how age, gender, race, and so on may influence supervisor–subordinate relationships. In some areas there may even be myths and misinformation associated with foreigners. Behavior that seems innocent and ordinary to you may be perceived as peculiar or even somewhat scandalous to locals, including your employees.

The advantages of a contract laundry service are that the hotel has more space for guest rooms. Also, there is no investment in equipment or additional employees. The negative side of a laundry service comes in the form of lack of quality control and loss of flexibility. The hotel has to work around delivery schedules. Any sudden changes in linen demand are very difficult to accommodate.

Having an on-premises laundry department has many advantages. The turnaround time is low. That is, the time between when an article is soiled and when it is washed, folded, and ready to use again is short. The hotel can purchase fewer sheets, tablecloths, and so on because no linens are ever in transit; they never leave the hotel. A laundry may even be used as a profit center by doing linen service for other properties. The negatives of an on-premises laundry room come in the form of high initial investment in equipment, space considerations, and an increase in utility and labor costs.

For many hotels in remote locations, there is no choice but to operate an on-premises laundry department. When contract services add long-distance transport charges to their bill, prices cease to be reasonable. On the other hand, some hotels, because of building design, city zoning, or other factors, *must* use a laundry service. Sometimes creativity finds a solution. For example, if a corporation owns four hotels in a close geographic area, one property may specialize in one activity for all four hotels. One property may be responsible for the laundry, another for bakery needs, and so on.

In most cases, housekeeping managers inherit an existing laundry situation when they begin a new job. If they are involved when a new property is being designed, they can request that the laundry be integrated into the housekeeping operations area. At this stage a laundry consultant can be hired to help in planning the laundry facility. Many variables have to be measured: What will the laundry volume be? How much space will be required? What about location within the building and the build-up of noise and heat? How about utility requirements such as water, electricity, and gas?

EXHIBIT 8–6

The size and cost of operating an on-premises laundry depends on the size of the property. The condition of linens is something guests notice immediately.

Photo by James L. Morgan, 85283.

Inside an On-Premises Laundry.   The remainder of this section will concentrate on on-premises laundry operations.

Any hotel laundry will have the basic requirement of washing and drying guest-room linens. This includes sheets, pillowcases, bath towels, and washcloths. Many hotels with food and beverage outlets have additional laundry requirements such as table linens and kitchen and server uniforms. The laundry may also be responsible for cleaning groundskeeper, maintenance, and engineering uniforms.

When purchasing washing and drying machines it is important to stay with name brands (e.g., Speed Queen, Univac). A no-name bargain may prove costly in the long run when parts cannot be easily found or repair technicians are stumped by unfamiliar assemblies.

Most new commercial washers are computer programmable. An operator need only push buttons that correspond to the proper washing formula for that particular type of linen. These programmable machines can regulate length of cycles, amount of detergent, softener, and bleach—along with length and duration of rinse and wash cycles. The commercial washing machine must be a very versatile piece of equipment, since it may be required to wash both delicate server uniforms and heavily soiled kitchen aprons. Commercial washing machines come in various sizes from 25-pound machines to ones that can wash more than 1,000 pounds of laundry. These machines are very heavy and have special installation restrictions. Most commercial machines, due to their weight and strong vibrations while in operation, are bolted down tightly to six-inch-thick concrete slabs. Failure to secure the washing machine will result in damage to the floor as well as to the washing machine.

Dryers are the next piece of equipment needed for the laundry department. It is important to note that the general rule for drying to washing is 2 to 1. That is, if you have 100 pounds of washing capacity, you will need a dryer

EXHIBIT 8–7

Approximate cost of operating an in-house laundry.

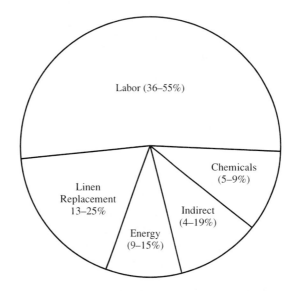

TO APPROXIMATE LAUNDRY COSTS

Percentages in the above chart are based on national averages.

For example, an account spending $3,600 a year on detergent costs would equal $45,000 in total laundry costs.

Calculate this by using detergent cost as your control point and estimating the other costs ($3,600 ÷ .08 = $45,000). For example, listed below are the dollar equivalents for the five areas assuming the following percentages per area:

Labor	46%	(45,000 × .46)	$20,700
Linen replacement	18	(45,000 × .18)	8,100
Energy	13	(45,000 × .13)	5,900
Indirect	15	(45,000 × .15)	6,700
Chemicals	8	(45,000 × .08)	3,600
	100%		$45,000

Courtesy: Ecolab, Inc., St. Paul, Minnesota.

with 200 pounds of drying capacity. Dryers are either totally electric or use a combination of electricity and gas. Gas may be either natural or propane. Where applicable, a gas dryer is always preferred over a totally electric one. This is due to the extremely high energy cost of a totally electric dryer.

A critical factor in the operation of a clothes dryer is lint removal. Lint causes two major problems. First, lint build-up is an incredible fire hazard. Lint is a dry material that is extremely flammable. The other problem with lint is that it drastically reduces the efficiency of the dryer, because the dryer has to work harder and longer to achieve the same results.

Other essential equipment needed for a commercial-type hotel laundry includes the following: a soak sink to soak stained linens, a set of mobile storage racks for clean linen, a "third-hand" sheet folder, a set of mobile hampers to sort and store soiled linens, and an adequate folding table. These additional items increase the laundry's efficiency and help keep clean linens clean as they are sorted, folded, and stored.

Managers can further improve a laundry's operation by developing an efficient laundry flow. Needed is an organized system that begins with the picking up of soiled linens from any area of the property, and continues through the washing, drying, and folding areas to the restocking process. Laundry flow patterns work best when updated and refined according to machinery capacities and labor availability .

Exhibit 8–7 illustrates the approximate costs of operating an in-house laundry. As you can see, labor is highest, with chemicals being the lowest. Choosing a laundry chemical vendor is an important operational decision. Ideally, the goal is to use chemicals that work well in local water, with as little harshness as possible. Using harsher-than-necessary chemicals reduces linen life and may irritate employees' and guests' skins.

When reviewing laundry operations, managers carefully examine monthly customer service reports, as shown in Exhibit 8–8. These reports establish a performance record of how each washer is operating, what maintenance has been done, and what tests have been run. Here, patterns or problems can be noted and adjustments made. These laundry reports are dated and signed by the vendor and the laundry supervisor.

On-premises laundries can add speed, flexibility, and quality control to the washables process. They can also generate revenue in slow times by offering laundry services to other hotels in the area.

Purchasing

If you ever want to find out how many salespeople there are in any area, just open a business—because that's when they come out of the woodwork. The vendors these salespeople represent can be valuable resources, since they are product or service specialists. Their salespeople often know not only their own, but also the competition's products and prices. Because of these and other reasons, *vendor relations* are important.

Some items—guest room linens, sheets, and towels—are a direct reflection on the quality of the hotel. They also have limited life spans. The linen supplier to the hotel will, therefore, come calling quite often, if not to sell new linens, then to check on how the present products are holding up. Conversations with the manufacturer's or vendor's representative are perfect opportunities to discuss needs—for a tighter weave or longer lasting dye on napkins, or better stitching on the edges of sheets. These items are examples of quality standards and purchasing specifications, characteristics you can specify when you order. Let's examine some other products and quality standards, in this case, for the purchasing of linens.

The standard hotel bed sheet is a t-180, percale, flat sheet. The *t-180* indicates there is a thread count (or density) of 180 threads per square inch. *Percale* refers to the production finish of the material. This process is what gives the sheet its feel. *Flat sheet* means that the sheet has no elastic in the corners. The reason for using flat sheets in hotels and hospitals is that they are washed on a daily basis and without elastic they will last much longer. The

EXHIBIT 8–8

An example of monthly customer service report.

CUSTOMER SERVICE REPORT **LAUNDRY**	Ecolab Inc. Ecolab Center St. Paul, MN 55102

DISTRICT MANAGER	TERR. MANAGER	TERR. NO.	REPORT CONTROL NUMBER

DISTRICT MGR. PHONE NO.   TERR. MGR. PHONE NO.

ACCOUNT	ACCOUNT NO.	TIME-IN	TIME-OUT	MONTH	DAY	YEAR	EMERGENCY	NIGHT
		TO						
	CHAIN NO.	MACHINE MAKE			MODEL			
		DISPENSER			LOCATION			

OPERATION & EQUIPMENT SECTION RESULTS
CIRCLE-INDICATE OPERATING CONDITIONS FOUND AND ACTION TAKEN IN SECTION BELOW AND REASON FOR FAIR OR POOR RESULTS

RESULTS:		TEST KIT			PROCEDURES		OK	TRAINING
1	Appearance	7	℃	☐ ℉ ☐ No	12	Pre-sorting		☐ Correct Pre-sorting Procedures
2	Superior 1 2 3 4 5 6 7 8 9 20 POOR	8	km	☐ Yes ☐ No	13	Loading		☐ Proper Use of Suppliers
3	Odor	9	Linen pH:		14	Wash Formulas		☐ Wash Machine Loading Procedures
4	Feel	10	Wtr Hrdns	grg	15	Extract Times		☐ Proper Linen Handling & Folding Procedures
5	Stain Removal	11	Wettability		16	Wash Charts		
6	Wrinkling		☐ Good ☐ Poor					

EQUIPMENT CONDITIONS FOUND

WASH MACHINE NO.	1	2	3	4	5	WASH MACHINE NO.	1	2	3	4	5
17	Titration %						21	Timers					
18	Water Levels						22	Wash Charts					
19	Temperature						23	Lint Traps					
20	Drain Valves						24	Wash Count					

NO.	CONDITIONS FOUND, ACTION TAKEN & OTHER COMMENTS

DESCRIBE OTHER CUSTOMER NEEDS

PRODUCT											
STOCK ON HAND											

REORDER DATA	CUST. ORDER NO.	☐ FUTURE N.L.T.	☐ DELIV. ON	☐ C.O.D. $

QTY	CODE	PRODUCT AND SIZE	QTY	CODE	PRODUCT AND SIZE

WARRANTIES OF FITNESS AND MERCHANTABILITY, IF ANY, AS WELL AS ANY EXPRESS WARRANTIES COVERING THE ABOVE PRODUCT SHALL NOT BE EFFECTIVE UNLESS THE PRODUCTS ARE USED AS DIRECTED BY ECOLAB INC.

CUSTOMER'S SIGNATURE _____   ECOLAB REP. _____   TERR. NO. _____

ST. PAUL

Courtesy: Ecolab, Inc., St. Paul, Minnesota.

color of the standard hotel sheet is white. Some hotels may purchase ''seconds,'' sheets with minor imperfections, at a great savings with little perceptible loss in quality. Many upscale hotels use an off-white (natural or cream colored) sheet to add ambience to their guest room decor.

Towels and washcloths vary in cost and quality. A budget motel located next to an interstate highway whose guest towels are often stolen will buy the cheapest linens available. An upscale resort will have the softest, most absorbent towels available—some even with monograms. These towels will be expensive but will reflect the quality of the property. Most properties fall somewhere between the two extremes. Most guests are satisfied with a towel that feels comfortable against the skin and absorbs moisture adequately.

Bedding is a critical area for the success of a hotel and a very important purchasing decision. A great hotel must start with a comfortable bed; after all, the main service a hotel offers is a good night's sleep. This means the hotel will have to purchase quality name-brand box springs and mattresses. Quality name brands, though more expensive, usually pay off in the long run because of consistent construction and durability. Manufacturers of name-brand goods also offer factory warranties of some sort. This is an area where a hotel can't look for cheap substitutes.

Cleaning chemicals are an important purchase for the housekeeping department, too. The vendor of these products should be able to train the housekeeping department in the proper use, storage, and supply of all safety-related materials. A simple dispensing system with color-keyed bottles and chemicals, and pictures of what the chemical cleans, helps housekeepers with a literacy or language problem figure out what product cleans what.

The housekeeping department will also purchase equipment ranging from simple vacuum cleaners to complete carpet-care machines. Vacuum cleaners used in cleaning guest rooms are, of course, an essential part of housekeeping, and greatly affect the guest's impression of a room's cleanliness. Vacuum cleaners take a lot of abuse so they must be durable. It is better to buy a $400.00 machine that will last a couple of years than to buy three $125.00 machines that will wear out in a few months. It's wise to take some time to find out what other hotels in the area use and what type of service can be expected from local equipment dealers. This is another area in which a bargain may cost a lot more money in the long run, especially if you make the mistake of buying a home-consumer model rather than a commercial quality machine.

A few final comments on purchasing. The vendors who work for respectable companies are, in general, a very reliable source of information. Vendors have experience in solving most of a hotel's cleaning problems and are generally very willing to help in training people on how to use their equipment. Even so, remember that vendors are dedicated to making sales. For this reason, purchases should always be spread between at least two vendors. When a vendor knows that you regularly buy some products from a competitor, he or she is motivated to keep trying to please you in hopes of persuading you to reassign some of those sales. Competition between vendors will benefit you in two ways: First, the service will be good, and second, the prices will be fair.

Maintenance and Engineering

This section deals with the department that keeps the building from falling down. The size and responsibilities of this department are very similar to those of the housekeeping department. The size of the unit, the complexity of the construction, and the property's type directly affect the number of people needed in the maintenance/engineering departments. A small bed and breakfast operation will, more often than not, have only the owner to perform routine maintenance. He or she will paint, cut the grass, and do minor electrical and plumbing repairs. When something major breaks, he or she will have to rely on outside help. A large resort hotel, on the other hand, may need hundreds of maintenance personnel for all phases of the operation. A hotel with 3,000 rooms, a 36-hole golf course, a convention center, four swimming pools, six restaurants, three bars, and a 10-acre parking lot will definitely require a great deal of care. There will be thousands of lightbulbs to change, hundreds of toilets to plunge, and thousands of square yards of carpets to repair.

Maintenance

The terms *maintenance* and *engineering* are often used interchangeably but they have two distinct meanings.

Maintenance is simply defined as the work involved in keeping something in good working order. Maintenance comes in many forms, from routine to preventive, and from emergency to scheduled. In the case of hotels and restaurants, there are a great many things to keep in good working order. Routine maintenance can range from simple housekeeping tasks such as lubricating squeaky doors and shoveling snow, to changing air filters and smoke detector batteries. These simple tasks make up a majority of the tasks that are generally considered to be maintenance.

Preventive maintenance, also known as *PM,* is done specifically to avoid a major breakdown of equipment. These activities include regular lubrication of moving parts, testing of backup and emergency equipment, changing machine belts, and, most importantly, finding minor problems before they become major ones. The old axiom "an ounce of prevention is worth a pound of cure" describes exactly what preventive maintenance attempts to accomplish.

Emergency maintenance activities are performed in situations where a property suffers or may stand to suffer loss of revenue. If a toilet is broken, stopped up, or leaking, the room cannot be sold. If a busy restaurant has one large dishwasher that fails and prevents clean dishware and silverware from being set at a table, this may result in revenue loss. Emergency maintenance is developed to solve money-losing problems quickly. This is also the most expensive type of maintenance because all phases come at a premium price. Labor, parts, and the "fix it at any cost" attitude push costs to the extreme.

Many times, PM activities are done with particular seasons in mind. In late spring, most swimming pool maintenance is completed. Heating boilers are serviced before winter sets in, and refrigeration units are serviced before the heat of summer. If the hotel has an off-season, this is the ideal time to close down rooms for painting and repairs. When an area or unit is not in use, scheduled maintenance can occur. Scheduled maintenance is the preplanned repair or replacement of major components of working systems.

Eye on the Issues

Technology

Managers of engineering and housekeeping departments should make every effort to stay abreast of advancements in pertinent technology. Monthly trade publications, trade show attendance, and membership in professional associations provide avenues for keeping current. The major goal of adopting new technology is to increase efficiency and safety. For example, recent advances in bug-control technology have made termite and roach control both safer and more efficient. By spraying hormone-related compounds in infested areas, pests can be prevented from maturing to the point where they can reproduce. This quickly reduces bug populations without the use of potentially hazardous toxic pesticides.

Engineering

Engineering is the department wherein employees need a thorough knowledge of all the working systems in a hotel. These systems include the following:

Water and wastewater.

Lighting.

Telecommunication.

Waste management.

Energy management.

Electricity.

Laundry.

Safety and security.

Food service equipment.

Heating, ventilation, and air conditioning (HVAC).

This department is another crucial one in the overall performance of the property. The guest in any hotel or restaurant expects the lights to go on, the toilets to flush, and room temperature to be pleasant. If any one of these creature comfort items fails, the property will appear not to care about the guest's comfort, and that is not the impression a hotel or restaurant wants to create.

Engineering is responsible for any renovation or new construction after the property is in operation. All systems inside and outside of the building are under the direction of engineering.

Water Systems.   Water and wastewater systems are essential in any building. In hospitality, the entire property is tied to some type of water system. Water can be divided into two types: potable and nonpotable. **Potable water** refers to water that is drinkable. Nonpotable water cannot be consumed by human beings. It has limited use. The most common use of nonpotable water is to supply the **fire suppression** system. The sprinklers, standpipes, and hose cabinets are supplied by a nonpotable water system. This includes the internal system and the outside fire hydrants.

The potable water supply comes in two forms: hot and cold. Hot water has two uses: for people and equipment. People need hot water for the following purposes: bathing, cooking, and washing. Equipment needs hot water for cleaning and for the operation of swimming pools, spas, and Jacuzzis.

Cold water is used by people for flushing toilets, bathing, cooking, and drinking. Equipment needs cold water in the kitchen, laundry room, swimming pool, heating and cooling systems, and the grounds division.

A guest does not think about the water system too much until it fails. But when a guest uses a water fountain, goes to brush his or her teeth, or take a shower, the water system had better be in working order!

Engineering is also concerned with water quality. Most of the trouble with water quality originates at the source. Water that comes from wells, inlets, streams, or the utility company varies greatly in makeup. Ideally, water should be colorless, odorless, and tasteless, and should contain no harmful bacteria. Local health agencies are required to test water quality several times a year.

Pollution at the source of water supplies can come in many forms. Industrial pollution in the forms of fuel spills, waste oil spills, and waste products from mining can alter the composition of water. Farming can pollute water through the use of excess fertilizers and pesticides that run off into the local water supply.

After water gets to the property, its mineral content (such as iron, manganese, and calcium) has a direct effect on its quality. High amounts of minerals causes **hard water.** This hard water, over time, will build up "scale" on the insides of boilers and heaters, reducing their efficiency.

Another problem caused by hard water is that more detergent is needed in washing machines to overcome the minerals and to clean properly. In the presence of hard water, soap will not lather and will leave a soap scum on plumbing fixtures, which makes them harder to clean. It then becomes necessary to use stronger chemicals and increase labor to get the cleaning accomplished. Obviously, hard water may create several problems that become costly if not addressed properly.

The best system for overcoming a hard water situation is the use of a water-softening unit. Water softeners use different types of salts to remove minerals. The cost of water-softening units is usually recovered through the longer life of heating units and lower amounts of detergents being used. When engineering is aware of a hard water situation in the area, a water-softening unit should be included as part of the water system.

Swimming pools pose several problems for engineering. A pool's location, and whether it is inside or outside a building, creates changing water conditions, which contribute to high maintenance costs. Pool water must be monitored and adjusted constantly. Outdoor pools must be kept in circulation or drained during periods of below freezing temperatures. Resorts may have several pools, both inside and out. If engineers had their way, all pools would be indoor pools since they are easier to maintain, may be used all year, and are not subject to extremes in climate. Unfortunately for them, sun-loving guests love outdoor pools and the chance to bask next to them.

The engineering department must also be concerned with wastewater generated by a hotel and its restaurants. What happens to everything that goes down the drain? A property that is located in the center of an urban area will be tied into the city sewer system. The property will pay for this access to the public sewer system with a per gallon charge from the local water treatment utility plant. Thus, water costs money not only as you bring it to your property, but also as you get rid of it.

Some (though very few) properties have their own on-premises wastewater treatment plants due to remote locations or strict local laws. Small privately owned wastewater systems are tightly regulated by state and county laws. If a property has a wastewater facility, it is usually required to have a technician on duty who is up-to-date on the rules and certifications needed for operation.

All properties need hot water, yet hotels and restaurants have different hot water requirements. Kitchens, by local health codes, are required to wash dishes at 180° F. Any place where dishes are washed must consistently produce this high temperature. Most commercial dishwashers have some type of booster that raises the temperature inside the washing unit.

Hotels have two major needs for hot water: bathing and clothes washing. Every sink, shower, and bathtub is expected to have running hot water. The temperature at these fixtures should not exceed 155° F. Any higher temperatures may burn a guest. To prevent burning, a hotel should have mixing valves in the showers and sinks to regulate the temperature (mixing cold water with the hot water keeps it from getting too hot). This prevents a common home experience: While you are in the shower, someone flushes a toilet or turns on the lawn sprinklers. This forces the shower temperature up to where you scream and jump out of the shower. Needless to say, this cannot happen at a commercial property.

An on-premises laundry will increase demand for hot water, normally in the 150° F. and under range. Since most guests take a shower or have a bath early in the morning or late in the evening, these are times hotels do not want the laundry running with high hot water demands. Consequently, most hotels operate their laundry in nonpeak times of the day.

Electrical Systems.   A modern hotel cannot function without electricity. Because of the demands made by electrical appliances, large machines, and cooling and heating equipment, hotels must have access to dependable sources of electricity. The power needed for lighting alone is simply amazing. Look around the classroom complex you are in and notice the number and different kinds of lighting that are available. There may be simple lamps with 100-watt incandescent lightbulbs, an assortment of fluorescent lightbulbs, and sodium or mercury vapor parking lot lights. These are just three of the many types of lighting found in any commercial building. Soft light in dining rooms, exit sign lights, and heat lamps are some other examples of lights found in a hotel. Each type of lighting has a specific purpose and energy requirement.

High-rise hotels all have some type of elevator system powered by electricity; some also have escalators. Guests and employees need a fast and safe way to move up and down several floors of the buildings. Hotel guests are not going to check into a hotel and walk up 30 or 40 flights of stairs. The operation of the elevators places a high energy demand on the hotel's electrical system.

The use of computers in every hotel department causes another substantial demand for electricity. If your computerized reservation system goes down because of a power loss, this could mean hundreds of dollars being lost per minute because rooms cannot be booked. Computers track many other day-to-day operations such as purchasing, payroll, maintenance orders, check-in, check-out, and billing. Without electricity none of these operations can be performed.

In restaurants located inside a hotel property, all appliances are electrically powered. The list is almost endless and can include the following: coffeemakers, meat slicers, blenders, dishwashers, microwave ovens, mixers, timers, and steam tables. The most important electrical devices in the kitchen are the refrigeration units. If the power goes off, thousands of dollars can be lost due to food spoilage.

The guest room has many electrical outlets and guest appliances. Televisions and, in some cases, VCR units are requisite entertainment equipment. Guests also expect to be able to use electric-powered hair dryers, irons, razors, personal computers, and battery packs.

You now know something about a hotel's electrical demands, but do you know where the electricity comes from? The vast majority of hotels buy their electricity from a utility company. Some remote properties produce their own power with generators that run on steam, gasoline, or other fuels. Whatever power source a hotel uses, the electric current flows into the building and is distributed throughout. Electricity is similar to plumbing in that it must be directed to different areas according to demand. National and local building codes regulate the quality, size, and type of material used in all phases of designing electrical systems. Inspectors monitor construction of commercial buildings to ensure that they comply with these standards.

Cost, as reflected by monthly utility bills, is of great concern to the engineering department. Excessive use of electricity can be caused by undersized equipment or old, worn-out electric motors. By closely examining the electric usage, the engineering department can make the necessary changes to upgrade equipment and increase efficiency.

HVAC.   *HVAC* is seen all the time in conjunction with commercial buildings. The letters stand for *heating, ventilation,* and *air conditioning.* **HVAC** systems have unique demands placed on them in hospitality situations. One guest might turn the heat on in August when the outside air temperature is above 90° F. Another guest may open a guest room window in the dead of winter. A cold banquet room heats up quickly after 300 guests arrive and start to socialize with each other. A kitchen may start off the morning cold, but as soon as the bakers start baking bread in the oven the whole area heats up. A tour group of senior citizens may ask for warmer meeting and sleeping room temperatures, while a group of college students on spring break may crank the air conditioning up as far as it will go.

The control of the climate throughout the building is regulated by HVAC, from the stairwells, to the guest rooms, and to all other parts of the building where guests and employees can be found.

Heating the building is critical for two reasons. The guest's comfort is important. However, the protection of the building is the most critical function of the heating system. If the heating system fails on a cold winter day with the temperature below freezing, pipes can break. This could mean that entire sections of the water system may need to be replaced at a tremendous cost. When pipes burst, there is usually attendant damage to walls, ceilings, carpets, furnishings, and so on. Also, some fire suppression systems that rely on a water ''charge'' can be rendered inoperable and thus constitute an additional major hazard.

Heat needs some type of fuel source. The most common fuels for heating are electricity, natural gas, liquified petroleum, fuel oil, and steam. Each different fuel has benefits and drawbacks. In some cases, due to local rules or availability, there is no choice and only one type of fuel can be used. When there is a choice of fuel types, cost, storage, and availability must all be considered.

Air-conditioning requirements vary from one climate to another. The most important fact to remember about air conditioning is ''cold is not produced; heat is taken away.'' This is the basic principle of air conditioning. A refrigerant, when converted from a liquid to a gas in a condenser, produces a temperature change. As the liquid turns to a gas, it absorbs heat from the immediate environment. The cold that is felt actually comes from the transformation of heat to another form of energy.

Ventilation is simply understood by looking at a building as though it were a living thing that needs to breathe. Fresh air needs to be brought into a building, filtered, and moved to areas requiring fresh air. The ventilation system also exhausts air that is too hot or foul smelling. It does this through a series of fans, ducts, and filters. These are all high-maintenance items. Fan belts break and wear out, and filters eventually clog and become inefficient. This system is always placed on a scheduled maintenance program to prevent any problems.

Protecting Assets, People, and Property

This section of the chapter will discuss the protection of people and property. The *safety and security* of the people and property within a hotel operation are fundamental. Safety entails protecting individuals from injury and property from damage by fire or other types of disasters. Security entails providing freedom from the fear of negative or harmful interactions. Another way to look at this is that safety is related to protecting people from disasters and security deals with protecting them from other people who may harm them.

Safety

Most local building codes in each city, county, and state strictly regulate safety beginning at the time of construction. Fire prevention and protection are a local responsibility. Materials used to build hotels and restaurants must be of a certain quality, and fire walls are required in certain building sections to prevent fire from spreading.

Smoke detectors are another basic form of fire safety built right into the design of the building. Fire suppression units are also part of many building codes and are found in two types. The most common type is the **heat-activated sprinkler system** that dumps water at a high pressure onto the heat source. This type of fire suppression system is found in many modern hotels and restaurants, especially in commercial kitchens and high-rise hotels. The second type of fire suppression system uses a sprinkler that sprays a chemical on the heat source. The **chemical-type sprinkler** is used in computer rooms where water damage to the equipment could run into millions of dollars.

Most modern hotels have a central computer that controls all aspects and elements of the fire safety system. If a smoke detector goes off in the 14th floor hallway, an alarm will sound. The central fire computer will alert the front desk and/or the security department, pinpointing the exact location of the problem. With this information, immediate action can be taken.

An important part of fire codes relates to the number and location of fire exits. Familiarity with their locations can be of the utmost importance in times of emergency. Look around the building you are in right now. Do you notice the location of existing signs? Are they visible? Could you find your way out of the building if a fire started? Elevators should not be used in case of fire, so fire escapes, internal sets of stairs usually located at both ends of the building, are the main means of exit from upper floors. If you walk into any commercial building, notice that all exterior doors open outward. This is a code written to allow fast evacuation of buildings. Many hotels and restaurants, when inspected by fire marshals, are fined for locked or blocked fire exit doors.

Fire damage is fast and far reaching. The cost of preventing fires is much cheaper than the costs of repairing fire damage. Local fire codes are written for the protection of everyone. Failure to follow these codes can result in criminal and civil judgments against the corporation as well as the individual. You might also think of the public perception of your hotel should you be held responsible for a fatal fire—either through failure to comply with local codes or, worse, through deliberate disregard of them.

Many fire codes include laws designed specifically to protect hotel guests. These include the following: fire escape maps in each guest room, fire alarms, easily accessible fire extinguishers, and fire protection equipment that can operate under a power outage. All codes mandate minimum levels of protection; most properties of large corporations exceed what is required to increase the level of safety and protection.

Hospitality establishments should take the time to practice fire drills. Employees should know how to evacuate the building and assist guests in case of an emergency. It makes little sense to spend money on fire safety equipment and not take the time to train employees in its proper use. All personnel should be familiar with the operation of portable fire extinguishers. Most local fire departments are more than willing to help teach classes and participate in fire safety training. The firefighters in your area do not want to visit your hotel or restaurant for the first time when it is on fire.

A major fact to remember about fire is that most people who die in fires are killed by smoke inhalation. Smoke rises during a fire, so training employees to crawl along the floor where there is a supply of fresh air can save lives. The most important thing employees need to be aware of in an emergency fire situation is not to panic, although that is easier said than done. The difference between the life and death of employees and guests may be staff calmness and control. The better trained and prepared the staff is, the greater the chances they, and your guests, will survive an emergency situation.

While fire is a universal problem, some disasters that may affect a property will be natural ones unique to the specific location of the property. Beach properties in Florida and the Caribbean are keenly aware of hurricane season. Areas with active volcanoes make plans to prepare for eruptions. California no longer considers earthquakes a rarity. Properties close to bodies of water are subject to flooding. Blizzards can happen in mountain and northern regions of the country, and tornadoes occur in flat areas. Each one of these disasters can force a property to take emergency measures, because they may result in a lack of fresh water, loss of electricity and/or heating fuel, and so on. Knowing what problems may occur in your locale can help you better prepare your staff to deal with disasters.

Safety is also related to human-made problems. Many accidents and injuries happen on site at hotels and restaurants. These incidents are expensive for a business. Insurance claims due to guest injury drive up premiums and may result in lawsuits. When an employee is hurt on the job, workers' compensation insurance rates also increase, investigations occur, and lawsuits may, once again, be the result.

EXHIBIT 8–9

Every business should be prepared for fire emergencies. Because guests at lodging properties may be asleep and groggy, it's particularly important for hotels and motels to keep a fire escape route posted on doors where guests can find it.

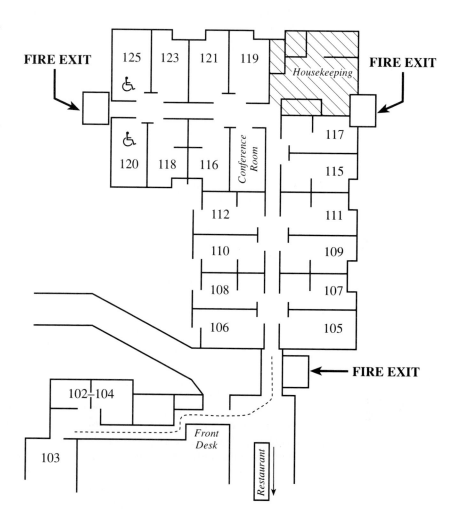

FIRE ESCAPE ROUTE
1st Floor

Many accidents/injuries occur because of lack of training on the part of the employer. Let's look at some situations where proper training could prevent serious injury.

- The kitchen supervisor sends a new employee to slice meat without proper training on the slicing machine.
- A child walks by a housekeeping cart, grabs an open unlabeled bottle of cleaning chemical, and drinks it, thinking it is lemonade.
- A housekeeping supervisor skips reading directions on new cleaning chemicals. The housekeeping staff is exposed to harmful, maybe fatal, doses of fumes.

- A guest checks out of the guest room leaving a fully loaded gun. A housekeeper finds it, drops it, and shoots himself.
- A groundskeeper fails to lock the gate to the swimming pool and a toddler wanders into the pool and drowns.
- A new busperson, thinking the last guest has been served, fills the iced tea dispenser with cleanser. A server comes back to the serving station, fills two glasses from the iced tea dispenser and serves two guests.
- A new houseperson mops the marble floor in the front desk lobby area without putting up "Caution, Wet Floor" signs. A man, in a hurry, runs to check in and slips, breaking his hip.
- The sous chef sends a kitchen worker into the freezer for a box of shrimp, forgetting to tell her that the freezer door sticks.
- After the lobby fireplace is cleaned by the housekeeper, the still hot ashes are deposited into the dumpster.

Security

Security in hospitality means protecting people and property. The protection of guests and employees while on the property is a great responsibility. Property has to be guarded against theft and vandalism.

Guest security varies with the type of hotel. A budget hotel may have only a night auditor on property between 11 PM and 7 AM. An exclusive resort with $400 per night suites will have a security force patrolling 24 hours a day.

Methods for protecting guests, employees, and property from potential harm take many forms, but one important one is the unofficial deputization of all employees as watchdogs. Employees should immediately report any suspicious activity to their supervisor. They should be encouraged to take an active role in the protection of people and property.

Many properties issue photo identification badges to their employees, with clearly visible name, photo, and department. This is a great way to discourage people from wandering into zones where they do not belong. It has the secondary benefit of putting guests at ease, since they can easily identify employees of the property if they need assistance.

Common areas and walkways should be well lit. Hallways, stairwells, and parking lots must also have adequate lighting. Escorts should be provided to employees and guests going out to the parking lot after dark.

As emphasized in Chapter 13, "Hospitality Law," one of the essential requirements of a hotel is that all guest rooms have doors that lock in a secure manner. Any problem with a guest room door justifies its being removed from service until repairs are made.

Guest room key control is an area for strict policy. A housekeeper should never let a person into a guest room with his or her pass key. A person claiming to have lost his or her room key should be sent to the front desk. Before issuing a key, the front desk requires the person to provide identification. Even if a true guest ends up being somewhat inconvenienced, he or she will generally appreciate the extra attention paid to security. This is definitely preferable to breaching the security of the hotel.

Every time a television news magazine talks about the lack of hotel security, reporters dwell on room key control. Time and again, news hawks send impostors to front desks to ask for room keys. Far too many times, without checking, the front desk gives the keys out—to people who are not even registered. Another problem is that of missing room keys. If a guest key is lost, the hotel should put the room out of order until the key has been found or the lock changed.

Hotels generally establish a good relationship with local police departments. Part of this relationship includes cooperation whenever police are called. If their errand requires that they arrest someone at a hotel, whether an employee or a guest, employees should back them up. If police request management or staff to file charges or testify in court, hotel policy should make it simple for the employee to do so. It is counterproductive to a hotel's security to hinder police business or make officers feel unwelcome. In fact, many 24-hour restaurants go out of their way to make on-duty police feel welcome—offering free coffee and discounted meals. This policy helps create a secure atmosphere at a very low cost. If criminals know a property is frequented by police, they will think twice before they burglarize it.

It is important to maintain all built-in security components. Doors that are supposed to be locked should be checked regularly and frequently. Fire escape doors must be kept closed. Guest-room sliding glass doors need to be secured. Employee entrances should be monitored. Anything related to building security must be kept in top condition. Breakages or malfunctions should be repaired immediately, since security devices are sometimes sabotaged for the very purpose of making a planned robbery easier. Hotel properties are by nature easy targets for burglars and muggers. New faces are an everyday occurrence, so thieves have an automatic protective cover. Proper security measures will thwart crime and give guests a feeling of comfort and protection.

Employee Theft

Billions of dollars are lost every year to employee theft. Sad to say, unscrupulous employees will steal from a property unless the property makes it difficult to do so. Sometimes, employee theft escalates to the point where it cripples a hotel's chances to make a profit. To prevent theft, employees must be given clear instructions on acceptable behavior. Without them, some may think that walking home with pockets full of guest-room amenities is no big deal. It's important that they know that this is considered stealing and that thieves will be prosecuted.

Perhaps a hotel will have a policy of letting employees take home discarded items instead of throwing them out. If so, it must be very clear what those items are. It's also important to control the area around trash disposal systems and dumpsters. Hotels that check such trash receptacles often find that usable items have been deliberately thrown out by employees who expect to collect them at shift's end.

There are several other simple measures a hotel or restaurant can take to curb employee theft. The easiest one is limiting the entrances and exits employees use. If all employees enter and leave the building through designated doors, they are less likely to walk out with company property. Standard operating procedures should be in place regarding who may sign for deliveries, pass keys, and storage area access. Another good precaution is tagging personal items brought onto the property by employees. Security should issue a multicopy pass that describes the personal item, including its color, model, and serial number. When the employee removes the item from the property, there will be a reliable record of ownership.

Employee parking areas should be located well away from the building with a well-lit path directly to the parking lot.

''Contamination'' is another problem that results from employee theft. Good employees who would never steal anything may watch other employees take things at will. The good employees often become contaminated by the actions of others and begin to steal things themselves.

A very important part in prevention of employee theft is setting an example from the general manager down the line. If members of upper management walk out the door with hotel property, watching employees will figure that they are stealing . . . and that this is normal practice. Rules that are written about ethics and honesty apply to all employees. Those at the top must lead by example.

Conclusion

Housekeeping is a complicated business. Staffing and training are two ongoing housekeeping functions. Establishing high standards for cleanliness is essential to the success of any property.

The many systems in a hospitality building are complex. Guests expect plumbing, heating, and all other creature comforts to work and work well. To monitor all the building's functions as well as control costs is a very important responsibility of the engineering and maintenance department.

This general overview of property management, was just that—general. Your curriculum may include one or more property management courses. Many students find these among their most interesting courses, since through them they explore the out-of-sight back areas of hotels. Some aspects of property management are becoming more and more automated, but overall, this area will continue to be labor intensive. Technology can and has, however, greatly improved the internal communications systems necessary for good property management. Managers in this area will continue to need both exceptional people skills and detailed logistical skills. Though many future housekeeping and property services executives begin their careers in hotels, opportunities are not limited to the lodging sector. All segments of hospitality, including restaurants, theme parks, casinos, and night clubs, require ongoing maintenance, cleaning, and inspection. There are also institutional opportunities in hospitals, correctional facilities, and supervised living communities.

Keywords

executive housekeeper   246
rooms report   247
codes of appearance   252
standard operating procedure   254
preventive maintenance   263
potable water   265

fire suppression   265
hard water   265
HVAC   268
heat-activated sprinkler system   269
chemical-type sprinkler   269

Core Concepts

demographics of the applicant pool   251
scheduling employees   252
key control   255

time card control   256
vendor relations   260

Discussion Questions

1. Describe some of the problems a hotel has in staffing the housekeeping department. What are some of the solutions?

2. When purchasing services and equipment from vendors, what are some major factors that should affect from whom you buy?

3. What are the most common areas of the physical plant for which the engineering and maintenance department is responsible, and why are these areas important to the success of the hotel?

4. Why should all departments in a hotel be involved in the safety and security of the people and property in a hotel?

5. In what ways can a hotel establish a policy that can be viewed as environmentally friendly?

6. Write a short (one page or less) procedure to be posted in a guest room regarding fire/emergency procedures. Describe the hotel/motel structure—number of rooms, stories, staircases, fire stairs, elevators, and so on—and specify whether there are interior hallways.

PART IV

Introduction to the Food and Beverage Industry

The food and beverage industry is fast-paced, challenging, rewarding, demanding, and a very large part of the hospitality industry. Just consider the following facts about the size and scope of the food service industry in the United States:

- The food service industry will reach sales of an estimated $275 billion in 1995.
- There are over 720,000 locations in the United States that might qualify as food service establishments.
- Most food service establishments in the United States are ''small businesses,'' whose average annual sales per unit are about $425,000.
- More than 8 million people are presently employed in the industry, and experts expect this number to go up to over 11 million by the year 2000.

With regard to the food service market—that is, all the people that visit or are expected to visit a food service outlet—whether it be table service or fast food, two important statistics are worth mentioning:

- Consumers spend almost 45 percent of every dollar they have available for food on meals and other food *away from home.*
- Almost 50 percent of all adults in the United States visit a food service establishment on any typical day.

Sales in the food service industry have been growing ever since they were first tracked on a national basis. Growth slowed down in times of economic hardship, of course; yet overall we have seen a consistent increase in revenues over the years. This is a reassuring fact if you are considering investing money in the food service industry or making it your career.

With regard to market demand for food service products, once again, it can be called very reassuring. Behavior patterns among consumers have been changing in favor of the industry in the last few years. More families will have dual incomes or will be single households, which leads to an increased demand for meals away from home because they can afford it or because they do not have the time to prepare meals at home. More women have entered and are still entering the full-time work force, which has already caused demand for food service products to go up. In short, more and more people are willing to spend more of their food dollars away from home.

And then we haven't even looked at the explosion that has occurred internationally. New markets are being opened every day (just think about the former Soviet Union, the rest of Eastern Europe, and Vietnam, to name a few). Worldwide, there is great interest in American culture, which, in turn, creates a demand for American food service products. In many foreign countries the demand is so "pent-up" that new food service outlets cannot be built fast enough to supply all of the demand. People in those new, foreign markets just cannot wait for new products to be introduced. Where do you think the biggest McDonald's outlets are in the world? In Moscow and Beijing.

There are negative aspects attached to all these positives. For instance, it has been determined that more than half of all newly established food service operations will go out of business within two years after opening.

Employee turnover, the rate at which employees in a particular job or operation are replaced, is still much higher in the food service industry than in other industries. It is not uncommon to see 100 percent turnover rate for a restaurant, meaning that every employee will have been replaced by another within a year. For certain positions that number might even be as high as 300 percent!

If you weigh all the positives and negatives, the food service industry is still extremely challenging, with enormous growth potential, and offers many opportunities for personal advancement. The industry needs thousands of managers every year and you might become one of those. Managing a food service establishment, whether it be a fast food franchise, a full-service restaurant, a microbrewery with a food service outlet, or a store selling specialty coffees, requires some unique skills, as the following chapters will show.

Obviously, food service managers must have technical skills. They have to be able to read, create, and understand financial reports, for instance, and possess the ability to react to the information those reports present to them. Also, they must have an understanding of production methods. Cooks, chefs, kitchen staff, and bartenders have to have the expertise to create the perfect chicken Parmesan or the best banana daiquiri in the world. A manager, though, must also have some knowledge of the ingredients, the contents, and the service methods involved, a knowledge he/she can convey to the customer and share with his/her employees.

Food service managers should also have people skills. Managing a restaurant means managing employees: understanding their needs and desires; dealing with their whims and peculiarities; listening to their concerns;

correcting their mistakes; accepting their suggestions; offering them a healthy, safe, and pleasant work environment; and helping them make the most of their jobs and their lives. Employees are the lifeblood of any restaurant. They cook the food, mix the drinks, clean the rest rooms and the kitchen, and serve the guests.

People skills also refer to dealing with customers and providing them with a comfortable, healthy dining experience. Ultimately, these skills are the ones that provide the food service operation with the revenue that makes it successful.

And then there are some particular personal skills that are needed to become a successful food service manager: determination, resourcefulness, patience, pride in oneself and the business, integrity, and leadership traits.

Not everyone has the personality or the skills needed for food service management. It is a demanding and, at times, peculiar industry. Not all of the skills necessary to become successful can be learned. Education can give you most of the technical skills you will need. Even some of the people skills can be acquired in general management and human resource classes. Work experience and internships can give you a feel for what it takes. Yet whether or not you have the personality of a food service manager is something you will find out only when you actually work in the industry. How do you really deal with a dissatisfied supplier, an angry regional vice president, a confused employee, or a happy customer?

The chapters in this section will present you with a picture of what it is like to *manage* a food service operation. Chapter 9, ''Food Service Management,'' looks at a food service operation as a system of interrelated elements. It argues that none of the elements of the system can be regarded independently. Safety and sanitation in a restaurant are just as important as the quality of preparation and production, the speediness and grace of service, or the satisfaction level of the employees. Only when all the elements work together smoothly will the restaurant function the way it should. This chapter emphasizes the human resource or people skills in particular. Included in the chapter is a brief discussion of bar management, which highlights some of the differences between selling food and selling alcoholic beverages.

Chapter 10, ''Food Preparation,'' discusses the back of the house. Although food service managers do not need to know all the details of how to prepare a menu item in most restaurants, they have to be aware of what it takes to produce the actual meal, with regard to the equipment required and the production methods involved. Ultimately, customers come for the food, and food is prepared in the kitchen.

You might be tomorrow's food service manager. Maybe you are destined to become president of a large fast-food chain; you might be fortunate enough to become the owner of multiple restaurants or franchises; maybe you will end up as a food and beverage director for a hotel. The following chapters will give you an impression of what food service management amounts to and will help you to find the answers to some of the maybes. As they say in the food service industry: Enjoy!

9 Food Service Management

Today's food service manager must possess many skills in order to fulfill the tremendous responsibilities inherent in food service management. Financial skills, human resources skills, planning and organization skills, and food safety skills have always been essential. Yet, as competition has increased, managers have realized that they must add marketing skills to their repertoire.

Traditionally, food service managers have been brought up through the ranks and simply did what their managers before them had done. However, as the world has changed, passed-down management techniques and strategies work less and less well. On-the-job experience is useful, and most professional management programs require work experience, but it is only through professional management training that students can expect to successfully manage food service operations in the future.

This chapter introduces the student to some of the responsibilities of food service management and the approach necessary to meet those responsibilities.

Outline

Introduction

Food is much more than fuel for the body. The social contexts in which food is eaten are part of what bonds a society together, whether in groups of family, friends, or strangers. We use the sharing of food as a metaphor to express welcome, friendship, familial love, and concern for the ill. We mark important occasions with special foods and celebrate with people via gifts of food. Holidays are identified with traditional feasts. Most occasions in our lives are experienced and perhaps enhanced with food.

The hospitality industry is, in many ways, like an extension of families. Hotels and restaurants house and feed people when they are away from home, as do hospitals, schools, and prisons. Special occasions are often celebrated at restaurants or at banquet facilities. It's hard to imagine baseball games without hot dogs, airline flights without meals or snacks, meetings without refreshments, or day trips without lunch stops.

It seems that just about everything we do incorporates food, and if we're not preparing the food at home, a food service operation is involved. A **food service operation** is an organization outside the home that prepares food for people, either for sale, as in a restaurant, or as part of a service, as in a hospital. Food service operations do the very same things we do at home to produce meals for our families.

In our homes, we decide what to serve for dinner, perhaps looking at some specific recipes. We then prepare a shopping list of all the items that we don't already have in the refrigerator or in the cupboard. We go to the grocery store and buy exactly what is needed to prepare the recipes we chose. Upon bringing the food home, we put it away so that it stays as fresh as possible until we are ready to start cooking. We then prepare the meal and serve it to our family. We finally clean up the mess and put away any leftovers. On a more institutional scale, this is roughly the model all food service operations follow. The stages of the process may have different names, yet the process is essentially the same.

Food Service Operations Model

MENU PLANNING
↓
PURCHASING
↓
RECEIVING
↓
STORING/INVENTORY
↓
PREPPING/COOKING
↓
SERVING
↓
CLEANING

The difference is, of course, volume. Food service operators do not plan and prepare meals for a family of four, but rather for a ''family'' of perhaps 100 or 1,000! Because of these high volumes, there is a lot more room for error, waste, illness, injury, and customer dissatisfaction. Thus, a food service manager's job is seldom one that involves wearing an apron and chef's tocque. Instead of (or in addition to) cooking skills, a manager needs a different set of skills—human resource management skills—so that he or she can direct employees to prepare and serve meals.

Competition

Food service is big business and has become so complex that it is less and less feasible for nonprofessionals to succeed using ''seat-of-the-pants'' methods. One in three restaurants fail in their first year, often because their creators naively believed they could succeed through optimism or by ''winging it.'' Professional training takes much of the guesswork out of food service management, and thus, much of the risk. Professional managers learn to look for and recognize trends. That requires reading trade journals, magazines, and newspapers, and generally keeping up-to-date, paying attention to what consumers say and do.

Food service industry profit margins are small. Success often depends on cutting out waste in all areas of operation. High **personnel turnover** (the rate at which an operation loses workers) can also be seen as a form of waste, since it is very costly and also results in lower service levels.

Competition in food service is increasing. Hospital food outlets, convenience stores, and grocery stores now compete with casual restaurants, fast-food restaurants, and cafeterias. On another front, long-term care and skilled-nursing facilities now use upgraded food-service departments to attract patients.

Competition requires that we meet the needs of our customers. As tastes change or the population changes, it is good business to change with them. It is easier to sell people what they want than to try to sell them something they don't want. In most cases, they can go elsewhere—and will.

Types of Food Service Operations

Food service operations are either commercial or institutional. **Commercial food service operations** seek to be profitable, and customers may directly pay for the food and service, as in restaurants. **Institutional food service operations** usually do not seek to make a profit and may not directly charge for food and service. An institutional food service operation may be part of some larger package—such as meals served to patients in hospitals or low-cost meals served in elementary and secondary schools.

Some institutions hire *food service contractors* to operate their in-house food services. These look like institutional or nonprofit food service operations, but are actually commercial because the contractors' goal is to make a profit.

The National Restaurant Association groups food service operations into three categories as Exhibit 9–1 shows.

Food Service Operation Classifications

Commercial or institutional food service operations may also be classified by their means of food preparation.

Conventional versus Convenience Food Service Operations.   A **conventional food service operation** prepares most menu items from scratch using raw ingredients, while a **convenience food service operation** uses mostly convenience (processed) foods to prepare its menu items. One isn't necessarily better than the other. The decision whether to use raw ingredients or convenience ingredients is based on budget, staff abilities and schedules, equipment availability, and customer preferences. Many food service operations' menus offer some combination of conventional items and convenience foods, so that it is often difficult to label an operation one or the other.

EXHIBIT 9–1   Categories of Food Service Operations

---

1. Commercial food service
   a. Eating places.
      (1) Restaurants, lunchrooms.
      (2) Limited-menu restaurants, refreshment places.
      (3) Commercial cafeterias.
      (4) Social caterers.
      (5) Ice-cream, frozen-custard stands.
      (6) Bars and taverns.
   b. Food contractors.
      (1) Manufacturing and industrial plants.
      (2) Commercial and office buildings.
      (3) Hospitals and nursing homes.
      (4) Colleges and universities.
      (5) Primary and secondary schools.
      (6) In-transit food service (airlines).
      (7) Recreation and sports centers.
   c. Lodging places.
      (1) Hotel restaurants.
      (2) Motor-hotel restaurants.
      (3) Motel restaurants.
   d. Other.
      (1) Retail-host restaurants, such as restaurants or delis in grocery stores or gas stations.
      (2) Recreation and sports.
      (3) Mobile caterers.
      (4) Vending and nonstore retailers.
2. Institutional food service (organizations that operate their own food service)
   a. Employee food service.
   b. Public and parochial elementary/secondary schools.
   c. Colleges and universities.
   d. Transportation.
   e. Hospitals.
   f. Nursing homes, homes for the aged, visually impaired, orphans, and the mentally and physically disabled.
   g. Clubs, sporting, and recreational camps.
   h. Community centers.
3. Military food service
   a. Officers and noncommissioned officers (NCO) clubs (''Open Mess'').
   b. Food service—military exchanges.
   c. Defense personnel.

Source: National Restaurant Association.

Commissary Food Service Operations.   **Commissary food service operations** may be commercial or institutional, and may or may not use convenience foods. Their distinguishing characteristic is that they prepare all meals in a central kitchen and then transport them to various serving sites. Some community school systems use a centralized kitchen to reduce the costs involved with individual kitchens and staffing.

Positions in Food Service

As you can surmise from Exhibit 9–1, given the scope of food service operations, there is an equivalent range of employment opportunity. For the most part, food service job titles vary from operation to operation, but the responsibilities and roles remain largely the same. Back-of-the-house positions usually fall into three groups: managerial, production, and service. Larger food service operations, which are often organized into subdepartments, generally employ a hierarchy of chefs and managers. More details on these types of positions are provided in Chapter 10, ''Food Preparation.'' Later in this chapter, we discuss the organizational structure of a typical bar/beverage outlet.

Food Service Systems Management

Managing a food service operation can be overwhelming. There are so many things that need to be done, seemingly simultaneously. Trying to manage such a complex, multiphase process intuitively is next to impossible. This is why the use of *models* and *systems management* approaches helps us better grasp the large picture and use the tools available. Imagine the difficulty of making a beautifully tailored suit without a pattern or preparing a scrumptuous torte without a recipe. In both cases we stand a much better chance of success if we consult a plan or model. Trying to manage a food-service operation without a systematic approach or model is equally difficult and generally results in far less than perfection.

A model of an airplane is made up of a lot of little parts that, when glued together according to the directions, look like the picture on the box. A dress pattern is also a model. We place the pattern pieces on fabric, cut them out, and sew them together according to the directions. The way parts work together to make a whole is called a *model*. We can make a model of the whole of food service and break it into its parts or components. This is a useful way to manage work and orchestrate performance so that one is effective and efficient.

Environment

Energy conservation, hazardous chemical disposal, and waste management are important to food service managers. How these agents are used and disposed of affects the health and safety of the staff and the health of the planet. Many companies are seeking ways to reduce excess waste *before* purchasing. Though we aren't likely to see purchasing agents carrying string bags and canvas totes, we are already seeing them weigh waste factors in the bidding process. If purchasing agents specify biodegradable packaging or choose packaging with less waste, their operations soon find they have less waste to dispose of. Biodegradable ''peanut'' packaging is one such spec that is gaining popularity.

Food Service Operations Model.   Now let us return to the food service operations model presented at the beginning of this chapter.

Food Service Operations Model

MENU PLANNING

↓

PURCHASING

↓

RECEIVING

↓

STORING/INVENTORY

↓

PREPPING/COOKING

↓

SERVING

↓

CLEANING

It's important to address each component in the food service operations model whether it is handled in-house or contracted out—otherwise we see only part of the picture. We know that some food service operations use convenience foods exclusively and do no preparation (''prep'') at all. That doesn't mean the costs and responsibilities go away. Instead, the food service operation pays for the convenience of having a manufacturer do the prep for it. Most people realize that an individual Burger King or Olive Garden does not develop its own menu. Nonetheless, the step in the model still takes place, though someone else performs it. The step is still important, since the menu affects all of the subsequent steps. (Chapter 10 will discuss more about menus, including types and cycles.)

Using the food service operations model, we can take an entire food service operation and break it into components to better examine what is working well and what is not. Then, when we've fitted it back together, we should find we're ready to produce and serve an improved food product to our customers.

Our ultimate goal in the food service industry is to satisfy our customers. This means, at the very least, they should not become ill or die from eating our food. It is not enough, however, that they simply survive the dining experience. Our customers must also be pleased with the service and the food. Food safety and sanitation must be built into and around the food service operations model, and need to be addressed first.

Sanitation

The 24-hour flu we've all suffered through at one time or another was more than likely a food-borne illness. We become more aware of a food-borne illness outbreak when it occurs after a family get-together or in an institution when everyone gets sick. Food-borne illness contracted at restaurants may go unreported because people often incorrectly assume that it's just a "touch of the flu," not realizing that everyone who ate that particular dish got the same unwelcome "touch." Children and the elderly can easily die from food-borne illnesses. For others, the symptoms range from extreme discomfort, to, in some cases, death.

Once word gets out in the community that a particular restaurant's food makes people sick, it is extremely difficult for it to ever regain consumer trust. (See Exhibit 9–2 showing headlines about *e coli* contamination.) In fact, restaurants often close after a publicized outbreak of food-borne illness. In health care institutions, outbreaks of food-borne illness are particularly dangerous because the patients may not be strong enough to recover from its effects. Aside from the obvious moral implications, avoiding food-borne illness is good business.

Fortunately, most food poisoning can be avoided. Most food-borne illnesses are caused by **bacteria,** which are microscopic one-celled plants. Like most plants, bacteria need food, moisture, and a comfortable environment to grow in. To ensure the production of safe food in our food service operations, our job is either to kill the bacteria or to make the environment inhospitable enough to severely retard their growth.

Bacteria are spread by carriers. A knife that was used to cut up raw chicken and then not washed and sanitized can spread bacteria to other foods. This is called **cross-contamination.** Insects or rodents that may have been walking

EXHIBIT 9–2

Incidents of E. coli 0157:H7 and salmonella contamination in restaurant-prepared foods have prompted heavy media coverage and stimulated tighter government regulation of potentially hazardous foods.

Chicken Linked to Millions of Cases of Food Poisoning

Food Poisoning: The New Epi...

Dangerous

FISH

Food Safety: A Growing Concern

Food-poisoning crisis at burger c... becomes PR disaster.

Mystery Illness Identified as E coli-caused

Meat Safety Comes Under Fire: Recent E. coli Outbreak Prompts Fears

Scientists Puzzled— Well-cooked meat may not be sole answer: E. coli shows up in salami.

Beef Gone Bad Kills Four

around in rotting garbage (or worse) can track bacteria into a kitchen. Bacteria can grow in standing water or be carried in the air. The most common carrier of bacteria, though, is the food service staff.

Since the manager in a food service operation is responsible for serving food that is safe to eat, he or she is also responsible for instructing the staff in safe food-handling procedures. A good manager conducts ongoing inspections to maintain the standards of sanitation required for the production of safe food and monitors the personal hygiene of all people involved in the handling of food.

Every state has its own state board of health. Written regulations are available and must, by law, be followed. State and local inspections are conducted by appropriate agencies. These agencies have the power to impose fines and to force compliance. All food service operators are responsible for knowing the health department regulations in their own cities and states. Adherence to the state regulations results in safe food. You'll learn more about sanitation in conjunction with food preparation in Chapter 10.

Safety

Food service operators are also required by law to provide a safe working environment for their employees. Food service is an inherently dangerous occupation, but most accidents can be avoided if all staff are trained in and follow the rules of safety. The federal government enacted the Occupational Safety and Health Act **(OSHA)** to ensure employment ''free from recognized hazards'' to all employees. Every work environment (not just food service operations) must adhere to OSHA regulations. OSHA can impose fines and/or jail sentences for failure to comply. It should be noted that although managers can make safety training and compliance a priority, no one person can guarantee a safe shop. This requires conscientious and voluntary caution on the part of employees.

A conscious practice of safety rules benefits a food service operation in several ways:

- By reducing time and money loss.
- By reducing breakage (china, glassware, equipment).
- By reducing staff stress and frustration.
- By producing a safer and more pleasant work environment.

Safety and sanitation are closely related. Food-borne illness and accidents are both costly and unfortunate, especially since both can be avoided.

Eye on the Issues

Ethics

The law requires that managers treat employees fairly and equally, avoiding discrimination on the basis of race, sex, national origin, age, and religion. However, professional management goes beyond the bottom-line moral requirement of the law; it requires managers to behave with integrity in all their business dealings. Personal integrity, or the lack of it, is the result of all the decisions a manager makes over the years.

Personal integrity is essential for employees engaged in purchasing, receiving, and issuing, areas where an unscrupulous person can permanently damage an organization's bottom line through acceptance of bribes, kickbacks, or other ''incentives.''

Food service managers also face decisions on whether to serve foods that may have been irradiated, come from animals that have been fed growth hormones, or contain controversial food additives. (Popular as these issues are, the Food Marketing Institute indicates that food-borne illness, described earlier in this chapter, constitutes the greatest danger to the public.)

Hazard Analysis

At each point in the food service operations model, safety and sanitation rules and checks must be incorporated so that meals are not only tasty, attractive, nutritious, and appreciated, but also safe to eat. This is accomplished by identifying *critical control points* as the food flows through the components of the model. Critical control points are established at any place along the food flow where something could go wrong that could result in food poisoning or illness. The **HACCP** (hazard analysis critical control point) process overlays and becomes part of the food service operations model. HACCP flowcharts can be seen as quality assurance tools that help assure the delivery of safe food in the best condition possible.

Hazard analysis is accomplished by constructing flowcharts for specific recipes that have the potential to become hazardous. While all foods *can* become hazardous, some are more hazardous than others. Dry cereal can become contaminated with bacteria from some other source but ordinarily would not be considered a hazardous food. Due to their susceptibility to spoilage and/or contagion, high-protein foods such as meat, poultry, fish, eggs, and dairy foods are especially hazardous.

Ideally, a manager will construct an HACCP flowchart for any recipe that contains one or more hazardous ingredients. The flowchart would begin at the receiving point (the third component of the food service operations model). Critical control points would be checked during the receiving function, and then the flowchart would continue on through each step of the model, identifying critical control points in storage, prepping, cooking, and serving. Managers also use HACCP flowcharts when developing step-by-step procedures for employees in each functional area.

Menu Planning

Menu planning is the first component of the food service operations model and is the basis of the entire food service operation. The menu is often the deciding factor in the consumer's restaurant selection. How often have you made lunch or dinner plans based on whether you fancy a Chinese, Mexican, Italian, or otherwise ''American'' menu? If you lived in a town with just one restaurant, the menu wouldn't make much difference. Today, however, that's seldom the case; we are used to many choices. Even in the smallest communities, there are several options. If we don't like the options, most of us can drive to where there are more desirable choices. In today's competitive market, the menu matters. We must offer our customers what they want, at a price they are willing to pay, and in a style that suits them. Otherwise, they will go elsewhere.

Many nonprofessional would-be restaurateurs open restaurants with little thought as to whom they will be serving. The menus they write may match only their own tastes, or may be very generic with the idea of meeting everyone's needs. Writing a menu that competes head-on with other restaurants is rarely a good idea unless there is a surplus of customers. To succeed with a copycat menu, a food service operation would have to differentiate itself significantly from its competitors (perhaps by service or ambience) or offer the same products more cheaply (perhaps by reducing its cost per item).

As food service operators, we must ask ourselves: Whom do we wish to serve? What do they want? Is anyone else already doing this? Can we really compete? At the same time we must identify our own resources and what we are capable of doing. Dissatisfied customers in restaurants not only don't come back, they tell all their friends for years afterwards of their dissatisfaction.

People who are institutionalized (e.g., in hospitals, schools, prisons) may have little or no control over their food choices, but that does not alter the institution's responsibility to provide healthy, nutritious food. Captive audiences (such as long-term patients or prisoners) crave more than adequate nutrition. They want food that is not only appealing but sufficiently varied. Imagine the reaction if you served baked chicken, Waldorf salad, broccoli, and bread pudding every day! Though tasty and nutritious, the monotony would soon cause problems. People in institutions who are dissatisfied with the food may be vocal and disruptive, may choose to go to other institutions, or in the case of prisoners, may hunger strike or riot. The type of clientele will influence the form the menu takes and how often it will be repeated.

Nearly every aspect of the operation of a food service business depends on the menu. Purchasing, production, sales, cost accounting, labor management, kitchen layout, and equipment selection are all based on the menu. The menu must be constructed to build sales by offering attractive choices to the customer, while at the same time promoting efficiency and productivity in the kitchen. Prices must be kept in line with the ability and willingness of customers to pay.

Once we determine what our customers want, we can develop menus by keeping the following questions in mind:

- Is the menu nutritionally adequate?
- Are the foods seasonal, available, and within price range?
- Are there contrasts in color, texture, flavor, consistency, shape or form, type of preparation, and temperature?
- Can the foods be prepared with the personnel and equipment available?
- Are the workloads balanced for personnel and equipment?
- Is any one food item or flavor repeated too frequently during the menu period?
- Are the meals attractive and suitably garnished?
- Do the combinations make a pleasing whole and will they be acceptable to the customer?

The development of a food service operation's menu is so important that it should be done before basic operating activities are addressed. In most cases, a "final" menu will never be written. Constant updating and revision are necessary if a menu is to respond to changing customer demands. Menus should be dynamic marketing tools.

Exhibit 9–3

Menu planning and restaurant theme go hand-in-hand. The growth of ethnic cuisine reflects changing tastes in society.

Courtesy: Busarakamwongs Intl., Inc., Phoenix, Arizona.

Menu Design.   The design, layout, and physical condition of a menu make a statement about management's standards and project an image. This image should complement the price structure. For instance, a menu dominated by higher priced items should incorporate an upscale design—not the brightly colored, thickly laminated plastic style popular for coffee shops.

Classes in food and beverage management will introduce design options and many menu-pricing strategies. The method, or combination of methods, depends on a chain's (or individual outlet's) objectives. The outlet's image and the desires of its target markets must also be factored in.

The menu, as the basis of the entire operation, is determined by considering the target market, the budget, the staff, the facilities, the competition, the availability of ingredients, equipment, and so on. Quality and quantity standards are set for (and by) the menu. Controls are then designed to ensure that the prepared items and the service system are consistent with the standards of the menu.

A menu item that reads, "a sizzling 8-oz. choice cut of beef surrounded with colorful, crisp-cooked fresh baby vegetables ☛$14.95," establishes standards for *quantity* in terms of beef size, *quality* in terms of beef grade, *quality* of cooking in terms of the vegetables, *quantity* in terms of the size and type of vegetables, and *quality* in service because the beef is served "sizzling." The description on the menu implies a level of quality. A cold 7-oz. choice-cut of beef with a scoop of olive-green overcooked canned beans would not meet the standards the consumer would expect from reading the menu.

Standardized Recipes.   A **standardized recipe** is a set of instructions describing the way an establishment prepares a particular dish. A recipe is a formula. Measured ingredients are combined in a specific procedure to give predetermined results of a known quality and quantity.

A recipe is a written communication tool, passing information from the food service manager to production personnel. A recipe is also a cost control tool. Since the ingredients and amounts of each ingredient will be the same each time the recipe is used, raw food costs can be determined from a standard recipe. Recipes help control waste by preventing overpurchasing or overproducing. Inventories can be maintained at adequate levels and storage space kept at a minimum.

By using standardized recipes, we can improve quality and quantity assurance for the foods we produce. The final product should be the same quality each time the item is prepared. A McDonald's Big Mac is an outstanding example of quality and quantity assurance. Every food service operation, regardless of its menu's pedigree, should aspire to giving its customers a consistent product that satisfies their needs.

Eye on the Issues

International

Food service operations have traditionally included employees from many nationalities and cultures, but for many years, chef and kitchen management positions around the world were dominated by males. In America this trend has shifted somewhat, allowing competent women to practice leadership, too. On an international scope, it's important for managers to understand and work with cultural differences in the perception of appropriate gender roles. The "old world" may conflict with the "new world" when employees from different national backgrounds (or generations) are assigned together without introduction or human resource groundwork.

Food service operators must also be aware of the wide variance in international food-production standards. Produce, in particular, from other countries may be grown or shipped using chemicals that have been banned in the United States.

Labor hours, too, can be reduced with standardized recipes. Since recipes are written with clear instructions, it is not necessary to review them with the kitchen staff each time they appear on the menu. Because standardized recipes are written with precise measurements and sequencing, they eliminate time lost to backtracking and double-checking vague directions. The time spent on purchasing procedures can also be reduced. As a further bonus, kitchens that use standardized recipes find that the training curve for new production employees is smoother and faster. Cooks know exactly what to do and how to do it through clear instructions.

Recipes must be thoroughly tested to ensure the desired outcome and then written in a predetermined consistent format. The use of good standardized recipes takes the guesswork out of cooking and results in a consistent product. You'll read more about standardization in Chapter 10.

Quality Assurance.   Today's consumer is more sophisticated than ever before and demands a consistent, high-quality product, delivered efficiently and pleasantly. The production and delivery of this high-quality, consistent product, produced at a price acceptable to management and the consumer, is only possible when systematic controls are in place.

Management's job is to put the controls in place and then monitor them. A *control* is a checkpoint in a process designed to prevent mistakes or loss from occurring. We place these checks at critical control points where problems could arise. Controls are a form of preventive supervision and can reduce waste and mistakes when used properly. The hazard analysis critical control point (HACCP) flowcharting discussed earlier identifies critical control points relating specifically to food safety. Other control systems have been designed for cost, quality, waste, or other potential problems.

Purchasing

Purchasing is the second component of the food service operations model. The first component, menu planning, dictates the firm's purchasing requirements. Once the requirements have been determined, it becomes the goal of purchasing to obtain the right quality and right quantity at the right time and price from the right source.

Quality is based on the firm's target market's needs and may be defined in terms of government grades, packer's grades, brand names, trade names, and endorsements. Chemical or physical specifications and performance standards may be used to establish a product's quality. Once a standard of identity has been developed for a specific food item, that item must contain only the ingredients specified in the standard.

Quantity relates to the rate of usage and the product's intended use. This also affects the purchaser's selection of the right source. Such a selection involves research; the purchaser narrows down potential suppliers after methodically and objectively evaluating them based on service levels, financial stability, need anticipation, stock levels, credit terms, delivery schedules, and the range of products offered. Savvy purchasers also turn to their suppliers as excellent sources of ideas and product usage tips.

Purchasing, receiving, storing, and issuing are related operating activities where much waste and loss can occur. The manager must first know exactly what he or she needs to buy to prepare the menu items. **Standard purchase specifications** are *control tools* that communicate the firms' needs to potential suppliers. They are precisely written descriptions of the quality desired in a product. It is impossible for a purchasing agent to make valid price comparisons if vendors have not been given definitive specifications. Imagine the variety of products that might turn up on a delivery truck if all that had been specified was "five pounds of beef."

EXHIBIT 9–4   **HACCP Receiving Process**

Critical Control	*Hazard*	*Standards*	*Corrective Action if Standard Not Met*
Receiving beef	Contamination and spoilage	Accept beef at 45° F (7.2° C) or lower; verify with thermometer	Reject delivery
		Packaging intact	Reject delivery
		No off odor or stickiness, etc.	Reject delivery
Receiving vegetables	Contamination and spoilage	Packaging intact	Reject delivery
		No cross-contamination from other foods on the truck	Reject delivery
		No signs of insect or rodent activity	Reject delivery

Source: Reprinted with permission from *Applied Foodservice Sanitation: A Certification Coursebook, 4th ed.* Copyright 1992 by The Educational Foundation of the National Restaurant Association.

Receiving

The **purchase order** is another management control tool. It communicates to the supplier exactly what the order is to contain and when it is to be delivered. It also enables the kitchen receiving agent to check incoming orders for accuracy in content and price. Receiving is an extremely important activity because it is the point at which ownership is transferred from the supplier to the food service firm. If poor quality goods are accepted, it will be difficult to produce a high-quality product from them.

The receiving component of the food service operations model is where the food first enters the food service outlet. This is a critical control point. The person checking in the order, sensitized to the need to inspect and protect hazardous foods, should consult HACCP flowcharts for each incoming order. Exhibit 9–4 shows the details involved in the receiving function of the HACCP flowchart for beef stew.

It is at the receiving critical control point that delivered food products must be accepted, adjusted, or rejected. Decisions are made on the basis of the standards for receiving particular food types. The specific recipe is not important at the receiving checkpoint. The standards for receiving beef, cheese, eggs, vegetables, or any food do not vary from recipe to recipe.

For example, the receiving standards for fresh beef are always the same. The beef must arrive with a temperature of 45 degrees or lower, the packaging must be intact, and there can be no ''off'' odor or stickiness. If any of these standards are not met, the delivery must be rejected because the meat is very

Exhibit 9–5

Before the kitchen receiving staff sign the invoice, they verify quantity, quality, and price of products.

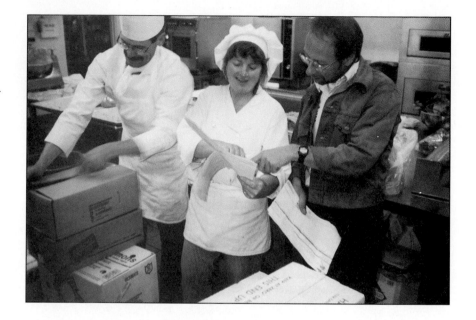

likely contaminated or alive with an unacceptable number of potentially dangerous bacteria.

Logically, there are different receiving standards for different types of foods. We check each item delivered to make sure that the particular receiving standard is met. We cannot hope to produce high-quality and safe meals if we begin with contaminated or questionable ingredients.

Storing/Inventory

Storage is designed to maintain product quality while minimizing losses due to pilferage, theft, and spoilage. It is important to remember that food products rarely improve in quality while in storage. Product spoilage and contamination will be minimized if proper sanitation procedures are adhered to in the storage areas. Theft and pilferage are controllable if the firm has a well-thought-out security system.

There are storage standards for each food type just as there are receiving standards for each food type. Recipes containing potentially hazardous foods have HACCP flowcharts. Exhibit 9–7 is an example of the storage HACCP flowchart for beef stew.

You will notice, in the beef stew example, that raw beef must be stored at a temperature of 45 degrees or below. Keeping food at proper temperatures throughout the entire flow through the food service model is vitally important. Bacteria grow rapidly in the **temperature danger zone,** the temperature range between 45 and 140 degrees. Thus, we keep hot food hot and cold food cold.

EXHIBIT 9–6

Product storage requires adherence to a long list of standards. For example, rotation of goods ensures freshness, dripping meats are always stored in a low place, and costly items are often locked away.

EXHIBIT 9–7   **HACCP Storage Process**

Critical Control	Hazard	Standards	Corrective Action if Standard Not Met
Storing raw beef	Cross-contamination of other foods	Store on lower shelf	Move to lower shelf away from other foods
		Label, date, and use FIFO rotation	Use first; discard if maximum time is exceeded or suspected
	Bacterial growth and spoilage	Beef temperature must remain below 45° F (7.2° C)	Discard if time and temperature abused
Storing vegetables	Cross-contamination from raw potentially hazardous foods	Label, date, and use FIFO rotation	Discard product held past rotation date
		Keep above raw potentially hazardous foods	Discard contaminated, damaged, or spoiled products

Source: Reprinted with permission from *Applied Foodservice Sanitation: A Certification Coursebook, 4th ed.* Copyright 1992 by The Educational Foundation of the National Restaurant Association.

Any time a potentially hazardous food is in the temperature danger zone, the risk of a food-borne illness increases.

Inventory.   Systems of inventory are developed to assure that appropriate ingredients are available when needed. A *physical inventory* is an actual count of what is in the storage areas, which include refrigerators, freezers, and dry storage. The inventory is generally used to determine the dollar value of food in storage. It is also a component of the *food cost percentage* equation, which is the cost of all the food used to prepare the menu items divided by the total sales of the menu items.

Issuing.   Issuing must be designed so that only authorized personnel may obtain food and beverage products from storage areas. Regulation is essential because the ownership or control of products is transferred from the storage to the production departments. Documentation is the key to controlling the issuing operating activity.

An issuing system that is under control will serve to reduce product waste, and will force production personnel to plan ahead. The system minimizes unauthorized access to storage areas. Obviously, if the system is to work, storage areas must be locked.

Storage area security is critical. If the firm and its employees view food and beverage products as money, the importance of strict product security becomes apparent. These assets must be protected at all times if the cost

control system is to remain viable. All the time spent in setting standards will have been wasted if the firm doesn't emphasize internal security.

No security system can work without key and lock control. Keys must only be issued to authorized personnel who need them to perform the responsibilities of their jobs. The number of master keys in circulation should be severely restricted. Locks should be changed if a key is lost or stolen or if an authorized key person leaves employment. It makes no sense to lock all storage areas and then freely permit anyone to use the keys to gain access.

For a firm to be competitive, it must design and use control systems for its purchasing, receiving, storing, and issuing areas. It is management's responsibility to train the staff in standardized procedures to maintain the integrity and security of these areas. Controls work only if they are used, so management must monitor use.

Prepping/Cooking

Food service directors, managers, supervisors, chefs, and workers produce meals under restrictions of time, money, facilities, equipment, and staff. Planning is essential to be able to get the work done on time and within budget. Such plans are based on an accurate forecast of the number of meals to be served; they consider factors such as employee workloads and equipment usage. Work schedules, cleaning schedules, and production schedules help employees work more efficiently.

Managers and workers must be aware of the principles of ***motion economy*** and work simplification to avoid wasting time and human energy. Motion economy is the same principle used by royalty and parade float beauty queens, for instance, to avoid tiring out the hand and arm with which they wave to admirers. When a small motion accomplishes the same function as a larger one but "costs" less in terms of exertion, it is usually preferred, especially when it must be repeated many times per shift.

Eye on the Issues

Technology

Many food service operations have automated their purchasing, inventory, sales, and human resources systems. Using bar codes in the purchasing and inventory department is an example of how technology can make tracking of foods faster and more efficient. It is important for managers to be current with available technologies, equipment, or methods that might be cost effective. The development of cash registers that use picture keys for items (such as milkshakes, sodas, orange juice) has been largely in response to illiteracy and innumeracy. Managers might want to consider whether such technology discourages employees from pursuing the literacies that would help them advance beyond their present competencies or whether the benefits to the company outweigh the disservice they may do to their employees.

EXHIBIT 9–9

There is an art and science to commercial food preparation. A chef has an eye for presentation—color and flavor combinations. He or she must also be cost-conscious and a master of time management so that all the details of a meal come together at once.

    Work simplification studies tasks and operations, or a group of operations, to determine the most efficient methods of performance. Operations are analyzed to reduce work time and to eliminate unnecessary aspects. Activities may also be analyzed to improve the quality of the product, and to help develop more skill in performing the task, so that the activity may be made more pleasurable, thus reducing stress. Motion economy considerations may be part of work simplification.

    In a food service operation, managers don't usually cook, but rather make sure that the cooks are able to do their jobs. The manager must provide the cooks and food service workers with good recipes, the necessary ingredients, supplies and equipment, and also the time and training to be able to excel.

    The prepping/cooking component of the food service model may have many critical control points when recipes with hazardous foods are being produced. The HACCP flowchart for this component is broken into two parts—the prepping and cooking functions—in order to carefully document all critical control points. The HACCP flowcharts for beef stew, shown in Exhibits 9–10 and 9–11, clearly identify hazards surrounding these functions.

    Since food is being handled during the prepping stage, it is essential that food service workers wash their hands often and have a very clear understanding of cross-contamination. Fortunately, heat is applied in the cooking stage and can kill many bacteria if proper temperatures are maintained for a long enough time.

Equipment.   Modern food service equipment allows the kitchen staff to be more efficient and productive. Food service equipment is, as mentioned earlier,

EXHIBIT 9–10   HACCP Preparation Process

Critical Control	Hazard	Standards	Corrective Action if Standard Not Met
Trimming and cubing beef	Contamination, cross-contamination, and bacteria increase	Wash hands	Wash hands
		Clean and sanitize utensils	Wash, rinse, and sanitize utensils and cutting board
		Pull and cube one roast at a time, then refrigerate	Return excess amount to refrigerator
Washing and cutting vegetables	Contamination and cross-contamination	Wash hands	Wash hands
		Use clean and sanitized cutting board, knives, utensils	Wash, rinse, and sanitize utensils and cutting board
		Wash vegetables in clean and sanitized vegetable sink	Clean and sanitize vegetable sink before washing vegetables

Source: Reprinted with permission from *Applied Foodservice Sanitation: A Certification Coursebook, 4th ed.* Copyright 1992 by The Educational Foundation of the National Restaurant Association.

EXHIBIT 9–11   HACCP Cooking Process

Critical Control	Hazard	Standards	Corrective Action if Standard Not Met
Cooking stew	Bacterial survival	Cook **all** ingredients to minimum internal temperature of 165° F (73.9° C)	Continue cooking to 165° F (73.9° C)
		Verify final temperature with a thermometer	Continue cooking to 165° F (73.9° C)
	Physical contamination during cooking	Keep covered; stir often	Cover
	Contamination by herbs and spices	Add spices early in cooking procedure	Continue cooking at least ½ hour after spices are added
		Measure all spices, flavor enhancers, and additives, and read labels carefully	
	Contamination of utensils	Use clean and sanitized utensils	Wash, rinse, and sanitize all utensils before use
	Contamination from cook's hands or mouth	Use proper tasting procedures	Discard product

Source: Reprinted with permission from *Applied Foodservice Sanitation: A Certification Coursebook, 4th ed.* Copyright 1992 by The Educational Foundation of the National Restaurant Association.

EXHIBIT 9–12

*Training is essential
to ensure safe
operation of
dangerous kitchen
equipment.*

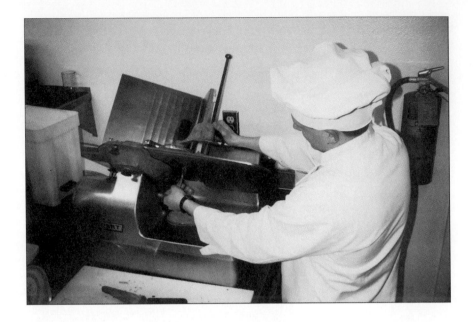

extremely dangerous, which makes it essential that employees be properly instructed in its use. No one should ever attempt to use a piece of equipment until he or she is thoroughly familiar with its operation and all its features. It is not safe to assume that an employee knows how to operate a particular piece of equipment, even if similar equipment is available in most homes. A commercial mixer (even a small one) is more powerful than a similar home model, and therefore more dangerous.

The equipment must be properly maintained. All equipment comes with manufacturers' maintenance and cleaning manuals. If the manuals are not on file in the food service operation, replacement manuals may be obtained from the manufacturer. The manufacturer knows best how its products should be cared for, and wise managers see that their kitchens' equipment is maintained according to manufacturer's instructions.

The production staff depends on the equipment to be in good working order to meet the demands of the particular job. Staff should be trained to use equipment properly and to notice when it is malfunctioning. For example, continuing use of a slicer that is making a metal-scraping-on-metal noise can ruin the blade. Any problems with the equipment must be reported to the supervisor or manager immediately, and arrangements to have the equipment fixed should be made as soon as possible.

Dirty equipment can contaminate food, may not run as efficiently as it should, does not inspire respect or encourage staff to take care of the piece of equipment, and may result in a citation or fine from an inspection agency. For all these reasons, staff should be trained to clean the equipment after each use. (Some larger jobs, such as cleaning ovens or refrigerators, can be performed on regular schedules.) Managers should systematically monitor the cleanliness of the kitchen and equipment.

Energy Conservation.   Energy conservation should be a way of life in a food service kitchen. Production should be planned so that equipment that uses a lot of energy is not on for long periods when not in use. Freezer and refrigerator lights should be turned on only when necessary, and the doors should be kept closed.

Machines are intended to be labor-saving devices. The usefulness of specialized processing equipment often depends on the volume of food they handle. It takes less time for a cook to slice one onion with a knife than to set up, use, clean, and sanitize a food slicer. Production may be planned, however, so that the cook can slice the one onion on the mechanical slicer when other slicing activities are taking place. Good manual skills remain important because equipment does not take the place of all hand work.

Serving

Restaurants, hotels, and institutions choose a type and style of service that meet the needs and desires of their clientele. Service personnel are performing a direct sales function by talking to clients and encouraging them to buy and/ or consume food. Good food, attractively displayed, is the key to merchandising and salespersonship. The effort put forth in producing good food can be lost if good merchandising techniques are not used. Merchandising should tempt people to buy and eat more menu items.

The overall responsibility for good merchandising belongs with the manager, as does the production of quality food. Some managers choose to become very involved with kitchen activities, but the kitchen is only half the food service operation. Managers need to evaluate the front of the house by experiencing the service regularly and conducting inconspicuous inspections.

It is management's responsibility to find and hire people who can be trained to become good servers. The CEO of Outback Steakhouses says, ''I don't think you can train for personality. We look for people who have outgoing personalities.'' (Outback then provides them with a formal training program.) Other desirable traits for successful servers are that they:

- Genuinely enjoy working with and for other people.
- Have high energy levels and enjoy a fast pace.
- View their job primarily as a sales position.
- Are flexible and can adapt to new demands and experiences.
- Can allow customers to be right (even if they aren't).

Once servers are hired, they must be trained. Training is essential. Managers must never assume that without training employees can somehow know what is expected of them. Front-line management is supervisory in nature.

EXHIBIT 9–13   **HACCP Holding Process**

Critical Control	Hazard	Standards	Corrective Action if Standard Not Met
Hot holding and serving	Contamination, bacterial growth	Use clean and sanitary equipment to transfer and hold product	Wash, rinse, and sanitize equipment before transferring food product to it
		Hold stew above 140° F (60° C) in preheated holding unit; stir to maintain even temperature	Return to stove and reheat to 165° F (73.9° C)
		Keep covered	Cover
		Clean and sanitize serving equipment and utensils	Wash, rinse, and sanitize serving utensils and equipment

Source: Reprinted with permission from *Applied Foodservice Sanitation: A Certification Coursebook, 4th ed.* Copyright 1992 by The Educational Foundation of the National Restaurant Association.

Since it is difficult to supervise a dining room from a secluded back office, managers must make it a practice to be out ''on the floor'' with their employees, making sure the atmosphere is conducive to excelling, and seeing firsthand that they have the tools, equipment, training, and support they need to do their jobs.

Since word of mouth can make or break a restaurant, it's important that all customers leave the restaurant happy and satisfied. Should complaints occur, they must be handled appropriately and immediately to defuse and appease the customer.

As in the other components of the food service operations model, there can be critical control points in the serving function. Exhibit 9–13 is the HACCP flowchart example for serving beef stew. It's important that servers, like kitchen staff, follow sanitation guidelines. Servers with unwashed hands who garnish plates or fill bread baskets could contaminate food and make customers sick. Servers with contagious diseases could breathe or sneeze germs onto food or tableware. This is not only unhealthy; it is unappealing.

Cleaning

Cleaning is the final component of the food service operations model. To **clean** is to physically remove soil and food. To **sanitize** is to reduce the number of microorganisms, such as bacteria, to safe levels. We cannot sanitize unless we also clean. In a food service operation, all food-contact surfaces must be

EXHIBIT 9–14

Although they begin in entry-level positions, dishwashers are essential to an operation's success. These people have been known to move on to dominant positions in the hospitality industry.

cleaned, then sanitized. (There's a further step, not often found in food service kitchens: sterilization. To **sterilize** is to remove all living microorganisms. Hospitals, for instance, sterilize operating room equipment.) An unclean food service operation can be assumed to be unsanitary. A clean food service operation can, however, still be unsanitary.

As you'd expect, food service outlets need to be both clean and sanitary. Professional managers identify the cleaning needs of the facility, determine the appropriate cleaning procedure, and then develop cleaning schedules that assign cleaning tasks to staff fairly. They then train employees to do the cleaning tasks in the prescribed manner and faithfully monitor the entire process to assure that the cleaning is being done when and how it is supposed to be done.

Each food service worker must be trained and encouraged to keep a neat and clean work area. Food service operations should be prepared for health department inspections at any moment—not because they are afraid of being caught, but rather because most people prefer working in a clean facility and like to take pride in their work and workstations.

EXHIBIT 9–15

Although potentially highly profitable, operating a bar also involves taking risks and assuming legal responsibilities.

Photo by James L. Morgan, 85283.

Beverage Operation Management

The preceding pages have discussed some of the prominent factors to consider in running a successful food service operation. Obviously, many similarities exist between managing a food service operation and managing a bar or beverage operation. Products are sold to customers who demand quality, by employees who need to be trained and managed, and who would like to work in a clean and safe environment. In that sense, a bar is not much different from a restaurant.

The purpose of this section, though, is not to dwell on the similarities, but to discuss the differences that exist between running an operation that serves alcoholic beverages and a food service operation, using the perspective of a bar manager. Several factors make the operation of bars and restaurants different:

- Issues surrounding alcohol.
- Purchasing.
- The increased risk of internal theft.
- The higher profitability of beverage operations.

Issues Surrounding Alcohol

Selling alcohol has both its positive and its negative sides. On the positive side, the alcoholic beverage industry is a great source of revenue for the government through taxes levied on alcoholic beverages. Moreover, alcohol is a profitable item for bars and restaurants. On the negative side, the abuse and misuse of alcohol cause many problems in our society.

Alcohol is an integral part of many of the celebrations and events of our culture. The new year is customarily welcomed with a glass of champagne or sparkling wine, and weddings are frequently celebrated with festive alcoholic beverages. Wine is part of the mass ceremony in Roman Catholic (and other) churches. Sporting events, such as football or baseball, are often enjoyed with a cup of beer in hand, whether the fan watches from stadium seats or the living room sofa. It is common practice for many to enjoy a glass of wine with dinner and a cordial or liqueur afterwards.

Since alcohol is consumed by such a broad cross-section of our society, it's perhaps not surprising that it has become our society's most abused drug. Unfortunately, some people cannot control their consumption of alcohol, and as a result, become dependent and/or dangerous after drinking it. The abuse of alcohol is a contributory factor to many of the problems of our society, including drunk driving. In fact, the majority of automobile deaths among American teenagers are alcohol-related. Because of its potential for abuse, alcohol is closely regulated.

Legal Factors

Regulations governing the beverage industry fall into three categories: federal, state, and local. The federal government controls the import of alcohol from foreign sources, and controls the production, labeling, packaging, and distribution of alcoholic beverages among states. State governments regulate the distribution and taxation of alcohol within their borders. This may include such things as the location of beverage operations, lawful times of operation, who may manage a bar, to whom alcohol may be sold, and whether alcohol may be consumed on the premises of an establishment or must be taken elsewhere.

Most states grant certain powers called *local option laws* to communities and counties. These laws allow local governments to control the sale of alcohol within their jurisdictions. Towns, cities, and counties may pass regulations that are even stricter than state laws, or which charge additional taxes. In fact, local governments may choose to ban the sale of alcoholic beverages altogether.

Operations that sell alcoholic beverages are some of the most heavily regulated businesses in the country, for two different reasons: (1) to protect the revenue source for the government and (2) to protect people from themselves.

Another law-related factor of great concern to bar operators is legal liability, which is discussed in greater detail in Chapter 13, "Hospitality Law." Legal liability impacts operating expenses through the high cost of liability insurance and through the potential for lawsuits involving sales to minors, sales by minors, and barroom liability.

Purchasing

The procedures for purchasing alcoholic beverages are different from those for purchasing anything else for a hospitality operation because of government control. While the buyer of general goods (such as olives or napkins) may buy from virtually anybody, beverage buyers must buy where states direct. States generally fall into two categories with regard to how they regulate alcohol purchases.

The majority of states (32) are "open" or "license" states. In these states, alcohol for bars and restaurants may be purchased only from licensed distributors who are granted rights to exclusive territories in which to sell their products. Thus, one company, United Distributors, may sell brands X and Y, while a second, Amalgamated Distributors, may sell only brands A and B. If a bar or restaurant wishes to purchase brand X, it must deal with United; if it wants brand B, it must deal with Amalgamated. If neither distributor carries a brand, the bar or restaurant will not be able to purchase it.

In a "control" or "monopoly" state, the state becomes the distributor and controls the distribution of alcohol to both food and beverage service operations and stores.

Increased Risk of Internal Theft

There are several factors that increase risk of theft in a bar operation, as compared to a restaurant. The main factors are the reduced number of people in the customer/employee transaction cycle, the intoxicating effect of alcohol on customers, the lack of tight inventory controls, and the different portion sizes served in most bars.

Opportunity: The Customer/Employee Transaction Cycle. Servers in bars have more opportunities to steal from their employers and their customers than do servers in a restaurant. To understand why, consider the following transaction cycles: In a restaurant, the server takes an order, delivers it to the kitchen where the cook prepares the food, which, once completed, is delivered to the guest by a server who may or may not be the one who took the order. Once the guest is finished eating, he or she generally pays a cashier. The customer/employee transaction may be handled by as many as four people, which greatly reduces the chance for theft.

This differs greatly from the customer/employee transaction cycle in a bar. The bartender is in charge of all aspects of the transaction: he or she takes

EXHIBIT 9–16

The bar from an employee's perspective.

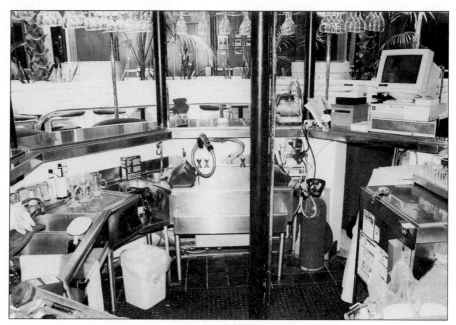

Courtesy: Pavilion Mesa Hilton, Mesa, Arizona. Photo by James L. Morgan, 85283.

the order, prepares the drink, serves the drink, and collects the money. Since all the segments of the cycle center on only one person, the chance for theft increases. Even if the guest is sitting at a table, rather than at the bar, only one more person (the server) is added to the transaction cycle, slightly reducing the opportunity for theft. The small number of people participating in the cycle increases the opportunity for theft, either from the bar or the customer, or both.

Opportunity: The Intoxicating Effects of Alcohol.   People, as they drink, become less aware of what is going on or what they are drinking, opening the door for the possibility of being defrauded. After several drinks, most people cannot tell the difference between the name-brand spirit they ordered and the non–name brand the bartender may have poured them. This allows the bartender to serve them a less expensive spirit and charge them for the more expensive spirit, pocketing the difference in price in the process.

Opportunity: Different Portion Sizes and Lack of Tight Inventory Controls.   Many beverage items in a bar are sold in multiple sizes, making it difficult to compare the amount sold with the amount that *should have been* sold. This is complicated by the fact that many bars use different-sized jiggers or shot glasses during the day (for example, a small jigger for happy hour, a larger one for other hours). Drink recipes may also call for fractions of jiggers (as in a ''Zombie,'' which requires ⅔ jigger of four different kinds of rum). Sales of draft beer, served from a keg, are hard to track, too, since foaming and head size affect the number of ounces poured. All these variables make it nearly impossible to detect differences between what should be in inventory and what is in inventory. As a result of such imprecision, theft may go undetected.

Increased Profitability

The selling and serving of alcoholic beverages is more profitable than the selling and serving of food, for several reasons. Since alcohol is far less perishable than food, much less is lost to spoilage, which reduces waste and cost.

Drinks require less space to prepare than food. Generally, 30 to 45 percent of the space in a food service operation is dedicated to the kitchen or preparation area. This space cannot be used to serve guests, yet it adds to the expense of the building and operation of the restaurant. In contrast, bars require much less space due to the fact that preparation goes on behind the bar in view of the guest. The reduction in the preparation space means that a bar can serve the same number of guests as a restaurant, using much less space.

Finally, the markup from cost to selling price of alcohol is higher than with food products. The average product cost for a food item is 35 to 45 percent of the selling price, while the product cost for beverage items ranges from 15 to 25 percent. The lower the product cost percentage, the higher the profit.

Conclusions about Beverage Operations

One of the main differences between bar and restaurant management is that bar managers have the additional responsibility of making sure that the consumption of their products does not get out of hand. People who eat spaghetti will obviously know when they have had enough. If they overconsume, no one blames the establishment. In contrast, people who drink alcohol may easily and rapidly overindulge, which *is* the legal concern of bar management.

Despite some of the negative factors associated with running a beverage operation (increased risk of theft, extensive regulation, and liability issues), bars, in general, tend to be more profitable than food service operations. This, as discussed, is due to a combination of factors, including low perishability, compactness of preparation and serving space, and high profit margin. Additionally, bar operations also tend to have fewer layers of staffing, since bartenders often do double duty as servers. Also, employers may pay bar staff lower hourly wages or salaries since their positions generate higher tip income than in food service establishments. Both of these factors can work to reduce payroll costs.

Many of the management skills highlighted in the food service section of this chapter also apply to bar management. Ultimately, managers in both operations have to take care of their customers, their employees, and their products.

Human Resource Management

The food service operations model describes steps in the production and service of the menu. However, because this process involves people (the manager directing the staff), there is another umbrella model in force here, the human resources model.

The success of a food service firm depends on its employees. The success of a food service manager depends on his or her ability to manage people. Technical skills are important for a food service manager, but people skills are essential. Part of the people skills portfolio is leadership. Managers set standards, and as professionals, set them high. They carefully choose their employees and systematically train them in the organization's standards and expectations. The best managers attempt to train (and to encourage) ground-level staff to move upwards through the organization. This requires the ability to motivate. (This is discussed more thoroughly in Chapter 11, ''Human Resource Management.'')

For the purposes of this chapter, let us note that managers must be aware of their employees' needs in order to provide a motivating atmosphere. Changing demographics have resulted in a new typical worker profile. The new typical worker may be a single, uneducated, 30-year-old woman with children. Job security and a paycheck may be her initial needs. As those needs are met, she may look to her job for social needs and later for self-esteem needs. A manager attuned to his or her employees' needs can increase employee productivity and job satisfaction, thus reducing turnover.

A manager can reinforce desired behavior. Just as people have different needs, they have different ideas of what a reward is. For one person a verbal ''that's good'' is a reward. Another person might respond to a more tangible reward such as increased responsibility or time off. By knowing their employees, managers are better able to understand their needs and thus offer the kinds of rewards that will increase their motivation.

Employees are not mind readers. Managers must tell employees what they are expected to do. To state the obvious, this requires that managers first know what it is that their employees are supposed to do. Only then can they show employees how to do it. Under the manager's (or trainer's) supervision, employees then try the tasks themselves, receiving immediate corrective feedback and encouragement. The manager must then monitor the employees consistently to make sure that the standards are maintained. Supervision is an ongoing process and is not as simple as most workers believe.

To recap, managers assure that standards are met by providing a good working atmosphere and good working conditions. Managers must provide good recipes, the ingredients called for in the recipes, and adequate equipment, supplies, and time to prepare the recipes.

Managers must also provide leadership. By demonstrating the company's philosophy at all times, managers can make it real to their employees. This is important, since every employee should clearly understand the company's philosophy and mission statement. Employees are strongly influenced by their manager's conduct. A manager who does not adhere to the rules and standards he or she sets indicates that the rules and standards are not important. If trainers, managers, and top management do not respect the rules, regulations, and standards they've set (and execute all of them with consistency and fairness), neither will their employees.

As emphasized before, the manager is responsible for seeing that the job gets done right. A manager can only do that by utilizing personnel to the fullest. This requires good communication, constructive feedback, and respect. Ultimately, it is the manager's behavior that tells the employee whether he or she is respected, and this perception profoundly affects the way an employee performs his or her job. For food service operations to be successful in an increasingly competitive environment, managers must be professional and must train and encourage professionalism at all levels. This includes the encouragement of mutual respect as well as self-respect among all employees.

Conclusion

Professionalism in food service management is essential in today's highly competitive market. This overview of food service management is intended to demonstrate the scope and seriousness of food service management and to underscore the importance of professional training/education for potential food service managers.

Food service management can be wonderfully satisfying, fulfilling, and fun, but only if we are properly prepared to manage. Managers must have firm foundations in marketing, financial management, and, perhaps most importantly, human resource management.

Meeting customers' needs, selecting and retaining a well-trained staff, and operating a safe and sanitary food service operation require professional management training. The traditional practice of promoting food service line workers into management positions has contributed to dissatisfied customers and turnover rates of up to 300 percent. The up-through-the-ranks manager may be less competitive today and in less demand in the current food service management market. Professional food service management training is a necessity in today's workplace.

Keywords

food service operation   282
personnel turnover   284
commercial food service operations   284
institutional food service operations   284
conventional food service operation   284
convenience food service operation   284
commissary food service operations   284
bacteria   288
cross-contamination   288

OSHA   290
HACCP   291
standardized recipe   294
standard purchase specification   295
purchase order   296
temperature danger zone   297
clean   306
sanitize   306
sterilize   307

Core Concepts

food service contractors   284
models   286
systems management   286
critical control points   291
control   295

control tools   295
physical inventory   299
food cost percentage   299
motion economy   301
work simplification   302

Discussion Questions

1. Why is professional training necessary for today's food service manager?

2. Why is it useful to use a model in food service management?

3. List and define the seven components in the food service operations model.

4. Construct an HACCP flowchart for any recipe containing a potentially hazardous food.

5. Describe why it is necessary to use HACCP flowcharting.

6. Describe the role of a food service manager and list his or her responsibilities.

References

The Educational Foundation of the National Restaurant Association. *Applied Foodservice Sanitation: A Certification Coursebook.* 4th ed. New York: John Wiley & Sons, 1992.

Farkas, D. "Abstract Thinking." *Restaurant Hospitality* 76, no. 4 (1992), p. 60.

Gordon, E. "Foodservice Employment to Top 12 million by 2005." *Restaurants USA* 12, no. 1 (1992), pp. 28–30.

"NRA 1993 Foodservice Industry Forecast." *Restaurants USA* 12, no. 11 (1992), pp. 13–32.

Food Preparation

Food service experience, and specifically food preparation experience, is essential for all hospitality management students, regardless of whether they plan to pursue a management career in hotels or restaurants. Students who prefer to pursue a career in the hotel segment of the industry often look with disdain toward the food service courses in their curriculum, unaware that the food and beverage area of a hotel can be a major profit center and can generate significant revenue. In fact, most major hotel companies require that their general managers have management exposure to food service as well as hotel operations. Students who wish to expand their career options cannot neglect this essential area.

The purpose of this chapter is to present the key components of the food preparation area of food service operations. This includes a discussion of some of the trends affecting food service preparation, the role of menus, food service equipment, methods of preparation, and the hierarchy of kitchen personnel positions.

Outline

Introduction

People are prompted to dine out by great food. While the service provided with the meal can have a direct impact on the customers' dining satisfaction, it is food that initially draws them to dine out. The food preparation area is a key area in food service operations—without a kitchen there would be nothing to serve. The food preparation area is often called the back of the house or the *heart of the house* due to its central role in the operation of the food service facility. The food preparation staff is generally responsible for all aspects of the food served, including planning the menu, ordering the food, preparing the food, and plating the prepared items for the servers to present to the guests.

Successfully managing a food production area requires a different set of skills than other areas of management, largely because of the many variables that can affect costs and profits. The perishability and seasonality of food products are just two of the concerns food service managers have. They must also avoid ordering too little food or too much food for their outlet's needs.

Ordering too little leads to lost business because customers tire of hearing, "We're out of that tonight." Underordering may also increase food costs if the chef, rather than disappoint customers, sends someone to the supermarket to buy the item at retail price (which may be 15 to 40 percent more than the wholesale price).

Ordering too much food leads to waste and loss. Most foods are purchased at the peak of their quality and flavor. The longer they are stored, the less suitable they become for use. Any food item that is purchased and not served to guests results in a loss of profit.

Because of all the variables involved in running a food service operation, it's often difficult to diagnose what's wrong when one facet is running poorly. What seems to be a purchasing problem may in fact be a *forecasting* problem. One food service management task is to determine or forecast the number of customers. Management must also predict how many guests will order each of the items on the menu (commonly called the *menu mix*). The accurate forecasting of customer counts and the menu mix is crucial. It determines not only how much food is purchased, but how much of it is pre-prepared for the meal period.

The food preparation area does not work alone. It must cooperate with the other areas of the establishment to ensure a smooth transition of products from the back of the house to the guest's table. A good relationship with the dining staff is essential; servers can offer valuable input on which items guests prefer. The dining room hosts or hostesses must update the kitchen on reservations and head counts so that the kitchen staff can plan accordingly. Both areas work together closely during meal service to ensure that the menu items are produced on a timely basis and served to the customers while they are still at the peak of their quality.

The food preparation area has been affected by a shift in the nation's demographics. Food service operations have always been labor intensive. The overall reduction of the 16- to 21-year-old age group has had a direct impact on the staffing of commercial kitchens, which have traditionally relied heavily upon this age group. This reduction in the available workforce has caused food service operators to increase their use of preprocessed food items beyond any past levels. As Chapter 9 discussed, this situation is neither positive nor negative. It simply allows food service operations to function with a reduced staff, since much of the preparation has been done elsewhere.

The trend toward healthier lifestyles has also affected food service, as customers seek healthier choices when dining out. Menus are being rewritten and kitchen personnel are pursuing retraining that will enable them to provide the type of foods their patrons demand. This chapter will look at how menus are written, what equipment is used to prepare the food, how food is prepared, and how kitchens are organized.

The menu of a food service operation is the hub around which many other factors revolve. The menu determines the number and skill level of both the kitchen and dining room staff, the set-up of the dining room, the amount of storage space needed, and the size and type of equipment required. Equipment serves a vital role in food service operations, and due to its expense, its selection requires conscientious management homework prior to purchase.

Recipes are the power behind the menu. They help to ensure food consistency, determine the cost of menu items, and dictate the training of new cooks.

The Role of the Menu

The success of most restaurants is often directly associated with the planning of the menu. The four goals of a successful restaurant are to:

1. Serve products of quality.
2. Increase the amount of money the customer spends.
3. Attract new customers and business.
4. Increase the frequency of visits by the customers.

A properly planned menu can help accomplish all four goals, when combined with good service, quality food, and a clean operation. The menu should do more than just convey what the operation offers for sale. When properly designed, the menu can both inform customers and influence their purchasing decisions.

The menu determines many of the key factors of both the back and front of a food service operation. In most new projects, *menu design* decisions drive kitchen design and are preceded only by the formulation of a project's concept or theme. When a new menu is being designed for an established food service, it is done so only after the existing kitchen equipment has been reviewed. Care must be taken that the existing equipment and work stations are adequate to meet the demand the new menu will put upon them. If any one area is overloaded, work flows will be inefficient and production delays will be inevitable.

The primary role of the menu is to communicate to the customer what the operation is offering for sale; it should act as a silent salesperson. Menu descriptions give information about items that the guest may not be familiar with and might be reluctant to ask about. ''Specialties'' alert the guests to the items that the operation wants to show off. ''Specials'' allow the kitchen to test new presentations, feature seasonal flavors, or use up specific products (i.e., leftovers). The menu, to be most effective, should be easy to read and be uncluttered.

Eye on the Issues

Environment

Food service operations generally produce large amounts of waste, in both the kitchen and the dining room. Disposable containers are a specific sore spot cited by environmentalists, particularly for the fast-food portion of the industry. A national consulting organization worked with McDonald's to help them reduce waste and increase the use of recyclable disposable containers. The program also required suppliers to use shipping boxes at least partially composed of recycled cardboard. The consultants theorized that suppliers, eager to do business with the giant chain, would begin to use recycled shipping materials voluntarily—or lose the opportunity to bid on its business. Other smaller companies are also more actively recycling waste, partially due to increasing fees charged by garbage collection companies. Whether driven by philosophy or economics, many food service operations are working to reduce their waste by sorting for recycling and/or by choosing recycled products whenever possible.

Four Factors that Determine the Menu

The Number and Skill Level of the Kitchen Staff.   Obviously, the more items on the menu, the more food service workers are needed to prepare them. Furthermore, the complexity of the menu items determines the skill levels of the kitchen staff. For example, a food service operation that serves primarily hamburgers and french fries would require a smaller, less-skilled kitchen staff than an operation with a more complex, continental cuisine menu.

The Amount of Storage Space.   A restaurant's menu and its storage space are also closely related. A hamburger restaurant, with a limited menu, would need only limited storage space. A restaurant with a fancier menu, however, will have more storage space, which will allow it to offer a more extensive menu.

The Size and Amount of Equipment in the Food Preparation Area.   The larger the menu and more varied the menu selections, the larger and more extensive the equipment needed to prepare the items. Once again, the limited-menu hamburger restaurant example would come out on the low side of the equation, while its high-end cousin would require more kitchen space and equipment.

The Set-Up of the Dining Room.   The type of menu dictates the type of seating and the set-up of the dining room. The seating found in fast-food restaurants tends more toward booths than tables and is generally less comfortable than the seating found in table-service restaurants. Harder, less comfortable seats discourage customers from staying at the table too long and promote higher *table turnover.* Since fast-food–type operations generally charge less for their food, thus making a smaller profit per customer, they must rely on a greater turnover (or number of guests during a meal period). Table-service operations, on the other hand, generally charge more for the food they serve, so they are less dependent on turnover. Table-service restaurants have more comfortable seats to accommodate longer dining periods, and their servers deliver the food to the guest's table rather than requiring the guest to pick it up at the front counter.

Five Types of Menus

Menu designers commonly recognize five basic types of menus. Most fast-food restaurants have fairly static menus. This is why they so heavily promote the addition of new menu items, because they signal significant change. Table-service restaurants may use a combination of menu types. It's relatively rare to find such a restaurant locked into a single kind of menu.

Static.   **Static menus** do not change. The advantage of a static menu is that the preparation staff gets familiar with making the items, return guests know

EXHIBIT 10–1

This is an example of a static menu. High-quality reproduction can be justified since the menu does not change often.

Here at Lyon's, we use only the freshest and highest-quality ingredients in everything we serve. Our Prime Rib, for example, is specially seasoned and slow-roasted to seal in the fullest flavor. Our fish and produce are always fresh, and we serve only 100% real russet mashed potatoes. Our hamburgers are freshly ground, and our dinners are served with your choice of two homestyle side dishes.

We take our desserts just as seriously. Try fresh-baked apple pie or our Mile High Mud Pie. Or, maybe you'd like to treat yourself to a rich, creamy, old-fashioned milk shake.

And coffee? We just brewed a big pot a few minutes ago, using fresh-ground 100% Arabica beans.

Because we want you to stay as healthy as your appetite, we will make every effort to accommodate your needs. We only cook with cholesterol-free oil and offer Egg Beaters®, Fleischman's® margarine, nonfat milk, sugar free sweetener and caffeine-free beverages.

Thank you for joining us. We hope your visit with us is absolutely delicious. Please tell us if we can do anything to make it more enjoyable. **Because At Lyon's...It's All About the Food**℠.

Burgers & Melts

Our burgers are 1/3 pound of fresh ground beef, cooked to order. Served with French fries or thick-cut potato chips and Kosher dill pickle. *Add homestyle soup, crisp green salad or homemade cole slaw for only 1.19.*

LYONBURGER®   5.69
With lettuce, tomato, mayonnaise and red onion. *add cheese for 39¢*

MONTEREY BURGER   6.69
With Monterey Jack cheese, bacon, avocado, lettuce, tomato, red onion and mayonnaise.

CHILI SIZE   6.69
Served open faced, smothered with our famous southwestern chili, and topped with melted Cheddar cheese.

MIGHTY LYON®   6.99
A California classic. A full 1/2 pound of lean ground beef, with Cheddar cheese and grilled onion. Served on a crusty French roll. *add bacon for 79¢*

CHEESE AND BACON BURGER   6.69
With choice of cheese and crisp bacon, lettuce, mayonnaise, tomato and red onion.

NEW-FASHIONED GRILLED CHEESE   4.69
Cheddar, Monterey Jack and Swiss cheeses with crisp bacon, sliced tomato and grilled onion. Served on grilled sourdough bread.

PATTY MELT   6.19
On grilled corn rye with melted American cheese and grilled onions.

TUNA MELT   5.99
Albacore tuna salad, American cheese and tomato on grilled corn rye bread.

New **MEATLOAF MELT**   6.19
Our famous meatloaf with sweet and mild chili sauce, fresh tomato, grilled onions and melted Cheddar cheese. Served on grilled sourdough bread.

New **TURKEY AND BACON MELT**   6.99
Sliced turkey breast with crisp bacon, fresh tomato, grilled onion and melted Cheddar cheese. Served on grilled sourdough bread.

REUBEN   6.69
Hot corned beef with Swiss cheese, sauerkraut and Thousand Island on grilled corn rye.

GARDENBURGER®   6.49
A vegetarian patty grilled and topped with fresh tomato, red onion, avocado and lettuce. Served on a whole wheat bun with honey mustard sauce.

Lyon's Sandwiches

© 1995 Lyon's Restaurants, Inc. 06/95

what to expect, and purchasing is easier. The disadvantage is that repeat guests may grow bored with the limited menu choices.

Cyclical.   Menus that change on a regular basis are called **cyclical menus.** They are common in cafeterias and are generally repeated every four to six weeks. The changes in the menu give guests more choice and allow the restaurant to plan ahead for purchasing purposes. A disadvantage of cyclical menus is that regular guests, familiar with the items of one cycle, may be displeased if their favorite item is not included when a new menu cycle kicks in.

Table d'Hôte.   Menus that include all the courses and accompaniments of the meal at one price are called **table d'hôte** or **prix fixe menus.** The chef and kitchen staff put together menu items that complement each other, thereby creating a carefully designed dining experience for the customer, who would otherwise have to order à la carte (see Exhibit 10–2).

À la Carte.   Menus that charge for each item separately are called *à la carte*. Guests may mix and match their own meals with complete freedom among the menu choices. On an à la carte menu, side dishes are usually ordered separately; for example, the price of a steak does not include a baked potato; the potato is ordered separately, if desired.

Du Jour.   Menus that change on a daily basis are called **du jour menus.** The food production staff puts menu items together based on freshness and availability. The success of du jour menu operations is largely dependent on the reputation of the chef, since guests do not generally know what menu items will be available on the night they dine and must trust that the chef will produce something they'll enjoy.

Most food service operations use a combination of menu types on their menu rather than a pure form of any of the types mentioned above. A dinner house restaurant, for example, will often feature a menu that is part static, part cyclical (with specials that are repeated over a set period of time), part table d'hôte or one-price meals, part à la carte (usually accompaniments and drinks), and still offer a du jour special. However, this approach does tend to keep the food preparation and planning area "hopping."

Periodic Menu Review

Menus should be reviewed and revised on a periodic basis. Items that are not selling should be replaced with ones that will. Care should be taken in the design of the menu, and staff suggestions should be incorporated. Servers can offer insights into the menu because they hear and respond to guest questions and preferences. The purchasing agent should also be consulted; he or she has the best idea of what ingredients are readily available at peak quality and

EXHIBIT 10–2

A table d' hôte menu offers diners a limited choice but an optimal dining experience.

Recommended Wines

Napa Valley

Johannisberg Riesling	15.50
Napa Valley Beringer Gamay Beaujolais	15.75

Washington State

Gewurtztraminer	16.00
Chase Limogere Sparkling Wine	16.00
Ariel Premium Alcoholic-Free Champagne	12.50

Other Wines You May Enjoy

Napa Valley Chenin Blanc	12.00
Napa Valley Pinot Noir	15.00
Imported Australian Shiraz Cabernet	20.00
Imported Banfi Chianti, 375 ml.	11.50

House Wines
by Morgan Vineyards—California

	Glass	1/2 Liter	Liter
Chablis	2.50	4.25	8.00
White Zinfandel	2.75	5.50	9.50
Chardonnay	3.50	6.00	11.00
Cabernet	3.75	7.00	14.50

Please ask us about the art around you ...
courtesy of John Waddell, sculptor, and Diane Eide, painter.

Table d'Hote

Zakuski
«« Russian-style buckwheat blini w/sour cream & golden caviar »»
«»

Asparagus Cream Swirl
«« with focaccia loaf »»
«»

Strawberry Radish Salad
«« with fresh lime and Mesclun greens »»
«»

Belon Oysters Maltese
«»

Midori Melon Ice
«»

Veal Saltimbocca
«« rolled slices of veal with fresh sage & prosciutto »»
Spinach Tortellini
«« with sun-dried tomato basil pesto & imported Romano »»
«»

Chocolate Sin

Coffee

$23.95

reasonable price. A menu based on just one person's perspective is likely to create problems of scope, production, or procurement.

Truth in Menu

Menu designers must ensure that all menu information is totally accurate. Because of ethical considerations and government regulations, management must be careful to avoid inaccurate statements on menus. Some states have passed **truth in menu legislation** to combat inaccuracy and misrepresentation. These laws are generally enforced by local watchdog agencies. The offending restaurant's penalties for violations are fines and court costs on one hand and adverse publicity on the other.

Every statement—written on the menu or made by the server orally—must be *completely* accurate. Management must be able to prove the claims made about the food they offer for sale. For example, fresh squeezed orange juice *must* be fresh. Ground sirloin must actually be made from sirloin and not another cut of beef. It follows that extreme care must be taken before using descriptions such as *imported, homemade, natural, real,* and *fresh.* This also means that the kitchen staff cannot vary from the standardized recipes upon which the menu descriptions are based.

Menu planners must consider the following points when writing a menu:

- List the points of origin of the ingredients only if they are sure of a steady supply.
- Specify the means of preservation (fresh, frozen, or canned) and the method of preparation.
- Represent the quantity accurately (Does the advertised quarter-pound shrimp plate really weigh four ounces?).

Conclusions about Menus

The menu of a food service operation has a direct effect on the success of the operation. The menu serves many functions and drives several other food service areas. The menu also silently sells by accurately (and temptingly) informing customers what is for sale. Menus serve as a marketing tool and a form of advertising. Other operational decisions are based upon the scope of the menu, such as the type of beverage service offered, the number and skill level of the staff, and the set-up of the dining room.

Equipment in Food Service Operations

The equipment used in a food service operation represents a major portion of its opening budget. This significant expense requires that managers or food service operators spend a significant amount of time and effort planning and researching their purchasing decisions. Selection is very important and errors are costly.

Food service operations depend on a vast variety of equipment to perform their many preparation tasks. Some food service equipment used in restaurants resembles home appliances; the major differences are the cost, capacity, durability, and the ability to be cleaned and sanitized. For example, consider the use time of a home appliance versus its commercial counterpart. A home kitchen may use a blender for five minutes a day, while a commercial kitchen may use its blender for several hours at a time to process mass quantities of food. To withstand heavier workloads, commercial operations need equipment with larger capacities and longer life spans.

The precise size, capacity, and type of equipment needed vary with the operation. Equipment purchases are usually made when a new operation is being built or when an existing operation is being remodeled (perhaps because of a change in concept or theme). Purchases are also driven by the need for greater capacity or for replacement of outdated or broken equipment. Not surprisingly, most decisions are based on the equipment type, model, or features that employees are familiar with.

Preparation Equipment

As explained earlier, the need for preparation equipment is directly related to the amount of preprocessed food that an operation uses. Though some of the pieces of equipment discussed next will not be found in operations that rely heavily on processed foods, many facilities will have some version of them.

Mixers.   The mixer is one of the most versatile pieces of preparation equipment in the kitchen. Mixers, with their assortment of implements, can do many things, including beat, whip in air, fold, mix two solids together, and develop gluten (the ''stretchy'' proteins in bread that give it its cohesiveness). Mixer attachments may be used to convert the basic machine into a shredder, grinder, or slicer (see Exhibits 10–3, 10–4, and 10–5).

Food Cutters or Choppers.   Food choppers were one of the first labor-saving devices used in food service operations. They were first developed for the food processing industry and then adapted for food service use. Food cutters help to free the cook from dicing items by hand on a cutting board.

Eye on the Issues

Ethics

The increase in the cost of some ingredients has prompted some unscrupulous operators to deceive customers by misrepresenting the products that they sell. Examples include serving an off-brand cola drink as Pepsi or Coke, serving artificial crab as real crab, or selling regular ground beef as ground sirloin. These practices are, of course, unethical.

Restaurants that offer all-you-can-eat deals for such popular items as crab legs or buffalo wings also face an ethical decision. By delaying delivery of refill items to guests, they can significantly reduce the amount of food consumed, and thus reduce their costs. This is partially due to the fact that guests begin to feel full as their first plate of food begins to digest. Waiting time is also a factor since many guests cannot stay two to three hours to eat as much as they might like. When restaurants double or triple their delivery time to thwart big eaters, are they acting ethically?

Food Slicer.   Food slicers fill the need for a tool that accurately and uniformly cuts slices of food, whether it be ham or tomatoes. The food slicer is a motor-driven metal disk with sharp, ground edges. Slicers may be mounted on a rolling table for satellite use or left stationary on a table.

EXHIBIT 10–3

This machine is basically a mixer.

Courtesy: Hobart Corporation, Troy, Ohio.

EXHIBIT 10–4

Converted, the same machine as in Exhibit 10–3 becomes a grinder.

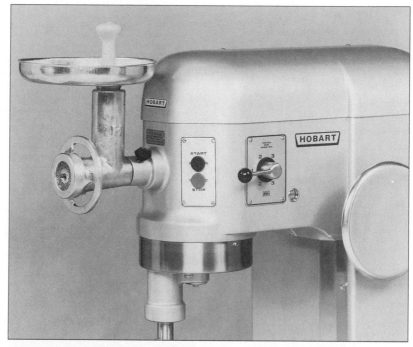

Courtesy: Hobart Corporation, Troy, Ohio.

EXHIBIT 10–5

One additional way the machine in Exhibit 10–3 can be converted is into a shredder.

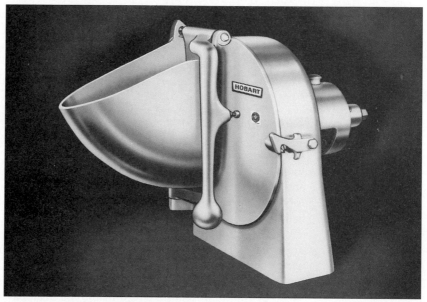

Courtesy: Hobart Corporation, Troy, Ohio.

Courtesy: Wolf Range Company, Compton, California.

Cooking Equipment

Ovens.   An oven is an insulated box with a heat source that is used to cook food. **Conventional ovens** are the most basic form of oven. They are basically an insulated box containing a heat source; heat passes from the source to the food via the cooking pan or the air. People have used this type of oven for nearly as long as they've cooked with fire.

Convection ovens (also known as *forced-air convection ovens*) were originally developed by the United States Navy to increase the efficiency of standard conventional ovens. Convection ovens are the main work horses of high-volume production kitchens, due to their higher capacity, efficiency, and speed of cooking. Heat is moved inside the oven cavity by a fan in the back of the oven. The movement of the hot air by the fan allows for more rapid cooking at a lower temperature, while allowing more food to be cooked at one time. An example of the convection process is shown in Exhibit 10–6.

Courtesy: Wolf Range Company, Compton, California.

Microwave ovens cook by producing short electromagnetic waves that vibrate food molecules, which causes friction and then heat. Unlike the ovens mentioned above, the cavity of this type of oven is not heated. Microwave ovens have limited application for food service operations due to the fact that cooking time increases as more food is put in the oven. Their use is generally limited to defrosting frozen items or reheating items.

Ranges and Broilers.   A range (often called a stove) is a versatile piece of cooking equipment. The unit can be heated either by gas or electricity and is designed to cook food in pots and pans as well as on a flat-top grill. Ranges are often paired with ovens as a base and/or with a broiler located above them (see Exhibit 10–7).

Broilers are used to cook individual portions of meat, poultry, or seafood. The broiler does a very good job of cooking steaks, chicken breasts, and some types of fish. The broiler's trademark is the crusty, almost charred taste it imparts to the food. Heat for a broiler can be generated either from above or below the food to be prepared.

Kettles and Steamers.   The majority of nonbaked or nonroasted foods produced in large-volume operations are produced in **steam-jacketed kettles.** Steam-jacketed kettles consist of two large curved-bottom kettles nested together. If you are familiar with a double boiler, you'll see a similarity in design and principle. Food is placed in the outside kettle; the inside kettle is filled with water or steam, which is then evenly heated to cook the food. Steam-jacketed kettles are often preferred over ranges because they allow food to be cooked over indirect heat rather than direct heat, reducing the chance for burning.

Compartment steamers are energy-efficient and versatile pieces of cooking equipment. Two of their advantages lie in their ability to cook items without the addition of fat and in their preservation of a high percentage of a product's nutrients. Moist heat makes steamers ideal for reheating leftovers, unlike ovens that tend to dry food out.

Conclusions about Food Service Equipment

Food service equipment can help workers be more productive and efficient. Equipment expense makes up a significant amount of a food service operation's opening budget. Managers in charge of the selection and purchase of equipment should consider such factors as expense and longevity; type, number, and capacity; ease of operation and cleaning; safety; and options that provide multipurpose use.

Preparation

The success of a food service operation will rise or fall based on the quality of the food produced by its preparation area. The keys to good preparation are quality and consistency. Both are, of course, the responsibility of management. As indicated in Chapter 9, kitchen staff must be trained in the proper methods to produce menu items, and be provided with the tools to do the job. The primary means of ensuring consistency is through tested and reproducible **recipes.**

Preparation is the procedure that transforms food from the state in which it was purchased to a form in which it is ready to be cooked. Foods may be purchased in various states of preparation ranging from the natural state to ready to cook. For example, suppose a food service wants to offer french fries on its menu. It can purchase:

- Frozen french fries, ready to be cooked to order.
- Fresh potatoes already peeled and cut into french fries.
- Fresh, unwashed potatoes in their skins.

Degrees of Preparation

The cost of an item generally increases with the readiness of the item, since the costs of labor and processing are passed on to the purchaser. But choosing a product (at whatever degree of preparation) doesn't end the decision-making process. How much pre-preparation will the kitchen be instructed to perform on the fries before the meal period?

Eye on the Issues

International

The nation's changing demographics have already caused changes in food service operations. As more Asians and Hispanics enter the workforce, food service operations will be forced to adjust their training materials and in-house communication. Population shifts will also drive changes in the kinds of foods consumers will look for on menus. This will, in turn, affect cooking methods and require the development of purchasing standards for the procurement of "exotic" ingredients.

America has been transforming its tastes and dining habits, and this has enlivened menus across the country, often through the addition of ethnic dishes. While many foreign cuisines (Thai, Caribbean, Vietnamese) have found their way to even small American cities, the familiar foreign cuisines, for example, Italian, Chinese, and Mexican (in order of popularity), have not lost their appeal. In fact, these standbys have infiltrated mainstream, nonethnic restaurants in the form of a variety of pasta and stir-fry dishes. When you can order stir-fry at JB's and Denny's, you realize just how far this trend has gone.

1. Frozen french fries require no pre-prep. They are taken from the box to the fryer, without thawing, and cooked to order.
2. Fresh potatoes already peeled and cut into french fries require one stage of pre-prep. They need to be blanched (partially cooked) before they can be cooked to order.
3. Fresh, unwashed potatoes in their skins require four transformations before they can be cooked to order: washing, peeling, slicing, blanching.

Kitchen A may choose to do all these steps prior to the meal period. Kitchen B may wait until they are ordered. Which method makes the most sense? Before you decide, consider part two of the preparation puzzle: *Food products generally diminish in quality once they have been prepared.* If you are the kind of operator who is concerned about **product degeneration** (loss of flavor, texture, color, nutrients, and so on), you might lean toward kitchen B's wait-till-they-order-it theory. However, this concern must be balanced against the rapid pace of meal service, which does not allow for too much time to elapse after a customer's order. All those last-minute steps can translate into a service lag.

Kitchen A's method and method 2 make sense, time-wise, but again bring up the concern of possible product degeneration. Method 1 is the one most food service operators choose due to simplicity, time savings, and predictability of quality. (Commercial freezing stabilizes product degeneration for most foods.) Unless your menu specifies french fries from scratch (remember truth in menu), method 1 will most reliably provide the consistent product to which your operation aspires.

Now multiply this decision making and planning dozens of times over for each menu item. This is the task that falls to the food production manager in ensuring that a consistent, high-quality product is speedily served to the guest.

Recipes and Formulas

As stated earlier, the most significant component of the preparation area is the recipe because it is the key to producing consistent products. Recall from Chapter 9 that a *standardized recipe* is a set of instructions that precisely describes the way a particular establishment prepares a particular dish. You've already learned that several areas in the back of the house use recipes, including the purchasing staff and the preparation staff. However, recipes can also be used as valuable training tools since they can orient and instruct new cooks.

A more specific form of recipe, called a **formula,** is used for bakery items. The delicate nature of bakery items requires more detail than is generally required for most food items, especially in terms of the ratio of ingredients. Because of this, bakery ingredients are measured by weight rather than by volume, in contrast to other foods. Most food recipes are somewhat tolerant of slight measurement variations. Not so with bakery items. For example, the amount of baking powder in a cake is crucial and requires precise measurement; any small amount over or under the specified amount could ruin the final cake. On the other hand, the amount of mushrooms in a recipe of mushroom gravy is not as crucial; if the recipe calls for 16 ounces and you only use 14 ounces, the gravy will not be greatly affected.

Part of the process of standardizing a recipe or formula is **kitchen-testing** it on site to confirm that the product it produces is consistent. This is important for several reasons. A recipe designed and tested in a humid or high-altitude kitchen, for example, will require some adjustment for use in arid climates or at lower altitudes. The testing process also allows the operation's cooks to practice the recipe's steps and procedures, detect any problems, and verify that the recipe does indeed produce the number of portions stated.

EXHIBIT 10–8   **Example of a Standardized Recipe**

RECIPE #34: Basic Vinaigrette Dressing
Yield: 1 qt.

Measurement	Ingredients	Procedure
1 cup	Red wine vinegar	1. Combine ingredients in a bowl and mix well with a wire whisk.
1 tsp	White pepper	
1 tbsp	Salt	
1.5 pint	Salad oil	2. Stir well before using.

Important Components of Recipes. A well-standardized recipe includes several important components that together help produce consistency (see Exhibit 10–8). Five of them are described below.

Name. The most basic component of a recipe is its name. Food service workers need the name of the item to identify the recipe precisely. There is a significant difference between ''Chicken à la King'' and ''Chicken à la Thermidor'' and an even bigger difference between ''filet'' mignon and ''fillet'' of sole. Accurately naming recipes prevents miscommunication.

Yield/Portion Size. It's also important for preparation staff to know how much food a recipe will yield, to avoid over- or underproducing. Knowing the yield allows the cook to adjust the size of the recipe and the ratio of ingredients so that only the amount needed is prepared.

Yield can be expressed in two forms: total yield and number of portions. Total yield is generally expressed in volume. For example, a soup recipe might have a yield of one gallon. Often, recipes provide a two-prong yield: ''one gallon/makes 21 six-ounce servings.'' Of course, *portion control* and bowl size become important in such cases. Six ounces of soup served in a 12-ounce bowl may look ''skimpy'' to the customer, or even to the staffer who ladles the soup. If portion control is not enforced, the yield of the recipe will still be one gallon, but the pot will be empty long before 21 bowls of soup have been served.

Cooking Time. Cooking times are hard to predict, due to fluctuations in oven temperatures, external environments, and nonuniform sizes of products. Though only approximate, cooking times give production personnel an idea when a product should be done cooking, which is important for planning purposes as well as cooking. Experienced cooks always check for doneness before the scheduled completion time in order to prevent overcooking. Conversely, they always test the product before removing it from the heat to make sure that it is, in fact, done.

List and Amounts of Ingredients.   Standardized recipes list ingredients in the order of use rather than randomly or alphabetically. Ingredients are specified as precisely as possible to ensure that the final product is consistent. A recipe that calls for beef is obviously imprecise. The specific cut of beef, such as chuck or round steak, should be mentioned in the recipe. Precision is also important for seasoning and measuring. Terms such as *splash, dash,* or *to taste* leave too much to chance and to the personal palate of the preparer. Scales and measuring cups should be accessible and accurate if a consistent outcome is to be expected.

Procedures.   Instructions or procedures are perhaps the most important component of a recipe. The finest ingredients on the market can be ruined if confusing procedures cause cooks to mix up preparation procedures or skip steps. Good procedures should be written as simple as possible—containing no more or no less detail than needed—so that the most basically trained cook can follow them. The steps should be sequential with suggestions of which steps can be done ahead. If a step is ''tricky,'' a note of caution should alert the user.

Conclusions about Preparation

Recipes are the key to consistency and cost control in a food service operation. Management uses recipes to determine the cost of food items, which form the basis of menu prices. Precise recipes enable purchasing agents to make good buying choices. Recipes, with their written steps and procedures, provide much of the information necessary to train new personnel in the preparation of an item.

Production

Whereas preparation is the procedure that transforms food from the state in which it was purchased to a form where it is ready to be cooked, **production** is the process wherein the food is converted to the state in which it will be served.

In a food service operation, production may involve one or many steps, depending on the nature of the products or the recipes that the operation uses. Production often includes cooking (the addition of heat to) an item. Some products, even some that are served cold, are cooked prior to being served. Before discussing the various methods of cooking used in food service operations, we need to discuss how heat is transferred—how it moves from the source (range, oven, or broiler) to the food product.

Heat Transfer

Heat transferred to food causes reactions in the food, such as firming of the protein or browning, and causes changes in color, texture, and flavor. It generally makes food easier to eat. The type of heat, coupled with the amount of heat, affects the final product. There are several ways in which heat is transferred to the food, and some methods of cooking use more than one form of heat transfer to change the food from raw to cooked. There are three basic forms of heat transfer: conduction, convection, and radiation.

Conduction.   The transfer of heat by direct contact is **conduction.** Conduction is a very efficient form of heat transfer. The gas flame or electric coil heats the pan, the food product is placed in the pan, and heat is transferred by contact with the hot pan. Omelets cooked in sauté pans or Japanese vegetables stir-fried in a wok are examples of foods prepared through conduction.

Convection.   The transfer of heat by liquid or air is **convection.** Convection heat transfer is effective, but not as efficient as heat transferred by conduction. With convection, the heat source heats up air or water, which, in turn, transfers the heat to the product. The browning of the exterior of a turkey roasting in the oven is an example of heat transfer by air, while the cooking of eggs in simmering water (poached eggs) is an example of heat transfer by a liquid.

There are two ways that heat can be transferred by convection: natural or forced. You'll remember from high school science that heat naturally rises; this is a form of natural convection. Water boiling in a pot is another example of this. The hot range burner heats the bottom of the pot, which heats the water in the bottom of the pot; this hot water then rises to the top of the pot.

To increase the efficiency of natural convection, mechanical or forced convection methods have been developed. A fan placed in an oven to rotate the air causes the oven to cook faster by moving the heat around. The stirring of a pot of stew, another form of forced convection, transfers the heat from the bottom of the pan to the top, spreading the cooking, and reducing the burning at the bottom of the pan.

Radiation.   The transfer of heat by waves is radiation. Radiated heat waves cause reactions in food molecules. There are two forms of radiation common to cooking: microwave and infrared. Microwave ovens have a microwave generator that produces waves of energy that are absorbed by the food. The waves vibrate the water molecules in the food so fast that they generate heat and cook the food. Infrared radiation transfers heat from a very hot source to the surface of the food; the heat is then transferred from the exterior of the food to the interior by conduction. As demonstrated in this last example, infrared heating is almost always used in conjunction with some other form of heating.

Let's look at another combination method of heat transfer. A steak broiled on a barbecue relies on several forms of heat transfer to be cooked. In the spots where the steak touches the hot grill, it is cooked by conduction. The areas of the food that do not come in contact with the hot grill are cooked by both convection and radiation. Heat is directly transferred to the steak from the heat source below by radiation. While most of the heat is transferred directly to the steak, some is also transferred to the air, which, in turn, heats the product by convection.

Cooking Methods

Due to the varying nature of their chemical makeup, different foods react differently when cooked by different methods. Some foods are suited to only one cooking method; others are more versatile, revealing varied textures and flavors depending on the way that they are cooked. Most recipes use one of three basic cooking methods: moist heat, dry heat, and combination.

Moist Heat.   The transfer of heat to the food by a liquid (other than fat)—or in the presence of moisture or steam—is called **moist heat.** Moist heat generally works best for cooking vegetables and tougher cuts of meat. Exposure to hot liquids breaks down the tough components and tissues of these foods, making them more digestible. The most common forms of moist heat cooking are boiling, simmering, poaching, and steaming. Though the first three forms share the common trait of cooking food by submerging it in water or a seasoned liquid, they differ in terms of water temperature and speed of cooking.

Dry Heat Methods.   The methods of cooking food products without the addition or presence of moisture are **dry heat** methods. Please note that in food preparation and cooking methods fat is not considered a liquid or a form of moisture, but simply acts as the medium to transfer the heat to the food from the source. Dry heat is generally best suited for tender food products. Common methods are broiling, grilling, griddling, roasting, baking, sautéing, deep-frying, and pan-frying.

Combination Cooking Methods.   Some food products are more appetizing if a combination of methods is used to transform them to their finished state. Moist-heat methods do a remarkable job of breaking down the tough components of food, but do not produce the attractive brown exterior diners prefer. So, to make the food more appealing, the food is first browned in hot oil or seared by a grill or broiler. Large tough cuts of meat benefit from this latter method, called *braising.* In braising, a food's exterior is browned using dry heat methods, then cooked by submerging it in a liquid to break down tough components. The end product of this process is appealing and appetizing both because of the robust color and the tender interior.

EXHIBIT 10–9

*A gas range with an
oven base, flat top,
and four open
burners is pictured
here.*

Courtesy: Wolf Range Company, Compton, California.

Eye on the Issues

Technology

Generally, the food-preparation industry lags behind other industries in the use of technology. Technology has found its best advocates among national quick-service chains, which place high value on standardized production in all stores. Smaller and independent operations that aim to distinguish themselves precisely *because of* their unique products and personal service resist such technology. In the nonproduction area, computers have gained popularity as tools for tracking inventory and analyzing menu items.

Sanitation in Food Service Operations

Customers judge the cleanliness of a food service operation before they even enter a food service outlet, drawing conclusions from its lighting and exterior. Consciously and unconsciously they use their senses of smell and sight to rate an operation's condition. Their judgments may extend to the staff's personal hygiene, grooming, and the state of their uniforms. Through these cues, customers feel justified in forming an overall feeling about an operation's desirability.

The problem or benefit, depending on how you look at it, is that the customer is permitted to see only a portion of the food service operation and its employees. Customers are generally not allowed to see back-of-the-house food preparation areas and staff. Instead, they see only the front-of-the-house staff—the host/hostess, the servers, and the buspeople. Fair or not, customers will deduce the cleanliness and personal hygiene of the kitchen and kitchen staff based upon the areas and staff they are allowed to see. The saying, ''You can judge the cleanliness of a restaurant kitchen by the cleanliness of its rest rooms,'' is based on this same logic. If management allows a customer-visible area, such as the rest rooms, to become dirty or to fall into disrepair, customers may assume that the same conditions apply in the areas of the operation they are not allowed to view.

The National Restaurant Association conducted a survey to determine how important the cleanliness of a food service operation is to customers. The NRA chose customers of three types of restaurants (quick service, moderate service, and full service) and asked them to rate the importance of a group of characteristics they considered when choosing a place to dine. Customers rated cleanliness the most important characteristic for quick-service and moderate-service outlets. For full-service outlets, they placed it second to food quality and preparation. These results indicate that customers *expect* a clean operation when they dine out.

Chapter 9 discussed some of the causes of food-borne illness, particularly in terms of temperature danger zones. Because of the painful and memorable symptoms of food poisoning, most people are wary of eating in places that appear dirty or unsanitary. They connect the appearance of cleanliness with the probability of safe food, and the lack of cleanliness with potential danger.

Everyone generally agrees that a food service operation must be kept clean. What food service managers know is that their operations should be both *clean* and *sanitary*. There are legal, monetary, and moral reasons why this is so. Before we progress any further, please review the basic terms found in Exhibit 10–10. You may recognize some of them from Chapter 9. However, they are so important they bear emphasizing a second time.

The rash of publicity on food safety problems at national restaurant chains has pushed the issue of food safety to the front burner again. In most cases, the food, tainted at a processing plant, is delivered to a food service operation that, failing to detect the contamination, serves the food to guests, who consume it and become ill. Often the restaurant takes the blame for a problem generated by suppliers. Since the restaurant is the point of guest contact, it is inevitably held responsible, whether it contributed to the problem or not.

Food safety problems seem to occur periodically, causing media ''flaps'' and public dismay. Typically when problems arise, food handling policies are

EXHIBIT 10–10   Sanitation Terminology

Biological hazards	Harmful, disease-causing bacteria, viruses, or parasites that can be supported by, or transmitted in, food.
Chemical hazards	Contamination of food with toxic substances, such as cleaning and sanitizing chemicals and substances.
Clean	Free from visible soil.
Contamination	The unintended presence of harmful substances or microorganisms in food or beverages.
Cross-contamination	Allowing harmful substances from one food product to come in contact with other food products.
Food-borne illness	A disease that is carried or passed to human beings by food.
Food-borne illness outbreak	A reported incident when two or more people report that they have become ill from a common food, which is confirmed through laboratory analysis as the source of the illness.
Physical hazards	Contamination of food with nonfood items, such as pieces of glass, staples from cartons, or metal shavings from can openers.
Sanitary	Having had many or most disease-causing bacteria removed.
	Wholesome food handled and prepared in such a way that the food is not contaminated with disease-causing bacteria or chemicals.
Sanitation	The creation and maintenance of healthful conditions.
Spoilage	Damage to the edible quality of food.

reevaluated and extra precautions are taken. Then, when no new cases develop, guards are slowly let down, opening the door for future outbreaks. Exhibit 10–10 lists some basic sanitation terms.

Hazards to Safe Food

All food service employees must understand how easily food hazards can ruin safe, wholesome food. The need for sanitation is sometimes a ''hard sell'' to employees since they may not see the connections between cause and effect. This is why many states require food employees to obtain food handlers' certificates. As part of the certification process, employees view explicit videos that show how, for example, the casual wipe of a knife on a soggy sponge can lead to 25 sick customers.

The Goals of an Effective Sanitation Program

The goals of an effective sanitation program, one that ensures that the operation will serve safe food, are relatively simple and straightforward. They are:

- To protect food from contamination through safe handling procedures.
- To reduce the effects of contamination.

What Bacteria Need to Survive

The three factors that have the *greatest* influence on bacterial growth are: moisture, the availability (or lack) of oxygen, and the amount of time the food is left exposed to bacteria.

Bacteria require adequate moisture to survive. When the amount of moisture is lowered, bacterial activity decreases. Dried fruit, such as apples or bananas, will last much longer than fresh produce due to the reduced moisture levels in the food.

Bacteria fall into three categories with regard to oxygen requirements. Some grow only in environments that have plenty of available oxygen. Some can grow only in closed containers where there is *no* free oxygen. However, most bacteria fall into the *facultative* category. They can survive and grow with or without oxygen.

Most organisms, including bacteria, function most effectively within a certain range of conditions. The bacteria that have the most detrimental effect on food grow best in the 60–110° F temperature range—which, conveniently for them, is the temperature range of most commercial kitchens. Care must be taken by food production personnel to reduce the amount of time that potentially hazardous food remains in the 60–110° F range.

Potentially Hazardous Food

Virtually any food can carry and transmit food-borne illness, but some foods, due to their composition, are more susceptible to harmful bacteria. The majority of food-borne illness outbreaks have been traced to a group of potentially hazardous foods. These include foods that contain milk products, eggs, meats, poultry, fish, and shellfish. These high-protein foods require the greatest attention from food service operators. The best protection is refrigeration, which inhibits bacterial growth by keeping food below the temperature danger zone.

The Importance of Sanitation for a Food Service Operation

Sanitation is important to a food service operation for legal, monetary, and moral reasons. Food service operations do not have a choice whether they want to keep their facilities clean or not—they are obligated by law to do so. Government agencies at several levels set minimum standards and regulations; it is the responsibility of the food service operator to abide by them.

Though the federal government has little to do with the daily internal operations of a food service operation, it does play an important role in protecting the quality of food products that an operator may purchase. The three federal agencies that have the greatest impact are the USDA, FDA, and CDC.

The United States Department of Agriculture (USDA) inspects and grades meat, poultry, dairy products, eggs, and produce that are shipped across state lines. The Food and Drug Administration (FDA) helps state and local health departments develop health and food safety ordinances and regulations. It also reviews and controls the use of potentially hazardous chemicals, such as fertilizers, pesticides, dyes, and other additives, in food production and processing. The U.S. Centers for Disease Control (CDC) investigates and compiles data on food-borne illness outbreaks, and examines the causes and controls of disease.

State, county, or local health departments have the greatest influence on the daily operation of commercial food service operations. Depending on an operation's location, it may fall under the jurisdiction of one or all of these regulatory entities.

It also makes monetary sense to maintain a clean operation with proper sanitary procedures. An operation that covers and dates refrigerated food and conscientiously rotates its pantry stock saves money by reducing waste. Equipment that is properly cleaned and maintained not only reduces the spread of harmful bacteria, it lasts longer and runs better. Operators are painfully aware that an outbreak of food-borne illness will result in a loss of revenue if the establishment's reputation is tarnished. Lawsuits are also a disturbing and expensive possibility.

Besides the legal and monetary reasons discussed above, commercial operations have a moral obligation to serve the public food and beverages that are safe from harmful bacteria and contaminants. This is part of an unspoken contract between customers and food providers. Customers are seeking to be nourished, not poisoned. Food service operators must do all within their power to protect the safety of the food that they serve. For them to knowingly serve spoiled or unsafe food is unforgivable.

Summary of Sanitation in Food Service

Food service customers rank cleanliness and sanitation high on their list of priorities when dining out. Sanitation is important to food service operators for legal, monetary, and moral reasons. To maintain a clean and sanitary operation, food service managers must understand how and where bacteria thrive and how sanitation techniques can hinder their growth. They must make sure all food service employees in their charge share this understanding and use proven methods to prevent food contamination.

Classification of Kitchen Positions

Food service job titles vary from operation to operation, but the responsibilities and roles remain pretty much the same. Back-of-the-house positions usually fall into three groups: managerial, production, and service.

Managerial Positions

The person in charge of the kitchen and its staff is called either the *kitchen manager* or *chef*. Larger food service operations, which are often organized into subdepartments, generally employ a hierarchy of chefs (this may be necessary if the food service kitchen serves several restaurants, as in full-service hotels or multioutlet campus facilities). Smaller restaurants more frequently employ kitchen managers.

The **executive chef** is the person in charge of the chefs who run the kitchens of a food service operation. The executive chef oversees the executive sous chef or second chef, who, in turn, supervises the other **sous chefs.** (*Sous* translates to "sub" or "under," but is commonly used to mean assistant.) In larger operations the executive chef and executive sous chef very seldom cook or prepare food. Instead, they spend most of their time doing both long-term and short-term planning and supervising the staff. The hands-on management of the individual operations becomes the realm of the individual sous chefs. Large hotels may even employ a separate sous chef for their catering and banquet departments. Thus, a person holding the title sous chef at a large hotel may, in fact, have more responsibility than an executive chef at a smaller operation (see Exhibit 10–11).

There are several other career opportunities in the food service industry. These include dietitian, test kitchen chef, food scientist, and noncommercial food service careers.

Dietitians primarily work in hospitals, nursing homes, and extended care facilities. They are the connective link between the food service department and medical care staff. Dietitians work with the medical staff of a facility to plan meals that satisfy the nutritional and medical needs of the patient and with the food production department to ensure the food is properly prepared.

Corporate test kitchen chefs and food scientists work in an assortment of settings for a number of different types of employers. Most major food processing, food service, and hotel companies operate test kitchens to develop, test, and refine new products and recipes. Food magazines often operate kitchens to test recipes for possible publication. Test kitchen staffs need knowledge and training in both cooking and food chemistry. The ideal candidate for the position also needs imagination, creativity, and awareness of trends in the food service industry.

Noncommercial food service segments of the hospitality industry also offer many career opportunities. Noncommercial operations include school, college and university, hospital, and prison food service. These operations have similar positions as their commercial (hotel dining and restaurant) counterparts. They employ managers, cooks, and dining room personnel. Although these positions may not be viewed as glitzy, they offer several advantages. A major advantage is the fact that noncommercial food service operations generally work on a Monday–Friday schedule, as do their employees. Additionally, the noncommercial food service segments of the industry have undergone very rapid growth in recent years, offering many management and career advancement opportunities.

Production Personnel

Back-of-the-house employees who are responsible for the preparation of food items are classified as production personnel. They are the workers in charge of procuring, storing, and preparing and producing foods. Though the majority of their work is done out of sight of guests, it is important that they still keep the guest as their top priority. Exhibit 10–12 shows several typical production job titles and duties.

Service Personnel

Food production personnel cannot work without the support of service personnel, such as dishwashers and pot washers. Without clean dishes, tableware,

EXHIBIT 10–12   Examples of Production Personnel

Entry Level (requires minimal or no prior training)

Kitchen assistant (prep cook)	Assists cooks, chefs, and bakers in measuring, mixing, and preparing ingredients.

Midlevel (requires minimum training and experience—on-the-job training is often provided)

Cook	Prepares and places food on plates. In larger operations may be responsible for specific foods, such as soups, vegetables, meats, or sauces.
Pastry chef	Bakes cakes, cookies, pies, and other desserts, as well as bread, rolls, and quick breads.
Pantry supervisor	Supervises salad, sandwich assistant. Should be able to create attractive food arrangements.

Upper Level (requires both education and experience—job descriptions may vary from one operation to another)

Food service manager	Responsible for profitability, efficiency, quality, and courtesy in all phases of the food service operation.
Assistant manager	Performs certain supervisory duties under the manager's direction.
Executive chef	Responsible for all quantity and quality food preparation for the entire operation, supervision of sous (support) chefs and cooks, and menus and recipe development.
Food production manager (sous chef)	Responsible for all food preparation and supervision of the kitchen staff. Knowledgeable in food preparation techniques, quality and sanitation standards, and cost-control methods.

kettles, and skillets, a food service operation will soon come to a grinding halt. Because the work environment in the dish room or pot room is hot and steamy and the work is dirty and messy, these workers generally need the support and protection of management.

Conclusion

Training in food preparation is important for those who plan careers in kitchen management, restaurant management, and hotel management. No future manager should narrow his or her training to exclude either back-of-the-house or front-of-the-house experience.

Careers in the food preparation area are exciting and offer many opportunities, and they can be approached through a number of avenues. Students may:

- Attend a culinary school or chef training program.
- Complete a degree program in HRIM (hotel, restaurant, institutional management).
- Participate in an apprenticeship program sanctioned by the American Culinary Federation (the national association of chefs).

• Work their way up a career ladder gaining knowledge and experience in the operations where they work.

The individual who pursues a career in food preparation can expect plenty of job opportunities in a variety of types of food service operations. Trained food preparation professionals can find work in any part of the country they desire.

This career requires physical stamina, since it involves standing and working for long hours, often in an expanded workweek that includes nights, weekends, and holidays. A well-rounded training in management is important, and should include cost control, purchasing, the selection of food and nonfood items, menu planning and design, and a thorough knowledge of food preparation. Future managers should also school themselves in those basics not normally expected of management, such as dishmachine operation. This not only equips them to assist their kitchen staff in busy periods or emergencies, but it can also contribute to a positive cooperative bond between managers and their food service team.

Keywords

static menu   320
cyclical menu   322
table d'hôte menu   322
du jour menu   322
truth in menu legislation   323
conventional oven   328
convection oven   328
microwave oven   329
steam-jacketed kettle   330

compartment steamer   330
recipe   330
preparation   330
formula   332
production   334
conduction   335
convection   335
moist heat   336
dry heat   336

Core Concepts

forecasting   318
menu design   319
table turnover   320
product degeneration   332

kitchen-testing   332
portion control   333
executive chef   342
sous chef   342

Discussion Questions

1. Explain the difference between and give an example of both forced and natural convection.
2. Which is the most efficient form of heat transfer? Which is the least efficient? Please explain.
3. What is the definition of clean? Sanitary? Can an item be clean but not sanitary? Explain.
4. What are the three goals of a food service organization? Explain how a properly designed menu can help an operation achieve those goals.
5. List three foods that are potentially hazardous. Explain why some foods are potentially hazardous and some are not.

PART V

Introduction to Hospitality Operations

Managing hospitality businesses requires special knowledge and skills. A manager must know how to manage people and money; how to apply new technology to hospitality operations; how to market hospitality products and services to potential customers; and how to comply with government laws that govern hospitality operations. This section introduces these specific hospitality management responsibilities.

Because they discuss a specific topic of hospitality management and operations, these chapters are specialized and technical in nature. However, the topics apply to all sectors of the hospitality industry. The discussions of these topics are thus not confined to just one sector of the hospitality industry. Great efforts have been made by the authors to include as many different examples across the industry as possible in order to demonstrate the importance of these hospitality management topics to the industry in general.

Chapter 11 discusses human resource management in the hospitality industry. Hospitality management is highly people oriented: It means serving guests, managing employees, and dealing with purveyors. Working well with people is an essential skill for a manager. Clearly outlined are the strategic human resource management process for any hospitality operation and the human resource laws that govern employment practices. The chapter offers practical knowledge every human resource manager should have in order to manage people in the hospitality industry.

Chapter 12 deals with the topic of hospitality accounting and finance. This chapter first introduces students to the generality of accounting practice in commercial business. It then focuses on accounting practice and management in the hospitality industry with current examples from both hotel and restaurant operations. It discusses various issues of financial planning and budgeting for hospitality operations. A clear distinction is made in this chapter between accounting and finance for students' better understanding.

Chapter 13 analyzes the legal aspects of hospitality management operations. Federal, state, and local governments are all involved in the relationship between a hospitality business and its guests. This chapter discusses how laws are enacted and what laws have a direct impact on lodging and food and beverage operations, as well as on their labor practices. It points out that laws pertaining to the hospitality industry vary among states and that the understanding of federal and local laws is essential to a successful hospitality operation.

Chapter 14 talks about how technology is used in the hospitality industry. Systematic management requires a systematic way of gathering, processing, and storing information for decision making. Rising labor costs often force the hospitality industry to look for more efficient alternatives to operate business. Technology has proven to be one of the best answers. This chapter describes in detail how computer systems are used in the various aspects of both lodging and food service operations. This chapter explains and emphasizes management applications of computer operations, and introduces the most up-to-date technological developments in the hospitality industry.

Marketing is a business practice that brings buyers and sellers together. It is particularly challenging in the hospitality industry because the industry sells both tangible products and intangible services. In Chapter 15, the unique characteristics of service marketing are clearly differentiated from those of product marketing. It explains comprehensively the different marketing elements that make up an effective and successful hospitality marketing program.

These five chapters combine to present some of the specific skills a future manager needs to develop. The effective management and control of these areas is vital to the success of any hospitality business operation.

Human Resource Management

Hospitality managers are primarily people managers. The United States' 50 percent divorce rate is an indication that the possession of people skills (so necessary for people management) is not a necessarily inherent human quality. Human resource management requires professional training to be able to address all the needs of today's diverse workforce. The ''I'm the boss'' mentality is not an effective management strategy. Employees are no longer content to be treated like cogs on a gearwheel. They want respect and participation in their company's future.

Many line workers, such as cooks, servers, and housekeepers, often believe that they can be better managers than the managers for whom they are working. They perhaps could be, given training and a long-term perspective, the one who takes into account not just the day's, week's, or even year's success, but instead looks at the long term. However, management is far more difficult than it appears. This chapter describes the long-term planning effort needed to assure adequate staffing into the future. It also details the day-to-day personnel functions and the tools hospitality managers must master to achieve and maintain the standards set by the organization.

Outline

Introduction

University hospitality management programs are graduating prospective hospitality managers who are technically skilled. Graduates can design and price menus, read balance sheets, design operations, use relevant computer information systems, market and promote their facility or destination, cook and serve foods and beverages, and select and buy equipment. These graduates know the hospitality business, and most have the capabilities to operate a small business almost single-handedly. Most graduates, however, will not single-handedly operate small businesses. Rather, they will be working as managers in large operations, and their major responsibilities will include directing and instructing others in the functions of the operation.

Students at universities may be educated and trained to perform most of the jobs of the employees they will manage. However, being able to perform a particular job is different from being able to direct and train someone to do that particular job.

Historically, hospitality managers have been promoted from the ranks and learned management practices from senior managers. As the hospitality industry has become more complex and more competitive and as the labor pool has grown less skilled and decreased in size, these handed-down management practices have come to be seen by some as marginally effective. Some question whether these practices were ever effective, but, with less competition in the past, poorly selected or poorly trained employees could easily be replaced because of an abundance of cheap, unskilled labor.

Most of the new jobs and most of the new wealth in the next decade will be from the service industry. The hospitality industry is growing at a phenomenal rate, and by the year 2000, some experts predict that the hospitality industry will be the largest industry in the world. More hotels and restaurants are being built, and the industry is becoming more competitive. Qualified workers must be recruited and, more important, be retained. It is imperative that professional human resource management address these needs and issues to operate successfully in today's competitive market.

Strategic Human Resource Management

Employees are human resources. Resources are things of value, for example, natural resources such as oil, coal, water, or fertile topsoil. While most of us have long agreed that it is wrong to squander our natural resources, we have not always made the parallel assumption that it is wrong to squander human resources. Since it is our employees who deliver the service to our customers, our success as an organization is therefore directly tied to our employees' effectiveness. If we do not adequately and appropriately staff our operation, our employees will not be able to effectively deliver service to our customers. This requires long-term planning.

Strategic human resource management is a process whereby human resource decisions and strategies are made with the intent of facilitating a company's long-term objectives. This assumes that the company has long-term objectives that indicate where it, as a company, wants to be in the future. It is important that these objectives be consistent with the company's self-identity and what is important to its owners, so it must first define itself in writing. This is normally done in the company's mission statement or statement of philosophy.

Mission Statements

We hear sad stories of students who went to college to become lawyers or doctors because their parents wanted them to be lawyers or doctors, and how they failed or persevered and were miserable. Their personal *mission statements* (definitions of who they wanted to be) were incorrect, not true to whom they really were.

It is very important that mission statements be true definitions of companies (or individuals) because many, if not all, decisions are based on these definitions. If a mission statement is wrong, the decisions based upon it will also be wrong, which will result in friction and cross-purposes. (See Exhibit 11–1)

EXHIBIT 11–1

A mission statement reflects the values and beliefs of its organization. What do the words in bold in the mission statement tell you about Restaura?

MISSION S T A T E M E N T

RESTAURA PROVIDES AN **exceptional** LEVEL OF CULINARY **excellence** AND PROFESSIONAL MANAGEMENT THROUGH PERSONALIZED **service** FOR BUSINESS, LEISURE, AND OTHER **select** CUSTOMERS.

WE PROVIDE OUR **customers** WITH HIGH **quality** CUSTOMIZED DINING, VENDING, AND RELATED SERVICES IN A **professional** MANNER THAT CONSISTENTLY **exceeds** THEIR EXPECTATIONS.

WE AGGRESSIVELY SEARCH OUT NEW WAYS TO BETTER **serve** OUR CUSTOMERS AND PROVIDE A **challenging** AND PROFESSIONAL WORKING **environment** FOR ALL RESTAURA TEAM MEMBERS.

WE ACHIEVE GROWTH AND PROFITABILITY BY KEEPING OUR **promise** TO EACH CUSTOMER TO PROVIDE A TOTAL **experience** THAT IS REFLECTIVE OF OUR **commitment** TO EXCELLENCE.

Ⓡ Restaura.

Courtesy: Restaura, Incorporated, Phoenix, Arizona.

Long-Term Objectives

If a company's mission statement defines it as a fine-dining restaurant with a strong emphasis on elegant, personal service, one of its long-term objectives might be to open similar establishments in several cities in a particular region of the country. Its focus would be on this goal, and it would make decisions to reach it. It might forgo investing in a "great deal" such as a sports bar, for instance, because it would lose its focus and perhaps deter itself from its long-term goal.

Long-term objectives have to be more than just a wish list. They have to be realistic. Strategic human resource management requires that planners look at their company's labor force to determine its strengths and weaknesses. While the company may want to emphasize elegant, personal service, it may not have any employees capable of that type of service, even with training. In that case, it would have to modify either its plan (so that it reflects what it is capable of doing) or its staff (so that it becomes capable of achieving the type of service it has identified).

Long-term objectives also have to be realistic in terms of availability of future workers. If a company wishes to expand with restaurants in other cities, it must determine whether there will be adequate capable workers available there to fill job openings, not only this year, but also five years from now. On the other hand, it must also consider the possibility of losing customers and what it would then do with the excess staff.

External Environments

Businesses operate in controllable and uncontrollable environments. The only things they can control are their own decisions. They must be realistic about their competition since they cannot change it. Can they compete on all fundamental fronts? It's a given that they will compete for workers from the same labor pool. Will workers choose to work for company A rather than company B? Will they choose to stay with either company after being hired? Businesses can control the working conditions and the style of management in their operations, but not the composition of the labor pool.

Long-term human resources planning must also take into consideration some of the other uncontrollable environments in which companies operate, such as the social environment. For example, fast-food companies have recently returned to paper wrappers in response to changing social values concerning the natural environment. Also, society's views towards smoking and drinking alcohol have changed considerably over the last 20 years. It's hard for any one business to fight these changes. Instead, business managers must figure out how to deal with them.

Social changes have a way of becoming legislative changes over time. Society's negative views on smoking have recently resulted in new laws banning smoking in public buildings. Legislation is another uncontrollable environment within which businesses must work, following the numerous laws related to human resource management.

The technological environment is a third uncontrollable environment in which human resource managers must operate. Changes in technology require an awareness because failure to grow and improve technologically can result in the loss of competitiveness.

There are economic cycles that must be anticipated, because they affect our business. Population shifts, geographical concerns, natural disasters, political changes, and international events can all affect business and must be considered when making any long-term plans or decisions.

Forecasting

Businesses want to anticipate the future and be proactive rather than reactive to crises. Forecasting involves using various anticipatory and predictive methods to identify expected future conditions and needs, based on past and present conditions and needs. Forecasts must identify the supply of workers and compare it with expected demand for workers on a short-term and long-term basis.

Environment

Managing can be very enjoyable. However, with management comes tremendous responsibility. Managers are responsible for their employees, and their decisions affect many lives. Employees look to managers for guidance. Managers can therefore have a very positive influence on their behavior, decisions, attitudes, and beliefs. Managers are directly responsible for creating a work environment that is conducive to helping employees excel in their work. If managers show genuine environmental concern, some of that concern might ''rub off'' on the people who work for them.

Strategic Human Resource Management Process

To review the steps up to this point: Businesses first define who they are and then base long-term objectives on that definition. Next they compare their objectives' feasibility with the company's strengths and weaknesses, with external uncontrollable environments, and with forecasted conditions and needs.

The next step in the process is to develop strategies for achieving the objectives. If a company had a long-term goal of operating a chain of elegant fine-dining restaurants, and the goal was feasible in terms of the competition, the company's strengths and weaknesses, and all the known uncontrollable environments, it could then devise a specific plan or strategy to realize that goal. It could then implement those strategies and monitor them to determine their effectiveness, revising them if necessary. (See Exhibit 11–2.)

EXHIBIT 11–2

Strategic management model

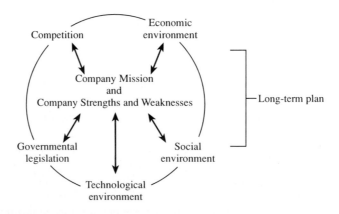

Changes in the Workforce

Demographics

Hospitality managers must be prepared to manage the workers of today and tomorrow. Yesterday's hospitality workers were primarily young, white males. Today the pool of available workers is, for one thing, older. The United States population is aging. The average age of the population is increasing as the baby boom generation (born between 1946 and 1964) ages. In 1970, the supply of workers in the 16- to 34-year age bracket made up 42 percent of the population and totaled 34,818,000. Projections for the year 2000 are that the same 16- to 34-year age bracket will make up just 38 percent of the population (though it will account for 53,374,800 people). It is expected that the labor force will continue to grow at this slower post–baby boom pace in the future.

The hospitality industry has traditionally relied on teenagers to fill many of its entry-level positions. As this labor source is decreasing, people over the age of 55 are and will be available to fill many of the job openings. In the past, older workers were often dismissed as a potential labor source because of stereotypical beliefs and the availability of teenagers and young adults for entry-level hospitality jobs. These incorrect stereotypes asserted that older workers could not easily learn new skills, that they were not interested in learning, and that they had diminished problem-solving skills. Happily, these narrow-minded myths have been exploded, and employers are finding that, in many cases, older workers offer advantages such as improved attendance, punctuality, and a positive service orientation.

Consider some other changes. There were 21 million women in the workforce in 1960. By 1985, that number had increased to 51 million. Today, women make up 45 percent of the workforce, and 43 percent of those women earn wages below the poverty level. Presently, almost one-half of the women in the workforce are primary income earners. The average wage of women is only about 69 percent of the average wage of men. The percentage of the workforce made up of women represents a 60 percent increase in overall employment over the past 30 years, and women are projected to represent 64 percent of the workforce by the year 2000.

The black, Hispanic, and Asian portions of the U.S. workforce are growing at faster rates than the white workforce. White males will make up only 15 percent of the new entrants into the labor force from now until the year 2000. Ninety percent of the growth in the labor force over the next 10 years will be represented by minorities and women.

Increases in immigration have resulted in increases in the number of people who speak English as a second language. People with different languages, different social customs, different standards, and different cultural backgrounds are entering the workforce in great numbers. At the same time, more socially, educationally, and financially disadvantaged people are also entering the workforce.

The expectations of workers have been changing throughout this century. Workers are less willing to be humble and obedient and prefer some latitude, recognition, respect, and input into how ''their'' company is managed. Workers are less willing to perform boring jobs, and they depend increasingly on their work for personal fulfillment. Managers have to be aware of these changes and accommodate them if possible.

Illiteracy

Twenty percent of American adults cannot read, write, or compute adequately to be productive workers. Up to one-half of this group may be totally illiterate. It is reasonable to expect that many of these people are and will be employed in the hospitality industry.

Illiteracy is often hidden and not easily detected. Some hospitality companies in the United States have begun to question whether training programs can be effective when they are delivered to an illiterate audience. In response, some are experimenting with in-house literacy programs to provide illiterate employees with the basic skills necessary to benefit from training.

Another trend in the hospitality industry has been to redesign jobs for illiterate people by making the jobs easier and reducing decision-making demands. However, jobs without variety and diversity have the unfortunate side effect of tending to decrease the ability of people to make decisions. Entry-level jobs in the hospitality industry often involve the delivery of service to customers. Successful service requires employees to be able to respond to situations and take action, so this practice (which some have uncharitably called *dumbing down* a job) ends up being a disservice to all concerned.

In cities across the country, planners and activists are looking at chronic unemployment and chronic labor shortages in tandem—as two problems that might be tweaked into helping solve each other. After all, there are jobs going unfilled (for want of skilled labor) and people unable to find jobs (for want of appropriate skills). Some hospitality corporations are attempting to produce a pool of skilled workers for entry-level positions by seeking the chronically unemployed who are physically able to work. This group is then trained for job-specific skills (like serving or making beds), basic skills (reading, writing, arithmetic), and life skills (how to behave on the job, how to get along with others, how to manage money, and so forth). Graduates of the training program are then available for entry-level positions.

Industry and community-related programs are responding to the idea that business and community are directly related; businesses are less likely to be healthy in an unhealthy society. The chronically unemployed and/or homeless people participating in training programs experience increased self-esteem and self-confidence, which, in turn, enables them to become more effective and loyal employees.

EXHIBIT 11–3

Training is particularly important in the quick-serve restaurant segment, where consistency is a priority. Here, in a White Castle system training poster, proper methodology is demonstrated with a strong visual example.

PROPER AMOUNT OF ONIONS
SPREAD EVENLY OVER ENTIRE GRIDDLE

PROPERLY COLORED MEAT PATTIES
PLACED IN EVEN ROWS TO COVER
ENTIRE GRIDDLE

PROPERLY BAKED BUNS PLACED SQUARELY
ON MEAT PATTIES AND PROPERLY
STAGGERED

White Castle

HOW THAT ONE-OF-A-KIND-TASTE STACKS UP

WHAT YOU CRAVE

HOW NOT TO STACK UP A WHITE CASTLE

■ NOT ENOUGH ONIONS — NOT SPREAD EVENLY

■ TOO MANY ONIONS — NOT SPREAD EVENLY

■ ONIONS NOT SPREAD EVENLY

■ MEAT PATTIES NOT IN EVEN ROWS

■ MEAT PATTIES NOT EVENLY SPACED

■ MEAT PATTIES TOO CLOSE TOGETHER — NOT COVERING ENTIRE GRIDDLE

■ DEFINITELY NOT — THIS IS A TOTAL MESS

■ BUNS NOT SQUARELY ON MEAT PATTIES

■ BUNS AND MEAT PATTIES TOO CLOSE TOGETHER — NOT COVERING ENTIRE GRIDDLE

Courtesy: White Castle System, Inc., 1995.

Human Resource Laws

Discrimination means to give preferential treatment to members of certain groups. In the United States, young white males have, over time, often been given preferential treatment in human resource situations such as hiring and promoting. Because of this preferential treatment, other groups have been discriminated against and have been determined by the federal government to be in need of protection. These protected groups are minorities, women, older people, Vietnam veterans, and those with disabilities, and all have been given protection under the Equal Employment Opportunity laws.

Yet, even without the EEO laws, hospitality managers would really have no choice about hiring women, older workers, minorities, and workers with disabilities. In today's labor market, there simply aren't enough young white males to fill all the entry-level hospitality positions.

That's the pragmatic or practical side, but philosophically, it is in our best interest to be free of discrimination. If we hold negative stereotypic views of African-Americans, Asians, Hispanics, older people, women, and others, we are less likely to be able to see the real strengths and weaknesses of any given individual. Thus, we are less likely to be able to inspire the best effort of that particular employee, and he or she will be less likely to feel any loyalty or commitment to us and our organization.

Eye on the Issues

Ethics

Though it hasn't been labeled as such, this entire chapter has dealt with ethics. Ethics has to do with doing the right thing, always, even if it is not the easiest or most expedient thing. Ethics boils down to treating others as we like to be treated. Few of us like to be lied to or cheated or taken advantage of. Most of us like to be respected and treated kindly and fairly.

The fact that some businesspeople are unethical does not make it necessary or okay for us to be unethical, too. In the not-too-distant future, you will make the decisions that will affect all your employees and society as a whole. The decisions you make today determine the decisions you will make in the future. Integrity and strength of character are developed over time. If you make unethical decisions today, you will have no integrity tomorrow.

Our country is founded on the principles of equality and fairness. The mission statement of the United States of America, the Constitution, affirms the right of equal opportunity. Laws are generally enacted because people fail to do the right thing voluntarily. Discrimination on the basis of race, age, sex, national origin, or religion is morally wrong, legally wrong, and just plain bad management.

Motivation

Our task as hospitality managers is to hire people capable of doing the jobs we wish them to do. If they are not capable of doing the jobs, no amount of training will make them effective. Moreover, they must also be *willing* to do the job. They can have the ability to do the job, but if they don't really want to do it, they probably won't be effective. The third part of this interconnection is this: Employees can be willing to do the job and perfectly capable of doing the job, but if they are not shown how to do the job, they still may not be effective.

Once we have capable, willing, and trained employees, our ongoing challenge is to figure out how to get them to do *what* we want them to do, *when* we want them to do it, *how* we want them to do it, and for them to do it graciously, since we are, after all, a service industry. In order to do this, we need to understand why people do what they do, to know what motivates them.

Motivation comes from within people. We cannot motivate people to do things. They must have a reason for wanting to do what we want them to do, and that comes from within them. Our task as hospitality managers is to figure out what motivates our employees. To be able to do that, we must know them. We need to create a delicate set of conditions wherein they can somehow meet their needs while doing what we want them to do.

Teachers want students to study and get good grades. But teachers can't make students do that if they don't want to. Students may do what teachers want them to do if studying hard and getting good grades meets some needs the students have, such as pleasing parents, obtaining scholarships, and obtaining jobs. Only if the desires of teachers and the needs of the students are similar can good results come about. Similarly, workers' needs and management's desires must be aligned.

There are numerous theories of motivation that address the question of why people do things. Money is often thought to be a motivator. The lack of adequate or equitable compensation can have a very negative effect on employee productivity and attitude. However, in the long run, money alone will rarely be enough to make up for insufficient support or unsatisfactory job matches.

Another view is that satisfied or happy workers will be motivated. It is true that people who are satisfied with their jobs will be absent less often and will tend to hold their jobs longer. In this view, inadequate compensation and lack of job satisfaction are seen as negative motivators; adequate money and good job satisfaction are seen as positive motivators.

The third view is that most people strive to reach their full potential. How far they have advanced toward reaching their full potential will determine what motivates them. The idea here is that if we as managers know where on this spectrum of potential they are, we will know what motivates them and can therefore provide the appropriate incentives that will encourage them to do the tasks associated with their jobs. The most well-known theory of this third view is ***Abraham Maslow's hierarchy of needs,*** shown in Exhibit 11–4.

EXHIBIT 11–4

Maslow's hierarchy of motivational factors.

Maslow contends that people are motivated at the lowest level first. People first need food and shelter. When those needs are met, they are then motivated at the next level, which is a desire for safety and security. For example, people who are homeless and do not have enough food will do almost any job if it will enable them to buy or obtain food.

Once people are no longer in that very precarious, scary position, they become a little more choosy and are motivated by desires for safety and security. If employees are at this level, a manager can offer incentives appropriate for this level, such as letting them know their work is appreciated and telling them that they can expect to keep their jobs and perhaps even move upward over time.

People who feel safe and secure desire a social life and want to feel part of something. (Starving people aren't terribly concerned with popularity or social activities.) But if we know our employees have progressed to this level, we might offer activities such as employee parties or softball games to give them a feeling of belonging. They can then conclude that working for us gives them access to acceptance and affiliation, which is what they need or desire.

The next level of need is esteem. At this point we can offer employees such things as employee-of-the-month awards, special recognition, enriched jobs, or more authority as incentives.

At the highest level on Maslow's hierarchy (self-actualization), employees are self-motivated. They need no incentives to do their best work.

People may be at various levels at the same time, or may change levels, going back to a previous level (as in the case of a family crisis or divorce). We need to know where our employees are in their lives. Maslow's theory is a theory—not a fact. It is, however, a useful tool for us to get to know our employees better and thus help them to meet their needs while meeting ours.

Service Industry

As you have heard and will hear echoed throughout this text, the hospitality industry's product is service. As competition increases, guests have more choices, and hospitality managers must be able to assure good service. Repeat business is a result of positive guest experiences. Guests expect servers and other hospitality workers to be technically proficient. Good service is technical proficiency delivered with a smile, a remembered name, or a friendly attitude. Studies show that guests who have positive experiences are each likely to tell five to nine other people. Guests who have negative experiences, on the other hand, are each likely to tell between 10 and 30 people.

The technical aspects of service can be transmitted through training. It is more difficult or even impossible to train a worker to have a friendly attitude, so it is important to hire people who are hospitable to begin with. While a good match between worker and job is necessary, a positive working environment and job skills training can improve the worker's attitude.

Workers who are expected to care for guests must be cared for by management. Successful hospitality corporations regard their workers as their greatest assets. Employees are as important to an operation as guests are and should be treated in the same way management would like their employees to treat guests. Also, today's workers expect to be treated with respect. When workers and managers clearly understand that the success of their operation is directly related to the quality of the employees' work effort, respect can be fostered.

It has taken time, but hospitality organizations are finally beginning to see the light: Unhappy workers are not motivated to give good service. Neither are poorly treated or unacknowledged workers. It is through trust and caring that people are empowered to be better, more responsible workers, and, therefore, find the satisfaction today's workers expect from their jobs.

The successful management of an increasingly diverse workforce requires enhanced communication and leadership skills and an ability to teach and train individuals with varying degrees of experience and understanding. The focus in management must be on accommodating change, rather than on resisting it.

Hospitality Industry Turnover

Turnover is the rate at which a business replaces workers. A 25 to 30 percent rate of turnover is considered too high in most industries. The hospitality industry, however, has turnover percentage rates ranging well up into the low hundreds! Turnover directly and indirectly increases a company's expenses, due to search and selection costs, hiring and training costs, separation costs such as severance pay, production losses, waste, accidents, decreases in morale, faltering service levels, and loss of customers.

Management Turnover

Hospitality industry management turnover is very high, with poor communication between managers and their superiors given as the most important reason why managers leave their jobs. Low pay, long hours, high pressure, and aggravation may be keeping potentially high-caliber managers away from hospitality management positions. One-third of all hospitality management graduates may defect from the hospitality industry five years after graduation.

Managers who choose to stay in the hospitality industry often change jobs in order to advance. The most common reason given for changing jobs, however, is the lack of appreciation managers feel they receive from their supervisors. The hours, the pay, the lack of support, and the lack of adequate training can overwhelm even those managers who are already employed in the hospitality industry. They may feel ''used'' by upper management, and it is this upper management ''user'' mentality that is at the heart of burnout. Burnout is more likely to result in a manager leaving a particular property or job than leaving the entire industry.

Today, 80 to 90 percent of hospitality managers are married as compared to the 1960s when most managers were single. Managers with families are naturally more concerned with quality-of-life issues. The hospitality industry may have to consider the effect that hours worked per week, pay, and benefits have on their management staff from the quality-of-life perspective.

Worker Turnover

The turnover rate among nonmanagers is higher because of low wages, lack of challenge, and lack of interest. Operators know that they should sell an appealing image of their establishment to customers; however, not all understand that they must also sell an appealing image of the establishment as a good place to work to prospective and current workers. For customers to return, the service experience must match the advertisement. Likewise, for workers to stay, the work environment must be positive and rewarding.

As mentioned before, many workers may be seeking a sense of belonging or a sense of self-worth. Managers who are able to encourage and foster a team spirit and a sense of family can reduce turnover. Providing ongoing comprehensive training may enable workers to become and feel more competent, which can raise self-esteem. People working together as a team share responsibility, rely on each other, support each other's efforts, and realize common interests in improving performance and being part of a successful operation.

Eye on the Issues

International

This chapter describes the workforce of today and the future. Many of the industry's workers are and will be from countries other than the United States, having English as a second language and having completely different customs and standards. The present job standards don't have to change, but as managers we must understand and accommodate their differences in order to help this diverse workforce meet the industry's standards.

Additionally, the opportunities for us to manage hospitality operations in the international market keep increasing. As with international workers in our national industry, we must be aware of different cultures and intrinsically different standards to be able to get people to do what we want them to do graciously.

Cross-training—training employees to do tasks outside their own job description—has been demonstrated to be an effective strategy for sharing responsibility and understanding among staff members, while at the same time helping to fill gaps left by labor shortages. Cross-training can also be a means for encouraging teamwork.

Retention Tactics

Leadership

To build teams, managers must continuously develop their own leadership skills. Traditional authoritative management styles are ineffective with today's workers, because today's workers do not respond positively to autocrats. Managers must attempt to foster a positive sense of partnership with employees. Managers who wish to retain employees must attempt to meet employee needs by providing an atmosphere in which personal creativity, decision making, and employee input are encouraged.

Increasing competition has magnified the importance of a service orientation, not only externally (to customers), but also internally (to employees). A corporate culture where guests and employees are valued with a similar esteem can act as a positive "escalator," lifting a business to new heights. You can almost picture the upward movement: Employees feel valued and are given chances to become more valuable through further training. Being contented and better trained, they produce better service. Guests are delighted by their courtesy and efficiency and return again and again, producing strong revenues. The business does well in the market and retains its excellent employees. Everyone in the organization, however, must buy into the culture for it to work. If some factor in the culture "pushes people off the escalator," the upward momentum can be lost.

It isn't easy building such a positive, healthy corporate culture, and managers who hope to do so (by building teams, motivating employees, coaching, training) must possess certain character traits. If a manager initially lacks the necessary people skills, he or she needn't give up; such skills *can* be taught. Unfortunately, true and real concern for employees cannot be taught, yet is equally essential.

Career Planning

Many employees leave jobs and organizations to accept better jobs. Companies that desire to retain excellent employees are discovering that it is mutually beneficial to assist employees in career planning—by identifying career paths within the organization that match the abilities and aspirations of the employees with the needs and requirements of the organization. Company-assisted career planning helps employees avoid costly and painful career decision mistakes, and demonstrates company commitment to employee development. At the same time, it helps the company find excellent successors for those employees who do leave the organization, and this assists long-range planning.

Development Programs

Development programs are important for managers as well as for workers to improve current and future job performance. Ongoing management development programs can help prevent management burnout while providing a succession of managers for top-level jobs.

Training

Lack of proper training is consistently cited in surveys as one of the top reasons for turnover. Sixty percent of employee resignations are given during the first month of employment. Employees who resign due to a lack of adequate training may have been directly or indirectly serving guests. The likelihood of positive guest experiences that promote repeat business during this period is questionable, to say the least.

One of management's goals should be to help employees stay in their jobs. Employees who become *part of* the company, as opposed to merely *working for* the company, are more likely to stay with the company. It is far easier for an employee to feel part of a company (and embrace its service orientation) if he or she is given adequate and encouraging training. Good managers feel an obligation to provide training that enables workers to perform their service roles successfully.

Personnel Functions

Strategic human resource management involves making long-term plans for an organization based on its identity, its strengths and weaknesses, and the uncontrollable environments in which it operates at present (and in the future). Upper management determines long-term plans. It is line management, however, that determines the short-term plans that ultimately result in achieving the long-term goals planned by upper management.

The day-to-day running of a hospitality operation requires adequate and appropriate staffing to deliver the expected service. Personnel functions, short-term by nature, are the ongoing activities of managing human resources and include the following (see also Exhibit 11–5):

- Job analysis.
- Job description/job specification.
- Recruiting/selection.
- Orientation/training.
- Performance appraisal.

EXHIBIT 11–5

Personal functions

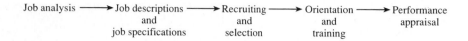

Twenty years ago, most hospitality corporations had ''personnel'' departments rather than ''human resource management'' departments. But as the competitive environment intensified and the labor pool became more diverse and less skilled, companies had to use a more global and long-term (strategic) approach to stay competitive.

The personnel functions now fall under the umbrella of strategic human resource management. Personnel policies are administered on a day-to-day basis, but are in line with the long-term game plan. It is through the personnel functions that managers incorporate motivation theories, knowledge of the labor force, and adherence to the equal employment opportunity laws in order to operate systematically and successfully.

Job Analysis

Job analysis is the systematic investigation of the scope and duties of a job as they should be performed to result in the desired level of service. We do job analysis in order to write job descriptions and job specifications.

A **job description** is a list of the significant duties and responsibilities of a job. It simply ''describes'' the job. The person we hire must be able to do all the items listed on the job description. The **job specification** is a list of all the skills and characteristics a person must already have in order to be hired for the job.

All the personnel functions are based on data collected during a job analysis. If we skip the job analysis component, all our operating documents and plans are based on guesswork, albeit educated guesswork. This is similar to the concept of opening a restaurant without doing market research to determine customer preferences. Professionals remove as much of the risk as possible.

Job analysis should be done for every position in the operation. In a restaurant we would do job analyses for cooks, servers, buspersons, and so forth. Ideally, job analysis is done before a new operation opens or if job descriptions have never been written or are out of date. We want answers to the following questions for each position:

1. What does this person do in this job?
2. What should this person be doing in this job?
3. What kind of training is necessary for this job?
4. What qualifications are necessary for this job?
5. What should the scope of this job be?

EXHIBIT 11–6

A thorough initial screening of applicants may help the recruiting and selection process.

Recruiting and Selection

Part of the personnel function is the development of recruiting and selection plans that can be used every time there is an opening. Because we have a job specification and know exactly what we need to fill the position, we can write accurate and appropriate advertisements ahead of time. We want to be specific so that recruits will self-select and we won't have to bother weeding out all those who don't have the necessary qualifications.

We then analyze incoming applications to determine whether any are a likely match for the job. We can notice job histories, looking for gaps in employment and job jumping, and then choose the best matches to be interviewed. In the interview we can ask questions raised from analyzing the application. It is in the interview that we clarify and assure ourselves of the rightness of the match. However, we should caution that even the toughest interviewers realize that life is difficult, and the presence of a gap, a variety of jobs, or even a firing doesn't necessarily mean a person could not become a superb long-term employee. Job jumping may raise questions, but should not necessarily be immediate cause for rejection.

Interviewing

We may experience job interviews where the interviewer obviously hasn't even looked at the application before the interview. He or she may do most of the talking and then ask us, ''Do you have any questions?'' This interviewer has missed the opportunity to make a wise selection—to make a good match. If an employee works out under such circumstances, it is due to luck.

EXHIBIT 11–7

Interviewing is an important skill for managers to master.

Here again, we must keep the focus on the job and be able to really see and hear the applicant. We often see and hear what we *wish* to see and hear. Many interviewers decide to hire an applicant before they even talk to the person. We must be aware of our own biases so that we are not viewing the person through our own perceptions. We must be aware of common interviewing errors so that we do not make them:

1. Interviewers assume that an applicant's reaction to one situation will be the same in all situations.
2. Interviewers prefer to hire applicants who seem more like themselves in background, style, and/or attitudes.
3. Interviewers form an opinion before meeting the applicant.
4. Interviewers like one thing about an applicant and assume everything else is good too.
5. Interviewers make selection decisions before analyzing the various candidates and information and checking references.
6. Interviewers stereotype people of protected groups.

Interviewers make these mistakes without awareness and assume they are making thoughtful selections. They may not be. Such mistakes keep them from really seeing who they are interviewing, which makes it very difficult to match job and applicant. Some of these pitfalls can be avoided through awareness and practice, and it's important to make the effort, whether the job is high level or entry level.

Nonprofessionals often think that the selection process doesn't matter because "it's just a dishwasher." It does matter, though. If the person hired to do dishes has the characteristics listed on the job specification, he or she will be able to get along better on the job and stay longer. This makes everyone's job easier, including that of the manager.

Unfortunately, the hospitality industry has been known for the "warm body syndrome." This describes conditions wherein a manager hires the first person available for a job. If he or she is lucky, the warm body works out. Too often, though, things do not work out and the carelessly hired employee becomes one of the company's many turnover statistics. Unnecessarily high turnover costs this industry a fortune in money, time, customers, service, and aggravation.

Orientation

Our human resource task is to hire the right people for our jobs and then keep them. Reputation is one way to attract the right people, since prospective employees may have heard, through the grapevine, which are the good places to work in town. The prospective employee's first encounter with us can set the tone for the entire working relationship. That first inquiring phone call or stop in for an application can determine an applicant's perception of the company's suitability as an employer. If we are rude, or too busy to listen, or make the applicant wait too long, we are making a statement to the employee—a statement about how we treat our employees in general.

Eye on the Issues

Technology

There are many computer applications available for payroll, tracking employees, and scheduling, that have considerably simplified human resource paperwork, thus freeing managers to be with their employees doing their job, which is supervising.

Supplementing more traditional methods of training with technological methods (mediated training) can cost-effectively provide consistent, convenient training that is easily monitored. Some companies are taping their own customized training videos. Videos used in conjunction with written texts or workbooks and self-test questions can provide a comprehensive, interactive, inexpensive, and consistent approach to training. Interactive videodisks combine the strengths of computer-assisted instruction and videotapes. These growth areas will continue to make headlines over the next decade.

After having spent the time and money making a good selection, it makes sense to "protect our investment" by acknowledging new employees as they arrive for their first day at work. We want new employees to feel welcome and pleased that they have joined our team. If we don't make some kind of connection with them from the very beginning, we may well lose them. More employees quit in the first month of work than later. They do so because they do not feel like they belong, and they decide they do not want to belong.

A good first-day orientation is a simple way to welcome new employees into the organization—and it's simple hospitality, which is our business anyway. A first-day orientation may include:

- Showing the employee around.
- Introducing him or her to fellow workers, perhaps assigning a mentor or ''big brother or sister.''
- ''Pre-answering'' all the questions they need to ask but might be too embarrassed to ask (where the bathrooms are, when they can take breaks, what food they can eat, and whether they have to pay for it).
- Showing them where to put their coats and gear, and how to punch or sign in.
- Putting them at ease; helping them to feel comfortable.

A complete company policy orientation should be done after the employee has gotten his or her ''sea legs'' and achieved a basic comfort level. The first day on the job is too overwhelming to assail a new employee with insurance plans and company history and policies.

Training

Orientation is showing people how to *get along* on the job. Training is showing people how to *do* the job. These are not the same.

Shadowing, which consists of following an experienced worker around for a shift or two, is often called *training,* but it, too, is no substitute. Watching a highly skilled employee doesn't necessarily translate into an understanding of the tasks he or she is performing. The experienced employee may be an excellent worker, but may not have the interest and/or skills to effectively train other employees. Trainers pulled from the ranks who have not been trained to train often deliver inconsistent or incomplete training. This is primarily because they do not know how to transfer knowledge to other people. To be effective, potential trainers must become acquainted with the technology of teaching, that is, the principles of learning, the design of instruction, and teaching methods. Without this grounding, they may deliver new employees ''out on the floor'' or ''on the desk'' before they are ready. This can be disastrous in terms of both customer experience and employee esteem. No customer wants to be ''practiced on'' by a green employee—especially when he or she is paying for professional service.

Performance Appraisal

A performance appraisal is an evaluation of an employee's job performance for the purpose of improvement and works in conjunction with training. The strengths and weaknesses of an employee are documented over a regular period of time, such as a quarter, six months, or a year. At the end of this period, the employee and the manager discuss the results of this evaluation in a performance appraisal interview.

Progressive Discipline

If we've hired the right people for the jobs, welcomed them into our operations, given them consistent formal training, ongoing supervision, and thoughtful performance appraisals, we may not need to worry about discipline and terminations. Often, though, we are hired as managers of an already existing staff. We deal with people, and there are no certainties with people. Even if we cut down the margin of error by using professional methods of management, we will still have to deal with disciplinary problems at times.

Progressive discipline is another form of ongoing training. The purpose is to improve an employee's performance—to get him or her back on track.

Employees have to know rules and standards in order to be able to adhere to them. The rules and standards and the consequences for failure to follow them should be spelled out at some time during the orientation period. It is not enough to give employees policy manuals and assume they will read them. Even if they sign a "have read and understand" form, we cannot assume that they have actually read it and did understand its intent.

As emphasized above, managers should not spend their energies trying to catch employees doing wrong things. Instead, they should help employees avoid wrong behaviors. This can be done by helping employees to understand rules, making sure the rules are consistent and fair, making sure the rules are implemented and administered fairly, and making sure there is a grievance procedure for both parties to follow.

Progressive discipline begins when a new problem arises or when ongoing training (coaching) has failed to make the appropriate change in the employee's performance. The first step is a verbal warning. The employee is told that it is a verbal warning and the warning will be documented in writing. If the deviant behavior continues, the next step is a written warning. The infraction is detailed in writing, the employee signs the written warning, and a copy is put in the employee's file, joining the documentation of the verbal warning.

If the behavior persists, a final written warning is given to the employee describing the consequences for failure to comply. One commonly used consequence is suspension; the strongest (and final) step in progressive discipline is termination.

Health and Safety

The Occupational Safety and Health Administration (**OSHA**) was created by the U.S. Congress "to assure, so far as possible, every working man and woman in the Nation safe and healthful working conditions, and to preserve our human resources." Kitchens are particularly dangerous places to work. Boiling water, powerful equipment, toxic chemicals, knives, wet floors, and rushed employees make for very hazardous working conditions. Most accidents are caused by human error and can be avoided.

The costs of accidents and illnesses in terms of absenteeism, morale, customer service, workers' compensation, lawsuits, and medical expenses have compelled many organizations to institute employee safety programs and **wellness programs** to help their employees improve their health through diet, exercise, stress reduction, and other preventive measures.

It is so costly to replace employees that many organizations are attempting to help troubled employees through trying times with **employee assistance programs** where employees are referred to various agencies to deal with emotional problems, addiction, and family disturbances. Since most people have personal problems at some time in their lives, it is in management's best interest to work with good employees during difficult periods. It is, however, never good policy to allow employees to flagrantly break rules or ignore company policies, despite the personal and professional compassion you, as a manager, may feel.

Conclusion

Beyond our daily goals of profit and superior service, our day-to-day operations must also move us toward our long-term goals and objectives—as determined by upper management. When determined methodically, long-term goals and objectives are feasible because they are based on an organization's strengths, weaknesses, likes, dislikes, resources (financial and human), and the uncontrollable environments of today and the future.

The hospitality industry is growing at a tremendous rate. At a time when the demand for workers is increasing, there are fewer workers available to take low-level minimum wage jobs. Entry-level jobs increasingly require computer skills, decision-making skills, math, and reading skills, yet many of the workers available to take entry-level jobs have fewer rather than more of these basic skills. Twenty percent of American adults cannot read, write, or compute adequately to be productive workers. This means that we must first keep the workers we already have, which may require providing them with higher pay, better benefits, improved working conditions, and better and more training.

As an industry, we will be hiring more women, seniors, disabled, and disadvantaged people, and those for whom English is a second language. We will have to be sympathetic to each of these groups' individual needs, and accommodate physical restrictions, language difficulties, need for child care, and so forth.

The tools of the personnel function can be used to assure efficient, effective, fair, equitable, and non-discriminatory management of our human resources.

Management in the hospitality industry is the management of people. It is essential that we, as hospitality managers, understand ourselves so that we can also understand others. This includes actively cultivating leadership and team-building skills. It is essential that we be able to hire the right people for the right jobs, give them excellent training, and supervise them in an effective manner that will enable them (and us) to maintain our company's standards. It is our task to help our employees excel. This requires professional management, an important dimension of preparation for a degree in hospitality, tourism, or travel.

Keywords

illiteracy   356
discrimination   358
turnover   361
cross-training   363
job analysis   365

job description   365
job specification   365
OSHA   371
wellness programs   371
employee assistance programs   371

Core Concepts

strategic human resource management   351
mission statements   351

Abraham Maslow's hierarchy of needs   359
progressive discipline   370

Discussion Questions

1. Describe the relationship between strategic human resource management and personnel functions.

2. List and describe the uncontrollable environments in which hospitality organizations operate.

3. What is a mission statement and why is it important?

4. List and describe the personnel functions.

5. Describe how the personnel functions work together.

6. Explain Maslow's hierarchy of needs. How can it relate to human resource management?

7. What are the common interviewer errors? Give examples.

8. What is the difference between orientation and training?

9. Why is formal training necessary? What are the possible problems associated with shadowing as a training method?

10. What is the purpose of a performance appraisal?

References

Bernadon, N. L. *Workforce 2000*. Alexandria, VA: Hudson Institute, 1988.

Elmont, S. E. "Foundations . . . Trust, Caring, and Empowerment." *Arizona Hospitality Trends* 31, no. 1 (1992), pp. 20–21.

Ford, D. J. "Toward a More Literate Workforce." *Training and Development* 46 (1992), pp. 52–55.

Herlong, J. "The ABCs of Literacy: Programs from the Workplace to the Classroom." *Restaurants USA* 10, no. 1 (1990), pp. 12–15.

Keegan, P. O. "Quality Training Doesn't Have to Be Bankbreaking." *Nation's Restaurant News* 25, no. 22 (1991), p. 56.

Meyer, R. A., and H. H. Shroeder. "Rewarding Non-productivity in the Hospitality Industry." *FIU Hospitality Review* 7, no. 1 (1989), pp. 1–12.

Pavesic, D. V., and R. A. Brymer. "Job Satisfaction: What's Happening to the Young Managers?" *The Cornell Hospitality & Restaurant Administration Quarterly* 30, no. 4 (1990), pp. 90–96.

Sullivan, J. "How to Use Knowledge as a Main Tool for Training." *Nation's Restaurant News* 24, no. 36 (1990), p. 46.

Hospitality Accounting and Finance

This chapter introduces the student to the areas of hospitality accounting and finance. After explaining and distinguishing the terms *accounting* and *finance*, it explores the general accounting model and explains how it serves as the foundation for accounting reports in the hospitality industry. The chapter then explains business transactions and how they form the building blocks of an accounting system. The chapter concludes by looking at the careers available in the hospitality finance area and the educational requirements needed.

Outline

Introduction

Finance and *accounting* are two distinct terms. In an industry setting, ***finance*** is the management of a company's monetary resources and income. The perspective of a financial manager covers the past, present, and future of the company. The financial manager is concerned with finding the best ways to manage the company's monetary resources and income so that the company may prosper.

Accounting, by contrast, is a tool used in financial management. Its perspective is principally historical: It asks, ''What has happened to the company's financial resources and income up to the present time?'' A financial manager uses the historic financial information of the company provided by the company's accounting system to assist in making the decisions that will affect the company's financial health in the future.

Finance is a discipline concerned with the monetary affairs of the company. Companies have many of the same concerns that we as individuals do. We are all concerned with money. How will we pay our daily living expenses? How much income and savings do we need to meet these expenses? Can we handle emergency expenses? Just as individuals are concerned with their financial affairs, hospitality companies must also be disciplined in the management of their financial dealings. These companies sell goods and services to their customers at market prices. Their total sales receipts must cover payroll costs, goods and services, interest expense, taxes, other expenses, and profits for the owners of the company. If sales are insufficient, the company will lose money and eventually go bankrupt. Company managers are responsible for maintaining the good financial health of their organizations.

Accounting reports and systems supply the information that managers and investors need to manage and evaluate the financial condition of their business.

Accounting is a process whereby the receipts and disbursements of an organization are measured, recorded, and analyzed. It reports on the resources (***assets***) controlled by an organization and the claims (***liabilities***) against those resources.

Accounting, like finance, permeates all of our society. Your checkbook is a simple **accounting system** used to keep track of payments, receipts, and balances in your checking account. Federal and state governments have elaborate accounting systems to help them manage their cash receipts and disbursements.

Businesses monitor their operations through the use of accounting records and reports. Business managers rely on accounting information to answer a multitude of questions: How much revenue did our company earn? What were our net profits for the year? How much money do we owe? Business managers use accounting information to make decisions. The results of their decisions are ultimately reflected in subsequent accounting reports and thus provide feedback about the correctness of their decisions. Accounting systems come in all sizes. A small business can manage with a very simple accounting system, whereas a large corporation needs a more complex one.

In this chapter we will examine accounting in industry in general and the hospitality industry in particular. We will look at the role of finance and make some comments on educational requirements and careers for future general and financial managers in the hospitality industry.

Accounting

The financial affairs of any organization need to be managed and evaluated. The primary tool for doing this is through the organization's accounting system. A company cannot determine if it has made a profit or a loss unless it has some kind of score keeping or accounting system. All phases of a business's operation are monitored through various types of accounting records. Without reliable accounting information, it would be impossible to manage the financial affairs of any organization, for profit or nonprofit. We will first consider how accounting operates in for-profit companies in general and then focus our attention on the peculiarities of the hospitality industry.

Accounting in Industry

The primary distinction between industrial organizations and other organizations in society is their profit motive. All profit-making companies have one objective in common: increase the value of the owner's investment in the company by generating revenues that exceed expenses. The accounting methodology used in business is designed to measure this objective. Accounting reports are designed with the user of the accounting information in mind. The two major categories of users of accounting reports are the company's managers and persons external to the organization, such as stockholders and creditors.

Description and Definition.   Accounting is a process of measurement in monetary units, such as dollars and cents, of what is going on in the business and the reporting of this information to interested parties. Accounting information is reflected from two perspectives:

1. Resources controlled by the organization and claims against those resources. These categories are more commonly referred to as assets and liabilities.
2. Flow of resources into and out of the organization. Examples of resources flowing in would be revenues; resources flowing out would be expenses.

Accounting procedures need to be established in order to collect, process, and evaluate this information.

Objectives of Accounting Systems.   Businesses have broad objectives that must be met by the accounting systems they use.

1. The information produced by the accounting system should be useful to investors, creditors, and managers when they make decisions concerning the business. Reports should be tailored to the needs of the user. One type of summarized report might be adequate for investors and creditors, whereas another more detailed report might be needed for management.

2. Accounting reports should reflect the results of past decisions. For example, individuals might invest in a company based on the information they read in the financial reports of the company. Subsequent reports would reflect the financial progress of the company and would provide feedback to the investors as to the wisdom of their decision. Another example might be the management of a restaurant company that decides to open a new restaurant. The progress of the new restaurant would be reflected in subsequent financial reports. How much were the revenues and the profits of the new restaurant? Were the results up to management's expectations? Was the feasibility study done accurately? (See also the appendix to Chapter 5.)

3. Accounting records should provide detailed information on items about which managers, investors, or creditors need to know or that need to be controlled. Some examples might be cash in banks and on hand; amounts receivable from customers; amounts invested in land, buildings, and equipment; and amounts payable to creditors.

The Accounting Model.   To obtain a basic understanding of how accounting works, we need to examine the **accounting model.** We use the term *model* to indicate that accounting is a financial representation of what the firm is. A company at a certain point in time possesses resources such as cash, equipment, land, buildings, and other tangible items. The company could also possess intangible items such as amounts due from customers and investments. We call these possessions *assets*.

At this same point in time the company might owe money to persons and organizations. These could include **accounts payable** to (owed to) suppliers, loans payable to a bank, and wages payable to employees. We call these items *liabilities*. If we deduct the total of the liabilities from the total of the assets, the remaining amount would be the equity belonging to the owners of the business. We call this remainder or residual *owner's equity.* Thus, we can define owners' equity as the excess of a company's assets over its liabilities. Let us illustrate this with some numbers. On December 31, 1993, company A has a total of $100,000 in assets and a total of $80,000 in liabilities. The owners' equity at the same point in time would be $20,000. We can show this relationship by the following formula:

$$\text{Assets} - \text{Liabilities} = \text{Owners' equity}$$

$$\$100,000 - \$80,000 = \$20,000$$

We can eliminate the minus sign by moving Liabilities to the other side of the equation, giving the following equation:

$$\text{Assets} = \text{Liabilities} + \text{Owners' equity}$$

$$\$100,000 = \$80,000 + \$20,000$$

The above formula represents one of the basic financial reports of a company: the *balance sheet.* The balance sheet is prepared as of a particular point in time. The numbers we cited above for company A were as of December 31, 1993, for example. The balance sheet of a company reflects in dollars the assets the company owns, the liabilities it has to others, and its owners' equity. Information on the balance sheet is presented in summarized form. A line reporting ''Cash in banks and on hand'' summarizes total cash rather than giving a detailed list of all the bank accounts and cash funds.

Remember, a balance sheet reflects the condition of a company *at a particular point in time.* As a company conducts its business affairs and generates profits (or unfortunately, sometimes, losses) the values on the balance sheet change. This business activity is summarized in another accounting report called the *statement of income.* The statement can be represented by the following formula:

$$\text{Revenue} - \text{Expenses} = \text{Net income}$$

$$\$50,000 - \$45,000 = \$5,000$$

The net income is added to the owners' equity and equals the change in assets less the change in liabilities. To continue our example of company A, assume that it earned revenues of $50,000 and incurred expenses of $45,000 during the year ending December 31, 1994; the resulting net income would be $5,000. The effect on the balance sheet might be as follows:

COMPANY A
Balance Sheets
As of December 31, 1993, and 1994

	As of 12/31/93	Changes during 1994	As of 12/31/94
Assets	$100,000	$10,000	$110,000
Liabilities	$ 80,000	$ 5,000	$ 85,000
Owners' equity	20,000	5,000	25,000
Liabilities + Owners' equity	$100,000	$10,000	$110,000

Notice that owners' equity went up by $5,000, the amount of net income that company A earned during 1994. We assume that the changes in assets and liabilities were $10,000 and $5,000, respectively. The difference between the two amounts must equal the change in the owners' equity. It would be possible for the changes in these two categories to change by any amount as long as the total change in assets, less the total change in liabilities, was equal to the change in owners' equity of $5,000. This equality is fundamental to the balance sheet accounting model. If the difference were any amount other than $5,000, there would be an error somewhere in the numbers.

Later in your school career when you take courses in financial and hospitality accounting, you will learn more about how this accounting model is developed into accounting records and reports. We have included a sample of a balance sheet and income statement in this chapter's Appendix A.

Now consider how transactions build into the accounting process.

Transactions and the Accounting Process.   One of the most valuable commodities required for the operation of our economic system is information. Decision makers, such as investors or corporate managers, execute their business choices based on financial and other business information, coupled with their own expertise and experience. Accounting data is the raw material out of which financial information is produced. In order to decide what to invest in, investors review critical information such as security market activities, performances of various corporations, government taxing and spending, interest rate levels, and other data. Hospitality managers might review the same information, plus other specific information on their own company's operations, in order to determine whether the company should construct a new hotel or open a new restaurant.

Financial information is based on accounting reports, which in turn are built upon numerous business transactions. To better understand how this all fits together, consider the flowchart in Exhibit 12–1.

Let us start at the top with business activities. Business activities can encompass a broad range of actions, ranging from opening a business in a new location to conducting normal day-to-day and week-to-week business affairs.

EXHIBIT 12–1

An example of a transaction flow chart.

Transaction Flow Chart

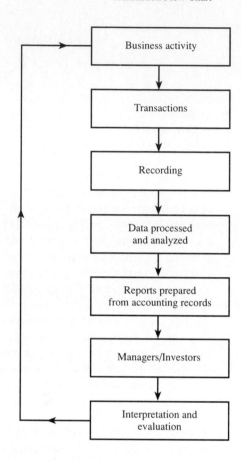

Businesses produce products or services and sell them to customers, with a goal of generating sufficient sales to cover their costs and produce a profit equal to or in excess of their objectives. This process goes on continuously in all areas of the free market economy. From large corporations, such as McDonald's and Hilton, down to the local motel and restaurant, all companies participate in this economic process.

All company sales and expenditures are called **business transactions.** For example, each sale at a restaurant constitutes a transaction: A meal is served to a customer who, after completing the meal, pays the bill; the cash is deposited in a cash register, which completes the sales transaction. Business expenditures are another form of transaction. Two examples are: an employee who works for a company by providing specific services and then, on payday, receives payment in the form of a payroll check; or a vendor who ships raw food products to a restaurant and receives payment for the goods. From these examples, we can define *business transactions* as exchanges of goods and

EXHIBIT 12–2

Reports for stockholders are highly summarized and do not provide the fine detail and complexity included in management reports.

Photo by James L. Morgan, 85283.

services for money that take place continuously and in all areas of our economy. The sum total of all these transactions represents the total dollar activity of our economy.

In order to understand the collective impact of a period's transactions, a business must first create a record of each transaction. This is the recording process. Business records are numerous and varied: cash register receipts, sales tickets, payroll time cards, invoices from vendors, canceled bank checks, hotel room ledger accounts, and so on. Accounting transactions are often recorded electronically in computer data files.

After a business records its transactions for a period of time, such as a month, the data must be processed and analyzed into information. Businesses process most of these transaction data automatically through routine accounting procedures, often assisted by computers. Full-time accounting managers oversee the processing of transaction data into useful financial reports. The primary financial reports of a profit-making company are the balance sheet, income statement, and cash flow statements.

Accounting managers then tailor financial reports to fit the needs of the particular parties to which the reports are addressed. For example, reports produced for stockholders are highly summarized and do not provide detailed information of company operations. Thus, when publishing a brochure for its stockholders, a hotel chain might report sales from all its hotels in one total amount without giving a breakdown of the sales by its individual hotels. Exhibit 12–2 shows several annual reports that hospitality companies publish.

In addition to producing reports for parties external to the corporation, the accounting department will spend considerable time and energy producing reports to meet the specific needs of its managers. Management reports are more complicated and detailed than reports produced for outsiders, such as stockholders. The accounting department of a hotel chain might produce a complete set of financial reports for each of its hotels but make them available only to corporate management. The same hotel chain, in reporting to its shareholders, would probably produce one set of consolidated financial reports reflecting in total numbers the activities of all its individual hotels.

Once the accounting information has been summarized into financial reports, management and investors need to interpret and evaluate these reports. Often managers make critical decisions based on the information in accounting reports. For example, a restaurant chain's management reports might reveal that one of its locations is losing money. Management will need to evaluate the operation of this restaurant in detail and ultimately may change procedures or personnel. Although the losing restaurant might be a hopeless cause and need to be closed, the same restaurant chain might have other individual restaurants that are highly profitable. Management will want to analyze the success of the strong locations to determine if this pattern can be replicated at other locations and thus improve overall company profitability.

Business activity is a dynamic process rather than a static one. Change is constant and managers need to be flexible. If they are to make the right decisions for their corporations, managers need accounting reports that provide meaningful, accurate, and timely information. The consequences of their decisions, both good and bad, will be reflected in the company's financial performance as reflected in future accounting reports. This process goes on month to month and year to year.

Accounting in the Hospitality Industry

In addressing the topic of hospitality accounting, we need to keep in mind that there is considerable similarity among the financial reports and accounting records of all companies in all industries. Of course, there are also notable peculiarities in the accounting records and financial reports of different industries. For instance, the income statement of an airline company will normally show a large amount of fuel expense and aircraft maintenance expense, and consumer goods companies will have large amounts of marketing expenses. Banks will have a high proportion of their assets tied up in loans and investments and a small proportion invested in property and equipment. The hospitality industry is not exempt from this pattern. We have provided you with some examples of hotel financial statements in Appendix A at the end of the chapter.

The hospitality industry is divided into two major subcategories each made up of diverse markets: lodging and restaurants. In lodging there are large full-service hotels, medium-size hotels, motels with and without restaurants, resort hotels, and gaming hotels. This diversity also holds true in restaurants, a category that includes gourmet restaurants, family restaurants, specialty restaurants, fast-food operations, and concession food services that handle ball parks, hospitals, schools, and other institutions.

Professional organizations within the hospitality industry have developed accounting systems tailored to the needs of hospitality managers. One such system is the **Uniform System of Accounts and Reports for Hotels** (USARH). This system was first developed in 1926 and has been revised many times to keep it current with industry needs. The industry's purpose in developing the USARH was two-fold: (1) to provide a flexible accounting system that could be used by all hotels, large and small, and (2) to provide standardized accounting and reporting that would facilitate comparison of operations between hotels and the hotel industry in general. The system provides for the production of financial reports that are specialized to the needs of the hotel industry. This common statement format has permitted the development and publication of industry statistics. Arthur Andersen, an international consulting firm, publishes hotel operating statistics in its annual ''Host Report.'' The report compiles revenues, expenses, operating income, and operating statistical data from 2,300 full-service, limited-service, and all-suite hotels. A sample from this report appears in Exhibit 12–3. The table analyzes income and expenses as a ratio or percentage of total sales, per available room and per occupied room, broken down by hotels with the following average room rates: under $50, $50 to $75, and over $75. Without the USARH, the ''Host Report'' would not be available. With it, hotel managers are able to compare the operations of their hotels with industry averages, and with other similar hotels.

The National Restaurant Association developed the *Uniform System of Accounts and Reports* (USAR) for use by restaurant businesses. The USAR was developed for the same purpose as the hotel system: ease of use and standardized reporting in the restaurant industry. The USAR is divided into four parts:

1. A list of standard financial statements and supporting schedules for use with a restaurant operation.
2. Examples of financial statements from a full-menu, table-service restaurant; a large full-menu, table-service restaurant; and a limited-menu, no-table-service restaurant.
3. Description of simplified record keeping for a typical restaurant operation along with suggested forms.
4. Procedural controls for running a restaurant.

How Accounting Information Is Accumulated.   Before we look at some examples of financial statements, let us review the transaction flow chart

EXHIBIT 12–3   **These are some of the most current data available on the financial performance of the U.S. lodging industry.**

Full-Service Hotels—Statements of Operating Income & Expenses—1994

	Total U.S. Results			Chain-Affiliated			Independent		
Occupancy	70.8%			71.4%			65.7%		
Average Size of Property (Rooms)	293			299			241		
Average Rate	$78.67			$76.67			$95.75		
	Ratio to Sales	Per Available Room	Per Occupied Room Night	Ratio to Sales	Per Available Room	Per Occupied Room Night	Ratio to Sales	Per Available Room	Per Occupied Room Night
REVENUE									
Rooms	67.6 %	$20,092	$ 78.67	68.6%	$19,861	$ 76.67	59.2%	$22,081	$ 95.75
Food	19.0	6,427	26.09	18.5	6,107	24.17	22.9	9,184	42.63
Beverage	5.1	1,763	7.19	4.9	1,644	6.54	6.7	2,791	12.79
Other Food & Beverage	2.4	802	3.18	2.5	815	3.18	1.7	687	3.12
Telephone	2.6	809	3.14	2.7	809	3.11	2.1	806	3.39
Minor Operated Departments	2.1	892	4.00	1.8	724	3.02	4.9	2,350	12.53
Rentals & Other Income	1.2	427	1.77	1.1	340	1.36	2.4	1,184	5.34
Total Revenue	100.0%	$31,214	$124.04	100.0%	$30,300	$118.05	100.0%	$39,083	$175.55
DEPARTMENTAL EXPENSES									
Rooms	26.4%	$ 5,247	$ 20.80	26.2%	$ 5,148	$ 20.06	28.7%	$ 6,087	$ 27.08
Food & Beverage	82.2	7,163	29.15	81.6	6,777	26.86	86.5	10,475	48.77
Telephone	60.5	442	1.77	57.1	432	1.69	90.3	564	2.48
Other Departmental Expenses	1.6	693	3.08	1.4	555	2.28	3.9	1,883	9.99
Total Departmental Expenses	42.0%	$13,545	$ 54.80	41.3%	$12,912	$ 50.89	47.9%	$19,009	$ 88.32
Total Departmental Profit	58.0%	$17,669	$ 69.24	58.7%	$17,388	$ 67.16	52.2%	$20,074	$ 87.23
UNDISTRIBUTED OPERATING EXPENSES									
Administrative & General	9.8%	$ 2,919	$ 11.77	9.7%	$ 2,790	$ 10.93	10.7%	$ 4,035	$ 18.98
Marketing	5.9	1,886	7.66	5.8	1,799	7.14	6.7	2,640	12.17
Franchise Fees	1.4	333	1.35	1.5	366	1.48	.2	46	.21
Energy	4.9	1,384	5.63	4.9	1,350	5.36	5.0	1,683	8.04
Property Operations & Maintenance	5.3	1,610	6.54	5.2	1,529	6.09	6.1	2,313	10.45
Total Undistributed Operating Expenses	27.2%	$ 8,132	$ 32.95	27.0%	$ 7,833	$ 31.00	28.7%	$10,717	$ 49.85
GROSS OPERATING PROFIT	30.8%	$ 9,537	$ 36.29	31.6%	$ 9,555	$ 36.16	23.4%	$ 9,358	$ 37.38
Management Fees	2.1%	$ 646	$ 2.60	2.1%	$ 638	$ 253	1.8%	$ 708	$ 3.19
INCOME BEFORE FIXED CHARGES*	28.7%	$ 8,891	$ 33.69	29.5%	$ 8,917	$ 33.63	21.6%	$ 8,650	$ 34.19
Property taxes	3.2%	$ 989	$ 4.04	3.2%	$ 981	$ 3.95	2.9%	$ 1,092	$ 4.83
Insurance	.9	255	1.08	.9	245	1.01	1.0	331	1.59
Reserve for Replacement	1.3	378	1.51	1.3	363	1.43	.9	355	1.49
AMOUNT AVAILABLE FOR DEBT SERVICE & OTHER FIXED CHARGES	23.3%	$ 7,269	$ 27.06	24.1%	$ 7,328	$ 27.24	16.8%	$ 6,872	$ 26.28
Total Fixed Charges* (Including Property Taxes & Insurance)	21.9%	$ 6,952	$ 28.56	21.0%	$ 6,373	$ 25.53	21.4%	$ 8,569	$ 39.18
Pre-Tax Income (Loss)*	6.8%	$ 1,939	$ 5.13	8.6%	$ 2,543	$ 8.10	.2%	$ 81	$ 4.99
PAYROLL & RELATED EXPENSES									
Rooms	17.3%	$ 3,385	$ 13.44	17.0%	$ 3,282	$ 12.83	20.0%	$ 4,133	$ 18.57
Food	54.4	3,369	14.15	54.4	3,245	13.16	54.4	4,392	22.26
Beverage	47.5	435	1.31	50.5	360	1.11	22.4	1,203	3.82
Telephone	12.6	126	.50	12.0	124	.48	18.1	155	.69
Other Operated Departments	1.2	539	2.36	1.1	475	1.91	2.0	1,008	5.66
Administrative & General	5.0	1,534	6.18	4.9	1,468	5.75	5.5	2,091	9.82
Marketing	2.5	779	3.17	2.4	740	2.95	3.1	1,136	5.19
Property Operations & Maintenance	2.6	822	3.38	2.6	786	3.17	2.9	1,095	4.94
Total Payroll & Related Expenses	33.0%	$10,988	$ 44.49	32.5%	$10,477	$ 41.35	37.7%	$15,144	$ 70.60

*Income before fixed charges is priced in deducting Reserve for Replacement, Depreciation, Rent, Amortization and Income Taxes. Total Fixed Charges and Pre-Tax Income (Loss) do not include a deduction of the Reserve for Replacement.
Totals may not add due to rounding. Departmental expenses are expressed as a percentage of respective departmental revenue. All other expenses are presented as a percentage of total revenue.
Source: Smith Travel Research, Hendersonville, Tennessee.

EXHIBIT 12–4   Description of Five Classic Business Transactions

Type of Transaction	Example of Transaction
Sales	Customer checks into hotel. For each day the customer remains in the hotel, revenue is recorded and the customer's room account is charged. Other revenues such as restaurant sales, room service, and telephone usage are recorded and charged to the customer's room account.
Cash receipts	When the customer checks out of the hotel and pays the balance on his or her account, cash receipts are recorded and the room account is credited, bringing its balance to zero. Cash collections are accumulated and deposited in the hotel's bank, at least on a daily basis.
Purchases of products and services	The hotel receives the utility bill for the month, records the charge as an expense, and sets up a liability to the utility company.
Payroll	The time cards for two weeks are listed in a record by employee and the amounts of pay due each employee less payroll taxes are calculated. Total payroll expenses and payroll tax expenses are recorded as expenses with the liability for the amounts payable to employees and tax authorities recorded.
Cash disbursements	The hotel prepares a check to the utility company and mails it so as to reach the utility company by the due date. Checks are prepared for employees based on information on the payroll journal. In addition, checks are disbursed to the appropriate tax authorities for the payroll taxes withheld.

illustrated in Exhibit 12–1 to see how it applies to a hotel operation. The business activities of a hotel will generate many transactions. We can categorize these transactions into five parts and illustrate them with some examples (see Exhibit 12–4).

As business is conducted during the month, hotel employees record each transaction onto a physical document or a computer record. The hotel accounting department processes and analyzes these transactions into meaningful totals. At the end of the month, after all transactions have been recorded, processed, and analyzed, the accounting department will prepare monthly financial reports for management. Examples of what these reports might look like appear in Appendix A at the end of this chapter.

The final step in the accounting cycle is management's review of operations. Financial statements give managers feedback on how well their operations are performing. They can use this information to direct their inquiries and investigations into the departments in the hotel that seem to be performing poorly (see Exhibit 12–5). For example, to eliminate an operating loss in telephone communications, management may want to change the way guest

EXHIBIT 12–5

Managers do not have to reinvent accounting procedures; one is already in place.

CONTENTS

Uniform System of Accounts for Hotels.

telephone calls are handled. If management handles this review process wisely and makes the necessary changes to improve the hotel's operations, future accounting reports will provide more feedback as to how well they have utilized the reports currently in use.

Utilization of Computers in the Accounting Process

Computers have had a significant effect on the accounting process, in the hospitality industry in particular. As previously discussed, the accounting process involves the recording of transactions, and the analysis and processing of the transaction data into useful information in the form of accounting reports. Computerization has revolutionized this process. These changes are reflected in a number of ways:

- Accounting reports are now more sophisticated and informative than were previously available.
- Accounting departments are more productive and able to meet their responsibilities with smaller staffs.
- With the availability of personal computers, sophisticated accounting systems are now being used by small hotels and restaurants.

- Management has access to accounting information on a more timely basis.
- The software industry has developed specialized hotel and restaurant accounting and information systems that have translated into higher profits for the users. These systems include but are not limited to hotel front office systems, reservation systems, restaurant point-of-sales systems, and food and beverage cost control systems.
- Computer technology continues to revolutionize the accounting process. Computer companies are producing more powerful computers at lower and lower costs (a personal computer used today has as much computer power as a mainframe computer in use 10 years ago). In tandem with computer hardware technology progress, the software industry continues to develop systems for the hospitality industry. Tomorrow's hospitality manager will need the knowledge and self-reliance to be able to exploit this information in a wise manner.

Eye on the Issues

Ethics

There are many ethical issues that manifest themselves in the financial affairs of a hospitality business. One issue is the question of how management balances the rights of stockholders (the owners of the business) with other stakeholders, such as employees, management, creditors, and the local community. It is incumbent upon management to have policies in place to deal with such issues *before* they arise. Such a crisis might be a hostile takeover offer by another company that benefits the stockholders, but hurts management and the employees.

Financial Management

The **financial management** of a corporation is a process that involves the handling of all the monetary affairs of the corporation and the coordination of this activity with the other parts of the organization. Large companies usually have a vice president of finance who is a senior officer of the corporation who reports directly to the chief executive officer. Sometimes referred to as the *chief financial officer,* or CFO, the vice president of finance is responsible for the functions we discuss next.

Accounting

Accounting is one of the prime responsibilities of the vice president of finance. The chief accounting officer of the corporation, sometimes called the vice president–controller, heads up this responsibility and reports to the vice president of finance. The controller manages the corporation's accounting system and oversees the preparation and release of its financial reports. In a hospitality corporation, the controller's department might consist of accounting staff at the headquarters level plus field accountants at each of the hotel or restaurant locations.

Budgeting and Forecasting

Budgeting and forecasting are critical to the long-term success of a corporation. One of the main budget documents, the *operating budget,* is an income statement of the corporation and its constituent parts projected one to five years into the future. This document is prepared for all levels of the corporation and involves the input of all levels of the operation's management. The operating budget serves two main purposes: (1) to assist top management in strategic corporate planning, and (2) to serve as a control mechanism in order to hold the various departments and divisions of the corporation accountable for meeting specific revenue, expense, and income targets. Capital budgets are used to evaluate and control capital expenditures, especially large projects such as the opening of a new hotel or a new restaurant location. The finance department evaluates these projects using sophisticated financial techniques to assure that the project will contribute to the long-term profitability of the corporation and enhance the value of the shareholders' capital stock.

Cash Management

This function controls the flow of cash between the many parts of a corporation. Under the direction of the cash management officer, surplus funds from one location can be transferred to other locations in need of cash. This department invests surplus corporate cash in marketable securities that provide some return but that can also be quickly sold to provide cash as needed. Specialists in cash management must be experts in short-term cash budgeting and forecasting. Their function is essential in managing a corporation's cash.

Raising Capital Funds

This is a primary responsibility assigned to the vice president of finance. An expanding corporation frequently has investment cash needs that exceed its cash flow as generated by its profit-making operations. The vice president of finance must see that funds are available for capital projects such as opening new hotels, casinos, and restaurants. The finance department can raise these funds through a number of sources:

- *Public financing.* A corporation can obtain investment funds through the sale of its common stock, bonds, or debt instruments to the public

EXHIBIT 12–6

Publicly held hospitality stocks are traded on national and international stock exchanges, such as this one in Chicago.

at large (see Exhibit 12–6). The vice president of finance will usually perform this function with the assistance of outside accounting, legal, and investment banking firms.

- *Banks.* A corporation can raise capital through short-term to intermediate-term loans (payable up to five years) from bank institutions. Banks can also provide credit lines that the corporation can use, as needed.

- *Other financial institutions.* Insurance and leasing companies are other sources of financing. These usually provide mortgage loans and other types of long-term loans.

Tax Compliance

This department prepares and files the tax returns that the corporation is required to file. These returns cover U.S. federal income taxes, state income taxes, payroll taxes, state sales taxes, and other municipal and local taxes. If a corporation operates internationally, it must comply with the tax laws of each of the countries in which it operates. The tax department is staffed by tax accountants and lawyers. When large and complex tax issues arise, the corporation may employ the services of outside accounting and law firms.

Bank Relations

This function involves the opening and closing of bank accounts as required by the corporation. The banks range from large institutions that handle major corporate needs down to the local banks that service each location where the corporation operates.

Risk Management

This function oversees corporate insurance needs in order to protect the corporation from casualty, property, and liability losses.

Internal Audit

The internal audit department's main responsibility is to audit selected locations and departments of the corporation. Staff auditors of the department might be supervised by an officer titled *general auditor* or *vice president–audit*. Auditors review the operations of the department they are auditing to assure that it is complying with company procedures; their audits can cover both financial and operational activities. A main purpose of internal audits is to make sure the company's internal controls are adequate and to prevent fraud. Auditors, upon completion of their audit review, issue a report stating their findings and recommendations for improvement of department operations. Internal auditing has become a more important function in the eyes of corporate management because of an increased emphasis on the need for good internal controls. In recognition of this greater importance, a number of companies have their internal audit departments reporting directly to the chief executive officer of the company, or even to the board of directors rather than to the vice president of finance.

As you can see from this review, a company's finance department has broad and important responsibilities.

Eye on the Issues

 # International

In hospitality finance, as in other disciplines, the world is getting smaller. Most large hospitality companies now operate in one or more foreign countries. Finance department managers need to be knowledgeable about the tax laws, currency regulations, and financial markets of each of the countries in which they operate. Standards of accounting in foreign countries are usually different from standards in the United States. The finance manager and departmental staff need to be able to handle the demands of operating in an international world. Hospitality companies often operate on a worldwide basis, placing an added burden on its finance managers.

Education Requirements and Career Opportunities

As you continue your education with the objective of a career in hotel and restaurant management, you will need to take some courses in accounting. Students looking at general hospitality management should expect to take a course in the principles of financial accounting and another course in hospitality managerial accounting. Related courses such as corporate finance and food and beverage cost control will also be needed. Students who would like to work in hospitality accounting and finance should take elective courses in accounting and auditing, or minor in accounting, along with their major in hotel and restaurant management.

Once you are out working in the hospitality industry, you will be exposed to various kinds of managerial reports and accounting records. By grounding yourself in the basic content of such reports while in school, you can become proficient in the use of this valuable managerial information and gain an edge toward becoming a successful manager.

Eye on the Issues

Environment

Strange as it may seem, even the hospitality finance manager often needs to be concerned with environmental matters. When opening new hotels or restaurants, companies need to consider the environmental effects of the new property on the locality. As part of the feasibility study that is prepared to examine the economic soundness of a new property, management initiates an environmental impact report (as the appendix on lodging development describes in detail). While the finance department does not get directly involved in the preparation of such a report, it does have an obligation to see that such a report is prepared. Since minimizing a new property's adverse environmental effects may often add construction and development costs, finance officers must be involved and aware of related plans and purchases.

Eye on the Issues

Technology

Technology has had a significant impact on the hospitality industry and the finance department in particular. Rapid changes in computer and software technology continue to affect the accounting and information systems of hospitality corporations. Improvements in telecommunications permit managers at many distant locations to keep in close touch with headquarters. Also, computers at a hospitality corporation's many locations throughout the world can "talk" to the home office computer. Large hospitality companies can now operate with smaller headquarters staffs, but put a greater demand on local operating managers in doing so. While the local manager has greater access to management information and technology, his managerial skills need to be broader.

Conclusion

We can now return to the original question considered at the beginning of this chapter: What is the distinction between hospitality accounting and hospitality finance?

Hospitality management is a broad discipline that includes many specialties. The financial manager is concerned with the monetary affairs of the company and how they relate to all the other operations of the company. The ultimate objective of the financial manager is the prosperity of the company. The perspective of finance is the present and future condition of the company. Within the finance department there are many subdisciplines: accounting, budgeting, cash management, capital fund raising, tax regulation compliance, maintenance of proper relations with the banks, insurance coverage, and internal audit.

Accounting's perspective is primarily historical: developing the financial report information that reveals how the company has operated in the past. This historic information is essential for proper management.

While the general hospitality manager does not need to be an expert in accounting, he or she does need the skills to read and interpret accounting reports. These reports provide valuable feedback to hospitality managers, telling them how well their business is performing. Managers use this information to help plan for the future.

Keywords

accounting report   375
accounting system   376
accounting model   377
accounts payable   378

business transaction   380
Uniform System of Accounts and Reports
  for Hotels   383
financial management   387

Core Concepts

finance   375
accounting   375
assets   375
liabilities   375

owner's equity   378
balance sheet   378
statement of income   378

Discussion Questions

1. Define the term *finance* as it applies in a business setting.
2. Define the term *accounting*.
3. Give at least three examples of questions that a business manager might get answered through the information provided by an accounting system.
4. The two major groups who make use of a business's accounting information are persons external to the business, such as stockholders and creditors, and _____ ?
5. The accounting model can be expressed by the following formula:

$$\text{Assets} = \text{Liabilities} + ?$$

6. What financial statement is represented by the formula in question 5?

7. The income statement can be represented by the following formula:

$$Revenues - Expenses = ?$$

8. As of December 31, 1994, company A has assets of $150,000 and liabilities of $75,000. What is company A's owners' equity at December 31, 1994?

9. Company A experiences the following changes during the calendar year 1995: assets increase by $25,000 and liabilities decrease by $10,000. How much are company A's assets, liabilities, and owners' equity as December 31, 1995?

10. What is the Uniform System of Accounts and Reports for Hotels and why did the hotel industry develop such a system?

11. What are some of the benefits provided by the utilization of computers in the accounting process?

12. List five functions for which a hotel vice president of finance might be responsible.

APPENDIX A
SAMPLE HOTEL FINANCIAL REPORTS

In this appendix we will illustrate a typical set of hotel financial reports using the California Resort Hotel as an example (any similarity to a company is purely coincidental). We will look at an income statement, a statement of cash flows, a balance sheet, and a common size income statement.

The income statement for the year ending December 31, 19X4, appears in Exhibit 12–A1. The statement breaks out the hotel's three revenue-producing departments: rooms, food and beverage, and telephone. Each revenue-producing department is presented showing revenues minus direct operating expenses (cost of sales, payroll and related expenses, and other direct expenses) equaling departmental operating income. Next, undistributed expenses and fixed expenses are deducted from departmental operating income to arrive at income before income taxes. Undistributed expenses are operating costs that apply to more than one income-producing department and that cannot be reasonably allocated solely to any one of them. Fixed expenses are costs that will be incurred irrespective of operating levels. Finally, provision for income taxes is deducted, giving a bottom line net income of $301,249.

The next report is the cash flow statement for the year ending December 31, 19X4 (Exhibit 12–A2). This report provides information on the change in cash that took place during the accounting period. The report is broken down into three sections:

1. *Net cash flow from operating activities.* This section reconciles the net income, of $301,249, on the income statement to the actual cash, of $517,649, that was generated by operations.

2. *Net cash flow for investing activities.* This section reports the amount spent for new property and equipment of $15,000.

3. *Net cash flow for financing activities.* This section reflects cash receipts and disbursements from and to long-term creditors and stockholders. Repayment of long-term debt and dividends amounted to $250,000.

The net increase in cash of $252,649 is added to the beginning cash of $317,600, equaling the ending cash balance of $570,249. Both these numbers agree with the amounts appearing on the balance sheet, which we look at next.

The balance sheet as of December 31, 19X4, and 19X3, appears in Exhibit 12–A3. This report gives information on the carrying value of assets, liabilities, and stockholders' equity. These are comprised of:

EXHIBIT 12–A1   A Typical Income Statement from a Resort Hotel

CALIFORNIA RESORT HOTEL
Income Statement
Year Ended December 31, 19X4

	Net Revenue	Cost of Sales	Payroll and Related	Other Expenses	Income (Loss)
Operating departments:					
Rooms	$2,260,750		$ 452,150	$248,683	$1,559,918
Food and beverage	3,090,000	$1,081,500	988,800	401,700	618,000
Telephone	109,500	114,975			(5,475)
Total operating departments	$5,460,250	$1,196,475	$1,440,950	$650,383	2,172,443
Undistributed operating expenses:					
Administrative and general expenses					377,615
Marketing					382,218
Guest entertainment					123,600
Property operation, maintenance, and energy cost					188,700
Total undistributed operating expenses					1,072,133
Total income before fixed charges					1,100,310
Rent, property taxes, and insurance					157,250
Interest					240,600
Depreciation					239,000
Income before income taxes					463,460
Provision for income taxes					162,211
Net income					$ 301,249

1. Assets of $6,273,049, made up of $605,049 in current assets (cash or assets that will turn into cash within one year); $5,588,000 of property and equipment (based on original cost less depreciation expense recorded to the date of the balance sheet); and $80,000 other assets (miscellaneous items such as trade names and organizational expense).

2. Liabilities of $1,959,000, made up of $244,000 of current liabilities (liabilities that are to be paid within a one-year period) and $1,715,000 of long-term liabilities (liabilities that are not to be paid until after a one-year period).

3. Stockholders' equity of $4,314,049, representing the accounting equity that shareholders have in the company. (This amount does not necessarily agree with the market value of the company; the reason why will have to wait until you take your

accounting and finance courses.) This section of the balance sheet is broken down into the amount shareholders have invested in the hotel of $3,500,000 (made up of capital stock and additional paid-in capital) plus the retained earnings the company has earned since its origin, in the amount of $814,049. The balance of retained earnings for the two years is reconciled as follows:

Balance as of December 31, 19X3		$617,800
For the year ending December 31, 19X4		
Add net income	$301,249	
Deduct dividends paid	105,000	
Net change		196,249
Balance as of December 31, 19X4		$814,049

EXHIBIT 12–A2   **A Typical Statement of Cash Flow from a Resort Hotel**

CALIFORNIA RESORT HOTEL
Statement of Cash Flows
Year Ended December 31, 19X4

Net cash flow from operating activities:	
Net income	$301,249
Adjustment to reconcile net income to net cash flows from operating activities:	
Depreciation	239,000
Increase in accounts receivable	(6,000)
Increase in inventory	(5,000)
Increase in prepaid expenses	(600)
Increase in accounts payable	10,000
Decrease in accrued expenses	(1,000)
Decrease in income taxes payable	(20,000)
Net cash flow from operating activities	517,649
Net cash flow for investing activities:	
Purchase of equipment	(15,000)
Net cash flow for investing activities	(15,000)
Net cash flow for financing activities:	
Dividends paid	(105,000)
Payment of long-term debt	(145,000)
Net cash flow for financing activities	(250,000)
Net increase in cash	252,649
Cash at beginning of year	317,600
Cash at end of year	$570,249
Supplemental disclosure of cash flow information:	
Cash paid during the year for:	
Interest expense	$240,600
Income taxes	182,211

Exhibit 12–A3   A Typical Balance Sheet from a Resort Hotel

CALIFORNIA RESORT HOTEL
Balance Sheet
December 31, 19X3, and December 31, 19X4

	12/31/X3	*12/31/X4*
Assets		
Current assets		
Cash	$ 317,600	$ 570,249
Accounts receivable	7,000	13,000
Inventories	15,000	20,000
Prepaid expenses	1,200	1,800
Total current assets	340,800	605,049
Property and equipment, at cost		
Land	900,000	900,000
Buildings	5,000,000	5,000,000
Furniture and equipment	390,000	405,000
	6,290,000	6,305,000
Less accumulated depreciation	478,000	717,000
Property and equipment—net	5,812,000	5,588,000
Other assets	80,000	80,000
Total assets	$6,232,800	$6,273,049
Liabilities and Shareholders' Equity		
Current liabilities		
Current maturities on long-term debt	$ 145,000	$ 145,000
Accounts payable	40,000	50,000
Accrued expenses	10,000	9,000
Income taxes	60,000	40,000
Total current liabilities	255,000	244,000
Long-term debt, less current portion	1,860,000	1,715,000
Shareholders' equity		
Common stock, par value $0.50, 500,000 shares authorized, 350,000 shares outstanding	175,000	175,000
Additional paid-in capital	3,325,000	3,325,000
Retained earnings	617,800	814,049
Total shareholders' equity	4,117,800	4,314,049
Total liabilities and shareholders' equity	$6,232,800	$6,273,049

APPENDIX B

THE TALE OF JOE COLLEGE AND THE BUSINESS THAT GREW

The Working of an Accounting System Shown through a College Student's Part-Time Business Experience

Let's see how some of this chapter's important concepts are illustrated in the case of Joe College, who is starting his first year of college. Joe plans to major in hotel, restaurant, and institution management. To help finance his education, Joe's father has given him a $2,000 gift. Along with some partial scholarship aid and part-time work, Joe hopes to finance his four years of college. While waiting for his funds to arrive, Joe starts looking for a bank where he could deposit the funds and earn some interest. The best deal he can find is a credit union paying a quite miserly 2 percent per year. Joe calculates that this interest would amount to only about $40 per year. Naturally, he finds this less than exciting and starts looking at alternative ways to invest his money.

After looking at a number of possibilities, Joe comes upon an opportunity to invest in a candy machine business. He finds three student dormitories where he can place candy vending machines paying a rent based on 10 percent of machine revenues. A local candy vendor offers to sell variety candy in 500-bar cases at a cost of $.15 per candy bar. Joe believes he can charge $.50 per bar dispensed from the candy machines, thus achieving a profit of $.30 per candy bar after paying for the candy ($.15) and rent (10% of $.50). Joe checks with a number of candy machine manufacturing companies and finds a machine that will do the job. The machine holds 100 candy bars, is of the right size for the space allocated to him at the three dormitories, and has the proper electrical hookup. The machines cost $1,000 per unit, or a total of $3,000. Joe calls his dad and discusses the proposed business venture. His dad likes the proposition and agrees to lend Joe $2,000 on the following terms: interest at 1.5 percent per month (equivalent to 18 percent per year) plus monthly principal payments of $100 in order to pay off the loan. Thus, the loan will be paid back in 20 months (20 × $100 = $2,000).

Filled with an entrepreneurial urge, Joe decides to proceed with his candy machine venture.

The next day Joe opens a bank checking account for a new business he names "Joe College Student Candy Machines." He deposits his $2,000 of education funds plus the $2,000 loan from his dad for a total deposit of $4,000. He then orders the three machines from the manufacturer, who promises delivery to the three dormitories within two weeks. He then orders one case of candy containing 500 candy bars. He sets August 31 as the startup date. The machines arrive on time. Joe loads each machine with 100 candy bars and sets aside the remaining inventory of 200 bars to be used to replenish the machines as needed. Joe writes a check of $3,000 to the machine company. He has until the end of September to pay for the candy. Joe is ready to start collecting his sales.

However, Joe is somewhat uneasy. He believes he should have some kind of record-keeping system to keep track of all his business transactions. His new roommate, Lawrence Ledger, is an accounting major starting his second year at college. Lawrence agrees to give Joe some assistance. After reviewing the bank accounts and the invoices from the machine company and the candy vendor, Lawrence develops the following balance sheet for Joe's business:

JOE COLLEGE STUDENT CANDY MACHINES
Balance Sheet as of August 31, 19x1

Assets

Cash	$1,000
Candy inventory (500 bars @ cost of $.15) . .	75
Machines—at cost (three @ $1,000 each) . . .	3,000
Total assets	$4,075

Liabilities and Owners' Equity

Accounts payable—candy vendor	$ 75
Loan from father	2,000
Owners' equity (gift from father)	2,000
	$4,075

After Lawrence prepares the balance sheet, he reviews Joe's business assets (totaling $4,075) described as follows:

1. Cash balance of $1,000. This consists of the original $2,000 gift that Joe received from his father, plus the loan of $2,000, less the $3,000 payment made to purchase the three new candy machines.

2. Inventory of $75. This represents the cost of the 500 candy bars shipped by the candy vendor (300 candy bars being in the machine, and 200 candy bars being held in reserve). Lawrence tells Joe that one of the accounting principals he has learned is that inventory is to be carried on the balance sheet at cost; therefore, the 500 candy bars are valued at 15 cents per bar rather than 50 cents per bar retail value.

3. Machines and equipment are carried at $3,000. Like inventory, equipment is to be recorded on the balance sheet at cost. Lawrence indicates to Joe that this cost should be allocated as an expense against the business's monthly profits over the useful life of the machine. The manufacturer has indicated that the machine should have a life of 5 years or 60 months. Lawrence suggests writing the equipment off over the 60 months as a monthly expense of $50 ($3,000 divided by the 60-month life). This is referred to in accounting terminology as *depreciation.*

On the other side of the balance sheet, the total of liabilities and equities amounts to $4,075 and consists of the following:

1. $75 payable to the candy vendor. This bill will need to be paid off by September 30.

2. The $2,000 loan payable to Joe's father. Joe will need to pay $100 to start reducing the loan, plus interest of $30 (1.5% of $2,000) by September 30.

3. $2,000 owners' equity. This is the amount of Joe's gift from his father and his original investment. Lawrence explains that this amount will not change until the business starts operating.

Lawrence explains to Joe how the balance sheet was put together using the accounting model by the following schedule:

	Assets	= Liabilities +	Equity
Joe's investment . .	$2,000	—	$2,000
Father's loan . . .	2,000	$2,000	—
Candy inventory . .	75	75	—
Purchase of equipment	—	—	—
Total balance 8/31/x1	$4,075 =	$2,075 +	$2,000

During the month of September, Joe checks his machines at the end of each week. For the first week, the three machines yielded sales of 198 candy bars. Joe deposits the cash sales in the bank and replenishes the machines. Since sales are very strong, he orders two more cases of candy (1,000 units) as back-up inventory. The sales continue to be strong for the rest of September. By the end of the month, Joe has sold 800 candy bars, yielding $400 in sales, which he deposits in the business bank account. He writes the following checks to take care of his expenses:

1. $75 to the candy vendor to pay for the initial shipment of candy.

2. $40 as rent expense, representing 10 percent of the sales for the month.

3. $130 to his father for the month's interest and principal payment on the loan.

The bank account now contains $1,155.

Joe calls on Larry to help him sort out what had happened in September. Lawrence first develops a statement showing what happened to the cash. He called it a *cash flow statement.*

JOE COLLEGE STUDENT CANDY MACHINES
Cash Flow Statement
Month of September 30, 19x1

Sales of candy bars	$400
Less cash payments:	
Payment to candy vendor	75
Rent	40
Interest on loan	30
Principal payment on loan	100
Total cash disbursements:	245
Net increase in cash	$155

Joe has no problem understanding the cash flow statement. It reflects an increase in cash of $155, which agrees with his current cash balance of $1,155.

Lawrence then shows Joe the income statement for the month of September.

JOE COLLEGE STUDENT CANDY MACHINES
Income Statement
Month of September 30, 19x1

Sales of candy bars	$400
Less	
Cost of candy bars sold	120
Rent (10% of sales)	40
Depreciation of machines	50
Interest on loan	30
Total expenses	240
Net income	$160

After reviewing the income statement, Joe feels a little confused. "Why was the net income on the income statement $160, rather than the $155 increase in cash?" he asks. Lawrence replies that as a profit-making venture, his business should keep its accounting records on an "accrual basis" since this method gives a more accurate calculation of monthly income. Lawrence defines *accrual basis accounting* for Joe: "Under the accrual accounting method, revenue should be recognized when it is earned rather than when the resultant cash is collected." In the case of Joe's business there is no problem since cash is earned and collected at the same time. "However, expenses, under the accrual method, should be recognized *when incurred* rather than when paid for." This definition reflects the accrual basis method of accounting as contrasted with the cash basis. Lawrence then explains the difference between the income statement and cash flow statement, item by item:

1. The cost of candy bars sold should reflect the number of actual candy bars sold, not the candy bars paid for. Since 800 candy bars were sold, the cost of candy bars sold should be $120 (800 units × 15 cents).

2. Of the $130 paid to his Dad for a loan, only $30 interest should be shown on the income statement as an expense. The remaining $100 is a repayment of principal and should be a reduction of the liability.

3. Depreciation expense of $50 shown on the income statement is not a cash payment but is

an allowance, or an allocation, of part of the original $3,000 machine cost. "Remember," Lawrence says, "we estimated the machines would have a 60-month life; if we record depreciation expense at $50 per month over the 60-month life of the machines, we will ultimately write the original cost of $3,000 down to zero."

Joe reflects on these comments for a moment. "What you say makes sense, but how can we keep track of all this?" Lawrence replies that they will not have a difficult time keeping track of the transactions if they rely on the accounting model. "It's a 'double-entry' system that requires each transaction to be in balance." Each entry must adhere to the principal: *assets equal liabilities plus owners' equity.* Lawrence then pulls out a work sheet on which he has listed all the entries for the month of September.

Lawrence's work sheet started out in the left-hand column showing the balances for the August 31 balance sheet. All September entries were listed in the columns to the right of the August 31 balance sheet and showed their effect on the various balance sheet items. The first five columns related to the income operations. The sales column reflected the increase in cash of $400 for the month's sales balanced by an increase of the same amount in owners' equity. Cost of candy bars reflected the $120 decrease in inventory for the candy sold balanced by a decrease of the same amount in owners' equity. Rent and interest expenses were shown by reductions in cash and owners' equity. Depreciation expense was recorded with a $50 reduction in the machine account (accumulated depreciation) and owners' equity. Collectively, the first five columns reflected the business income activities and amounted to a net increase of $160 to owners' equity; this $160 increase is the month's net income. The entries in the remaining three columns related to other transactions. These included:

1. The $75 payment for the initial shipment of inventory recording a reduction in cash and accounts payable.

2. The $100 payment reducing cash and loans payable to his father.

3. The $150 of candy bars purchased recording an increase in inventory and accounts payable.

Lawrence then pulled out the September 30 balance sheet and reviewed it with Joe.

JOE COLLEGE STUDENT CANDY MACHINES
Balance Sheet
As of September 30, 19x1

Assets

Cash		$1,155
Candy inventory		105
Machines—cost	3,000	
Less accumulated depreciation . .	50	
Machines—net		2,950
Total assets		$4,210

Liabilities

Accounts payable—candy vendor . .		$ 150
Loan from father		1,900

Owners' equity

Owners' equity September 1, 19x1		$2,000
Add net income month of September 19x1		160
Owners' equity September 30, 19x1		2,160
Total liabilities and owners' equity . . .		$4,210

Larry reviewed each of the items on the September 30 balance sheet item by item (Note: the balance sheet agrees with the right-hand column of Exhibit 12–B1). Assets totaled $4,210 and consisted of the following:

1. $1,155 in cash.
2. A candy inventory balance of $150 representing 700 candy bars at 15 cents each. This was reconciled to the beginning balance inventory using the following information:

The machine account cost of $2,950 representing the original cost less one month's depreciation. With monthly depreciation expense of $50, the machine would be written down to zero by the end of its five-year life.

The items on the other side of the balance sheet were as follows:

	Inventory	
	Units	Cost @ $.15 per unit
Balance as of August 31, 19x1	500	$ 75
Balance as of August 31, 19x1	500	$ 75
Purchases	1,000	50
(Less) Sales	(800)	(120)
Balance as of September 30, 19x1	700	$105

1. Accounts payable reflected a balance of $150 representing the cost of shipments made during September. This would need to be paid during October.
2. Loan balance of $1,900. $128.50 would have to be paid at the end of October, consisting of one month's interest and the $100 principal. With the loan balance now down to $1,900, interest at 1.5% equals $28.50.
3. Owners' equity of $2,160. This consists of the original investment of $2,000 plus the $160 profit earned in September.

Joe was very impressed with all this information. He had a better understanding of how his business was going, and looked forward to his operations for the following month. He felt that with more coaching from Lawrence, he could start maintaining his own business accounting records.

CHAPTER 13

Hospitality Law

This chapter introduces the body of law that governs the relationships between a hospitality operation and the guest, the government, and the legal system. The chapter also includes a discussion of how and where the laws of the United States are generated. Through the use of several scenarios, the chapter examines a hotel's obligation to provide accommodations and privacy to its guests, and to protect both guests and their property. A section on restaurant and bar operations explores the legal issues that affect that side of the industry. This chapter also contains a brief explanation of the laws pertinent to human resources and labor.

Outline

Introduction

Throughout your hospitality education you will no doubt hear many professors at the beginning of each semester say that their course is the most important course you will take in college. Well the truth of the matter is that hospitality law *is* the most important course you will take in college. Without an understanding of the ***liabilities,*** that is, the risks associated with operating a hospitality operation, you are likely to make costly mistakes. These could result not only in you or the company for which you work being forced to pay large sums of money to persons whom you injure or to whom you cause damage, but also result in criminal sanctions: you could go to jail!

Perhaps an example will help to clarify this idea. Imagine that you just recently graduated from a school of hotel and restaurant management and have begun your first job in the industry. You were recruited by one of the big international hotel chains and accepted a position as a front desk clerk. It is 5:00 PM on a Friday afternoon. A woman approaches you and states that her husband obtained a double room in your hotel on a month-to-month basis because he often does business in the area. She states that she frequently joins him on weekends and holidays and that he is expecting her. She asks that you give her a key to his room. You try to reach the husband but he is not available. The husband did not tell you or anyone else at the hotel that should his wife show up, she was to be given a key.

You have a decision to make. Do you give her the key as requested? (Think about it: if you do, who knows what she may discover when she enters the room.) Or do you deny her request and risk her getting angry and upset, and, of course, taking it out on you?

With some basic knowledge of the law, which you will obtain after taking a hospitality law course, you will know what to do. A case just like this occurred in the state of Louisiana. In *Campbell* v. *Womack* the court held that a hotel was not liable for damages for refusing to admit a wife to her husband's room when she was not a registered guest. The court stated that the hotel had an affirmative duty, an obligation, stemming from a guest's rights of privacy and peaceful possession of the room not to allow unregistered and unauthorized persons to gain access to the rooms of its guests. The court went on to state that the fact of the couple's marriage did not imply the husband's authorization for her access to his room, noting that a hotel would never be able to know whether a marriage was on good terms or not.

It does not take a great deal of imagination to picture what the wife might have discovered upon her surprise entry into the husband's room. Perhaps the situation could have become violent. If so, the hotel's problems would have increased.

In your imaginary **scenario,** you now can relax. Since you know what to do, you would prevent the problem from escalating by politely refusing to give the woman the key.

U.S. Government: A Source of Law

From the example above, you can see that a court is referred to as the authority from which the law comes. Does a court make law? Where does our law come from? Who is it that makes up the rules that govern our conduct? This short review of some of the basics regarding the U.S. government may touch on some points you never considered before.

In the 1700s, when the (future) United States was a British colony, the King of England made its laws. Whatever the King thought the law should be, was, in fact, the law. If the King wanted to place a tax on tea, nobody had the power to stop him. What if you, as a tea drinker, refused to pay the tea tax? What could the King do to you? Well, the King's army was just that: the *King's* army—it did as the King directed it. If you did not do what the law required, the army would be sent to force you to do it, or escort you to jail. As you remember, some colonists became so disenchanted with this system that they revolted against it. The Revolutionary War was largely fought in protest of the King's unchecked power to make unreasonable laws and set arbitrary taxes on the colonists, who had no say or representation in the matter. After winning their struggle, the colonists vowed that the new United States of America would be based on both law and representation. They had had enough of all-powerful monarchs meddling in their affairs.

To keep power from falling into the hands of any one leader, they decided to divide up the powers of government so that no one person or group of persons could rule the country without limitation. Their strategy was to create three branches of government, each with the ability to review what the other two branches might propose as law or try to do (with or without law). These are the familiar branches you learned long ago: the legislative branch, the executive branch, and the judicial branch. No one branch is supreme. Each must act only within the authority given to it by the United States Constitution, the document that created this tripartite system.

Since the colonists assigned each of the branches certain lawmaking powers, it isn't surprising that each, in its own way, does make law. Let's briefly review their lawmaking powers.

The Legislative Branch

The legislative branch of the U.S. government is the Congress. This bicameral (composed of two parts) body consists of the House of Representatives and the Senate. A state's representation in the House is based on its population. The greater a state's population, the more representatives to which it is entitled, and therefore the more influence it wields. Every state, regardless of its size, has two senators.

Congress cannot make law by itself. Even if Congress passes a bill (meaning that both the House and the Senate voted on and approved it), it cannot become law until the executive branch acts on it. The bill must then go to the office of the president. If he or she approves it and signs it, it then becomes law. If the president does not agree with Congress and feels it should not be the law, he or she will veto it. This puts the bill in a kind of limbo; it is not law, but it is not ''dead,'' either. Congress reviews the bill once more and if it concludes the president is wrong, it can override the presidential veto and enact the bill into law. This, however, requires a ''supermajority'' of Congress, that is, a two-thirds majority.

Notice the interaction between the two branches of government. They check and balance each other's powers. The president cannot ignore what the 530+ men and women of Congress propose, but neither can they ignore the president. If Congress *does* override the executive veto, it is considered to be the voice of the ''many'' prevailing over the voice of ''one.'' In this way, the representative nature of government is further protected. A law that is passed by the legislative branch of government is called a **statute.**

Eye on the Issues

Environment

Environmental law has taken on a new sense of urgency today. From air and water quality to toxic waste disposal, new laws are greatly increasing the legal liabilities for damage done to the environment. Suffice it to say that prior to purchasing a hotel or restaurant, or modifying its waste- or fuel-related procedures, hospitality entrepreneurs should seek proper legal advice regarding environmental issues.

Thirty years ago, concepts such as ''light pollution'' and responsibility for reflected building glare or structural light blockage were unheard of. Today, in some locales, operators may be held responsible for any of these environmental impacts if they are seen to affect neighboring businesses or the community. Operators may also be required to control such environmental concerns as litter or noise. They may even be prohibited from developing a site if local government determines that it will create unacceptable levels of traffic density, which contributes to air pollution.

The Executive Branch

The executive branch is headed by the president of the United States. We've already discussed its relationship to the legislative branch, with one exception. This is the question of presidential lawmaking power. The president *can* make law all by him- or herself; however, that power is limited. By issuing executive orders the president can set forth law on a wide variety of topics. However, checks and balances still apply. If Congress, or anyone else for that matter, believes that the president has gone too far and has exceeded the powers described in the Constitution, an executive order can be challenged.

EXHIBIT 13–1   **Key Legislation that Affects the Hospitality Industry**

Americans with Disabilities Act (ADA)	Prohibits discrimination in the workplace and in access to public places of accommodation based upon ''disabilities,'' which is broadly defined.
Civil Rights Act	Prohibits discrimination on the basis of race, religion, sex, and national origin.
Fair Labor Standards Act	Sets minimum wage.
Immigration Reform and Control Act	Prohibits the employment of persons not authorized to work in the United States.
National Labor Relations Act	Regulates the relationship between management and labor (various).
Dram Shop Statutes	Regulate the liability of a seller of spirituous liquor to a person damaged as a result of a sale (see state, not federal law).

The Judicial Branch

The judicial branch of government was created to resolve disputes between people and even between the branches of government. In theory, the three branches of government are equal; one branch does not possess more power than the others. Whether this is true in practice has been debated among legal scholars for 200 years and that debate will doubtless continue. Some commentators believe that the judicial branch does indeed have more power because when a dispute arises as to whether an act of Congress (a statute) or an act of the president (an executive order) is within the grant of power given that branch by the Constitution, it is up to the judicial branch to make that determination. In other words, the judicial branch has the power to review the actions of the other branches of government and rule on their constitutionality. If the judicial branch feels that the statute or executive order goes beyond the powers granted, the act is said to be unconstitutional. By so ruling, the judicial branch of government is ''making law.'' Law created by the judicial branch of government is called **common law.**

Through common law, executive order, or statute, the government makes law that affects not only individuals, but how those individuals may relate to each other—as employers and employees, as business entity to business entity, and as citizens of the United States in relation to each other and the world. Exhibit 13–1 presents some key legislation as it pertains to the hospitality industry. Other laws or regulations that influence the industry directly or indirectly include: tax legislation that controls the deductibility of business expenses (such as restaurant meals); bed, booze, and board taxes (levied by some states and many cities); and smoking ordinances that affect airlines and restaurants.

Legal Aspects in the Hospitality Industry

The hospitality industry has characteristics that differentiate it from other industries. Just as manufacturers or oil companies have laws that apply specifically to their industries, so, too, does hospitality. And, since the hospitality industry itself includes several important segments under its umbrella, you can be certain there are many specialized legal aspects to be aware of. This is why most hospitality management programs require their students to complete at least one full semester of hospitality law.

One of the largest segments of the industry is the lodging segment, the segment that provides lodging to people while they are away from home. If you think about it, providing accommodations to a person is quite unique. You are providing one of the basic human needs, shelter. As a shelter provider, do you have certain responsibilities or are you free to pick and choose your customers? Consider this scenario.

What if you were to turn a person away from your hotel who was in need of a place to rest? Perhaps it is extremely cold outside, or perhaps the person is in some type of danger, or, as is more probable, the person is simply weary from a long day of traveling. Suppose, for no reason at all, you refuse to give this person a room. Further suppose that that person, forced to leave, is injured or even killed because in his or her fatigue, he or she falls asleep at the wheel and is involved in a fatal accident. Could your hotel be held responsible? The answer (you may be surprised to learn) is yes.

Must a hotel accept all persons seeking a room? Again the answer is yes. Certainly there are exceptions to that rule (law, like grammar, and sometimes even football, is filled with exceptions), but common law notably applies here. Over the years, the common law rule has evolved thusly: A hotel is under an obligation to accept all comers. That is somewhat unique. How did such a law evolve?

Even before the passage of civil rights laws, the government made a distinction between a hotel's ''product'' (a room to sleep in) and other types of products (let's use gasoline as an example). Before civil rights laws outlawing various forms of discrimination, the gasoline seller was under no legal obligation to sell gas to any person who wanted it. If the gas seller was racist or **xenophobic** (afraid of strangers or those ''different'' from oneself), he or she could refuse to sell gas to a potential customer. Even in such unenlightened times, though, a hotelkeeper *was* obliged to sell hotel rooms to all comers. It was the nature of the industry and the service that was being provided that led to the development of that rule. A hotel is considered to have an *affirmative duty* to accept all persons as guests.

Of course, exceptions do apply. If a person has no money to pay for a room or if your hotel has no vacancies, you may refuse a person a room. Likewise, if the person is carrying contraband (animals, explosives, and so on) or is drunk or disorderly, you may refuse that person a room. In addition, if the person is a carrier of a contagious disease, a hotelier may deny him or her a room. But there's a delicate line to walk. You must be especially cautious about refusing a room to a person based upon that last criterion. You could be found liable for illegal discrimination if you deny a person a room for the wrong reason.

What if you abide by your duty and do accept persons as guests but it later turns out that perhaps you should not have accepted them because they were carrying contraband? The question arises, may you evict them? The answer is yes. Before going on, let's clarify a potentially confusing difference: *tenants versus guests.*

Suppose you live in an apartment and your lease with your landlord requires that you pay $500 per month in rent, payable on the first day of each month. You fail to pay your rent as required and on the second day of the month the landlord opens your apartment door with his or her pass key and informs you that, due to your failure to pay rent, you are being evicted immediately and must vacate the premises. Is that legal? May a landlord **summarily,** on his or her own initiative, evict a tenant? The answer in most states is no. A landlord must first go to court and get a judge to sign an order of eviction. In short, the landlord must sue the tenant and seek from the judge an order that the person vacate the apartment. The landlord may not, on his or her own, evict a tenant.

What about a hotel? Does the same rule apply to the eviction of a hotel guest by a hotelier? The answer is no. A hotelier need not get a court order prior to evicting a guest. If the guest has not paid his or her hotel bill, the hotelier may inform the guest of that fact and order the person to leave. If the person refuses to leave, the hotelier may use reasonable force (security personnel) to evict the guest. Extreme care must be taken in this regard; if too much force is used, the potential liabilities are great.

A problem remains, however. How do we tell the difference between a ''guest'' and a ''tenant''? If you think about it, there is one overriding similarity between the two. Are not both, the guest and the tenant, paying another (a landlord or a hotelkeeper) for accommodations? Yes. The law, however, recognizes a substantial difference between the treatment of a guest and of a tenant, namely, the proper method of eviction. A landlord must first go to court to evict a tenant; a hotelkeeper need not go to court to evict a guest.

If the two are so similar, how do we decide which category a given person falls under and which method of eviction is therefore proper? In most cases it is not too difficult to differentiate. If a person makes a reservation for a three-day stay and will pay for his or her room on a daily basis and will be receiving traditional hotel services such as housekeeping, it is pretty clear that the person is a guest. On the other hand, if the person signs a lease for a two-year period and agrees to pay on a monthly basis and no other services are provided, the person is clearly a tenant.

There can be occasions, however, when the distinction becomes blurred. Do people ever ''live'' in hotels? Are there not cases where people rent a suite in a posh New York hotel and stay there for years with the hotel providing housekeeping and perhaps even room service? Is such a person a guest or a tenant? What about the situation wherein the hotel accommodates persons who pay on a monthly schedule and also people who pay on a daily basis? The point is that it is not always immediately clear which method of eviction will be proper. Your job as the hotelkeeper is simply to recognize that the distinction does have to be made if you are contemplating evicting a person and, if any questions exist as to the proper status of that person, the advice of an attorney should be solicited. In this, and in other instances, the recognition of when you need legal advice may be your most important managerial responsibility. If you understand the **intent of the law** (the actual meaning of the law, as opposed to the spirit of the law) involved, you can consult someone to advise you on the *extent* to which it applies.

Ethics

Ethical conduct is a subject of great concern in hospitality-related law. For example, is it ethical to place a no vacancy sign on your hotel when you have rooms available—just so that later in the day when all the other hotels in town are full, you can raise your rate, based on scarcity? Can you prominently advertise a low ''blowout price'' that prompts customers to select your motel only to find that the rate applies to only three or four rooms (which have conveniently been sold)?

Ethics also applies to more serious problems, such as bribes and kickbacks to health, safety, zoning, or other public officials. Because the public relies on hospitality operators to provide the essentials of food and lodging, they must have confidence that such items will be provided in an honest, safe, and forthright manner.

The Hotel's Duty to Protect Guests

As stated above, the relationship between a hotel and its guests is somewhat unique in the commercial world. It is unlike the relationship between most sellers of goods and services and their customers. A hotel provides lodging and safety from the elements, and also from other hazards that exist in the real world.

With that in mind, imagine the following scenario: Ms. Smith, a corporate executive with a large international corporation, is on a business trip to your city. She books a room at the hotel at which you are general manager. After a long day of meetings, she returns to her room after dark. While getting ready to retire for the night, she hears the door to her room being tampered with from the hallway. All of a sudden the door flies open and an unknown assailant bursts in and robs her of her money and jewelry at gunpoint. Even though she does not put up any resistance, she is hit on the head with a blunt object that causes severe head injuries. After months of medical attention and rehabilitation, she recovers from her injuries.

In an attempt to try to apprehend the assailant, the local police contact her but she is unable to identify the person and he will most likely never be caught. The police question her as to whether or not she had used all of the locking devices on the door of her guest room after she had entered her room that evening. She declares that she used all the locks. An investigator is sent to the room to inspect the locks. His review reveals that the main lock was not operating properly. He finds that simply putting pressure on the door knob from the outside would result in the lock failing. In addition, the screws that held the door chain in place were not tightened properly when installed and would not withstand even the lightest pressure. The investigator tells Ms.

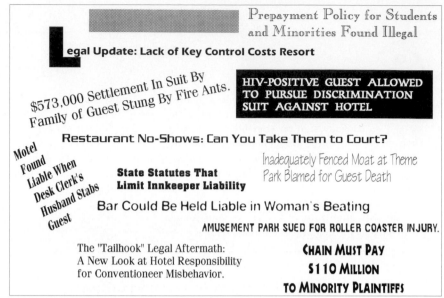

Collage by Marilyn McDonald

Smith that if the locks had been operating properly, the assailant would never have been able to gain entry into the room and the attack would not have taken place.

What do you think of this scenario? Certainly, if anyone caused Ms. Smith's injuries, it was the criminal who hit her on the head. However, did anyone else do, or *fail to do,* something that, if properly done, would have prevented this from occurring? What about the malfunctioning locks? Do you think that it is unreasonable for a hotel to provide a room to a guest with door locks that do not operate properly while knowing that there are ''bad people'' out there who, if given the opportunity, would do to Ms. Smith exactly what this assailant did? Of course it is! Do you think that your hotel was at least partially at fault for causing Ms. Smith's injuries and should be required to compensate her for her injuries? Certainly she incurred large medical bills and also missed months of work, and paychecks, which but for your failure to maintain the locks would not have happened. According to the decision in *Kiefel* v. *Las Vegas Hacienda,* the answer is yes, the hotel is at least partially at fault.

This example illustrates the basic principle behind the law of torts. A *tort* is a civil wrong. One commits a *tortious* act when one acts, or fails to act, as any reasonable person in the same circumstances would have. Is it right (i.e., reasonable) to provide a room to a guest with locks that do not work? Would not a reasonable hotelkeeper inspect the locks on guest-room doors on a regular basis to assure that they work properly? After all, we all know that there are bad people out there in the world (especially if your hotel is in a

EXHIBIT 13–4

The hotel has a duty of care to post notice of a wet floor. Does this seem reasonable to you?

neighborhood with a high crime rate) who will prey on innocent people. Is it not right for the law to expect that, once you know of a potential harm, you will take steps to try to prevent that harm from occurring?

Think of it in very simple terms. Suppose you work at a frozen yogurt store and the display cooler malfunctions, leaking water on the floor. Once you learn that the floor is wet, would you not conclude that there is potential harm to customers who might walk in that area, unaware of the wetness? Of course you would. It is pretty easy to foresee that a person might slip on a wet floor and get hurt. Therefore, what would you do once you became aware that the floor was wet? What would any reasonable person do? The answer is: mop it up as soon as possible. But that brings up another point. What about the time that ticks away before it can be mopped up? Wouldn't a reasonable person *warn* others about the wet floor by placing a sign in that area stating, ''Caution Wet Floor.'' Of course he or she would.

That is what the law of torts requires. The law places a duty of care on us to avoid **negligence,** that is, to act as a reasonably prudent person would act in the same circumstances. This duty of care is placed upon hotelkeepers with regard to their guests. If you do not repair inoperable locks or if you do not mop up wet floors, you are failing to act as a reasonable person would act in the same circumstances—and if that failure causes injury to another, you will be held liable for those injuries.

What lesson can we learn from this discussion? It is simply this: We must all be aware of potential harms that exist and do what common sense tells us is reasonable in the circumstances to prevent those harms from occurring. We cannot bury our heads in the sand and ignore the very real dangers that might exist.

Liability for Guest Property

Consider the following scenario: You are the executive housekeeper of a very posh Beverly Hills hotel. Some of the richest people in the world routinely stay at your hotel, including movie stars, royalty, and sports celebrities. One evening, Elizabeth Taylor and her entourage check into the hotel. A bodyguard accompanies her and you notice the extraordinary diamonds she is wearing. After she has checked in, she goes for dinner in the hotel restaurant only to return to her room later and find her jewelry, valued at over $2 million, missing. The general manager asks to see you to discuss what role any of your staff, the housekeeping personnel, might have had in the mysterious disappearance of Ms. Taylor's jewelry. You inform the general manager that, due to the evening schedule, you have only a skeleton housekeeping crew on duty and you have no idea how the jewelry could have been taken.

The police are called to the scene and their investigation reveals that the lock on Ms. Taylor's room door was defective. The door would yield to even a very small amount of pressure, even if attempts had been made to secure the door upon leaving the room. The police conclude that some criminal(s) probably entered the room, took the jewelry, and disappeared. They file their theft report but it seems unlikely that the perpetrator will be found.

A few days after the incident, the general manager (GM) of the hotel receives a letter from Ms. Taylor's attorney stating that the theft was the fault of the hotel due to its having an inoperable lock and further demanding that the hotel immediately reimburse her in the amount of $2 million. The GM, unsure of what to do, refers the letter to the corporation's legal counsel.

In such a situation, what do you think the hotel should be required to do under the law? Should the hotel be forced to pay? After all, the hotel did not steal the jewelry; a criminal did. On the other hand, if the room's doorlock had operated properly, the criminal would never have gotten in and Ms. Taylor's jewelry would be safely in her possession. You might argue that Ms. Taylor had no business coming to the hotel with such incredibly valuable jewelry. In other words, you might assert, ''This is a hotel. We are in the business of selling guest rooms for a profit. We are *not* in the business of safeguarding people's valuables—that is a task for banks or 'rent-a-cops,' who are equipped to do so. A hotel should not have to take on that kind of responsibility.'' In other words, if Ms. Taylor travels around carrying such valuable items, she does so at her own risk and no hotel, restaurant, or anyone else should be responsible if the items are lost or stolen.

That last position is, for the most part, the one with which the law agrees. Back in the days of old England, the rule of law was that if a guest came to a hotel with valuables and they were lost or stolen, the hotel was responsible—even if the items were lost or stolen through no fault of the hotel. This arrangement could encourage dishonest guests to commit fraud by claiming they checked in with valuables, when, in fact, they did not. Even in cases like that, the hotel would have to pay.

EXHIBIT 13–5

The housekeeping staff can contribute to hotel security by controlling access to guest rooms. Also, by positioning the cart across the door they can avoid uninvited guests.

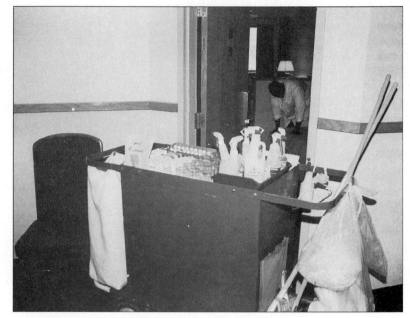

Photo by James L. Morgan, 85283.

Such was the rule at common law. Remember, common law is law that is created by the courts, the judicial branch of government. What if the people, through their elected representatives, express dissatisfaction with the rules of common law created by the courts? In this instance, suppose a hotel owner had been required by a local judge to pay a large sum of money to a guest who claimed to have lost property at his or her hotel. Suppose that hotel owner complained to his fellow hotel owners and warned them that they could easily suffer the same fate. Could they do anything about it? Could the law be changed? The answer is yes, but how?

Under our form of government, the legislative branch can, in some cases, change the law created by the judicial branch. In this case, the hotel owners would need to convince their elected representatives to sponsor a bill that would change the common law rule and instead state that hotels would not be liable for the loss of guest property. And that is what has happened in the United States.

Today, all 50 states have enacted statutes (remember, a statute is a law created by the *legislative* branch of government) that in some manner limit the liability of a hotel for the loss of guest property. These statutes vary quite a bit from state to state. For example, the operative provisions of the California statute actually set dollar limits for the loss of various types of luggage. It further states that if the hotel provides a safe on the premises for the storage of valuables and guests choose not to use the safe, the hotel will not be liable for their loss.

EXHIBIT 13–6

The security of guests and the property becomes even more pressing in casinos: The ''eye in the sky'' and omnipresent security personnel are featured prominently to avoid security and liability issues.

Courtesy: Cow Creek Indian Gaming Center, Canyonville, Oregon.

The Arizona statute is somewhat different. It basically states that if a hotel has a fireproof safe on the premises, and posts a notice in the room of each guest that the safe is available for the placement of valuables, if the guest does not put his/her valuable items in the safe, the hotel will not be liable for their loss *unless the hotel commits some act(s) that causes the item to be lost.*

To many commentators, that last phrase of the Arizona statute is troubling. To illustrate this problem, let's use the set of facts outlined above with regard to Ms. Taylor's diamonds. You'll recall two things: She did not put her jewelry into the safe provided by the hotel; and the items were stolen due to a defective were lock. Based on the California statute, do you think the hotel would be responsible for the jewelry? The answer is that the total liability of the hotel would be no greater than the amount set forth in the statute, that is, $1,000. Even though the hotel was at least partially at fault for causing the loss of the items by not having an operable lock on her guest-room door, the liability of the hotel is limited to no more than $1,000, pursuant to the above-quoted statute.

Now, let's take the same set of facts and apply them to the Arizona statute. Would the same result occur? Not necessarily. Remember, the Arizona statute states that if the hotel provides the safe and the guest does not put the items in the safe, the hotel will not be liable *unless the hotel in some manner causes the loss of the items.* Do you think that the hotel caused the loss of Ms. Taylor's jewelry? Perhaps the answer to that question is yes. In that event, the Arizona hotel might be held fully responsible for the jewelry, while based upon the same set of facts, the California hotel might be held liable for only $1,000.

As you can see, the law, and the words used in a statute, can have an enormous impact on hotels and hoteliers. The importance of knowing the law in the state or country in which your hotel will be operating cannot be over-stated. That is why some basic knowledge of hospitality law is important to you at this introductory level. As you progress through the curriculum, you will not only become aware of the law, but you will also learn how to find out what the law is, and, most importantly, how to read and understand what it means.

International

More and more hospitality operations are expanding their operations overseas. Tempted by the opening up of China, the former Soviet Union, and even the Republic of Vietnam, Western companies are grabbing the opportunity to participate in these growing economies. In such countries, it's extremely important to remember that wholly different sets of laws apply. There is an enormous danger in assuming that the laws to which you are accustomed (which you may consider ''natural'') will be valid in a foreign country. The movies have gotten a lot of mileage out of exaggerating ''native'' laws, taboos, and the consequences. (''The foreigner saw the chief's daughter without her ceremonial mask on—now he must marry her.'') While such portrayals have trivialized different cultures' laws and traditions, today's managers should not. Without sufficient knowledge, the risks are significant and may doom a naive entrepreneur, investor, or manager. Americans are especially prone to assuming that rights they have always enjoyed are guaranteed elsewhere.

Restaurants and Food Service

Perhaps this has happened to you—or perhaps you've heard the nightmarish stories of alien objects being consumed by unsuspecting diners. Here's a blood-curdling example. After taking two bites of a hamburger you feel a sharp pain in the roof of your mouth. You stop chewing and put one finger in your mouth to investigate. To your surprise, you discover a large amount of blood and a shard of glass lodged in your gums. You leave in horror and upon your arrival at the emergency room you are told by the oral surgeon that you will need extensive reconstructive surgery to repair the deep wound in your mouth. After months of visits to the surgeon and indescribable suffering, your mouth begins to feel better, but it will never be the same.

How did a piece of glass get into that hamburger? Are the injuries you suffered the fault of the establishment from which you purchased the hamburger? Maybe the glass was there when they received the meat from their supplier. What about your enormous doctor bills and all of the time you missed from work due to your surgeries? These are questions that might arise when you bring a civil suit against the restaurant for your damages.

It's beyond the scope of this course and this text to describe the various remedies of law that you might rightfully pursue in such a case—though you're likely to be treated to such fascinating details if you take one or more courses in hospitality law. Suffice it to say that such unfortunate occurrences do happen all the time. There is a very real possibility that you or your company will at some point serve food to a customer that might be termed "unfit for human consumption." It is also true that restaurants are often found liable if their customers are injured by an item of food that the restaurants served to them. Needless to say, proper inspection and preparation of food products is essential. (See Chapters 9 and 10 for more discussion on food safety.)

Liquor Liability

Spirituous Liquors.   As you are all no doubt aware, the sale of spirituous liquors forms a very large segment of the hospitality industry. From the five-star resort that offers an upscale piano bar, beer service to golfers on the course, and minibars in each guest room to the hole-in-the-wall neighborhood tavern, the sale of liquor is a huge industry. From a legal standpoint, there are two main issues regarding the selling of liquor.

Licensing.   Every state has laws that regulate the sale of alcoholic beverages. Basically, according to these laws, it is illegal to sell liquor without first obtaining a license from the state. States offer many different types of licenses; it is essential that you obtain the type of license that will permit the type of sales in which you intend to engage. For example, you can obtain an on-premise sale license for a bar. For a liquor store, an off-premise license would be required. A restaurant license allows operators who derive most of their income from food to also sell liquor. Licenses may be granted to hotels, microbreweries, or even excursion boats.

To obtain a license, you must apply to the state liquor authority. If a license is granted, you may then engage in the activities that are permitted by that license. Each state will have detailed rules and regulations with which you must comply. If you do not, the state will either suspend or revoke your license. These rules vary greatly from state to state, but usually they specify the following:

- The hours of the day during which sales are permitted.
- The number of drinks one person may be served at a time.
- Whether or not employees are permitted to drink or even purchase drinks for patrons.

Needless to say, you must know the rules in the state where you operate very well and strictly comply with them, and obey federal regulations. (See exhibit 13–7.)

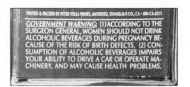

Photos by James L. Morgan, 85283.

Dram Shop Liability. The other issue that surfaces all too often is that of **dram shop liability.** To understand what is meant by dram shop liability, we must look at a simple set of facts. Picture this: After dinner one evening you get into your car and are on your way to basketball practice. It is dark outside, but the roads are dry, and visibility is good. You are on a two-lane highway and see a car approaching you. For the most part it is staying on its side of the road, but you do observe that it is swerving within its lane. As it gets closer, it strays across the double yellow line. You do what you can to avoid the oncoming vehicle and swerve to your right. However, a head-on collision is unavoidable. Fortunately, you did wear your seat belt and you were not ejected from the vehicle. You did sustain serious back, neck, and leg injuries. After a number of months of rehabilitation you recover but are told you will suffer some permanent leg problems that will cause you to walk with a slight limp.

The police send you a copy of their accident report. Upon reading it, you discover that on the night of the accident the driver of the vehicle that hit you (let's call him Mr. Drunk) had been at a local bar. He would have been arrested for drunk driving except, unlike you, he did not wear a seat belt, and was killed in the accident.

You become curious as to why Mr. Drunk lost control of his car. Did his steering fail? Did one of his tires blow out? The accident report does not indicate any such problem. You wonder if he simply had too much to drink at the local bar. You go to the bar and speak to the bartender who was on duty that night. He informs you that between the hours of 4:00 PM (the beginning of happy hour) and 6:00 PM, when Mr. Drunk left the bar, he had consumed six double scotches. Prior to being served drink number six, he had tried to stand up to go to the restroom but had fallen flat on his face. Upon being helped to his seat, he said, "Gee, I should not have fallen like that. I must need another drink!" He was promptly served double scotch number six. He left the bar after that drink and the accident occurred 10 minutes later.

Now, with that story in mind, do you think that the bar, not just the drinker,
should be held responsible to you for your injuries? The liability of the bar
for those injuries is what we refer to as *dram shop liability.* (*Dram shop* is
another term derived from old England. A dram is a unit of liquid measurement
equal to approximately one ounce or one shot. A dram shop was a bar, a shop
that served liquor by the dram. Hence the term.) Each state has its own laws
regarding a bar's liability to an innocent victim of a person to whom they
served liquor. Some states take the position that the bar should have no responsibility. Their reasoning is that it was not the bar that caused the injuries;
it was the person that got in his or her car and drove while impaired. Other
states take the position that the bar can be liable if it served the drinker a drink
when he or she was already drunk. Their reasoning is that it should be obvious
to bartenders that if they serve a patron who is already intoxicated, he or she
may operate a motor vehicle irresponsibly and cause an accident injuring another driver or pedestrian. Therefore, the bar must not serve such persons; they
must be ''cut off.''

Unfortunately, our Mr. Drunk scenario is all too real. It is imperative that
all hospitality operators be familiar with the dram shop liability imposed upon
them by the state in which they operate and that they strictly comply with the
law. The service of alcoholic beverages is a very important part of the hospitality industry and can be very profitable. However, due to the nature of
alcohol as a drug that can cause severe impairment, it must be dealt with
properly.

Technology

As technological advances occur, new legal problems are created. An example is computer software. A hospitality operator might spend thousands of dollars developing a software program that is unique and gives that operator a competitive advantage over others. That final product is protected from ''thieves'' by copyright laws that give a creator of a new work the exclusive right to its use.

Ownership of customer databases is another example. One computer disk may contain customer mailing addresses, credit information, and buying history—data that cost thousands of dollars to accumulate. One disgruntled employee can cost a company a fortune in lost time and clientele by copying such information or sabotaging it. The legalities surrounding technology are changing daily.

The Hospitality Operation and Its Employees

As you will soon find out in your studies, not only is the hospitality industry extremely labor intensive, it also has one of the highest employee turnover rates of any industry. Therefore, as a manager, one of your constant duties will be to hire personnel, fire personnel, and act as the mediator of disputes between your personnel and various governmental entities. As an employer, you are also bound by a growing number of laws regarding your relationship to employees before, during, and after their terms of employment. The laws relating to the personnel (or human resource) function of a hospitality operation are many and complex.

Discrimination.   It is now illegal for an employer to discriminate against a person with regard to terms of employment based upon:

- Race
- Religion
- National origin
- Sex
- Disabilities

It is important to understand what is meant by the term *discrimination.* An example may make this concept clearer: Let's assume that you are the food and beverage manager of a hotel. You have five employees on your staff. Four of the employees are very competent and responsible employees—they always show up for work on time, their work is excellent, and you've never had a customer complain about their performance. The fifth employee, however, is a different story. He is habitually late for work and rude to customers, and you receive at least one complaint per week about him. If you were to fire that fifth employee, would you have discriminated against him? The answer is yes.

EXHIBIT 13–9   **Main Points of the ADA Legislation**

- Hotels, restaurants, theaters, stores, offices, transit stations, museums, social service agencies, parks, schools, and gyms must not discriminate against individuals with disabilities.
- Barriers in existing facilities must be removed when removal can be accomplished without undue difficulty or expense. If not, alternative methods of making goods and services available must be in place.
- Altered facilities must be accessible. In major structural alterations, a path of travel to the altered area and restrooms serving the altered area must be accessible.
- New facilities must be accessible, unless structurally impractical.
- Auxiliary aids and services are required, unless the business can demonstrate undue hardship.
- Elevators need not be provided in buildings with fewer than three floors or with less than 3,000 square feet per floor, other than in shopping centers and health-care buildings.
- Bona fide private clubs and religious groups are not covered by these provisions.

Source: The President's Committee on Employment of People with Disabilities.

The question is, was your act of discrimination (firing him) illegal? No. You did not illegally discriminate against him because you did not fire him *because* of his race, religion, and so on; you fired him because of his poor job performance. There is no law forbidding discrimination on the basis of job performance.

Let's change the facts: Let's assume you fire employee number four, one of the competent, hard-working employees, because he refused to work on Saturdays, the Jewish Sabbath. He is Jewish and he told you that he could not work on Saturdays. Instead of trying to schedule around his religious needs, as you might have been able to do, you dismiss him immediately. Did you discriminate against him? The answer is yes. Was that illegal discrimination? The answer is again yes. Exhibit 13–9 shows the main points of the ADA legislation, as they affect the hospitality industry.

From these two examples you can see that the same act (firing an employee) can in one case be illegal discrimination and in another be perfectly legal. The difference is the *reason* behind your act. Did you do it because of the person's race, religion, and so on, or did you do it because of poor job performance? The reasons *why* you acted as you did become all important. Obviously, therefore, as an employer, you must be careful to act nondiscriminatorily. In addition, you must **document** the reasons for your actions. If you get complaints, such as lateness, about an employee, you should note them in a personnel file or report. This serves as evidence that will later support your motivation for acting as you did.

Exhibit 13–10

Inside the courtroom, the plaintiffs make their cases against the defendant (hotel). Assuming the operation has properly met its duty of care, there should be nothing to worry about.

Other Employment-Related Laws.   Other laws that affect the personnel function are *tax laws*. Employment-related taxes such as FICA (the Social Security tax) and FUTA (the unemployment tax) must be paid to the government based upon the earnings of your employees.

Labor laws affect how unionization of your workplace may prohibit certain actions you might wish to take, such as lowering wages. In turn, *minimum wage laws* dictate the amount of money you must pay employees—unionized or not. *Immigration laws* will affect your hiring not only of illegal aliens, but of all employees. The basic ways in which all of these laws affect hospitality operations are covered in more detail in college-level hospitality law or hospitality human resource management classes.

Conclusion

We began this chapter by stating why a hospitality law course is the most important course you will take in your college career. In today's litigious society, being able to avoid lawsuits should be one of your two top priorities (along with profit making).

It must be said, however, that before your career as a hospitality operator or manager is over, you will almost certainly become acquainted with the inside of a courtroom. Very few hospitality operations are run so perfectly that some customer, sometime, will not bring a lawsuit. It's hoped that with heightened awareness, proper education, and knowledge, you'll be able to minimize such occurrences. It's also assumed that, when you *do* enter the courtroom, you will be better prepared and, with proper legal counsel, will be more likely to win.

Keywords

scenario   402
statute   404
common law   405
xenophobic   406

summarily   407
intent of the law   408
dram shop liability   417
document   420

Core Concepts

liabilities   402
affirmative duty   406
tenants versus guests   407

tort   410
negligence   411
discrimination   419

Discussion Questions

1. Must a hotel accept all potential guests? Under what circumstances may a hotel refuse a room to a guest?

2. Will a hotel always be liable to a guest who gets injured on its property? Or to a guest who loses valuables at the hotel?

3. What is the liability of a bar to a person injured by a patron who drank liquor at that bar?

4. Are there any restrictions on an employer's firing an employee?

5. What are checks and balances in terms of the federal government? Can you think of any checks and balances that might exist in a hospitality operation?

6. Are all persons who stay overnight at hotels "guests"? Why is it important to distinguish between a guest and a tenant?

7. Do all states have identical statutes regarding the licensure of sellers of alcoholic beverages? Why would knowing this be important?

Hospitality Automation

CHAPTER 14

The hospitality industry has witnessed a dramatic increase in computer use in the last 20 years. It is almost impossible to find any organization that has not been affected by computer information technology. Even the so-called mom-and-pop restaurants and motels have been caught up in the flow of technology, even if only through the use of desktop publishing, electronic cash registers, or faxes. In the larger world of nationally and internationally owned lodging, computers and other technologies are now a given. Though hardware and software vary from chain to chain and country to country, certain basic principles apply to all.

Courses on hospitality automation generally include a discussion of hardware and software, exposure to general software applications used in the industry, and practice in applications specific to the hospitality field. This chapter will touch on all of these areas. While many instructors include an overview of computer basics to help put later details in perspective, it is beyond the scope of this chapter to cover the history and development of computers. It is important, however, to know how and why computers work—otherwise you will have unrealistic expectations of what they can and can't do. Your future hospitality automation courses will give you this perspective.

With regard to industry-specific programs, this chapter includes a discussion of property management systems, accounting applications, computer-based food and beverage systems, and property management system interfaces, and a look at computer system selection and technology trends.

Outline

423

Introduction

In their book, *In Search of Excellence,* Thomas J. Peters and Robert H. Waterman, Jr., write:

> We had decided, after dinner, to spend a second night in Washington. Our business day had taken us beyond the last convenient flight out. We had no hotel reservations, but were near the new Four Seasons, had stayed there once before

and liked it. As we walked through the lobby wondering how best to plead our case for a room, we braced for the usually chilly shoulder accorded to latecomers. To our astonishment, the concierge looked up, smiled, called us by name, and asked how we were. She remembered our names![1]

Since this is a chapter on hospitality automation, you're probably guessing that this neat trick was somehow done with computers. This example is used precisely because this is a chapter on automation. The concierge used no computer to amaze her two late-night guests. Her performance was the result of excellent training, a good memory, and well-developed people skills. There's a point here: As incredible as hospitality technology can be, it is still a partner with people skills. Some things machines do best; other things people do best; still other things are best done by some combination of hardware, software, and "warm-ware" (as some "techies" refer to people). As you read about the technologies that have swept into the lodging industry, please keep this truth in mind.

As you've already read in earlier chapters, changes are taking place in the way the world does business. The hospitality industry has to incorporate and respond to these changes, just like any other industry. Many of the changes are the result of changing business conditions; others are being brought about by new technology, which is being introduced almost daily.

You have only to look around you to see how technology has changed modern life. Whereas hardly anyone had a computer 15 years ago, computers are now an aspect of nearly every part of your life. From the moment you wake up and fix your breakfast in the microwave, to starting your car, driving to school or job, all the way to doing your laundry, and going to the bank or ATM, your life is affected by computer technology.

As a result of these tremendous changes in technology, the business world and the hospitality industry, in particular, needs workers who are familiar with and able to use this technology on a daily basis. Indeed, you will have an edge in the workplace if you are familiar with and know how to use computers and a variety of software.

Lodging and restaurant operations have seen (and will continue to see) technology-driven changes that include:

- More efficient operations due to more powerful (and better-utilized) computers.
- Better management information.
- A better ability to track and react to guests and their needs.
- Empowerment of lower level staff members to make technology-based decisions.
- The use of technology as a training tool for employees.

Information technology will soon engulf all the departments of a hotel or a restaurant, from the front desk to housekeeping, and from the cash register to the kitchen. Large centralized organizations, such as Hilton, Sheraton, or McDonald's, already have management information departments as part of their corporate structure to control and manage information. Their recruiters have come to realize that any person dealing with information technology will need the following skills:

- An understanding of how information system hardware and software function and interrelate.
- An understanding of how to design a system for optimal performance.
- The capacity to evaluate system performance.
- The ability to train system users.
- The ability to guard and preserve the system from unauthorized access.
- The capacity to maintain a system documentation library.

Information in the hospitality industry world is a resource and as such must be managed well and used properly. Information may give the manager of one property an edge over the manager of a property down the street who does not have access to that same information.

This chapter will present you with an overview of some of the hardware and software used in the hospitality industry, and touch upon some of the technological advances we can expect in the near future.

The Computer System

Information is a finished, useful product consisting of **data.** Data are the raw materials that are processed to become meaningful and useful information. This transformation process, the making of data into information, is generally referred to as the *data processing cycle* (see Exhibit 14–1). Let's look at a simple example. A ''W'' and a ''2'' on their own do not mean much to you unless you have very specific background knowledge. They are data, not really information. Yet, as soon as they are combined through a process, they become information to you: W-2 (the form that those of you who work are familiar with, particularly around April 15 each year; it is used for income tax purposes).

A **computer** is a tool capable of processing large quantities of data into information more quickly and accurately than any other data processing method. A computer system streamlines the process of collecting and re-cording data and expands the ways in which information is organized and reported.[2]

Hardware

A computer hardware system is made up of four basic components: an input device, a central processing unit (CPU), an output device, and a storage device.

Together these items are what is called ***hardware.*** As users, we interact with
the system through input devices such as keyboards and scanners and output
devices such as monitors and printers. The CPU processes the data into useful
information, and the storage devices retain that information for future use.

Software

For the computer to do the work we would like it to do, it needs instructions.
A **program** is a set or sequence of instructions. All programs together are
referred to as ***software.*** Software are the computer programs that control the
hardware and that perform the processing tasks for the user. There are two
basic types of software we use in a computer system: (1) **system software,**
the master control programs informing the computer how to function; and
(2) **application software,** the programs designed to perform specific tasks
(also called *applications*). Most of you are probably familiar with programs
such as word processing, electronic spreadsheets, and database management
systems. Yet, you are probably not familiar with hospitality industry–specific
applications used in the front office, accounting, central reservations, and food
and beverage departments. This chapter discusses both general or generic software applications and the industry-specific ones.

Eye on the Issues

Environment

The earth's environment is a resource that we need
to protect and one where computer technology can
help. By using computers to communicate via electronic mail and by linking computers together in
networks, operations can greatly reduce the amount
of paper they use. Communicating electronically
will impact the environment by reducing the
amount of mail that needs to be transported by
trucks and airplanes, thus reducing air pollution
and the use of nonrenewable resources such as oil.

Computer hardware manufacturers are responding to our environmental concerns by producing computers that save energy by reducing the
power used if left on over long periods of time and
by using components that can be recycled.

Computer systems are tools for solving problems. The systems used in the hospitality industry help us solve our problems by enhancing our resource utilization, which in turn improves our profitability. Some of the key advantages of a computerized information system include:

- Improved labor productivity and organizational efficiency.
- Enhanced decision-making capabilities.
- Reduced operating costs.
- Increased information accuracy.
- Increased revenues.
- Greater guest satisfaction.
- Improved controls.[3]

The next section will look at generic application software. Whether you are familiar with it or not, you will undoubtedly be asked to use some of it in your future management career.

Generic Application Software.   *Word processing software,* the most popular type of application software program, allows us to automate the task of typing, storing, editing, formatting, correcting, and printing text. As text is typed into the computer, it is displayed on the screen and can be manipulated in many ways before printing or storage. It is possible to insert words, move words, and delete words. Documents can be combined and electronically checked for spelling and simple grammatical errors. Writers can also usually access add-ons such as electronic thesauruses, dictionaries, and other references. With word processing software, users can create letter documents and mailing lists and then automatically merge them together.

Electronic spreadsheet software stores numerical data in cells, performs calculations, and produces reports. Once data are entered into the spreadsheet, it can be manipulated by the user and graphs can be created from the data entered. This allows us to present financial and other numerical data in an easily understandable format, which is useful when a picture is worth a thousand words or, in this case, a thousand numbers.

Spreadsheets are one of the most commonly used software packages in the hospitality industry. Hospitality managers base their decisions largely on numerical information such as occupancy percentages, sales volumes, and average checks. Information is presented in income statements, balance sheets, and budgets. Once all of these data have been input properly, managers can experiment with the data and explore different ''what if'' scenarios, examining the effects that different situations might have on their bottom line.

Database management software provides the user with a way to manage large amounts of information. Once data are entered into the database program, it can be manipulated to create reports using selected criteria. Database software can create and maintain records, extract records according to certain criteria, sort records, and link files. In the hospitality industry, database software can be utilized, for instance, to maintain client lists in the sales department, frequent guest lists for the reservations office, or travel agent lists for the accounting department. As needed, these lists can be used to generate labels for mailings, such as promotional materials, rate announcements, or commission payments.

Property Management Systems

The lodging segment of the hospitality industry consists of many different types of properties (resorts, commercial hotels, transient hotels, motels), and all of them have varying computer needs. **Property management systems (PMS)** are software applications that assist managers in the day-to-day operation of their properties and that address almost every phase of the lodging operation. A PMS normally performs both back and front office functions and supports a variety of other functions such as housekeeping, sales, catering, energy management, and call accounting. The types of technology and systems selected by hotels are influenced by factors such as:

- Departmental needs.
- Service level—quality of guest/employee interaction.
- Facility size and layout.
- Guest amenities—entertainment, minibars, and so on.
- Organizational structure of the property.
- Financial capacity.

Exhibit 14–2 shows you the various components or modules of the PMS. As you can see, the PMS is actually a set of programs that work together but that also have individual, specific tasks.

Front-Office Applications

Reservation Applications.   A *reservation module* typically performs the following basic functions:

- Sell individual reservations.
- Sell group reservations.
- Display room availability.
- Track advance deposits.
- Track travel agent information.
- Generate reservation reports.

EXHIBIT 14–2

The main menu screen of a property management system shows a number of various functions.

EXHIBIT 14–2

The main menu screen of a property management system shows a number of various functions.

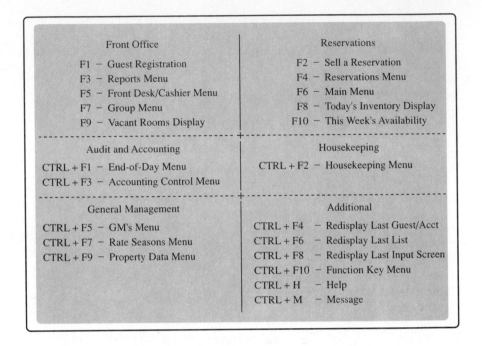

Front Office		Reservations	
F1	Guest Registration	F2	Sell a Reservation
F3	Reports Menu	F4	Reservations Menu
F5	Front Desk/Cashier Menu	F6	Main Menu
F7	Group Menu	F8	Today's Inventory Display
F9	Vacant Rooms Display	F10	This Week's Availability

Audit and Accounting		Housekeeping	
CTRL + F1	End-of-Day Menu	CTRL + F2	Housekeeping Menu
CTRL + F3	Accounting Control Menu		

General Management		Additional	
CTRL + F5	GM's Menu	CTRL + F4	Redisplay Last Guest/Acct
CTRL + F7	Rate Seasons Menu	CTRL + F6	Redisplay Last List
CTRL + F9	Property Data Menu	CTRL + F8	Redisplay Last Input Screen
		CTRL + F10	Function Key Menu
		CTRL + H	Help
		CTRL + M	Message

Central Reservation Systems.   In the majority of the lodging properties that use a PMS, the reservation module may be interfaced (connected) to a central reservation system (CRS). A CRS connects individual lodging properties with a computer reservations center that is usually staffed 24 hours a day. Guests access the center through a toll-free telephone number. Each guest reservation created by the CRS staff is sent through the computer system to the individual property.

Central reservation systems have been in existence since the 1960s and were first installed by major chains in their properties. Most property management systems (PMSs) can be and are interfaced with a CRS, reducing the labor required to handle reservations and allowing for better control over room availability. It is, of course, essential that the CRS and the PMS constantly update each other, so that neither sells a room that has already been sold by the other. (See Exhibit 14–3, which details how a PMS links all departments together.)

Property Reservation System.   A PMS reservation system allows the hotel to enter, review, modify, or cancel a reservation. Unless a guest uses a CRS, the reservation process normally starts with a phone call to the property and ends with a complete guest reservation record. (The actual process of guest reservation handling was discussed in Chapter 7.)

Since rooms availability information is crucial to the process of selling reservations, most PMSs have the ability to display room availability in many

Exhibit 14–3

A well-interfaced system links many departments.

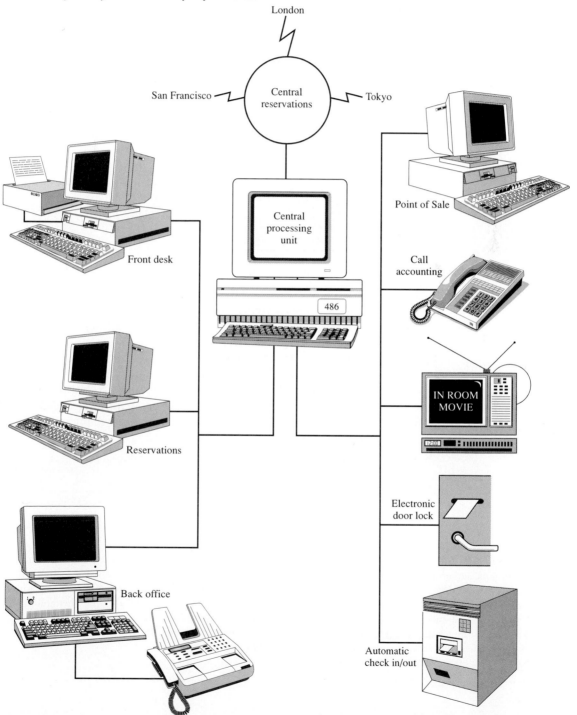

EXHIBIT 14–4

A PMS availability screen shows rooms remaining unsold (available) by date. Note May 5 is oversold on queen bed/queen rooms by three rooms.

Room Type	THU MAY 05	FRI MAY 06	SAT MAY 07	SUN MAY 08	MON MAY 09	TUE MAY 10	WED MAY 11	1per Rates 2per * = Higher Rate * = Lower Rate
QBQR	-3	1	1	1	1	1	1	74.00 79.00
QBRS	1	1*	1*	1*	1*	1*	1*	66.00 71.00
QBQP	0	10*	10*	10*	10*	10*	10*	66.00 71.00
DDPH	1	2*	2*	2*	2*	1*	2*	66.00 71.00
PRES	0	1*	1*	1*	1*	1*	1*	66.00 71.00
QBDB	1	4*	4*	4*	4*	4*	4*	66.00 71.00
Total:	4	19	19	19	19	18	19	

Action: 1 = Forward 1 Week   2 = Back 1 Week   3 = Forward to Rate Change

formats (such as queen, double, king, disabled-accessible, and facing golf course). Exhibit 14–4 shows you an availability screen.

In addition, guest name lists can be displayed on the screen or printed according to special requests or specific criteria (nonsmoking room request, special package rate, registrant of XYZ convention). (See Exhibit 14–5.)

Reservations can be guaranteed in many different ways. Guests may give the reservationist their credit card number, arrange advance billing, or send money in advance. This form of guarantee is called an *advance deposit*. Advance deposits received by the hotel are also recorded through the reservations module. Exhibit 14–6 displays a reservation screen.

Eye on the Issues

Ethics

All those involved in the hospitality industry—the guest, unions, government, stockholders, management, owners, and the vendors of information technology—need to promote the issue of responsible and ethical use of information technology. If we provide our guests with electronic data links, we must ensure that such links are secure and private. It would be highly unethical for lodging operations

to eavesdrop on guests' personal business transactions, or use "smart" room sensors to spy on guests. Beyond having a responsibility for their own employees' use of information technology, hotels will also have to act as guardians of their guests' electronic security by taking steps to prevent external snooping.

EXHIBIT 14–5

This information menu lists all functions that access guest data.

```
                            Guest Information Menu

        F1 – Arrivals for Date              F6 – Canceled Arrivals for Date
        F2 – Checked-in on Date             F7 – Guests Now In-House
        F3 – Expected Departures for Date   F8 – All Guest Records for Date
        F4 – Departed on Date               F9 – Reservation Booked on Date
        F5 – No-Shows for Date              F10 – Guest Database
    -------------------------------+-------------------------------------
                        Select List Number: .
                      For Date Range from: ... ... (Today)
                                       to: ... ... (Same Day)
                                    Print: . (N)
    -------------------------------+-------------------------------------
    Include Guest Records With:

         Request Code: ....         Guest ID: ...........        Info: ........
           Group Code: ....       Source Code: .        Address 1 Name: ........
          Market Code: ....      Overried Rate: . (+ or -)     Company: ........
            Room Type: ....               Rlwy: . (+ or -)       Street: ........
            Rate Code: ..                 Crib: . (+ or -)         City: ........
      Gtd/Pay by Code: ..                 Pets: . (+ or -)        State: ..
       Travel Agent ID: ........        VIP ID: ....               Zip: .....
```

EXHIBIT 14–6

A blank reservation screen. Some data are mandatory (e.g., guest name). Other data are optional (e.g., address).

```
                            Sell a Reservation
            Source: .
          Operator: ..        Arrival Date: ... ..   Nights: ..   Depart: ... ..
        Room Type: ....   Nbr of Rooms: ..
        Guest Name: ...........................   Adults: ..   Kids: ..
            Phone: . (...)...-....    .............

    Gtd By: .. ...........................  Exp: ../.  Rlwys: ..  Cribs: ..   Pets: ..
        Rate Code: ..      Print Confirmation: . (N)    Complimentary: . (N)
      Override Rate: .......   Deposit Required: . (N)   Deposit Amount:
        Group Code: .... Mkt: .... Rt Type: . Vip/Co: .... Requested By: ...........
      Travel Agt ID: ........     Corporate ID: ........       Guest ID: ...........
          Request: ...............................     Pay TA: . (Y)
             Info: ...........................................................
                   ...........................................................
        Adr1 Nm: ........................   Adr1 Nm: .......................
        Company: ........................   Company: .......................
          Street: ........................   Street: .......................
             Ct: ................ St: .. Zip: .....  Ct: ............... St: .. Zip: .....
    Other Names: ...................................
                 ...................................     Override Password: .....
                 ...................................
```

PMS reservations modules should also be able to track travel agent bookings and commissions. When travelers book their hotel accommodations through a travel agent, the hotel will often pay the travel agent a commission. It's therefore of some importance to keep track of travel agent accounts, not only to facilitate paying commissions, but to determine the amount of business generated by each agent.

Groups, conventions, and tour groups form a large percentage of the business for lodging properties. Group reservations require more attention and few extra steps. In a PMS, a room reservation for a group requires the creation of a *group master,* which sets up a block of rooms either by room type or by "run of the house" (which allows the guest to have any available room for the contracted group price). When dealing with room reservations for groups, reservation agents must pay close attention to the room block. Meeting planners often ask for room lists and counts on how many rooms have not yet been reserved. To accommodate groups efficiently, a PMS should be able to:

- Block a large number of rooms at one time.
- Establish group rates by room type.
- Set up charge instructions for the group account.
- Assign rooms prior to the group arrival.

When a PMS handles these tasks smoothly, the hotel staff will have a much easier job of servicing large or small groups. Efficient check-in and check-out of group blocks can make or break a group's satisfaction with the property's performance. Of course, the reservation process is crucial to all guests, regardless of whether they are members of a group. Accuracy is paramount, since once a guest is entered into the PMS, the system follows the guest throughout his/her stay at the hotel, referencing the initial entry many times.

Rooms Management. The rooms management module basically links the front desk to the other departments of the hotel, housekeeping in particular. As a guest with a reservation arrives at the front desk, reservation information is transferred from the reservation module to the rooms management module. The guest is assigned a room and a folio or guest account is created to keep track of charges and payments. Room assignment can be accomplished by displaying the available rooms via a computerized room rack (from which the desk agent selects a room) or by having the computer automatically pick the room based on the requested room type and features (see Exhibit 14–7). The room rack will display rooms available based on the criteria that are entered. After the room has been assigned, the front desk clerk will confirm a method of payment from the guest. Obtaining the method of payment and displaying the credit available to the guest are very important features in the PMS.

Room Rack Display					
Room	Type	Desc	Rate	Connected	Status
102	QBQR		42		VC
103	QBRS		42		VC
106	QBQP	C	42	Connects 108	VC
107	PRES	NC	42		VC
108	QBDB	C	42	Connects 106	VC
109	QBQP	NC	42		VC
110	QBQP		42		VD
111	QBQP	NC	42		VC
112	QBQP		42		VC
115	QBDB	N	42		VC
116	QBDB	C	42	Connects 118	VC
117	QBQP	NC	42		VC
118	QBQP	C	42	Connects 116	VC
119	QBQP	NV	42		VD
120	DDPH	H	42		VC
121	QBQP	NV	42		VC
123	QBQP	NV	42		VC
125	DDPH	HN	42		VC

The final step of the registration process is to verify the ***room status.*** This confirms the status of the room as ''occupied'' (or ''in-house''). Guests who have checked in and guaranteed their rooms are considered in-house. After check-in, the PMS informs all other departments whether the guest is allowed to charge services or purchases to the guest room account. Management can also use the PMS to monitor the guest's charges in relation to the account's credit limit.

The guest who arrives at the hotel without a reservation will spend a little longer at the front desk. The front-desk clerk first needs to check availability of the room type requested by the guest and then gather all the information about the guest to complete the registration record. After that the clerk proceeds through the same steps as with a guest who has a reservation.

In order to sell rooms, the front desk must have up-to-date and accurate room status information. This is provided by the housekeeping department. When a guest checks out, the status of the room he or she occupied changes. Once the housekeeping staff has cleaned and checked the room, the executive housekeeper changes its status once again. He or she may either inform the front desk of the room's new status or change the status via a PMS terminal in the housekeeping department.

Sometimes discrepancies in room status occur. A *discrepancy* occurs when a room is reported occupied when it is vacant, or clean when it is not made up (or vice versa). Discrepancies need to be cleared up speedily, since rooming a guest in a dirty room may harm the property's reputation and failing to sell an available room causes loss of revenue. If discrepancies recur, management should review procedures and training to see if some oversight in these areas is contributing to the problem. In this, as in all other interactions between the housekeeping department and the front desk, good communication is essential. Without such communication and cooperation, proper selling will not be able to take place and room revenue will suffer.

Guest Accounting.　In the guest accounting module, *folios* (or guest accounts) are created, transactions are posted, cashier shifts are opened and closed, and guests are checked out. There are four basic types of folios:

- *Individual folios* are created for each individual guest.
- *Master folios* are typically created for groups.
- *City ledgers/folios* contain lists of customers who owe the hotel money and nonguest accounts with in-house privileges.
- *Control folios* are set up to ensure that all revenues and payments become part of the daily report to management.

What happens when the guest wants to check out? The first step in the check-out process is to print a folio for the guest to review. The folio can be printed on command for the guest to look over before check-out. If there are any disputed charges, they can be resolved at this point and adjustments can be made. Once the guest has paid, the final payment is posted to the folio and one copy of it is given to the guest. Another copy is retained by the hotel. When the folio registers a zero balance, the PMS will prompt the clerk to inform the guest accounting module that the guest is checked out. The system does not "know" this until the clerk keys in the change in status. Once the clerk has done so, the system's guest check-out feature automatically updates the room status, the house count, and all pertinent reports.

As the rooms division chapter indicated, the *night audit* is a process that reconciles all the account postings that occur during the day and that closes the hotel's accounting books every 24 hours. In balancing all the accounts, the night audit function relies heavily on the accuracy of the guest accounting module. Reports generated by the night audit inform management about the hotel's revenue performance and its operating and marketing statistics.

General Management Applications

The front-office applications of the PMS provide information to front-line employees (front-desk clerks) and management alike, and both use them in their day-to-day decision making. The information can be incorporated into many different report formats depending on the needs of the property and its managers. Reports for such indicators as occupancy statistics and average

Exhibit 14–8

A basic back-office accounting system main menu.

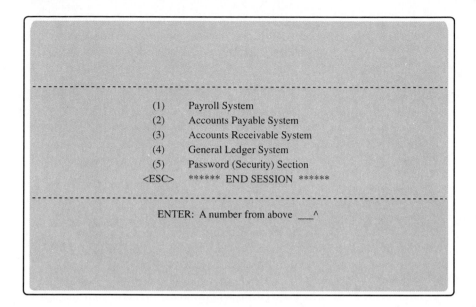

```
        (1)     Payroll System
        (2)     Accounts Payable System
        (3)     Accounts Receivable System
        (4)     General Ledger System
        (5)     Password (Security) Section
      <ESC>   ****** END SESSION ******

           ENTER:  A number from above ___^
```

daily rates for different room types can be generated on a daily, weekly, or on-demand basis and are generally referred to as *general management reports*.

Back-Office Applications

Accounting is a very important aspect of any business. As an owner or a manager, you will need to know how well your company is performing financially. Questions to be answered are: Are we making or losing money? How much money did we make yesterday? How much was spent on payroll, or on food? Answers to these questions depend partially on the way in which you monitor your revenues and expenses. You can use paper and pencil to keep track of them, or you can use computers and software. The accounting applications within the PMS can record all financial transactions that occur with customers, suppliers, employees, and other financial institutions. (See Exhibit 14–8.) They can help you manage your cash flow, collect monies owed by customers, control and track expenditures, evaluate your financial status, and track monies owed to creditors. With this brief introduction, we now discuss the most frequently used modules in a hospitality accounting system.

General Ledger Module

The *general ledger* is the primary ledger or account of a hospitality operation. It contains all of the property's balance sheet and income statement accounts.

The general ledger module is mostly used to produce a variety of financial reports. With it, detailed or consolidated financial reports can be generated by department, property, or company for a specific time frame. The three commonly found reports in the general ledger are:

- *Balance sheet*—summary of assets, liabilities, and equity accounts.
- *Income statement*—showing income and expenses incurred during a certain interval of time.
- *Comparative balance sheet and/or income statement*—comparing current period results with previous period(s).

When it comes time to present financial reports to higher levels of management or to investors, a trained user can import presentation software into the system to create graphs, charts, and other graphics that make comparisons of performance more understandable and visually powerful.

Accounts Receivable Module

The main purpose of the *accounts receivable module* is to monitor and improve the cash flow in an operation by making sure monies owed by customers are collected in a timely manner. It greatly reduces the amount of folder shuffling and the filing and refiling of physical paper records.

Eye on the Issues

International

Changes in computer technology and telecommunications are making the world smaller. Computer networks, fiber-optic cable, microwave technology, and satellites make it possible to send messages across the world at ever-decreasing cost and at ever-increasing speed.

The breakdown of communications barriers between countries, reduced cost of international telephone calls, increased competition in the telecommunications field, and global reach of toll-free numbers will all contribute to global data communication and the establishment of the ''information highway.'' The hospitality industry will also be affected by this in a major way.

Accounts Payable Module

The *accounts payable module* provides management with information on what the operation owes to creditors and what discounts are being offered by the creditors (for early payment, prepayment, and so on). By tracking due dates and deadlines, such modules increase the likelihood of timely payments to vendors, which helps to maintain credit ratings and to prevent interruption of supplies.

Payroll Module

The largest expense in hospitality industry operations is the cost of labor, since the industry is very labor intensive. Hospitality employees work different hours, in different capacities, and some receive tips, whereas others do not. One of the primary goals of management is to control this major expense; payroll modules offer useful assistance.

Payroll expense includes the direct cost of payroll (Hours worked × Pay rate) and the costs associated with the benefits provided to employees (such as health insurance, dental insurance, and retirement). The payroll module of the PMS is used to keep track of the hours worked, the pay rate, vacation days, sick days, bonuses or commission earned, and additional benefits or deductions such as taxes and social security.

The payroll module saves management time by performing the payroll calculations quickly and accurately, distributing payroll expenses among departments, printing checks, and producing payroll-related reports.

Inventory Control Module

Internal control is essential to efficient hospitality industry operations. An accounting system may use an inventory module for internal control. The *inventory control module* tracks product quantities and prices and provides accurate information on inventory activities, enabling management to control food cost better. The taking and extending of inventories and ordering and receiving tasks are made easier.

Purchasing Module

Effective purchasing methods are extremely important because cost savings at the purchasing stage affect a property's bottom-line profitability. A large percentage of sales income is spent on purchasing, so it is critical that effective controls are established in an operation. The purchasing report is the main report generated by this module and includes information on prices, allowing management to secure the best price possible. Data from this module can also be transferred to the accounts payable module in a fully integrated system.

Property Management System Interfaces

Property management system interfaces can be defined as automated systems that can function independently, such as a guest-room television, or have the capacity to connect with the property management systems. The advantage of being connected (or interfaced) with the PMS is that data can be transferred easily and automatically between interface and PMS. The best example here would be the in-room movie. If guests watch the movie in their room, and the television is interfaced with the PMS, their folio would be updated with the movie charge automatically. We discuss some of the most common hospitality interfaces in this section.

Point-of-Sale System

The point-of-sale (POS) system that a food service outlet in a hotel will have may be connected or interfaced with the hotel's property management system. This interface allows for direct posting of food and beverage charges to the guest folio without those charges first going to the front desk. It streamlines the operation and limits the chance of late charges, which occur when the food and beverage outlet posts charges to rooms that are checked out or vacant.

Call Accounting System

In 1981, AT&T was deregulated, which meant that everyone was allowed to sell telephone calls at whatever price they could get away with. Hotels, too, could sell telephone calls and charge their own rates for them. This transformed the hotel telephone department into a profit center overnight, whereas before it had traditionally been a loss department. This sudden shift to profitability is attributable not only to deregulation, but also to the development of *call accounting system* (CAS) technology. A CAS is a computer that is connected to the telephone switchboard. As is the case with any other interface, a CAS can be a stand-alone unit or can be connected to the property management system. As a call is made by each guest, the CAS generates a call record and charges the guest folio with the cost of the call. Not only does it improve labor productivity, it also eliminates late charges and clerical errors.

An additional advantage of the CAS is *least cost routing*. This feature sends calls over the lowest cost routes available, regardless of which long-distance phone carrier is used.

Hotels can add additional features to their telephone systems. The most common one is the automatic wake-up call system. Some hotels have added electronic messaging systems to their telephone systems, establishing a voice mailbox for each room, which is cleared automatically when the guest checks out.

Electronic Locking Systems

Guest security is a very important concern of management as several other chapters also indicate. One of the most important and most obvious elements of guest security is the door lock and key. Keys are often used but are actually not very safe. Keys in a mechanical key system can be lost and may end up in unauthorized hands. Hotels using mechanical key systems have to keep track of keys used and replace locks if necessary. This can prove rather costly and if not done promptly may lead to even costlier lawsuits. More and more, the insurance industry is forcing lodging properties to replace mechanical key systems with electronic locking systems. *Electronic locking systems* provide more adequate guest-room security, better liability control, and increased personnel accountability—and save money for the hotel in the long run. There are two basic types of locking systems on the market: one- and two-way communication locks.

One-Way Communication Locks.   This system uses a microcomputer (key-card console) with an electronic key encoder, a device used to encode a new lock combination on a guest keycard. In such a system, each door has its own battery-powered microprocessor and card reader (these are called *stand-alone locks*). When a keycard is inserted into the right door, the new combination automatically cancels the previous one. The keycard can be optically encoded (the card has holes punched into it) or magnetically encoded (the card has a magnetic strip on the back, like a credit card). Magnetically encoded keycards can be used over and over. The following are the advantages of this type of lock over a mechanical key system:

- The system tracks who issued each card.
- Keycards can be programmed with room restrictions—a card is valid during a certain time period or only for a group of rooms (maintenance or housekeeping).
- The expense of replacing the lock is eliminated.
- A lost card is replaced with a new one, wiping out the old combination.
- A history of use can be obtained by connecting a hand-held computer to the lock.

Two-Way Communication Locks.   In this system, all of the door locks are wired to a central computer. This system is more expensive than the one-way system, but it provides enhanced guest security control. When the keycard is made, the new lock combination is instantly transmitted to the lock's microprocessor. If someone attempts to use an old card, the computer alerts the front desk. The computer records every time the door is opened. It records forced door openings and unlocked doors. Two-way communication locks can be interfaced with the PMS, and special cards can be used to update the status of the room when it is cleaned. This system allows the housekeeping department to monitor the productivity of the housekeeping staff since the computer interface lets managers monitor the times of entry and exit from the room.

  In the future, guests may use their credit cards to access their room—without even having to stop at the front desk to register. Instead, the first part of registration would be taken care of when the reservation is made. Inserting the credit card into the lock would complete the registration process.

Energy Management System

Energy management systems have been installed by hotels to conserve energy, contain energy costs, and tighten operational controls over guest room and public space environments. Currently, the majority of the systems on the market are stand-alone ones and are not yet capable of interface with a PMS. An *energy management system* (EMS) is a computer-based control system designed to manage the operation of mechanical equipment on the property automatically and to save energy in doing so. The programming of the system allows management to determine what equipment is to be turned on or off or otherwise regulated. For instance, if a meeting room will not be used until 3 PM, it does not need to be air-conditioned all morning. An EMS could therefore be programmed to reduce or shut off the air-conditioning until one hour before the scheduled function. The EMS has a variety of features, but common energy control designs include:

- *Demand control.* The system maintains usage levels below a given limit by turning off equipment that can be turned off for varying periods without negatively affecting the comfort of the guest.
- *Duty cycling.* The system turns off equipment sequentially for a period of time each hour. Heating, ventilation, and air conditioning are systems that can be duty cycled.
- *Room occupancy sensors.* In guest rooms, either infrared or ultrasonic waves can be used to register the physical occupancy of the room. Sensors turn on such devices as lights, air-conditioning, and heating when a guest enters the space. When the guest departs, after a period of time, the sensors react and turn off lights and adjust the temperature back to preset levels.

The interface of EMS with PMS offers other opportunities to control energy use. Through the interface we can control room assignment so as to help in energy conservation (perhaps filling west-facing rooms last in a desert climate). As a room's status changes from vacant to occupied, we can remotely turn on its lights and heating/air-conditioning (HVAC); the same system can also control the environment in administrative and office areas when they are not occupied.

Guest Services–Related Automation

Self-Check-In/Check-Out Terminals.   These terminals can typically be found in hotel lobbies near the front desk and may include audio and video capabilities. Guests with advance reservations may check in by inserting a credit card and a keycard blank; they can then proceed to their room. A guest checks out by inserting his or her credit card into the terminal, reviewing the bill, settling it, and printing out a folio. These terminals are most appropriate for large hotels with business clientele who need to leave quickly and avoid the hassle of checking in and out.

Beverage Systems.   The in-room *minibar system* is a guest amenity that has gained popularity. The system monitors and posts sales transactions, determines refill quantities, and increases food and beverage profitability.

When you visit a hotel, you will find two different types of minibars. The first type is the *nonautomated honor bar.* The minibars are always open, which makes it difficult to monitor sales transactions and to conform to local liquor laws. To determine consumption, minibars in occupied rooms must be monitored by manual inspection. If products have been consumed, the attendant enters them into a bar computer via the telephone; charges are then posted to the guest folio as soon as the attendant hangs up the phone (if the bar computer is interfaced with the PMS).

Eye on the Issues

Technology

More and more, technology is becoming transparent to users; that is, users use technology without a clue as to how it works, or how to fix it if it fails. Alan Hald, chairman of MicroAge Computers, Inc., says that in the next decade technology will go beyond being user-friendly toward increasing transparency. He compares the process to that of driving a car. Early cars required considerable user knowledge about how engines worked; early drivers also had to be emergency mechanics and know step-by-step procedures for starting their vehicles (priming, cranking, choking, throttling). Today's drivers simply turn an ignition key. Today's computer users still use commands and desktop management techniques to operate their PCs. Tomorrow's transparent technology will have them simply performing the equivalent of turning the ignition key. If you think today's technology is exciting, just wait for tomorrow's!

The second system, the *automated minibar,* uses microprocessor-based vending machines. In this system, fiber optic sensors are used to record the removal of items from each closed compartment in the minibar. An on-board microprocessor time-stamps each sales transaction and records the exact product sold. This information is transmitted to the bar computer. If the system is interfaced with the PMS, the bar computer immediately charges the guest folio. When underage persons occupy the room, the compartments holding liquor can be locked through the bar computer, thus allowing compliance with local liquor laws. To prevent theft such bars can also be locked automatically when a guest checks out. (See Exhibit 14–9.)

EXHIBIT 14–9

An in-room minibar is both an amenity (guest convenience) and a valuable profit center for the hotel.

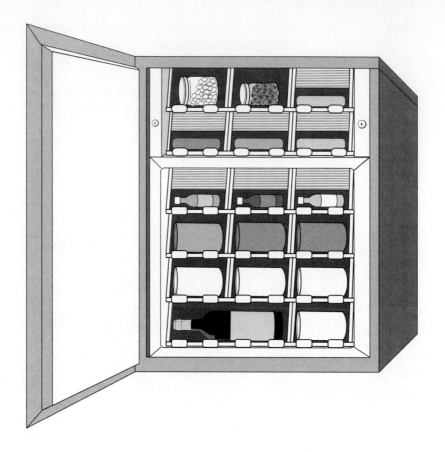

In-Room Movie System.   The in-room movie system or entertainment system provides the guest with pay-per-view movies and the hotel with additional revenue, as we have seen earlier. Again, if a pay-per-view system is interfaced with the PMS, movie charges do not have to be posted by hand; they are done automatically.

In-Room Safes.   In-room safes are most often found in resorts, casino hotels, and hotels in large urban areas. The purpose of these safes is to discourage employee theft and fraudulent guest claims, and to reduce insurance premiums and security-related costs. Safes can be digital (keyless) or card-accessed. The keyless safe allows the guest to select a four-digit code and enter it on the keypad for opening and locking the safe. This eliminates the need to track a key.

A safe card is similar in operation to an electronic locking system. A card is issued to the guest and the lock combination is encoded onto it. The guest inserts the key into the magnetic card reader to open the safe. Charges for the use of the safe can be posted automatically to the guest folio if the system is interfaced with the PMS. (See Exhibit 14–10.)

EXHIBIT 14–10

*In-room safes provide
convenience and
security.*

Life Safety Systems.   An integrated fire safety system saves lives, reduces
fire damage, lowers insurance premiums, and prevents costly litigation. More
and more hotel properties are starting to install these systems, which require
a centralized computer or a fire command console that uses electronic and
audio control devices for fire protection, alert, and response.

Interactive Television.   Interactive television allows a guest to complete
check-out by using the guest room TV and remote control. When guests are
ready to check out, they can ''call up'' their folio charges on the TV screen,
confirm these charges, and then automatically authorize payment through their
credit card. Through the interactive interface, guests can examine their folio
charges at any time, which allows them to clear up any questions they have
long before check-out time. Thus, interactive TV makes life easier, not only
for guests, but also for management, since it speeds up the check-out process,
reduces the front desk workload at peak times, and helps eliminate lines for
guests. Hard copies of their folio can be picked up at the front desk upon
departure or may be mailed upon request.

Many services that previously required a concierge may be done through interactive television or computer links. Guests may interact with a central computer system from the guest room using remote control and to access various video services on demand, including:

- *Automated wake-up service.* Guest can set up wake-up calls and confirm the time on the screen. At the requested time, the TV will turn on.
- *Room service.* Guests can review restaurant menus, place room service orders, and specify delivery time.
- *Room status.* Housekeepers can report when rooms are clean.
- *Automated message system.* The TV can be used to send personalized messages to individual guests or simultaneous messages to large groups. The guest can save or delete the message.
- *Customized viewer programming.* Allows guests to personalize the programs they watch by responding to questions and making choices posed by the program.
- *Information services.* Guests can access information about restaurants, attractions, shops, and events. In the future, guests will be able to use the TV for purchasing tickets to plays and other events.

Interactive Phones.   Guest-room phones have grown from simple line-in/line-out machines to easy-to-operate communications control centers. Sophisticated phones may have many features, including:

- Call waiting and forwarding.
- Speed-dialing buttons.
- Two-way speakerphones.
- Data port for attaching portable computers and fax machines.
- Digital clock.
- Hold button.
- AM/FM radio.
- Wake-up alarm with snooze bar.

Phones with wireless remote controls allow guests to control the lights, heat, air-conditioning, and television from their beds. When guest-room phones are interfaced with the property management system,

- Housekeepers can update a room's clean/dirty status from the room.
- The front desk can adjust lights and room temperature before and after guest check-in and check-out, which both conserves energy and allows a guest to enter a well-lit, climate-controlled room.

Sophisticated phone centers may also include a touch screen that displays instructions in several languages. In an attempt to eliminate communications problems for busy business travelers, some hotels offer their guests an in-room phone unit that includes a fax machine. Some have even gone so far as to supply guests with cellular phones through which they can access phone messages left on their in-room voice mail.

Computer-Based Food and Beverage Systems

To compete effectively in the markets of today, and tomorrow, all stages of the restaurant production and service chain must act in concert, so as to ultimately deliver quality products at the right prices to the right guests at the right times. Failure to do so can result in excess inventory, poor food quality, poor guest service, underutilized capacity, and unnecessary cost. Restaurant technology helps management monitor and coordinate these activities in a more timely and focused manner.[4]

Service Applications—Front of the House

ECR/POS Hardware.   The new technology available today changes the way in which restaurants process and monitor transactions. More and more often restaurants are choosing point-of-sale (POS) systems or its slightly simpler cousin, the electronic cash register (ECR). A POS system can enhance decision making, operational control, guest service, and revenues. Not all POS systems have the same capabilities and potential for improving revenue. This section will discuss the elements that are necessary for the selection of a POS system for a table-service restaurant. (See Exhibit 14–11.)

A *POS system* is a network of cashier and server terminals that typically handle food and beverage orders, the transmission of orders to the kitchen and bar, the settlement of guest checks, time keeping, and interactive charge posting to guest folios. POS information can also be imported to accounting and food cost/inventory software packages.[5]

The main components of the POS system are:

- *Server terminal.* This terminal is used by the server to enter a food or beverage order into the system and communicate the order to the kitchen or bar by means of a keyboard or touch screen. A display screen allows the server to monitor the order.
- *Cashier terminal.* The cashier terminal includes a cash drawer as well as a keyboard and a monitor and is primarily used for both entering and settling guest checks.
- *Printers* are the third essential component of the POS system and are used to print checks, orders, and reports on service areas and kitchens for management.

An additional feature of the POS system is the *magnetic stripe reader,* an input device for credit-card processing. As guests settle their checks with

EXHIBIT 14–11

This flowchart highlights the main steps in choosing a property computer system.

System Selection Flowchart

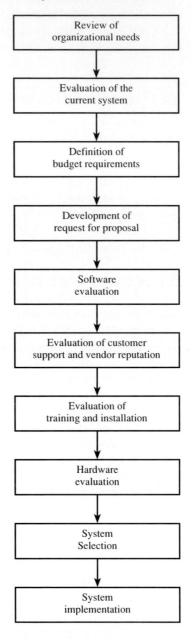

credit cards, all the cashier has to do is "swipe" the magnetic strip of the credit card through this reader and a credit card slip is printed automatically.

The selection of a POS system should be based on the needs of the restaurant. These needs should be evaluated in a systematic manner, preferably through a checklist. Several questions need to be answered in the selection process, such as:

* How quickly must orders be processed?
* Which system provides the most effective interaction?
* How will menu changes be handled?
* How many preset keys are needed?
* What should the POS terminal set-up be?

If the POS system is being added to an existing system, it is important to carefully verify compatibility and interface ability. The POS system will also need to be protected by passwords and secured against power fluctuations.

Some large operations are exploring the use of hand-held order entry terminals that allow the staff to enter orders while they are at the guest table. The system uses radio signals to communicate with a base station from where the order is sent to the appropriate preparation area. This allows the servers to spend more time with guests as they do not have to go back and forth to the kitchen or the terminal. A silent paging system informs the server when the order is ready.

ECR/POS Software.   The hardware of a computer cannot accomplish anything by itself; it needs instructions. There must be a set of software programs directing the system in what to do, how to do it, and when to do it. ECR/POS software programs not only direct internal system operations; they also maintain files and produce reports for management.

Automated Beverage Control Systems.   Automated beverage systems reduce many of the time-consuming management tasks associated with controlling beverage operations. While automated beverage systems vary, most systems can dispense drinks according to the operation's standard drink recipes and can count the number of drinks poured. Automated beverage systems can be programmed to dispense both alcoholic and nonalcoholic drinks with different portion sizes. With many of the systems, the station at which drinks are prepared can be connected to a guest-check printer that records every sale as drinks are dispensed. Automated beverage control systems can enhance production and service capabilities while improving accounting and operational control.[6]

Management Applications—Back of the House

Menu Management.   Menu management applications help management answer questions about pricing menu items; about the menu mix at which profit is maximized; whether any menu items need to be removed, repriced, or changed; and how menu changes can be evaluated. Information from the ECR/POS system and from other applications can be used to facilitate this process.

Recipe Management.   Recipe management applications maintain data on recipe ingredients, preparation methods, cost, and sales prices.

Sales Analysis.   Sophisticated ECR/POS systems can store files that contain important data regarding daily operations. When the ECR/POS system is connected to a fully integrated restaurant management system, this information can be accessed by computer-based management applications such as the sales analysis application. The sales analysis application can sort or combine data into a variety of reports to help management direct daily operations.

Integrated Restaurant Systems.   The limitations of nonintegrated restaurant systems are apparent. Since data must be entered several times, often at different stations, the time spent on this task is enormous and information may not reach managers on time. Integrated food service systems allow data to seamlessly pass from one application to another. Since data are entered only once, input time is saved, accuracy is increased, and decisions that hinge on these data can be made in a more timely manner. As a result, the operation can function more efficiently.

Other Hospitality Technology Applications

Hotel Sales and Food Service Catering Applications

The sales and catering department of a hotel generates large amounts of paperwork, and people spend major parts of their days managing this paperwork. Sales and catering contacts have to be recorded, client files maintained, function contracts prepared and distributed to different departments, correspondence sent out, and meetings conducted. Since one of the strong points of computers is the handling of large amounts of data, this area has been ripe for computerization. Sales and food service catering applications expedite many tedious tasks. Sales information can be accessed instantaneously, the risk of human error is reduced, and communication with clients (as well as with employees and other departments) is enhanced. Good systems can free sales or catering department staffers to concentrate on selling their department's services, instead of slogging through paperwork.

Yield Management

Yield management, sometimes also called *revenue management,* is a set of demand-forecasting techniques used to determine whether prices should be

raised or lowered and whether reservation requests should be accepted or rejected in order to maximize revenue. Yield management is based on supply
and demand principles. Prices tend to rise when demand exceeds supply; prices
tend to fall when supply exceeds demand. Since pricing is the key to profitability, computer software that can suggest optimal pricing can help management to determine optimal rates. Of course, this software does not make
decisions for managers; it provides them with information and supports their
decisions. The most important advantage of using computer technology for
yield management is the ability of the computer to retrieve, manipulate, and
store large amounts of data quickly.[7]

Presentation Packages

You are familiar with the saying, ''A picture is worth a thousand words.''
Presentation packages allow managers to transform numerical information
about operational performance into visual information. Visual (or graphical)
formats help audiences (such as employees or shareholders) understand large
amounts of data. Graphics created with presentation packages can be converted into overhead transparencies or slides and used in presentations to large
groups.

Data Communication

By now you have heard of the **information highway,** the technological interconnection of people all around the globe through computers, modems,
microwaves, and satellites. Until the information highway becomes a reality,
we are primarily linked to each other by wires that carry voice and computer
signals. This form of information delivery is called **data communication,** the
electronic transfer of information from one computer to another via direct
cable connections or via telecommunications links involving the telephone
system and modems. Despite the need for physical connecting hardware, this
network has brought about the internationalization of business.

Data communication is important to hospitality organizations because it:

- Offers quick access and transmission of information.
- Allows information to be stored in a central database. Any user can
  access this information, which eliminates duplicate processing,
  redundant information, delays, and errors.
- Provides speedy ways for businesspeople to be in touch with their
  customers.
- Improves organizational efficiency by linking independent computer
  networks or units. Information can be transmitted from individual
  units to headquarters and vice versa.

A *modem* enables us to transmit data between two computers at different
sites. A modem is a contraction of two words: *modulation* and *demodulation.*

Computers process data using *digital* signals, distinct pieces of data. Telephone lines carry data using *analog* signals. When a modem is connected to the computer, it converts (modulates) the digital signal from the sending computer and transmits it. At the receiving end, another modem converts the analog signal back to the digital signal (demodulation).

In the future, modems may become obsolete if telephone lines are converted into digital lines that will carry digital signals directly. When this happens, phone lines will be able to carry more information, pictures, and video, at much faster speeds than their present-day counterparts. The digital network will tie businesses, households, and computers into an integrated network called an *integrated service digital network* (ISDN). By then, many businesses will also use microwave transmission and satellites to communicate with each other all over the world. Right now, very few businesses have this capability.

Local Area Network.   The electronic transfer of information from one computer to another at a particular site over a direct cable connection is called a *local area network* (LAN). A LAN can connect computers in one department, several departments, or through an organization's whole building or complex.

Local area networks provide tremendous advantages to hospitality operations. The sharing of data and communication capabilities, and the ability for unlike devices to communicate with each other are the goals for which hotels and restaurants are now striving.

Wide Area Network.   A *wide area network* (WAN) is the linking of computers over a great distance (more than a mile) using telephone lines, satellites, microwave stations, or combinations of these devices. In the United States it is presently illegal for companies to install their own cables. Until such legal restrictions are relaxed, WAN users must make use of telephone company channels to establish communication.

System Selection and Implementation

The selection and implementation of a computer system (or any other technology purchase) for a hospitality operation is one of the most serious undertakings hotel or restaurant managers face. Their decisions will affect organizations over a long time, particularly since most operations purchase such big-ticket items infrequently. Managers must carefully consider needs, gather information, weigh alternatives, and try to maximize the "bang for their buck." Let's take a look at some of the steps organizations go through in selecting new information systems (see also Exhibit 14–11).

Developing an information plan takes first priority, as it provides management with a framework for making sound technology decisions. An information plan reviews the organization's needs and emphasizes the organization's mission, its goals, and its structure. Employees at all levels of the organization need to be involved.

In the second step of the process, managers must develop a complete understanding of the current system. How is information processed in the organization? What are the problem areas in the organization, or in a department? Is the current system adequate, and does it help in vital areas? After a thorough system evaluation, managers should formulate several objectives to guide the selection process.

In the third step, budget requirements are defined. Here, managers must evaluate the technology in terms of the cost of the investment and its annual savings. They ask themselves: What savings will my organization realize as a result of purchasing this technology? How long will it take to get the cost of the investment back in savings? Another decision factor may be that of whether to buy or lease a new system. This requires another thorough analysis of the benefits versus costs of the alternatives.

Step four kicks off with the formation of a committee, comprised of representatives from the various departments of the organization. Their first task will be to develop a property profile, describing the computing needs of the organization, and for this they will reference and build upon the information plan.

Once the needs have been agreed upon, a ***request for proposal*** (RFP) is drawn up. The RFP should include:

- The property profile.
- A detailed description of desired features and requirements for the software and hardware, including expectations regarding performance, vendor references, installation, postsale training, and customer support.
- Guidelines for bid submission.
- A description of how vendor responses will be evaluated.

The fifth step to be undertaken is system evaluation and selection. Selection of software precedes selection of hardware. Does the software meet system requirements? Can it be interfaced with existing systems? Is it easy to operate? Is it user friendly? Are there any logical flaws in the software? The selection of hardware components is also an important step. Hardware must be selected on the basis of:

- Its compatibility with the preferred software.
- Its ability to process data speedily.
- Its storage and memory capacity.
- Its ability to be upgraded or expanded in the future.

Of especial importance is the reliability and financial security of the vendor. While good vendors will offer an organized and well-structured training program, the RFP should also specify inclusion of a detailed plan for training and installation. Such plans should spell out time frames and turnaround time on repairs. Prices should be quoted for nonwarranty technical support services and maintenance agreements.

One Last User Concern.   The science that deals with the computer environment is called *ergonomics.* A well-designed computer system brings together people and computers in an environment that is comfortable, allowing people to work productively with the computer system. Ergonomics addresses such problems as poor lighting, glare, noisy printers, and cramped workspace, as well as heat and ventilation problems, which, if not addressed properly, can reduce efficiency dramatically. Ergonomics includes concern for work surface height and seating, which may have health implications in terms of high-tech maladies such as carpal tunnel syndrome, eye fatigue, and back strain.

System and Data Security

The failure of a computer system can paralyze an organization. Preventing computer failure and minimizing disruptions require planning. Such plans should include steps to secure the system, steps to maintain system performance, and procedures to follow in case of a natural disaster.

Hardware components can fail at any time. To prevent hardware failure or at least to minimize it, it is important to maintain an environment with proper temperature and humidity control. Regularly scheduled equipment maintenance also helps keep computers working and in top condition.

Computers rely on electrical power, but that same electricity can cause damage to hardware and software through power line irregularities. To avoid such problems, organizations can:

- Use surge protectors. A surge protector is a device that prevents unexpected increases in power line voltage.
- Properly wire and ground computers.
- Protect against a power failure by using an uninterruptible power supply (UPS) device. A UPS has a battery that provides power to a computer system during power outages.

Another threat to computer systems is posed by computer viruses. A computer virus is a program that can spread by copying itself from one program to the next, changing or destroying each program without the user knowing it. Virus detection and elimination software can protect computers against viruses when used faithfully. Unfortunately, new computer viruses, like their biological counterparts, often crop up and do damage before a ''vaccine'' has been developed. Keeping antivirus software current helps fight loss of data and information.

Also, all data and programs in a computer system should be copied and saved on another secondary storage device. This is called *backup.* If any damage occurs, the backup files can be used to restore the lost programs and data on the hard disk.

Perhaps the greatest threat to computer system integrity is hackers or other people who seek unauthorized access to or destruction of data. To protect their computerized records organizations must practice good security. Two effective ways of restricting access to data are: (1) the use of passwords and (2) the encryption or scrambling of data to make it unreadable to others. Other techniques include physically locking up computer system units and keyboards or installing alarms to protect against theft and fire.

Operator error such as improper handling of routine and lengthy procedures can be eliminated by proper training.

Technology Advances—Future

Predicting what is going to happen in hotel technology even one year from now is like gazing into a crystal ball at a carnival. Technology, in general, and hospitality technology, in particular, are changing with tremendous speed. According to Larry Chervenak, author of "Hotel Technology at the Start of the New Millennium," "Technology will literally alter how we work, play, study, and travel; how tall we grow; and how long we live. As such, it will have both a direct and indirect effect on the hospitality industry."[8]

The increase in the number and power of personal computers, the decrease in their prices, and the improvement in microprocessor speed will lead to improvements in how business is conducted. What will these new technologies mean to the hospitality lodging industry? The advances in technology and the increasing power and capabilities of the PC will allow for a more efficient operation, better management information, and a better ability to react to guest requests. Lodging properties will have a competitive edge based on the increased power of the computer—and well-trained "power" users.

Use of new technologies will lead to the restructuring of organizations and to the empowerment of their employees. With more and better information regarding guest needs at their disposal, employees will have the power to make more and better decisions regarding guest service.

The new generation of employees working in lodging and food service properties will have at least some familiarity with computers. Building on this computer literacy, human resources departments are developing or purchasing technology-based training tools. In the very near future new employees will probably be able to learn their jobs much easier and faster.

Revolution

There's no two ways about it. There is a revolution going on—a revolution in the way we communicate. The world is getting smaller and will get even smaller as worldwide communication networks become established. Let's discuss a few consequences of this here.

The development and constant improvement of fiber-optic cable technology will lead to better telephone systems, which will mean more telephone calls will be able to travel over fiber-optic cables. Better international communication will allow our guests to call 800 numbers from anywhere in the world.

Communication barriers between countries have started coming down and, as a result, it will be easier to establish communication networks in these countries. The cost of international communication will be reduced as well. Hotels will be able to extend their reservation services globally.

''Smart'' guest-room phones will provide a number of convenient features, ranging from data connections to portable PCs, and from faxes to bedside control of air-conditioning and remote turnoff of room lights. Even smarter phones will blend telecommunication, video, and computer capabilities together and will be used throughout the hotel.

Video phones may be available and hotels will have them on hand for guests wishing to call their homes or offices. Voice messaging will be a standard feature on all telephones in the hotel, changing the way hotels take messages forever. During the next few decades, the pocket phone will be improved in clarity of transmission, and its cost will be reduced. With a pocket phone you will be able to call anywhere in the world.

Rapid changes in audiovisual technology will soon impact lodging properties. The guest-room television set will be different and able to do more than just broadcast standard television fare. The TV will no longer be a ''set'' or a box, but rather a large, flat screen with interactive features. With high-definition picture technology, we can look forward to three-dimensional pictures; guests will be able to watch a telephone caller in full color and motion. Guests will ask for (and get) movies on demand; if the future follows history, guests will expect their in-room TV to offer the same number and variety of channels as their home equipment. At the same time, lodging marketers will tap the potential of interactive TV to conduct surveys, promote hotel outlets, and provide shopping and information services.

Videoconferencing will also have an impact on lodging properties. Videoconferencing has been around since the 1970s but the reduction in cost and improvement in quality now make videoconferencing more practical. The advances in videoconferencing will be merged in the future with advances in videophones and multimedia PCs. These advances may spell the demise of business travel as we have known it, since videoconferencing may become far more common than traveling to face-to-face meetings. Hotels will have to adapt in order to compensate for the meetings that no longer occur.

Yield management applications will be widely used; electronic locking systems will be a must. Some hotels may even install **biometric systems**— guest-room doors may use machine recognition technology to read personal characteristics, such as fingerprints or retinas of the eye, before allowing access. Technology used in the guest services area will include self-check-in and check-out, remote check-in from airport shuttle vans, electronic guest-room safes and bars, and guest-room office units (fax, copier, computer, printer, and phone in a single unit). Integrated services digital networks will make it a snap to communicate across the world.

In short, by the year 2000, practical knowledge of technology will be essential for a career and survival in the hospitality industry.

Conclusion

A computer is a tool that helps managers combine their many skills and enables them to interact with information. As the lodging industry is becoming increasingly more competitive, industry executives are realizing they need information technology to help them cope with the changing environment. Remember though, computers do not make decisions; people do. For future managers in the industry to make the right decisions, knowledge of information technology is essential.

Keywords

information   426
data   426
computer   426
program   427
system software   427

application software   427
property management system (PMS)   429
information highway   451
data communication   451
biometric systems   456

Core Concepts

hardware   426
software   427
word processing software   428
electronic spreadsheet software   428
database management software   428
group master   434
room status   435

folios   436
minibar system   443
POS system   447
modem   451
request for proposal   453
ergonomics   454

Discussion Questions

1. Describe and discuss the hardware components of a computer system.
2. Describe a property management system. What are the modules that are a part of the PMS? What function does each module perform?
3. Integration, or the interconnection between all the components of an organization, has been stressed in this chapter. What are the benefits of integration to a food service or lodging operation?
4. Describe some of the applications that can be interfaced with the property management system. What are the benefits of interfacing?
5. Describe the process that should be followed in selecting a computer system.

References

Chervenak, L. "Hotel Technology at the Start of the
  New Millennium." *Hospitality Research
  Journal* 17, No. 1 (1993).

Collins, G. *Hospitality Information Technology:
  Learning How to Use It.* Dubuque, IA: Kendall/
  Hunt Publishing Company, 1992.

Hall, S., S. J., ed. *Ethics in Hospitality Management,
  A Book of Readings.* East Lansing, MI:
  Educational Institute of the American Hotel &
  Motel Association, 1992.

Kasavana, M. L., and J. J. Cahill, *Managing
  Computers in the Hospitality Industry.* 2nd ed.
  East Lansing, MI: Educational Institute of the
  American Hotel & Motel Association, 1992.

Hospitality Marketing

Marketing is one of the essential ingredients in the overall success of any business. This chapter will help you gain an understanding and appreciation of the complexities involved in the marketing of products and services in the highly competitive hospitality industry. It will introduce basic marketing vocabulary and demonstrate the omnipresence of marketing in American society. The chapter will explore several kinds of marketing strategies and illustrate the many different components of a successful marketing campaign.

Outline

Introduction

Consider a day in the life of Kathryn. She gets up at 6:30 and turns on a news channel on the TV. Many of the ads on the station are for *business travel to hotels.* She flips to a weather channel, where the national weather is presented by *United Airlines.* As she drives to work she passes several fast-food restaurants offering breakfast specials before finally pulling into a *McDonald's* where she purchases an *Egg McMuffin* and a cup of coffee and reads the morning paper. In the paper is a coupon for a half-price meal at the *local seafood restaurant.* For lunch she and a friend go to that seafood restaurant. On the way home from work she stops by a *travel agency* where she picks up several *brochures* for a vacation in Mexico. After dinner, which includes the use of *Chi-Chi's* bottled taco sauce, she settles down to watch TV, including highlights of a tennis match sponsored by a *state office of tourism.*

All of the words and phrases italicized in the above paragraph are examples of the influence of marketing on Kathryn's life. In fact, it is almost impossible to imagine a situation where a person would be able to escape the influence of marketing. The marketing of hospitality products and services is a significant part of the overall marketing of products and services in the world today. (See Exhibit 15–1.) In this chapter we introduce the concept of marketing, and discuss why marketing is so important to the overall success of a hospitality business.

Marketing Defined

Because the role of marketing is so big, it's sometimes hard to come up with an exact definition of marketing. Basically, **marketing** is:

> All of the activities designed to move goods and services from the producer to the consumer.

As we will see, this short definition involves a considerable number of activities. In essence, the goal of a business, and therefore the goal of a marketing department, is to determine what it is that consumers want or need. The next step is to create a product or service that will fulfill those wants or needs. Then, consumers must be made aware of the product or service; and, finally, the product or service has to be made readily available to the consumers at a price they can afford. If all of these situations are handled correctly, there is hope that the business will prosper.

Hospitality Marketing as a Part of Services Marketing

The business industry overall can be divided into two separate categories. **Product industries** are those industries that are involved in the manufacturing of items that consumers use. Examples would be the manufacturing of cars,

EXHIBIT 15–1

These are just a few of the many restaurant products that are now cross-marketed through grocery stores.

Photo by James L. Morgan, 85283.

jeans, or soft drinks. **Service industries** are those industries involved in the performance of some activity or service for consumers. Examples would be hair salons, law firms, and transportation services such as airlines. The hospitality industry is generally considered a part of the service industry, as Exhibit 15–2 shows.

Differences between Products and Services

Since products and services are different, the ways in which they are marketed are also different. There are five major ways by which products and services differ, and each way causes some special marketing problems.

Intangibility. Services such as a hotel stay are intangible in the sense that they are not physical. If you buy a pair of jeans, you receive in return something that actually exists. On the other hand, when you sit in a classroom, you receive a service in return. When you leave the classroom, you take very little evidence with you that shows an exchange of some sort has occurred—maybe some notes.

A similar situation occurs when people rent a hotel room. When they leave the hotel, they generally take nothing physical home with them. (At least they are not supposed to; guests have been known to take just about anything out of hotel rooms, from towels to televisions!) Even in a restaurant situation, where there is the physical purchase of food, much of what guests pay for is intangible. They pay for *service*.

EXHIBIT 15–2

How hospitality fits into the business world

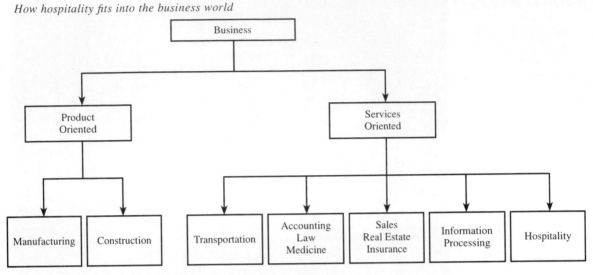

The problem for marketers is that, in an ad for a hotel stay, you can be shown a picture of the room, but not what is going on during the entire stay. Thus, it is hard for people to know exactly what it is that they are buying. How can you sell people something if they cannot see it in advance?

Inseparability.   This concept refers to the fact that services are often produced and consumed at the same time. You cannot get a haircut unless you go some place and get a haircut. Similarly, you cannot generally eat a restaurant meal unless you go to the restaurant and eat the meal. Compare these situations to one where a pair of jeans is produced in New York, sold at a store in Chicago, and ultimately worn by somebody living in Los Angeles.

 The marketing problem here is that the guest is always watching what the service people in the hotel or restaurant are doing. Guests are involved in the production of the service in that they are present while the service is being provided.

Nonstandardization.   Nonstandardization of a service means that, since people are involved, the service product cannot be created through automation in the way that many assembly-line products are. Services are variable; a service person in a restaurant will typically have good nights and bad nights. There will be some service persons that do a better job than others, and so on.

 The marketing problem is that the guests will never know exactly what to expect. Will the service in this restaurant be good tonight or not? Will the food be the way it was last time or not? Buying services such as a restaurant meal can be risky. Would you want to take your boss to dinner at a restaurant where the service *might* be good, but *might* also be bad?

Perishability.   One of the big problems with a service is that it cannot be stored for use at any time. If a car dealer does not sell a car on the lot today, it will be there to sell tomorrow. However, if an airline does not sell a seat on a plane today, that sale is lost forever. The seat will still be there tomorrow, but today's sale is lost. If a hotel misses selling a room today, the revenue for today is gone forever. The room will still be there tomorrow, but today's sale has "perished."

The marketing issue, then, is to make sure all hotel rooms and all restaurant seats are sold *today*. This is one of the most difficult marketing and management problems in the hospitality industry.

Eye on the Issues

Environment

The hospitality industry has long been considered a nonpolluting industry; yet, in fact, this is not so. Fast-food restaurants have produced enormous amounts of refuse. Popular attractions such as national parks constantly have long had to deal with air and noise pollution. Large hotels generate large amounts of waste water. Naturally, industry members do not go out of their way to point out their environmental failings. Instead, as laws have become stricter, and the public has become more aware of environmental issues, hospitality marketers have had to find ways to promote their companies as being environmentally active. Many fast-food restaurants now openly promote the fact that they use recycled materials. Many hotels and restaurants do not offer drinking water unless asked, and post tabletop notices hailing their efforts to conserve. National parks are restricting automobile traffic and publicly advertise their efforts.. In these efforts, marketing plays an important role, as indeed it has in selling the whole concept of recycling and environmental conscientiousness. Can you imagine the reaction of 1950s consumers if they were told that their hamburger was wrapped in coated tissue made from paper someone had already used once and thrown away? Unused to the idea of or the need for recycling, they would probably have been repelled. Marketing has not only made this important concept palatable, but dressed it in virtue.

Nonownership.   Nonownership of a service means that people seldom actually own the service they are using. Rather, they rent or hire the service. Consumers buy jeans and own them, but they do not buy the restaurant in which they are eating or the hotel in which they stay.

There are several problems that nonownership creates. First, guests are often more abusive to property that is not actually theirs. Also, problems between the actual owners and the users can arise, such as differences of opinion as to how the property should be treated. This is often a problem between hoteliers and their guests.

EXHIBIT 15–3

Elements of the marketing process

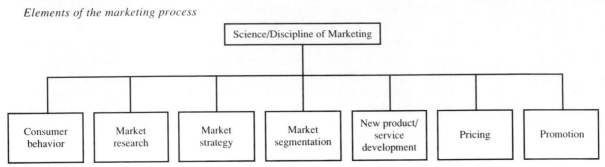

Services marketing and management are different from product marketing and management. Many of these differences are critical in the evaluation of hospitality marketing, and impact the way hospitality marketers do their jobs.

The Different Elements of Marketing

When a lot of people think of marketing, they automatically think of advertising and personal selling. Of course, advertising and sales are important parts of the overall marketing process, but they are by no means the only parts. There are many different elements of the marketing process that fit together into the discipline of marketing, as displayed in Exhibit 15–3. We will take a look at them in this section.

The Marketing Mix

Very often when we talk about marketing, we lump the elements together into what is called the **marketing mix.** The marketing mix has been defined as the controllable variables a company manipulates in order to achieve its overall objectives.

Everything that a hotel or restaurant could do to affect its success would be a part of its marketing mix. Traditionally, the marketing mix has been characterized as being composed of four parts (''four Ps'' of marketing): product, promotion, price, and place.

Product.   The product is the actual good or service being offered for sale. It could include all of the features of the good or service as well as the packaging and brand name of the good or service. Remember that the term *product* in this case does not necessarily refer to a tangible or physical thing. Rather, it is the total goods/service package that is being sold. In many industries such as the automotive industry, the *physical* product dominates the sale. However, in the sale of a hotel room the *service* product dominates the sale. The dual use of the term *product* as defined in the previous section and in this section can be confusing, but these are the definitions traditionally used in the marketing field.

Promotion.   This part of the marketing mix is concerned primarily with communication. How do we communicate with customers about what we have to sell? How do we convince them that what we are selling is what they want to buy? The promotional part of the marketing mix is what we normally refer to when thinking of advertising and personal selling. Actually, there are also two other promotional methods: sales promotions and public relations/publicity. Later in this chapter we will discuss the promotional mix in further detail.

Price.   The price of a product or service is one of the main considerations customers have when buying products or services. When we set prices, we have to consider whether our customers will think the price is fair, too high, or too low. Will all customers think the same way? Would a dinner priced at $100 affect sales to a millionaire in the same way that it would to a typical college student? These are the kinds of issues that make pricing very difficult to do. As with the area of promotion, we will discuss pricing from a marketing perspective in more detail later in the chapter.

Place.   Place refers to distribution: how we go about getting the product or service to the customer. A good restaurant will fail if customers are not available. A nice hotel will fail if no one likes the location. Ironically, a mediocre restaurant might be successful simply because it is in the right place at the right time. Can you think of any restaurants at which you have eaten that were not too good but had a wonderful location? One of the old sayings in hospitality marketing is that there are three important keys to success—*location, location,* and *location.* While this statement may be oversimplified, there is a certain amount of truth to it.

Consumer Behavior

One of the most important and time-consuming activities in which we all engage is the act of consuming. When you eat a meal, you are literally consuming it, and when you stay in a hotel you are consuming the experience. It's quite hard to think of any activity in which we engage that does not, at least in part, involve an aspect of consumer behavior. However, there is a lot more to the process than simply using a product or service you have purchased. *Consumer behavior* could be defined as: the process of purchasing, using, and evaluating products and services.

Exhibit 15–4 displays a typical consumer behavior process. This process has several stages and can become quite involved.

The process unfolds as follows. First there needs to be a reason for you to buy something. You are hungry, so you go to a restaurant. Or you are away

EXHIBIT 15–4

*The consumer
behavior process*

Need Arousal
↓
Evaluation of Alternatives
↓
Purchase
↓
Usage
↓
Evaluation of Usage

from home, so you check into a hotel. However, there are many restaurants and many hotels, so you must evaluate all of the relevant alternatives. You then purchase the restaurant meal or the hotel stay. You eat the meal or stay in the hotel, and then you have some sort of opinion as to how you liked what you just bought and used.

Hospitality marketing departments are responsible for analyzing each of these areas, but their task is not an easy one, since choices are seldom based on clear and simple logic. As human beings we do not always act rationally. It is very difficult to describe or forecast human behavior, yet this is what marketers are constantly trying to do. The more marketers know about human behavior, the better they can predict what products and services will sell the best.

All behavior is influenced by our culture and by the network of family and friends (in-group) that surrounds us. Understanding how our culture and our in-groups influence our behavior helps us understand how people behave. Our eating habits, whether at home or in a restaurant, are greatly influenced by who we are and where we come from, and any restaurateur needs to recognize and deal with these considerations. Is it any wonder that certain types of restaurants are more popular in certain areas of the country than others? Is it any wonder that culturally based eating habits of foreign travelers to the United States are often different than what we are used to? Or is it any wonder that different lodging facilities will appeal to different types of people? These are just a few reasons we need to improve our understanding of who we are and how we behave.

Market Research

To make good decisions, a marketing department must have good information at its disposal. Good-quality information is essential; garbage-quality data only muddy up the planning process. Consider some of the many decisions you might have to make as a member of a management team at a hotel operation:

- Should we build a new hotel?
- Should we remodel our hotel?

- What kinds of clientele do we have?
- What kinds of clientele do we want?
- What price(s) should we charge?
- What is the best kind of advertising for us to use?

In each of these cases, along with many others, it is necessary to predict how all of the types of people involved in your hotel would react to the various alternatives you are considering. Most of the people would be outsiders—guests, competitors, and suppliers—people over whom you have relatively little control. Therefore, you need to have as much relevant information as you can get *before* you make any decisions.

Eye on the Issues

Ethics

The issue of ethics in the marketing field is an important one, especially in view of stand-up comedians' lampoons and movie caricatures of marketers. Consider the following situations:

- You have a chance to win a big convention account that will mean a lot to you and your resort. The sales representative for the other company has hinted that he would be influenced by a ''gift.'' Your assistant recommends giving the sales representative a week's free vacation at your resort. What would you do?

- You are interviewing a former director of marketing for one of your major competitors and are thinking of hiring her. She would be more than happy to tell you all of the competitor's marketing plans for the next year. What would you do?

- Your property is 11 miles, via a busy freeway, from the metropolitan airport. Average transit time for the shuttlebus is 45 minutes. Your

intern figures that since the posted freeway speed is 55 mph, an 11-mile trip takes just 5 minutes. You'd like to attract the tired business traveler who seeks a hotel close to the airport. What would you do?

These are just three examples of situations that could come up in the marketing area. Because there is so much pressure to sell and be successful, marketers will sometimes try to gain an edge by exaggerating a claim, slightly misrepresenting the performance of a product or service, or intentionally doing something that may not be illegal, but would certainly be unethical. It is not the intent of this chapter to write a prescription describing the ethics you should follow, but rather to reinforce the idea that ethics are important to consider. Marketing is one of the areas of business in which ethics is very important, in dealing both with the public and with other members of the company.

Decisions are always risky to make; it is the goal of good market research to minimize that risk. **Market research** is, then, the formal means of creating, obtaining, and using information in the marketing decision-making process.

Ways to Do Market Research.   There are three basic ways in which hospitality companies do general market research. First, they can do *qualitative* *research.* Qualitative research is very general, and also very subjective, that is, influenced heavily by the views and opinions of the researcher. If we are interested in finding out if our guests are enjoying our restaurant, we can watch them, interpreting from our observations how they are feeling. Are they having fun? Do all types of our customers seem to be enjoying themselves? Does the restaurant atmosphere seem to be positive, or do we get a feeling that something is wrong? Managers generally do this kind of research automatically. It's relatively easy to do, and can provide some good information, but, as you can probably tell, it is not very scientific. What one manager considers a positive atmosphere, another might disapprove of completely.

The opposite of qualitative research is *experimental research.* This kind of research is often done in laboratory settings. Experimental research is carefully controlled research where precise measurements are taken. For example, in an actual experiment, researchers were interested in whether or not the name of a menu item could affect guests' perceptions of its taste. One group of people was given a plate of ''mudfish.'' Another group was given a plate of ''angelfish.'' In reality, both groups got the same fish. Now, which group do you think liked the fish better? The subjects concluded that the angelfish tasted heavenly, while the mudfish tasted ''dirty,'' that is to say, terrible. This type of research is very precise, but very hard to do; it is unnecessarily difficult for most hotel or restaurant research needs.

The third type of research method, called *survey research,* is the most common. Surveys are a convenient, economical way to collect information, and require relatively little skill to use. As a result, a large number of organizations now use survey research as the primary method of gathering marketing information.

We can do survey research over the telephone, by mail, and person to person. Every person reading this book has completed a number of surveys, probably of all three types. Perhaps the most common in the hospitality industry is the ''comment card'' placed on restaurant tables and in hotel rooms, asking guests how well they liked the food, the service, and the accommodations.

Market Strategy

Just as you probably have long-term objectives (such as having a good job, making a good living, and, in general, living a productive, rewarding life), hospitality companies have long-term goals. You have probably developed strategies and tactics (such as majoring in a hospitality curriculum and getting practical experience in some hospitality business) that will help you achieve your goals. The planning process that you are going through and will continue to go through is nothing more than an example of *strategic planning.* In business terms this can be defined as: the process of developing and maintaining a close fit between a company's goals and its present situation. Exhibit 15–5 provides a chart of how the basic strategic marketing process works.

EXHIBIT 15–5

*The strategic
marketing process*

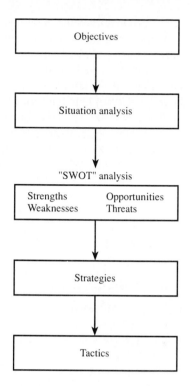

The first task in the strategic marketing process is to consider what *objectives* we have for our business. These objectives can be short term, such as filling our hotel this week or making sure there are enough food supplies on hand for next week's banquets, or long term, such as determining how many new hotels or restaurants to open in the next five years. When objectives are created, they need to be clearly stated, and also need to be realistic. It is easy to make the statement ''we will be the biggest hotel chain in the world in 10 years.'' It is a lot harder to reach that objective.

The next task is to perform a *situation analysis.* A situation analysis is a critical look at where our enterprise (hotel, casino, restaurant, attraction, and so on) is now. One common method of doing a situation analysis is called the *SWOT method.* SWOT stands for *strengths, weaknesses, opportunities,* and *threats.* We analyze what our strengths and weaknesses are compared to those of the competition. Perhaps we have better food service or a better location than the competition. On the other hand, perhaps our building is older and does not look as nice as our competitor's. When dealing with our strengths or our weaknesses we need to be realistic. Sometimes it is easier to point to our strengths than to notice our weaknesses.

We also need to analyze what *opportunities* for success we foresee and weigh them against possible *threats* to success. Is business booming in a certain area? Is our steakhouse restaurant concept one that people like?

Alternatively, does the economy look bad in the future, or is our steakhouse concept going to run into trouble with animal rights supporters and vegetarians? Again, a critical assessment is necessary.

After we have identified our objectives (where we want to be in the future) and done our situation analysis (where we are now), it is time to figure out how to accomplish our objectives. *Strategies* and *tactics* are the precise methods we use to achieve our objectives.

Developing marketing strategies may seem simple, but it actually isn't. Predicting the future is always difficult. There are too many variables that can influence events. Who, for example, really predicted the rapid changes that occurred in the former USSR in the early 90s? Who foresaw the sweeping behavioral changes brought about by the AIDS epidemic? Who would have thought that a children's puppet program on public TV would change the way American children learned to learn? Obviously, planning for the future requires a lot of time and thought.

Market Segmentation

How many different restaurant concepts are there? Hundreds? Thousands? From how many brands of hotels and motels can a traveler choose? Again, hundreds? Why do all of these different products and services exist? Americans have always assumed that free choice is a critical part of the American way of life, but does everyone want the same thing?

The answer is a resounding no, and leads us into the next area of marketing. We know that everyone is different. Products and services that sell well, such as a Big Mac or a room at Motel 6, do so because the buyer sees something of value in the product or service. The problem is that what one buyer sees as valuable may seem uninteresting to another. For example, some people go to a restaurant primarily to relax and have fun. Others may go to the same restaurant primarily to get away from the kids. Still others may go to the same restaurant because of its convenience. The point is that we, as individuals, are ultimately unique, and each one of us has a special set of likes and wants that separate us from everyone else. In a country of 275 million people like the United States this means that, taken to the absurd conclusion, there would need to be 275 million different restaurants tailored to each of us.

Obviously this situation could not occur. What marketers need to do is somehow group sets of individuals together, and sell their company's products and services based on characteristics of the group. Marketers go through a process called **market segmentation** and separate people into distinct groups based on their individual characteristics and buying habits.

The better the job we do in targeting what we sell to the correct group of consumers, the better our business should do. We use elements of the segmentation process to help us answer the following questions:

Courtesy: McDonald's Corporation, Oak Brook, Illinois.

- What different ways are there to segment our market?
- What are the different characteristics and buying habits of each of these market segments?
- Which segment or segments are the best ones for us to pursue?
- Why are these chosen segments the best ones for us to pursue?
- What do we offer that makes us the most attractive competitor to these chosen segments?

There are many ways to segment a market, and that is the problem. Even a small number of people can theoretically be divided in many different groups. What we need is a method of dividing the market into groups that are meaningful to us. In Chapter 6, ''Lodging: History, Supply, Demand, and Structure,'' some of the standard methods by which hotel markets are segmented were discussed. In this chapter we will take a more general look at how markets can be segmented.

Geographic.   Geographic criteria include categories such as climate or altitude. It should be obvious that people who live in warm climates will have different eating patterns from those who live in colder climates. Restaurant menus have to be tailored to the particular eating patterns of these different people.

Demographic.   Demographic criteria involve categories such as age or sex. Older adults have different eating habits and nutritional requirements than their teenage counterparts. Restaurants catering to a mature clientele simply cannot sell the types of fast food that teenagers eat. Similarly, males and females do not necessarily like the same things. Restaurants and lounges that have a dark, masculine decor may not attract females, who have been shown to like a lighter, cheerier atmosphere.

Psychographic.   Psychographic criteria relate to peoples' personality traits, lifestyles, and motivations. For example, some people tend to be more careful with their money than other people. A restaurant that emphasizes value (good, cheap food) would then be more likely to attract this market segment. Another example would be people called *belongers*. People in the belonger market segment need to be a part of their environment. Restaurant advertisements targeted to this group might emphasize that the in-crowd goes to the advertised restaurant.

Product Use.   Finally there are the product-use criteria. Here the focus is on how products and services are used. One example might be an ''ordinary'' versus a ''special'' situation. If you are going out to dinner and there is no special occasion to celebrate, your choice of a restaurant, or what you order at a restaurant, will likely be different from when, say, you are celebrating your birthday. When you are celebrating, you tend to buy different items, and spend more on them than in a normal, routine purchase situation.

Conclusions about Market Segmentation.   Five conditions must be met for market segmentation to work. First, the market segment has to be defined in such a way that all of its members share the same important characteristics. Second, the segments have to be identifiable; that is, they must be different from other segments. Third, different segments need to be comparable to each other, so that the best segment or segments can be picked. Fourth, at least one segment must have enough profit potential to be developed as a market. Fifth, we must be able to reach the segment or segments we have chosen; it does little good to identify a segment we cannot access.

New Product/Service Development

One of the significant differences in how American businesses operate today, as opposed to in the past, is in the area of the development of new products and services. If you can, think about all of the new products you have encountered in the past few years. Approximately 80 percent of all products that are on the shelves of stores today did not exist in their present form six or seven years ago. The pace with which new products and services enter the market is continually accelerating, and we, as consumers, are faced with an often bewildering array of products and services from which to choose.

However, most of these new products are doomed to mediocre sales lives, if not outright failure. Estimates vary, but somewhere in the neighborhood of 90 percent of all new products do not live up to the expectations their creators have for them. Even large, experienced, powerful companies like Coca-Cola are not immune to failure. In 1985 the Coca-Cola Company, after years of market research that cost an enormous amount of time and effort, launched their New Coke brand. All of the tests indicated that consumers liked the taste of New Coke better than the original Coke formula. After an initial period of high sales, a considerable consumer reaction set in, and the Coca-Cola Company was barraged by a tremendous amount of negative reaction to the new product. The company responded quickly to criticisms, and before long Coke Classic—the original Coke product—was again the number-one-selling cola drink, with the largest accounts, McDonald's and KFC, leading the way. What did Coca-Cola do wrong? Why did this prestigious company blow it with respect to New Coke if consumers actually liked the taste of New Coke so much? The answer lies in the company's lack of understanding about what the image of Coca-Cola meant to the American people. Yes, the taste of New Coke was perceived as better, but to change Coca-Cola was to tamper with Mom, apple pie, and the flag! Coca-Cola was and is an American institution, one that the American people feel very strongly about. In all of the new product development process that Coca-Cola went through, this vital issue was not addressed, with disastrous results for the company.

The process of developing any new product or service is obviously dangerous. How can companies like Coca-Cola or McDonald's minimize the likelihood that disasters like the introduction of New Coke will occur? There are a number of procedures used to develop new products and services.

Product Life Cycle.   We should note that the new product/service development process is only a part of what is called the *product/service life cycle*. A basic assumption in marketing is that all products and services over time exhibit the same types of characteristics that living organisms do. The product/service development process leads to the *introduction* phase of the life cycle—when the new product/service is first put on the market. At this point, sales are low and costs are high; many of the products that fail do so during introduction. New Coke in essence never made it beyond this point. The *growth* phase comes next. During this phase sales take off, and lots of people buy the product or service. After the growth phase comes the *maturity* phase, where sales peak. Finally there is the *decline* phase, where sales continuously drop, until they finally cease altogether and the product or service dies or disappears.

The new product/service process is so specialized that very few marketing graduates practice the discipline. Therefore, we will leave a detailed discussion of the new product development process to the marketing professors you'll encounter later on in your curriculum. Clearly, however, this is a process that is critical to the overall success of a company. Giants like McDonald's spend millions of dollars each year researching and developing new menu item concepts, but very few of those concepts actually make it as far as the introduction stage of the life cycle.

International

One marketing area that is growing rapidly is that of international marketing. The hospitality industry, like most industries, is experiencing a period of strong internationalism, with most U.S. companies getting into international markets, and many foreign companies entering the U.S. market. While many of the marketing practices described in the above sections are equally applicable to both the U.S. and most foreign markets, care has to be taken to recognize that foreign travelers have many cultural differences of which we need to be aware.

What sells in the United States may not sell overseas and vice versa. Many of the fast-food companies that attempted to enter the European market in the 1970s encountered considerable resistance to their products. Originally, most *did not* offer beer or wine, a familiar pattern to Americans.

However, Europeans generally would not even consider eating in a restaurant that did not sell beer and wine. Similarly, they did not appreciate the "eat and run" mentality of a typical fast-food restaurant. Meals are social occasions in Europe, not just a way to get nourishment. As a result of these (and other) problems, the introduction of fast-food outlets to the European market was not very successful initially. It was not until considerable research had been done that the American companies realized that they had to modify their product/service offerings to fit the European way of doing things; at that point they became relatively successful. In today's industry, knowing how to market overseas and to foreign travelers in the United States is a *very* important part of the overall marketing process.

Pricing

Of all the different elements of the marketing mix, perhaps the most difficult to deal with is the element of pricing. Hotel or restaurant marketers have a much more difficult time in setting their prices than do retailers or manufacturers. It is safe to say that, as an industry, we do not know much about how to set prices—which is dangerous, since price is generally the single most important factor influencing people's buying decisions.

Prices are all around us. You pay rent for your hotel room, a *fee* for a tennis lesson at a resort, a *fare* to a taxi driver taking you from your hotel to the airport, a *toll* on a highway as you drive on vacation, and *dues* to your country club. If you work as a salesperson, you receive a *salary* (the price an employer pays for an employee) plus a *commission*. The list goes on and on.

The main problem with pricing strategies is the determination of how prices are set. Historically, two or more people would haggle over the value of their items, and through negotiation arrive at a price that was agreeable to each of them. Today, in most business settings, this process no longer is used. Rather, the seller will often set one price that is applicable to all buyers. Can you imagine going to a restaurant and haggling over menu prices? It simply is not done. (There are some exceptions to this rule. You *can* negotiate on the price of an automobile or a house. Aficionados of garage sales and "park and

EXHIBIT 15–7

Each of these restaurants has successfully positioned itself in its respective market niche.

swaps'' often dicker over white elephants. However, in the hospitality business sector these exceptions are rare.)

Factors Influencing Price.   There are a number of factors that influence how prices are set. These fall under the realm of strategic, cost, and market demand considerations.

Strategic Objectives.   First, consider the strategic objectives of a company. What is it exactly that the company is trying to accomplish with respect to price? Survival of the company could be the main objective. If a hotel has low occupancy, lowering prices might help to fill the rooms and generate more revenue. Market leadership might be another objective. Market leadership means that the company has more business than any of its competitors. (McDonald's is a market leader in the fast-food business.) The advantage of being a market leader could be the image of being the best, as well as perhaps having lower costs than other companies. One way to become a market leader is to lower prices to get more business. Product/service quality leadership is another strategy. In this strategy, a company seeks to be seen as having the highest-quality product or service in the market; charging high prices contributes to this mystique. Ritz-Carlton hotels, for example, are very upscale, which is the image they want. Not surprisingly, they are also among the most expensive hotels around.

Costs.   Hotels and restaurants have costs of their own that affect the minimum prices they must charge for their products and services. These would include all of the costs for producing, marketing, and distributing their products or services. The lower a hotel's costs are in relation to the competition's, the lower price it can charge and still make a profit.

Market Demand.   While costs to a hotel or restaurant will set the *minimum* price that the hotel or restaurant must charge, market demand will set the *maximum* price. In fact, one of the most important aspects of the pricing process is determining how much guests are willing to pay. Actually, this is an important part of the segmentation process discussed earlier in the chapter; one very good way of creating market segments is on the basis of **price sensitivity,** or how much each segment is willing to pay.

Pricing Methods. There are three basic pricing methods used in the hospitality industry. The first, *cost-based pricing,* is essentially based on cost factors. Costs are determined and then a price that includes some profit is calculated. This probably seems quite logical, but before we leave the subject, we should mention that there is one damaging criticism about cost-based strategies. Does it make sense to set a price before finding out if people will pay that price? That is exactly what happens. Many times, price is based on costs to a hotel or restaurant, and not on what people are willing to pay.

Demand-based pricing strategies, on the other hand, look at what price guests are willing to pay, and then determine if the company can afford to produce the product or service at that price. If the price that people are willing to pay is less than what the product or service costs the hotel or restaurant to produce, then the product or service cannot be successful. No one can stay in business producing something that costs them $25.00 to provide if customers refuse to pay more than $20.00 to consume it.

Competition-based strategies are strategies applied when competitors are neck and neck. Follow-the-leader pricing is a common method. Pricing strategists for one hotel observe what other hotels charge, and adjust their prices based on the competitive advantages and disadvantages they see for their hotel. Yet think about it: If we set our prices based on another property, how do we know that they are not doing the same with us? This could be a case of the blind leading the blind. On the other hand, any fast-food restaurant selling hamburgers must consider what companies like McDonald's are charging, since they are so powerful in the fast-food restaurant industry.

Discounting. Once we have set prices, something interesting happens. We never charge those prices! Almost everything sold on the American marketplace, whether hospitality-related or not, will eventually be sold at a discount to its listed price. How many times do you buy items in a store at sale prices? How many times do you go to a restaurant with a discount coupon or because there are specials? It is entirely possible for a large hotel to sell 1,000 rooms on a given night and never charge the listed or rack rate for any room. This is because discounting is a tremendously powerful marketing technique that almost guarantees increased business.

Why do discount practices work? Consumers are always looking for a bargain, and if the price tag of a product or service is less than what appears to be the ''regular'' or normal price, then consumers feel as though they are getting a good deal. In this day and age, it seems that everyone discounts, and it would therefore seem logical that consumers would not ''fall'' for discounts, but they do.

Yet there are some negative elements to discounting. If you sell a hotel room at $20.00 off the regular rate, how do you know you couldn't have sold it for the full price? You are gambling that you will pick up more business, and, in the long run, come out ahead, but how can you ever be sure that you wouldn't have achieved the same overall occupancy without discounting? Discounting too much can also cause an image problem. If your room rate is too low, what might potential guests conclude about your property? Mightn't they wonder if there is something wrong with it? Finally, how far do you go with your discounting? (The ultimate discount would be 100 percent off, or a free room; this clearly makes no sense.) And, if everyone in the marketplace is discounting, who wins?

Promotions

In a famous advertisement done years ago, a businessperson was seen making the following statements to a salesperson:

> I don't know who you are. I don't know your company. I don't know your company's product. I don't know what your company stands for. I don't know your company's customers. I don't know your company's record. I don't know your company's reputation. *Now, what is it you wanted to sell me?*

The point of this advertisement is that people are not going to buy products and services unless they have a considerable amount of information about the purchase situation—the company selling, the products and services being sold, and so on. It is the goal of the **promotion** component of marketing to provide that information, as well as persuading the customer to buy.

Many people consider promotion to be the single most critical element in the entire marketing process. The complex nature of promotion makes it a very interesting element to evaluate. It is the one area where the producer and consumer are completely intertwined.

The two-part goal of promotion is to *inform* and *persuade*. Information means knowledge. We first have to know about a product or service before we can ever consider buying it. Persuasion means convincing people to buy the product or service. After we know about it, we need to be convinced that the product or service is worth buying. If the elements of informing and persuading are present, then the promotion has a good chance of being successful.

Like marketing in general, promotion has its own particular mix, composed of four elements: *advertising, personal selling, sales promotions,* and *public relations/publicity.*

Advertising.   *Advertising* involves the use of any form of nonpersonal communication about a product, service, or idea. The nonpersonal component of the definition means that mass media, such as television and magazines, are generally used to convey the message. Because of mass media's large audience, many potential consumers can be reached with each advertisement.

The amount of advertising done in the United States is phenomenal. On average we are exposed to somewhere between 1,000 and 1,500 ads each day!

EXHIBIT 15–8

Increasingly, modern hotels have had to develop and advertise amenities, such as indoor swimming pools and fitness centers, in their continuous efforts to increase market demands.

Courtesy: Palmer House Hilton, Chicago, Illinois.

If you consider just the hospitality field, how many ads would you be exposed to on a given day? The ads you see for restaurants and hotels in newspapers or on television add up to a considerable number. We are bombarded with ads everywhere. Billboards are ads. Labels on cans are ads. Logos on clothing are ads. This is not to mention the ads that pretend not to be ads, such as recipes that specify Campbell's Soup or movies that contain lingering shots of a Bacardi bottle or a pack of Camels. In point of fact, *you* are an ad—the way you dress, the way you style your hair, and the way you act are all methods of sending a message. It is impossible to escape the impact of advertising.

Personal Selling.   A second major form of promotion is ***personal selling***. Personal selling is a form of person-to-person promotion where the seller attempts to inform and persuade one person (or a small group of people) to buy a product or service. As a result, personal selling is almost the opposite of advertising. Not too many people can be reached at one time, but the influence of person-to-person contact is much greater than the impersonal methods used in advertising. Obviously, the cost of personal selling is high due to the small numbers of customers that can be reached and this technique is best used when each customer represents a large amount of business. In the hospitality field

EXHIBIT 15–8

Continued.

Courtesy: Palmer House Hilton, Chicago, Illinois.

personal selling approaches are generally used to sell conventions and other group business, while advertising is used to sell to the individual traveler.

Sales Promotions.   A third type of promotion has the repetitive name of ***sales promotion.*** This type of promotion is a little hard to define because it encompasses a number of different areas. Basically, sales promotions are any marketing activities designed to produce immediate sales or that provide an extra incentive to buy.

Perhaps the best way to understand what sales promotions are is by example. Half-price coupons that you see in newspapers are sales promotions. They are supposed to get you to buy *now* by limiting the offer to a certain short time period, *and* provide the extra incentive to buy since there is a special half-price deal. Table tents on restaurant tables that advertise special dinners, desserts, or wine service are also sales promotions for the same reasons. An example of a simple sales promotion in a hotel is the reader board in the lobby that advertises happy hours in the lounge or entertainment in the dining room.

Public Relations/Publicity.   The final element in the promotion mix is the area of public relations and publicity. The two concepts are related but are not the same. *Publicity* refers to any communication about a business for which that business does not directly pay. It is like advertising in the sense that it involves communication to a mass audience. The goal of every hospitality enterprise is to get the publicity for little or no cost. If you host a Christmas party for the local Boy and Girl Scouts at your hotel, a newspaper story about the party will cast your hotel in a favorable light. If you remodel your restaurant and have a grand reopening, and the local television station carries a story on the festivities, your restaurant receives considerable attention. These are examples of *positive publicity.* On the other hand, publicity does not necessarily have to be positive. If there is a fire in your hotel, the news reports of the fire could be considered *negative publicity.* Similarly, if your restaurant is cited for health violations, or worse, closed down because of them, any news report would be considered very negative. These situations point out two specific characteristics of publicity that are not characteristics of the other elements of the promotion mix: Publicity can be negative, and is hard to control in the sense that the negative stories will be aired or published whether we like it or not.

Eye on the Issues

 # Technology

The pervasiveness of credit cards, point-of-sale units, and electronic bar coding has, to some degree, simplified research into consumer purchasing patterns. Unbeknownst to many customers, bar-coding or POS technology can allow a business to create an electronic data sheet tied to a credit card number or address. This data record might list all purchases charged to the card (or paid for with your checking account). From these data, a restaurateur might know that you typically visit his or her establishment on Tuesday evenings as one of a party of three, generally order Mongolian Hot Pot and two Tsing Tao beers, and frequently leave a 14 to 18 percent tip on an average check of $43.25.

Based on this information, you might become the target of promotional mailings announcing Tsing Tao nights, Chinese New Year Specials, or customer appreciation discounts. Depending on the restaurant, your name may be sold to or "shared" with other local businesses, who, seeing that you are a little different from the average couch potato, may also send you promotional mailings.

There has been some controversy surrounding such purchase tracking capability. Some consider it an invasion of privacy. If a restaurant can collect a "dossier" on you, imagine what your grocery or drugstore purchases might tell someone.

As a result, hotels or restaurants may find a need to deal with the area of ***public relations.*** In public relations we try to maintain as positive an image as possible for the company, either by maximizing the effect of positive publicity or minimizing the effect of negative publicity. For example, if a hotel hosts the scouts, the public relations person's job is to maximize press coverage. On the other hand, if a hotel experiences a fire, the public relations person's job is to downplay, as much as possible, the negative effects of the fire, and divert the public's attention to other issues—a very interesting but challenging job!

There are many different ways to promote a hotel or restaurant. The promotional mix involves an almost infinite variety of methods, yet in almost all cases all four elements of the promotional mix—advertising, personal selling, sales promotions, and publicity—need to be utilized to best inform and persuade present and potential guests of a hotel's or restaurant's value.

Conclusion

Marketing is a broad discipline offering many options to hospitality professionals. Since hospitality firms are a part of the service industry, the HRM student with an interest in the field should work to differentiate between product-tied and service-tied marketing issues.

Subdisciplines within marketing include consumer behavior, market research, strategic marketing, market segmentation, new product/service development, pricing, and promotions. Individuals who wish to work in a hospitality marketing career need to have a variety of skills. An area such as market research requires a solid background in mathematics and statistics, while personal selling requires communication skills.

Keywords

marketing   460
product industries   460
service industries   460
marketing mix   464

market research   467
market segmentation   470
price sensitivity   476
promotion   477

Core Concepts

consumer behavior   465
advertising   477
personal selling   478
sales promotion   479

positive publicity   480
negative publicity   480
public relations   481

Discussion Questions

1. What are the major differences between the marketing of products and the marketing of services? What special kinds of problems do you see in marketing a hotel or restaurant?

2. What kinds of ads do you like? If you were going to develop an advertisement for a restaurant, what would you include in it?

3. Discuss some of the differences between marketing tangibles and intangibles.

4. Why do you go to a restaurant? Is it just for food? What could a restaurant ad contain that would appeal to you?

5. What kinds of positive publicity might a hotel or restaurant get? What kinds of negative publicity?

PART VI

Hospitality Management Career Opportunities

By now you have a fairly good idea what the hospitality industry is all about. You have read chapters that dealt with almost every aspect of the industry, from lodging to food service, from casino management to travel and tourism, from accounting to marketing.

As those chapters indicated, hospitality management takes a very special person, and not everyone may be suited to succeed in it. Terms such as *tenacious, hardworking, people oriented, dedicated, ethical,* and *open to change* were used to describe some of the characteristics of successful hospitality managers.

At this particular point in your life and your career you may not be certain whether or not you have what it takes to become successful in the hospitality industry. Rest assured. Many people working in the industry have that same problem! The difference between you and them, though, is that you have not started your career yet, and they, at least, are employed. Wouldn't it be nice, though, to have an idea about what kinds of careers are available for you? And wouldn't it be equally nice to know how to go about securing a job while you are still in school?

The last chapter in this book addresses these two questions in detail. It cannot give you absolute, foolproof answers, of course, but it will help you make some decisions about your education, career, and maybe even the rest of your life.

Chapter 16, ''Career Opportunities and Job Search Strategies,'' is divided into two parts. The first part will give you an idea as to what kinds of careers you can pursue in the hospitality industry. It will present you with a realistic picture of salaries, career ladders, and sources of information and discuss the time it will take for you to reach your goals. It is not wrong to set high goals for yourself; you can shoot for the moon and say to yourself: ''I want to be the chief executive officer of the largest hotel or food service company in the country.'' It is unrealistic though to expect to be at that position in seven years. Surely, you realize by now that most people will not become general managers within the first two years of their careers. It is not impossible, but reality tells us otherwise. There are several million people out there who have the same dream you have at this very moment.

You will read about some success stories from industry executives who have made it the hard way: through hard work and dedication. Instead of the ''super successes,'' you will read about people who are in positions you can aspire to in 10 years or so: a district manager of a restaurant chain, two regional vice presidents (of a hotel chain and an institutional food service company), a sales/marketing executive, and owners of restaurants and hotels. Altogether, these might be very helpful to you in your pursuit of that ultimate goal: a satisfying, rewarding, and challenging management position.

The second half of the chapter will give you some advice about how to become a manager from where you are at the moment. It will tell you what to do once you are ready to go out into the industry, what to expect and how to act during an interview, and how to write your résumé. Remember, the interview and the résumé might very well be the first contacts you make with your future employers; you'd better be prepared and they'd better be good! All that is left to say at this point is: Keep on dreaming and good luck on your job search and in your future career!

CHAPTER 16

Career Opportunities and Job Search Strategies

The key to making satisfying career choices is a clear sense of self, combined with a solid understanding of the options you are considering. As the chapter on managerial leadership, Chapter 2, indicated, there are several techniques for gaining self knowledge. This chapter will help you further clarify and understand your options and pave the way to begin making career choices. The first section contains information about opportunities in the hospitality industry. The second section introduces you to tools that may help you obtain employment in your chosen area of interest.

Outline

Introduction

Stop and think for a moment about your future. If you're an average person, not an heir to a great fortune or some lucky lottery winner, you are likely to spend the next 40 years working, eight or more hours a day, five days a week—the majority of your waking hours on the job. If you do not enjoy your work, this might feel like an endless prison sentence with no early release for good behavior! However, by investing some time in the decision-making process before you start out, work can be an exciting opportunity for growth and development.

The information and suggestions in this chapter are food for thought as you explore diverse opportunities in the hospitality industry. Throughout this process, we encourage you to keep an open mind, weigh risks, and ask yourself "Why not?" Based on what you learn and think, try to predict the future needs of the industry . . . and the ways *you* can meet those needs. Treat this process as an adventure of self-discovery as you begin charting a life of success and satisfaction.

Hospitality Industry Opportunities

Throughout this book you've read that the hospitality industry is the fastest growing industry in the world and that it offers some of the most exciting and challenging careers available. The potential rewards are extensive, and advancement can be rapid. But like most things in life, excitement and reward do not come without a price. The price in the hospitality industry comes primarily in the form of hard work and varying degrees of sacrifice in your personal life.

A Reality Check—Setting Yourself Up for Success

The hospitality industry is not for everyone. Long workweeks tend to be the norm rather than the exception. Hospitality operations are open long hours to cater to customers' needs. There are exceptions, some of which are described below, but they are truly not characteristic of the industry:

- Small motel operations that close their offices at night or during the off-season.
- Restaurants that are "breakfast and lunch only" operations.
- Ski or watersport resorts that operate seasonally, based on weather conditions.
- Business-district cafeteria operations.

Because of the industry's extended hours, you will most likely be working when others are having fun. Weekends and holidays are busy times for the industry, as are other times of celebration. You might easily find yourself working on Super Bowl Sunday or on your birthday or anniversary.

EXHIBIT 16–1

The hospitality industry is known for its extended hours of operation.

To balance things, remember that working with hotel and restaurant guests is rarely boring. Troubleshooting, checking on details, or acting as your company's ambassador will keep you stimulated and active, never chained to a desk or hidden away in a tiny cubicle. As a manager you will be mixing with the public, sometimes solving problems, other times preventing them, in a variety of environments and locales. During your early career years, you may be asked to relocate, often several times, since many companies have operations in a variety of locations.

The hospitality business is different from industries that produce tangible products. Hospitality is about people dealing with people. Since people are far less predictable than widgets and wires, this translates into a less controlled environment and a less standardized "product" than a manufacturing plant or a behind-the-scenes business. The hospitality industry is in a constant state of creating and delivering service.

The hospitality industry offers dynamic, exciting, and vibrant environments. A career in it can provide you with responsibility, advancement, diversity, and personal satisfaction. Perhaps the biggest challenge to be encountered in the pursuit of success will be achieving **balance.** If your career takes you into the high-glitz/high-pressure side of the industry, you'll need to stay grounded amidst constant change. As the following anecdotes will show, those who are most successful in the industry have made pleasing customers a career-long value, and they speak warmly of their like-minded colleagues and employees.

The following are testimonials from professionals in the hospitality industry who have found advancement and many rewards in their professions. Let their experience enlighten you about the field, as well as about yourself.

Life Stories . . . Success Stories

We all have been told that success does not happen overnight. This statement holds true for most of us, and the phrase ''paying your dues'' certainly rings true in this industry. Nevertheless, it can be difficult to be patient and understand that experience and expertise are gained over time and that they take a lot of dedication.

The following are six biographies that might inspire you to continue exploring career options in the hospitality industry. Our guests are:

> Ann Todd, corporate sales manager, Fountain Suites
>
> Roberta Schaffner, regional vice president, Marriott Education Services
>
> Robert Barger, multifranchise owner, Marie Callender's
>
> Kirk Michael, district manager, The Old Spaghetti Factory, International
>
> Mary Watson-Boswell, regional vice president, Wyndham Hotels
>
> Mary Jean Bublitz, owner and operator, Quality Suites and Quality Inn

Ann Todd, Corporate Sales Manager, Fountain Suites.   If I were to reflect back on the past 10 years of my work experience in the hospitality industry, I would have to admit that it has been an enlightening experience.

I began my career at the age of 16 working in the reservations headquarters of a major hotel chain. I started a business management degree at a large state university, but after two years of being addressed by my social security number, instead of my name, I decided to transfer to a smaller school and specialize in hospitality. My hotel and restaurant management degree program provided the education I needed to follow my aspirations. The following three years helped prepare me for the ''real'' world in a competitive, challenging, and changing industry.

During my college years, I continued to work at a local hotel as a lead agent at the front desk. This experience allowed me to apply the things I learned in school and showed me firsthand some important things that can't be absorbed from books—such as how it feels to work under managers with differing styles, and how politics and ethics complicate the workplace.

When it came time to graduate, in 1992, the economy was depressed, and on-campus recruiters were scarce. Determined not to get discouraged, I expanded my job search beyond the normal routes offered through the campus career planning and placement office. I tried to get as many contact names and leads as possible through friends, professors, industry publications, and professionals already in the workforce. I then sent out 250 letters and résumés to hotels across the country, hoping that some would be interested in my qualifications. This was an arduous experience, but helped me understand the importance of written communication as I drafted letter after letter. As the semester progressed, I took advantage of every interview opportunity I could. Through this, I gained useful practice in interviewing, and learned what kind of positions a new graduate could realistically expect.

I eventually chose to work for one of the few hotel chains that offered a structured management training program. My next two years were filled with both success and disappointment. My 12-month development program shrank to three months, but promotion came quickly. Soon I was a department head, overseeing front office operations. I continued in this position for nine months in Seattle, Washington; accepted a temporary assignment in Sunnyvale, California; and then transferred to a brand new property in Costa Mesa, California.

Working for a small but growing chain has its advantages, largely because of the opportunity for advancement. This particular chain was very profitable due to its management philosophy. It cross-trained its managers and empowered them at the property level. Guest satisfaction was the corporate credo, and the chain provided continuous training for both managers and line employees.

Small chains also have their drawbacks: Managers are responsible for the full operation of their departments, and for many this involves long hours, usually with minimal staffing. Workweeks of 80 to 100 hours were not uncommon (actually they were more of the norm)! After two years of never having two days off in a row and missing the normalcy of a social life, I decided to shift to a different facet of hotel work, one with fewer hours and less stress.

I gave six weeks' notice and moved to a city with a flourishing hospitality industry, hoping to find the change I craved. After a one-month job search, I was hired as corporate sales manager for a resort-like property. I was very fortunate to find an employer who believed that I could quickly adapt my operations experience and selling skills to my new position, and that I could succeed despite my lack of specific experience. Hospitality industry headhunters confirm that employers are reluctant to hire employees who have little or no directly relevant experience. To me, this only emphasizes the importance of student work experience and internships, and the need to polish interviewing skills. I was glad I had laid that groundwork while in college.

As a sales manager, I have found it important to stay involved and active in organizations for several reasons, including: networking, sales leads, training, and insight into future events that will affect tourism. I also believe that one must truly love this work to be successful in it. I do love it, but my direction has changed with experience. If someone had asked me three years ago what I wanted to be when ''I grew up,'' I would have told them I wanted to be a general manager; but if someone were to ask me that question today, I would have to admit that my interests have shifted—to training. By staying involved and active, I continue to grow, and so do my opportunities in the hospitality industry.

Roberta Schaffner, Regional Vice President, Marriott Education Services. When I began what was to become a wonderful career, life was very different. All it took to advance yourself was a lot of hard work and a fair amount of common sense. Times have certainly changed.

I dropped out of college in 1961, a move I deeply regretted. My father told me I had three days to find a job—or else. It made all the sense in the world to me to seek employment at the coffee shop where my friends and I had spent so much time.

I loved working as a waitress. The thought of getting what my parents called a ''real job,'' behind a desk from nine to five, filled me with horror! I wanted to stay in the business but needed to learn enough so I could advance past the waitress stage. Lacking the formal credentials that I knew were necessary to get into management with most restaurant firms, and not even realizing that colleges and universities offered hospitality degrees, I applied for a job with Howard Johnson's as a waitress at a large new restaurant in New York City. My plan was to learn all I could through the company's formal training program and to volunteer to do any and every job in the place until I mastered them all.

The plan worked! Two weeks after we opened, I was promoted to night hostess. Within one year, I was the head night hostess at the largest restaurant the company had on Long Island. A year later, I was head hostess and relief manager at a smaller store. At the time, there were not many women actually managing restaurants. Yet, I persevered and eventually became manager of a store.

From Howard Johnson's I went to work for Saga Corporation in the education division (dining services at colleges and universities). I began as a manager and progressed to food service director. Along the way I finished my college degree. Eventually, I became district manager in Ohio. Seven years later, after Saga was purchased by Marriott, I became vice president of marketing for the division. Now I am VP of regional operations in the southwest—the first woman vice president in our division!

What does it take to succeed in this industry? Commitment, integrity, and perseverance. The hours are long and you may never be rich. Why do I do it? The work can be great fun if you want it to be. The satisfaction of running your own piece of business is wonderful. Innovation and inspiration are welcomed and cherished. The instant gratification from satisfied customers is out of this world. Boredom and routine are rare. But most of all, it is a business that abounds with people, associates, and customers—always there and always hungry!

Robert Barger, Multifranchise Owner, Marie Callender's.   I am often asked how I first became involved in the restaurant business. The fact is that, for me, it started out as a part-time job after school.

In 1964, Marie Callender's was a very young company with only three retail pie shops. After working part time after school for about six months, they offered to train me for a management position while I attended college. Being chosen ahead of other tenured employees made me feel that there might be a long-term future for me in the company.

The company doubled in size by 1967. With only one year of college behind me, I made the decision to work full time at Marie Callender's. It was a big commitment, averaging 60 to 70 hours a week!

Time flew. I went from assistant manager to general manager and finally the opportunity came to own and operate my own restaurant. After two years of running the most successful restaurant in the company, the owners offered me a franchise and helped me finance it. The long hours, energy, and dedication paid off!

Since 1971, I have been a Marie Callender's franchisee in California. Even after 20+ years, I continue to stay active in the day-to-day operations. That is what keeps me going and my business growing. In 1980 I had an opportunity for another franchise in Colorado. I put a group of investors together for this second store. Nine years later I opened my third restaurant. Today, our California and Colorado operations together employ 250 people.

I have been very fortunate with the opportunities put before me. The rewards have been possible through working hard, continuing my education in the hospitality field, and surrounding myself with dynamic, energetic young people who want the same things I wanted when I was their age.

Over the years, my restaurants and I have received numerous awards. They have all been earned through dedication and labor. I am very involved in the Marie Callender's franchisee association and enjoy giving back some of what I have learned through the years.

If you are looking for a career in the service industry to last a lifetime, if you are dynamic, energetic, and aggressive, and find satisfaction working with and around people, the hospitality industry is for you!

Kirk Michael, District Manager, The Old Spaghetti Factory, International.
Growing up in a small town in Ohio, I never imagined myself as district manager for a restaurant company. But looking back over my career, I can think of nothing else I would rather do.

I graduated from college in 1982 with a degree in public administration from Miami University in Ohio. When I enrolled in school, my ambition was to be a city manager. While in college, I supported myself as a food server, a job at which I excelled and which I enjoyed a great deal. As graduation approached, I began to have second thoughts about a career in public service. I wanted to work in an environment where I could train and coach other people.

I wanted a position that offered a fast-paced challenge and where my decision-making and motivational skills could make a difference. After interviewing with many other companies, I decided to build my career with The Old Spaghetti Factory.

Even after 11 years, I am still attracted to The Old Spaghetti Factory because of the personal involvement of the owners of the company. I also selected The Old Spaghetti Factory because of the opportunity to travel. As a manager and general manager, I have lived and worked in nine different cities. A large part of my success today is the result of the ''living experience'' I gained while relocating.

My career path is atypical compared to many other food service professionals. Most of my colleagues have built their careers by moving frequently from company to company. I have worked exclusively for one company. After completing a three-month training program, I accepted my first assignment in Indianapolis. I later transferred to Denver, where I began to realize my potential, and was soon promoted to general manager in San Jose, Fullerton, and Atlanta. I had the opportunity to open new units before being promoted to district manager of the southwest.

My job is extensive. I work with a team of six managers in each unit, and I am responsible for the operation of five high-volume, full-service restaurants. Most of my time is spent assisting the local management teams with hiring, sales, maintenance, guest service, and daily operations. Recruiting, hiring, and training managers are also major responsibilities.

The activities I enjoy about my job are many. First, I receive great satisfaction from choosing and training our own management teams. Helping managers grow professionally and advance their careers has many rewards. Also, the decisions that I make are important ones and I am able to see their effects almost immediately. Finally, there is no greater satisfaction than a happy guest.

I began my career with many limitations. I had limited exposure to business, lacked professional grooming, and did not have much industry experience. However, the two characteristics that I recognize as my greatest assets can be demonstrated by anyone: hard work and persistence. Never give up and be willing to give whatever it takes, and you will reach your goals.

Mary Watson-Boswell, Regional Vice President, Wyndham Hotels. My first jobs in the hospitality industry were as a server and cocktail waitress during college summers. In 1978, when I finally settled down and needed a job after graduation, my summer-learned skills came to my rescue. Serving had taught me the basics of food and beverage and working at a front desk in a resort hotel one summer had introduced me to operations.

I applied at a resort hotel near Miami for a management position at the front desk, and despite my lack of management experience, I was given the opportunity to work in the reservations office. My first hotel position was as a reservationist handling group reservations at a 350-room hotel. From there,

I moved up rapidly in rooms division management. Four years later, I was resident manager at that same hotel, responsible for all rooms departments, security, recreational activities—and I was in charge of the hotel when the general manager was absent.

In 1984, I joined Wyndham to open an 800-room hotel in Florida. Two years later, I opened the first Wyndham Garden Hotel as a general manager. I was promoted to a regional manager's position and then to regional vice president in 1991.

The hospitality industry was not one I deliberately planned to enter. With all my practical job experience in that area, I entered the field because I needed work and I did not want to go to law school right away. Yet, from the first week, I never looked back and within months any thought of law school was gone.

What I love about the hospitality industry is the fast pace and high energy. Nothing ever stays the same—even though things are constantly changing, we are always focused on how to give better service and thereby increase revenue. What is challenging is to stay ahead of everyone else by always reviewing what you have done to see how it can be done better.

In my opinion, the most important skills and competencies you need to succeed in the hospitality business are dedication to service, communication, organization, delegation, and most importantly, leadership skills.

Mary Jean Bublitz, Owner and Operator, Quality Suites and Quality Inn. I was a junior in high school when I began my career, unsure of what I wanted to do with my life. Upon graduation, I received an academic scholarship for college to begin my studies towards a teaching career. However, after working in my parents' restaurant as a hostess, waitress, cook, and dishwasher I realized how much I enjoyed those jobs. As I learned more about the restaurant business, I became an asset to my parents and grew into the challenges of daily decision making.

Since 1962, my husband and I have developed, owned, and managed various businesses, including a delicatessen, candy store, motels, and hotels ranging in size from 20 units to more than 100 rooms. Today, our grown children work with us and as a family we own and operate a 96-room Quality Inn and a 102-unit, AAA 4-Diamond Quality Suites Hotel.

As a veteran in the industry, I must warn you: Be prepared to work nights, weekends, holidays, and even 12-hour days—these last are not uncommon. Though many careers require long hours and hard work for those starting out, hospitality is one of the more relentless.

Some measures of my success include serving on the Choice Hotels board of directors and on the advisory board of a school of hotel and restaurant management program. Furthermore, I was nominated for the Arizona Governor's Tourism Hall of Fame in 1993. My proudest achievement came in 1984 from the American Lung Association, an award for pioneering nonsmokers' rooms in the lodging industry.

I encourage each of you to follow the hospitality field if you are interested in a truly exciting world of opportunity, if you are not afraid of hard work, and if you enjoy working in an industry that is about people. If you are considering ownership as part of your future, you might consider the lower-cash-investment, easier-to-manage bed and breakfast opportunities.

Summary.   With one exception, our life story guests began their careers in the 50s, 60s, 70s, and 80s. Three of them completed college degrees immediately after high school, but only one earned an HRM degree. As Roberta Schaffner noted, ''Times have certainly changed.'' Today, more and more large companies are looking for evidence of commitment *before* they hire young managers. A college degree offers employers good evidence of persistence, organization, intellectual abilities, and motivation. A résumé showing summer or part-time jobs in the industry leads employers to deduce other qualities, such as reliability, presentability, and willingness to pay one's dues.

Hard work and persistence have always been required for success in hospitality; all the life stories referred to these in some way or another. In today's market, though, most management candidates must offer more. You are on the brink of following one of several possible paths to a hospitality career. Read on and see if it is the right one for you.

The paths and avenues to succeed in the hospitality industry are many. The following section will help you visualize the different routes and career ladders you may choose to take. Determination and purpose will prove helpful, because it's hard to keep climbing upward without them. The way to get to the top is by taking one step at a time.

Career Ladders in the Hospitality Industry

Appendix A at the end of the chapter presents samples of career ladders you may choose in the hospitality industry. Appendix B shows representative industry salaries, as well as lists of key management positions in lodging, food service, and tourism. Use this information as a tool to help you set realistic goals and expectations as you continue your career exploration. Once again, you'll be reminded that there is far more to the industry than hotels and restaurants. Here are some examples worthy of consideration:

- Country club management.
- Hospital or correctional facility food service.
- Corporate cafeteria food service.
- Airline in-flight food provision.
- School and university food service.
- Theme park management.
- Casino and gaming management.
- Cruise ship management.

- Military club management (civilians are employed to manage food service and lodging operations).
- City club management: athletic, dining, social, and professional.
- Hotel development management.
- Sales and marketing for hotels and restaurants.
- Golf course management.
- Executive chef/sous chef.

Current Trends

A trend denotes the dominant tendency in a given situation or environment. In the case of the hospitality industry, trends tell us the general direction of the industry at a given time. We are presently experiencing a somewhat giddy growth trend in employment. About 40 million new jobs will be created in the hospitality industry between 1990 and 2005 worldwide. This makes travel and tourism the fastest growing industry in the world!

Significant social, political, and economic changes have taken place and these have shaped and continue to shape the direction of the world. Some of the most prominent developments were the end of the Cold War, which opened up vast new markets, and the creation of several regional and multinational trade agreements intended to stimulate business and tourism between countries and regions. These changes have direct and powerful impacts on our industry. Some of the more recent trade pacts are:

- 1994—General Agreement on Tariffs and Trade (GATT).
- 1993—North American Free Trade Agreement (NAFTA).
- 1992—Association of Southeast Asian Nations (ASEAN).
- 1991—South American Southern Cone Common Market (Mercosur).
- 1957—European Community (EC).

Trends in the Hotel Industry.   One of the major trends in the hotel industry is a shift towards chain operations. In the past, most hotels were family owned and operated. However, as we approach the 21st century, almost half of the hotel industry is controlled and owned by about 25 hotel chains. One of the reasons why chains are well received by the American public is that their accommodations and service tend to be predictable and consistent. Guests can expect to find uniformity in any Holiday Inn or Sheraton hotel, no matter where they travel. In a world filled with uncertainty, predictability has its charm.

A second trend in the hotel industry is the shift towards catering to distinct customer bases with specific needs and expectations. Just as cars are available in a variety of models, colors, and prices, enabling people to choose according to their means, standards, and desires, so are hotels. As Chapter 6, ''Lodging: History, Supply, Demand, and Structure'' discussed, hotel chains are shifting towards specialization by serving specific segments of the market.

Exhibit 16–2

Chains are well received by the American public, largely because accommodations and service are predictable and consistent.

A third trend is the shift toward internationalization. American chains (food, lodging, theme park, reservation system) are expanding to countries around the world. Likewise, more travelers from overseas are visiting the United States, and more foreign companies are investing in American hospitality operations. Hotels have found it sensible to cater to international guests by providing such amenities as ethnic cuisine, currency exchange, and printed information translated into foreign languages.

What This Means to You.   The fact that hotel chains are expanding and shifting to an international level means that you may transfer to new locations and faraway cities, even abroad. On a worldwide basis, management candidates are not bountiful. In fact, according to the Harvard Business School, ''the demand is definitely greater than the supply when it comes to managers with international experience.'' Getting an education in hotel and restaurant management will benefit you wherever you venture, and due to the trend toward internationalization, speaking a foreign language will open many doors. For overseas positions, employers prefer broad-minded people who can listen and empathize, and foreign language ability may enhance those skills. Developing your powers of communication will always work in your favor.

Trends in the Food Service Industry.   It is not surprising that the trend toward take-out and drive-through meals continues to grow. We lead hectic and busy lives, and the idea of putting a roast in the oven after a long day at work sounds good only in concept. As a result, many table-service restaurants are adding take-out to their repertoires.

Even though the growth in fast-food restaurants in the United States is slowing, companies such as PepsiCo (Taco Bell's, KFC's, and Pizza Hut's parent company), McDonald's, and many others are expanding internationally at an enormous rate. Two-thirds of the growth of these companies occur outside the United States. Countries where consumerism is a novel concept, such as China and the former Soviet Union, are now fertile ground for business opportunities and market development.

What This Means to You.   To attract qualified food service employees, companies are offering full-time employment, benefits, higher pay, bonuses, additional training, and advancement opportunities for those who show commitment and dedication. More and more women and minorities are joining the food service workforce to take advantage of such benefits. This means, once again, an abundance of job and career opportunities.

Whatever field of specialization you pursue, it is important to remain aware of current events and trends. In today's dynamic global economy, you will need to be continually developing and upgrading your skills in order to meet the demands of the hospitality industry.

Industry-Specific Skills

Today's employers say they want well-rounded individuals with a willingness to work hard, a sense of focus, and a wide variety of skills. There are two areas that are critical to your success in the hospitality industry: technical and management skills.

Technical Skills.   The **technical skills** area includes all those skills needed to master the hands-on details of the job. All jobs have a technical component to them. The sooner you learn what is required of you technically, the faster you will be able to master a position and prepare for future challenges. The best way to improve any skill level is to practice and be persistent. The proverb, ''practice makes perfect,'' says it all. Some commonly required technical skills you'll find essential are the ability to:

- Operate computers (computer literacy).
- Perform financial analysis.
- Calculate hospitality statistics such as occupancy percentages, average daily room rates, average checks, overall revenue, and cost-to-revenue ratios.
- Take and extend inventory.

Management Skills.   The hospitality industry is a service industry. Our product is service; our customer base and delivery vehicle are people. Developing **management skills** that enable you to deal with people will save you time and energy and will help reduce turnover. Different management ''gurus'' and organizations may value slightly different sets of skills. Here are six that we have found to be well regarded by hospitality recruiters:

- Effective communication (listening, as well as speaking and writing).
- Innovation and creativity.
- Leadership.
- Critical thinking and decision making.
- Customer relations.
- Negotiation and conflict management.

As Chapter 11, ''Human Resource Management,'' advises, it is important to find a balance between technical and managerial skills; neither should be undervalued. Managers who focus their energy only on the technical aspects of their operation and disregard people management skills may find themselves alienating their employees and customers. On the other hand, managers who focus solely on people management skills, without attending to technical competencies, may fail to recognize trends or anticipate problem areas.

Avenues for Knowledge Development

The characteristics and skills needed to succeed in the hospitality industry can (and should) be developed throughout your life. Learning new skills (and refining existing ones) is not just for teens and ''20-somethings.'' The truth is, it is for everyone—veteran practitioners *and* those not-so-long-out-of-school. Professional development can take many forms: from degree programs, to hands-on learning, to management theory, to wine appreciation. As a manager it will be helpful for you to understand the different types of training available. This may help you select employees or, perhaps more importantly, help you suggest avenues through which your existing staff can grow professionally and personally.

EXHIBIT 16–3a

Do you have the necessary skills to turn this empty room into a dazzling banquet hall?

EXHIBIT 16–3b

If you do have the proper skills, a banquet room like this one—the Grand Ballroom at the Palmer House Hilton in Chicago, might be the result of your labor.

Courtesy: Palmer House Hilton, Chicago, Illinois.

Hospitality Training and Education.   During the first two-thirds of the century, few hotel managers, tourism directors, restaurant owners, or convention planners held specialized college degrees. Many entered their area of specialization at the bottom-most rung (often with little or no advanced education) and worked their way through layers of increasing responsibility before reaching property-, regional-, or chain-management positions. These veterans learned their business the hard way—through trial and error or under the wing of a mentor. Today, the complexity of competing in a world marketplace filled with increasingly sophisticated consumers requires more. It is still possible to succeed without credentials, but few attempt it after reviewing the odds. Even entrepreneurs benefit from a well-planned program of study that prepares them for possible pitfalls and known hazards.

So where to begin your training and/or education? Many people take their first step by starting out in an entry-level hospitality job. In such positions they usually receive specific training suitable only for the tasks for which they are directly responsible. A significant number of slightly older individuals may have received food service training during military service. For instance, military food service specialists receive nearly 400 hours of intensive institutional/culinary instruction geared for volume production. Those who do well in the specialty are offered further, more advanced instruction, and may be assigned to base facilities and officers' club operations.

Professional Certifications.   Programs such as those offered by the Educational Institute (EI) of the American Hotel and Motel Association (AH&MA), the International Association of Convention and Visitors Bureaus (IACVB), and the Educational Foundation (EF) of the National Restaurant Association (NRA) provide a valuable avenue for practicing hospitality managers (and aspiring managers) to pursue professional growth. Among EI's certifications are the certified hotel administrator (CHA), certified food and beverage executive (CFBE), and certified human resources executive (CHRE) designations. The IACVB offers certification in tourism marketing, convention marketing, and destination management, to name three. EF offers the NRA diploma in management development as well as certification in a variety of courses.

Technical Programs.   Technical or vocational programs, whether private or public, usually involve two years of full-time study (or equivalent coursework spread over a longer term for part-time students). Classes are tightly focused, and there are usually no requirements for competencies in English or exposure to the liberal arts courses. Such programs are often attractive to students who have already taken some college coursework and opted not to pursue a degree. Other candidates for such a concentrated approach are career changers anxious to gain expertise quickly en route to new employment. Students in such programs are given some exposure to management issues, but are not usually asked to demonstrate critical or abstract thinking skills.

Community College Programs.   Community college programs usually are two-pronged. They offer practical training in a short time period but also expect students to pursue a broader general education. Students who opt for a community college degree or certificate are required to demonstrate competencies in English, math, and general knowledge across the liberal arts. Community colleges have an advantage over most technical schools in the transferability of their credit hours toward a four-year university degree. This gives students the potential for "extra mileage" from their two years of coursework, should they decide to pursue a bachelor's degree.

Associate and Four-Year Programs.   This extra mileage advantage is shared by associate programs, a format offered by some four-year colleges. These, too, are usually two-year programs allowing the option of further work toward a bachelor's degree. Advantages include a degree or certification from a university (which some perceive as more prestigious than the equivalent from a community college). Disadvantages include a greater expense on average in enrollment costs per credit hour.

Four-year degrees from colleges and universities continue to be the most popular and perhaps financially viable degrees in the industry. Many fast-food chains now require college degrees for management recruits, as do many major lodging companies. Tourism development and management positions almost always require a minimum of a bachelor's degree. Four-year programs offer the advantage of extended contact with the same faculty throughout the student's academic career. This can result in a greater feeling of continuity, deeper bonding with fellow students, and opportunities for mentorship.

Graduate Programs.   Those who plan to pursue collegiate teaching and research or who aspire to executive positions in national and multinational corporations and agencies may continue their education with master's and/or doctoral degrees. CHRIE (The Council on Hotel, Restaurant, and Institutional Education) lists more than 30 member schools here and abroad that offer graduate degrees in hospitality management; hotel, restaurant, and/or institutional management; recreation and leisure; international tourism management; urban and regional planning; human nutrition and food systems; travel industry management, and so on.

There are several excellent references describing options for higher education in the relevant areas, including CHRIE's *A Guide to College Programs in Hospitality and Tourism,* the World Tourism Organization's *World Directory of Tourism Education and Training Institutions,* the American Society of Travel Agents' (ASTA) *Travel School Directory,* and the NRA's *Guide for Two- and Four-Year Foodservice/Hospitality Programs. Dun's Employment Opportunity Directory* provides listings (organized by industrial classification code) of companies that offer specialized training programs and internships.

Professional Organizations.   Before deciding which career field to pursue or which training or education to explore, you may find it helpful to contact some professional organizations. Every area of specialization has a professional organization designed to inform members of current trends and to monitor or establish industry standards of professionalism.

Membership in such organizations will expose you to specialized areas of interest, and put you in a position to collect solid information from both the association and its practicing members. These members will often become your first networking contacts—and sometimes role models. An additional incentive for joining professional organizations is that many offer students reduced membership fees.

Exhibit 16–4 lists some established organizations that you may want to contact.

Work Experience.   As you prepare to meet the demands of the hospitality industry, it is also important that you complement your education with work experience.

Acquiring work experience in the hospitality industry has many advantages. Because this is a hands-on industry, it is critical to have real-world training in addition to technical understanding and expertise. No book can substitute for the experience of working at the front desk of a hotel during peak season, or getting involved in the setting up for a 500-seat banquet.

Work experience gives you practice and allows you to learn on your own by seeing and experiencing through your own eyes and ears. Furthermore, getting the opportunity firsthand to see what takes place in hospitality establishments will help solidify your interest level and commitment to the industry. Firsthand experience in the industry will also increase your marketability and employment opportunities since recruiters place a high value on experience. And, finally, working in the industry can also afford you the pride and self-esteem of earning an income.

Internships.   One popular means of gaining work experience while going to school is through **internships.** These are supervised, structured learning experiences. As an intern, you are given the opportunity to gain hands-on experience in an organization or company. The best part is that it's agreed upon up front that your main purpose is to learn while you work. No one expects you to be a wizard or an expert; they know it's *your job* to ask questions and request direction.

As an intern, you'll gain knowledge not only about the host organization, but also about yourself. Your progress and development will be monitored by a designated individual. (Most colleges request a one-on-one relationship between intern and supervisor; establishing and maintaining open communication with this person is part of your learning experience.) Supervisors are also encouraged to include interns in a variety of meetings where they can observe decision-making and managerial styles—and offer input, if appropriate. It's not unusual for companies to implement changes in their policies or procedures based on interns' input.

An internship can be an excellent opportunity for an organization and a student to "test" each other. It can be a win-win experience for both parties.

EXHIBIT 16–4   Sources of Career Information

American Culinary Federation (ACF)
10 San Bartola Rd.
St. Augustine, FL 32085
Phone: (904)824-4468

American Dietetic Association (ADA)
216 W. Jackson Blvd., Suite 800
Chicago, IL 60606
Phone: (312)899-0040

American Hotel & Motel Association (AH&MA)
1201 New York Ave. NW
Washington, DC 20005
Phone: (202)289-3111

American Society for Hospital Food Service Administrators (ASHFSA)
840 North Lake Shore Dr.
Chicago, IL 60611
Phone: (312)280-6416

American Society of Travel Agents (ASTA)
1101 King Street
Alexandria, VA 22314
Phone: (703)739-2782

Association for International Practical Training (AIPT)
10 Corporate Center, Suite 250
10400 Little Patuxent Pky.
Columbia, MD 21044
Phone: (410)997-2200

CHRIE (The Council on Hotel, Restaurant and Institutional Education)
1200 17th Street NW
Washington, D.C. 20036–3097
Phone: (202)331-5990

Club Managers Association of America (CMAA)
1733 King St.
Alexandria, VA 22314
Phone: (703)739-9500

Dietary Managers Association (DMA)
One Pierce Place, Suite 1220W
Itasca, IL 60143
Phone: (708)775-9200

Educational Foundation of the National Restaurant Association (EF of NRA)
250 S. Wacker Dr., Suite 1400
Chicago, IL 60606
Phone: (312)715-1010

Educational Institute of the American Hotel & Motel Association (EI of AH&MA)
1407 S. Harrison Road
East Lansing, MI 48826
Phone: (517)353-5500

Foodservice Consultants Society International (FCSI)
304 W. Liberty St., Suite 201
Louisville, KY 40202
Phone: (502)583-3783

Healthcare Foodservice Management (HFA)
204 E. Street NE
Washington, DC 20003
Phone: (202)546-7236

Hospitality Sales & Marketing Association (HSMAI)
1300 L St. NW, Suite 800
Washington, DC 20005
Phone: (202)789-0089

Hotel Catering & Institutional Management Association (HCIMA)
191 Trinity Road
London SW17 7HN
United Kingdom
Phone: (081)672-4251

International Association of Conference Centers (IACC)
243 N. Lindbergh Blvd.
Saint Louis, MO 63141
Phone: (314)993-8575

International Association of Hospitality Accountants, Inc. (IAHA)
PO Box 203008
Austin, TX 78720
Phone: (512)346-5680

International Food Service Executives Association (IFSEA)
1100 S. State Rd. # 7, Suite 103
Margate, FL 33068
Phone: (305)977-0767

Meeting Planners International (MPI)
1950 Stemmons Hwy., Suite 5018
Dallas, TX 75207–3109
Phone: (214)746-5222

National Association of Catering Executives
304 W. Liberty St., Suite 301
Louisville, KY 40202
Phone: (502)583-3783

National Association of Colleges & Universities Food Service (NACUFS)
Manly Miles Bldg., Suite 303–305/1405 S. Harrison Rd.
Michigan State University
East Lansing, MI 48824
Phone: (517)332-2494

National Association of Food Equipment Manufacturers (NAFEM)
401 N. Michigan Avenue
Chicago, IL 60611–4267
Phone: (312)644-6610

National Executive Housekeepers Association (NEHA)
1001 Eastwind Dr., Suite 301
Westerville, OH 43081
Phone: (614)895-7166

National Restaurant Association (NRA)
1200 17th Street NW
Washington, DC 20036–3097
Phone: (202)331-5990

National Tour Association (NTA)
PO Box 3071
Lexington, KY 40596
Phone: (606)253-1036

Professional Convention Management Association (PCMA)
100 Vestavia Office Park
Birmingham, AL 35216
Phone: (205)823-7262

Professional Guides Association of America (PGAA)
2416 S. Eads Street
Alexandria, VA 22202
Phone: (502)583-3783

Society for Foodservice Management (SFM)
304 W. Liberty St., Suite 201
Louisville, KY 40202
Phone: (502)583-3783

Travel Industry Association of America (TIA)
2 Lafayette Center
1133 21st St. NW
Washington, DC 20036
Phone: (202)293-1433

Students get a chance to find out if their expectations about the industry are well founded and whether or not they would consider the organization as a place of permanent employment after graduation. The company has the opportunity to find out whether or not the intern has the qualities, skills, and characteristics it desires in its employees.

Most internships in the hospitality industry fall under one of three categories:

- Some corporations and larger operations have well-established, specially designed *structured internship programs.* Interns are provided with formal training in the form of seminars, meetings, and one-to-one supervision.
- Sometimes, operations offer students the opportunity to get involved in specific projects from beginning to end. These could include planning a promotion, launching an in-house employee program, converting departmental systems, or planning and helping execute a special event. Such *project-based internships* are invaluable, since interns become part of a team and see the results of their efforts by finishing a project.
- Most internships in the hospitality industry fall into the category of *rotational internships.* Interns are exposed to two or more aspects of an operation, either by rotating between departments or by rotating responsibilities within a single department.

Frequently, students are paid an hourly wage during their internships. Most internships are 12 to 15 weeks long, though longer internships are not uncommon. Participating in an internship can be one of the most beneficial and growth-provoking experiences of your education. Some students so enjoy them that they participate in two or three!

Summary.   By now, you have surely concluded that the hospitality industry is exciting, but demanding. This section has been intentionally blunt about workloads, hours, and pressures, for good reason. Those who enter this field without being aware of the challenges often burn out quickly. However, those who prepare themselves well and develop the right combination of interests, skills, and experience often thrive. Once you have acquired the know-how and experience, your next step will be to start an aggressive job search. The second part of this chapter will provide you with guidelines on how to find employment that will lead you up your chosen career ladder.

Marketing Your Assets

There is a much-quoted saying among employment counselors: ''It is not always the best qualified candidate who gets the job, but the most skilled job hunter.'' In other words, you may have the right skills and personality for a position, but if you don't know how to present them to an employer, someone less capable may get the job.

The first thing hotel or restaurant developers do when starting a new venture is establish a strong marketing plan for their enterprise. Job hunting is no different—you are the product and you need to establish an effective marketing plan. You must identify and analyze your customers (the employers), develop an effective advertising campaign (résumé and cover letters), and present the product (you) at the interview.

Information Gathering

One of the earliest steps in marketing yourself is to determine your target market. What do potential employers want? What are the industry's needs? How can I fulfill them? The first part of the chapter has emphasized the kinds of skills needed to succeed. Now the emphasis shifts to you and ''firsthand'' investigating. If you are going to devote most of your waking hours to a job, make sure it is a good fit.

Informational Interviewing.   The best way to learn about day-to-day life on a job is to talk to people doing the work you want to do. This is called **informational interviewing** and is valuable because it allows you to:

- See the environments in which you would work.
- Determine the personality types of the people who are likely to be your colleagues.
- Gain an understanding of the challenges you would face.
- Receive advice that could make your entry into the workforce easier.

Informational interviewing is the first step in what is called ***networking,*** the process of talking to people who may be able to offer information and suggestions about career plans and future employment opportunities (and who may eventually offer you opportunities). To begin the information-gathering process, first generate a list of people to interview. There are any number of ways to do this: get referrals from family, friends, and faculty members; go through the yellow pages; read the business section of newspapers and call people who are quoted or featured; ask your alumni office for assistance in locating former graduates; and so on. The list is endless if you are creative and resourceful.

Once you have established a list of professionals, write or call them to set up a 20- to 30-minute interview. You may want to say something like:

> Hi, my name is _____ and I was given your name by _____ . I am researching the hospitality industry to decide whether I would like to pursue a career in it. I understand you are actively involved in this area, and I would be interested in your personal perspectives. Could we arrange an appointment next week?

EXHIBIT 16–5   Sample Interview Questions for Informational Interviews

1. How did you get into this line of work?
2. How did you get your first job?
3. What has your career path been like? Is that typical in this industry?
4. What skills or personal qualities are necessary to succeed in this job?
5. What do you like most? What do you like least?
6. What do you do in a typical work day or week?
7. What type of people do you work with?
8. What is the biggest challenge facing your organization?
9. What is an average starting salary in this area? What variables determine salary and opportunity for advancement?
10. What schooling or experience was most beneficial in preparing you for this work?
11. What advice would you give someone wanting to break into this industry?
12. Could you give me the names of other individuals who might be willing to share their perspectives?

Prior to the interview, lay out a short list of questions. Ask about those things that are important to you and that would increase your understanding of the career. Exhibit 16–5 provides some sample questions.

Bear in mind that these people could become key members of your job search network and that you want to make a positive impression. Before ending the meeting, ask your interviewee to suggest one or two more individuals you might contact, and if you may use his or her name when you do. Thank the professional for his or her time and information, and follow up with a written thank you note as well.

Professional Organizations.   Professional organizations can offer a wealth of information and networking opportunities. It is well worth contacting some of the professional organizations listed in Exhibit 16–4; it's also the simplest way to begin networking.

Networking

As your job search progresses, the people you met in informational interviews can become the heart of a vital network. People sometimes associate the term *networking* with high-power wheeler-dealers socializing at cocktail parties and conferences. This false image can be intimidating to the first-time job hunter. In this context, networking simply means letting lots of people know who you are and what type of job you are pursuing, and then asking them to share information about any openings. It does not have to occur at an executive level. Your 16-year-old cousin, Vinnie, who works as a busperson at a fine dining restaurant, might be the contact who tells you about an opening for an assistant manager.

In order for networking to be effective, you need to be well organized, persistent, and resourceful. Make up an extensive list of everyone you could involve in your job search. Use the same suggestions provided earlier for generating a list of information providers. Remember to include the people you sought out for informational interviews. Let each person know that you have begun job hunting. Give them a copy of your résumé so they know what you are looking for and are capable of doing. Be persistent in contacting them every couple of weeks to ask if they have heard of anything new. Keep track of every referral they give you, and send them a thank you note letting them know how the contact went.

Job Search Correspondence

It is important to create a positive impression in all written correspondence with a potential employer. If your correspondence is unappealing and has mistakes, the employer may assume it is representative of the work you would produce on the job. The following information on résumé and letter writing is intended to offer guidelines for producing written materials that make a good impression. It is important to develop a résumé early on in your education, as early as your freshman year, to use for internship and summer employment opportunities.

Résumés.   The *purpose of a résumé* is not to get you the job, but to get you an interview. It should be well organized, concise, and written for a specific job target. Because everyone has different experiences and skills, there is room for individuality and creativity when writing résumés. However, there are certain standard categories and information common to most résumés, which we discuss next. The first four categories are the most pertinent information.

Heading.   Found at the top of the résumé, the heading includes your name, address, and phone number. It is a good idea to put both a current and a permanent address if you will be relocating within the next 6 to 12 months.

Career Objective.   The career objective tells the employer the type of position you are seeking. The career objective is like a thesis statement for a term paper: Every item on a résumé should serve to support it. If you have three career areas of interest, develop three different résumés. Some students worry that a career objective will limit their options, but employers repeatedly state they like to see one on a résumé because it shows a sense of focus and forethought. The career objective can be extremely brief, stating only the job title. Some sample career objectives for the hospitality industry include:

- Front-desk agent.
- Reservations agent.
- Sales representative.

- Assistant sous chef.
- Assistant housekeeper.
- Food & beverage controller.
- Human resource specialist.
- Meeting planner.

Education.   Recent graduates usually list education near the top of their résumés, since they are unlikely to have significant experience to cite. After a few years in the industry, your education section may move toward the bottom of the résumé, taking a supporting role to work experience. The education section should include the name of your graduating institution, degree title, major, and year received. High school and/or transfer school information does not need to be included.

Grade point average is optional; include it only if it works to your benefit. If working your way through school, you may want to include a statement about the percentage of college expenses you financed yourself.

Demonstration of Abilities.   This is the meat of the résumé, where the reader gets a taste of your potential based on your previous experiences. There are generally two formats used to present this information: the chronological format and the functional (or skills-based) format.

Chronological résumés focus on work experience, starting with your most recent employment and working backwards. Job titles, organization names, and job descriptions get the emphasis in this format. It is commonly used when your career direction is clear and your previous work history is directly related to your current objective. For an example, see Exhibit 16–14.

Functional résumés highlight accomplishments and skills while giving job titles and work history less emphasis. This format has more flexibility and can be used when a person is entering the job market for the first time or after a long absence. It is also a good format for a person making a career change. Examples of each format may be seen in Exhibits 16–14 and 16–16 at the end of this chapter.

To demonstrate your abilities, draw information from work experience, school activities, hobbies, academic projects, and community involvement. It is not important whether you were paid while gaining experience—employers are mainly interested in the skills developed.

Summary of Qualifications.   This category may be used to summarize personal characteristics that are not stated elsewhere in the résumé. This section, usually comprised of three to five concise statements, will generally follow the education section. An example of this can be seen in the sample résumé in Exhibit 16–14.

Honors and Activities.   If you have been extremely active in community or campus events or have received scholarships and distinguished honors, you may want to include them under this section.

Interests.   There is an ongoing debate about this category. Some employers like to have a fuller picture of you, including how you spend your free time. Other employers believe that personal interests are not relevant and that they reduce the seriousness of the résumé. Use your own best judgment as to whether to include this section. If your favorite pastime is getting tattooed or going skinny dipping, you'll be better advised to emphasize some other category option.

Options that may add to a positive impression are:

- Language ability.
- Multicultural experience, if you've studied or lived abroad.
- Computer skills.
- Military service.
- Research projects.

Summary.   How you arrange these suggested categories is up to you, but generally speaking, the flow of the résumé should be such that the most relevant information comes first on the page and tapers down to that which is of less importance to the employer. There are a few final tips that can make a good self-presentation on paper.

• Action verbs such as *coordinated, managed,* or *conducted* should be used to start every statement in your job or skill descriptions. This adds an energetic tone to the résumé. Use past tense action verbs unless you are describing a current position.

• Résumé paper is usually slightly textured and thicker than regular copy paper. Colored paper is an option, though most people prefer subtle shades to dark or bright colors. If you choose to use colored paper, the cover letter and any other enclosures should match the résumé paper.

• Laser-printed résumés are now the norm, and typewritten résumés do not make a comparable impression. It also makes sense to put your résumé on computer disk so that you can make changes quickly and easily.

• Length is usually limited to one page for recent graduates. However, if you have enough relevant material to fill two pages, that is acceptable. If information spills over to a second page, it should take up at least one-third to one-half of the sheet. If you want to fill up remaining space on a second page, you may list the names, titles, addresses, and phone numbers of three to five references.

• Personal information such as age, marital status, health, height, and weight were once standard information on résumés. This is no longer the case, largely because such factors should have no impact on a hiring decision.

It is a good idea to have your résumé critiqued. Ask members of your campus career center to look at it and give feedback. Ask professors and/or professionals working in the hospitality industry to share their opinions.

Letter Writing.   You will have occasion to write many letters in the course of a job search. The two most common types are cover letters and thank-you letters.

Résumés sent by mail should be accompanied by a **cover letter.** The purpose of the cover letter is to convey your interest and enthusiasm to an employer. It is also an opportunity to balance the professionalism of the résumé with an element of personal warmth.

Whenever you write a letter, try to address it to a specific person rather than to ''Dear Sir.'' If it is absolutely impossible to get a name, avoid using any *gender-based salutation.* Instead, use a functional title such as ''Dear Manager'' or ''Dear Selection Committee.''

The first paragraph of the cover letter should say why you are writing—in response to an ad or at the suggestion of a mutual friend, for example. The second paragraph should demonstrate that you have done some homework and know a little about the needs, priorities, or interests of the corporation. The third paragraph should state something about you that is relevant to the company and may distinguish you from other candidates. The final paragraph should state what you perceive the next step to be—and when you intend to follow up. Throughout the letter, you should remain brief and focused. Outline specifically what you are asking and offering. A sample cover letter is shown in Exhibit 16–6.

Thank-you letters are typically shorter and more personal than cover letters. Their size, though, is in direct contrast to their importance. It is critical throughout the job search that you express your appreciation for any assistance you receive. Not only does it demonstrate proper social etiquette, it is an opportunity to put your name out there one more time and leave a positive impression.

Always be specific in expressing your gratitude, whether it was for information, a referral, or an interview. A sample of a thank-you or follow-up letter is shown in Exhibit 16–7. This is a rather formal thank-you letter and represents a school of thought that approves of typing such letters. Many experts recommend a handwritten thank-you note.

The Art of Interviewing

Learning to interview effectively may seem a contradictory process. Experts stress that the key to good interviewing is ''to be yourself'' but then proceed to tell you how to act, what to wear, and what to say. It may help to think of interviewing as an art form. When people strive to be great artists, they often go through rigorous training that includes the history and basics of their art form. They may even be asked to imitate the masters. But the truly successful

EXHIBIT 16–6   Sample Cover Letter

Caitlin McKenzie
PO Box 1488
Denver, CO 81301

February 14, 19 _____

Ingrid Sanders
Director of Human Resources
Somerset Food Service
7080 North Melrose Place, Suite 600
Center, CA 90060

Dear Ms. Sanders:

A mutual friend, Harold Coil at the University of Denver student service office, suggested I write to you.

I am completing my bachelor's degree in Hotel Restaurant Management at Northern State University in May. I have worked in the campus food service industry while going to school. I have enjoyed my experience and am exploring career possibilities in food service management.

In researching your organization, I discovered that Somerset Food Service has undergone recent management changes. From what I understand, the organization is establishing a new reputation for ''nutritious and delicious'' food service. In order to accomplish this new vision, Somerset has made a commitment to a Total Quality Improvement plan encouraging teamwork and a ''can do'' attitude.

I would be interested in becoming a part of the Somerset team. I have experience in campus food delivery and have proven myself as an innovative and hard-working employee. I believe the Total Quality Improvement management style fits well with who I am personally and professionally.

I would appreciate any information or advice you could give me about my job search. I will call you next week to see if we might be able to schedule a meeting as I will be visiting your area in March. I have also enclosed a résumé summarizing my background.

Thank you for your time.
Sincerely,

Caitlin McKenzie

Caitlin McKenzie

enclosure

EXHIBIT 16–7   Sample Thank-You/Follow-Up Letter

Caitlin McKenzie
PO Box 1488
Denver, CO 81301

March 23, 19 _____

Ingrid Sanders
Director of Human Resources
Somerset Food Service
7080 North Melrose Place, Suite 600
Center, CA 90060

Dear Ms. Sanders:

Thank you for taking the time to talk with me last week. I thoroughly enjoyed the meeting and appreciate all the information you so generously shared.

I had not realized how different the food service industry can be from state to state. I still laugh about your statement that avocados are practically a food staple in the diet of California college students. I wish we were so fortunate in Colorado!

Your insights about food service management were very helpful. I have incorporated the changes you suggested in my résumé and have enclosed a "new and improved" copy.

I am sorry there are no current openings in your division. I will, however, take advantage of your invitation to keep in touch. Should anything open up, please keep me in mind.

Sincerely,

Caitlin McKenzie

Caitlin McKenzie

enclosure

artists are those who take this knowledge and then infuse it with their own style and personality. So it is with interviewing. You can study guidelines and gather information, but it is up to you to personalize the process.

The interview process can be divided into three parts:

* Preparation
* Performance
* Follow-up

Preparation.   If you are well prepared, your interview performance can be outstanding. Self-assessment, career exploration, and research on the interviewing company are the three essential areas of preparation.

Self-Assessment.   Before beginning the interview process, it's wise to reexamine your values, interests, and abilities. Recruiters have indicated that if you cannot verbalize a clear picture of who you are and what you want, they are unable to project where and how you would fit into their organization. In addition, employers question your maturity and ambition if you cannot present a strong sense of self in the interview.

Career Exploration.   Processing career information goes hand-in-hand with self-assessment. You must demonstrate to the interviewer that you know the career's demands, and that you have the confidence and ability to handle the challenges. This reassures potential employers that you will not be overwhelmed or disappointed with a job because you are entering it with unrealistic expectations. The information-gathering techniques mentioned earlier will help you gain a perspective on the day-to-day demands of any hospitality occupation.

Company Research.   The third area of preparation can be the most difficult. The research skills developed in school for term papers and projects can be directly applied to this process. Spend some time in campus or local libraries to track down information about the specific companies with whom you will be interviewing. Research is important because it allows you to speak in specifics about the company, and the position. More importantly, you will have a more realistic picture of the organization and be better able to judge how happy you would be working there.

There are several ways to obtain company data, including from inside the organization. You may wish to consult:

- The personnel department for job descriptions.
- Company newsletters, annual reports, or promotional literature.
- Menus, guest-services directories.
- Support staff.
- The present job holder.
- Others with similar jobs.

There are also sources outside the organization that can provide information about specific employers and job responsibilities:

- Professional journals
- Newspapers and magazines
- Competitor organizations
- Professional organizations (as shown in Exhibit 16–1)

EXHIBIT 16–8

A successful recruit researches corporate publications before the interview.

- Chambers of commerce
- Customers
- Vendors or suppliers

Before beginning the company research process, it is a good idea to develop a list of the details you would like to have. You may want to investigate answers to the following questions about each organization:

- Who is the company's targeted consumer?
- What kind of reputation does the company have among consumers and competitors?
- How does it differentiate itself from its competitors?
- What are the challenges facing the industry in the future?
- How does the company plan to address those challenges?
- What is the management style of the company and what are typical career progressions?
- What has its financial performance been?
- What other divisions and holdings does the company have?

The Final Preparation Step.   The final step of the preparation stage is practice. If you have never been through a formal interview, arrange some mock interviews. These are often available through campus career service offices. You can also ask friends or relatives to role-play an interview with you.

Performance.   If you have prepared yourself adequately, the interview will not be a terrifying ordeal. A little nervousness is normal and, in fact, good because it motivates you to perform at your best level. This section will cover appearance suggestions, typical interview structures, questions frequently asked by recruiters, and questions you might want to ask them.

Appearance.   In the weeks before your interviews, you will want to decide on your interview outfit so as not to be caught wearing white athletic socks with a new black suit. Research can help you decide what to wear for an interview by providing a sense of how formal or casual the company's clothing code is. When doing research, note how people are dressed in company brochures and videos, and try to find out what the recruiters are wearing when they visit campus.

As a rule of thumb, it is better to err on the side of being conservatively dressed in an interview. Look clean and well groomed. Some recruiters look at the "three Hs"—hair, hands, and heels. Hair should be clean and styled. Hands should also be clean with trimmed nails. Heels of shoes should not be scuffed or dirty. Women are encouraged to stay away from heavy makeup, bright nail polish, and excessive jewelry. Men are encouraged to be free of facial hair. If you absolutely refuse to shave a beard or mustache, make sure it is well trimmed. Avoid perfume and cologne, since interview rooms are often small and your lingering "Lagerfeld" may not be appreciated. Remember, many positions in the hospitality industry require front-line service with customers. Therefore, employers are often looking for individuals who can make an excellent first impression. Appearance counts, whether you like to think so or not.

Frequently Asked Questions.   There is no predicting what questions will be asked in an interview. CRS Recruitment Publications has compiled a list of the 50 most frequently asked interview questions, which we have included here in Exhibit 16–9. It is a good idea to review this list and mentally prepare answers, though we do not recommend writing down or trying to memorize detailed responses. This can result in a "canned" interview that lacks sincerity and spontaneity. Your best bet lies in the following five guidelines:

- Be positive.
- Personalize your answers.
- Take time to think.
- Avoid rambling.
- Relax and be human.

Let's look at these in greater detail:

1. Be positive. If asked about weaknesses, areas needing improvement, failures, disappointments, or examples of conflicts you have experienced, it is a good idea to be candid and honest. However, it is important that you answer in a positive way. For example, describe how you corrected a weakness or learned from failures, disappointments, and conflict.

EXHIBIT 16–9   **Fifty Most Frequently Asked Interview Questions**

1. Why did you choose to interview with our company?
2. Describe your ideal job.
3. What can you offer us?
4. Where do you want to be in five years? Ten years?
5. Do you plan to return to school for further education?
6. What skills have you developed?
7. Did you work while going to school? In what positions?
8. What did you enjoy most about your last employment?
9. What did you enjoy least about your last employment?
10. What did you learn from these college work experiences?
11. Have you ever quit a job? Why?
12. Why should we hire you rather than another candidate?
13. Why did you choose your major?
14. What do you consider to be your greatest strengths?
15. Can you name some weaknesses?
16. Do you prefer to work under supervision or on your own?
17. Would you be successful working on a team?
18. Of which three accomplishments are you most proud?
19. In which campus activities did you participate?
20. Have you ever dropped a class? Why?
21. Why did you select your college or university?
22. What do you know about our company (product or service)?
23. Which college classes did you like the best? Why?
24. Which college classes did you like the least? Why?
25. Who are your role models?
26. Do you think you received a good education at _____ ?
27. What is your overall GPA? What is your major GPA?
28. Do your grades accurately reflect your ability?
29. Were you financially responsible for any portion of your college education?
30. Have you worked under deadline pressure? When?
31. Are you able to work on several assignments at once?
32. Do you prefer large or small companies? Why?
33. How do you feel about working in a structured environment?
34. How do you feel about working overtime?
35. How do you feel about travel?
36. How do you feel about the possibility of relocation?
37. Do you have any hobbies?
38. What problems have you solved in your previous positions?
39. Are you willing to work flextime?
40. Have you ever done any volunteer work? What?
41. Define success. Failure.
42. Have you ever had any failures?
43. How does your college education or work experience relate to this job?
44. How did you get along with your former professors (supervisors and co-workers)?
45. How many classes did you miss because of illness or personal business?
46. What are your ideas on salary?
47. Tell me about yourself.
48. Do you have any computer experience?
49. Have you ever spoken to a group of people? How large?
50. Would you be willing to take a drug test?

Source: CRS Recruitment Publications/Cass Communications, Inc., Evanston, Illinois.

2. Personalize answers. Strive to make a lasting positive impression with recruiters by giving them a sense of your individuality. One way to do this is to provide specific examples that demonstrate your personality and skills. Paint a vivid picture; don't just give dry facts.

The following anecdote illustrates this point. During a mock interview, a student was asked ''What characteristics do you like in a supervisor?'' The student thought for awhile and then replied, ''I appreciate supervisors who are willing to work hard, communicate clearly, and enjoy their work.'' After the mock interview, the student was asked what questions she found difficult. She replied:

> The one about the supervisor was really hard. The only thing I could think of was when I first worked as a cook for a fishing crew in Alaska. My boss was this gruff captain with a bushy white beard. At first he scared me, but I came to respect him a great deal. He worked his fingers to the bone and would never ask anyone to do something he wouldn't do himself. He also was concerned about his crew and made sure everyone communicated. And he loved fishing. It wasn't just a job; it was something he took great pride in. But I didn't think I should mention him in the interview because he was just a blue collar worker so I struggled with that answer.

The student's second response was much more colorful and memorable. She could have told that story and then summarized with the statement she made in the mock interview to strengthen her answer.

3. Take time to think. If you don't have a ready answer to a question, say something along these lines: ''That's a good question. Let me think about that a minute.'' It is a good idea to pause before you answer *any* question so you can mentally compose what you want to say before you start speaking.

4. Avoid rambling. If you incorporate the above suggestion, you are less likely to fall into the rambling trap. Some people think out loud, and by the time they have arrived at the main point of their answer, they have lost the recruiter's interest. It is important to make your point and use enough detail to give a vivid picture, but don't spill over the fine line and say too much.

5. Relax and be human. Stress is inherent in the interview process. If you get flustered, stop and explain: ''I'm afraid I'm so nervous, I lost my train of thought. Can you repeat the question?'' Recruiters would rather get a sense of the real you, nervousness and all, than a wooden, impersonal interview response.

Responding to Difficult Questions.   There are certain questions that can prove troubling. For example, employers will sometimes ask what kind of salary offer you hope to receive. It is a good idea to avoid answering this directly because if you mention a low figure, you may be selling yourself short and get an offer lower than the employer initially intended to extend. Or you may request a salary so high the employer will consider you to be out of the company's price range. Some options in responding to questions related to salary include:

- After being in school so long, it is difficult for me to state a figure off the top of my head without doing further research. What do you typically offer entry-level people with my qualifications?
- I can't answer with a specific figure. It depends on job responsibilities, benefits, advancement potential, personal fit, and so on. Until I have all the information and have had a chance to digest it, I don't think I can answer that.
- If you have done your homework and are well prepared for this question, you may want to say something like, ''Salary will depend on many factors, but my understanding is that the current compensation for this position ranges from $ _____ to $ _____ . With my level of skill and experience and depending on other benefits, I would anticipate something within that range.''

There are other interview questions that may not only feel uncomfortable, but are illegal as well. Questions about ethnicity, religion, sexual preference, or age can be cause for discrimination. Therefore, the recruiter should not bring them up. If you get a question you feel uncomfortable with, there are several ways to handle it.

- Ignore your discomfort and simply answer the question.
- Tactfully confront the interviewer by responding, ''I'm afraid I don't understand how that question relates to my ability to do this job. Could you clarify what kind of information you are looking for and how it is relevant?''
- Answer what you believe are the concerns behind the question. For example, if asked about your religious affiliation, you might say, ''If you are worried I won't be able to work certain days or overtime due to religious obligations, I can assure you there will be no problem.''

Regardless of what route you take, it may be a good idea to report any unprofessional questions or actions to your campus career services office or the personnel office of the corporation.

Interviewing the Interviewer.   When interviewing, remember that the process is a two-way street. You can use the interview to determine whether or not the corporation is compatible with your interests, values, and aspirations. Asking the interviewer questions can provide this information as well as make a favorable impression.

Standard interview protocol suggests you avoid asking salary and benefit questions during the first interview. You do not want to give the impression that compensation is the only aspect of a job that is important. Consider the first interview an opportunity to get a better sense of the corporation and for the employer to get a sense of your personality. Shown in Exhibit 16–10 are some sample questions that can help you gain good information from the

---

EXHIBIT 16–10   **Sample Questions to Ask the Recruiter**

---

1. What is the organizational structure and where does this position fit?
2. Could you tell me who would be supervising this position and what his/her supervision style is?
3. What do you see as the greatest challenge facing this position?
4. Does your organization encourage interaction among employees outside the work setting such as softball teams or volunteer work? If so, what kinds of activities does the organization sponsor or encourage?
5. What is the typical career path for a person in this position?
6. _____ (writing, creative problem solving, organizing) is something I really enjoy. Would you anticipate an opportunity for me to utilize that skill in this position? How?
7. Many people believe organizations have a ''personality.'' How would you describe the personality of your company?
8. Can you describe the work environment and management style the person in this position would experience?
9. What type of person would be the ideal candidate for this job?
10. Can you describe your performance evaluation process?

---

interview process. The important point to remember is that the interview is a time to discover how much you really want to work for the company. Ask good questions to avoid accepting a position that you will be unhappy with in the long run.

Follow-Up.   The interview process does not end with the interview. There are several **follow-up** tasks left to be completed after the interview is finished.

Critique Your Performance.   Often, people react in one of two ways when an interview is over. They heave a sigh of relief and put it out of their minds. Or they concentrate on the negatives and berate themselves for not doing as well as they wanted. It can be more helpful to take some time to review the whole interview in your mind. Be sure to pat yourself on the back for the things that went well. For the less positive aspects, simply think about what you will do differently if the situation comes up again.

Send a Thank-You Letter.   In the previous information about correspondence, we provided a sample of a thank-you/follow-up letter. Don't forget this last step. One employer shared a story about two candidates who'd made it through the first round of interviews. The hiring committee liked both applicants equally well and brought them in for a property tour and a series of second interviews. Still, they could not decide between the two, so they put the decision on hold for a week. One candidate wrote a thank-you letter and followed up with a phone call to reiterate her interest in the job and inquire about the status of their decision. She was the candidate they hired because they felt she would show the same ability to follow through on the job.

Follow Up Rejections.   Avoid sinking into depression if you get a rejection letter from an organization. Instead, contact the employer and ask what you could do to make yourself more marketable or improve your chances for hire in the future. They may be willing to give you some advice that can help you do better in your next interview.

Cultural Issues.   Corporations, like any other group of people, have their own cultural norms, appropriate behaviors, and unspoken expectations. Research has shown that interviewers unconsciously like candidates who look, act, and think as they do; who demonstrate characteristics similar to those of their *corporate culture.* Often, interviewers unintentionally base their hiring decisions on this ''likability'' factor, giving more weight to it than to the applicant's specific abilities, and the result can be cultural bias.

The best defense against this is to be knowledgeable about the probable expectations of the recruiters. Behaviors and attributes usually valued by interviewers include good eye contact, a firm handshake, enthusiasm, and the ability to talk about individual achievements. For some individuals, these behaviors may feel unnatural and uncomfortable because they inherently clash with personal values or style. If this applies to you, you should begin to work now on developing alternate ways of expressing yourself. The best way to do this is to be open and honest.

For example, suppose you come from a culture that believes a gentle touching of the palms is more polite than a firm handshake and that limiting direct eye contact is a sign of respect. Or perhaps your cultural values teach that talking about your individual accomplishments is rude or that high-quality people have a quiet, reserved manner. You could be at a distinct disadvantage in the interview process unless you take a *proactive* stance, anticipating problems, change, or misinterpretations and acting ahead of time to prevent them.

To counteract unintentional bias, make a point of sharing your cultural norms with the recruiter and emphasizing the positive ways they might affect the work environment. Suppose the recruiter starts out with the standard question, ''Tell me about yourself.'' You might *proactively* respond with, ''In order to talk about myself, I think it would help first if I shared some information about my culture . . . '' Sharing insights about your heritage can also help you stand out as unique in the interviewer's mind. You may also create a positive side effect—clearing the recruiter's stereotypes.

Persistence.   The most critical element to a successful job search is tenacity—not giving up no matter how discouraged you may feel. One of the best ways to display tenacity is by adopting the attitude that one contact with

---

EXHIBIT 16–11   **Resources for Job Search Methods**

Asher, D. *From College to Career.* Berkeley, CA: Ten Speed Press, 1992.
Bolles, R. N. *What Color Is Your Parachute?* Berkeley, CA: Ten Speed Press, 1994.
Krannich, R. L., and C. R. Krannich. *Job Search Letters that Get Results.* Manassas
   Park, VA: Impact Publications, 1992.
Parker, Y. *The Damn Good Résumé Guide.* Berkeley, CA: Ten Speed Press, 1989.
Stoodley, M. *Information Interviewing.* Washington, MO: Paperbacks for Educators,
   1990.
Yate, M. J. *Knock 'em Dead with Great Answers to Tough Interview Questions.*
   Holbrook, MA: Bob Adams, Inc., 1990.
Yate, M. J. *Résumés That Knock 'em Dead.* Holbrook, MA: Bob Adams, Inc., 1990.

---

an employer is not enough. If you really want a job, keep going after it. Here's one famous story about a job hunter who did just that:

> A young man was having an incredibly tough time getting his first job. He finally convinced someone to let him work without pay for two weeks in a factory. His task was to sweep the floors every night. He not only swept the floors, but made sure the factory was cleaner than it had been in years. The owner was so impressed with the young man's work ethic, that he hired him full time. Later, the young man became the owner of the factory and went down in history as the father of the American automobile. His name was Henry Ford.

Though times have changed, one of Henry Ford's philosophies is as true today as it was in 1900, ''Whether you think you can . . . or you think you cannot . . . you are always right.''

You may think that the model of ''enthusiasm'' described above is not one that is right for you. This may be because the term is often associated with an outgoing ''cheerleading'' demeanor. But enthusiasm can also be expressed through quiet persistence. Send letters, make follow-up phone calls, and even volunteer to work without pay if necessary.

For more helpful information on job search methods, investigate the resources shown in Exhibit 16–11.

Conclusion

A great deal of information has been presented in this chapter. Like many careers, the hospitality industry is full of opportunities, but requires a great deal of hard work to succeed. Now is the time to begin building the skills and gaining the experience that will allow you entry into this dynamic profession. Choose your path of preparation, whether it be a two-year, four-year, or certification program. Develop a wide range of technical and managerial skills. Supplement formal education with on-the-job learning through intern, volunteer, or part-time employment.

When you are ready to begin looking for full-time career opportunities, prepare yourself well. Research potential employers and establish a network of helpful individuals. Develop a good résumé and be enthusiastic and professional in all your written and face-to-face contact with employers.

EXHIBIT 16–12

*And isn't this what we are all dreaming of . . . **hard** work and dedication may get you there!*

Courtesy: The Palmer House Hilton, Chicago, Illinois.

Keywords

Core Concepts

Discussion Questions

Following are two résumés, Exhibits 16–13 and 16–15, that need some work. Using the information presented in Chapter 16, what formats would you suggest and what changes would you make on these résumés? (Revised résumés are shown as Exhibits 16–14 and 16–16.)

EXHIBIT 16–13   Résumé Critique Assignment I

CAITLIN MARIE McKENZIE
PO Box 1488
South Bend, CO 81301
(303) 247-4227

CAREER OBJECTIVE:

An entry-level position in the food-service management area that would utilize my
education, skills, and experience.

EDUCATION

Northern State University, South Bend, CO
Bachelor of Science, Hotel Restaurant Management, May 15, 1994

HONORS AND ACTIVITIES

Eta Sigma Delta, secretary
S.A.D.D., member
Recipient of three local academic scholarships
Dean's list three semesters
International exchange student at the University of Granada, Spain
Annual Cancer Fun Run, volunteer

WORK EXPERIENCE

Camy's European Coffee House, 32 E. Butler, Tucson, AZ 85281
Baker and Counter Clerk, June–August 1988, June–August 1989, June–August 1990.
Supervisor: Tom Camy, (602) 526-1638
I was responsible for baking goods and providing front counter help with coffee.

Benny's Restaurant, 1717 W. Second Ave., South Bend, CO 81301
Busperson/Head Waitress, September 1990–May 1992.
Supervisor: Kathy Michaels, (303) 779-0286
Duties included waiting tables, scheduling employees, and general support in dining
area.

Tourram Food Service, Northern State University, South Bend, CO 81301
Student Manager, January 1993–May 1994.
Supervisor: Dan Nichols
Responsible for student employees and cash drawers for five campus dining halls.

PERSONAL DATA

Age: 21   Marital Status: Single, no children   Health: Excellent

EXHIBIT 16–14   Revised Résumé I—Chronological Format

Caitlin Marie McKenzie

Current Address:
PO Box 1488
South Bend, CO 81301
(303) 247-4227

Permanent Address:
3671 W. Pine Ave.
Tucson, AZ 86002
(602) 526-5792

CAREER OBJECTIVE
Food Service Management

SUMMARY OF QUALIFICATIONS
• Over six years' experience in food service industry.
• Demonstrated ability to work efficiently in high-stress, fast-paced environments.
• Productive and responsible; willing to learn and handle any new task.
• Develop rapport easily with staff, management, and customers.

EDUCATION
Northern State University, South Bend, CO, May 1994
Bachelor of Science, **Hotel Restaurant Management,** GPA 3.8
International Exchange Program, University of Granada, **Spain**
Fall Semester, 1992

EXPERIENCE
Tourram Food Service, Northern State University, South Bend, CO
Student Manager, January 1992–May 1994
• Staffed, trained, and managed crew of 50 part-time employees.
• Coordinated product output for five campus food operations.
• Supervised culturally diverse staff with a wide variety of backgrounds and skill levels.
• Audited all cash drawers.

Benny's Restaurant, South Bend, CO
Head Waitperson, September 1990–May 1992
• Started as busperson and earned three promotions because of consistently high performance.
• Organized and scheduled servers, buspeople, and cashiers for evening shift.
• Created customer awareness of menu items and increased check averages.
• Received high evaluations with mention of an ability to foster teamwork.

Camy's European Coffee House, Tucson, AZ
Baker and Counter Clerk, Summers 1988–1990
• Developed and prepared original pastry recipes for health-conscious clientele.
• Provided prompt and courteous counter service.
• Prepared specialty coffees including espresso, cappuccino, and latté.

HONORS AND ACTIVITIES
Eta Sigma Delta secretary (Hotel/Restaurant Honor Society)
Annual Cancer Fun Run volunteer
Students Against Drunk Driving volunteer
Recipient of three local academic scholarships

EXHIBIT 16–15   Résumé Critique Assignment II

MARK TERRENCE MARTINEZ

SC Box 2001
Andalusia, AL 36420
(205) 771-0881

EDUCATION

Southern College, Andalusia, AL, Dec. 1996
Associate of Applied Sciences, Hotel Management, GPA 2.3

WORK EXPERIENCE

House and Lawn Caretaker, Self-employed, 1992–Present
  Provide excellent house and lawn care for residential homes. Generate billing statements and handle all bookkeeping tasks. Utilize interpersonal skills in generating new clientele and maintaining established customers.

Resident Assistant, Southern College, August 1993–Present
  Planned educational programming for residence hall. Initiated and enforced residence hall procedures related to social activities, disciplinary procedures, and policy enforcement. Investigated reports of misconduct and resolved or eliminated conflict.

Previews Counselor, Southern College, Summer 1994
  Welcomed new students and parents to college campus. Provided tours and assisted in registration activities.

INTERNSHIP

Day Manager, The Inn (School Hotel Lab), Present
  Receive, compile, and organize reservations from hotel guests. Monitor cashier and shift reports for hotel lab and oversee house bank. Promptly and courteously greet and serve hotel guests.

ACTIVITIES

Special Olympics Volunteer

REFERENCES

Available upon request

EXHIBIT 16–16   Revised Résumé II

MARK TERRENCE MARTINEZ

Current: SC Box 2001, Andalusia, AL 36420   (205) 771-0881
Permanent: 321 W. Canyon, Holstream, AL 35420   (205) 882-5893

CAREER OBJECTIVE
Front desk hotel operations

EDUCATION
Southern College, Andalusia, AL
Associate of Applied Sciences in *Hotel Management,* December 1996
Financed 100% of college expenses through work and scholarships.

SKILLS SUMMARY
Organization Skills
- Received, compiled, and organized reservations from hotel guests.
- Monitored cashier shift reports for hotel lab and oversaw house bank.
- Handled all billing and collection responsibilities for own small business.
- Planned educational programming schedule for entire residence hall for the academic year.
- Maintained and balanced expense accounts for Special Olympics as secretary/treasurer.

Management Skills
- Trained lab students on check-in/check-out procedures and phone etiquette.
- Scheduled front desk, housekeeping, and reservation staff for day shifts.
- Initiated and enforced residence hall policies related to social activities, disciplinary procedures, and policy enforcement.
- Recorded maintenance and property damage reports for 30-room coed residence hall.

Interpersonal Skills
- Promptly and courteously greeted and served hotel guests.
- Demonstrated ability to interact with culturally diverse hotel patrons, co-workers, hall residents, new students, and Special Olympics participants.
- Developed loyal house and lawn maintenance clientele through friendly and reliable service.
- Investigated reports of misconduct and resolved or eliminated hall conflicts.
- Welcomed new students and parents to college campus; provided tours and assisted with registration activities.
- Recruited student volunteers and host families for the Andalusia Winter Olympics.
- Persuaded local vendors to donate prizes and refreshments for Winter Olympics activities.

EXPERIENCE

Day Manager	The Inn (School Hotel Lab)	Present
House and Lawn Caretaker	Self-employed	1992 to Present
Resident Assistant	Southern College	August 1993–Present
Previews Counselor	Southern College	Summer 1994
Assistant Coordinator	Andalusia Special Olympics	Winters 1993–1995

APPENDIX A
SAMPLE CAREER LADDERS

Front-office manager trainee, large chain-operated hotel

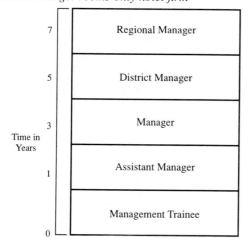

Time in Years	
10	General Manager (Usually after crosstraining in other functional areas)
8	Resident Manager
4	Front Office Manager
	Assistant Front Office Manager
1	Front Desk Shift Manager
0	Trainee

Food and beverage management trainee, large chain-operated hotel

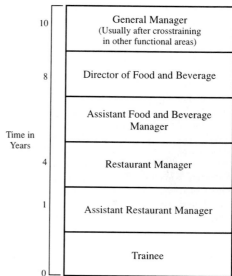

Time in Years	
10	General Manager (Usually after crosstraining in other functional areas)
8	Director of Food and Beverage
	Assistant Food and Beverage Manager
4	Restaurant Manager
1	Assistant Restaurant Manager
0	Trainee

Midscale/budget-rooms-only hotel firm

Time in Years	
7	Regional Manager
5	District Manager
3	Manager
1	Assistant Manager
0	Management Trainee

Chain restaurant firm

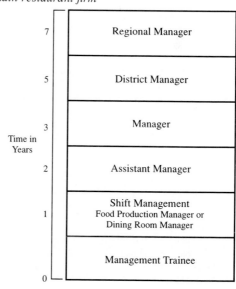

Time in Years	
7	Regional Manager
5	District Manager
3	Manager
2	Assistant Manager
1	Shift Management Food Production Manager or Dining Room Manager
0	Management Trainee

APPENDIX B
REPRESENTATIVE INDUSTRY SALARIES (in thousands of U.S. dollars)

Hotel Salary Guideline
Low represents 100–400 rooms
Median represents 400–700 rooms
High represents 700–1,000 rooms

Hotel Positions	Median
Vice President-Operations	66–92
General Manager	53–93
Assistant Manager	39–54
Front Office Manager	33–46
Auditor	24–26
Assistant Controller	27–36
Controller	46–57
Director of Sales	49–58
Sales Manager	33–39
Regional Sales Manager	41–62
Executive Housekeeper	32–42
Assistant Housekeeper	24–29
Chief Engineer	36–49
Food and Beverage Director	47–62
Beverage Manager	28–37
Restaurant Manager	30–38
Executive Chef	44–63
Chef	36–55
Sous Chef	32–41
Pastry Chef	35–42
Kitchen Manager (Steward)	29–31
Director of Catering	37–45
Banquet Manager	31–36
Banquet Sales	30–37
Director of Purchasing	33–46
Director of Sales & Marketing	44–46
Director of Human Resources	36–53
Conference Manager	33–39

Multiunit Foodservice Guideline

Low represents 3–25 units   FF = Fast Food Restaurant
Median represents 26–75 units   R-Non LIQ = Restaurant not serving liquor
High represents 75+ units   R-W/LIQ = Restaurant serving liquor

Foodservice Positions	Median
(Area) Regional Manager	42–52
District Manager	37–48
Cafeteria Manager	29–36
Chef Manager	26–32
Production Manager	27–29

Foodservice Positions	Median
Controller	32–38
Purchasing Director	28–39
Unit Manager	26–28
Assistant Manager	21–27
Director of Human Resources	29–41

Restaurant/Fast Food Positions	Median
ADMINISTRATIVE	
Marketing Director (Chain)	54–79
Controller (Chain)	47–75
Director of Human Resources	40–51
Training Manager	38–45
Controller (Single Unit)	29–36
Purchasing Director	37–48
EDP/MIS Manager*	29–41

Restaurant/Fast Food Positions	Median
OPERATIONS	
Division Managers (Corporate)	133–184
Regional Manager/Vice President	95–111
Operations Director (Chain)	52–85
District Manager (Multi-Unit)	46–61
General Manager (FF)	29–35
Assistant (FF)	26–28
Trainee (FF)	21–23
General Manager (R-Non LIQ)	26–34
Assistant (R-Non LIQ)	22–24
Trainee (R-Non LIQ)	21–22
General Manager (R-W/LIQ)	31–51
Assistant (R-W/LIQ)	27–33
Trainee (R-W/LIQ)	21–23
Chef	37–47
Sous Chef	27–36
Cook	20–22
Pastry Chef	26–31
Banquet Manager	32–41

County Club Manager (Golf)	Median
250–500 members	38–45
500+ members	79–115

*EDP/MIS = Electronic Data Processing/Management Information Systems.
Courtesy: Roth Young Wage and Salary Review, 1990.

Endnotes

Chapter 1

1. American Hotel and Motel Association, *Directory of Hotel and Motel Companies* (Washington, DC: Richard Turner, Editor-Publisher, 1994).

2. S. Clarke, "Helping Your Customers Want to Spend Money, *World's-Eye View on Hospitality Trends,* Summer 1993, p. 7.

3. R. Zemke with D. Schaaf, *The Service Edge* (New York: Penguin Books, 1989), p. 8.

4. H. Mackay, *Swim with the Sharks Without Being Eaten Alive* (New York: Ivy Books, 1988), p. 155.

5. D. Statt, *Concise Dictionary of Management* (London and New York: Routledge, 1992), p. 40.

6. W. D. Hitt, *The Leader-Manager: Guidelines for Action* (Columbus, OH: Battelle Press, 1988).

7. Somerset R. Waters, (*Travel Industry World Yearbook: The Big Picture,* Rye, NY: Child & Waters, Inc., 1983 and 1994), p. 9. and p. 11.

8. *Compendium of Tourism Statistics* (Madrid: World Tourism Organization, 1995).

9. E. G. Etess, *Arizona Hospitality Trends* 5, no. 2 (1991), p. 1.

10. *Working Woman,* September 1993, p. 104.

11. N. Hoyd-Fore, *Cornell Hotel and Restaurant Administration Quarterly* (Ithaca, NY: Cornell University, 1988), p. 9.

12. M. Cetron and O. Davies, *American Renaissance: Our Life at the Turn of the 21st Century* (New York: St. Martin's Press, 1989).

13. *Business Journal,* April 1, 1994, p. 00.

14. Dave Barry, *Arizona Republic,* January 9, 1994, p. F2.

15. R. Van Warner, *Nation's Restaurant News,* November 22, 1993, p. 21.

16. Professional Association of Innkeepers International, *So You Want to Be an Inkeeper . . .* (Santa Barbara, CA: Professional Association of Innkeepers, 1989), p. 19.

Chapter 2

1. Josephson Institute of Ethics, *The Ethics of American Youth: A Warning and a Call to Action* (Marina del Rey, CA: Josephson Institute of Ethics, October 1990), p. 1.

2. J. Patterson and P. Kim, *The Day America Told the Truth—What People Really Believe about Everything That Really Matters* (New York: Prentice Hall, 1991).

3. M. Josephson, *Making Ethical Decisions* (Marina del Rey, CA: Josephson Institute of Ethics, 1992), pp. 12–23.

4. M. Josephson, "Teaching Ethical Decision Making and Principled Reasoning," *Ethics: Easier Said Than Done,* Winter 1988, pp. 29–30.

5. Business Roundtable, *Corporate Ethics: A Prime Business Asset* (New York: Business Roundtable, 1988), pp. 20–22.

Chapter 3

1. Joseph Fridgen, *Dimensions of Tourism* (East Lansing, MI: The Education Institute of the American Hotel and Motel Association, 1991), p. 26.

2. Somerset R. Waters, *Travel Industry World Yearbook: The Big Picture* (New York: Child & Waters, 1992), pp. 143–45.

3. M. Bush, ''Understanding the $130 Billion Customer,'' *Hotels,* October 1993, p. 74.

Chapter 5

1. J. Scarnes, *Complete Guide to Gambling* (New York: Simon & Schuster, 1986).

2. S. Leonard, ''Study of Financial Reports on Casino Operations,'' in *U.S. Gaming Industry* (Los Angeles: Saul Leonard, Inc., 1992).

3. M. Rowe, ''Las Vegas—Big Gamble,'' *Lodging and Hospitality,* February 1994.

4. Scarnes, *Complete Guide to Gambling.*

5. James Crutchfield, comments made in conversation with the author, 1994.

Chapter 6

1. D. E. Lundberg, *The Hotel and Restaurant Business* (New York: Van Nostrand Reinhold, 1989).

2. R. C. Mill and A. M. Morrison, *The Tourism System* (Englewood Cliffs, NJ: Prentice Hall, 1985).

Appendix B

1. Laventhol and Horwath, *Hotel/Motel Development* (Washington, DC: The Urban Land Institute, 1984).

2. Ibid.

Chapter 14

1. T. J. Peters and R. H. Waterman, *In Search of Excellence: Lessons from America's Best Companies* (New York: Harper & Row, 1982), p. xvii.

2. M. Kasavana and J. J. Cahill, *Managing Computers in the Hospitality Industry,* 2nd ed. (East Lansing, MI: Educational Institute of the American Hotel & Motel Association, 1992).

3. G. Collins, *Hospitality Information Technology: Learning How to Use It* (Dubuque, IA: Kendall/Hunt Publishing Company, 1992), pp. 17–20.

4. Ibid., p. 207.

5. Ibid.

6. Kasavana and Cahill, *Managing Computers in the Hospitality Industry,* pp. 167–68.

7. Ibid., pp. 218–23.

8. L. Chervenak, ''Hotel Technology at the Start of the New Millenium,'' *Hospitality Research Journal* 17, no. 1 (1993), p. 115.

Glossary

accessibility Ease of access. This is a transportation-related factor that influences travel and tourism. Speed of movement is affected by accessibility, which in turn is related to infrastructure.

accounting model A representation of a business entity in terms of accounting data organized into two financial statements: balance sheet and income statement.

accounting reports Reports and systems that supply the information managers and investors need in order to manage and evaluate the financial condition of their business.

accounting system Activities, procedures, and records involved in producing accounting information and reports.

accounts payable Total of amounts owed to suppliers for goods or services received by a business but not yet paid for.

activity-based resort A resort that focuses on a single aspect of a destination or property as the key to identity. There are several types of activity-based resorts, including ski resorts, golf resorts, and tennis and water fun resorts.

advanced deposit reservations Reservations prepaid by the guest in an amount generally equal to the first night's room and tax. They represent the highest quality of reservation, since the guests have the highest likelihood of arrival.

Age of Exploration The historical period beginning with the sailing of Christopher Columbus in 1492 and marking a period of active exploration and the advent of capitalism and modern scientific thought.

agent A player employed by a dealer to help defraud the casino.

Airlines Reporting Corporation (ARC) A professional clearinghouse that represents airlines in the collection of airline ticket sales and commission payments to the travel agents. ARC's *Industry Agents' Handbook* describes the requirements of reservations, ticketing, and reporting for travel agents to follow.

American Plan A meal plan that includes three meals per day (breakfast, lunch, and dinner). Its price is included in the room rate.

application software Computer programs designed to perform specific tasks such as word processing and accounting.

baby boomers A demographic group of people born between 1946 and 1964. Estimated at 77 million, they currently represent about half of the working U.S. population. They will begin retiring in 10 to 15 years, shaking all leisure time norms to date.

back-of-the-house The part of a hotel operation generally considered guest support rather than guest service. Examples of back-of-the-house employees include: a groundskeeper, a housekeeper, a banquet set-up person, a comptroller, and a laundry room worker.

bacteria Microscopic one-celled plants that cause many foodborne illnesses.

bank hand A player acting as the bank in baccarat. Other players may bet on this hand or that of the "player hand."

Bermuda plan A meal plan that includes a more substantial full breakfast than a continental plan.

biometric systems Machine recognition technology that can read personal characteristics, such as fingerprints or retinas of the eye. This may be used instead of the present door lock.

business transactions All company sales and expenditures where goods and services are traded for money.

caravanserais Medieval lodging facilities. They were the predecessors to the stagecoach inn and later the motel and consisted of an enclosed courtyard for animals and spartan rooms for travelers.

cash flow statement An accounting report that explains the change in cash for the accounting period being reported on.

central reservations system (CRS) A system that acts on behalf of a hotel by taking reservations and forwarding the information to the specific property. This is the leading reason hotels choose to franchise or affiliate with a well-known brand. Some properties receive upwards of 75 percent of all their reservations through a CRS.

chemical sprinkler system A fire suppression system that uses a sprinkler that sprays a chemical on the heat source. Often used in computer rooms where water damage to the equipment could run into millions of dollars.

chronological résumé A brief, time line–based résumé accentuating previous experience, normally starting with the most recent experience.

clean To physically remove soil and food.

code of appearance Policy relating to employee appearance, for example, uniforms, makeup, hair length, jewelry, and type and color of footwear.

code of ethics A standard of conduct consisting of rules or principles (values) that individuals or organizations agree to uphold.

commercial food-service operations A food-service operation that seeks to be profitable.

commissary food-service operations A food-service operation whose distinguishing characteristic is that it prepares all meals in a central kitchen and then transports them to various serving sites. They may be commercial or institutional and may or may not use convenience foods. Customers may directly pay for the food and service as in restaurants.

common law Law created by court decision.

compartment steamer A closed compartment vessel wherein food is cooked by direct contact with steam.

computer A tool capable of processing large quantities of data into information quickly and accurately. It streamlines the process of collecting and recording data and expands the ways in which information is organized and reported.

conceptualization The first of the five stages in development of a hotel, restaurant, or attraction. During this stage the concept or idea about a particular project to be developed takes form. Later, the abstract idea must be transformed into a concrete plan or concept.

concierge A hotel's expert with regard to local activities and attractions. Concierges may help guests secure tickets to performances or sporting events, recommend restaurants or merchants, give directions, arrange tours, order flowers, or find baby-sitters.

concierge floor A limited access floor or wing in a hotel for guests who desire concierge services. Rooms on this floor are usually more expensive than equivalent rooms on nonconcierge floors.

conduction Heat transfer by direct contact.

conference center A lodging facility that earns the majority of its revenue (often as high as 95 percent) from conferences and meetings held by various organizations. Conference centers have a high proportion of meeting and function rooms relative to the number of sleeping rooms. They also offer access to sophisticated audio/visual equipment and specialized staff.

Continental plan A meal plan that includes a simple continental breakfast in the room rate.

convection Heat transfer by air or liquid.

convection oven A standard oven with an internal fan to circulate air for greater efficiency.

convenience food service operations Food service operations that use mostly convenience (processed) foods to prepare their menu items.

conventional food service operations Food service operations that prepare most menu items from scratch, using raw ingredients.

conventional oven An insulated box, heated by either gas or electricity, normally used to bake or roast foods.

cost of tourism The negative impact generated by tourists' contact with local societies and natural environments.

cover letter Introductory correspondence that accompanies a résumé.

cross-contamination A process by which bacteria are carried to foods from contaminated objects such as knives and cutting boards, from insects, or from other foods.

cross-training A type of training where employees are trained to do tasks outside their own job description. Cross-training can increase understanding among staff members, encourage teamwork, and fill gaps left by labor shortages.

cyclical menu A menu that changes on a periodic basis.

data facts or figures to be processed into useful information.

data communication The electronic transfer of information from one computer to another via direct cable connections or via telecommunication links involving the telephone system and modems.

decisiveness The ability to make decisions, often within time constraints.

demand Customer wants and needs, which are ever-changing and varied.

destination-management company (DMC) An enterprise that provides services for meeting planners, often serving as a local expert for off-site meeting planners. DMCs can arrange for speakers, entertainers, shopping excursions, airport pick-ups, VIP welcome, and many of the tiny-but-important details an out-of-towner would find time-consuming or difficult to arrange.

destination resort A place or location, rather than a single property. Resort cities, such as Miami, Orlando, and San Diego, are popular destinations because they offer a wide choice of activities, entertainment, and other diversions, along with their mild climates, beaches, and golf courses. In these cases, the location or the city itself is considered a resort, and individual properties are part of the total inventory of attractions that make the destination desirable. There may be a major attribute or activity that is at the core of the area's attractiveness, but the total array is what comprises the destination.

development club (developer-owned club) A club developed by a profit-seeking entity that sells club membership to the public. Members have no control over club operations. Many developer clubs are associated with real estate development. The presence of the club adds value to residents' homes and offers them amenities as homeowners.

discrimination To give preferential treatment to members of certain groups and to treat differently people who are similarly situated. It is illegal to discriminate against people based on race, religion, national origin, sex, or disabilities in employment or places of public assembly.

document To make record of an occurrence in a systematic or official way, at or near the time it takes place.

dram shop liability The liability of a server of alcohol to a person injured or killed as result of the serving of the alcohol.

dry heat cooking Cooking without the addition of water or steam.

du jour menu A menu that changes on a regular daily basis.

economic multiplier A statistical method used to estimate how tourist spending filters through the local economy and stimulates the growth of other sectors.

economies of scale Cost savings made by being able to make purchases or produce goods or services in high volume regularly; one of the advantages of larger businesses over small ones.

economy- or budget-lodging operations Hotel properties wherein the rooms division generates practically 100 percent of every dollar earned, (e.g., Motel 6, Sleep Inn, EconoLodge). Budget-lodging operations normally do not have restaurants, elaborate lounges, meeting rooms, or health spas.

ecotourism   That segment of tourism that has an interest in exploring how nature plays a part in the overall understanding of culture. It may include tourists seeking total submersion in a natural experience, or those who participate in ''adventure'' style recreation.

employee assistance programs (EAP)   Employer-sponsored programs designed to help troubled employees through trying times via referrals to agencies offering help in dealing with emotional problems, addiction, family disturbances, and so forth.

equity club   A club whose members buy a share in the ownership of the club's assets. Most clubs own valuable land and buildings, and each member thus owns a proportional share of the assets. Since the purpose of such clubs lies not in the seeking of profits but in the service of its members, they are usually exempted from income taxes.

European plan   Room only. Hotels that offer lodging only without any meals included in the rate are said to provide European plan accommodations.

excursionist   Any visitor who stays at a destination for less than 24 hours, such as day trippers and cruise passengers.

executive housekeeper   The member of middle management in a hotel responsible for overseeing housekeeping employees and delivering clean guest rooms.

experiential tourism   A segment of tourism whose main objective is to learn and experience the history and culture of the area visited.

Eye-in-the-Sky   An elaborate system of closed circuit television used by casino security to track the gambling activities of dealers and guests within the casino.

feasibility study   A study that attempts to determine whether or not a particular project is feasible (i.e., whether it has a chance to not only survive, but to have sufficient revenues to cover all expenses and gain profits). Feasibility studies give lenders an indication as to what can be expected in terms of their return on investment (ROI).

financial management   The process of managing the monetary affairs of an enterprise, including the coordination of this activity with the other parts of the organization.

fire suppression system   An important safety system for controlling fires, usually heat sensitive and using either chemicals or water for control.

floorwalker   A casino executive who has the primary responsibility of assuring that the games are conducted fairly and that no cheating is occurring by dealers or players.

follow-up   A strategy used to maintain close contact with a customer or future employer, to get a feel for his/her preferences, and to learn about previous contacts. In job hunting, follow-up activities are those accomplished after an interview, including a self-critique, a thank-you letter, and direct employer contact.

food service operation   An organization that prepares food for people outside the home, either for sale, as in a restaurant, or as part of a service, as in a hospital.

formula   A more detailed form of a recipe, used primarily for bakery items.

franchise   An agreement between a franchisee (in this case the developer of the new hotel or restaurant) and a franchisor (a renowned hospitality chain). The franchisor grants the franchisee the right to sell food or rooms by using their name. Along with the name the franchisee gets marketing assistance, operational guidelines, and, most importantly, a tested and successful operational approach.

front-of-the-house   The part of a hotel operation considered more guest-service oriented. Its employees are involved in direct and frequent contacts with the guests. These contacts require the front-of-the-house employee to be well-versed in such guest-service skills as complaint handling, and in providing the guest with a well-rounded customer experience.

front office   One of the three departments in the rooms division, and the primary guest service department of the entire hotel. Front office activities include guest check-in and registration; selection and assignment of guest room; establishment of credit and method of payment; opening, posting, and closing of the guest account; cashing of personal checks, travelers' checks, foreign currency; handling of guest complaints; and guest check-out.

full-service lodging Hotel operations that generate considerable revenues from other than rooms departments, such as gaming, and food and beverage. They attempt to provide their guests with more than just a room; they aim to provide a complete experience. Examples include Four Seasons, Ritz-Carlton, Marriott, and Sheraton.

functional résumé A résumé emphasizing skills, education, and achievements rather than experience.

global distribution system An integrated system of major global airline, hotel, and car rental central reservation systems that enables travel agents to make airline, hotel, and car rental reservations around the world electronically.

Golden Rule ''Do unto others as you would have them do unto you.'' Variations of the Golden Rule have been found in the revered writings of Christians, Muslims, Jews, Hindus, and Buddhists, as well as in the works of philosophers and social theorists dating back to 500 BC.

graveyard shift The shift between the hours of 11 PM and 7 AM. Generally this is the slowest period for a hotel.

guaranteed reservation A reservation guaranteed either to the guest's credit card or to the guest's account. In either case, if the guest fails to arrive, the hotel may charge the guest for one night's room and tax. Guaranteed reservations are of fairly high quality since the guests have a very strong likelihood of arrival.

HACCP (Hazard Analysis Critical Control Point) Critical control points are established at any place along the food flow where something could go wrong that could result in food poisoning or illness.

handle An accurate counting of the total amount wagered in a casino.

hard water Water with a high mineral content, such as iron, manganese, and calcium. Over time, hard water will build up ''scale'' on the insides of boilers and heaters, reducing their efficiency.

health status An important part of a personal inventory, this item relates to mental and physical stamina and emotional stability.

heat-activated sprinkler system A fire suppression system that dumps water at a high pressure onto the heat source. Found in many modern hotels and restaurants, especially in commercial kitchens and high-rise hotels.

high season The time when demand, occupancy, and rates are highest. The time when the property's attractions are at their peak, staffing is at its highest level, and activity and revenue crest.

holistic approach An approach that looks at a situation or idea as a ''whole,'' or system, not simply as disconnected pieces of a puzzle.

hospitality ethics Ethics as they apply to the hospitality industry, a segment of the business world. Those involved in hospitality ethics aim at developing reasonable ethical standards for our industry.

HVAC Acronym standing for *heating, ventilation* and *air-conditioning,* the systems that control the climate throughout a building.

illiteracy The inability to read. Twenty percent of American adults cannot read, write, or compute adequately to be productive workers. Up to one-half of this group may be totally illiterate.

industry The desire and ability to work for long hours, maintaining concentration until a task is done.

information The finished product made out of data that have been processed to have meaning and usefulness.

information highway The technological interconnection of people all around the globe through computers, modems, microwaves, and satellites.

informational interviewing A learning tool used to acquire insight into a specific job or career path. The individual searching for the information acts as the interviewer.

infrastructure The system of roads, harbors, bridges, tunnels, airports, and so on, necessary for vehicle movement. Infrastructure is also used to include services sufficient to service the populations using an area, be they residents or visitors. These include utilities, such as water, electricity, and gas; health care; sanitation and sewage; and services such as traffic control, police, and emergency personnel.

initiative A quality important to leaders, often equated with being a ''self-starter.'' Involves seeing what needs to be done and what could be improved, and anticipating problems and working to prevent them, without being directed by someone else.

institutional food service operations   Food service operations that usually do not seek to make a profit and may not directly charge for food and service. An institutional food service operation may be part of some larger package such as meals served to patients in hospitals or low-cost meals served in elementary and secondary schools.

intent of the law   The actual meaning of the law, as opposed to the spirit of the law.

intermediary   A "go-between" who connects end-users with sources of supply. These include meeting planners, travel agents, incentive travel specialists, destination management companies (DMCs), and wholesale tour operators.

internship   An on-the-job, supervised, structured, time-specific, learning experience.

inventory   Product items in a business that have been bought or produced and not yet sold; can be materials used in a product or partially finished or finished products.

job analysis   The systematic investigation of the scope and duties of a job as they should be performed to result in the desired level of service. Job analysis should precede the writing of job descriptions and job specifications.

job description   A list of the significant duties and responsibilities of a job; simply "describes" the job.

job specification   One of all the skills and characteristics a person must already have in order to be hired for the job.

knowledge and intelligence   Important parts of a manager's profile. They involve skills, technical knowledge, and the ability and willingness to learn new things. They are related to open-mindedness and the ability to study to acquire missing skills.

late charges   Charges that, for whatever reason, arrive late at the front desk, so that they miss being totaled in the guest folio before check-out.

leadership   A combination of skills and qualities that combine to persuade or inspire others to join or follow your direction. More than "bossing" people, it requires sensitivity, fairness, integrity, strength of character, and responsibility.

length of stay   A measurement of how long guests or tourists stay at a hotel or in an area. This is an important indicator of economic impact on destination areas. The longer tourists stay at the destination, the greater the economic contribution they make to local residents, because tourists spend money on local lodging, food, and entertainment, and in other retail businesses.

management   The act or skill of conducting the affairs of a business. Some call it art; some call it science. It is the effective and efficient use of materials, labor, capital, and equipment to produce goods or services at a profit. The word is also used as a collective noun to refer to the persons responsible for it in a business.

management skills   The skills needed to understand, direct, and motivate subordinates. They are normally divided in technical skills, human skills, and conceptual skills.

market research   The formal means of obtaining information used in the marketing decision process.

market segmentation   The process of separating people into distinct groups based on individual characteristics and buying habits.

marketing   The business technique of presenting goods or services in the market. Factors in marketing include price, advertising and promotion, salesmanship, and product quality and distinction, in short, all the activities designed to move goods and services from the producer to the consumer.

marketing information system   All the people, equipment, and resources needed to create timely and accurate information.

marketing mix   The many variables that must be manipulated for a company to achieve its objectives.

microwave oven   A fast-cooking compartment heated by very short electromagnetic waves.

Modified American Plan   A meal plan that offers two meals per day (breakfast and dinner). Prices are included in the room rates charged.

moist heat   Cooking in, or in the presence of, hot water or steam.

moral character   A person's internal makeup that guides his or her response to challenges, trials, and circumstances.

morning line   The odds of participants in a sporting event to actually win that event, as published by handicappers the morning of the event.

networking   Interacting with people who can impact your career options or advancement.

night audit   One of the subdepartments found at the front desk. It is so called because it is a nightly audit of hotel accounts and departments. The night audit is generally conducted between the hours of 11 PM and 7 AM.

no-show   A guest who does not show up to honor his or her reservation, whether at a hotel, restaurant, or golf course.

nonguaranteed reservation (also known as a "6 PM hold" reservation)   A reservation that is not secured with a deposit or any other form of guarantee. If the guest fails to arrive by 6 PM, the hotel has the right to sell the room to someone else.

Occupational Safety and Health Administration (OSHA)   A federal government agency charged with regulating personal safety and health aspects of working conditions in places of business. Also, OSHA stands for the Occupational Safety and Health Act, a Federal Government act authorized to provide employment "free from recognized hazards" to all employees. Every work environment (not just food service operations) must adhere to OSHA regulations.

off-season   A seasonal time period during which the attractions that "magnetize" a resort in the high season are usually not available. It is the time of year when occupancy and demand are down and tourist visits are low.

overbooking   To take more reservations than the actual number of rooms available. Although this is risky, it is a generally accepted practice in the hotel industry, because there will always be a number of no-show reservations.

overbuilding   A market condition in which supply greatly surpasses demand. Most often used to describe a market area has that far more hotel rooms than it has customers, though the term can also be used to describe markets containing too many competing restaurants, office buildings, and apartments. Overbuilding usually results in rate "wars" and an aggressively competitive market.

peek   A marketing concept employed to keep patrons interested in the games of a casino by placing the games in positions so that patrons will be encouraged to explore more of the casinos.

perishable inventories   Hotels, attractions, theaters, amusement parks, and, in some cases, airlines have what can be called perishable inventories. This means, in the case of a hotel with 200 rooms, that on a given night there are 200 perishable opportunities for revenue. Come nighttime, if the room has not been sold, the hotel has lost the revenue it might have earned.

personnel turnover   The rate at which an operation loses workers. A 25 to 30 percent turnover rate is considered high in most industries, yet the hospitality industry is known for rates as high as 300 percent. A 100 percent turnover rate means that every position in an operation is filled by a different person once a year.

pivot point   A department around which the entire hotel operation revolves. The rooms division is the pivot, "heart and soul," "focal point," or "lifeline" of hotel operations for three main reasons: economics, customer service, and departmental forecasting.

positive ethics   An intentional commitment to doing what one should do simply because it is the right thing to do. It requires knowing the difference between what is right and what is expedient.

pot   The bets in a game of poker that remain in the center of the table until a winner has been declared; the amount wagered in each hand.

potable water   Drinkable water. Nonpotable water cannot be consumed by human beings. The most common uses of nonpotable water are to supply fire suppression systems and to water the hotel's lawns and grounds.

preparation   The procedure that transforms food from the state in which it was purchased to a form where it is ready to be cooked.

preventive maintenance (PM) The maintenance done to avoid a major breakdown of equipment and the deterioration of the physical plant. These activities include regular lubrication of moving parts, testing of backup and emergency equipment, and changing of machine belts.

price sensitivity A factor in market segmentation; determining how much members of a market segment are willing to pay for a good or service.

product industries Those industries that are involved in the manufacturing of items that consumers use. Examples would be the manufacturing of cars, jeans, or soft drinks.

production The process following preparation wherein food is converted to the state in which it will be served.

program A set or sequence of instructions that tell a computer how to perform a task. All programs together are referred to as software.

promotion The marketing activity implemented to encourage buying by customers. Sales promotion includes advertising, public relations, display, and personal selling effort.

pull factor The drawing power of a destination area, such as spectacular scenery, friendly people, nice climate, and gourmet food.

purchase order A management control tool that communicates to suppliers exactly what an order is to contain and when it is to be delivered. Used by a receiving agent to check incoming orders for accuracy in content, quality, and price.

push factor Internal forces that drive an individual away from his or her everyday life and routine work schedules.

qualifying leads A process used by sales managers to determine if a lead has a reasonable probability of becoming a piece of business with a lodging facility. A contact may be "qualified" based on his or her authority to make decisions, how often his or her organization is likely to use hotel services, good credit history, or freedom from contracts with competitors.

rakeoff The percentage of a poker pot kept by the casino as a charge for hosting the game.

recipe Set of procedures and ingredients needed to produce a food item.

responsibility An important trait for managers that enables them to deliver on promises dependably and reliably.

return on investment (ROI) A measure of the effectiveness of the operation of a business or a division of one based on the relationship between its profit and the amount of capital in it. ROI can be compared to the interest charged to borrowers on a car loan or a mortgage that accrues to the lender by virtue of its risk.

rim credit Credit given to a player by a casino executive at the time of play. This is done to keep the action moving and to allow the guest to continue to gamble after he or she has spent his or her current stakes.

rooms division The division in a hotel operation that houses three separate departments: *reservations, front office,* and *uniformed services.* Often considered the heart of the hotel, due to its central position and its direct guest contact and revenue-generating functions.

rooms report A written (or electronically transmitted) document given to the housekeeping department by the front desk to indicate the number of guests checking out or staying over. It also includes special requests from guests, such as a late check-out or early make-up.

sanitize A procedure to reduce the number of microorganisms, such as bacteria, to safe levels.

satellite ticket printer An on-site unit in a corporate office that can print out tickets when a travel agent activates it through a telephone line hookup. This technology allows a business traveler to pick up a ticket "in-house," saving time and money.

scenario An imaginary or projected set of events used to illustrate a problem or form a plan of action and reaction.

screening questions A technique used by sales managers when prospecting for new customers. These questions help the sales manager to "qualify" a potential customer.

self-image An individual's perception of himself or herself. It involves liking oneself and taking pride in one's appearance and ability. Confidence is often based on self-image.

sensitivity   A character trait that includes concern, respect for others' feelings and beliefs, compassion, and kindness. It includes respect for the rights and interests of all stakeholders.

service industries   Those industries that are involved in the performance of some activity or service for consumers. Examples would be hotels, restaurants, or transportation services such as airlines.

shoulder season   The periods before and after the high season. During the shoulder season, properties are usually gearing up for or gearing down from the high season; and weather and activities are often attractive, but not prime. During these weeks or months, occupancies and rates are somewhat lower than during peak seasons, but still reflect the desirability of the location and property at that season.

6 PM hold (also known as a nonguaranteed reservation)   A reservation that is not secured with a deposit or any other form of guarantee. If the guest fails to arrive by 6 PM, the hotel has the right to sell the room to someone else.

skimming   The stealing of money by casino owners or employees before it is counted and recorded.

spas   Health resorts in locations with natural hot springs believed to have a therapeutic effect. One of the most famous ones, The Spa Resort in the city of Spa in Belgium, was established in the 13th century.

standard operating procedure (SOP)   A clear, concise description of how to perform a specific task. It contains ''how to'' information and may include a list of all equipment needed and all safety precautions that need to be taken to complete the task.

standard purchase specification   A management control tool that communicates a firm's need for products to potential suppliers. Without these precisely written descriptions, it is impossible for a purchasing agent to make valid price comparisons.

standardized recipe   A set of instructions describing the way an establishment prepares a particular dish. A recipe is a formula. Measured ingredients are combined in a specific procedure to give predetermined results of a known quality and quantity.

static menu   A menu that remains constant.

statute   A law passed by the legislative branch of government.

steam jacketed kettle   A double kettle setup wherein the space between the two kettles is heated with hot water or steam.

sterilize   A procedure to remove all living microorganisms.

supply   The tangibles provided in response to demand, such as hotel type and physical amenities, and intangibles such as the many personal services provided by the lodging staff.

system software   The master control programs informing the computer how to function, and providing the link between the computer hardware and the application software.

table d'hôte menu   A complete menu for a fixed price.

technical skills   Skills that allow individuals to master the ''hands-on'' details of their jobs.

temperature danger zone   The temperature range between 45 and 140 degrees. Any time a potentially hazardous food is in the temperature danger zone the risk of a food-borne illness increases, because bacteria thrive in this environment.

Thomas Cook   The father of modern travel agency operations who realized that industrial societies held great potential for multinational travel. His first organized tour took place on July 5, 1841, in England.

tourism attractions   Places that attract tourists to an area, generally categorized as either physical (or natural) attractions, cultural/historic attractions, and theme parks.

tourist   Any visitor who stays at a destination for more than 24 hours and less than one year.

travel and tourism industry   All the aspects of the service businesses that serve the needs and wants of people who are away from home.

trip   A unit used in the study of tourism, yet open to many different interpretations. The United States Travel Data Center defines a person trip as a person who travels away from home for at least 100 miles (160 km) one way. Statistics Canada defines a trip as anyone who travels a minimum of 50 miles (80 km).

truth in menu legislation   Regulations that require food service operators to be truthful about all aspects of the menu items that they serve.

uniform system of accounts and reports A standardized accounting system developed by the hospitality industry for use by hospitality companies. Uniform systems of accounts exist for both hotel and restaurant operations.

uniformed services The department where employees wear distinct uniforms to assist guests in identifying them as hotel front-of-the-house employees. Uniformed services employees include bell staff, concierge staff, hotel security force, and doorpeople (also known as the guest services department or the hotel services department).

walk To send a guest to another hotel due to lack of available space. Walking is a side effect of overbooking.

walk-in guests Guests who arrive without a reservation and hope to find an available room.

way ticket A keno ticket that is marked in many ''ways'' to increase the probability of winning. Actually this is a marketing technique to increase the sale value of each ticket; the chances of winning will not increase from marking more numbers.

wellness programs Employer-sponsored programs designed to help employees improve their health through diet, exercise, stress reduction, and other preventive measures.

xenophobic Fearing or hating strangers, foreigners, or those who are outwardly ''different'' from oneself.

Index